Archie®

THE MARRIED LIFE

TWO WORLDS. TWO LOV[…] DESTINIES.

Book Five

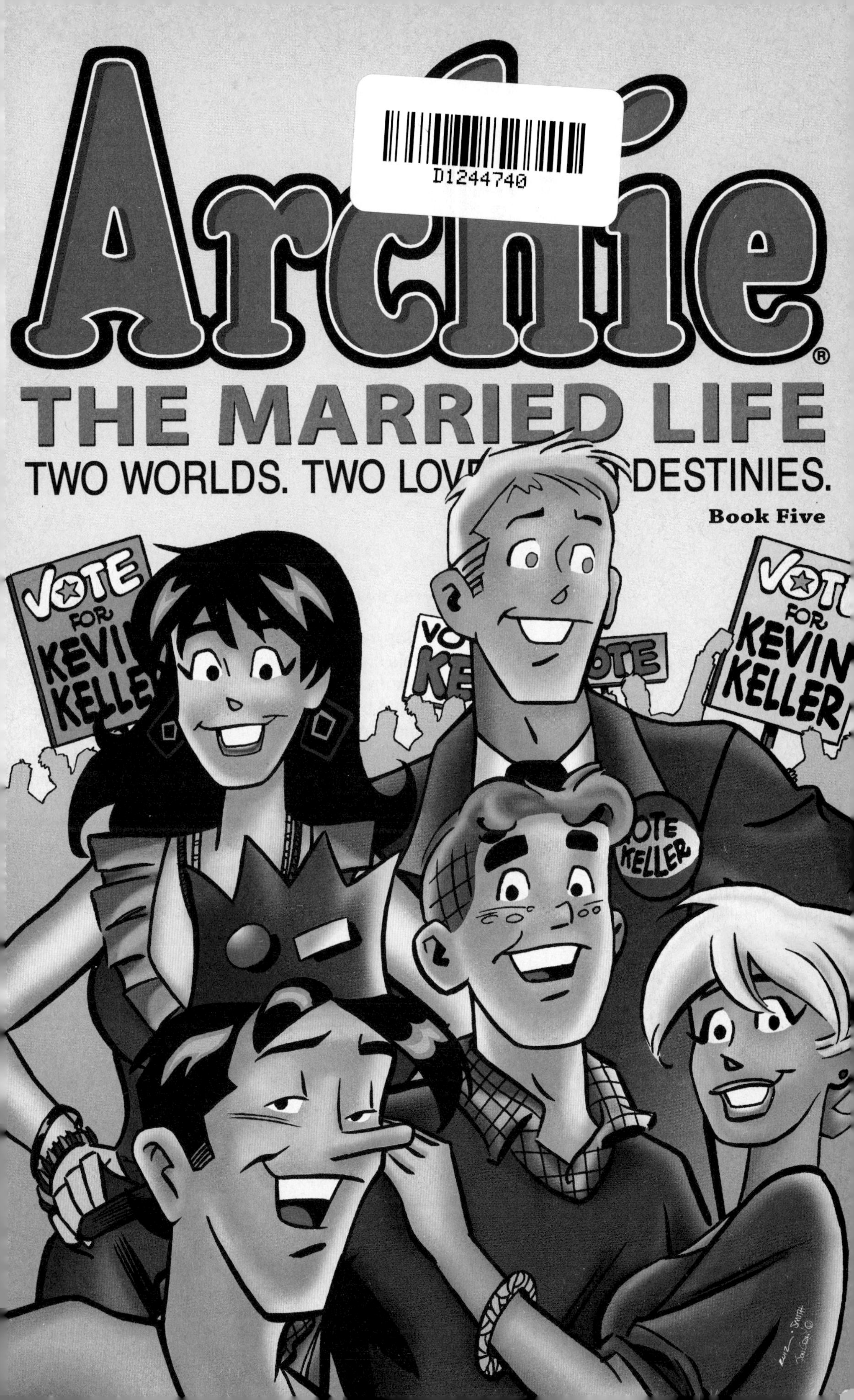
VOTE FOR KEVI KELLE
VOTE FOR KEVIN KELLER
VOTE KELLER

Archie®

THE MARRIED LIFE

TWO WORLDS. TWO LOVES. TWO DESTINIES.

Book Five

ARCHIE: THE MARRIED LIFE. BOOK FIVE
Published by Archie Comic Publications, Inc.
325 Fayette Avenue, Mamaroneck, New York 10543-2318.

ISBN: 978-1-61988-902-6
FIRST PRINTING.

Printed in U.S.A.

Publisher/Co-CEO: Jon Goldwater
Co-CEO: Nancy Silberkleit
President: Mike Pellerito
Co-President/Editor-In-Chief: Victor Gorelick
Chief Creative Officer: Roberto Aguirre-Sacasa
SVP - Sales & Business Development:
Jim Sokolowski
SVP - Publishing & Operations: Harold Buchholz
SVP - Publicity & Marketing: Alex Segura
Executive Director of Editorial: Paul Kaminski
Production Manager: Stephen Oswald
Project Coordinator & Book Design: Joe Morciglio
Editorial Assistant / Proofreader: Jamie Lee Rotante
Production: Tito Peña, Jon Gray

Archie®
THE MARRIED LIFE
TWO WORLDS. TWO LOVES. TWO DESTI...

Book Five

Written by:
Paul Kupperberg

Pencils by:
Fernando Ruiz
and
Pat & Tim Kennedy

Inking by:
Bob Smith
and
Jim Amash

Letters by:
Jack Morelli

Coloring by:
Glenn Whitmore

Cover by:
Norm Breyfogle

Based on the
Archie Wedding Series
originated by Michael Uslan

Two Worlds. Two Loves. Two Destinies. In an alternate universe where anything can happen and what you think is familiar is anything but...

Archie Marries Veronica

Previously...

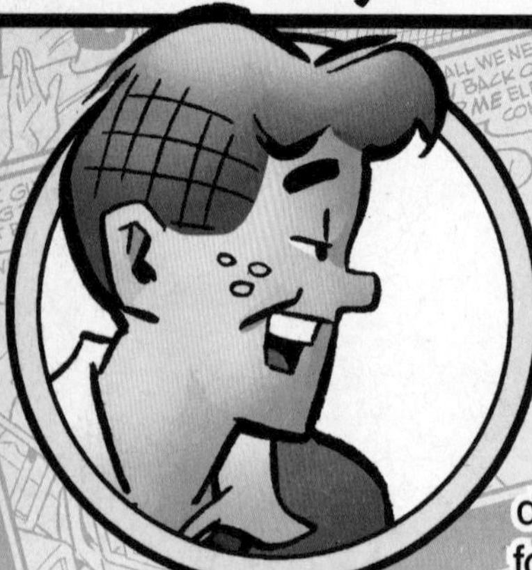

When we last saw our red-headed hero, it looked as though things were finally picking up for him and Veronica. He's been offered the job of a lifetime—the chance to run a brand new record label! There's just one, small problem: the record label is run by ruthless tycoon Fred Mirth, whose checkered past has had quite an effect on Riverdale! Could Mirth have finally changed his ways, or is this just another detail in his next evil plan? And how will Archie working for Mr. Lodge's number one enemy affect his marriage?

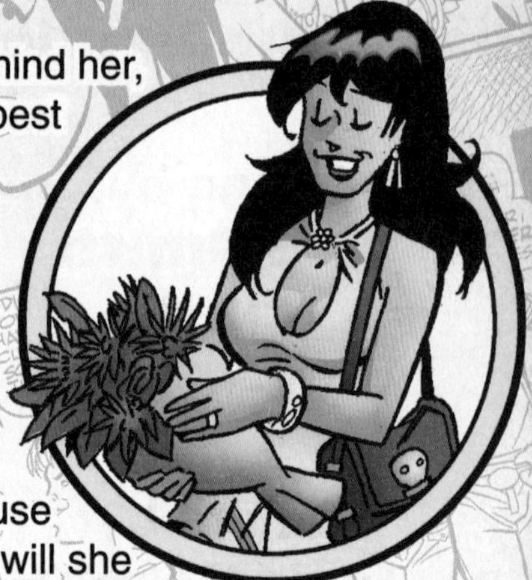

With what seems to be the worst of her legal woes behind her, Veronica's ready to take charge of her life and be the best wife she can be to her faithful and caring husband, Archie. But starting over is never easy, and rebuilding her life, her reputation, and her marriage is going to take some time and effort. While she and her father have improved their relationship, she's going to have to step out from daddy's watchful eye if she really wants to be independent. Thankfully Daddykins has taught her a lot—especially about business! Can she use her business know-how to branch out on her own? Or will she be in over her head?

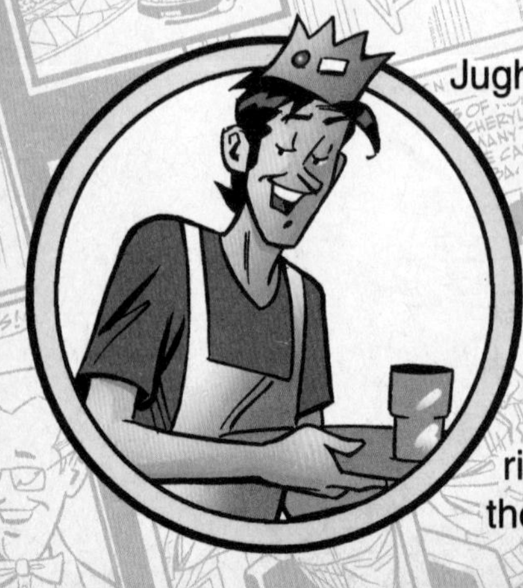

Jughead's living his dream, owning his favorite restaurant, meeting new people every day, seeing all of his old friends on a regular basis, and getting to eat as many burgers as he wants! Though he hit a rough patch when he almost lost Pop's, and definitely lost his girlfriend, Midge, things have started to turn around for everyone's favorite slacker, but what could be the next big step in his life? Could it be—love? That's right, love is in the air for the former girl-hater, and with the one person everyone least expected—Ethel Muggs!

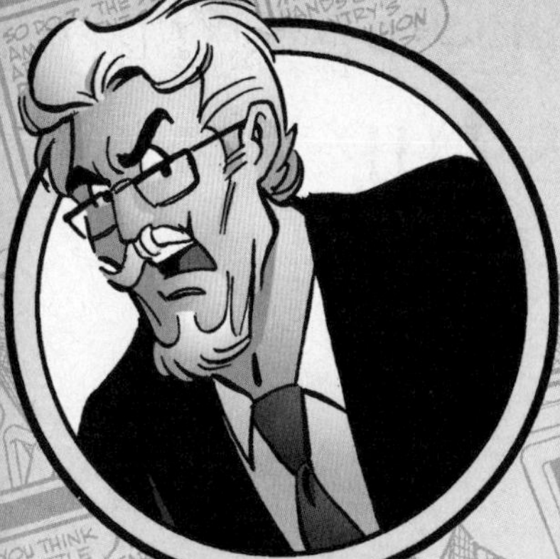

With Lodge Industries no longer in danger, and his daughter no longer living off the rails, Hiram Lodge should be feeling better—but is he? It seems that even though his life situation has improved, his health—both mental and physical—has been deteriorating. Now that Veronica's no longer working for the family business, and he's no longer capable to take charge, the workload is falling on his wife, Hermione. Will Mr. Lodge ever be able to face his fears and run his business alongside his wife?

Mayor Mason has been approached to run for state Senate! However, Moose has learned a lot of things from politics—the main one being that a politician's work is never done! There's still so much to be improved upon in Riverdale, running for Senate would mean that he'd have to virtually abandon the town that he loves. His girlfriend and campaign manager Ilana has faith in him and thinks he should go for it anyway, but Moose thinks there's someone else better suited for the position…

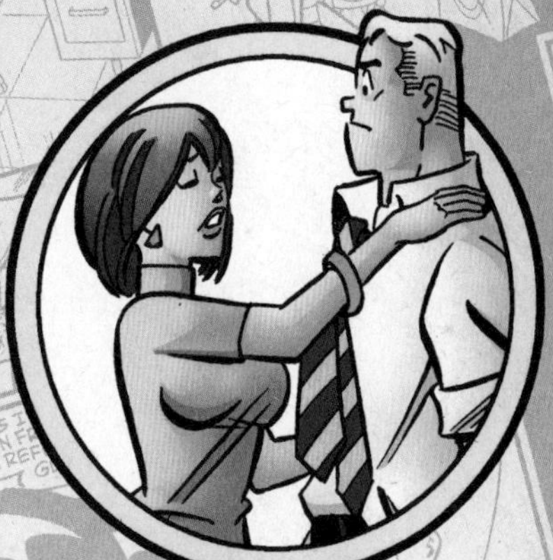

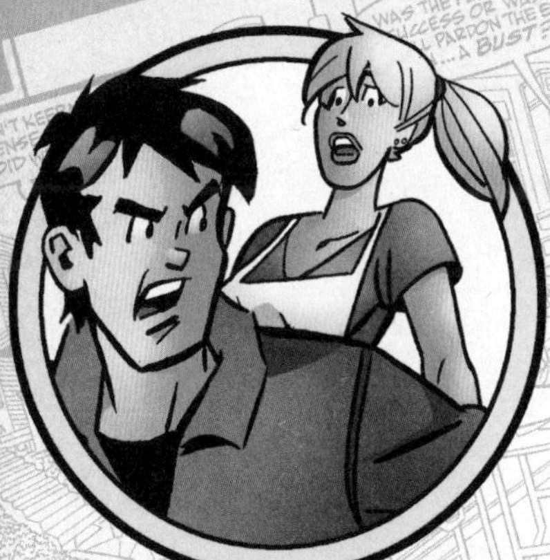

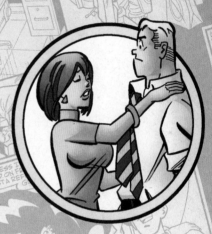

These two lovebirds have gotten their first taste of fame—with the premiere of their very own reality series *Betty Loves Reggie*! They've had their big debut, but that's just the beginning of their career in superstardom! But is being a celebrity all it's cracked up to be? How much longer can they have cameras on them 24/7 before it starts to put a strain on their relationship? And how long will fans be enamored with the everyday lives of Betty and Reggie before they start wanting to see some drama? Will the money be worth all the potential trouble?

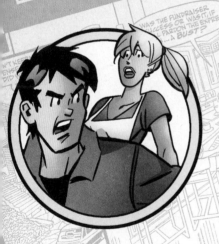

Kevin's husband Clay has been on a road to recovery since he was shot trying to stop a holdup at Jo's Garage. While he's seeing what life is like on the other side of physical therapy, Kevin is contemplating his big career shift into the world of politics. It seemed easy enough for Moose—but how tough will campaigning for Senate be for a newbie like Kevin? And how much will it affect his relationship with his recovering husband? Maybe if he gets some help from a close friend things won't be so bad…

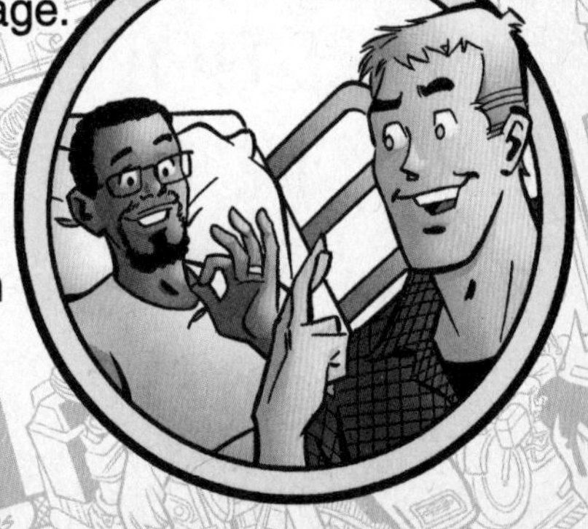

"THINGS WERE **STARTING** TO PICK UP BEFORE THAT, BUT I GUESS THE ADDED EXPOSURE DIDN'T HURT!"

"I JUST HOPE THEY DON'T **FORGET** ABOUT US *NEXT WEEK*!"

-*BETTY COOPER*

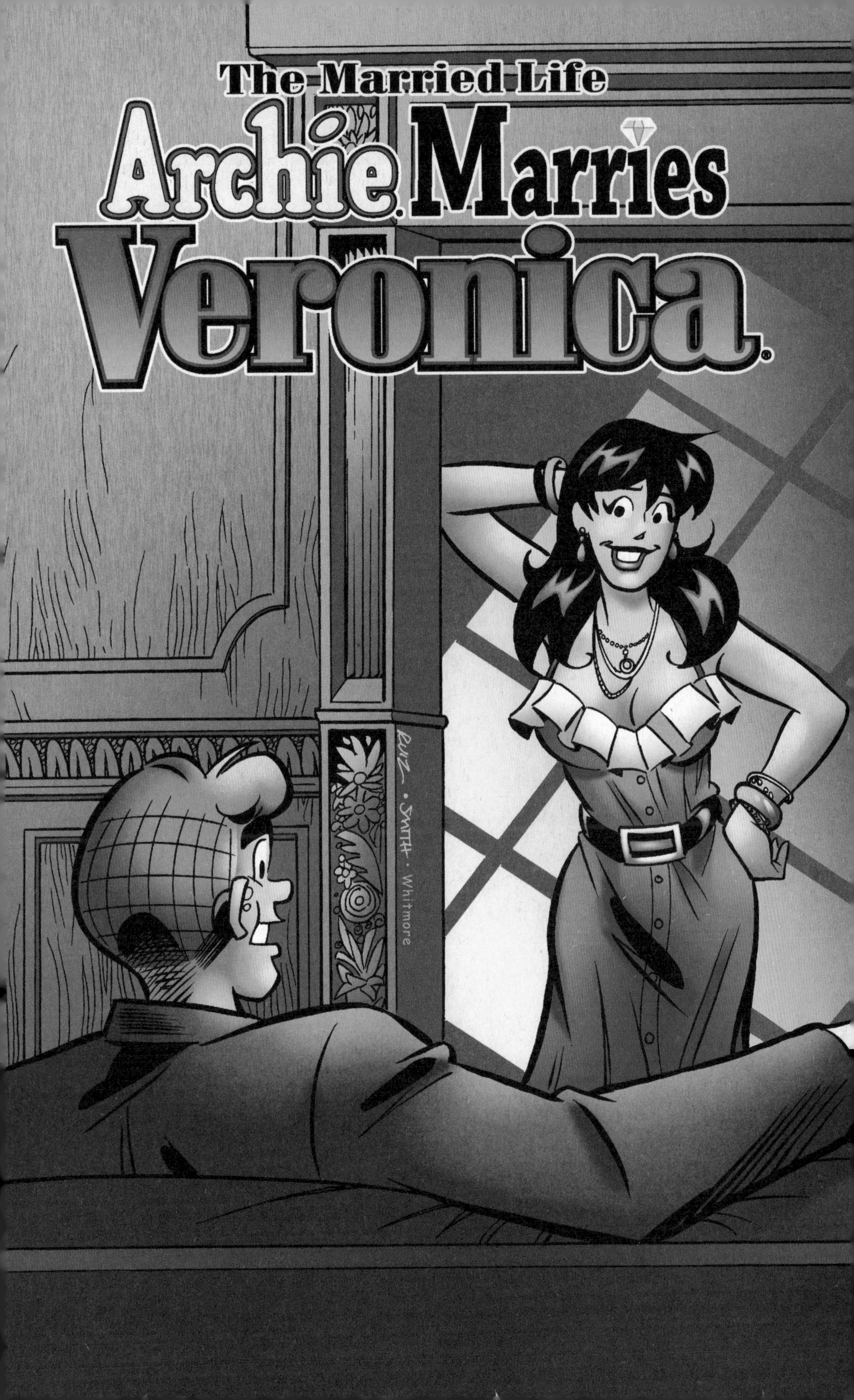

The Married Life
Archie Marries Veronica
Ruiz • Smith • Whitmore

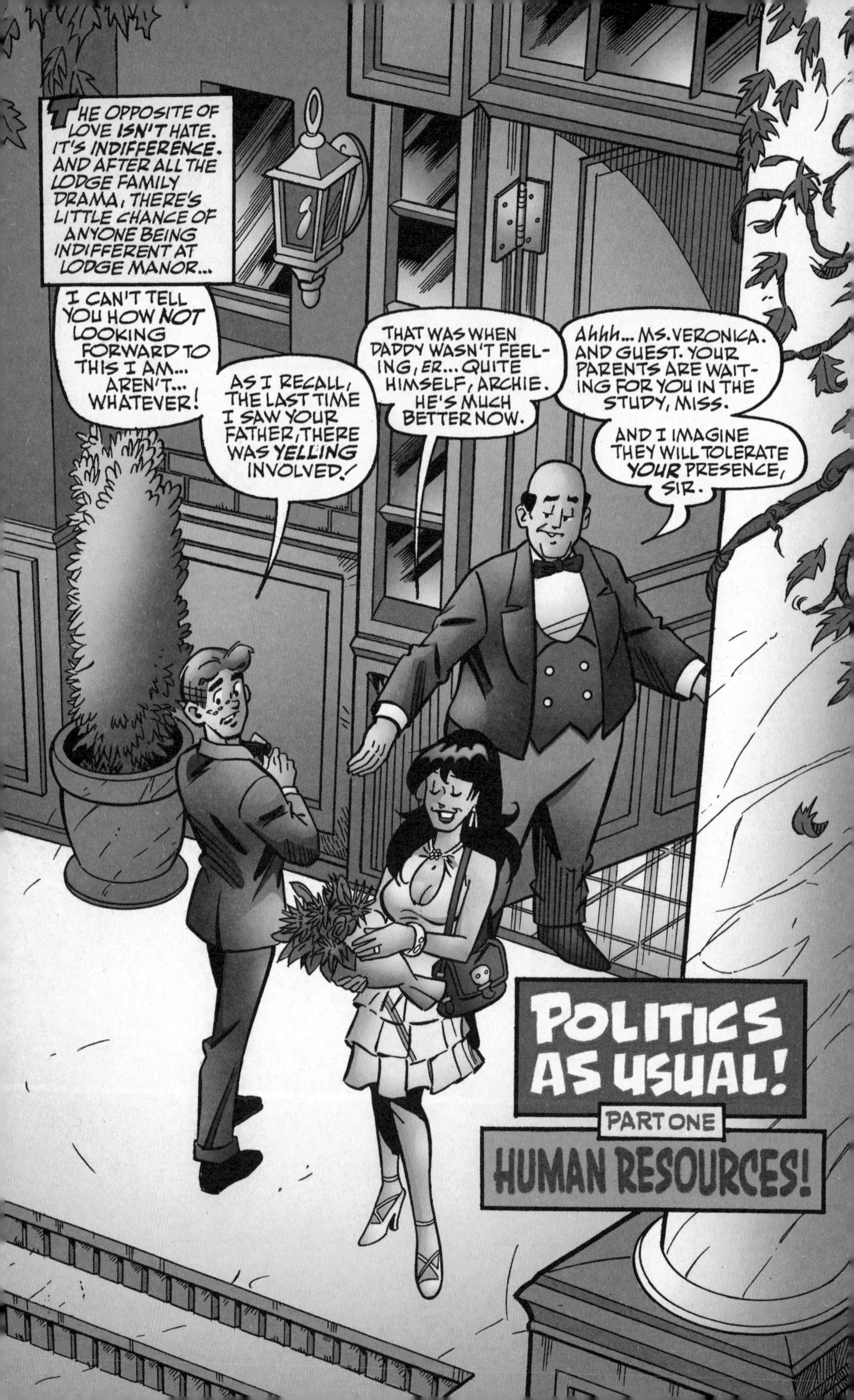
THE OPPOSITE OF LOVE ISN'T HATE. IT'S INDIFFERENCE. AND AFTER ALL THE LODGE FAMILY DRAMA, THERE'S LITTLE CHANCE OF ANYONE BEING INDIFFERENT AT LODGE MANOR...
I CAN'T TELL YOU HOW NOT LOOKING FORWARD TO THIS I AM... AREN'T... WHATEVER!
AS I RECALL, THE LAST TIME I SAW YOUR FATHER, THERE WAS YELLING INVOLVED!
THAT WAS WHEN DADDY WASN'T FEELING, ER... QUITE HIMSELF, ARCHIE. HE'S MUCH BETTER NOW.
Ahhh... MS. VERONICA. AND GUEST. YOUR PARENTS ARE WAITING FOR YOU IN THE STUDY, MISS.
AND I IMAGINE THEY WILL TOLERATE YOUR PRESENCE, SIR.
POLITICS AS USUAL!
PART ONE
HUMAN RESOURCES!

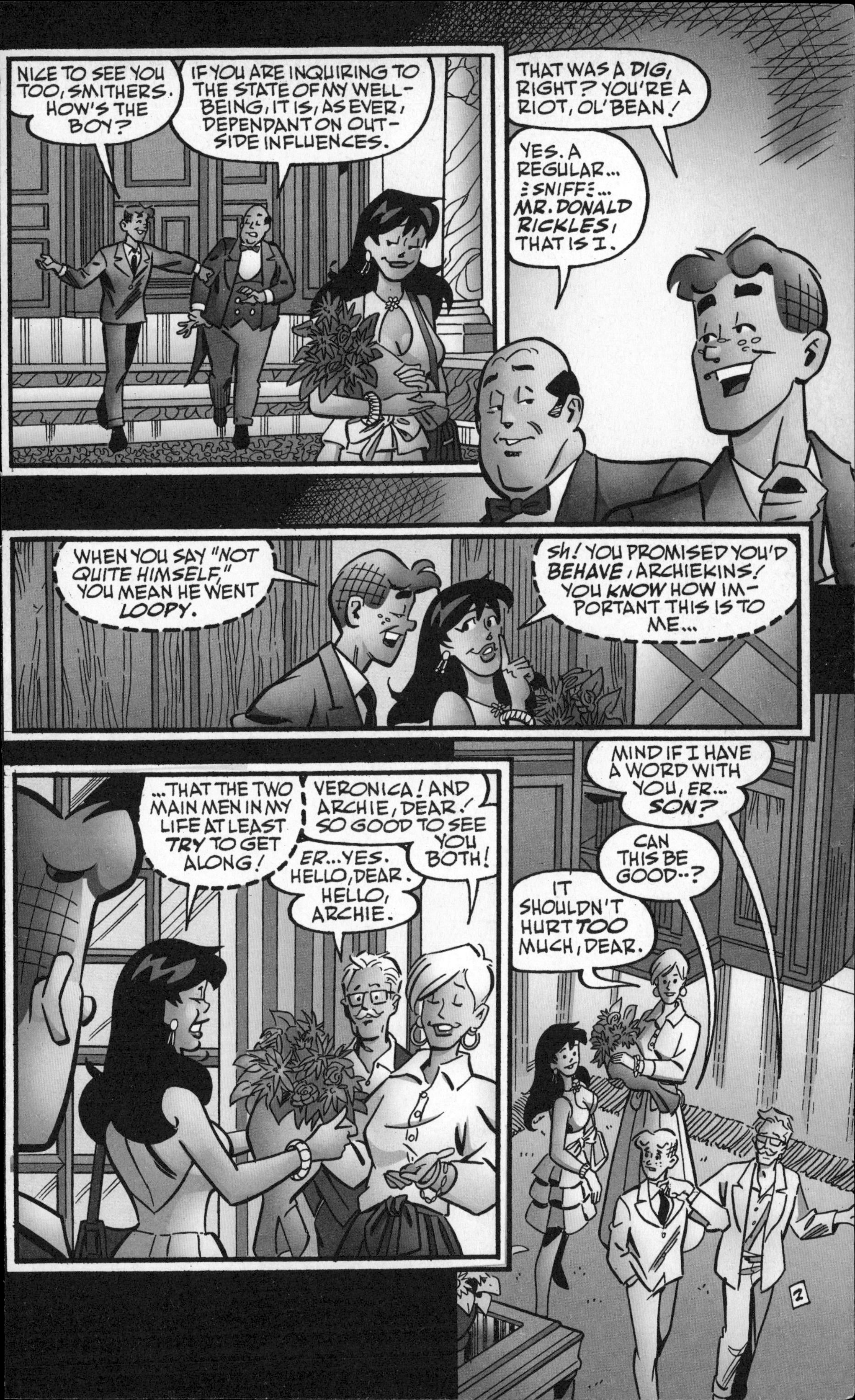
NICE TO SEE YOU TOO, SMITHERS. HOW'S THE BOY?
IF YOU ARE INQUIRING TO THE STATE OF MY WELL-BEING, IT IS, AS EVER, DEPENDANT ON OUTSIDE INFLUENCES.
THAT WAS A DIG, RIGHT? YOU'RE A RIOT, OL' BEAN!
YES. A REGULAR... SNIFF... MR. DONALD RICKLES, THAT IS I.
WHEN YOU SAY "NOT QUITE HIMSELF," YOU MEAN HE WENT LOOPY.
SH! YOU PROMISED YOU'D BEHAVE, ARCHIEKINS! YOU KNOW HOW IMPORTANT THIS IS TO ME...
...THAT THE TWO MAIN MEN IN MY LIFE AT LEAST TRY TO GET ALONG!
VERONICA! AND ARCHIE, DEAR! SO GOOD TO SEE YOU BOTH!
ER...YES. HELLO, DEAR. HELLO, ARCHIE.
MIND IF I HAVE A WORD WITH YOU, ER... SON?
CAN THIS BE GOOD..?
IT SHOULDN'T HURT TOO MUCH, DEAR.
2

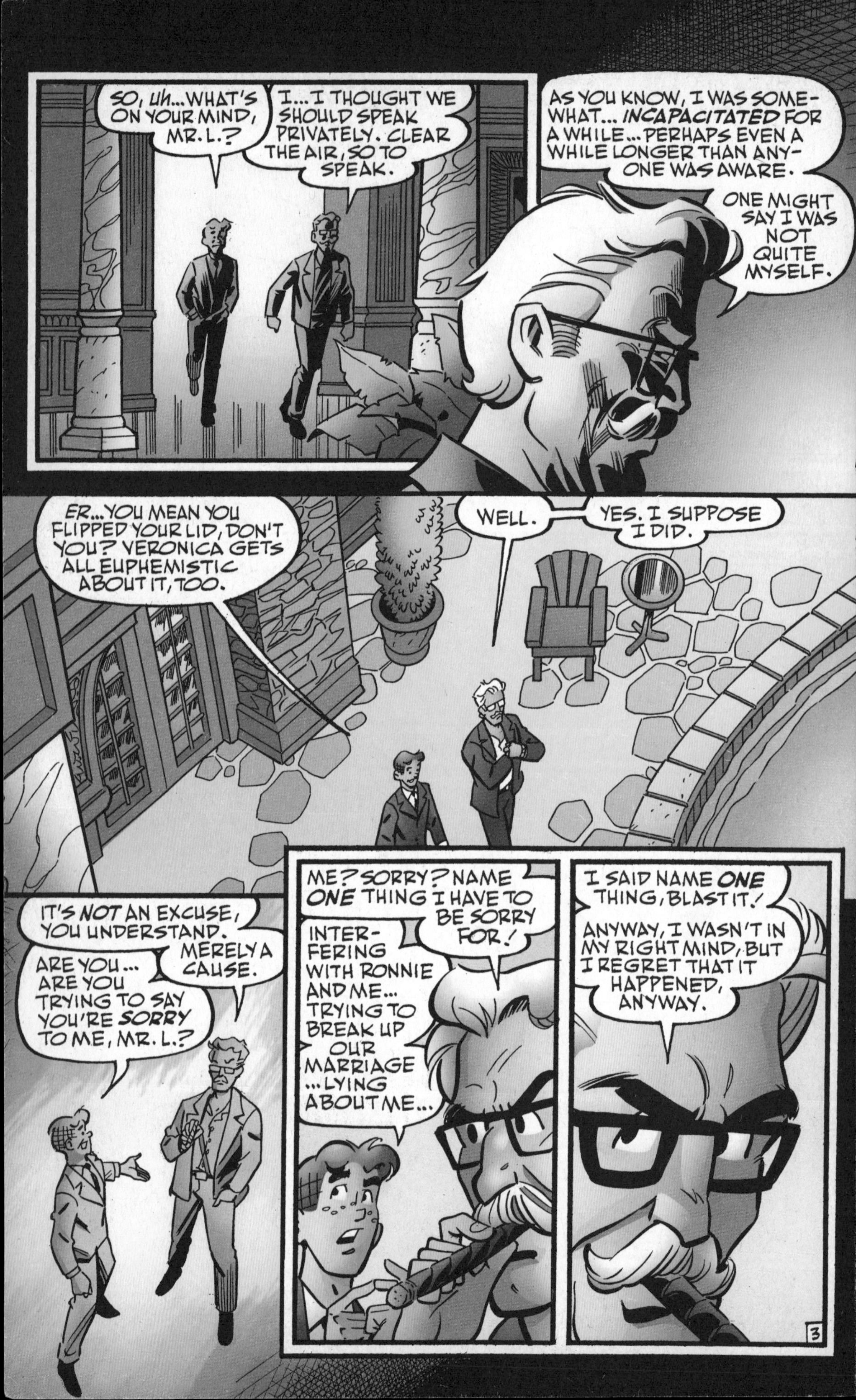
SO, UH...WHAT'S ON YOUR MIND, MR. L.?
I... I THOUGHT WE SHOULD SPEAK PRIVATELY. CLEAR THE AIR, SO TO SPEAK.
AS YOU KNOW, I WAS SOMEWHAT... *INCAPACITATED* FOR A WHILE... PERHAPS EVEN A WHILE LONGER THAN ANYONE WAS AWARE.
ONE MIGHT SAY I WAS NOT QUITE MYSELF.
ER...YOU MEAN YOU FLIPPED YOUR LID, DON'T YOU? VERONICA GETS ALL EUPHEMISTIC ABOUT IT, TOO.
WELL.
YES. I SUPPOSE I DID.
IT'S *NOT* AN EXCUSE, YOU UNDERSTAND.
MERELY A CAUSE.
ARE YOU... ARE YOU TRYING TO SAY YOU'RE *SORRY* TO ME, MR. L.?
ME? SORRY? NAME *ONE* THING I HAVE TO BE SORRY FOR!
INTERFERING WITH RONNIE AND ME... TRYING TO BREAK UP OUR MARRIAGE ...LYING ABOUT ME...
I SAID NAME *ONE* THING, BLAST IT!
ANYWAY, I WASN'T IN MY RIGHT MIND, BUT I REGRET THAT IT HAPPENED, ANYWAY.
3

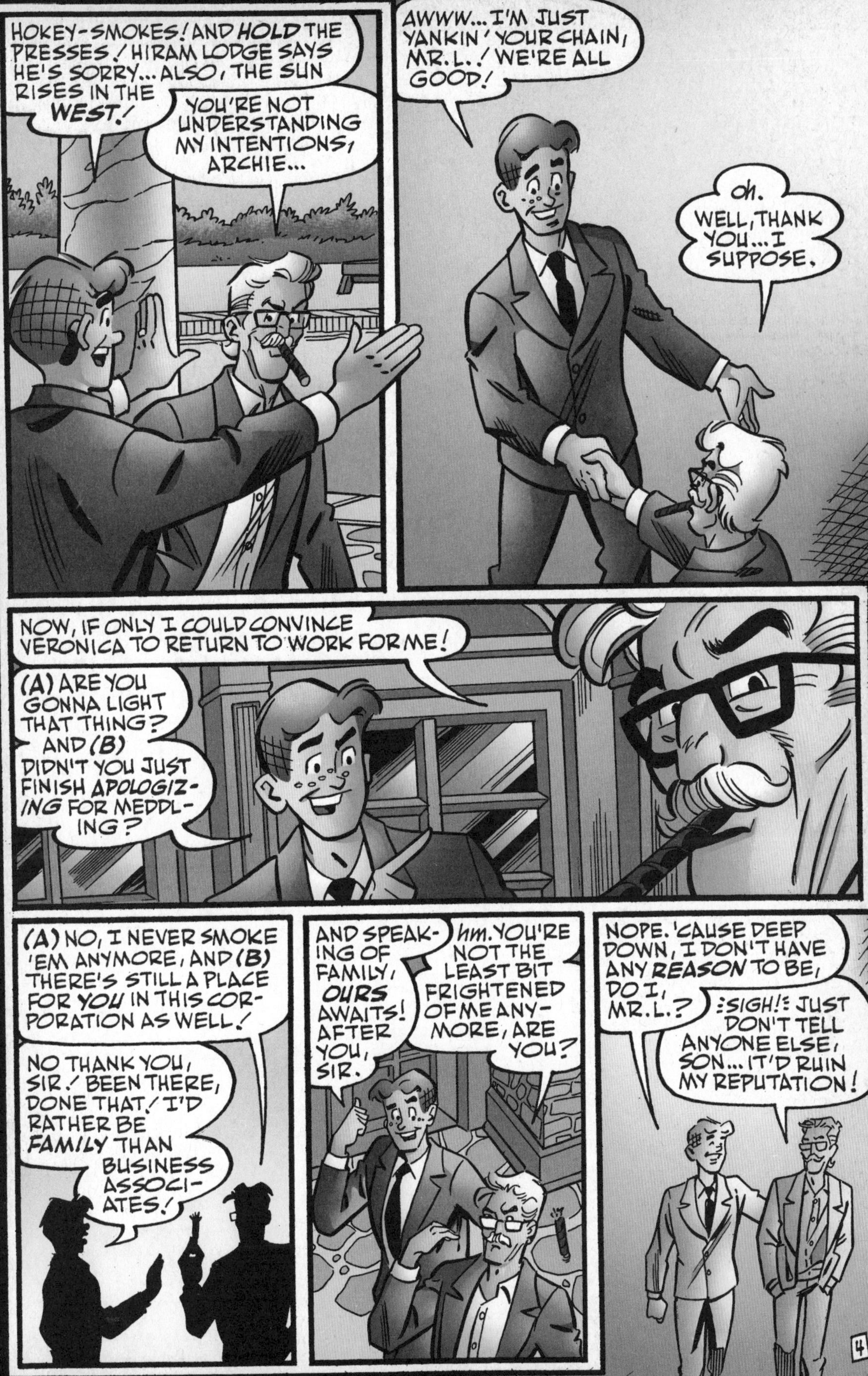

HOKEY-SMOKES! AND HOLD THE PRESSES! HIRAM LODGE SAYS HE'S SORRY... ALSO, THE SUN RISES IN THE WEST!
YOU'RE NOT UNDERSTANDING MY INTENTIONS, ARCHIE...
AWWW... I'M JUST YANKIN' YOUR CHAIN, MR. L.! WE'RE ALL GOOD!
oh. WELL, THANK YOU... I SUPPOSE.
NOW, IF ONLY I COULD CONVINCE VERONICA TO RETURN TO WORK FOR ME!
(A) ARE YOU GONNA LIGHT THAT THING? AND (B) DIDN'T YOU JUST FINISH APOLOGIZ-ING FOR MEDDL-ING?
(A) NO, I NEVER SMOKE 'EM ANYMORE, AND (B) THERE'S STILL A PLACE FOR YOU IN THIS COR-PORATION AS WELL!
NO THANK YOU, SIR! BEEN THERE, DONE THAT! I'D RATHER BE FAMILY THAN BUSINESS ASSOCI-ATES!
AND SPEAK-ING OF FAMILY, OURS AWAITS! AFTER YOU, SIR.
hm. YOU'RE NOT THE LEAST BIT FRIGHTENED OF ME ANY-MORE, ARE YOU?
NOPE. 'CAUSE DEEP DOWN, I DON'T HAVE ANY REASON TO BE, DO I, MR. L.?
:SIGH!: JUST DON'T TELL ANYONE ELSE, SON... IT'D RUIN MY REPUTATION!
4

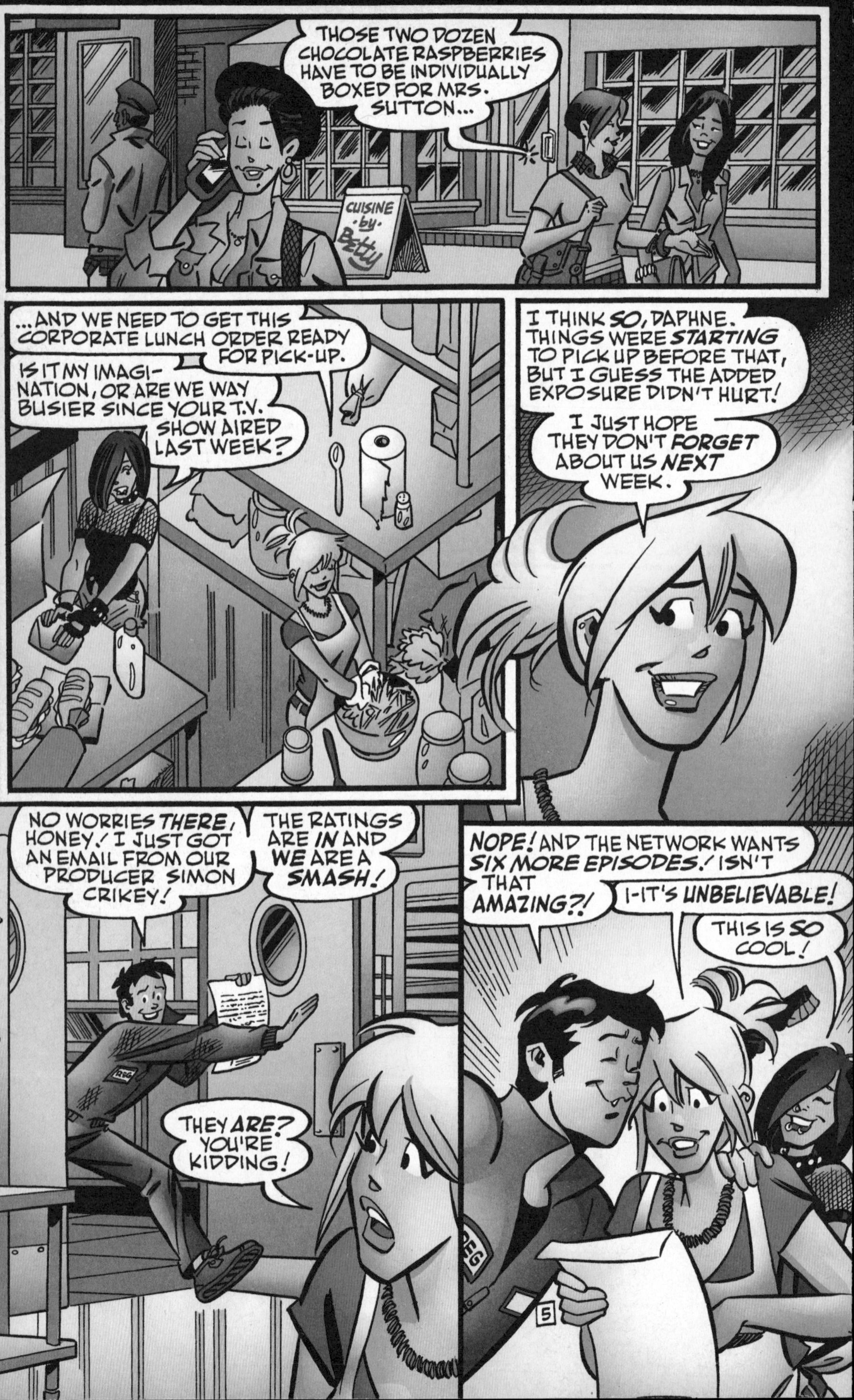
THOSE TWO DOZEN CHOCOLATE RASPBERRIES HAVE TO BE INDIVIDUALLY BOXED FOR MRS. SUTTON...
CUISINE ·by· Betty
...AND WE NEED TO GET THIS CORPORATE LUNCH ORDER READY FOR PICK-UP.
IS IT MY IMAGINATION, OR ARE WE WAY BUSIER SINCE YOUR T.V. SHOW AIRED LAST WEEK?
I THINK SO, DAPHNE. THINGS WERE STARTING TO PICK UP BEFORE THAT, BUT I GUESS THE ADDED EXPOSURE DIDN'T HURT!
I JUST HOPE THEY DON'T FORGET ABOUT US NEXT WEEK.
NO WORRIES THERE, HONEY! I JUST GOT AN EMAIL FROM OUR PRODUCER SIMON CRIKEY!
THE RATINGS ARE IN AND WE ARE A SMASH!
THEY ARE? YOU'RE KIDDING!
NOPE! AND THE NETWORK WANTS SIX MORE EPISODES! ISN'T THAT AMAZING?!
I-IT'S UNBELIEVABLE!
THIS IS SO COOL!
5

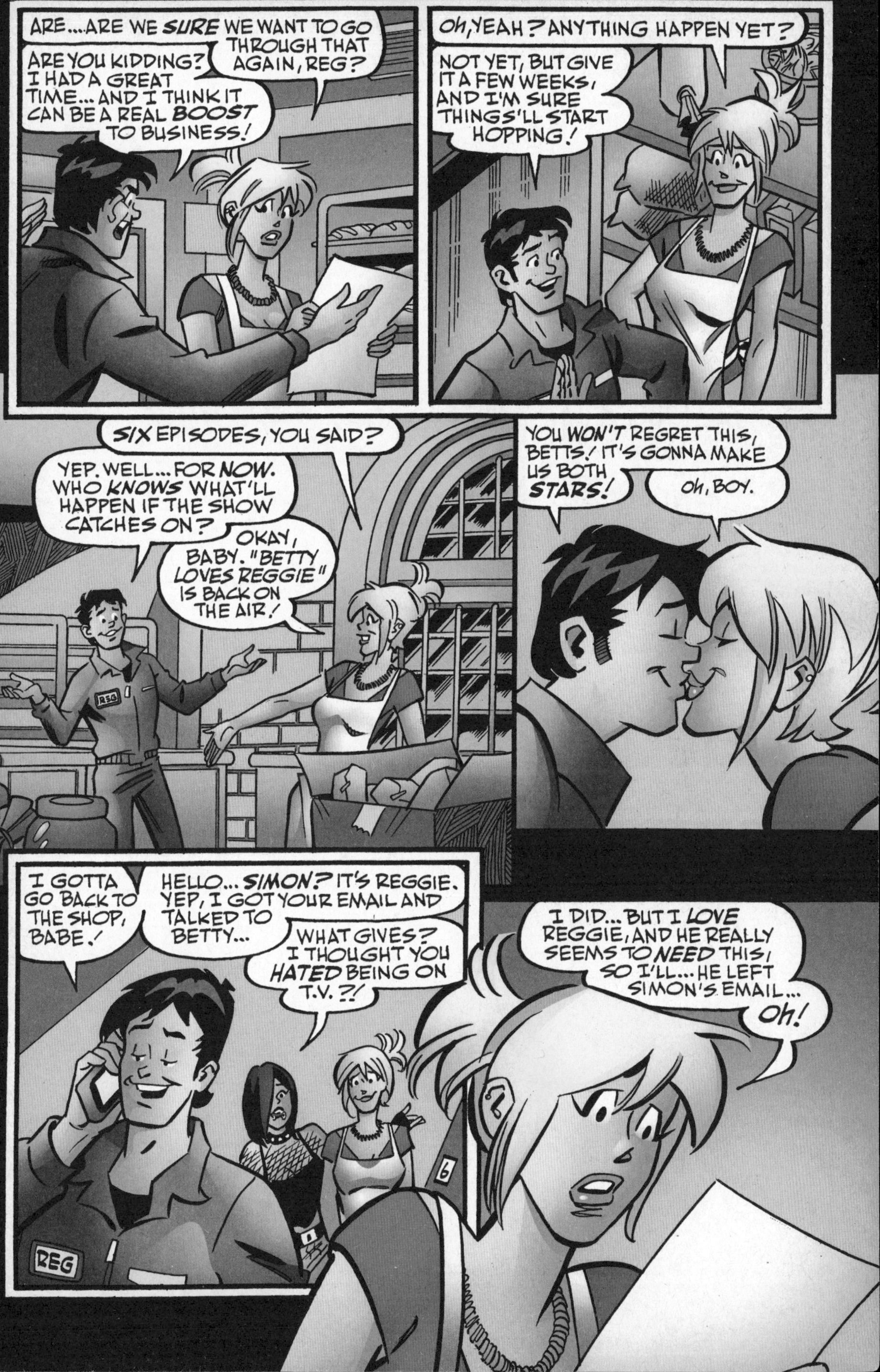

ARE...ARE WE SURE WE WANT TO GO THROUGH THAT AGAIN, REG?
ARE YOU KIDDING? I HAD A GREAT TIME... AND I THINK IT CAN BE A REAL BOOST TO BUSINESS!
OH, YEAH? ANYTHING HAPPEN YET?
NOT YET, BUT GIVE IT A FEW WEEKS, AND I'M SURE THINGS'LL START HOPPING!
SIX EPISODES, YOU SAID?
YEP. WELL... FOR NOW. WHO KNOWS WHAT'LL HAPPEN IF THE SHOW CATCHES ON?
OKAY, BABY. "BETTY LOVES REGGIE" IS BACK ON THE AIR!
REG
YOU WON'T REGRET THIS, BETTS! IT'S GONNA MAKE US BOTH STARS!
OH, BOY.
I GOTTA GO BACK TO THE SHOP, BABE!
HELLO... SIMON? IT'S REGGIE. YEP, I GOT YOUR EMAIL AND TALKED TO BETTY...
WHAT GIVES? I THOUGHT YOU HATED BEING ON T.V.?!
I DID... BUT I LOVE REGGIE, AND HE REALLY SEEMS TO NEED THIS, SO I'LL... HE LEFT SIMON'S EMAIL... OH!
6
REG

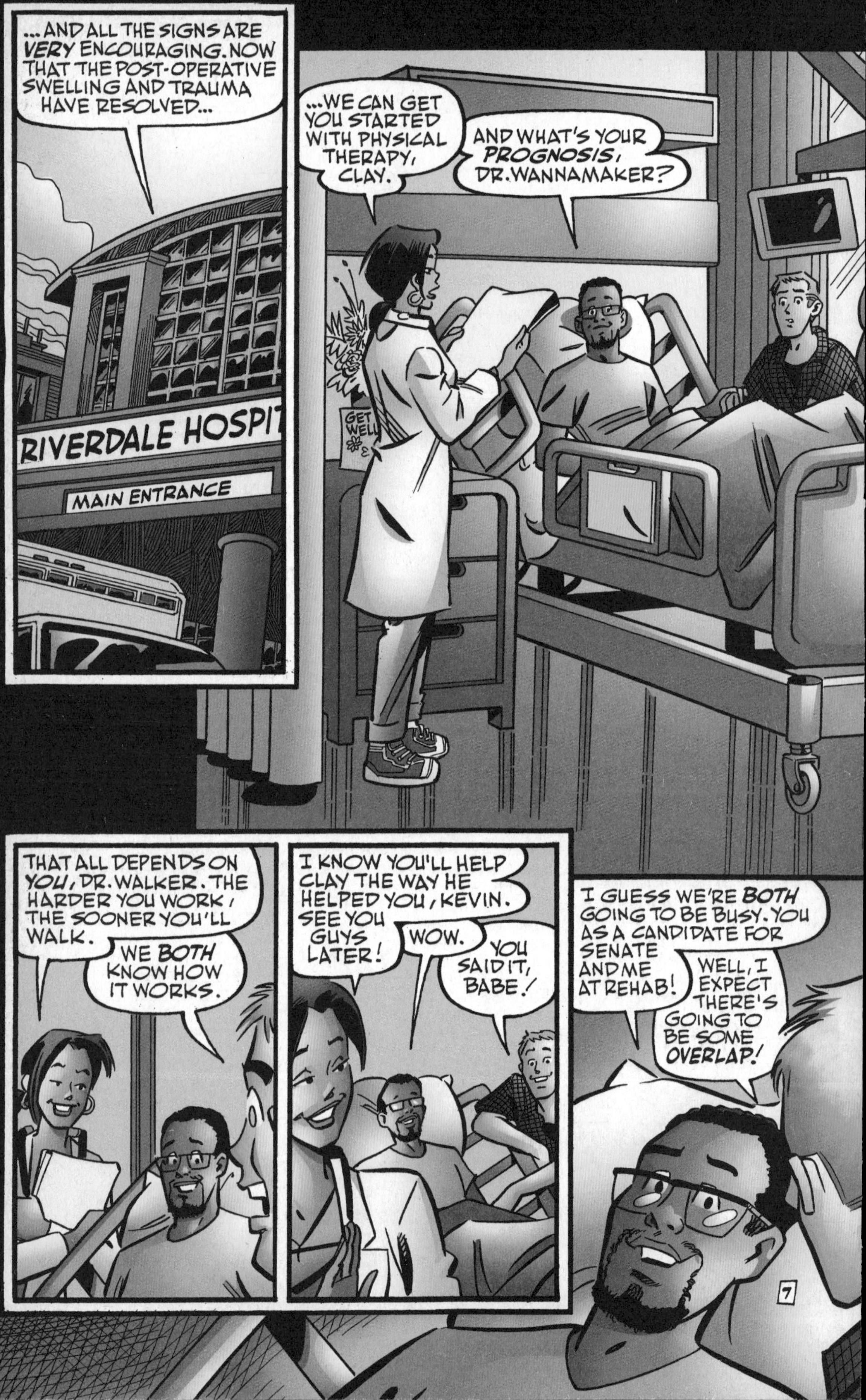
...AND ALL THE SIGNS ARE VERY ENCOURAGING. NOW THAT THE POST-OPERATIVE SWELLING AND TRAUMA HAVE RESOLVED...
RIVERDALE HOSPIT
MAIN ENTRANCE
...WE CAN GET YOU STARTED WITH PHYSICAL THERAPY, CLAY.
AND WHAT'S YOUR PROGNOSIS, DR. WANNAMAKER?
GET WELL
THAT ALL DEPENDS ON YOU, DR. WALKER. THE HARDER YOU WORK, THE SOONER YOU'LL WALK.
WE BOTH KNOW HOW IT WORKS.
I KNOW YOU'LL HELP CLAY THE WAY HE HELPED YOU, KEVIN. SEE YOU GUYS LATER!
WOW.
YOU SAID IT, BABE!
I GUESS WE'RE BOTH GOING TO BE BUSY. YOU AS A CANDIDATE FOR SENATE AND ME AT REHAB!
WELL, I EXPECT THERE'S GOING TO BE SOME OVERLAP!
7

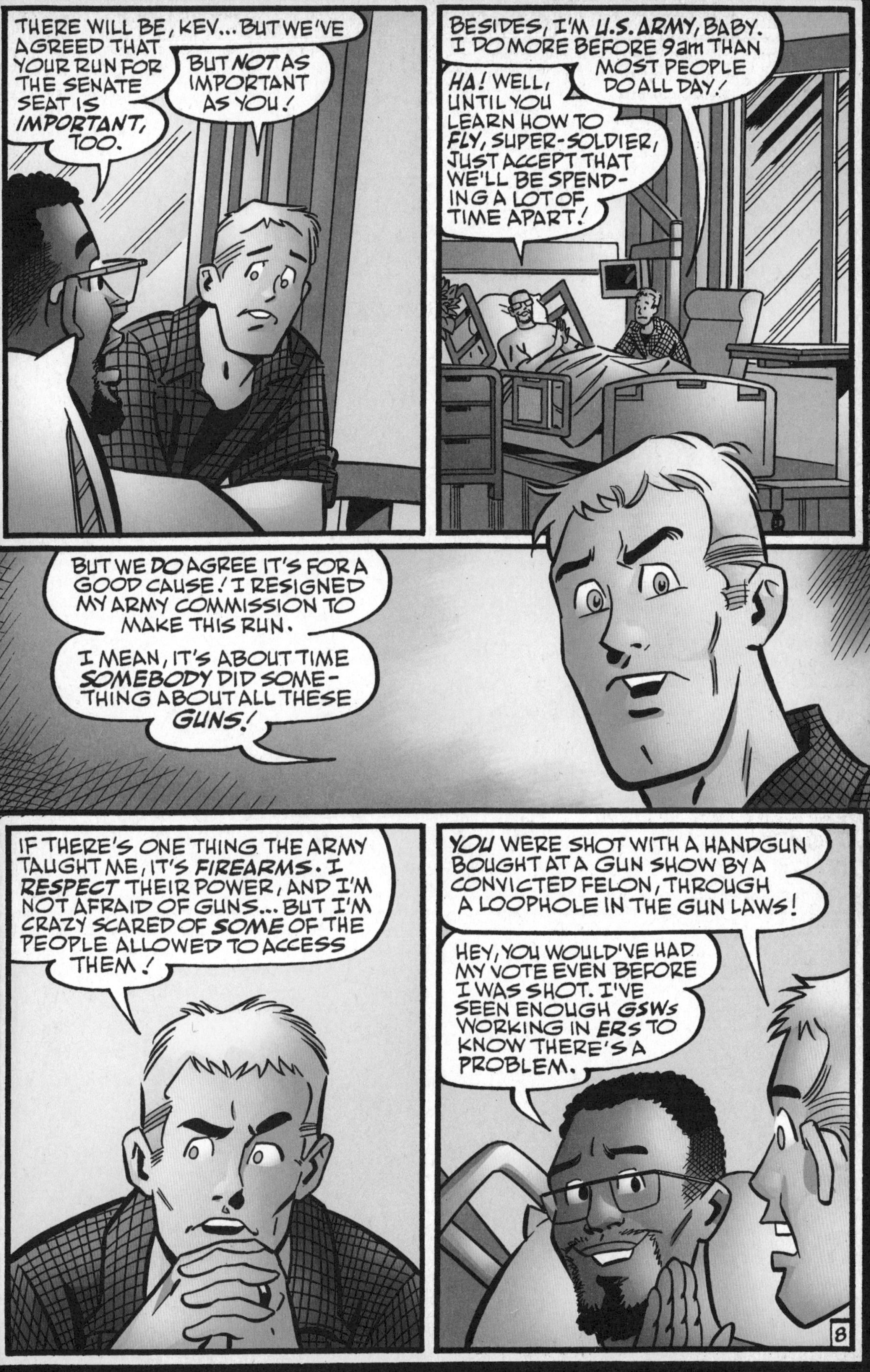
THERE WILL BE, KEV... BUT WE'VE AGREED THAT YOUR RUN FOR THE SENATE SEAT IS IMPORTANT, TOO.
BUT NOT AS IMPORTANT AS YOU!
BESIDES, I'M U.S. ARMY, BABY. I DO MORE BEFORE 9am THAN MOST PEOPLE DO ALL DAY!
HA! WELL, UNTIL YOU LEARN HOW TO FLY, SUPER-SOLDIER, JUST ACCEPT THAT WE'LL BE SPENDING A LOT OF TIME APART!
BUT WE DO AGREE IT'S FOR A GOOD CAUSE! I RESIGNED MY ARMY COMMISSION TO MAKE THIS RUN.
I MEAN, IT'S ABOUT TIME SOMEBODY DID SOMETHING ABOUT ALL THESE GUNS!
IF THERE'S ONE THING THE ARMY TAUGHT ME, IT'S FIREARMS. I RESPECT THEIR POWER, AND I'M NOT AFRAID OF GUNS... BUT I'M CRAZY SCARED OF SOME OF THE PEOPLE ALLOWED TO ACCESS THEM!
YOU WERE SHOT WITH A HANDGUN BOUGHT AT A GUN SHOW BY A CONVICTED FELON, THROUGH A LOOPHOLE IN THE GUN LAWS!
HEY, YOU WOULD'VE HAD MY VOTE EVEN BEFORE I WAS SHOT. I'VE SEEN ENOUGH GSWs WORKING IN ERs TO KNOW THERE'S A PROBLEM.
8

MAYBE IF MORE PEOPLE HAD TO SEE THAT, THEY'D BE A BIT MORE REASONABLE ABOUT GUNS.

I DON'T KNOW, KEVIN. PEOPLE FEEL PRETTY *STRONGLY* ABOUT THE ISSUE!

SO DO *I*. THE SECOND AMENDMENT SAYS GUNS ARE OKAY IN A *"WELL REGULATED MILITIA"* -- WHICH ARE THE MILITARY AND THE POLICE!

YES, DEAR.

SO WHY DO WE NEED AN ESTIMATED *200 MILLION* GUNS IN THE HANDS OF THIS COUNTRY'S *300 MILLION* CITIZENS?

Whoa! DON'T YOU THINK THE CROWD'S A LITTLE *SMALL* FOR A CAMPAIGN SPEECH?

Uh... YEAH, SORRY. GUESS I GOT CARRIED AWAY.

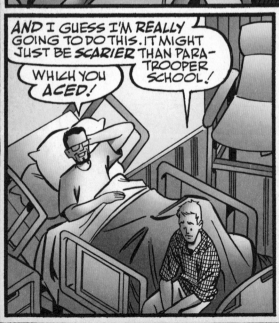

AND I GUESS I'M *REALLY* GOING TO DO THIS. IT MIGHT JUST BE *SCARIER* THAN PARATROOPER SCHOOL!

WHICH YOU *ACED!*

RIGHT! SO ALL WE NEED TO DO IS GET *YOU* BACK ON YOUR FEET AND *ME* ELECTED TO CONGRESS...

IS *THAT* ALL? *EASY!*

9

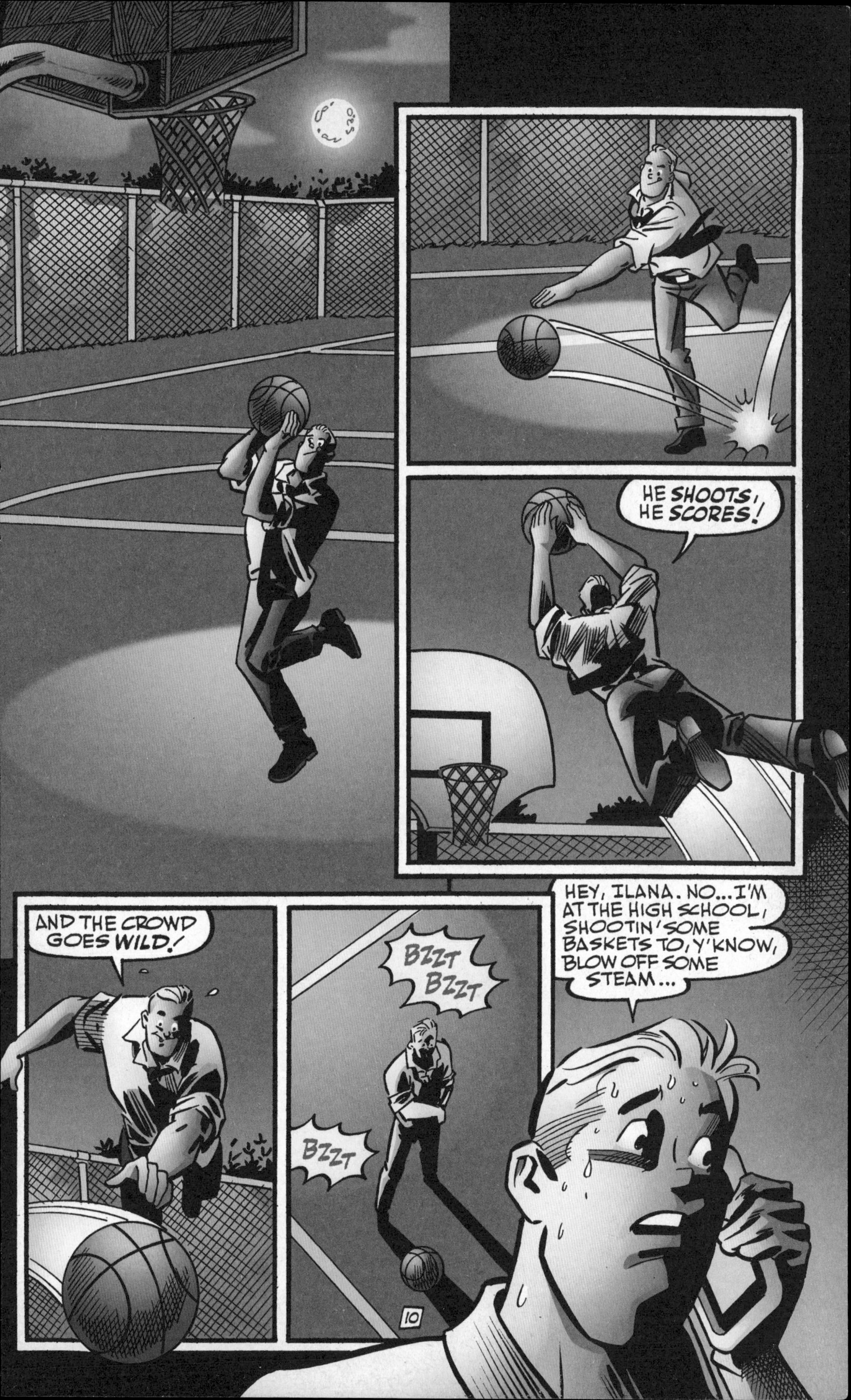
HE SHOOTS, HE SCORES!
AND THE CROWD GOES WILD!
BZZT BZZT
BZZT
HEY, ILANA. NO...I'M AT THE HIGH SCHOOL, SHOOTIN' SOME BASKETS TO, Y'KNOW, BLOW OFF SOME STEAM...
10

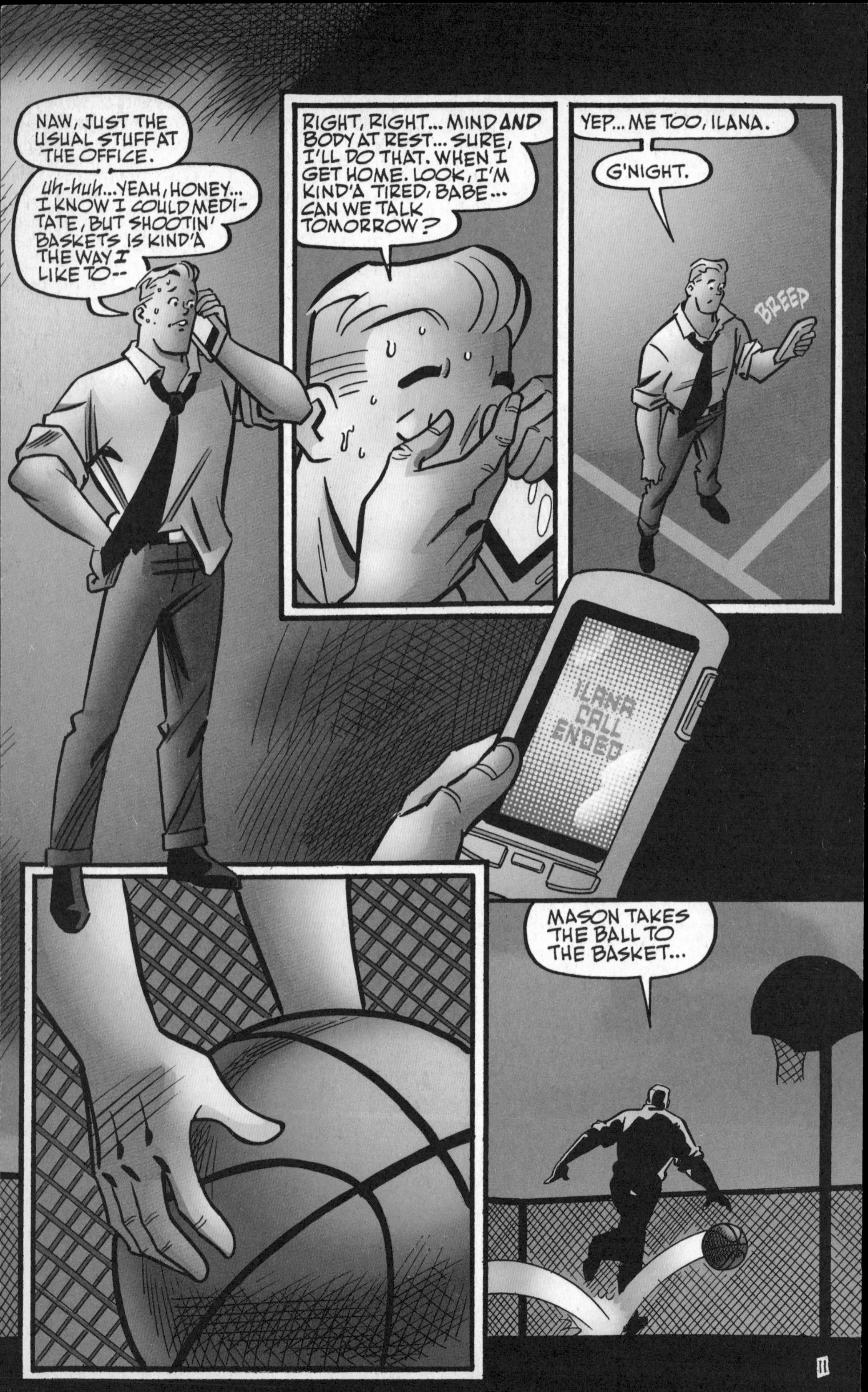
NAW, JUST THE USUAL STUFF AT THE OFFICE.
uh-huh... YEAH, HONEY... I KNOW I COULD MEDITATE, BUT SHOOTIN' BASKETS IS KIND'A THE WAY I LIKE TO--
RIGHT, RIGHT... MIND AND BODY AT REST... SURE, I'LL DO THAT. WHEN I GET HOME. LOOK, I'M KIND'A TIRED, BABE... CAN WE TALK TOMORROW?
YEP... ME TOO, ILANA.
G'NIGHT.
BREEP
ILANA CALL ENDED
MASON TAKES THE BALL TO THE BASKET...

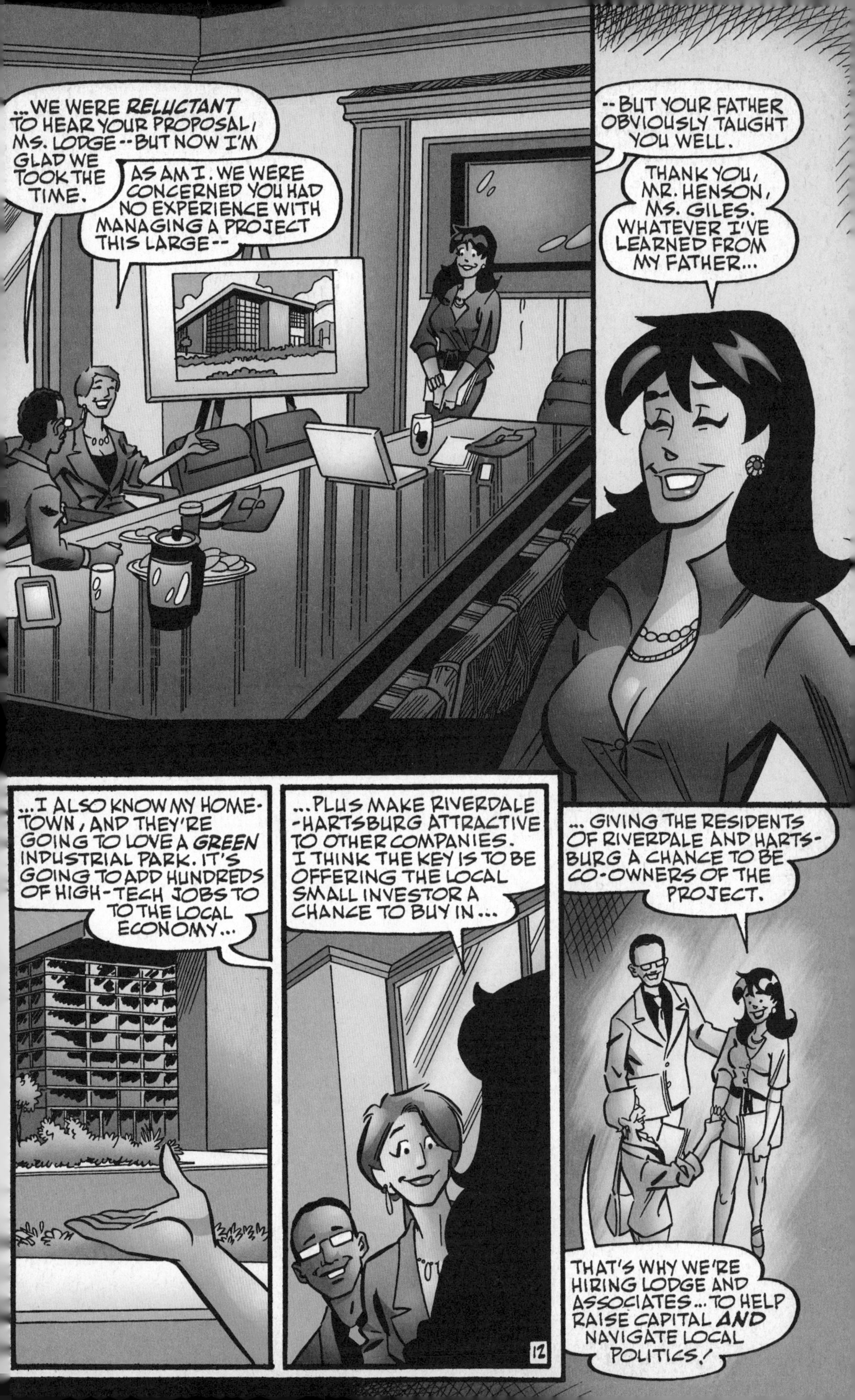
...WE WERE RELUCTANT TO HEAR YOUR PROPOSAL, MS. LODGE -- BUT NOW I'M GLAD WE TOOK THE TIME.
AS AM I. WE WERE CONCERNED YOU HAD NO EXPERIENCE WITH MANAGING A PROJECT THIS LARGE --
-- BUT YOUR FATHER OBVIOUSLY TAUGHT YOU WELL.
THANK YOU, MR. HENSON, MS. GILES. WHATEVER I'VE LEARNED FROM MY FATHER...
...I ALSO KNOW MY HOME-TOWN, AND THEY'RE GOING TO LOVE A GREEN INDUSTRIAL PARK. IT'S GOING TO ADD HUNDREDS OF HIGH-TECH JOBS TO TO THE LOCAL ECONOMY...
...PLUS MAKE RIVERDALE -HARTSBURG ATTRACTIVE TO OTHER COMPANIES. I THINK THE KEY IS TO BE OFFERING THE LOCAL SMALL INVESTOR A CHANCE TO BUY IN...
... GIVING THE RESIDENTS OF RIVERDALE AND HARTS-BURG A CHANCE TO BE CO-OWNERS OF THE PROJECT.
THAT'S WHY WE'RE HIRING LODGE AND ASSOCIATES... TO HELP RAISE CAPITAL AND NAVIGATE LOCAL POLITICS!

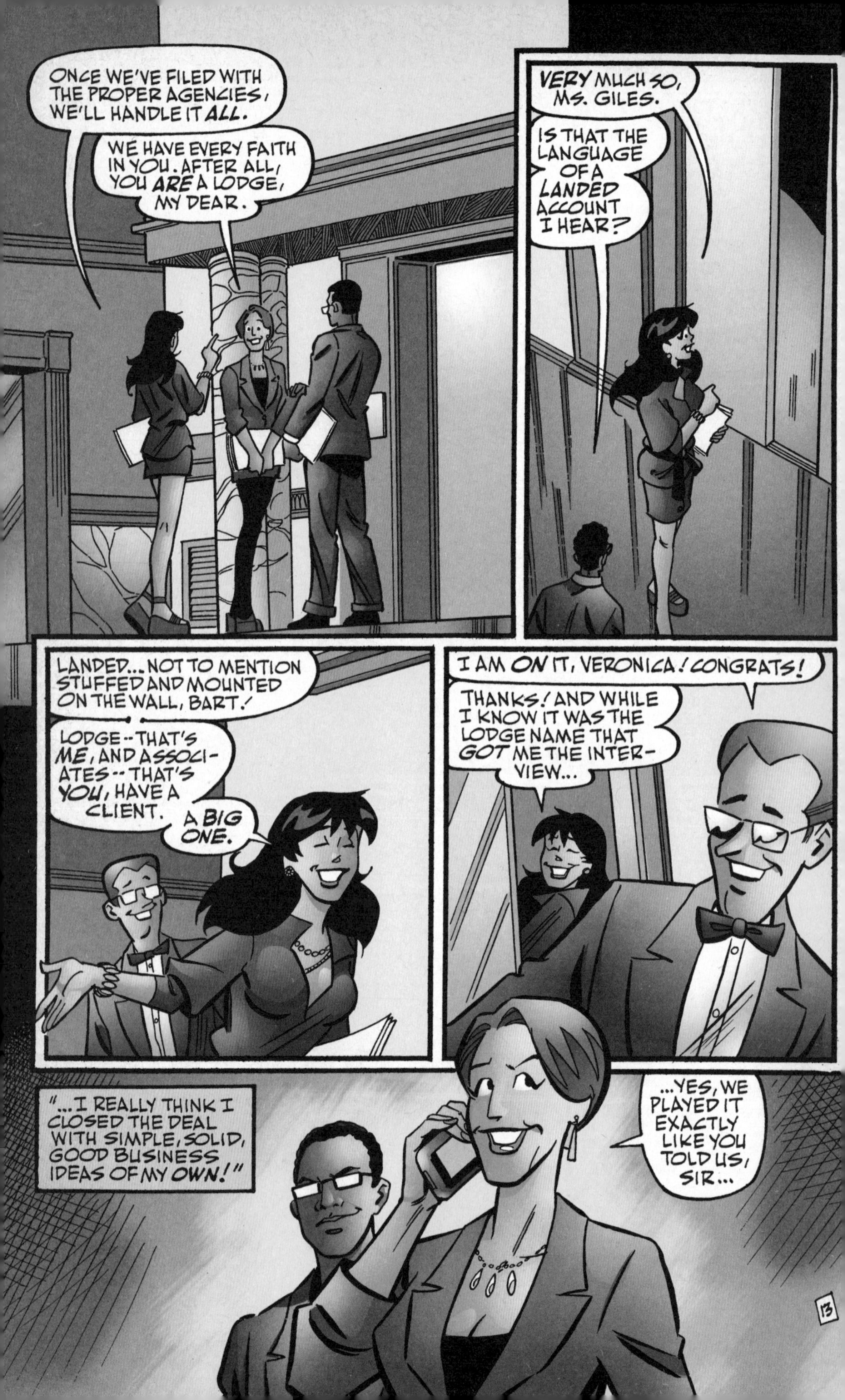
ONCE WE'VE FILED WITH THE PROPER AGENCIES, WE'LL HANDLE IT ALL.
WE HAVE EVERY FAITH IN YOU. AFTER ALL, YOU ARE A LODGE, MY DEAR.
VERY MUCH SO, MS. GILES.
IS THAT THE LANGUAGE OF A LANDED ACCOUNT I HEAR?
LANDED... NOT TO MENTION STUFFED AND MOUNTED ON THE WALL, BART!
LODGE--THAT'S ME, AND ASSOCIATES--THAT'S YOU, HAVE A CLIENT.
A BIG ONE.
I AM ON IT, VERONICA! CONGRATS!
THANKS! AND WHILE I KNOW IT WAS THE LODGE NAME THAT GOT ME THE INTERVIEW...
"...I REALLY THINK I CLOSED THE DEAL WITH SIMPLE, SOLID, GOOD BUSINESS IDEAS OF MY OWN!"
...YES, WE PLAYED IT EXACTLY LIKE YOU TOLD US, SIR...

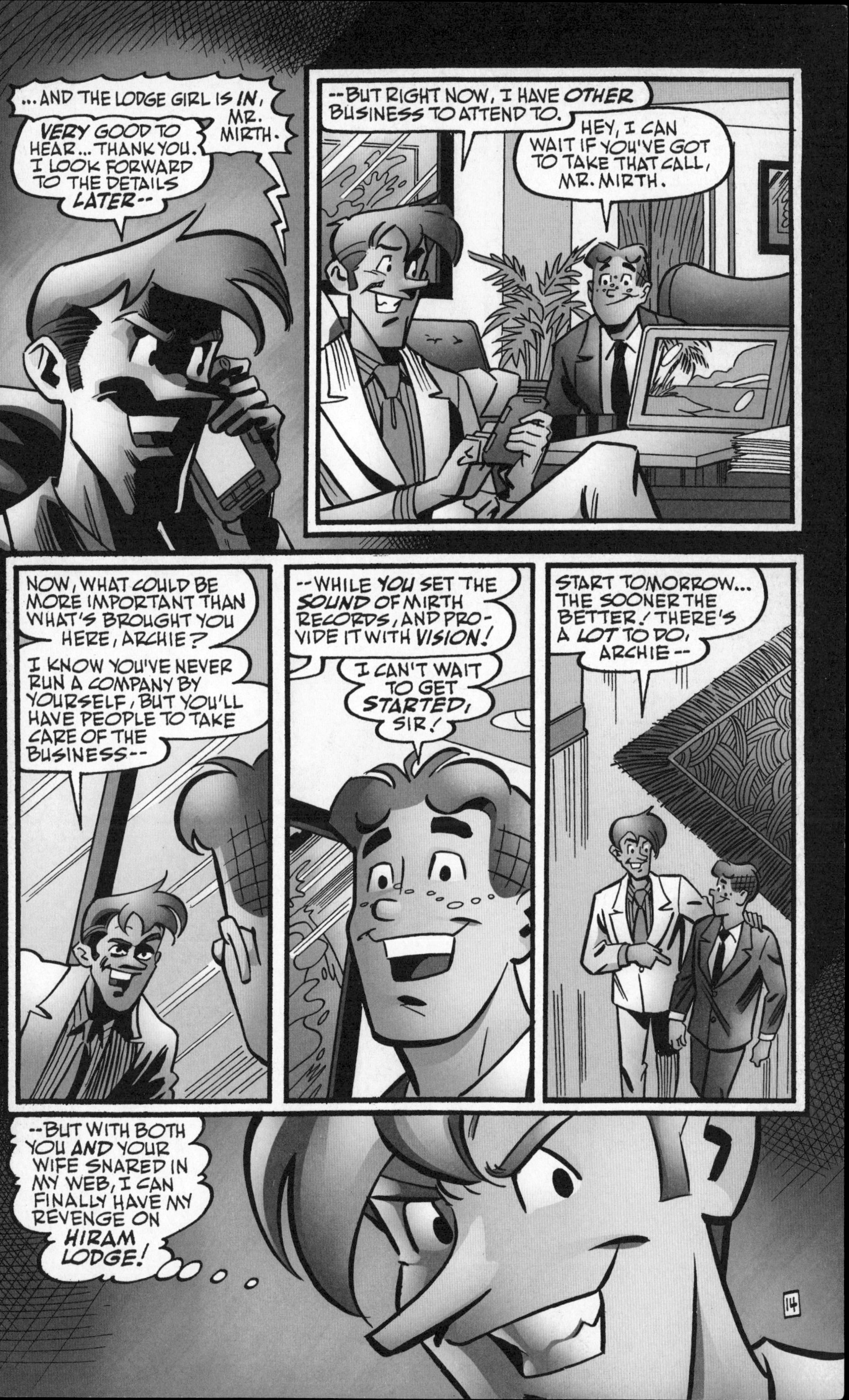
...AND THE LODGE GIRL IS IN, MR. MIRTH.
VERY GOOD TO HEAR... THANK YOU. I LOOK FORWARD TO THE DETAILS LATER--
--BUT RIGHT NOW, I HAVE OTHER BUSINESS TO ATTEND TO.
HEY, I CAN WAIT IF YOU'VE GOT TO TAKE THAT CALL, MR. MIRTH.
NOW, WHAT COULD BE MORE IMPORTANT THAN WHAT'S BROUGHT YOU HERE, ARCHIE?
I KNOW YOU'VE NEVER RUN A COMPANY BY YOURSELF, BUT YOU'LL HAVE PEOPLE TO TAKE CARE OF THE BUSINESS--
--WHILE YOU SET THE SOUND OF MIRTH RECORDS, AND PROVIDE IT WITH VISION!
I CAN'T WAIT TO GET STARTED, SIR!
START TOMORROW... THE SOONER THE BETTER! THERE'S A LOT TO DO, ARCHIE--
--BUT WITH BOTH YOU AND YOUR WIFE SNARED IN MY WEB, I CAN FINALLY HAVE MY REVENGE ON HIRAM LODGE!
14

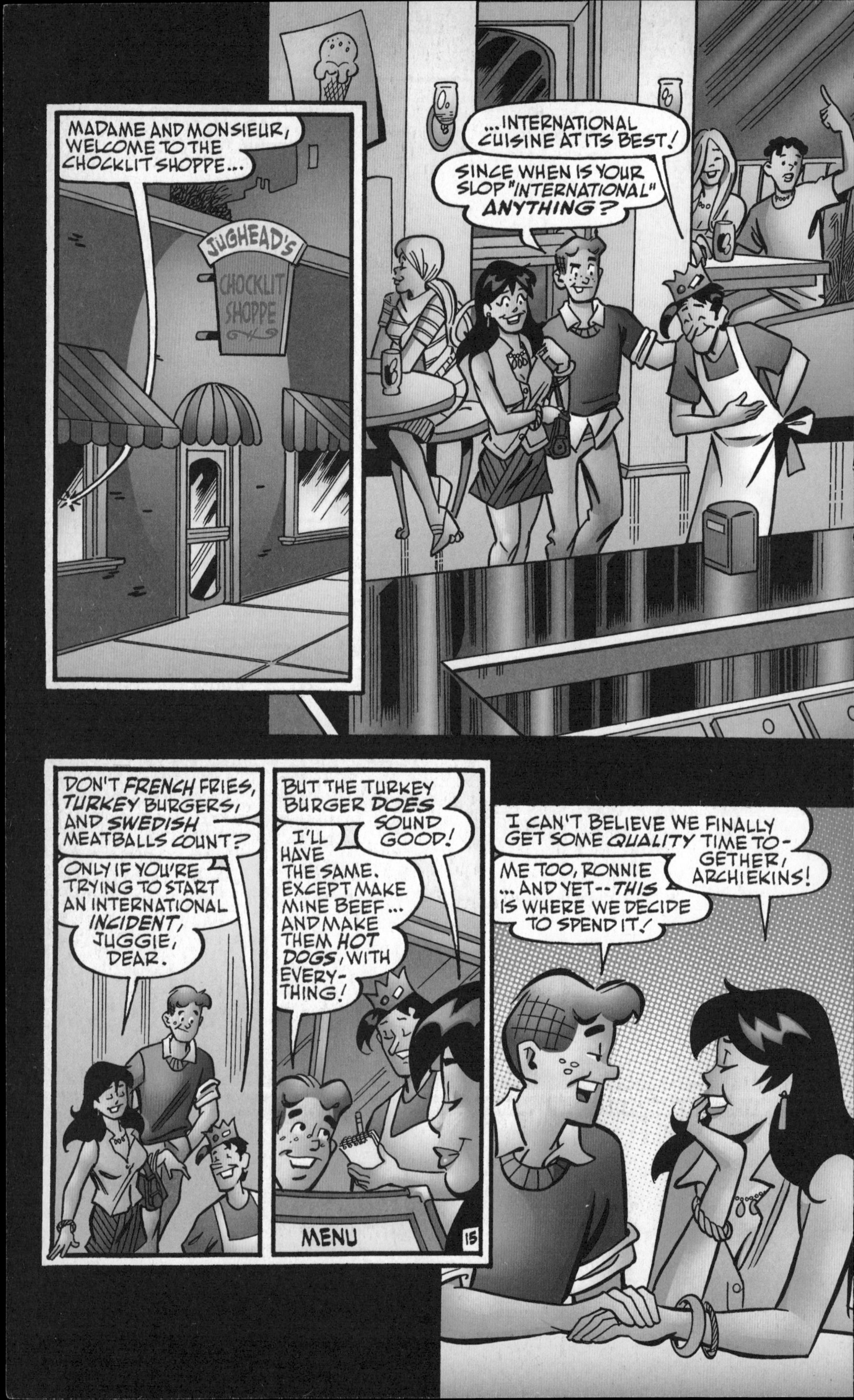
MADAME AND MONSIEUR, WELCOME TO THE CHOCKLIT SHOPPE...
JUGHEAD'S
CHOCKLIT SHOPPE
...INTERNATIONAL CUISINE AT ITS BEST!
SINCE WHEN IS YOUR SLOP "INTERNATIONAL" ANYTHING?
DON'T FRENCH FRIES, TURKEY BURGERS, AND SWEDISH MEATBALLS COUNT?
ONLY IF YOU'RE TRYING TO START AN INTERNATIONAL INCIDENT, JUGGIE, DEAR.
BUT THE TURKEY BURGER DOES SOUND GOOD!
I'LL HAVE THE SAME. EXCEPT MAKE MINE BEEF... AND MAKE THEM HOT DOGS, WITH EVERY-THING!
MENU
15
I CAN'T BELIEVE WE FINALLY GET SOME QUALITY TIME TO-GETHER, ARCHIEKINS!
ME TOO, RONNIE ...AND YET--THIS IS WHERE WE DECIDE TO SPEND IT!

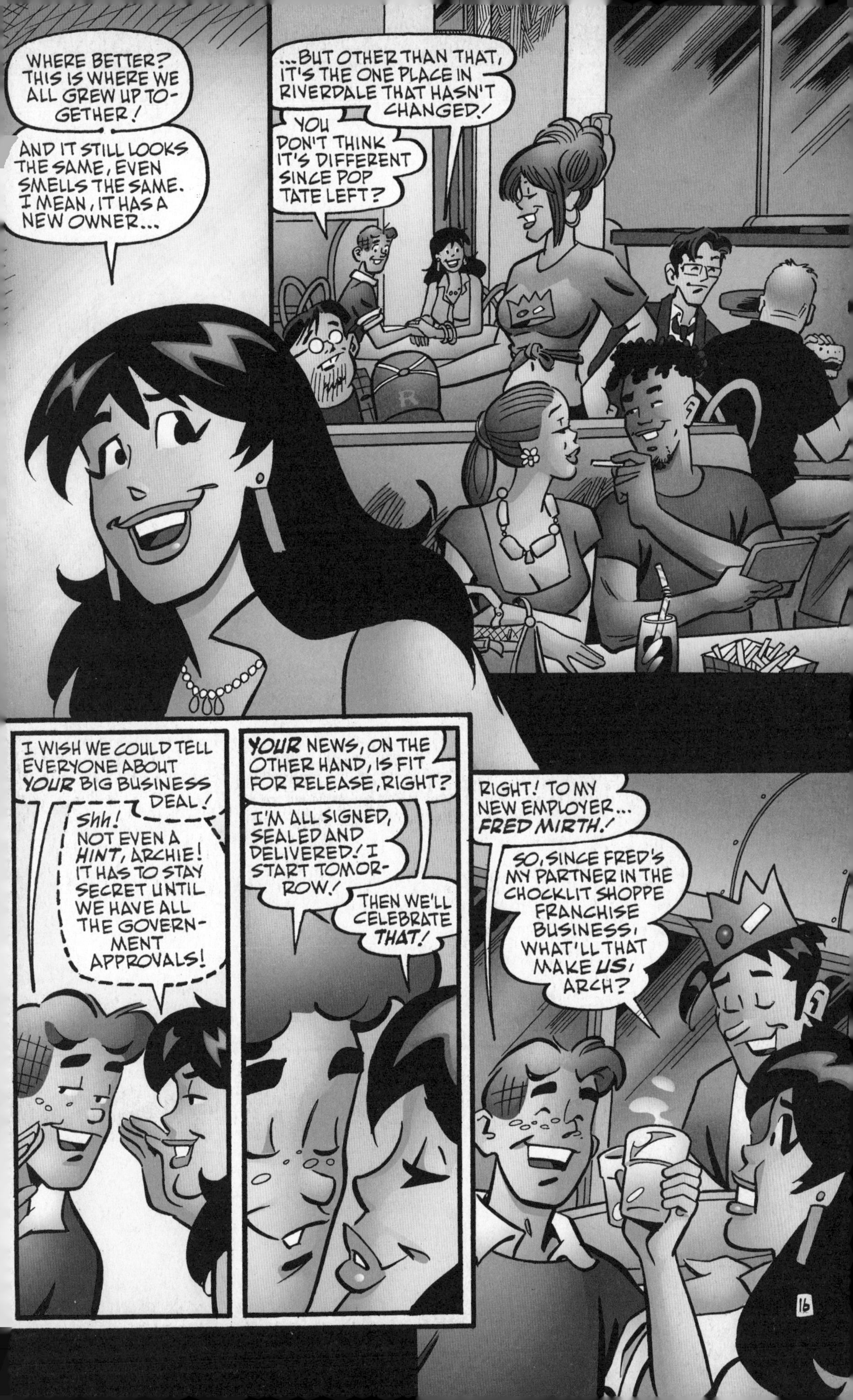
WHERE BETTER? THIS IS WHERE WE ALL GREW UP TOGETHER!
AND IT STILL LOOKS THE SAME, EVEN SMELLS THE SAME. I MEAN, IT HAS A NEW OWNER...
...BUT OTHER THAN THAT, IT'S THE ONE PLACE IN RIVERDALE THAT HASN'T CHANGED!
YOU DON'T THINK IT'S DIFFERENT SINCE POP TATE LEFT?
I WISH WE COULD TELL EVERYONE ABOUT YOUR BIG BUSINESS DEAL!
Shh! NOT EVEN A HINT, ARCHIE! IT HAS TO STAY SECRET UNTIL WE HAVE ALL THE GOVERNMENT APPROVALS!
YOUR NEWS, ON THE OTHER HAND, IS FIT FOR RELEASE, RIGHT?
I'M ALL SIGNED, SEALED AND DELIVERED! I START TOMORROW!
THEN WE'LL CELEBRATE THAT!
RIGHT! TO MY NEW EMPLOYER... FRED MIRTH!
SO, SINCE FRED'S MY PARTNER IN THE CHOCKLIT SHOPPE FRANCHISE BUSINESS, WHAT'LL THAT MAKE US, ARCH?
16

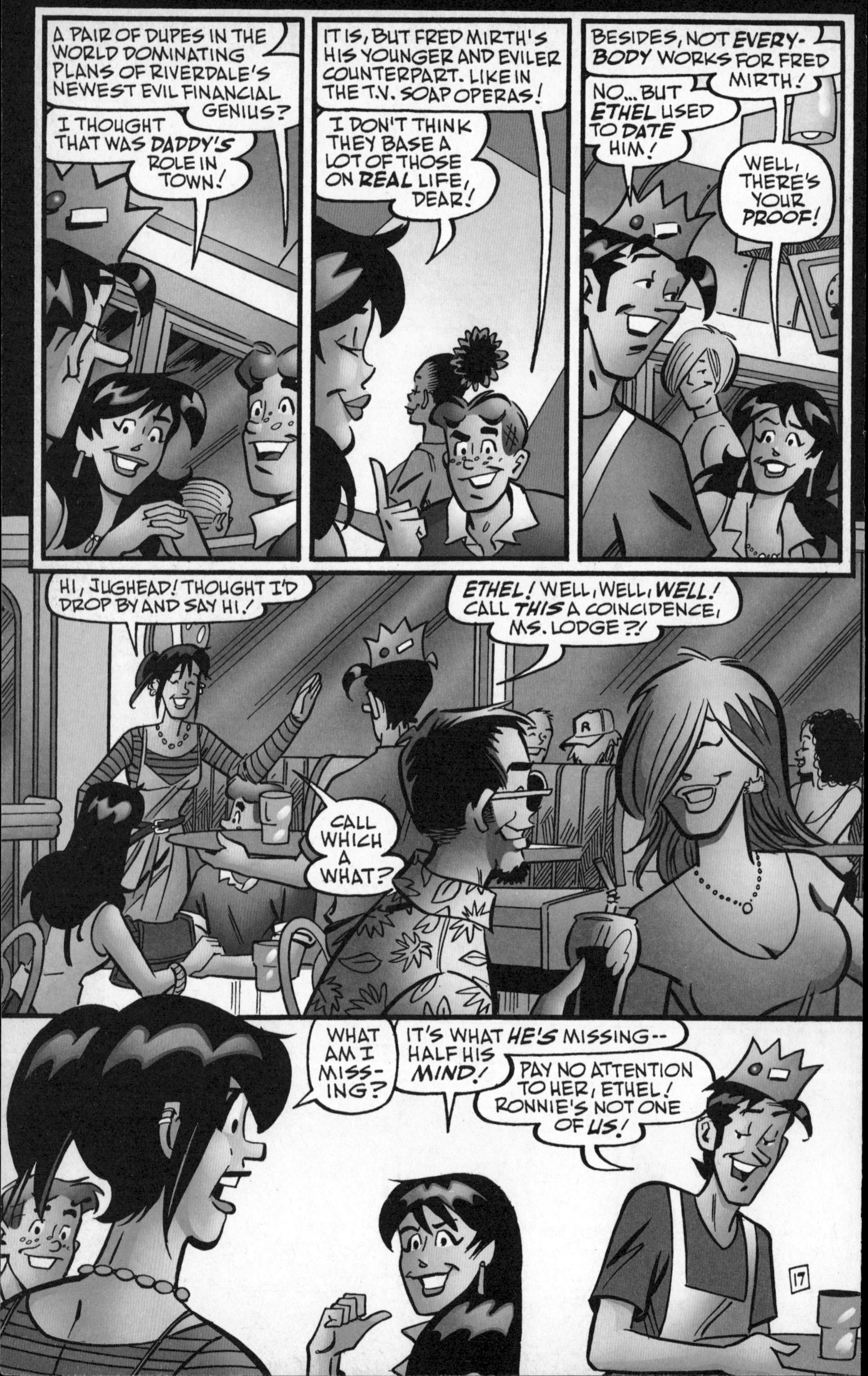

A PAIR OF DUPES IN THE WORLD DOMINATING PLANS OF RIVERDALE'S NEWEST EVIL FINANCIAL GENIUS?
I THOUGHT THAT WAS DADDY'S ROLE IN TOWN!
IT IS, BUT FRED MIRTH'S HIS YOUNGER AND EVILER COUNTERPART. LIKE IN THE T.V. SOAP OPERAS!
I DON'T THINK THEY BASE A LOT OF THOSE ON REAL LIFE, DEAR!
BESIDES, NOT EVERY-BODY WORKS FOR FRED MIRTH!
NO... BUT ETHEL USED TO DATE HIM!
WELL, THERE'S YOUR PROOF!
HI, JUGHEAD! THOUGHT I'D DROP BY AND SAY HI!
ETHEL! WELL, WELL, WELL! CALL THIS A COINCIDENCE, MS. LODGE?!
CALL WHICH A WHAT?
WHAT AM I MISS-ING?
IT'S WHAT HE'S MISSING-- HALF HIS MIND!
PAY NO ATTENTION TO HER, ETHEL! RONNIE'S NOT ONE OF US!
17

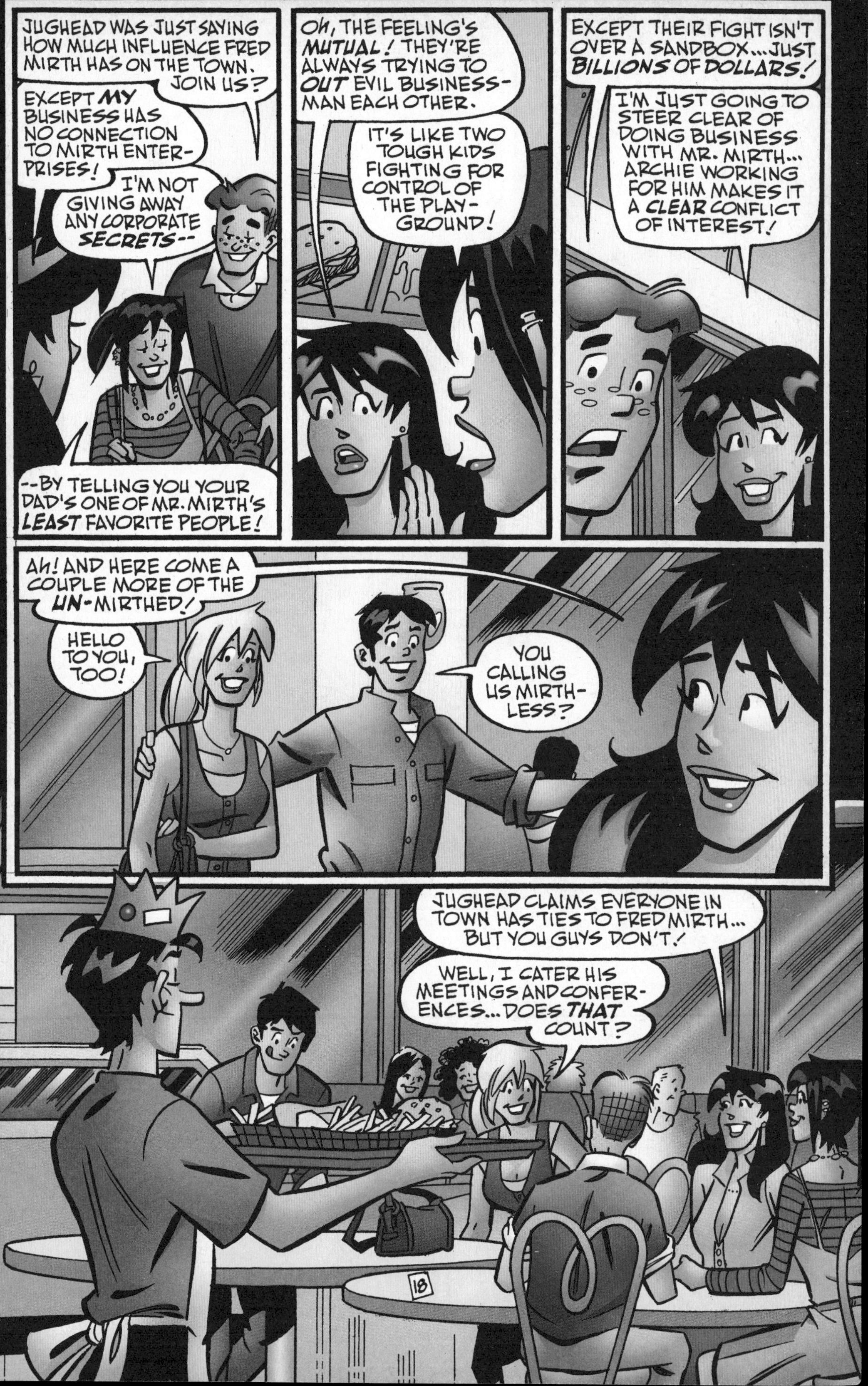
JUGHEAD WAS JUST SAYING HOW MUCH INFLUENCE FRED MIRTH HAS ON THE TOWN. JOIN US?
EXCEPT MY BUSINESS HAS NO CONNECTION TO MIRTH ENTER-PRISES!
I'M NOT GIVING AWAY ANY CORPORATE SECRETS--
--BY TELLING YOU YOUR DAD'S ONE OF MR. MIRTH'S LEAST FAVORITE PEOPLE!
OH, THE FEELING'S MUTUAL! THEY'RE ALWAYS TRYING TO OUT EVIL BUSINESS-MAN EACH OTHER.
IT'S LIKE TWO TOUGH KIDS FIGHTING FOR CONTROL OF THE PLAY-GROUND!
EXCEPT THEIR FIGHT ISN'T OVER A SANDBOX... JUST BILLIONS OF DOLLARS!
I'M JUST GOING TO STEER CLEAR OF DOING BUSINESS WITH MR. MIRTH... ARCHIE WORKING FOR HIM MAKES IT A CLEAR CONFLICT OF INTEREST!
AH! AND HERE COME A COUPLE MORE OF THE UN-MIRTHED!
HELLO TO YOU, TOO!
YOU CALLING US MIRTH-LESS?
JUGHEAD CLAIMS EVERYONE IN TOWN HAS TIES TO FRED MIRTH... BUT YOU GUYS DON'T!
WELL, I CATER HIS MEETINGS AND CONFER-ENCES... DOES THAT COUNT?
18

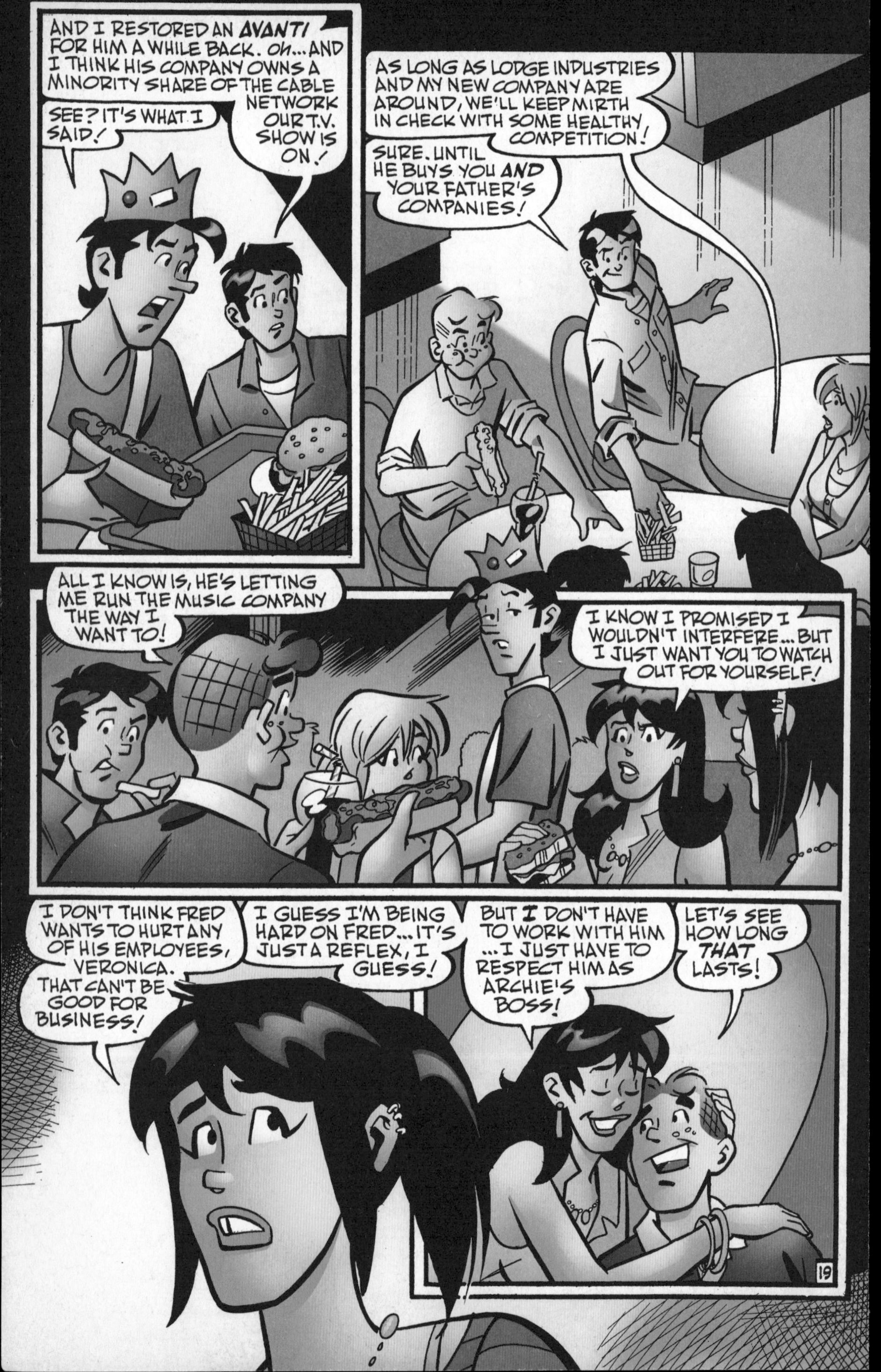
AND I RESTORED AN AVANTI FOR HIM A WHILE BACK. OH... AND I THINK HIS COMPANY OWNS A MINORITY SHARE OF THE CABLE NETWORK OUR T.V. SHOW IS ON!
SEE? IT'S WHAT I SAID!
AS LONG AS LODGE INDUSTRIES AND MY NEW COMPANY ARE AROUND, WE'LL KEEP MIRTH IN CHECK WITH SOME HEALTHY COMPETITION!
SURE. UNTIL HE BUYS YOU AND YOUR FATHER'S COMPANIES!
ALL I KNOW IS, HE'S LETTING ME RUN THE MUSIC COMPANY THE WAY I WANT TO!
I KNOW I PROMISED I WOULDN'T INTERFERE... BUT I JUST WANT YOU TO WATCH OUT FOR YOURSELF!
I DON'T THINK FRED WANTS TO HURT ANY OF HIS EMPLOYEES, VERONICA. THAT CAN'T BE GOOD FOR BUSINESS!
I GUESS I'M BEING HARD ON FRED... IT'S JUST A REFLEX, I GUESS!
BUT I DON'T HAVE TO WORK WITH HIM ...I JUST HAVE TO RESPECT HIM AS ARCHIE'S BOSS!
LET'S SEE HOW LONG THAT LASTS!
19

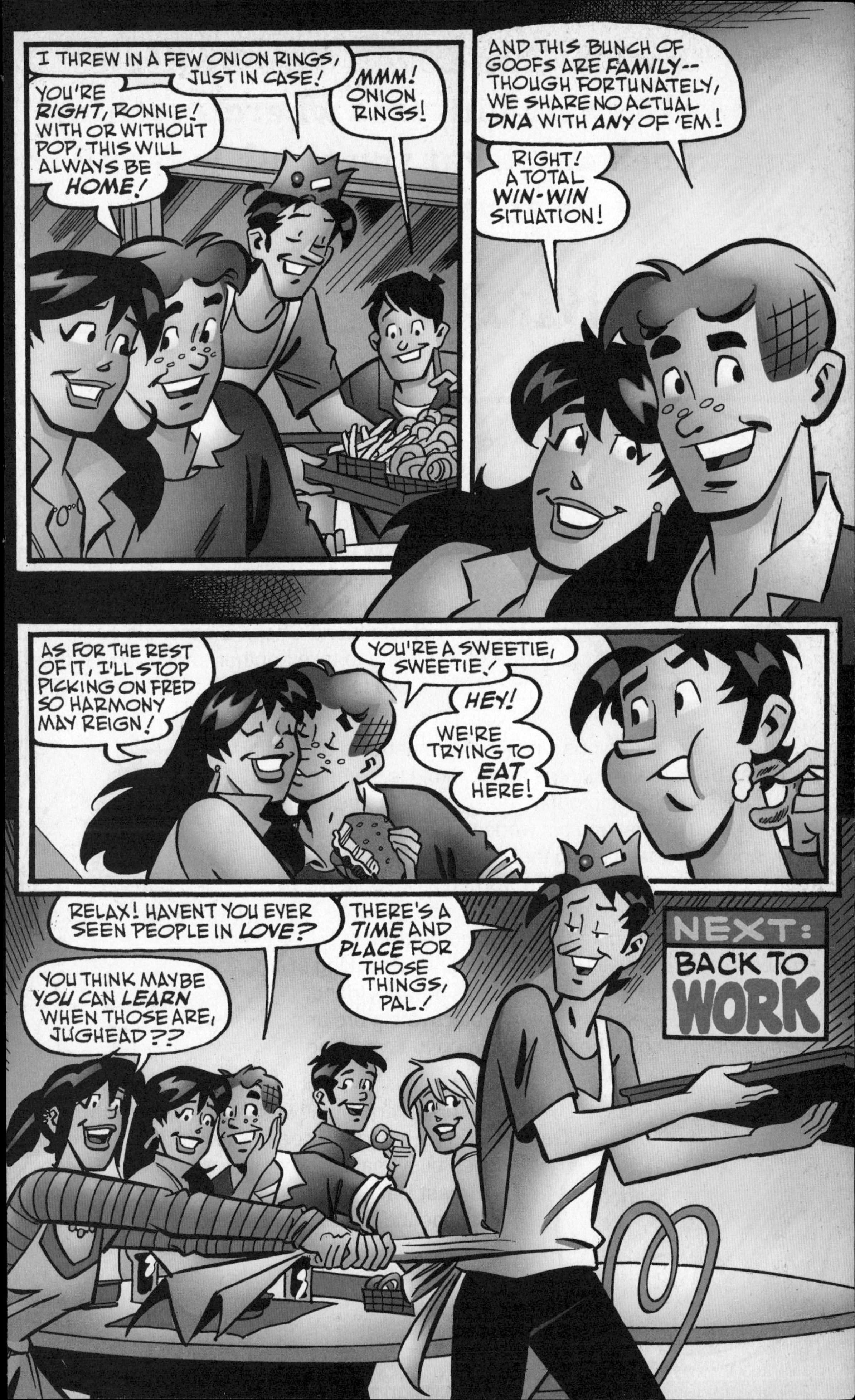
I THREW IN A FEW ONION RINGS, JUST IN CASE!
YOU'RE RIGHT, RONNIE! WITH OR WITHOUT POP, THIS WILL ALWAYS BE HOME!
MMM! ONION RINGS!
AND THIS BUNCH OF GOOFS ARE FAMILY-- THOUGH FORTUNATELY, WE SHARE NO ACTUAL DNA WITH ANY OF 'EM!
RIGHT! A TOTAL WIN-WIN SITUATION!
AS FOR THE REST OF IT, I'LL STOP PICKING ON FRED SO HARMONY MAY REIGN!
YOU'RE A SWEETIE, SWEETIE!
HEY!
WE'RE TRYING TO EAT HERE!
RELAX! HAVENT YOU EVER SEEN PEOPLE IN LOVE?
YOU THINK MAYBE YOU CAN LEARN WHEN THOSE ARE, JUGHEAD??
THERE'S A TIME AND PLACE FOR THOSE THINGS, PAL!
NEXT:
BACK TO WORK

Two Worlds. Two Loves. Two Destinies. In an alternate universe where anything can happen and what you think is familiar is anything but...

Archie Marries BETTY

Previously...

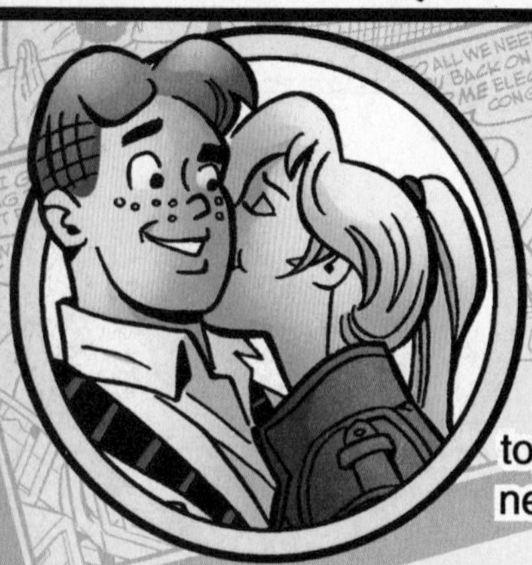

Archie and Betty have been busy, busy, busy! While Archie's been caught up with upkeep of the new Chowhouse restaurant as well as his teaching gig, Betty's been working overtime on the school committee! How much more could they possibly pile onto their already full plates? Fortunately, the two were able to take a break from their busy schedules to come together for their old friend Cheryl Blossom in her time of need—but is it going to take another tragedy to get these two to finally spend some time together?

Jughead's been a nervous wreck—the impending birth of his baby has been really taking a toll on him! He's employed kid sis Jellybean to help out at the Shoppe, but he's still overwhelmed by that and his workload at the new Chowhouse! It doesn't help that a recent string of robberies in Riverdale has him worried sick about his shop being hit next! He doesn't know who could be behind the bad stuff going on in his hometown, but he's becoming distrusting of many people. Speaking of which, he's not too fond of Jellybean's new boyfriend, Davey. Is he just being an overly protective big bro and overreacting, or could he actually be on to something...?

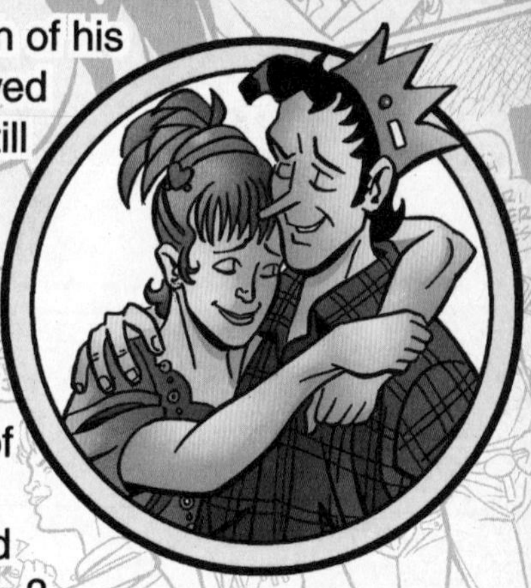

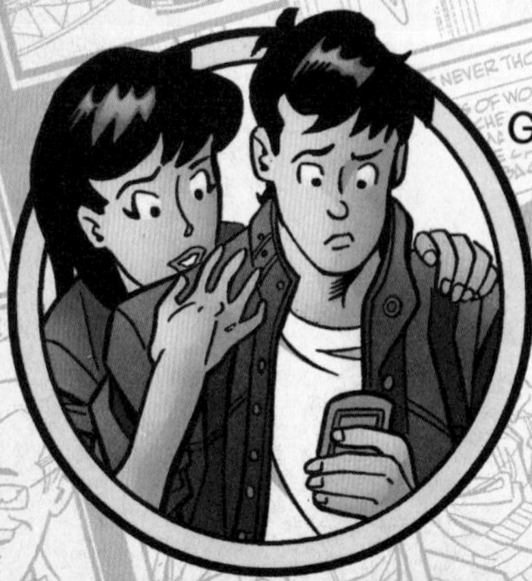

Reggie's discovering that working with his father at the Gazette isn't as easy as it seems! Meanwhile, Veronica's been busy making strides for the Cheryl Blossom Breast Cancer Foundation on top of her work at Lodge Industries. Despite their busy schedules, Reggie and Veronica still manage to make time for each other. This power couple seems to have found the perfect balance between work and love! But could something disrupt their harmonious union?

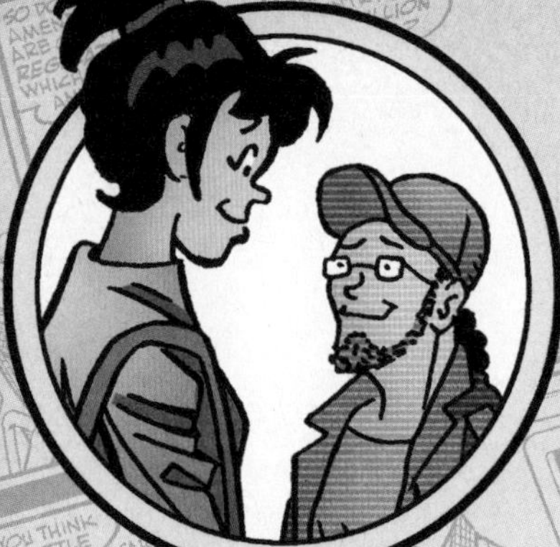

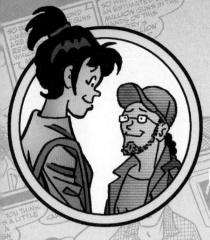

Ethel's had a hard time adjusting to life back in Riverdale. Her boss, Fred Mirth, seems to have disappeared off the face of the planet, leaving her without a job and without any sense of security! She's had to watch from the sidelines as her former love Jughead lives happily with his wife Midge. Fortunately, her budding relationship with resident genius Dilton Doiley seems promising—but will he be too involved in his technology to acknowledge their relationship? And just what is Dilton working on in that little shop of his?

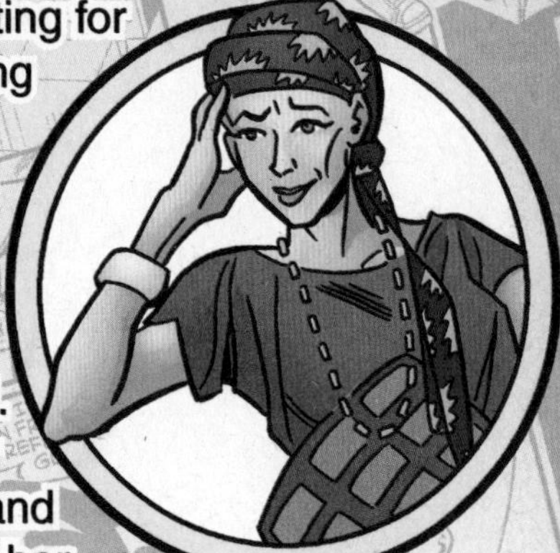

Cheryl's staying positive about her fight against an aggressive form of breast cancer. With everyone in Riverdale rooting for her recovery, and with former foe Veronica Lodge being by her side both financially and as a friend, Cheryl's confident that she can make a full recovery. And even in her time of sickness, she's taking charge as the face of her very own breast cancer foundation, which works to raise money for those not fortunate enough to have the financial help and love that she's received. Her chemo may make her weak—but Cheryl's forever a head-turner, and she's still strong enough to travel and make new acquaintances while raising awareness for her cause!

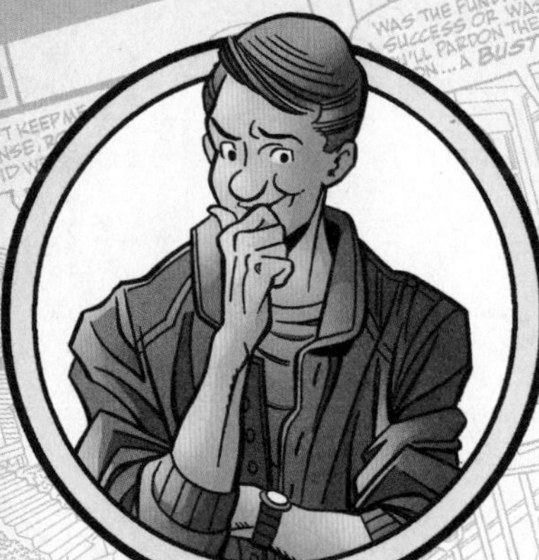

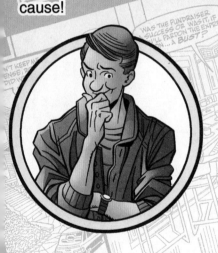

Ambrose is the proud owner of both the Chowhouse in New York City AND the Chowhouse II in his hometown of Riverdale! Thanks to The Archies and Josie & the Pussycats' successful gig at the Chowhouse II, it looks like Ambrose's hard work has put his restaurant/venue on the map! But with both partners Jughead and Archie preoccupied with their own lives and hectic schedules, will he be able to manage TWO restaurants all on his own?

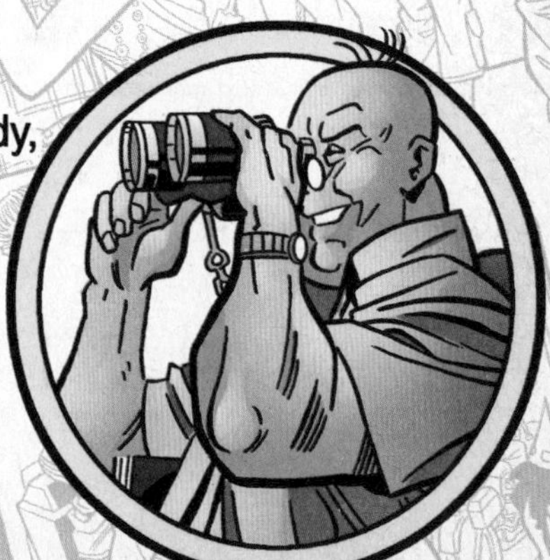

Though still coping with the loss of his wife, Ms. Grundy, Mr. Weatherbee is filled with hope and happiness witnessing his former students make such huge strides in their lives. He couldn't be prouder to see the big things going on around him—but what about his own life? Will he ever find someone who made him as happy as Geraldine did? Does he want to?

"OH, WE **ALL** FIGHT BACK...
IN OUR OWN WAYS."

"I JUST WENT *PUBLIC* WITH MY BATTLE,
BUT I'VE ALWAYS BEEN A BIT OF
A **HAM**, HAVEN'T I?"

-*CHERYL BLOSSOM*

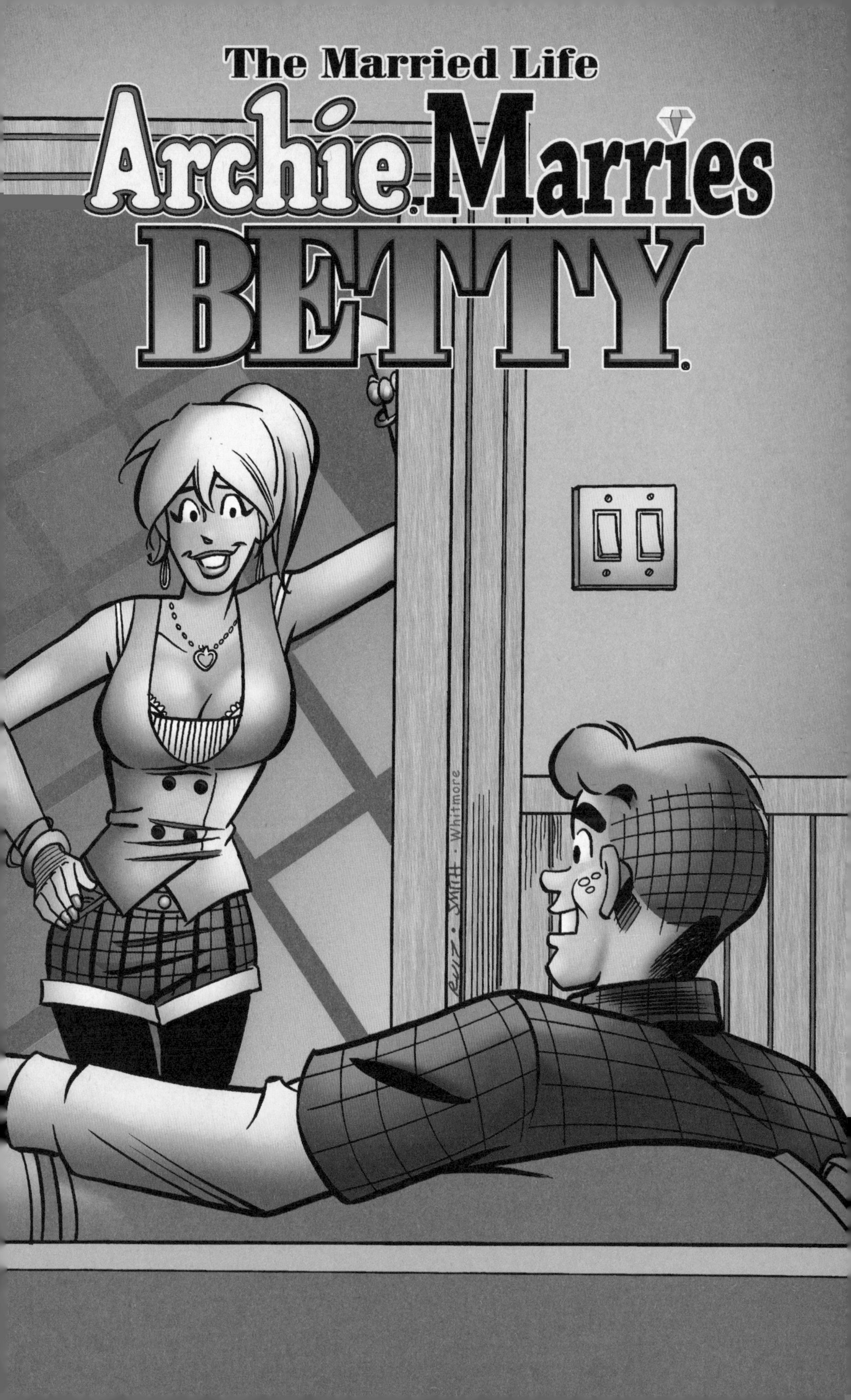
The Married Life
Archie Marries
BETTY
RUIZ • SMITH • Whitmore

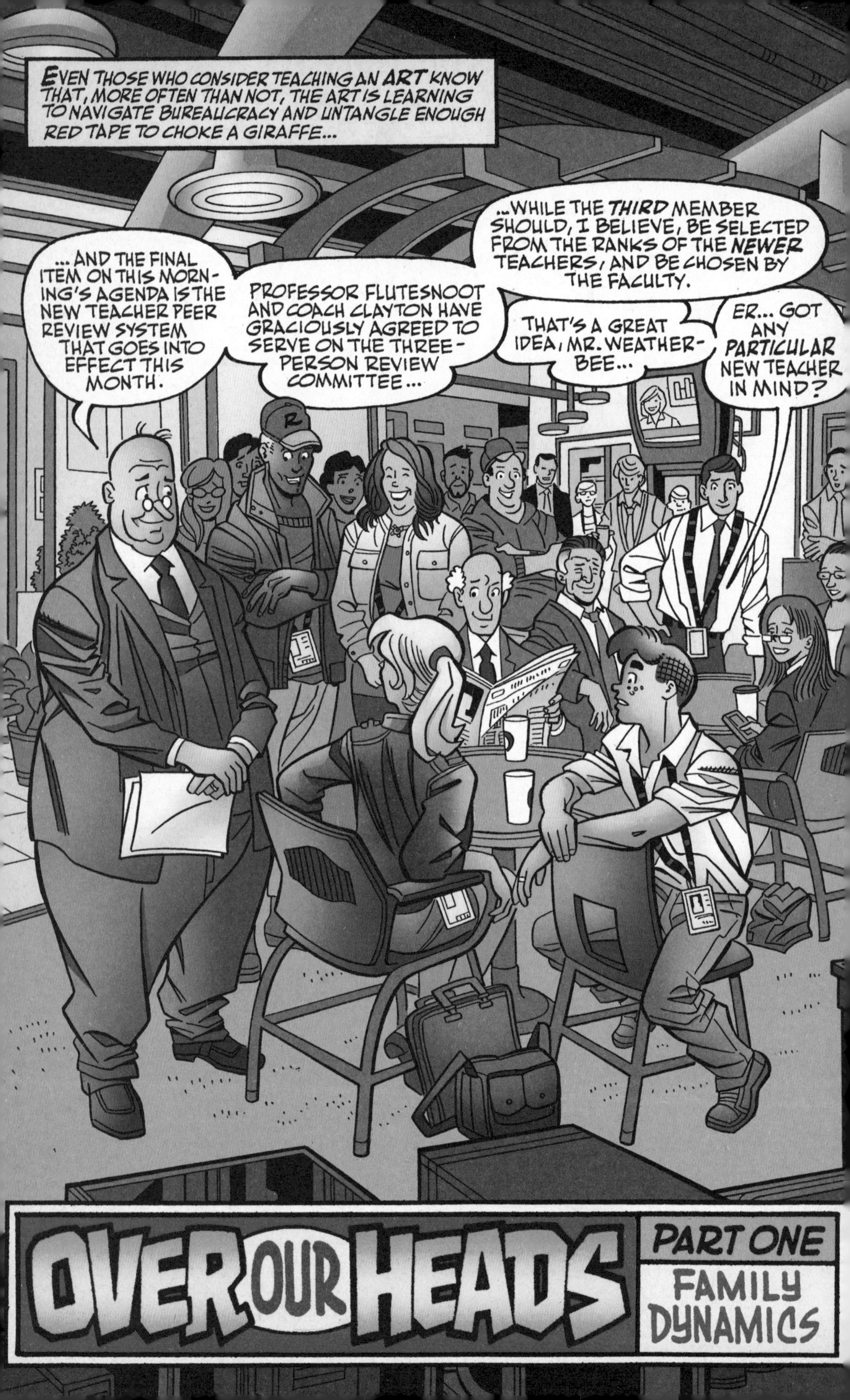
EVEN THOSE WHO CONSIDER TEACHING AN ART KNOW THAT, MORE OFTEN THAN NOT, THE ART IS LEARNING TO NAVIGATE BUREAUCRACY AND UNTANGLE ENOUGH RED TAPE TO CHOKE A GIRAFFE...
... AND THE FINAL ITEM ON THIS MORNING'S AGENDA IS THE NEW TEACHER PEER REVIEW SYSTEM THAT GOES INTO EFFECT THIS MONTH.
PROFESSOR FLUTESNOOT AND COACH CLAYTON HAVE GRACIOUSLY AGREED TO SERVE ON THE THREE-PERSON REVIEW COMMITTEE...
...WHILE THE THIRD MEMBER SHOULD, I BELIEVE, BE SELECTED FROM THE RANKS OF THE NEWER TEACHERS, AND BE CHOSEN BY THE FACULTY.
THAT'S A GREAT IDEA, MR. WEATHERBEE...
ER... GOT ANY PARTICULAR NEW TEACHER IN MIND?
OVER OUR HEADS
PART ONE
FAMILY DYNAMICS

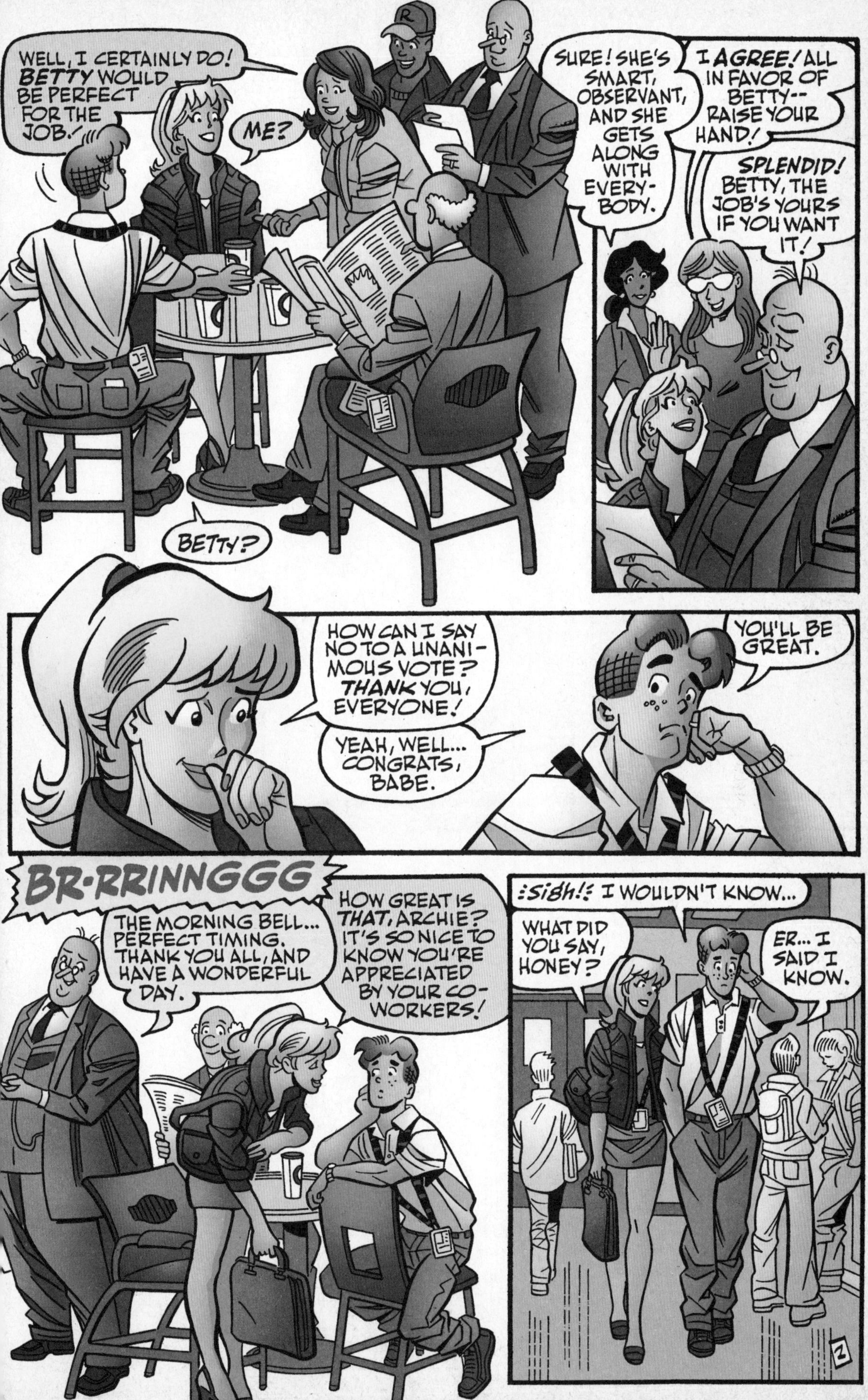
WELL, I CERTAINLY DO! BETTY WOULD BE PERFECT FOR THE JOB.
ME?
BETTY?
SURE! SHE'S SMART, OBSERVANT, AND SHE GETS ALONG WITH EVERYBODY.
I AGREE! ALL IN FAVOR OF BETTY-- RAISE YOUR HAND!
SPLENDID! BETTY, THE JOB'S YOURS IF YOU WANT IT!
HOW CAN I SAY NO TO A UNANIMOUS VOTE? THANK YOU, EVERYONE!
YEAH, WELL... CONGRATS, BABE.
YOU'LL BE GREAT.
BR-RRINNGGG
THE MORNING BELL... PERFECT TIMING. THANK YOU ALL, AND HAVE A WONDERFUL DAY.
HOW GREAT IS THAT, ARCHIE? IT'S SO NICE TO KNOW YOU'RE APPRECIATED BY YOUR CO-WORKERS!
:SIGH!: I WOULDN'T KNOW...
WHAT DID YOU SAY, HONEY?
ER... I SAID I KNOW.

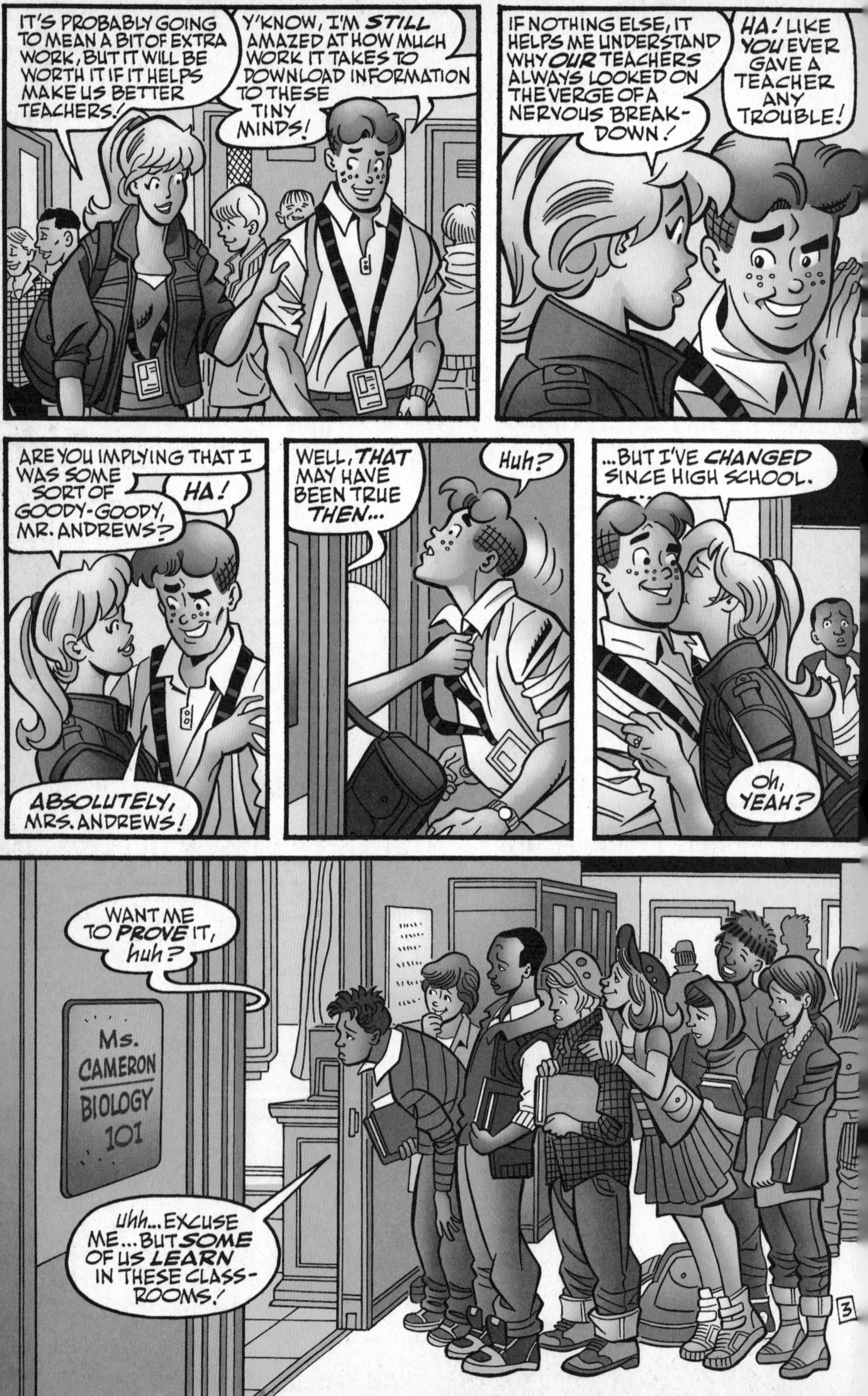
IT'S PROBABLY GOING TO MEAN A BIT OF EXTRA WORK, BUT IT WILL BE WORTH IT IF IT HELPS MAKE US BETTER TEACHERS!
Y'KNOW, I'M STILL AMAZED AT HOW MUCH WORK IT TAKES TO DOWNLOAD INFORMATION TO THESE TINY MINDS!
IF NOTHING ELSE, IT HELPS ME UNDERSTAND WHY OUR TEACHERS ALWAYS LOOKED ON THE VERGE OF A NERVOUS BREAK-DOWN!
HA! LIKE YOU EVER GAVE A TEACHER ANY TROUBLE!
ARE YOU IMPLYING THAT I WAS SOME SORT OF GOODY-GOODY, MR. ANDREWS?
HA!
ABSOLUTELY, MRS. ANDREWS!
WELL, THAT MAY HAVE BEEN TRUE THEN...
Huh?
...BUT I'VE CHANGED SINCE HIGH SCHOOL.
Oh, YEAH?
WANT ME TO PROVE IT, huh?
Ms. CAMERON BIOLOGY 101
uhh... EXCUSE ME... BUT SOME OF US LEARN IN THESE CLASS-ROOMS!
3

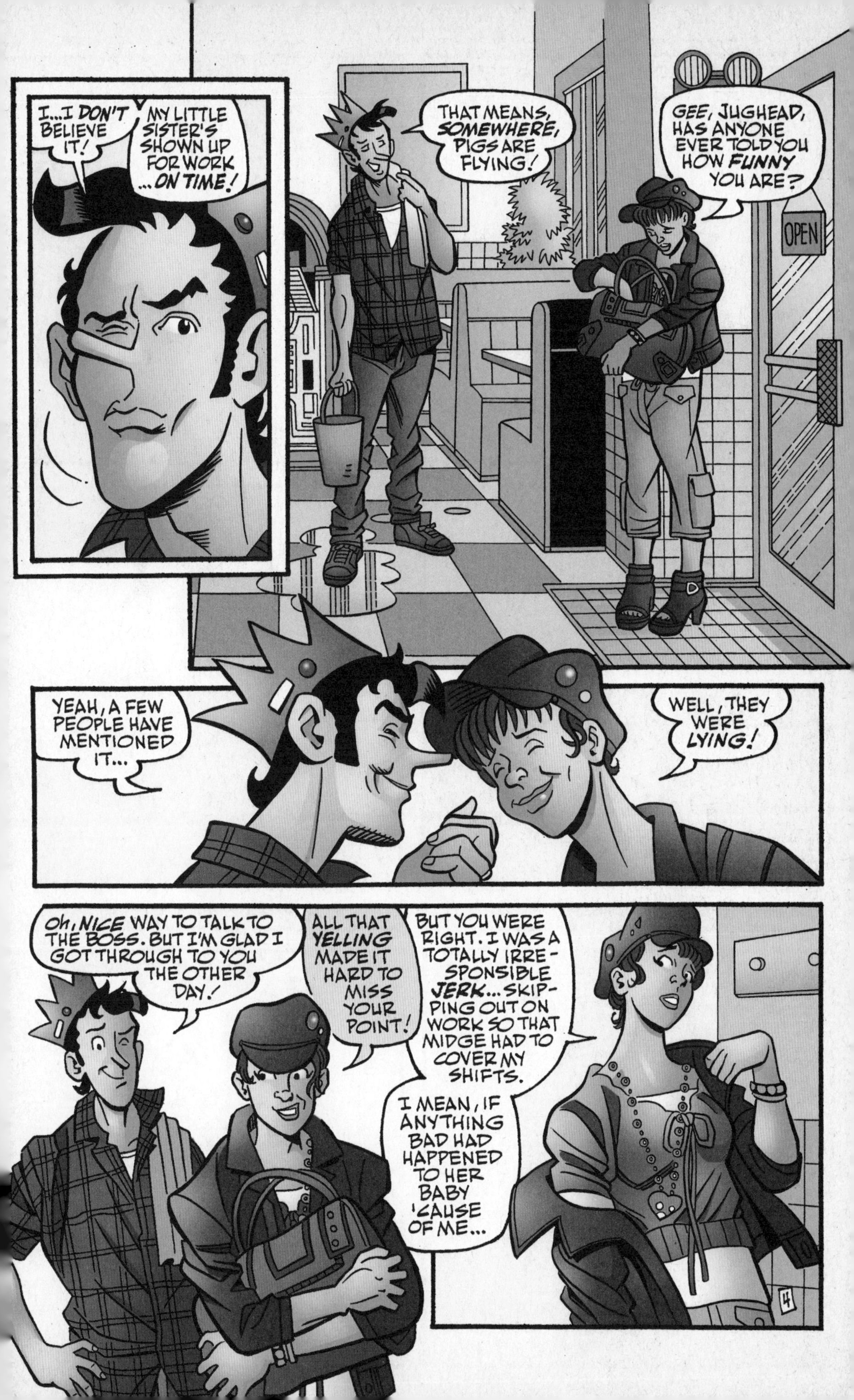
I...I DON'T BELIEVE IT!
MY LITTLE SISTER'S SHOWN UP FOR WORK ...ON TIME!
THAT MEANS, SOMEWHERE, PIGS ARE FLYING!
GEE, JUGHEAD, HAS ANYONE EVER TOLD YOU HOW FUNNY YOU ARE?
OPEN
YEAH, A FEW PEOPLE HAVE MENTIONED IT...
WELL, THEY WERE LYING!
Oh, NICE WAY TO TALK TO THE BOSS. BUT I'M GLAD I GOT THROUGH TO YOU THE OTHER DAY!
ALL THAT YELLING MADE IT HARD TO MISS YOUR POINT!
BUT YOU WERE RIGHT. I WAS A TOTALLY IRRE-SPONSIBLE JERK... SKIP-PING OUT ON WORK SO THAT MIDGE HAD TO COVER MY SHIFTS.
I MEAN, IF ANYTHING BAD HAD HAPPENED TO HER BABY 'CAUSE OF ME...
4

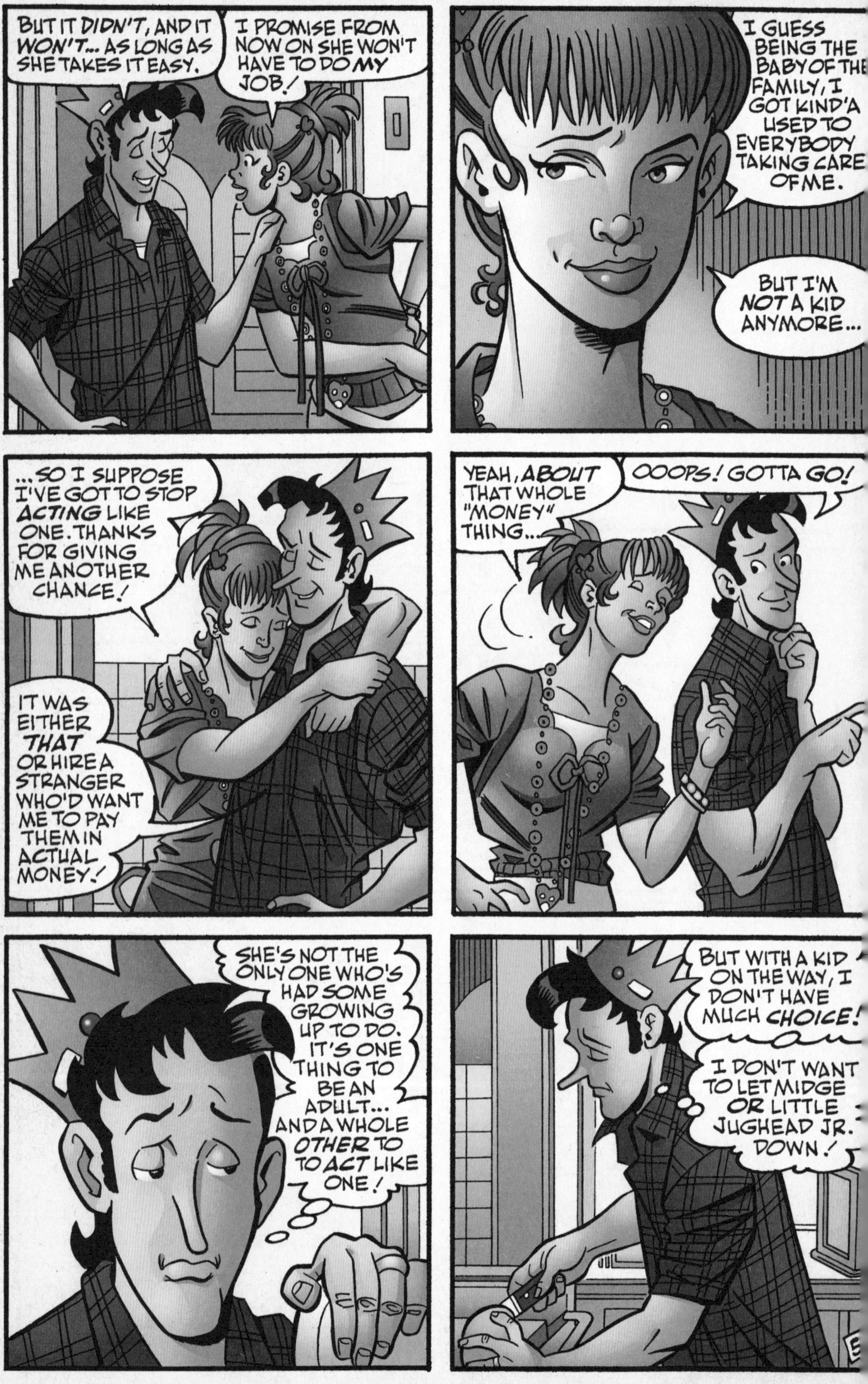
BUT IT DIDN'T, AND IT WON'T... AS LONG AS SHE TAKES IT EASY.
I PROMISE FROM NOW ON SHE WON'T HAVE TO DO MY JOB!
I GUESS BEING THE BABY OF THE FAMILY, I GOT KIND'A USED TO EVERYBODY TAKING CARE OF ME.
BUT I'M NOT A KID ANYMORE...
...SO I SUPPOSE I'VE GOT TO STOP ACTING LIKE ONE. THANKS FOR GIVING ME ANOTHER CHANCE!
IT WAS EITHER THAT OR HIRE A STRANGER WHO'D WANT ME TO PAY THEM IN ACTUAL MONEY!
YEAH, ABOUT THAT WHOLE "MONEY" THING...
OOOPS! GOTTA GO!
SHE'S NOT THE ONLY ONE WHO'S HAD SOME GROWING UP TO DO. IT'S ONE THING TO BE AN ADULT... AND A WHOLE OTHER TO TO ACT LIKE ONE!
BUT WITH A KID ON THE WAY, I DON'T HAVE MUCH CHOICE!
I DON'T WANT TO LET MIDGE OR LITTLE JUGHEAD JR. DOWN!
5

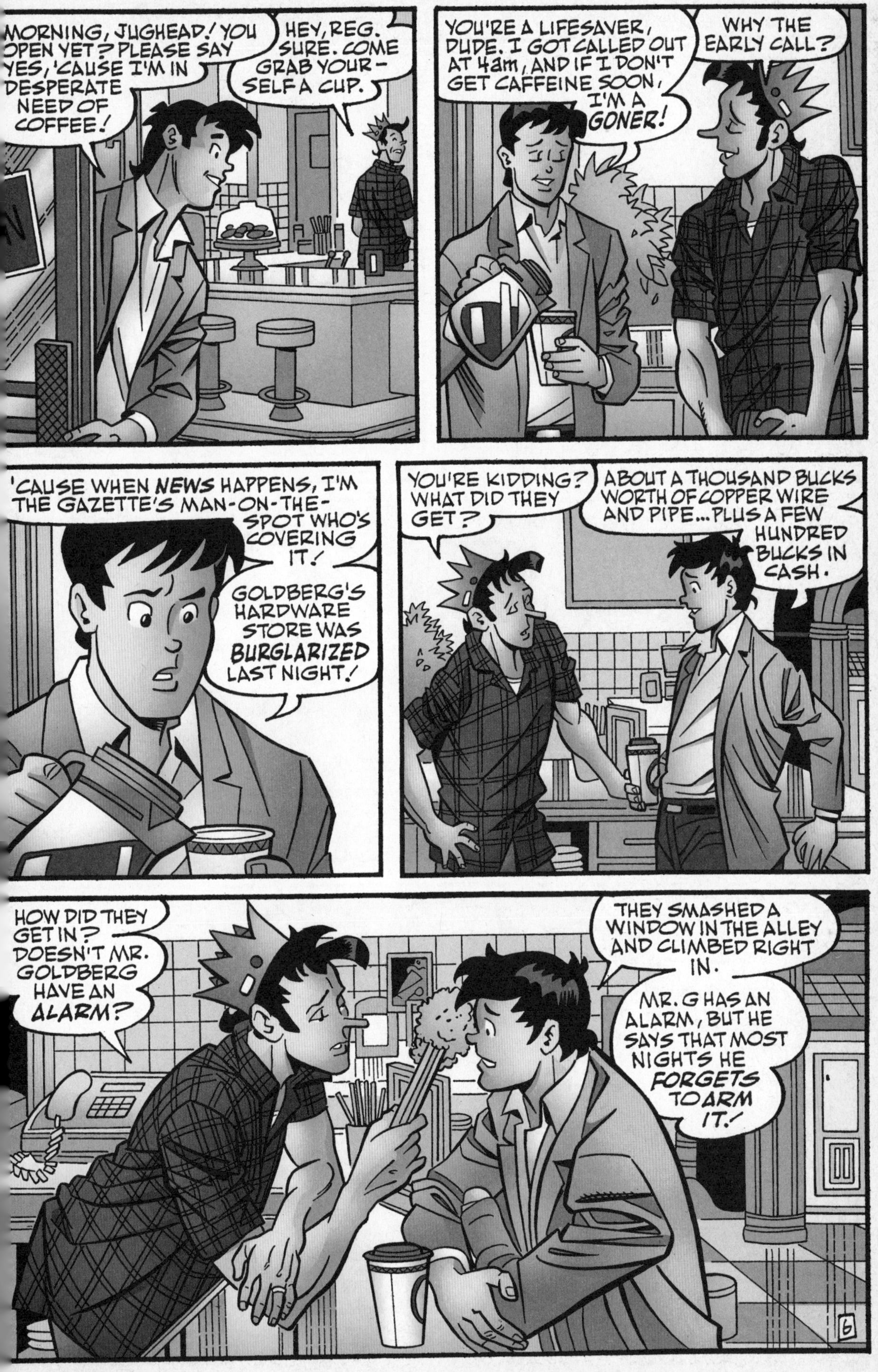
MORNING, JUGHEAD! YOU OPEN YET? PLEASE SAY YES, 'CAUSE I'M IN DESPERATE NEED OF COFFEE!
HEY, REG. SURE. COME GRAB YOURSELF A CUP.
YOU'RE A LIFESAVER, DUDE. I GOT CALLED OUT AT 4am, AND IF I DON'T GET CAFFEINE SOON, I'M A GONER!
WHY THE EARLY CALL?
'CAUSE WHEN NEWS HAPPENS, I'M THE GAZETTE'S MAN-ON-THE-SPOT WHO'S COVERING IT!
GOLDBERG'S HARDWARE STORE WAS BURGLARIZED LAST NIGHT!
YOU'RE KIDDING? WHAT DID THEY GET?
ABOUT A THOUSAND BUCKS WORTH OF COPPER WIRE AND PIPE... PLUS A FEW HUNDRED BUCKS IN CASH.
HOW DID THEY GET IN? DOESN'T MR. GOLDBERG HAVE AN ALARM?
THEY SMASHED A WINDOW IN THE ALLEY AND CLIMBED RIGHT IN.
MR. G HAS AN ALARM, BUT HE SAYS THAT MOST NIGHTS HE FORGETS TO ARM IT!
6

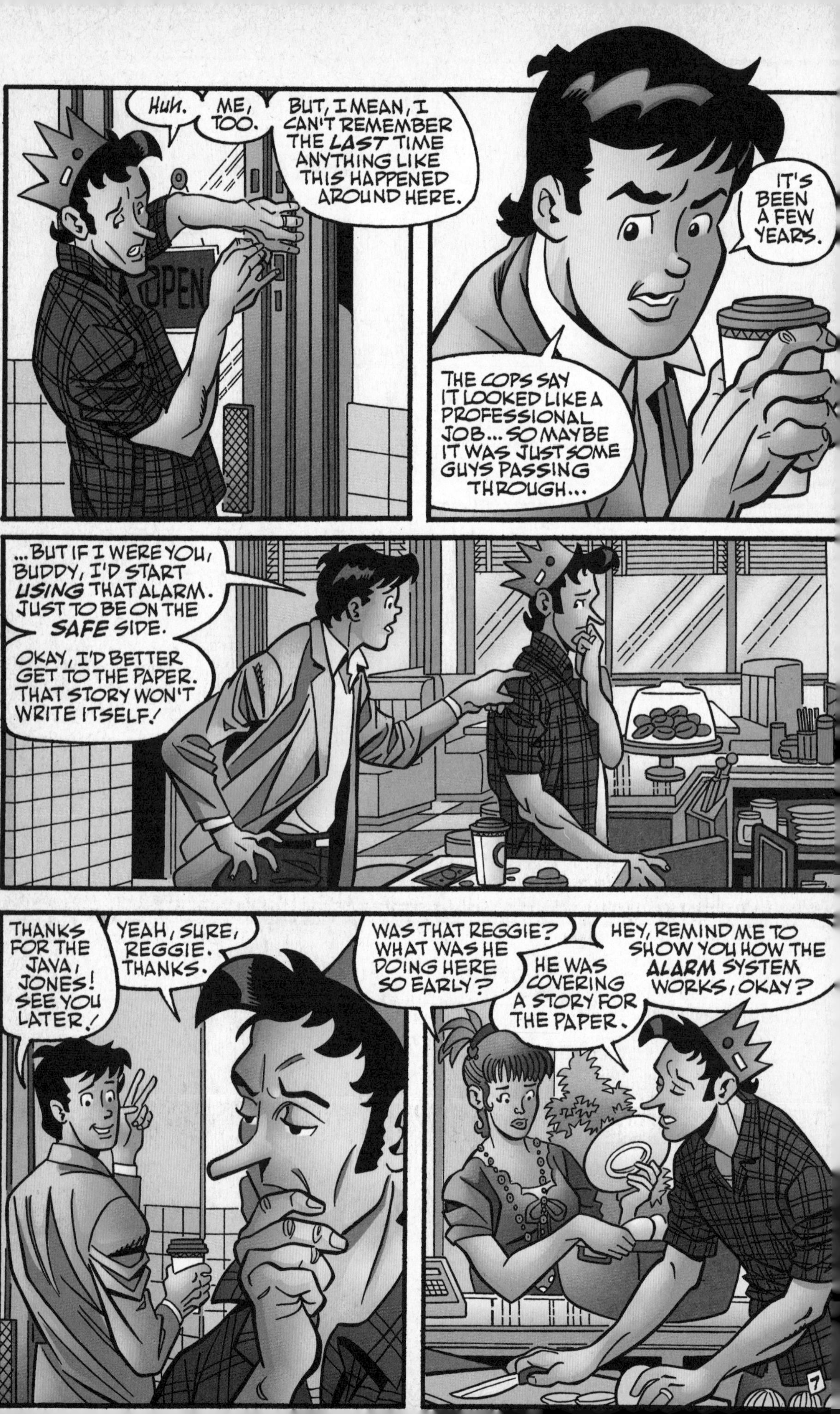
HUH.
ME, TOO.
BUT, I MEAN, I CAN'T REMEMBER THE LAST TIME ANYTHING LIKE THIS HAPPENED AROUND HERE.
OPEN
IT'S BEEN A FEW YEARS.
THE COPS SAY IT LOOKED LIKE A PROFESSIONAL JOB... SO MAYBE IT WAS JUST SOME GUYS PASSING THROUGH...
...BUT IF I WERE YOU, BUDDY, I'D START USING THAT ALARM. JUST TO BE ON THE SAFE SIDE.
OKAY, I'D BETTER GET TO THE PAPER. THAT STORY WON'T WRITE ITSELF!
THANKS FOR THE JAVA, JONES! SEE YOU LATER!
YEAH, SURE, REGGIE. THANKS.
WAS THAT REGGIE? WHAT WAS HE DOING HERE SO EARLY?
HE WAS COVERING A STORY FOR THE PAPER.
HEY, REMIND ME TO SHOW YOU HOW THE ALARM SYSTEM WORKS, OKAY?

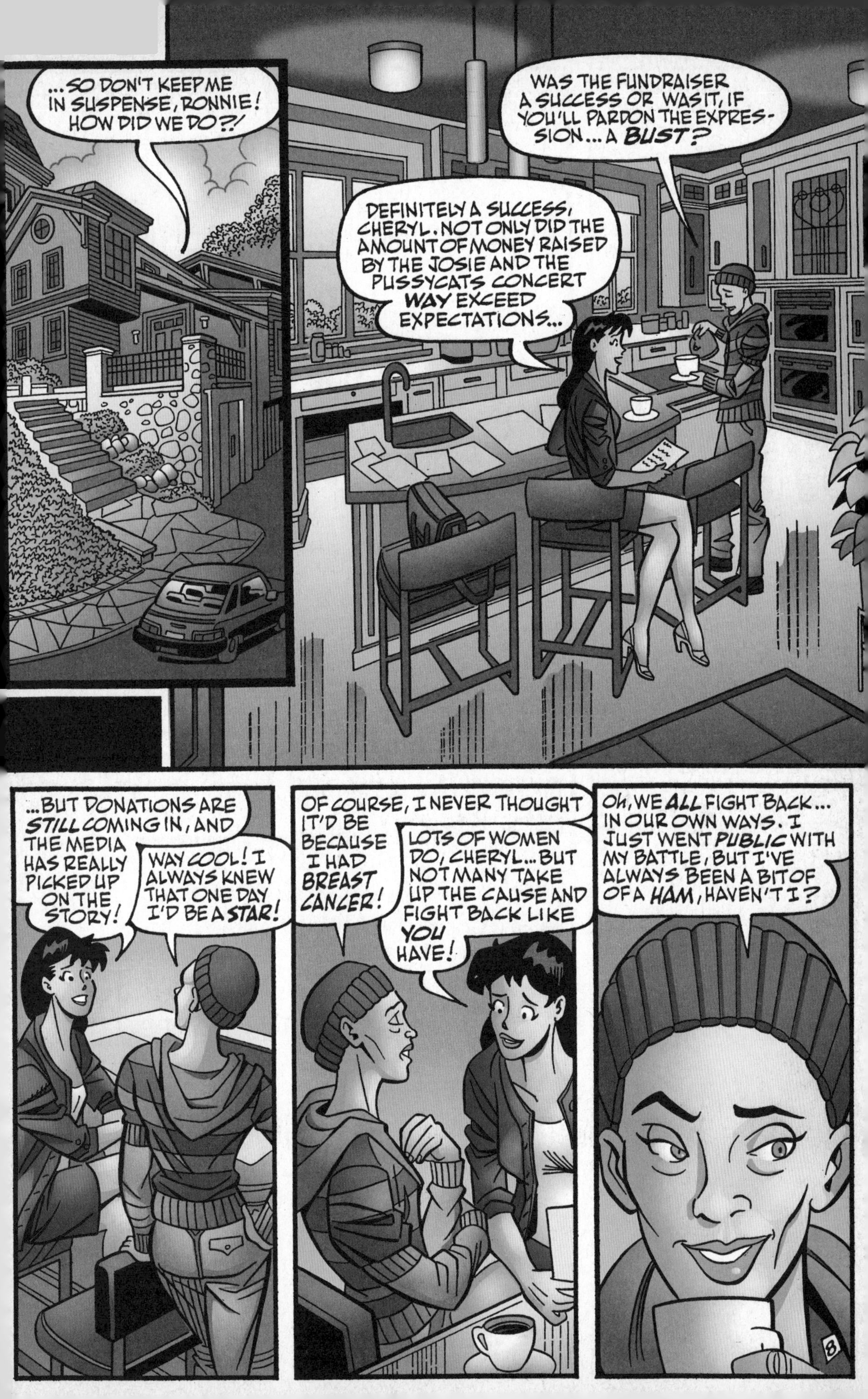
...SO DON'T KEEP ME IN SUSPENSE, RONNIE! HOW DID WE DO?!
WAS THE FUNDRAISER A SUCCESS OR WAS IT, IF YOU'LL PARDON THE EXPRESSION... A BUST?
DEFINITELY A SUCCESS, CHERYL. NOT ONLY DID THE AMOUNT OF MONEY RAISED BY THE JOSIE AND THE PUSSYCATS CONCERT WAY EXCEED EXPECTATIONS...
...BUT DONATIONS ARE STILL COMING IN, AND THE MEDIA HAS REALLY PICKED UP ON THE STORY!
WAY COOL! I ALWAYS KNEW THAT ONE DAY I'D BE A STAR!
OF COURSE, I NEVER THOUGHT IT'D BE BECAUSE I HAD BREAST CANCER!
LOTS OF WOMEN DO, CHERYL... BUT NOT MANY TAKE UP THE CAUSE AND FIGHT BACK LIKE YOU HAVE!
Oh, WE ALL FIGHT BACK... IN OUR OWN WAYS. I JUST WENT PUBLIC WITH MY BATTLE, BUT I'VE ALWAYS BEEN A BIT OF OF A HAM, HAVEN'T I?
8

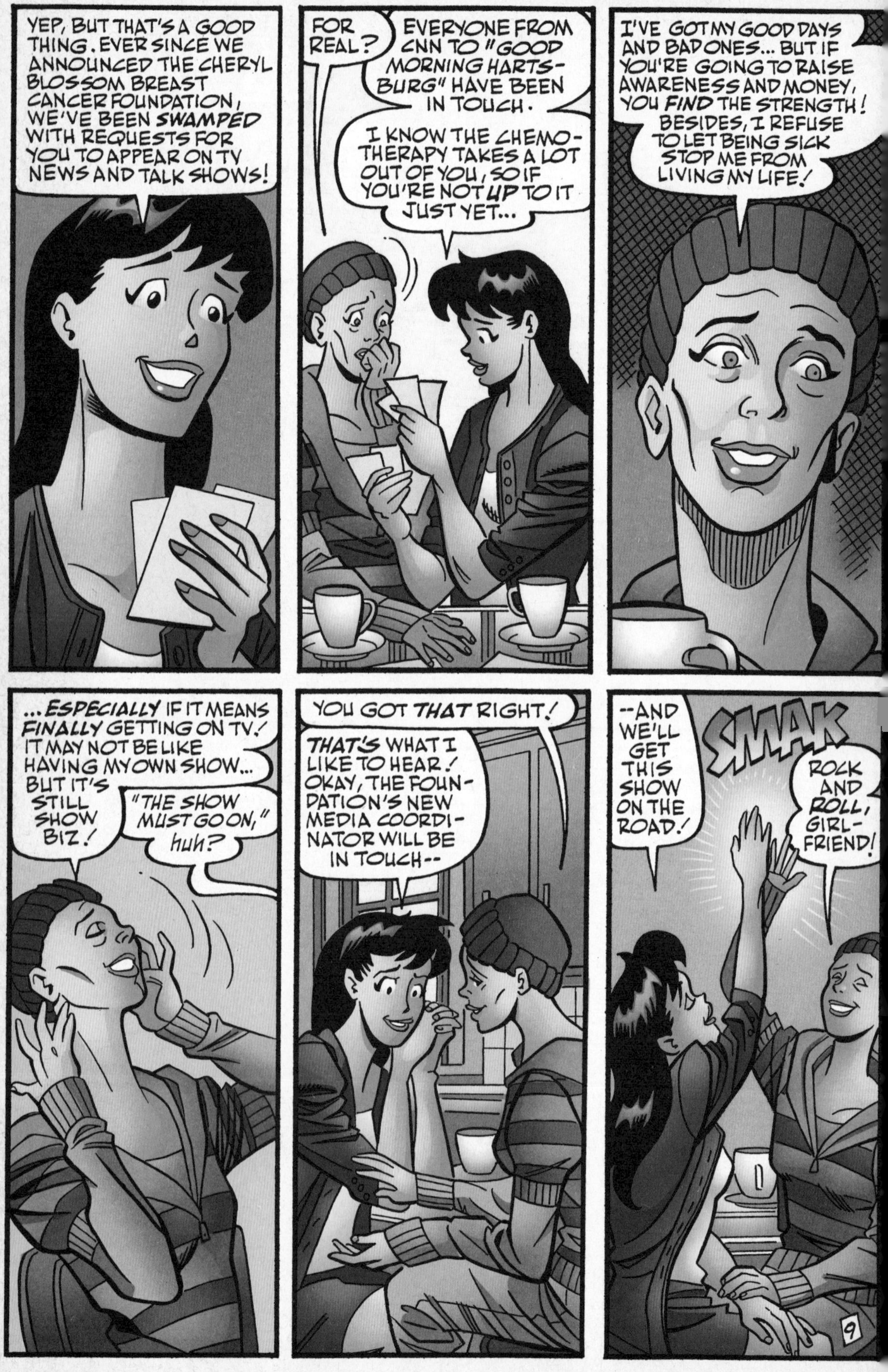
YEP, BUT THAT'S A GOOD THING. EVER SINCE WE ANNOUNCED THE CHERYL BLOSSOM BREAST CANCER FOUNDATION, WE'VE BEEN SWAMPED WITH REQUESTS FOR YOU TO APPEAR ON TV NEWS AND TALK SHOWS!
FOR REAL?
EVERYONE FROM CNN TO "GOOD MORNING HARTSBURG" HAVE BEEN IN TOUCH.
I KNOW THE CHEMOTHERAPY TAKES A LOT OUT OF YOU, SO IF YOU'RE NOT UP TO IT JUST YET...
I'VE GOT MY GOOD DAYS AND BAD ONES... BUT IF YOU'RE GOING TO RAISE AWARENESS AND MONEY, YOU FIND THE STRENGTH! BESIDES, I REFUSE TO LET BEING SICK STOP ME FROM LIVING MY LIFE!
...ESPECIALLY IF IT MEANS FINALLY GETTING ON TV! IT MAY NOT BE LIKE HAVING MY OWN SHOW... BUT IT'S STILL SHOW BIZ!
"THE SHOW MUST GO ON," huh?
YOU GOT THAT RIGHT!
THAT'S WHAT I LIKE TO HEAR! OKAY, THE FOUNDATION'S NEW MEDIA COORDINATOR WILL BE IN TOUCH--
--AND WE'LL GET THIS SHOW ON THE ROAD!
SMAK
ROCK AND ROLL, GIRL-FRIEND!

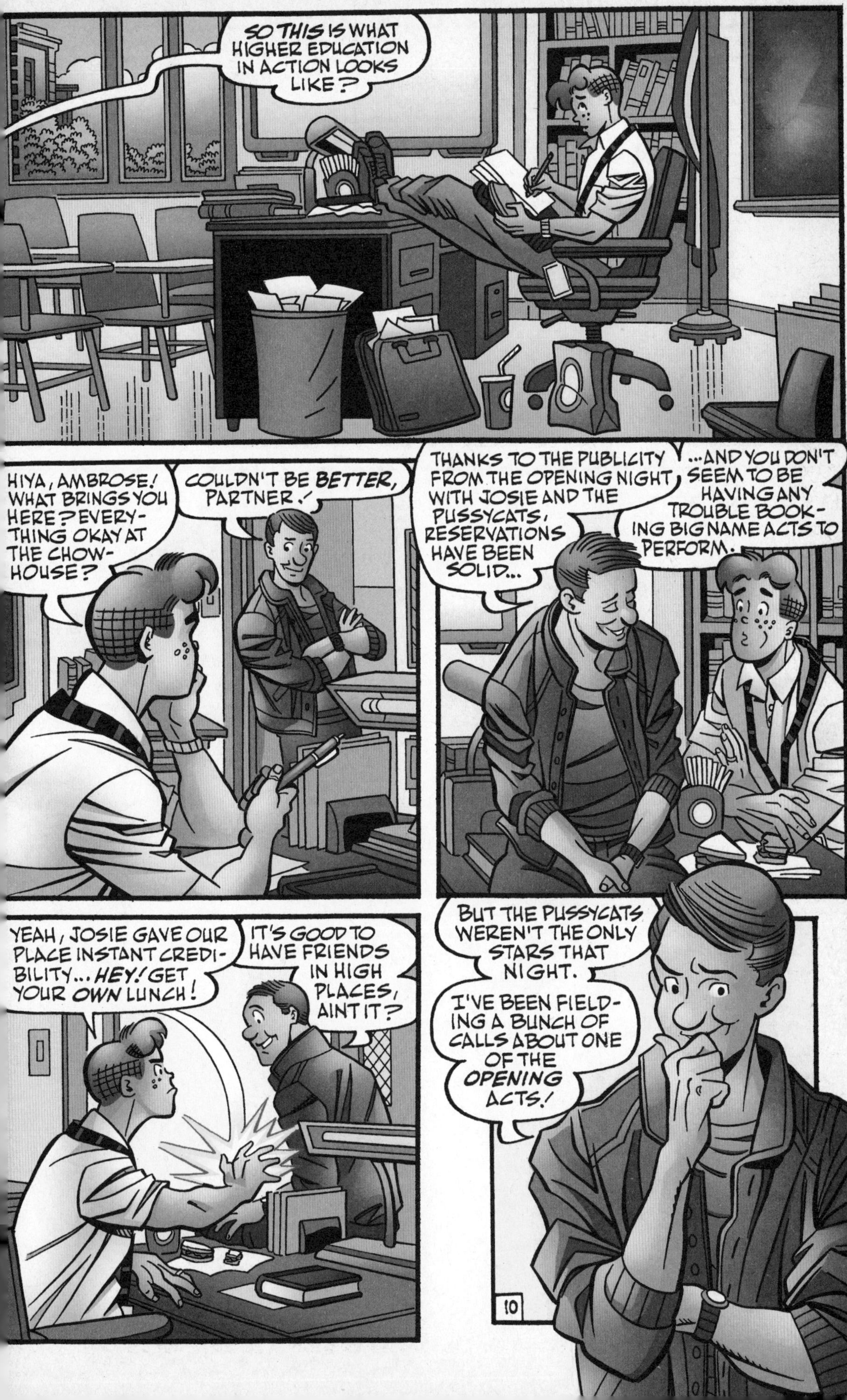
SO THIS IS WHAT HIGHER EDUCATION IN ACTION LOOKS LIKE?
HIYA, AMBROSE! WHAT BRINGS YOU HERE? EVERYTHING OKAY AT THE CHOW-HOUSE?
COULDN'T BE BETTER, PARTNER!
THANKS TO THE PUBLICITY FROM THE OPENING NIGHT WITH JOSIE AND THE PUSSYCATS, RESERVATIONS HAVE BEEN SOLID...
...AND YOU DON'T SEEM TO BE HAVING ANY TROUBLE BOOKING BIG NAME ACTS TO PERFORM.
YEAH, JOSIE GAVE OUR PLACE INSTANT CREDIBILITY... HEY! GET YOUR OWN LUNCH!
IT'S GOOD TO HAVE FRIENDS IN HIGH PLACES, AINT IT?
BUT THE PUSSYCATS WEREN'T THE ONLY STARS THAT NIGHT.
I'VE BEEN FIELDING A BUNCH OF CALLS ABOUT ONE OF THE OPENING ACTS!
10

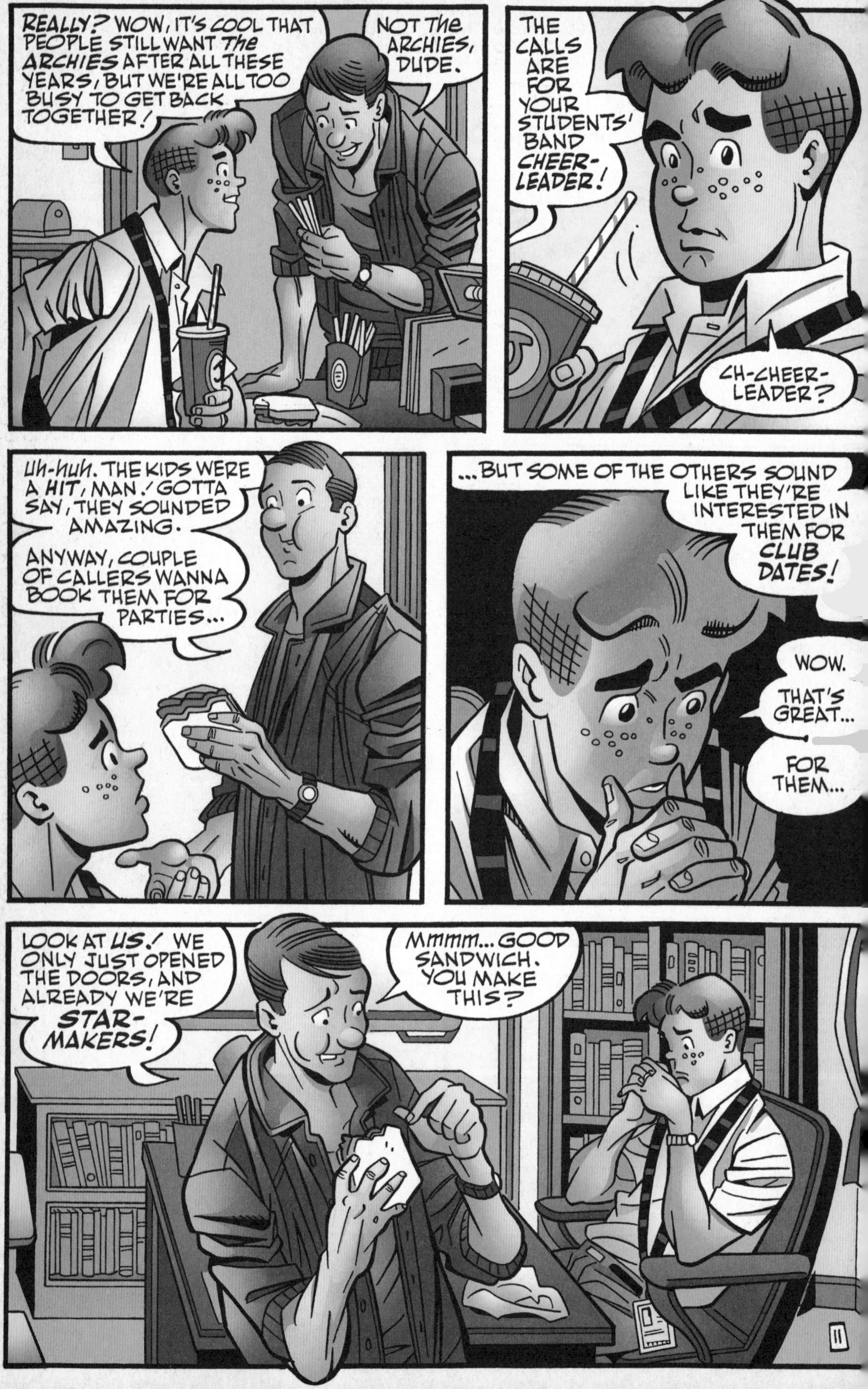
REALLY? WOW, IT'S COOL THAT PEOPLE STILL WANT THE ARCHIES AFTER ALL THESE YEARS, BUT WE'RE ALL TOO BUSY TO GET BACK TOGETHER!
NOT THE ARCHIES, DUDE.
THE CALLS ARE FOR YOUR STUDENTS' BAND CHEER-LEADER!
CH-CHEER-LEADER?
UH-HUH. THE KIDS WERE A HIT, MAN! GOTTA SAY, THEY SOUNDED AMAZING.
ANYWAY, COUPLE OF CALLERS WANNA BOOK THEM FOR PARTIES...
...BUT SOME OF THE OTHERS SOUND LIKE THEY'RE INTERESTED IN THEM FOR CLUB DATES!
WOW.
THAT'S GREAT...
FOR THEM...
LOOK AT US! WE ONLY JUST OPENED THE DOORS, AND ALREADY WE'RE STAR-MAKERS!
MMMM... GOOD SANDWICH. YOU MAKE THIS?
11

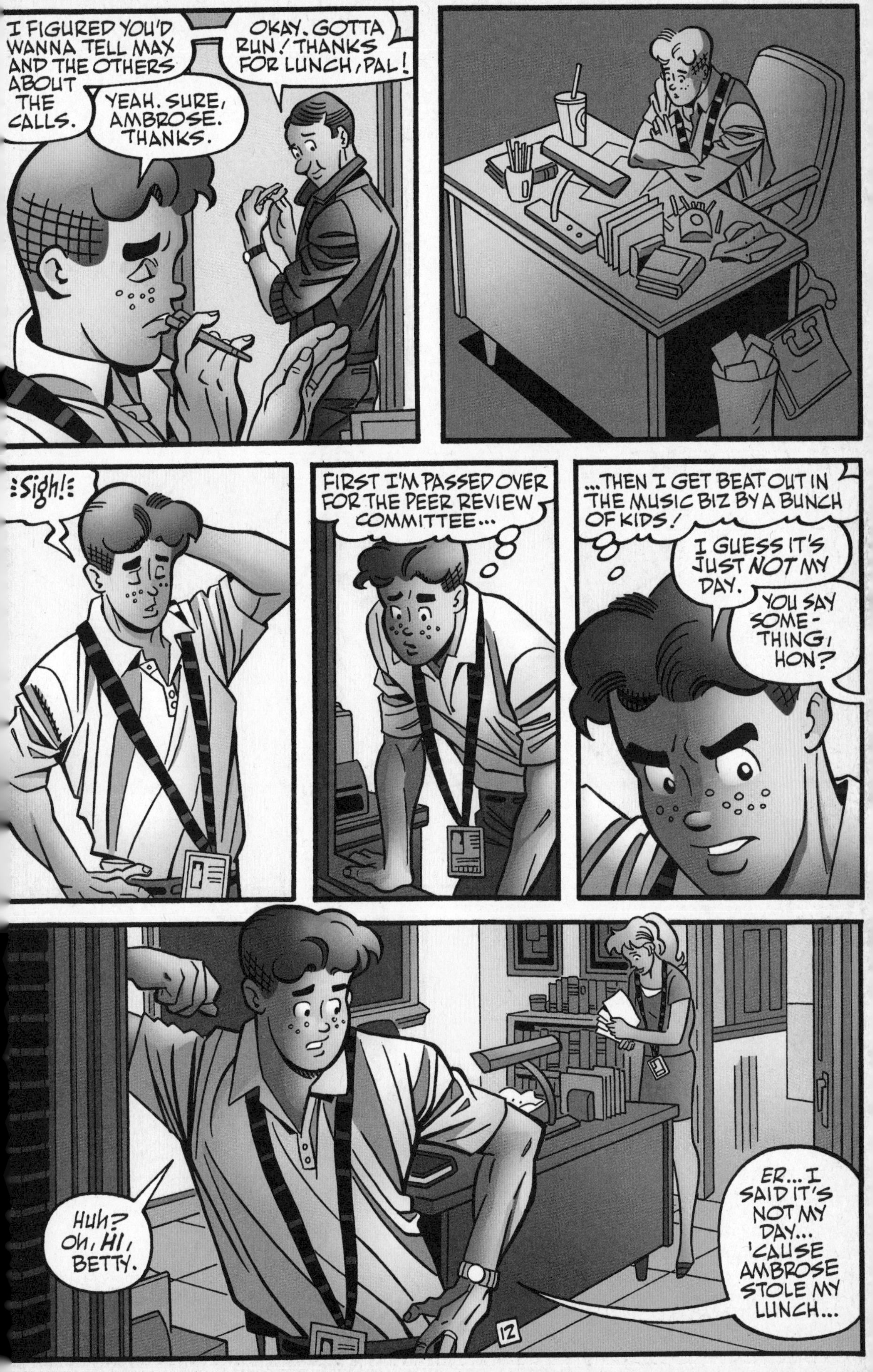

I FIGURED YOU'D WANNA TELL MAX AND THE OTHERS ABOUT THE CALLS.
OKAY. GOTTA RUN! THANKS FOR LUNCH, PAL!
YEAH. SURE, AMBROSE. THANKS.
Sigh!
FIRST I'M PASSED OVER FOR THE PEER REVIEW COMMITTEE...
...THEN I GET BEAT OUT IN THE MUSIC BIZ BY A BUNCH OF KIDS!
I GUESS IT'S JUST NOT MY DAY.
YOU SAY SOME-THING, HON?
Huh? Oh, HI, BETTY.
ER... I SAID IT'S NOT MY DAY... 'CAUSE AMBROSE STOLE MY LUNCH...
12

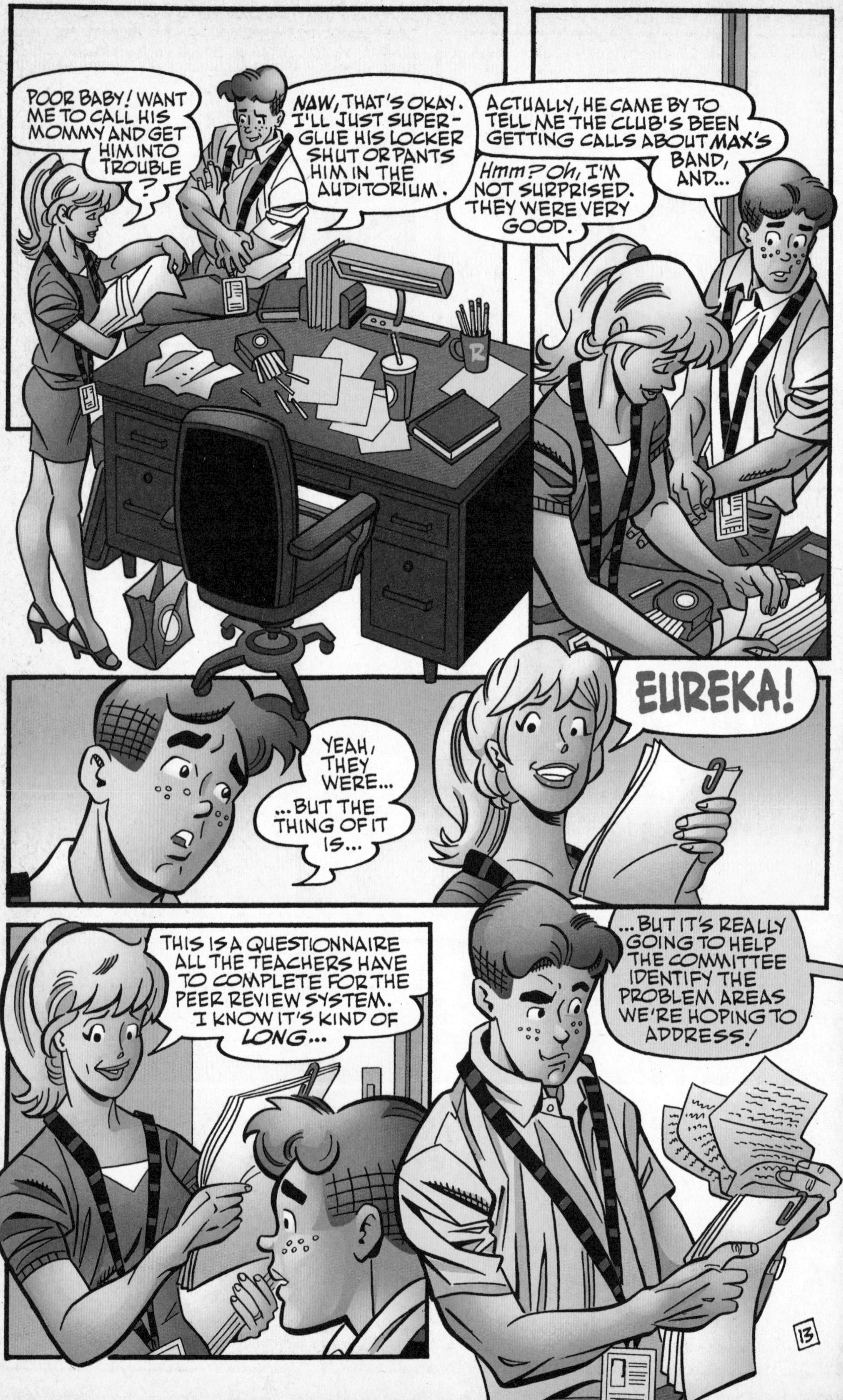
POOR BABY! WANT ME TO CALL HIS MOMMY AND GET HIM INTO TROUBLE?
NAW, THAT'S OKAY. I'LL JUST SUPER-GLUE HIS LOCKER SHUT OR PANTS HIM IN THE AUDITORIUM.
ACTUALLY, HE CAME BY TO TELL ME THE CLUB'S BEEN GETTING CALLS ABOUT MAX'S BAND, AND...
Hmm? Oh, I'M NOT SURPRISED. THEY WERE VERY GOOD.
YEAH, THEY WERE... ...BUT THE THING OF IT IS...
EUREKA!
THIS IS A QUESTIONNAIRE ALL THE TEACHERS HAVE TO COMPLETE FOR THE PEER REVIEW SYSTEM. I KNOW IT'S KIND OF LONG...
...BUT IT'S REALLY GOING TO HELP THE COMMITTEE IDENTIFY THE PROBLEM AREAS WE'RE HOPING TO ADDRESS!
13

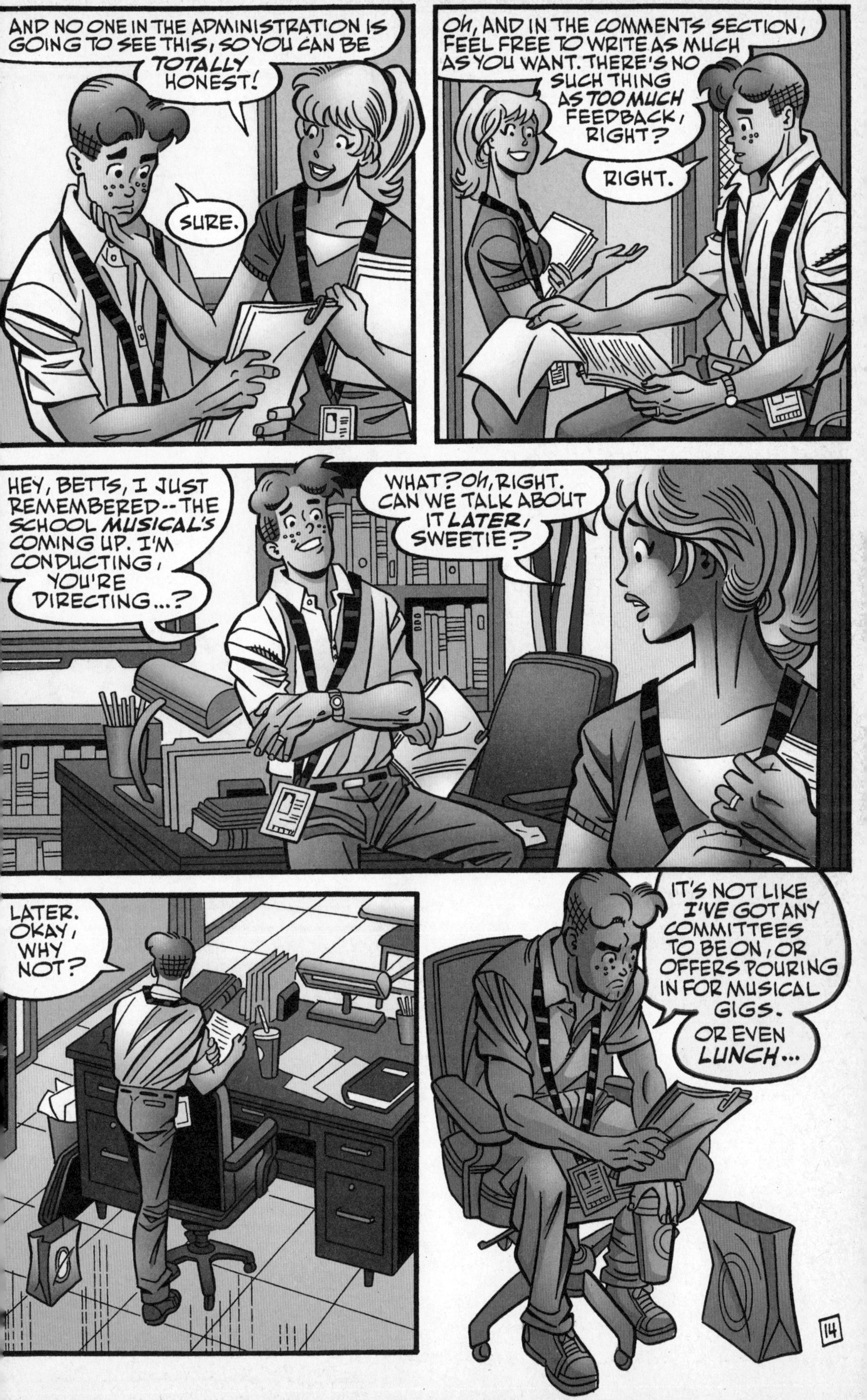
AND NO ONE IN THE ADMINISTRATION IS GOING TO SEE THIS, SO YOU CAN BE TOTALLY HONEST!
SURE.
OH, AND IN THE COMMENTS SECTION, FEEL FREE TO WRITE AS MUCH AS YOU WANT. THERE'S NO SUCH THING AS TOO MUCH FEEDBACK, RIGHT?
RIGHT.
HEY, BETTS, I JUST REMEMBERED-- THE SCHOOL MUSICAL'S COMING UP. I'M CONDUCTING, YOU'RE DIRECTING...?
WHAT? OH, RIGHT. CAN WE TALK ABOUT IT LATER, SWEETIE?
LATER. OKAY, WHY NOT?
IT'S NOT LIKE I'VE GOT ANY COMMITTEES TO BE ON, OR OFFERS POURING IN FOR MUSICAL GIGS. OR EVEN LUNCH...
14

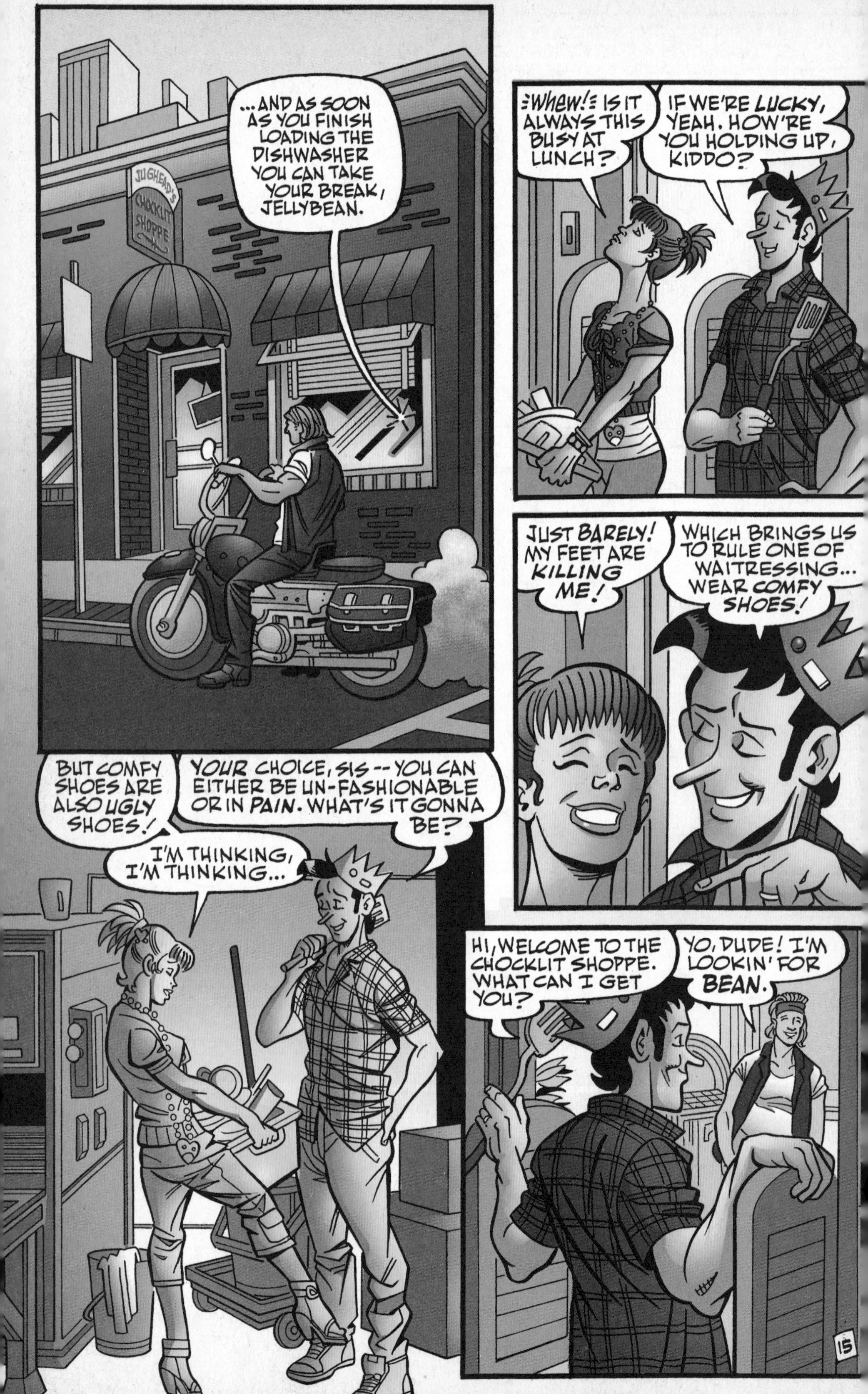
JUGHEAD'S CHOCKLIT SHOPPE
...AND AS SOON AS YOU FINISH LOADING THE DISHWASHER YOU CAN TAKE YOUR BREAK, JELLYBEAN.
=WHEW!= IS IT ALWAYS THIS BUSY AT LUNCH?
IF WE'RE LUCKY, YEAH. HOW'RE YOU HOLDING UP, KIDDO?
JUST BARELY! MY FEET ARE KILLING ME!
WHICH BRINGS US TO RULE ONE OF WAITRESSING... WEAR COMFY SHOES!
BUT COMFY SHOES ARE ALSO UGLY SHOES!
YOUR CHOICE, SIS -- YOU CAN EITHER BE UN-FASHIONABLE OR IN PAIN. WHAT'S IT GONNA BE?
I'M THINKING, I'M THINKING...
HI, WELCOME TO THE CHOCKLIT SHOPPE. WHAT CAN I GET YOU?
YO, DUDE! I'M LOOKIN' FOR BEAN.

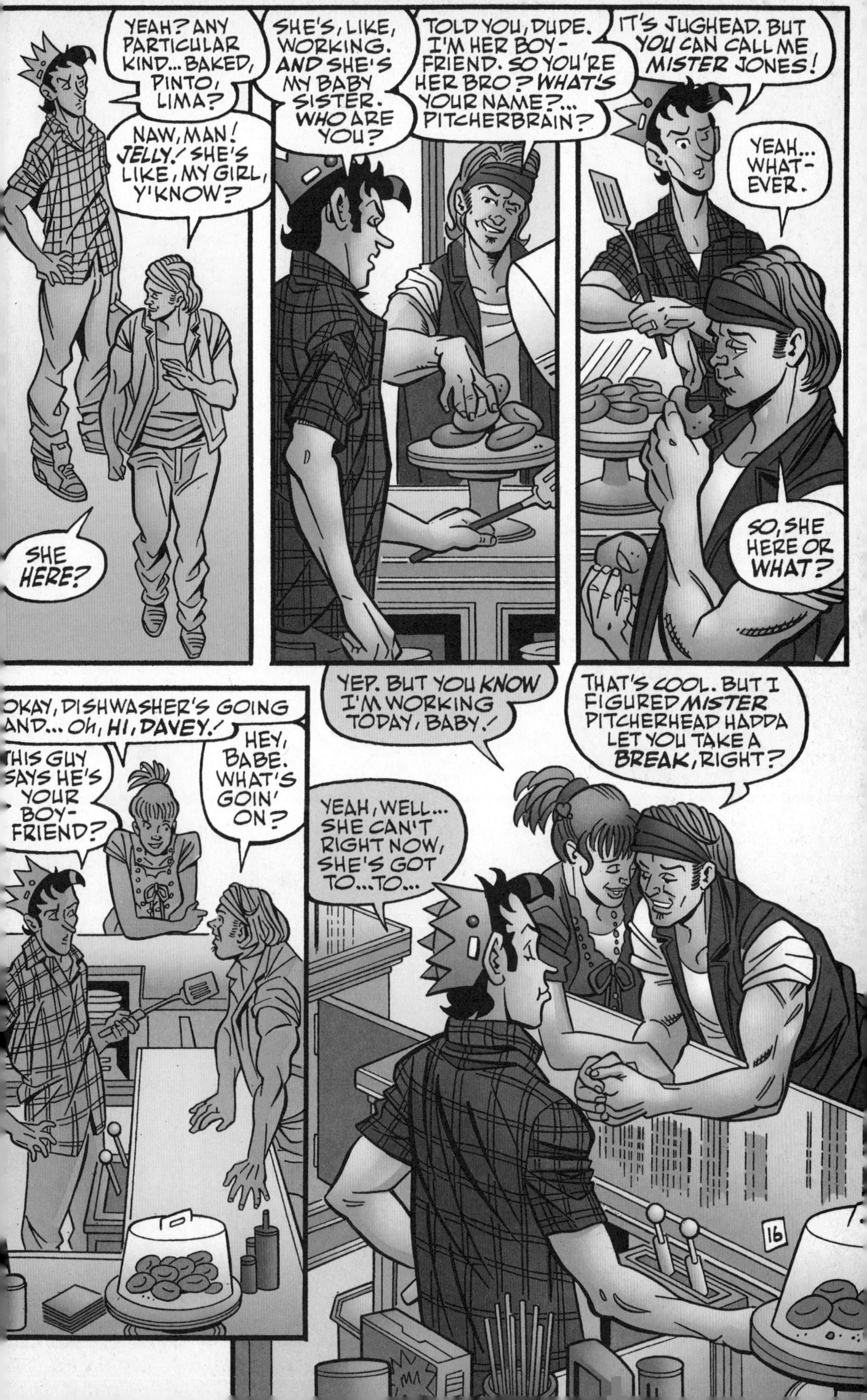
YEAH? ANY PARTICULAR KIND... BAKED, PINTO, LIMA?
NAW, MAN! JELLY! SHE'S LIKE, MY GIRL, Y'KNOW?
SHE HERE?
SHE'S, LIKE, WORKING. AND SHE'S MY BABY SISTER. WHO ARE YOU?
TOLD YOU, DUDE. I'M HER BOY-FRIEND. SO YOU'RE HER BRO? WHAT'S YOUR NAME?... PITCHERBRAIN?
IT'S JUGHEAD. BUT YOU CAN CALL ME MISTER JONES!
YEAH... WHAT-EVER.
SO, SHE HERE OR WHAT?
OKAY, DISHWASHER'S GOING AND... OH, HI, DAVEY!
THIS GUY SAYS HE'S YOUR BOY-FRIEND?
HEY, BABE. WHAT'S GOIN' ON?
YEP. BUT YOU KNOW I'M WORKING TODAY, BABY!
THAT'S COOL. BUT I FIGURED MISTER PITCHERHEAD HADDA LET YOU TAKE A BREAK, RIGHT?
YEAH, WELL... SHE CAN'T RIGHT NOW, SHE'S GOT TO... TO...
16

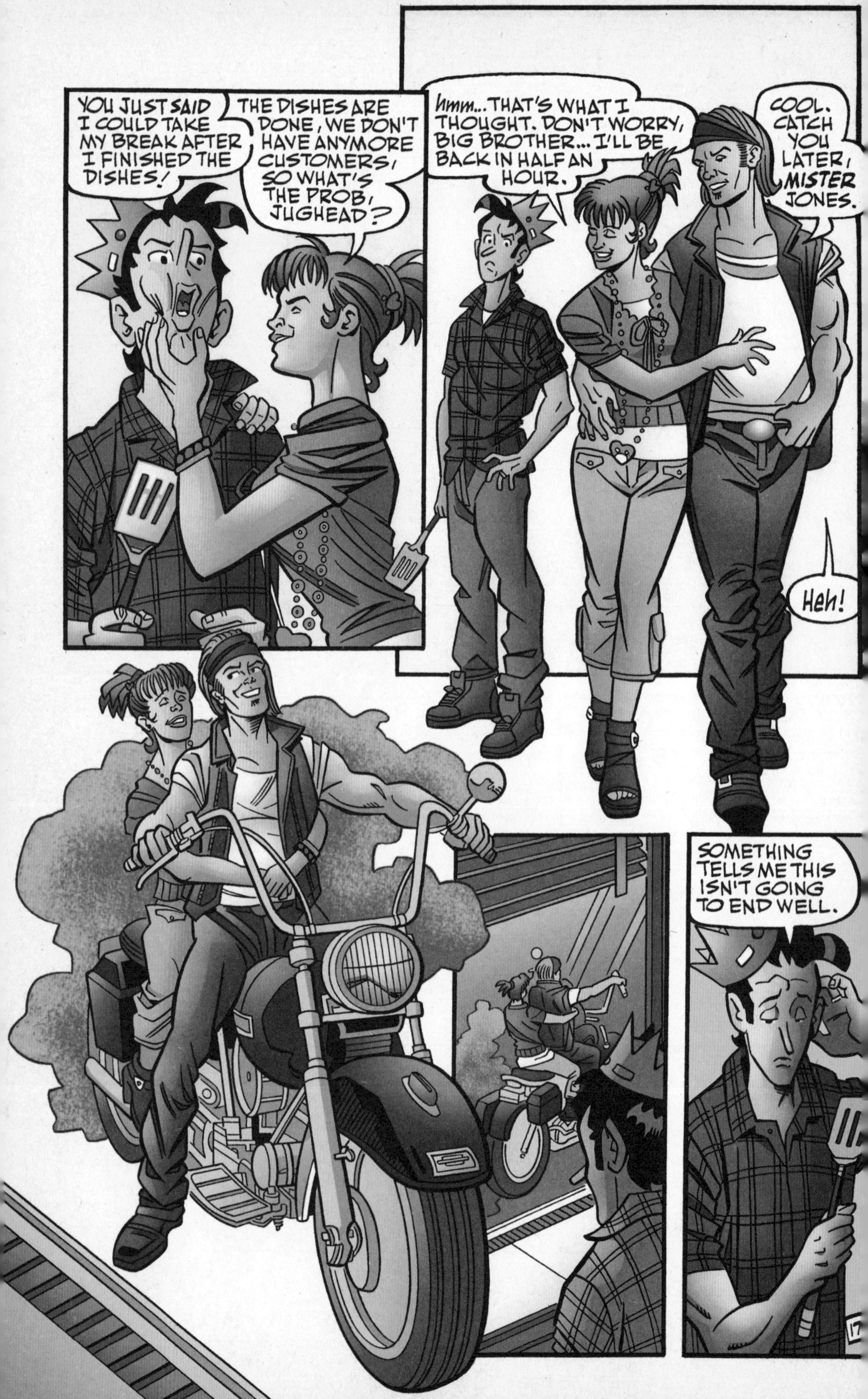
YOU JUST SAID I COULD TAKE MY BREAK AFTER I FINISHED THE DISHES!
THE DISHES ARE DONE, WE DON'T HAVE ANYMORE CUSTOMERS, SO WHAT'S THE PROB, JUGHEAD?
hmm... THAT'S WHAT I THOUGHT. DON'T WORRY, BIG BROTHER... I'LL BE BACK IN HALF AN HOUR.
COOL. CATCH YOU LATER, MISTER JONES.
Heh!
SOMETHING TELLS ME THIS ISN'T GOING TO END WELL.

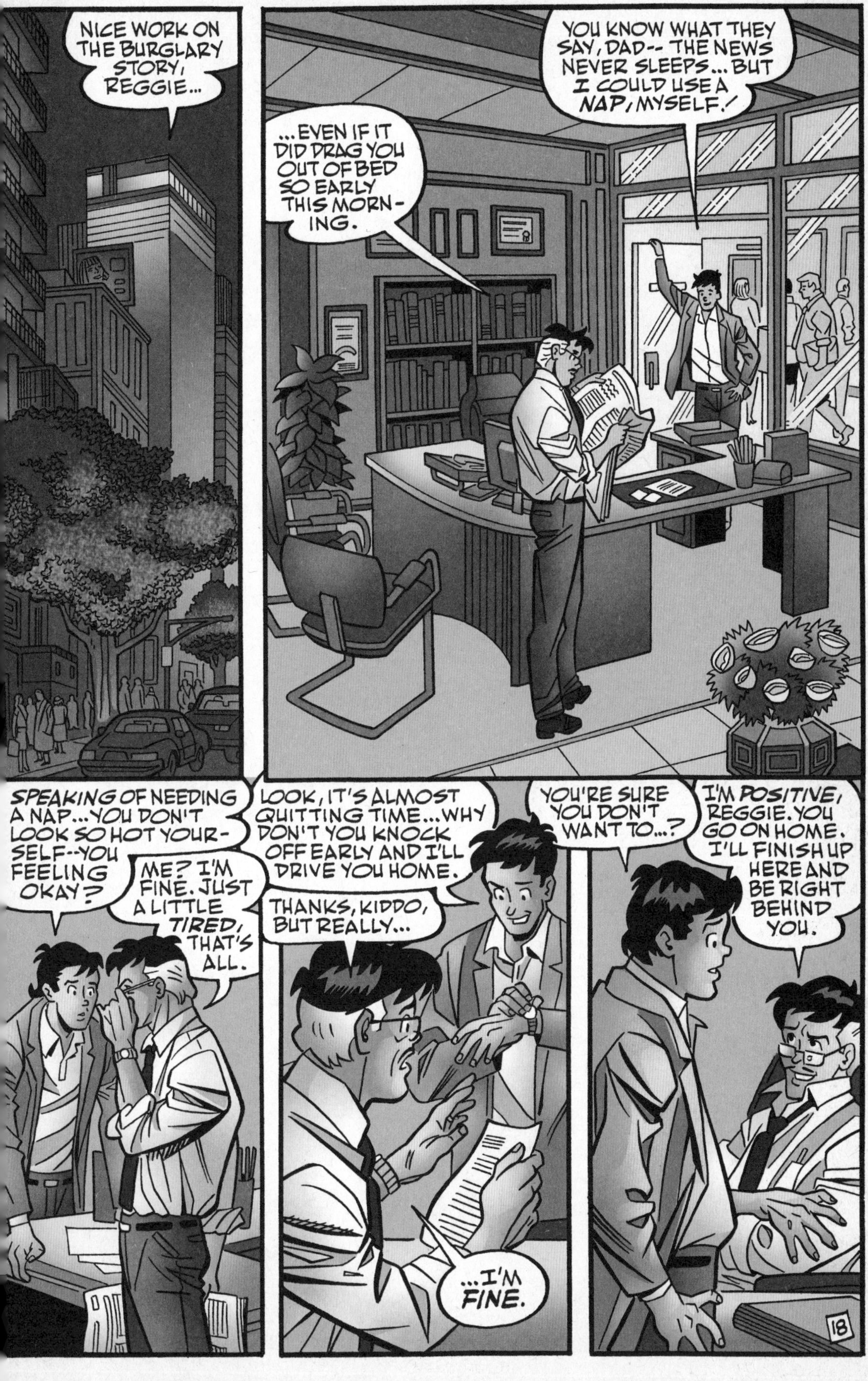
NICE WORK ON THE BURGLARY STORY, REGGIE...
...EVEN IF IT DID DRAG YOU OUT OF BED SO EARLY THIS MORN-ING.
YOU KNOW WHAT THEY SAY, DAD-- THE NEWS NEVER SLEEPS... BUT I COULD USE A *NAP*, MYSELF!
SPEAKING OF NEEDING A NAP... YOU DON'T LOOK SO HOT YOUR-SELF--YOU FEELING OKAY?
ME? I'M FINE. JUST A LITTLE *TIRED*, THAT'S ALL.
LOOK, IT'S ALMOST QUITTING TIME... WHY DON'T YOU KNOCK OFF EARLY AND I'LL DRIVE YOU HOME.
THANKS, KIDDO, BUT REALLY...
...I'M *FINE*.
YOU'RE SURE YOU DON'T WANT TO...?
I'M *POSITIVE*, REGGIE. YOU GO ON HOME. I'LL FINISH UP HERE AND BE RIGHT BEHIND YOU.

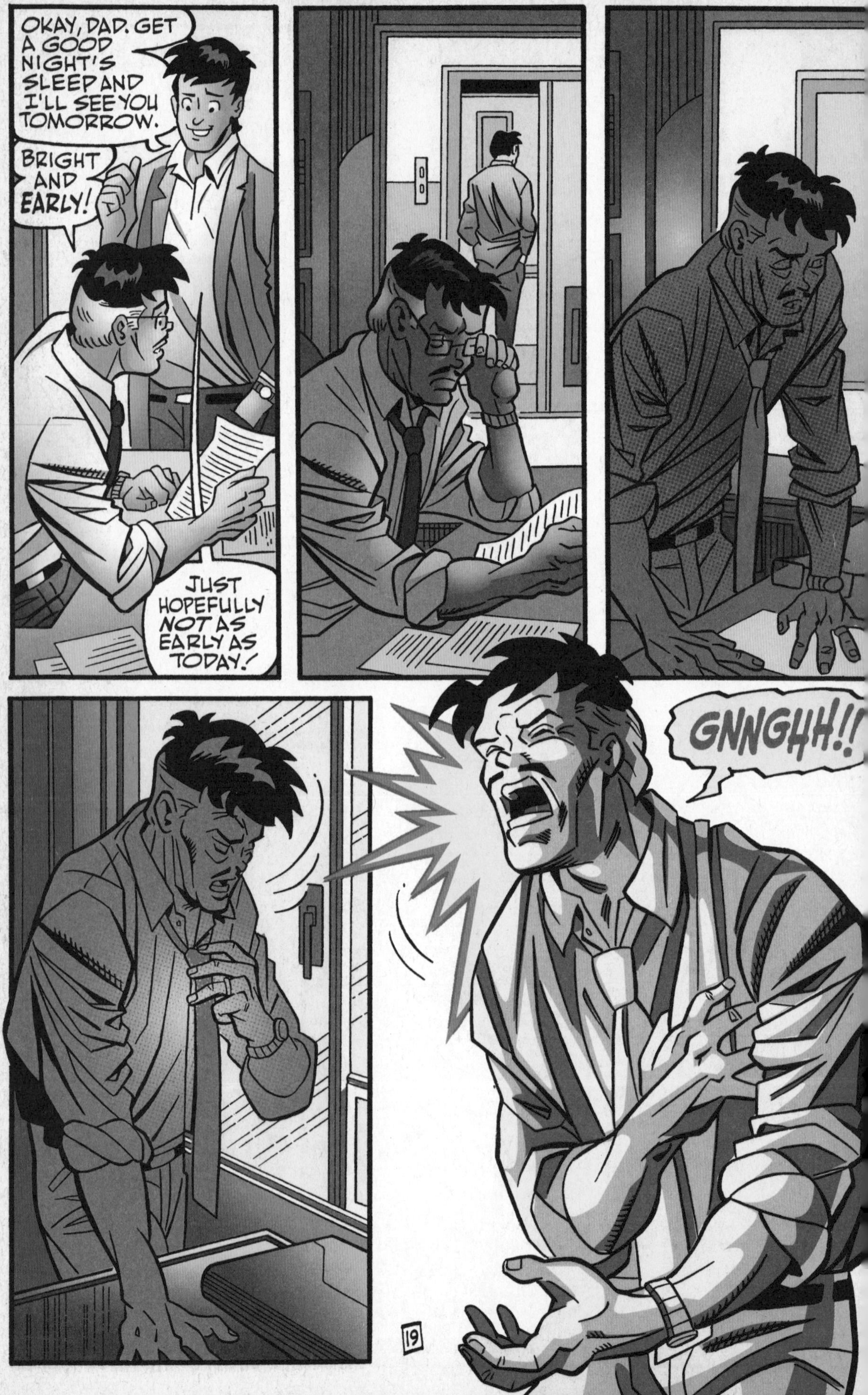
OKAY, DAD. GET A GOOD NIGHT'S SLEEP AND I'LL SEE YOU TOMORROW.
BRIGHT AND EARLY!
JUST HOPEFULLY NOT AS EARLY AS TODAY!
GNNGHH!!

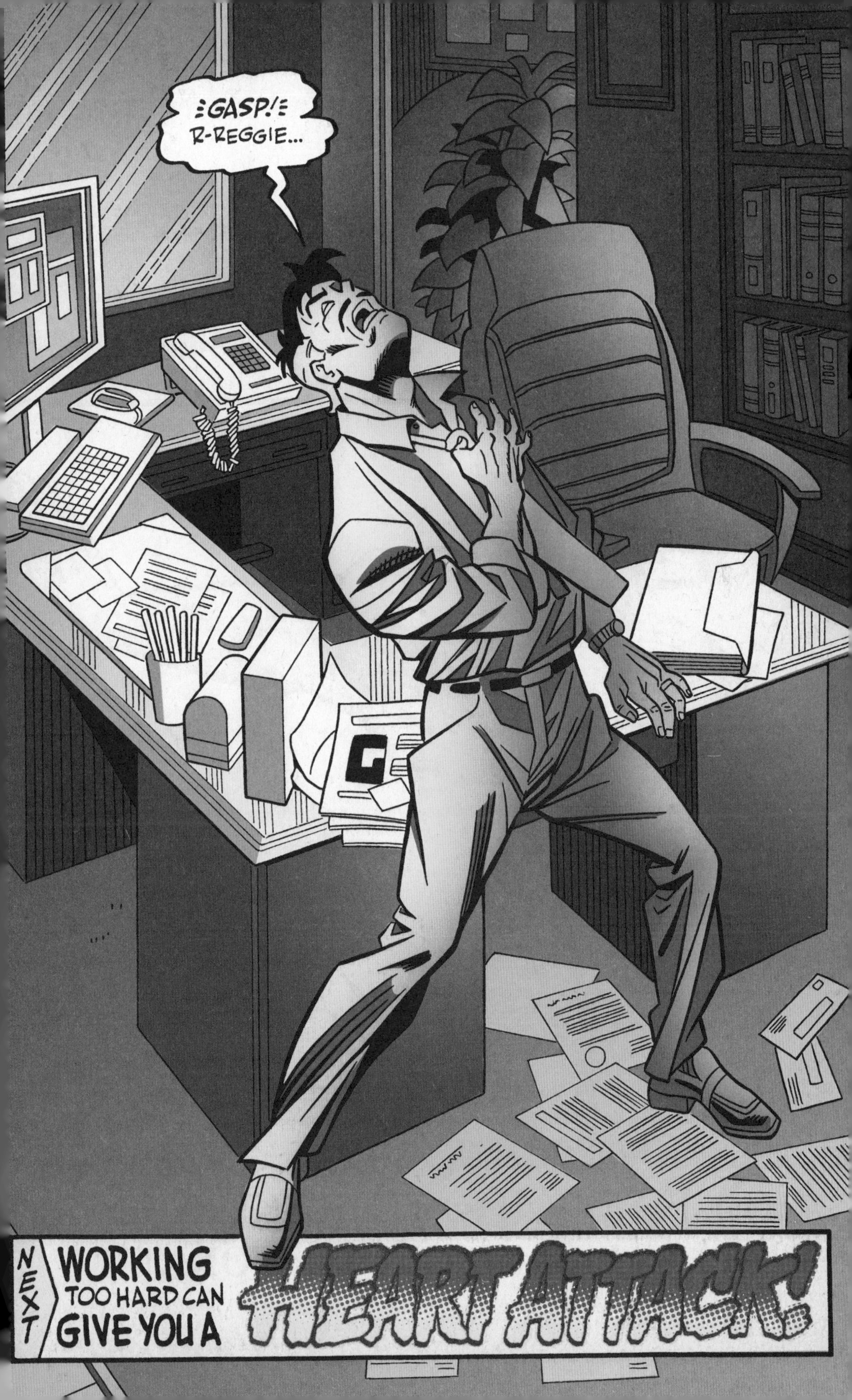

GASP!
R-REGGIE...
NEXT
WORKING TOO HARD CAN GIVE YOU A
HEART ATTACK!

"DAVE, I'M NOT TRYING TO TELL YOU HOW TO DO YOUR JOB--"

"--EXCEPT THAT I'VE ACTUALLY **DONE** YOUR JOB!"

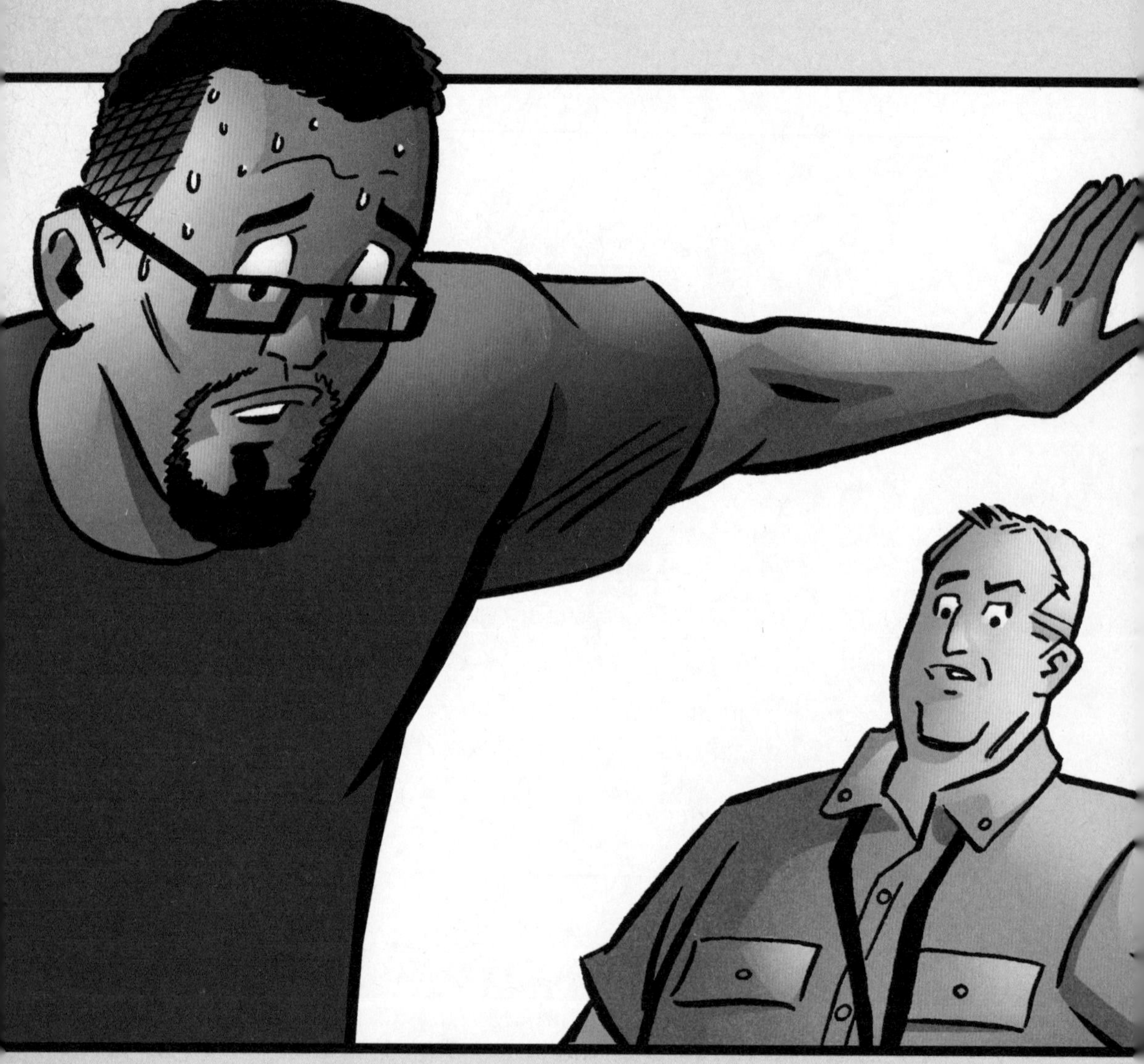

"...SO, NO OFFENSE, BUT IF YOU DON'T MIND, I'D MUCH RATHER **SKIP** THE SMALL TALK AND GET TO **WORK**!"

-DR. CLAY WALKER

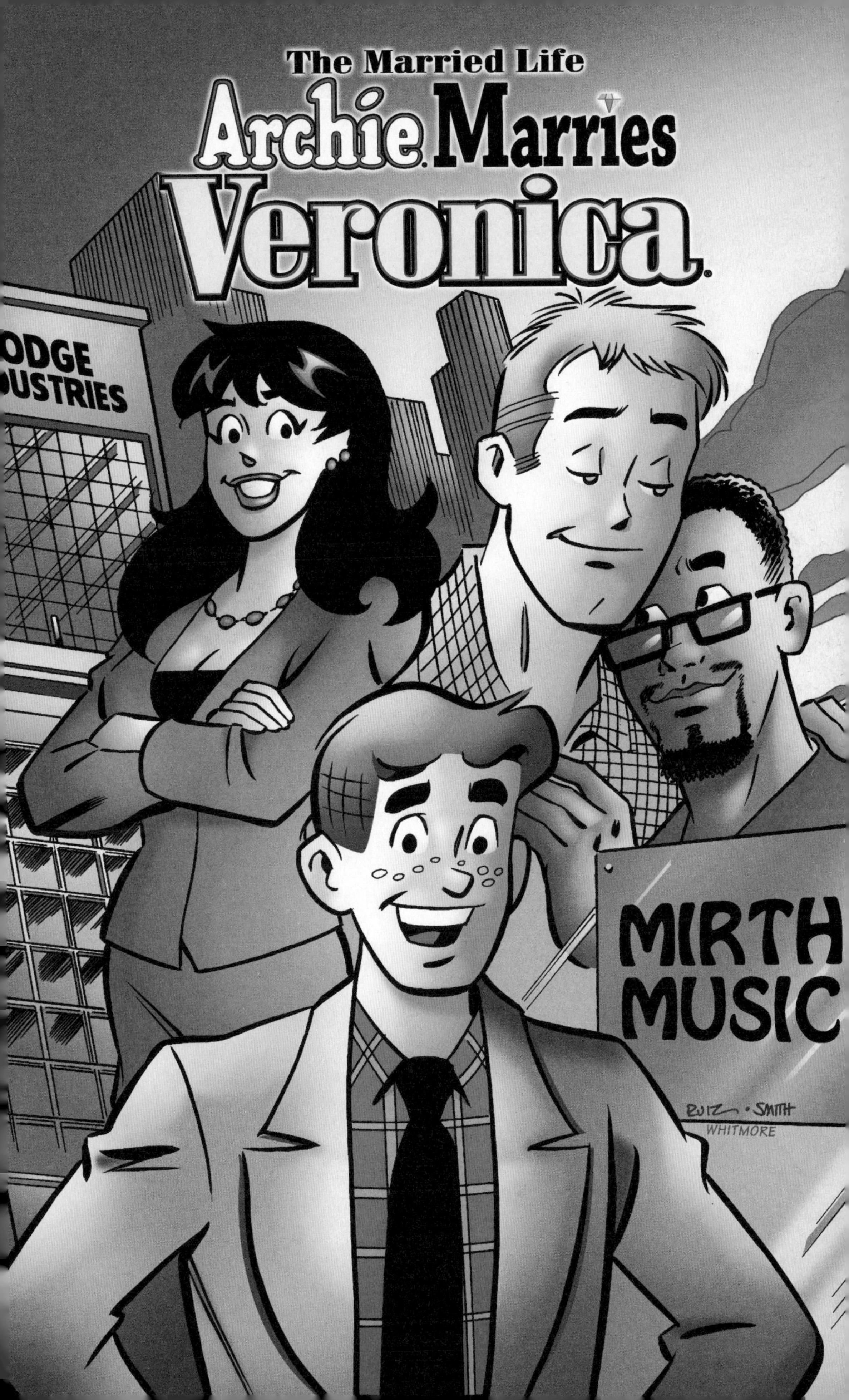
The Married Life
Archie Marries Veronica
ODGE
USTRIES
MIRTH MUSIC
RUIZ • SMITH
WHITMORE

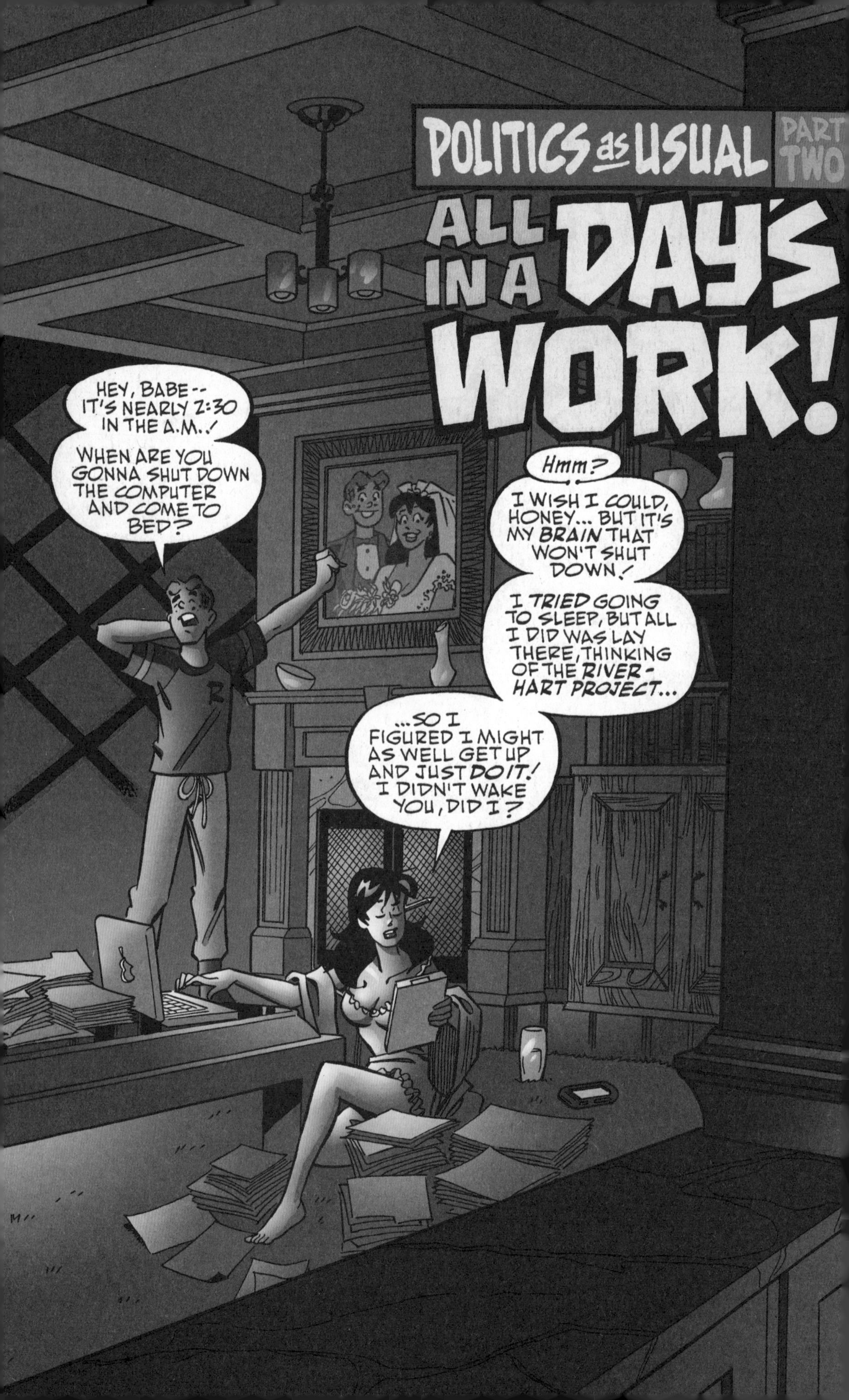
POLITICS as USUAL PART TWO
ALL IN A DAY'S WORK!
HEY, BABE-- IT'S NEARLY 2:30 IN THE A.M..!
WHEN ARE YOU GONNA SHUT DOWN THE COMPUTER AND COME TO BED?
Hmm?
I WISH I COULD, HONEY... BUT IT'S MY BRAIN THAT WON'T SHUT DOWN!
I TRIED GOING TO SLEEP, BUT ALL I DID WAS LAY THERE, THINKING OF THE RIVER-HART PROJECT...
...SO I FIGURED I MIGHT AS WELL GET UP AND JUST DO IT! I DIDN'T WAKE YOU, DID I?

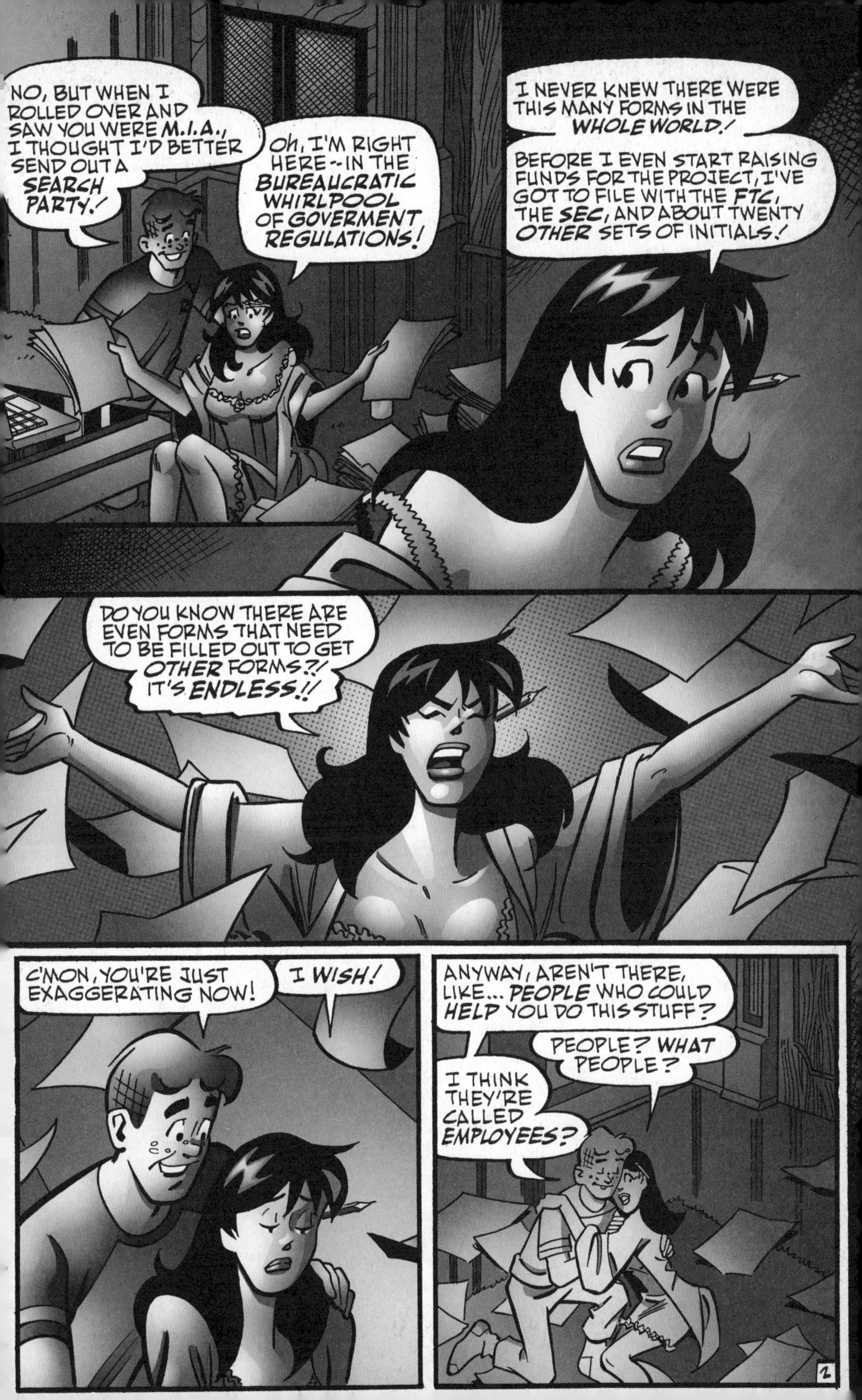
NO, BUT WHEN I ROLLED OVER AND SAW YOU WERE M.I.A., I THOUGHT I'D BETTER SEND OUT A SEARCH PARTY!
Oh, I'M RIGHT HERE--IN THE BUREAUCRATIC WHIRLPOOL OF GOVERMENT REGULATIONS!
I NEVER KNEW THERE WERE THIS MANY FORMS IN THE WHOLE WORLD!
BEFORE I EVEN START RAISING FUNDS FOR THE PROJECT, I'VE GOT TO FILE WITH THE FTC, THE SEC, AND ABOUT TWENTY OTHER SETS OF INITIALS!
DO YOU KNOW THERE ARE EVEN FORMS THAT NEED TO BE FILLED OUT TO GET OTHER FORMS?! IT'S ENDLESS!!
C'MON, YOU'RE JUST EXAGGERATING NOW!
I WISH!
ANYWAY, AREN'T THERE, LIKE... PEOPLE WHO COULD HELP YOU DO THIS STUFF?
PEOPLE? WHAT PEOPLE?
I THINK THEY'RE CALLED EMPLOYEES?
2

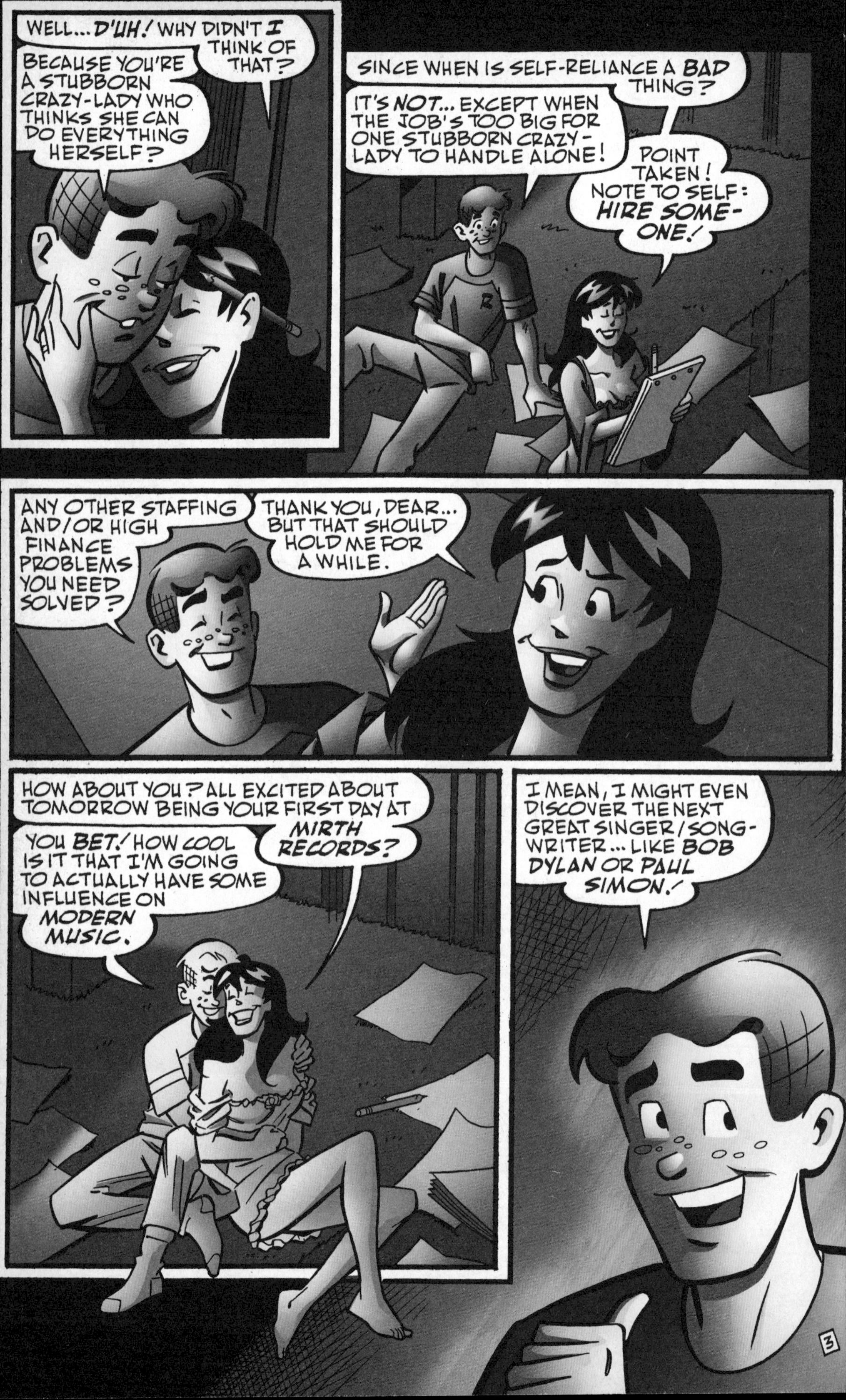
WELL... D'UH! WHY DIDN'T I THINK OF THAT?
BECAUSE YOU'RE A STUBBORN CRAZY-LADY WHO THINKS SHE CAN DO EVERYTHING HERSELF?
SINCE WHEN IS SELF-RELIANCE A BAD THING?
IT'S NOT... EXCEPT WHEN THE JOB'S TOO BIG FOR ONE STUBBORN CRAZY-LADY TO HANDLE ALONE!
POINT TAKEN! NOTE TO SELF: HIRE SOMEONE!
ANY OTHER STAFFING AND/OR HIGH FINANCE PROBLEMS YOU NEED SOLVED?
THANK YOU, DEAR... BUT THAT SHOULD HOLD ME FOR A WHILE.
HOW ABOUT YOU? ALL EXCITED ABOUT TOMORROW BEING YOUR FIRST DAY AT MIRTH RECORDS?
YOU BET! HOW COOL IS IT THAT I'M GOING TO ACTUALLY HAVE SOME INFLUENCE ON MODERN MUSIC.
I MEAN, I MIGHT EVEN DISCOVER THE NEXT GREAT SINGER/SONGWRITER... LIKE BOB DYLAN OR PAUL SIMON!
3

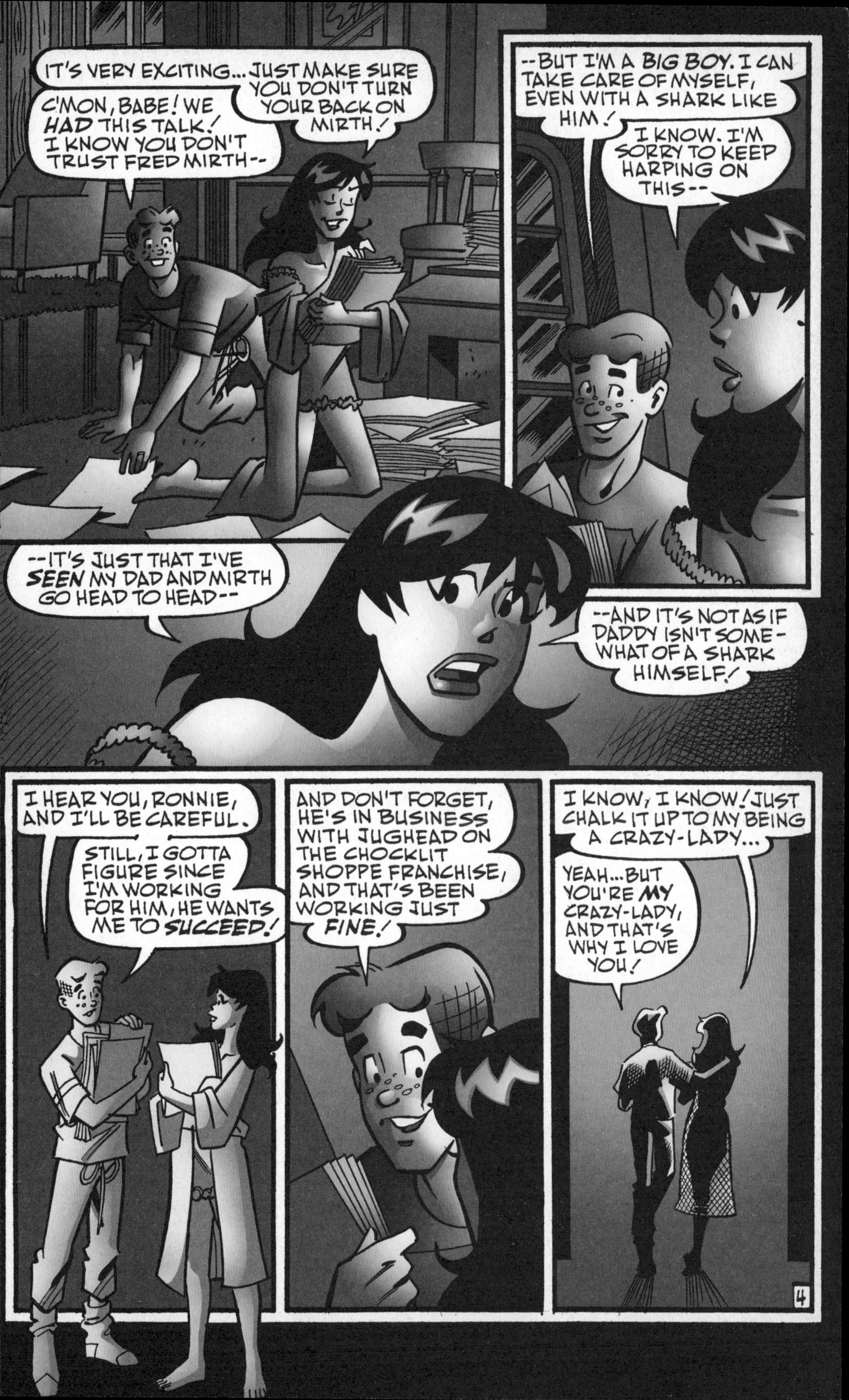
IT'S VERY EXCITING... JUST MAKE SURE YOU DON'T TURN YOUR BACK ON MIRTH!
C'MON, BABE! WE HAD THIS TALK! I KNOW YOU DON'T TRUST FRED MIRTH--
--BUT I'M A BIG BOY. I CAN TAKE CARE OF MYSELF, EVEN WITH A SHARK LIKE HIM!
I KNOW. I'M SORRY TO KEEP HARPING ON THIS--
--IT'S JUST THAT I'VE SEEN MY DAD AND MIRTH GO HEAD TO HEAD--
--AND IT'S NOT AS IF DADDY ISN'T SOME-WHAT OF A SHARK HIMSELF!
I HEAR YOU, RONNIE, AND I'LL BE CAREFUL.
STILL, I GOTTA FIGURE SINCE I'M WORKING FOR HIM, HE WANTS ME TO SUCCEED!
AND DON'T FORGET, HE'S IN BUSINESS WITH JUGHEAD ON THE CHOCKLIT SHOPPE FRANCHISE, AND THAT'S BEEN WORKING JUST FINE!
I KNOW, I KNOW! JUST CHALK IT UP TO MY BEING A CRAZY-LADY...
YEAH...BUT YOU'RE MY CRAZY-LADY, AND THAT'S WHY I LOVE YOU!
4

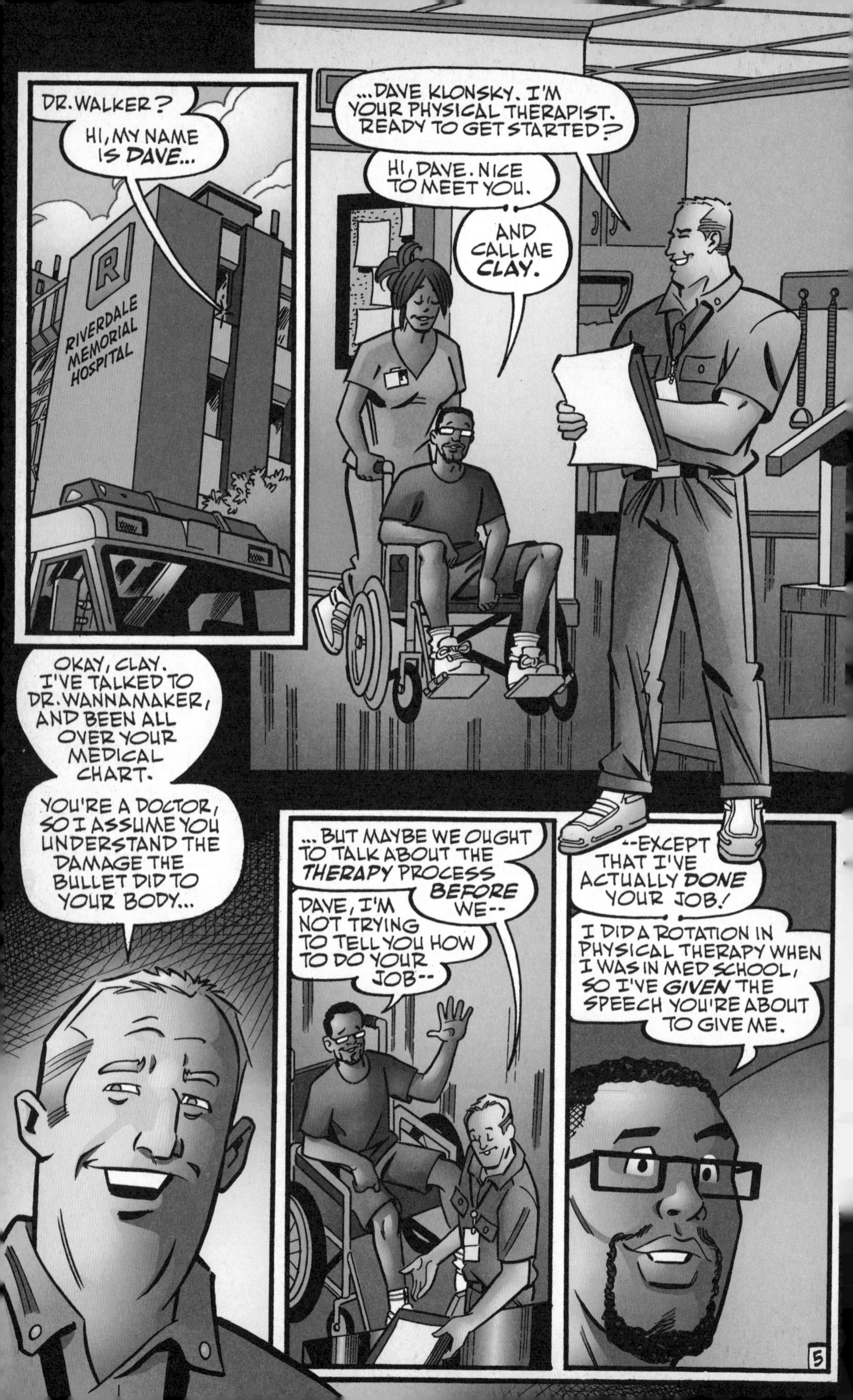
DR. WALKER?
HI, MY NAME IS DAVE...
RIVERDALE MEMORIAL HOSPITAL
...DAVE KLONSKY. I'M YOUR PHYSICAL THERAPIST. READY TO GET STARTED?
HI, DAVE. NICE TO MEET YOU.
AND CALL ME CLAY.
OKAY, CLAY. I'VE TALKED TO DR. WANNAMAKER, AND BEEN ALL OVER YOUR MEDICAL CHART.
YOU'RE A DOCTOR, SO I ASSUME YOU UNDERSTAND THE DAMAGE THE BULLET DID TO YOUR BODY...
... BUT MAYBE WE OUGHT TO TALK ABOUT THE THERAPY PROCESS BEFORE WE--
DAVE, I'M NOT TRYING TO TELL YOU HOW TO DO YOUR JOB--
--EXCEPT THAT I'VE ACTUALLY DONE YOUR JOB!
I DID A ROTATION IN PHYSICAL THERAPY WHEN I WAS IN MED SCHOOL, SO I'VE GIVEN THE SPEECH YOU'RE ABOUT TO GIVE ME.

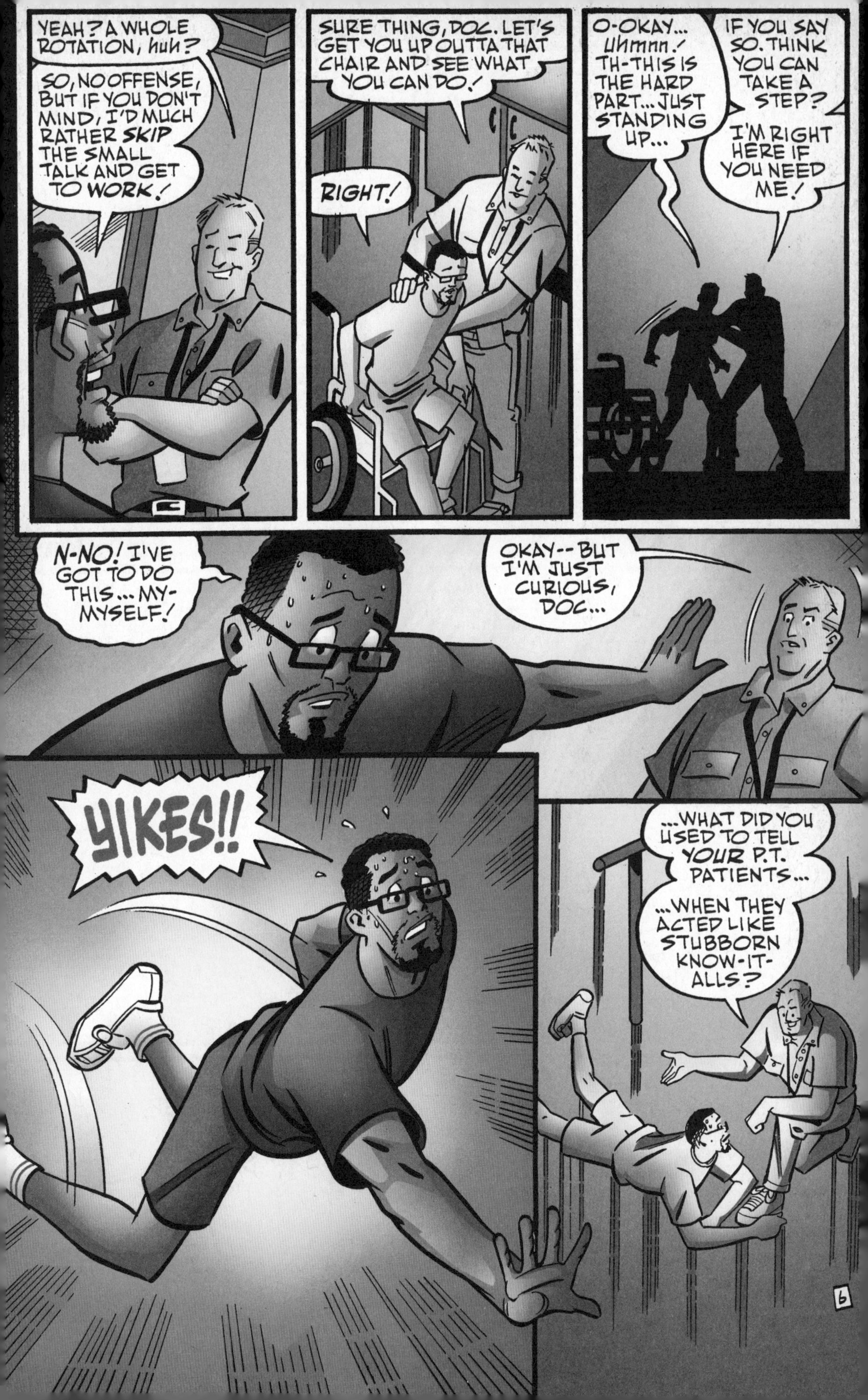
YEAH? A WHOLE ROTATION, huh?
SO, NO OFFENSE, BUT IF YOU DON'T MIND, I'D MUCH RATHER **SKIP** THE SMALL TALK AND GET TO **WORK**!
SURE THING, DOC. LET'S GET YOU UP OUTTA THAT CHAIR AND SEE WHAT YOU CAN DO!
RIGHT!
O-OKAY... uhmnn! TH-THIS IS THE HARD PART... JUST STANDING UP...
IF YOU SAY SO. THINK YOU CAN TAKE A STEP?
I'M RIGHT HERE IF YOU NEED ME!
N-NO! I'VE GOT TO DO THIS... MY-MYSELF!
OKAY-- BUT I'M JUST CURIOUS, DOC...
YIKES!!
...WHAT DID YOU USED TO TELL *YOUR* P.T. PATIENTS...
...WHEN THEY ACTED LIKE STUBBORN KNOW-IT-ALLS?
6

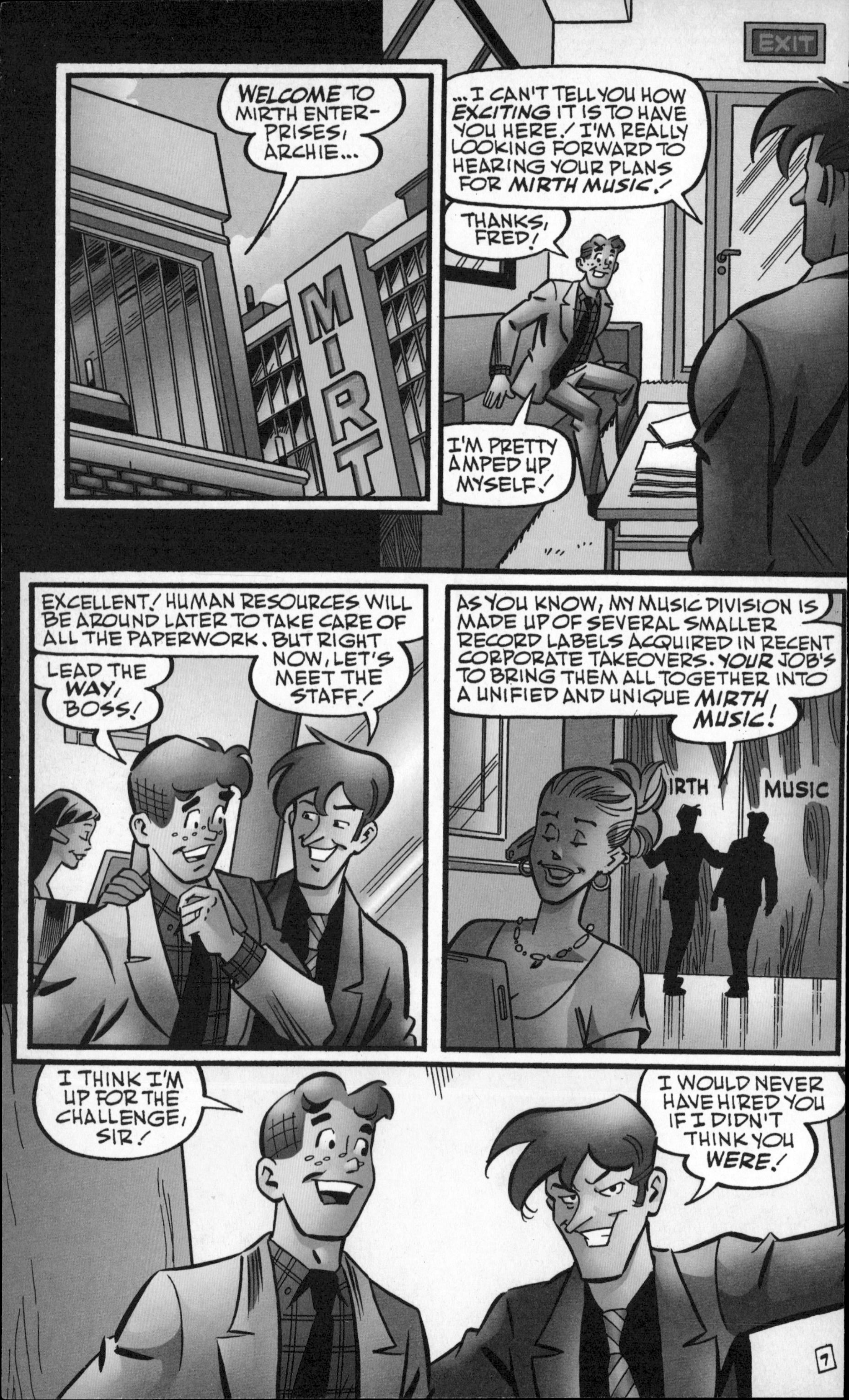

EXIT
WELCOME TO MIRTH ENTERPRISES, ARCHIE...
MIRT
...I CAN'T TELL YOU HOW EXCITING IT IS TO HAVE YOU HERE! I'M REALLY LOOKING FORWARD TO HEARING YOUR PLANS FOR MIRTH MUSIC!
THANKS, FRED!
I'M PRETTY AMPED UP MYSELF!
EXCELLENT! HUMAN RESOURCES WILL BE AROUND LATER TO TAKE CARE OF ALL THE PAPERWORK. BUT RIGHT NOW, LET'S MEET THE STAFF!
LEAD THE WAY, BOSS!
AS YOU KNOW, MY MUSIC DIVISION IS MADE UP OF SEVERAL SMALLER RECORD LABELS ACQUIRED IN RECENT CORPORATE TAKEOVERS. YOUR JOB'S TO BRING THEM ALL TOGETHER INTO A UNIFIED AND UNIQUE MIRTH MUSIC!
IRTH MUSIC
I THINK I'M UP FOR THE CHALLENGE, SIR!
I WOULD NEVER HAVE HIRED YOU IF I DIDN'T THINK YOU WERE!

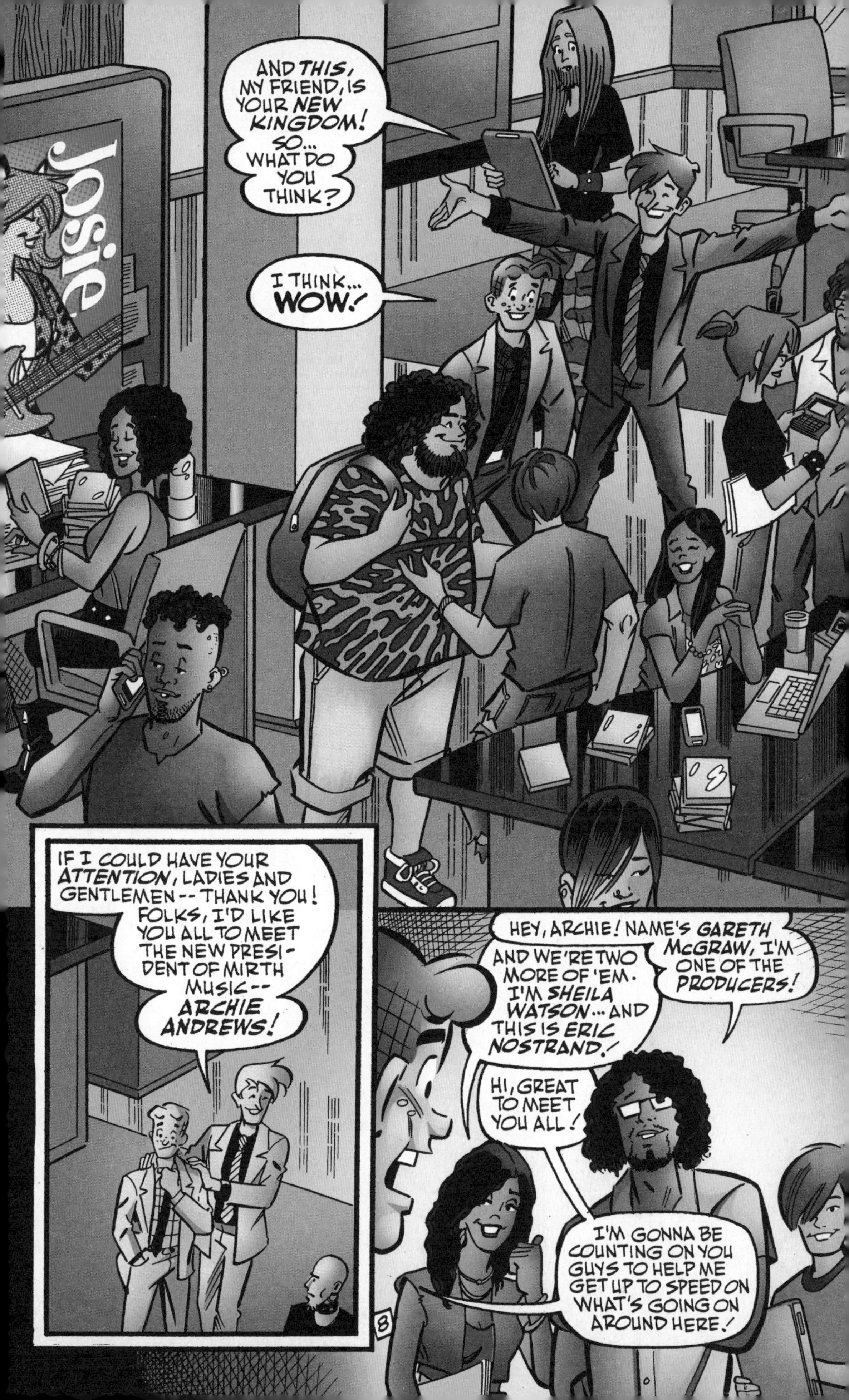
Josie
AND THIS, MY FRIEND, IS YOUR NEW KINGDOM! SO... WHAT DO YOU THINK?
I THINK... WOW!
IF I COULD HAVE YOUR ATTENTION, LADIES AND GENTLEMEN -- THANK YOU! FOLKS, I'D LIKE YOU ALL TO MEET THE NEW PRESI-DENT OF MIRTH MUSIC -- ARCHIE ANDREWS!
HEY, ARCHIE! NAME'S GARETH McGRAW, I'M ONE OF THE PRODUCERS!
AND WE'RE TWO MORE OF 'EM. I'M SHEILA WATSON... AND THIS IS ERIC NOSTRAND!
HI, GREAT TO MEET YOU ALL!
I'M GONNA BE COUNTING ON YOU GUYS TO HELP ME GET UP TO SPEED ON WHAT'S GOING ON AROUND HERE!
8

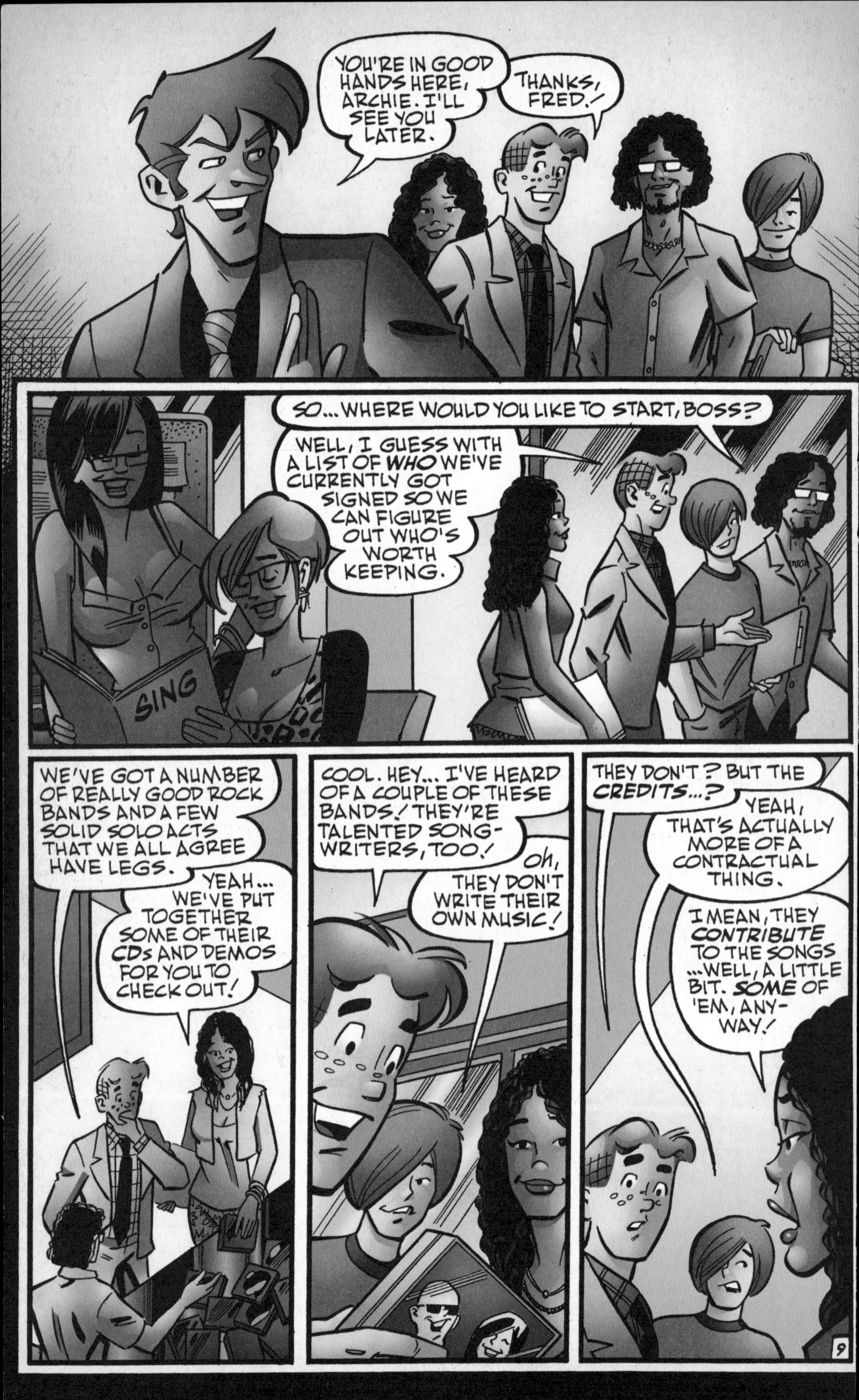
YOU'RE IN GOOD HANDS HERE, ARCHIE. I'LL SEE YOU LATER.
THANKS, FRED.!
SO... WHERE WOULD YOU LIKE TO START, BOSS?
WELL, I GUESS WITH A LIST OF WHO WE'VE CURRENTLY GOT SIGNED SO WE CAN FIGURE OUT WHO'S WORTH KEEPING.
SING
WE'VE GOT A NUMBER OF REALLY GOOD ROCK BANDS AND A FEW SOLID SOLO ACTS THAT WE ALL AGREE HAVE LEGS.
YEAH... WE'VE PUT TOGETHER SOME OF THEIR CDs AND DEMOS FOR YOU TO CHECK OUT!
COOL. HEY... I'VE HEARD OF A COUPLE OF THESE BANDS! THEY'RE TALENTED SONG-WRITERS, TOO!
OH, THEY DON'T WRITE THEIR OWN MUSIC!
THEY DON'T? BUT THE CREDITS...?
YEAH, THAT'S ACTUALLY MORE OF A CONTRACTUAL THING.
I MEAN, THEY CONTRIBUTE TO THE SONGS ...WELL, A LITTLE BIT. SOME OF 'EM, ANY-WAY!
9

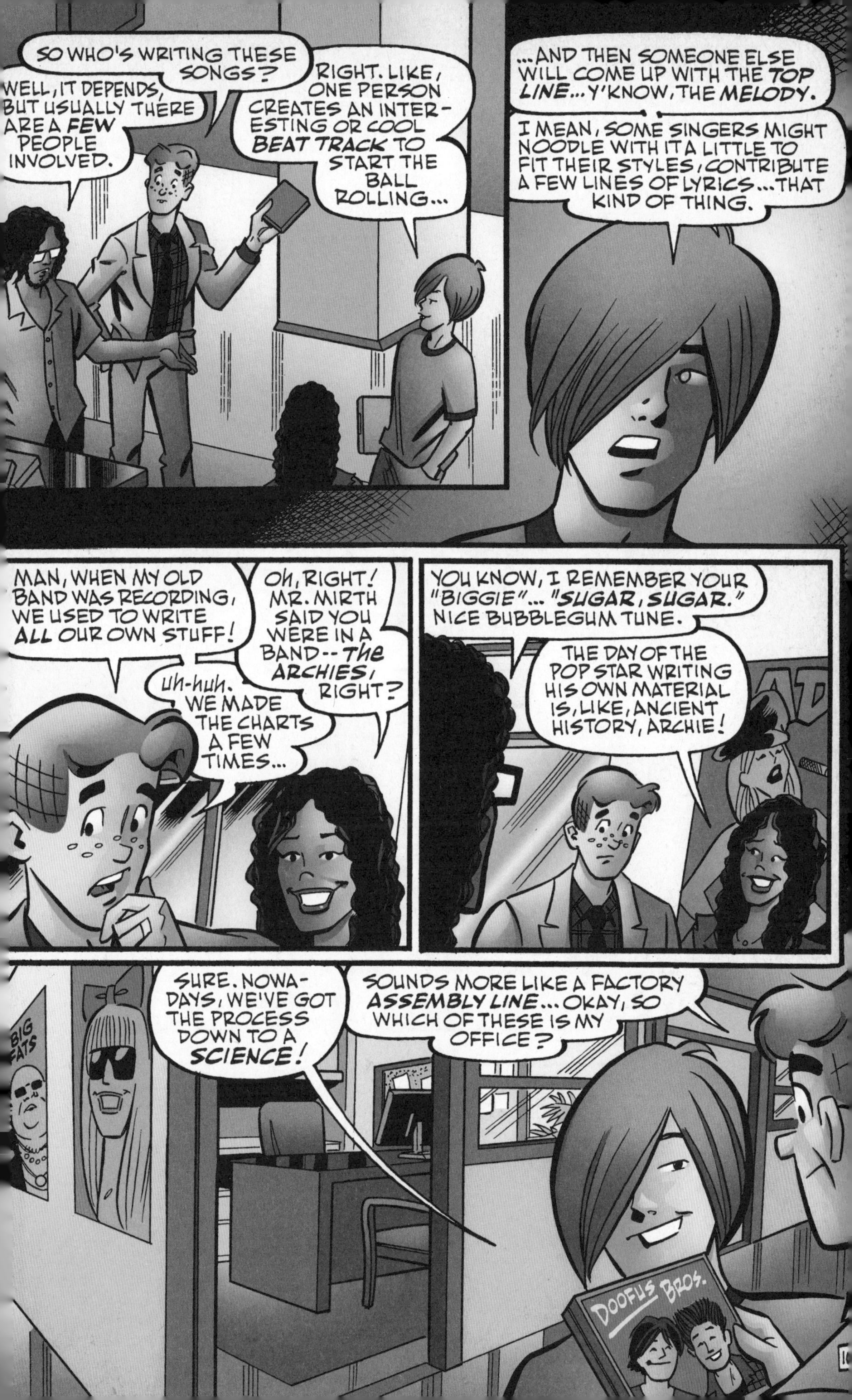
SO WHO'S WRITING THESE SONGS?
WELL, IT DEPENDS, BUT USUALLY THERE ARE A FEW PEOPLE INVOLVED.
RIGHT. LIKE, ONE PERSON CREATES AN INTERESTING OR COOL BEAT TRACK TO START THE BALL ROLLING...
...AND THEN SOMEONE ELSE WILL COME UP WITH THE TOP LINE... Y'KNOW, THE MELODY.
I MEAN, SOME SINGERS MIGHT NOODLE WITH IT A LITTLE TO FIT THEIR STYLES, CONTRIBUTE A FEW LINES OF LYRICS... THAT KIND OF THING.
MAN, WHEN MY OLD BAND WAS RECORDING, WE USED TO WRITE ALL OUR OWN STUFF!
Oh, RIGHT! MR. MIRTH SAID YOU WERE IN A BAND-- THE ARCHIES, RIGHT?
UH-HUH. WE MADE THE CHARTS A FEW TIMES...
YOU KNOW, I REMEMBER YOUR "BIGGIE"... "SUGAR, SUGAR." NICE BUBBLEGUM TUNE.
THE DAY OF THE POP STAR WRITING HIS OWN MATERIAL IS, LIKE, ANCIENT HISTORY, ARCHIE!
BIG FATS
SURE. NOWADAYS, WE'VE GOT THE PROCESS DOWN TO A SCIENCE!
SOUNDS MORE LIKE A FACTORY ASSEMBLY LINE... OKAY, SO WHICH OF THESE IS MY OFFICE?
DOOFUS BROS.

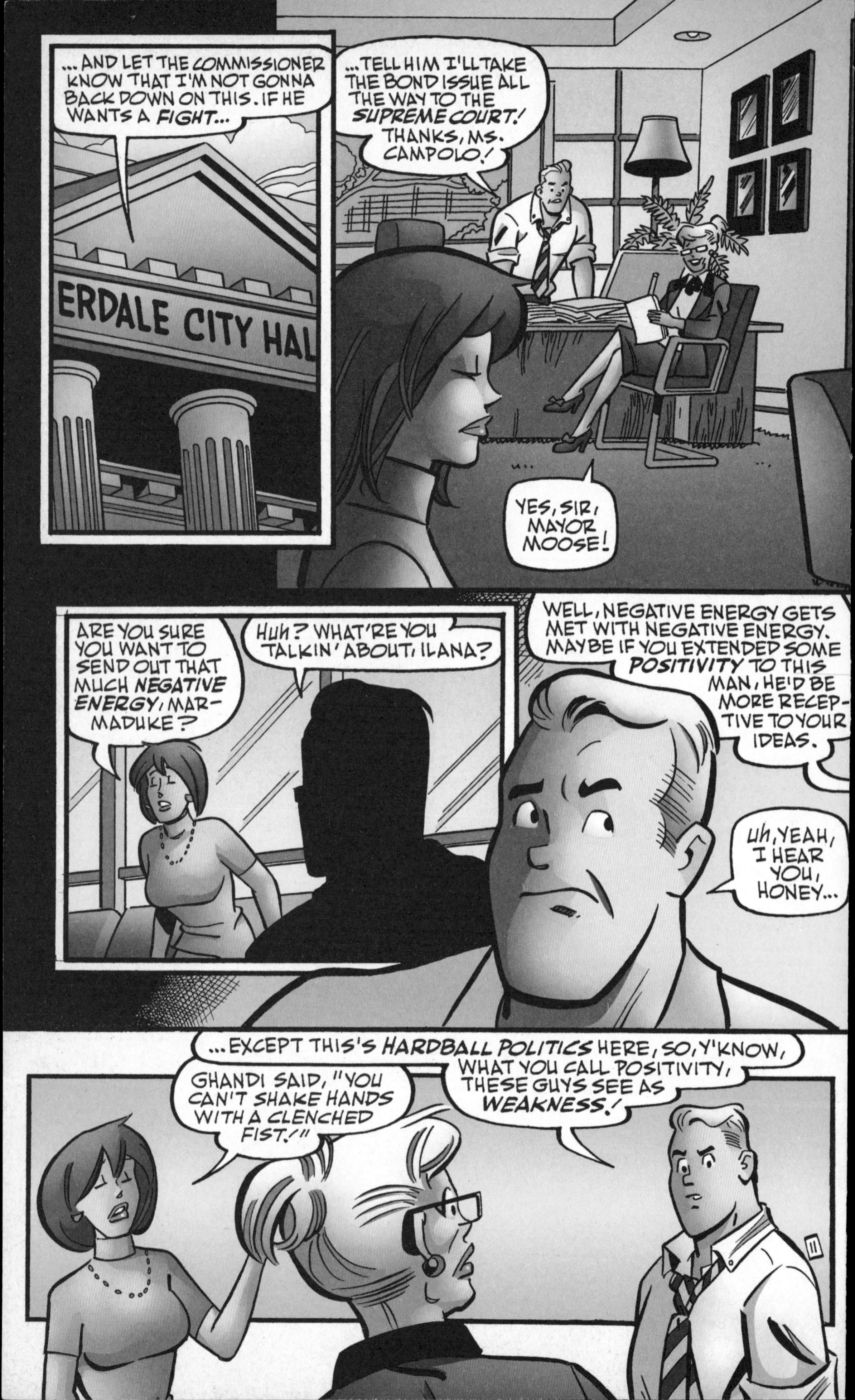

ERDALE CITY HAL
...AND LET THE COMMISSIONER KNOW THAT I'M NOT GONNA BACK DOWN ON THIS. IF HE WANTS A FIGHT...
...TELL HIM I'LL TAKE THE BOND ISSUE ALL THE WAY TO THE SUPREME COURT! THANKS, MS. CAMPOLO!
YES, SIR, MAYOR MOOSE!
ARE YOU SURE YOU WANT TO SEND OUT THAT MUCH NEGATIVE ENERGY, MARMADUKE?
HUH? WHAT'RE YOU TALKIN' ABOUT, ILANA?
WELL, NEGATIVE ENERGY GETS MET WITH NEGATIVE ENERGY. MAYBE IF YOU EXTENDED SOME POSITIVITY TO THIS MAN, HE'D BE MORE RECEPTIVE TO YOUR IDEAS.
UH, YEAH, I HEAR YOU, HONEY...
GHANDI SAID, "YOU CAN'T SHAKE HANDS WITH A CLENCHED FIST!"
...EXCEPT THIS'S HARDBALL POLITICS HERE, SO, Y'KNOW, WHAT YOU CALL POSITIVITY, THESE GUYS SEE AS WEAKNESS!
11

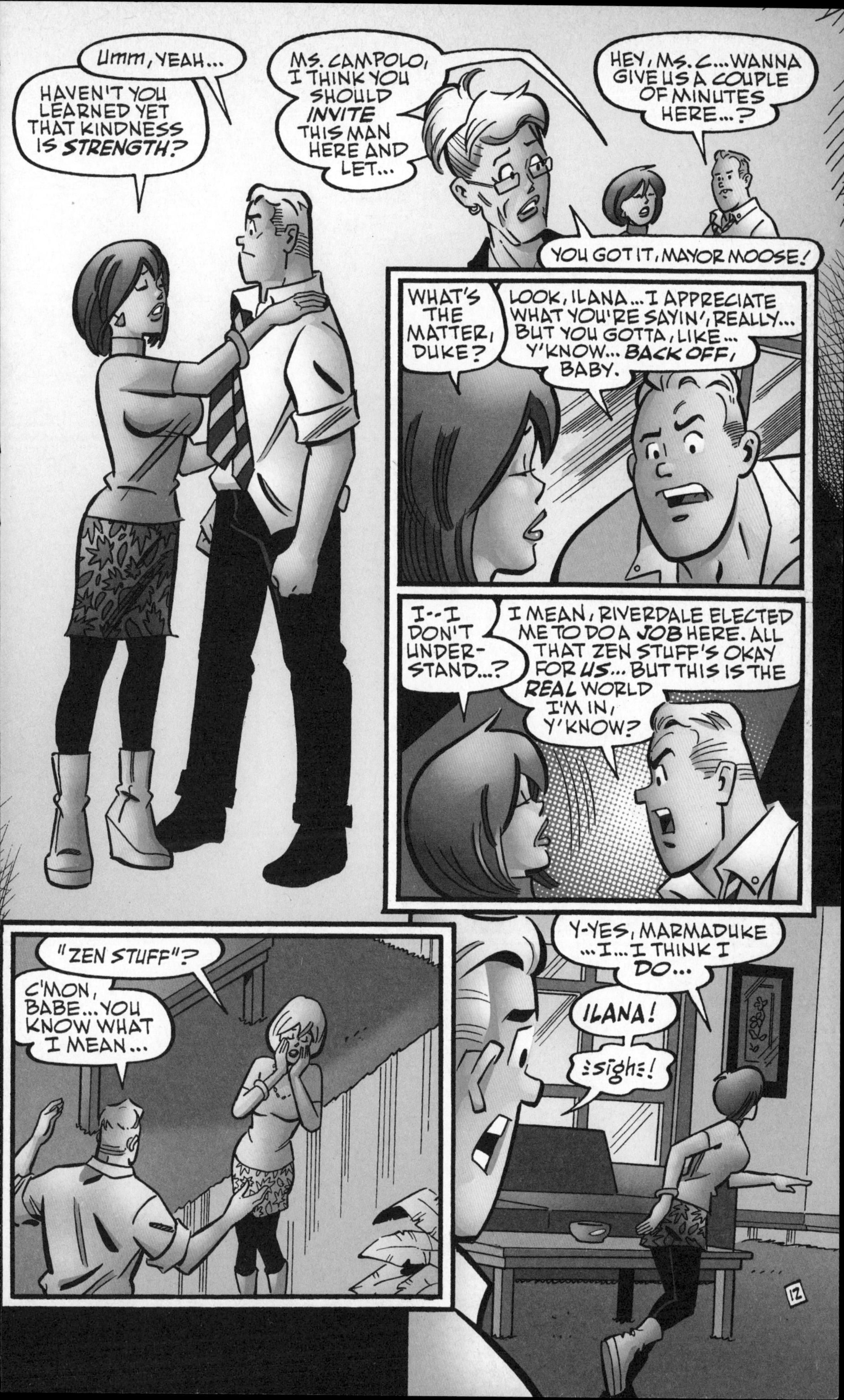
UMM, YEAH...
HAVEN'T YOU LEARNED YET THAT KINDNESS IS STRENGTH?
MS. CAMPOLO, I THINK YOU SHOULD INVITE THIS MAN HERE AND LET...
HEY, MS. C...WANNA GIVE US A COUPLE OF MINUTES HERE...?
YOU GOT IT, MAYOR MOOSE!
WHAT'S THE MATTER, DUKE?
LOOK, ILANA... I APPRECIATE WHAT YOU'RE SAYIN', REALLY... BUT YOU GOTTA, LIKE... Y'KNOW... BACK OFF, BABY.
I--I DON'T UNDER- STAND...?
I MEAN, RIVERDALE ELECTED ME TO DO A JOB HERE. ALL THAT ZEN STUFF'S OKAY FOR US... BUT THIS IS THE REAL WORLD I'M IN, Y'KNOW?
"ZEN STUFF"?
C'MON, BABE... YOU KNOW WHAT I MEAN...
Y-YES, MARMADUKE ...I...I THINK I DO...
ILANA!
:sigh:!
12

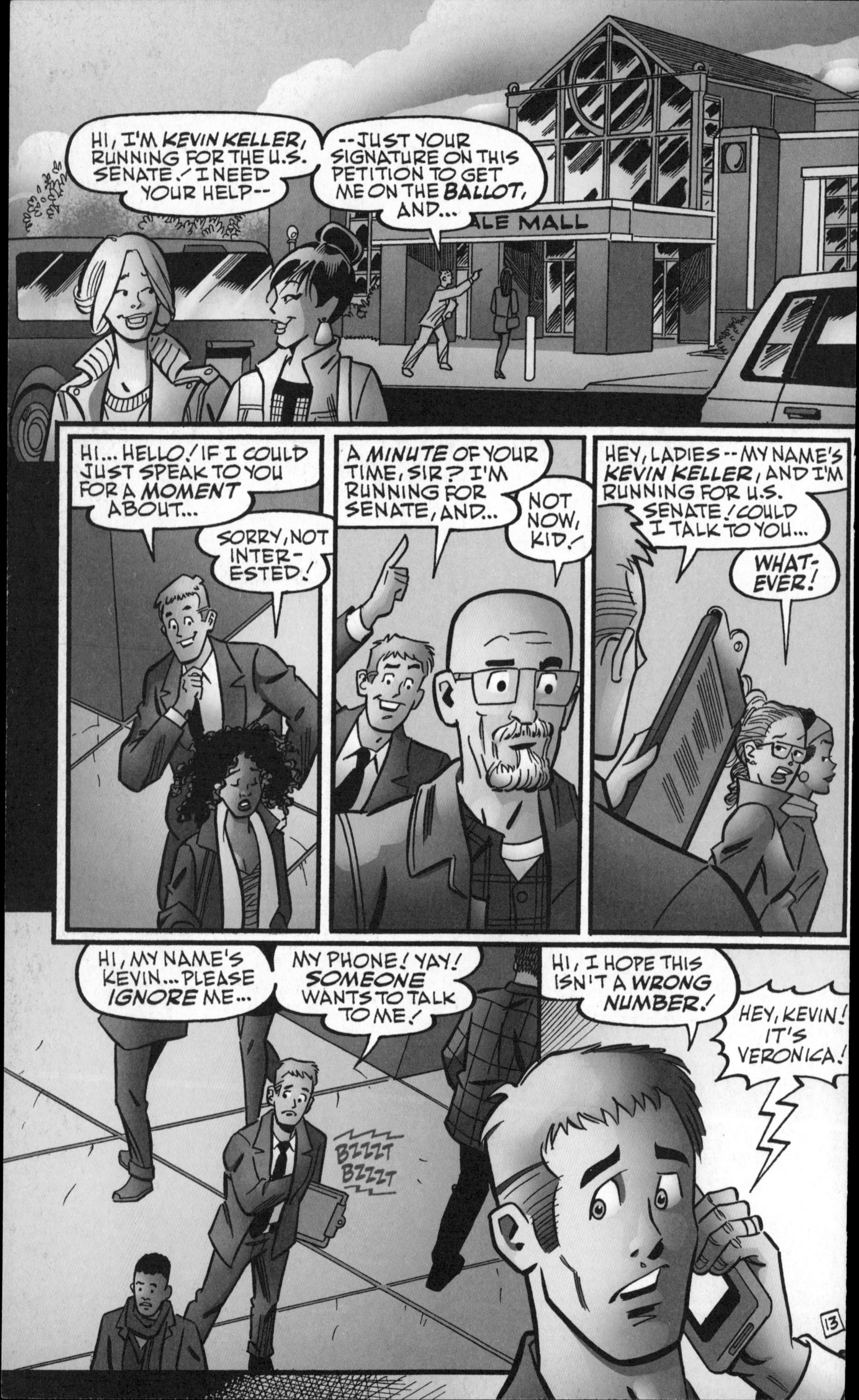
HI, I'M KEVIN KELLER, RUNNING FOR THE U.S. SENATE! I NEED YOUR HELP--
--JUST YOUR SIGNATURE ON THIS PETITION TO GET ME ON THE BALLOT, AND...
ALE MALL
HI... HELLO! IF I COULD JUST SPEAK TO YOU FOR A MOMENT ABOUT...
SORRY, NOT INTER-ESTED!
A MINUTE OF YOUR TIME, SIR? I'M RUNNING FOR SENATE, AND...
NOT NOW, KID!
HEY, LADIES--MY NAME'S KEVIN KELLER, AND I'M RUNNING FOR U.S. SENATE! COULD I TALK TO YOU...
WHAT-EVER!
HI, MY NAME'S KEVIN... PLEASE IGNORE ME...
MY PHONE! YAY! SOMEONE WANTS TO TALK TO ME!
BZZZT BZZZT
HI, I HOPE THIS ISN'T A WRONG NUMBER!
HEY, KEVIN! IT'S VERONICA!
13

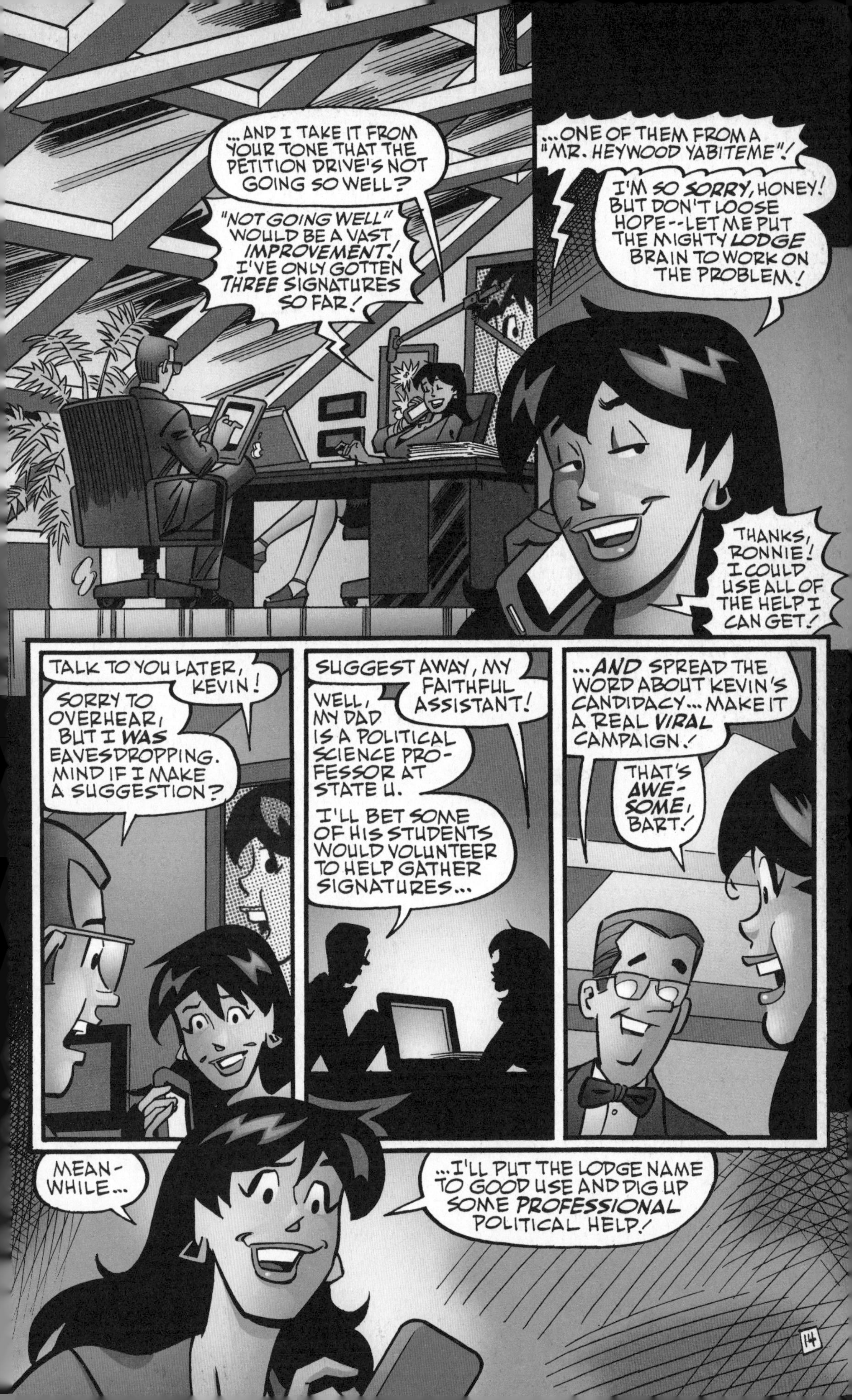
...AND I TAKE IT FROM YOUR TONE THAT THE PETITION DRIVE'S NOT GOING SO WELL?
"NOT GOING WELL" WOULD BE A VAST IMPROVEMENT! I'VE ONLY GOTTEN THREE SIGNATURES SO FAR!
...ONE OF THEM FROM A "MR. HEYWOOD YABITEME"!
I'M SO SORRY, HONEY! BUT DON'T LOOSE HOPE--LET ME PUT THE MIGHTY LODGE BRAIN TO WORK ON THE PROBLEM!
THANKS, RONNIE! I COULD USE ALL OF THE HELP I CAN GET!
TALK TO YOU LATER, KEVIN!
SORRY TO OVERHEAR, BUT I WAS EAVESDROPPING. MIND IF I MAKE A SUGGESTION?
SUGGEST AWAY, MY FAITHFUL ASSISTANT!
WELL, MY DAD IS A POLITICAL SCIENCE PROFESSOR AT STATE U.
I'LL BET SOME OF HIS STUDENTS WOULD VOLUNTEER TO HELP GATHER SIGNATURES...
...AND SPREAD THE WORD ABOUT KEVIN'S CANDIDACY... MAKE IT A REAL VIRAL CAMPAIGN!
THAT'S AWESOME, BART!
MEANWHILE...
...I'LL PUT THE LODGE NAME TO GOOD USE AND DIG UP SOME PROFESSIONAL POLITICAL HELP!
14

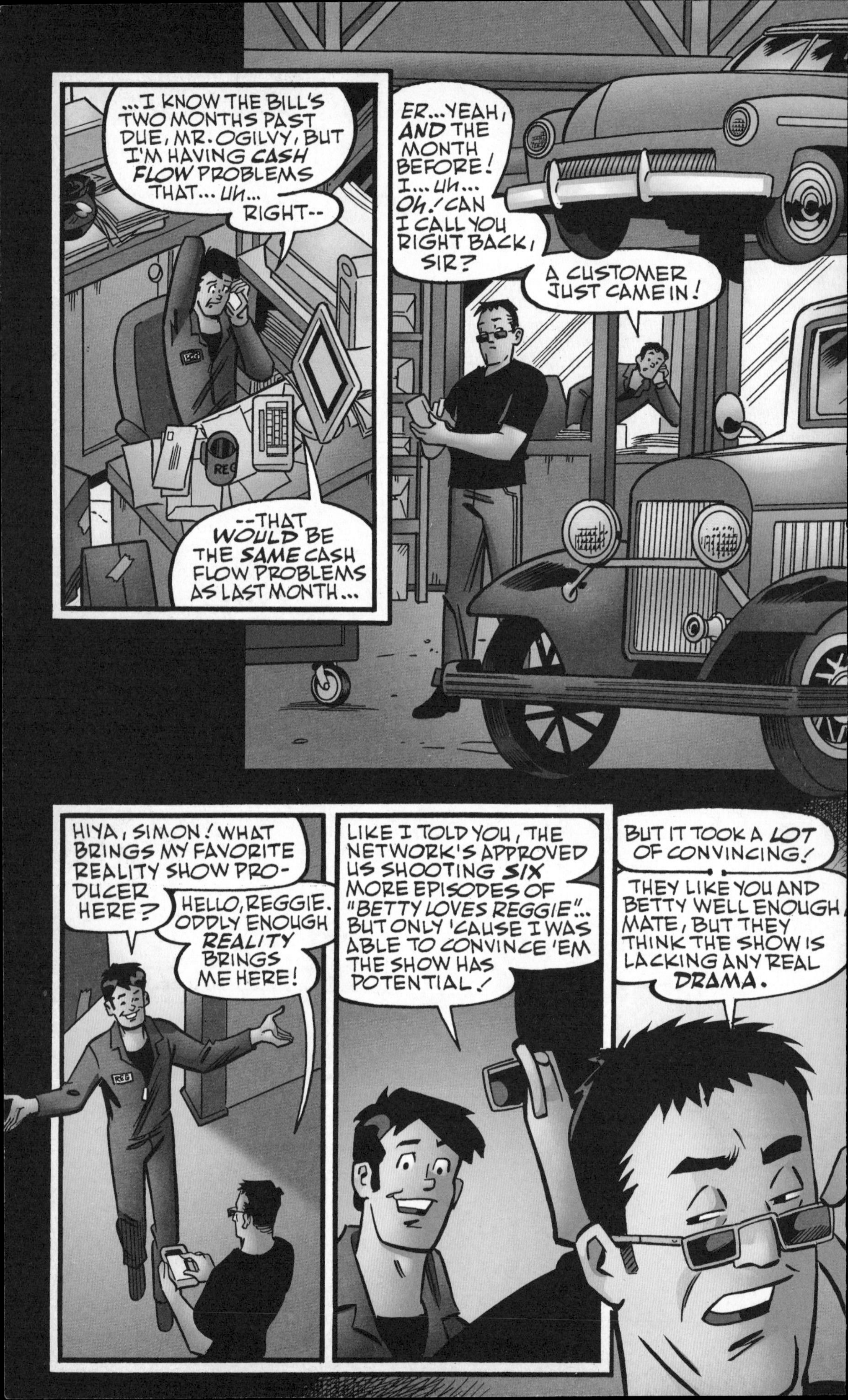
...I KNOW THE BILL'S TWO MONTHS PAST DUE, MR. OGILVY, BUT I'M HAVING CASH FLOW PROBLEMS THAT... UH...
RIGHT--
--THAT WOULD BE THE SAME CASH FLOW PROBLEMS AS LAST MONTH...
ER...YEAH, AND THE MONTH BEFORE! I... UH... OH! CAN I CALL YOU RIGHT BACK, SIR?
A CUSTOMER JUST CAME IN!
REG
REG
HIYA, SIMON! WHAT BRINGS MY FAVORITE REALITY SHOW PRO-DUCER HERE?
HELLO, REGGIE. ODDLY ENOUGH REALITY BRINGS ME HERE!
LIKE I TOLD YOU, THE NETWORK'S APPROVED US SHOOTING SIX MORE EPISODES OF "BETTY LOVES REGGIE"... BUT ONLY 'CAUSE I WAS ABLE TO CONVINCE 'EM THE SHOW HAS POTENTIAL!
BUT IT TOOK A LOT OF CONVINCING!
THEY LIKE YOU AND BETTY WELL ENOUGH, MATE, BUT THEY THINK THE SHOW IS LACKING ANY REAL DRAMA.

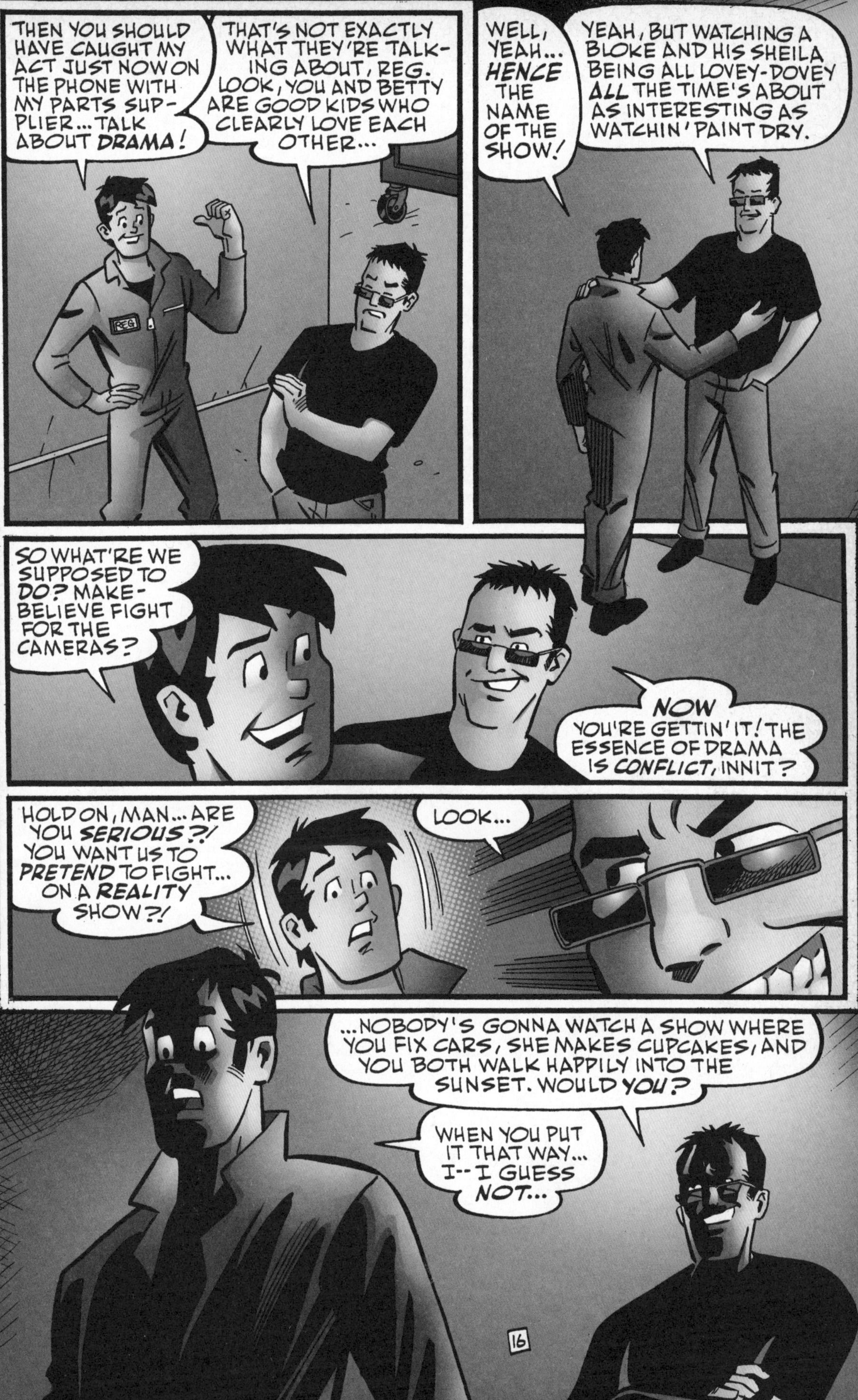
THEN YOU SHOULD HAVE CAUGHT MY ACT JUST NOW ON THE PHONE WITH MY PARTS SUPPLIER... TALK ABOUT DRAMA!
THAT'S NOT EXACTLY WHAT THEY'RE TALKING ABOUT, REG. LOOK, YOU AND BETTY ARE GOOD KIDS WHO CLEARLY LOVE EACH OTHER...
WELL, YEAH... HENCE THE NAME OF THE SHOW!
YEAH, BUT WATCHING A BLOKE AND HIS SHEILA BEING ALL LOVEY-DOVEY ALL THE TIME'S ABOUT AS INTERESTING AS WATCHIN' PAINT DRY.
REG
SO WHAT'RE WE SUPPOSED TO DO? MAKE-BELIEVE FIGHT FOR THE CAMERAS?
NOW YOU'RE GETTIN' IT! THE ESSENCE OF DRAMA IS CONFLICT, INNIT?
HOLD ON, MAN... ARE YOU SERIOUS?! YOU WANT US TO PRETEND TO FIGHT... ON A REALITY SHOW?!
LOOK...
...NOBODY'S GONNA WATCH A SHOW WHERE YOU FIX CARS, SHE MAKES CUPCAKES, AND YOU BOTH WALK HAPPILY INTO THE SUNSET. WOULD YOU?
WHEN YOU PUT IT THAT WAY... I-- I GUESS NOT...

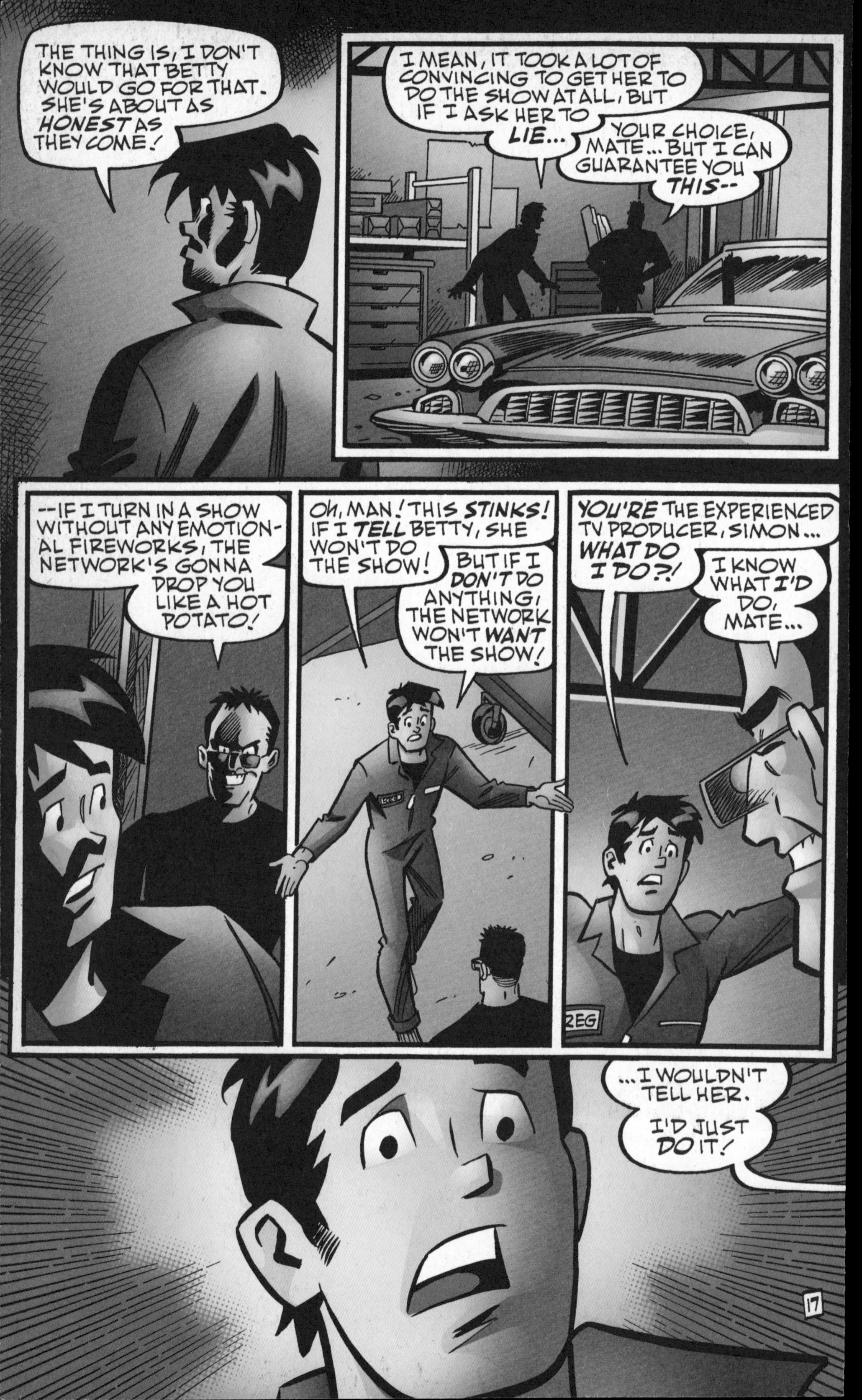
THE THING IS, I DON'T KNOW THAT BETTY WOULD GO FOR THAT. SHE'S ABOUT AS HONEST AS THEY COME!
I MEAN, IT TOOK A LOT OF CONVINCING TO GET HER TO DO THE SHOW AT ALL, BUT IF I ASK HER TO LIE...
YOUR CHOICE, MATE... BUT I CAN GUARANTEE YOU THIS--
--IF I TURN IN A SHOW WITHOUT ANY EMOTIONAL FIREWORKS, THE NETWORK'S GONNA DROP YOU LIKE A HOT POTATO!
OH, MAN! THIS STINKS! IF I TELL BETTY, SHE WON'T DO THE SHOW!
BUT IF I DON'T DO ANYTHING, THE NETWORK WON'T WANT THE SHOW!
YOU'RE THE EXPERIENCED TV PRODUCER, SIMON... WHAT DO I DO?!
I KNOW WHAT I'D DO, MATE...
REG
...I WOULDN'T TELL HER.
I'D JUST DO IT!

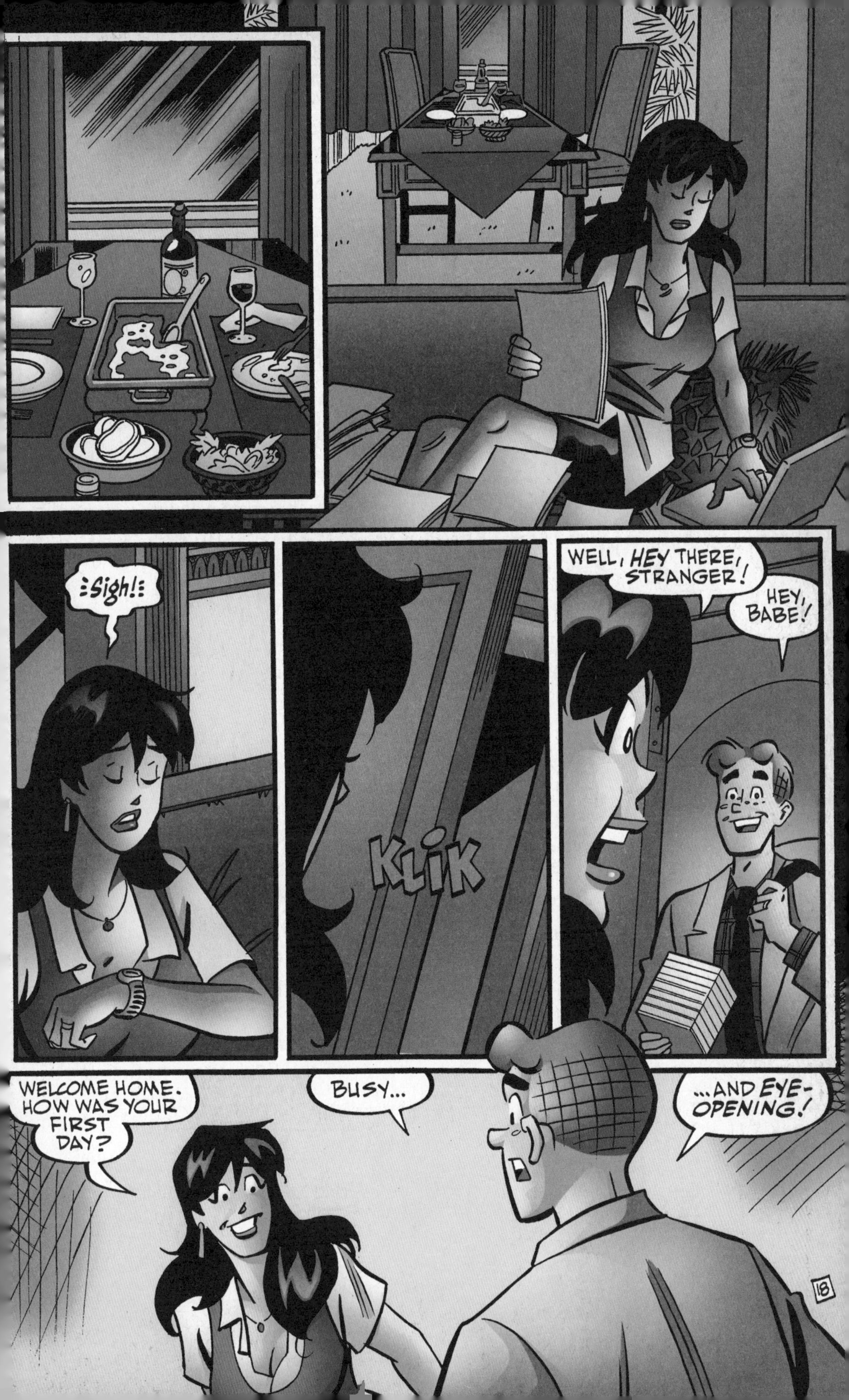
SIGH!
KLIK
WELL, HEY THERE, STRANGER!
HEY, BABE!
WELCOME HOME. HOW WAS YOUR FIRST DAY?
BUSY...
...AND EYE-OPENING!
18

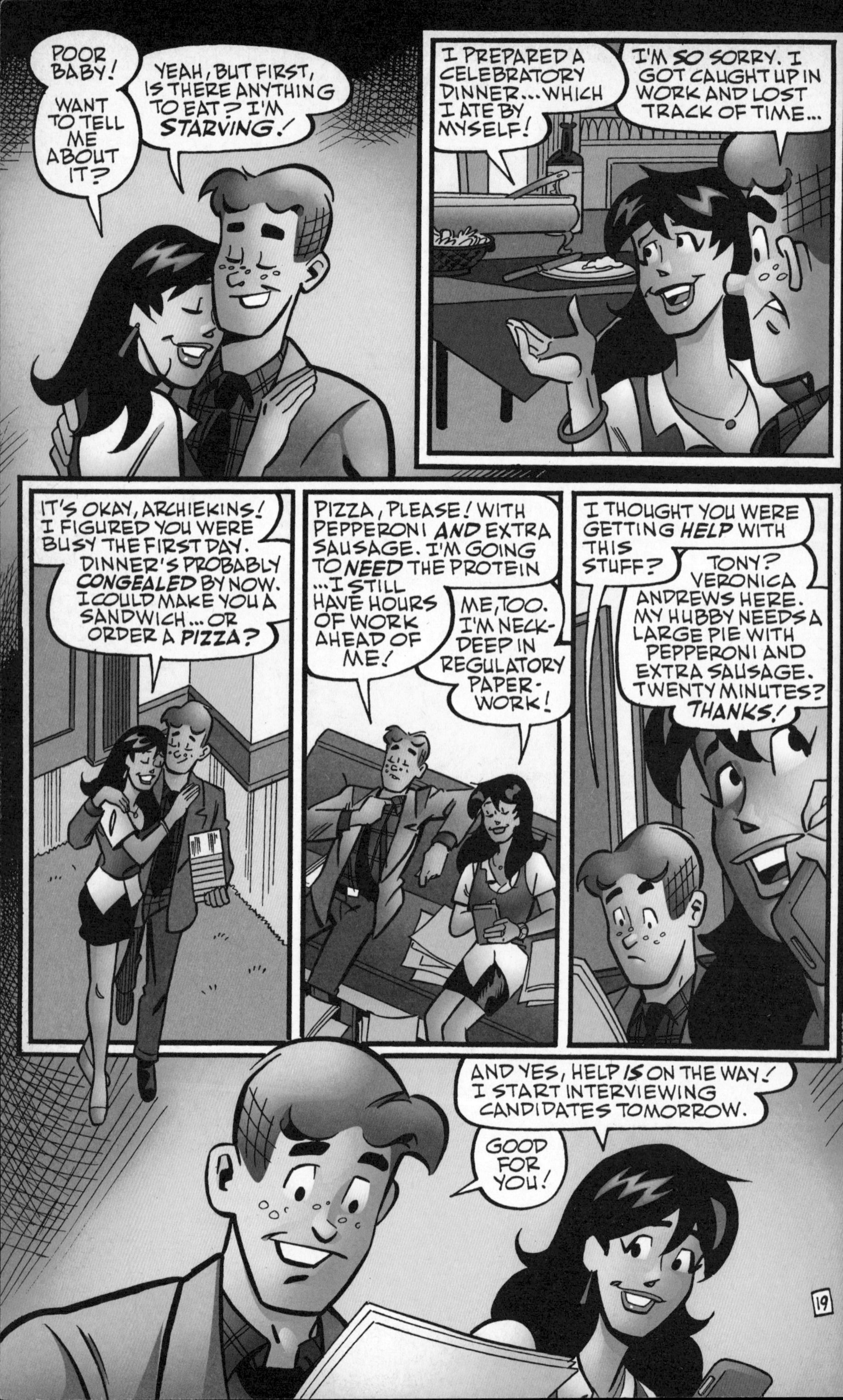

POOR BABY!
WANT TO TELL ME ABOUT IT?
YEAH, BUT FIRST, IS THERE ANYTHING TO EAT? I'M STARVING!
I PREPARED A CELEBRATORY DINNER... WHICH I ATE BY MYSELF!
I'M SO SORRY. I GOT CAUGHT UP IN WORK AND LOST TRACK OF TIME...
IT'S OKAY, ARCHIEKINS! I FIGURED YOU WERE BUSY THE FIRST DAY.
DINNER'S PROBABLY CONGEALED BY NOW. I COULD MAKE YOU A SANDWICH... OR ORDER A PIZZA?
PIZZA, PLEASE! WITH PEPPERONI AND EXTRA SAUSAGE. I'M GOING TO NEED THE PROTEIN ...I STILL HAVE HOURS OF WORK AHEAD OF ME!
ME, TOO. I'M NECK-DEEP IN REGULATORY PAPER-WORK!
I THOUGHT YOU WERE GETTING HELP WITH THIS STUFF?
TONY? VERONICA ANDREWS HERE. MY HUBBY NEEDS A LARGE PIE WITH PEPPERONI AND EXTRA SAUSAGE. TWENTY MINUTES? THANKS!
AND YES, HELP IS ON THE WAY! I START INTERVIEWING CANDIDATES TOMORROW.
GOOD FOR YOU!

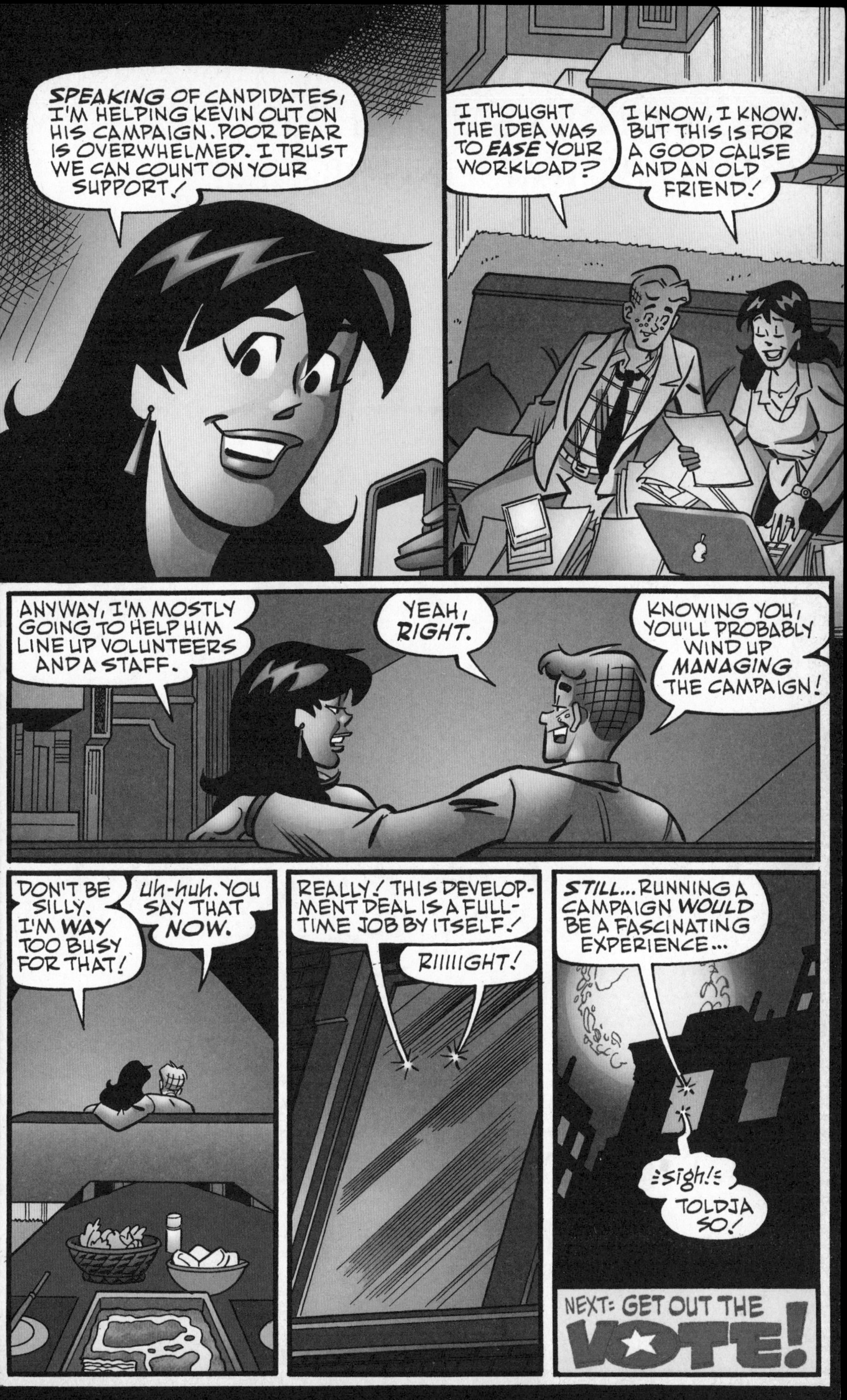
SPEAKING OF CANDIDATES, I'M HELPING KEVIN OUT ON HIS CAMPAIGN. POOR DEAR IS OVERWHELMED. I TRUST WE CAN COUNT ON YOUR SUPPORT!
I THOUGHT THE IDEA WAS TO EASE YOUR WORKLOAD?
I KNOW, I KNOW. BUT THIS IS FOR A GOOD CAUSE AND AN OLD FRIEND!
ANYWAY, I'M MOSTLY GOING TO HELP HIM LINE UP VOLUNTEERS AND A STAFF.
YEAH, RIGHT.
KNOWING YOU, YOU'LL PROBABLY WIND UP MANAGING THE CAMPAIGN!
DON'T BE SILLY. I'M WAY TOO BUSY FOR THAT!
Uh-huh. YOU SAY THAT NOW.
REALLY! THIS DEVELOPMENT DEAL IS A FULL-TIME JOB BY ITSELF!
RIIIIIGHT!
STILL... RUNNING A CAMPAIGN WOULD BE A FASCINATING EXPERIENCE...
sigh!
TOLDJA SO!
NEXT: GET OUT THE VOTE!

"A HEART ATTACK. MAN!
THE DOCTORS SAID THERE
HAD TO BE WARNING SIGNS..."

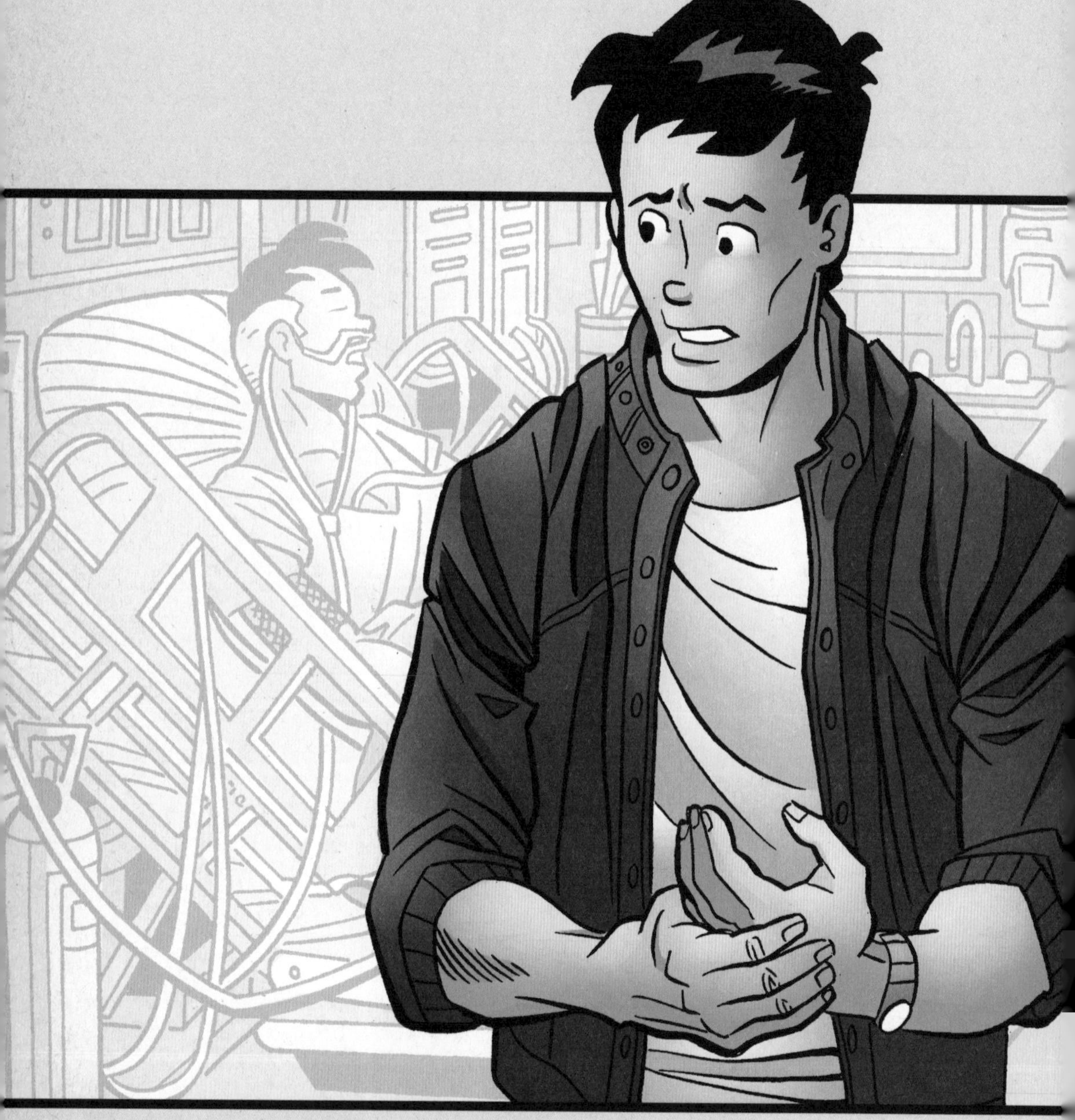

"...BUT HE ***IGNORED*** THEM!"

-REGGIE MANTLE

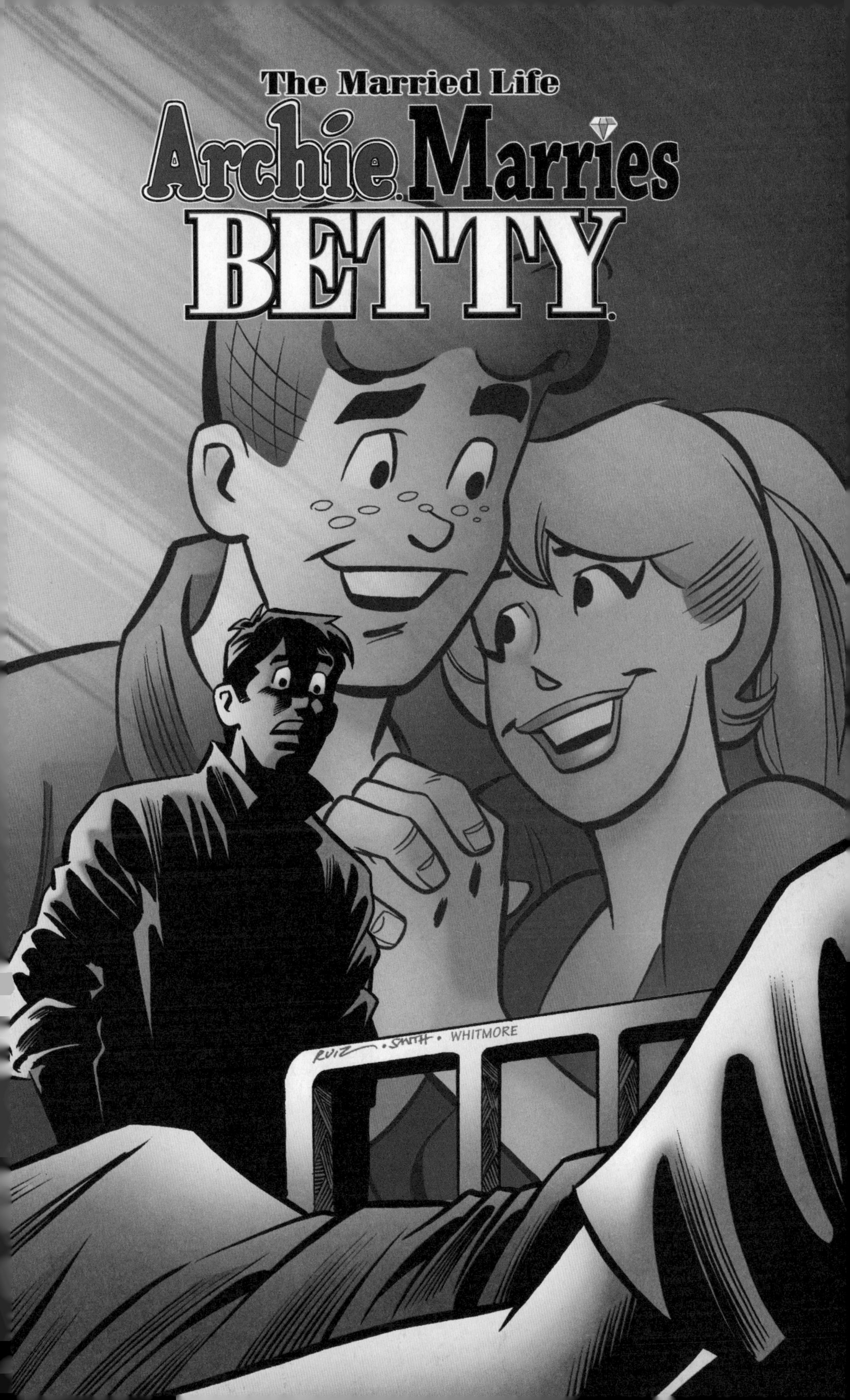
The Married Life
Archie Marries
BETTY
RUIZ • SMITH • WHITMORE

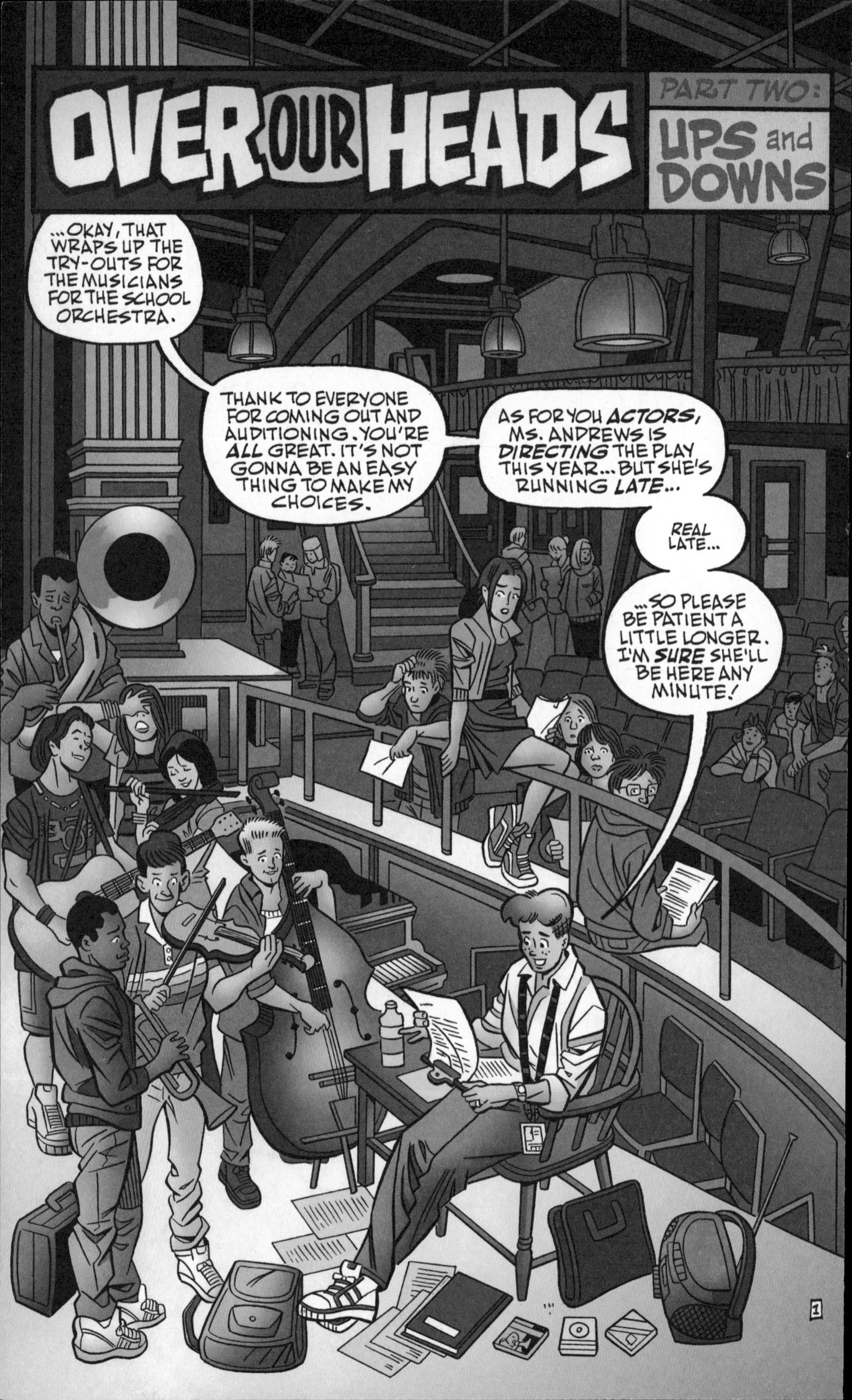
OVER OUR HEADS
PART TWO:
UPS and DOWNS
...OKAY, THAT WRAPS UP THE TRY-OUTS FOR THE MUSICIANS FOR THE SCHOOL ORCHESTRA.
THANK TO EVERYONE FOR COMING OUT AND AUDITIONING. YOU'RE ALL GREAT. IT'S NOT GONNA BE AN EASY THING TO MAKE MY CHOICES.
AS FOR YOU ACTORS, MS. ANDREWS IS DIRECTING THE PLAY THIS YEAR... BUT SHE'S RUNNING LATE...
REAL LATE...
...SO PLEASE BE PATIENT A LITTLE LONGER. I'M SURE SHE'LL BE HERE ANY MINUTE!

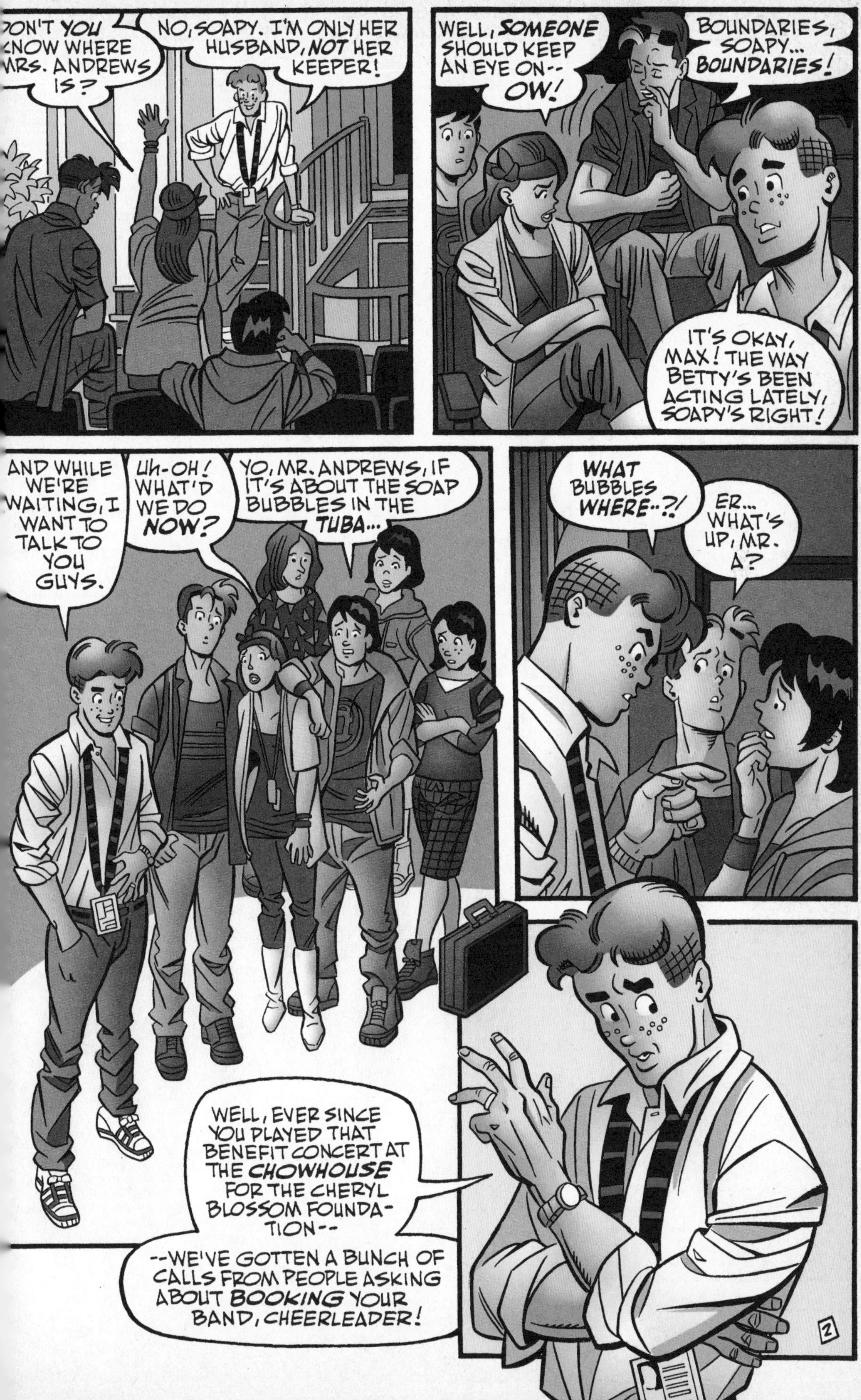
DON'T YOU KNOW WHERE MRS. ANDREWS IS?
NO, SOAPY. I'M ONLY HER HUSBAND, NOT HER KEEPER!
WELL, SOMEONE SHOULD KEEP AN EYE ON-- OW!
BOUNDARIES, SOAPY... BOUNDARIES!
IT'S OKAY, MAX! THE WAY BETTY'S BEEN ACTING LATELY, SOAPY'S RIGHT!
AND WHILE WE'RE WAITING, I WANT TO TALK TO YOU GUYS.
UH-OH! WHAT'D WE DO NOW?
YO, MR. ANDREWS, IF IT'S ABOUT THE SOAP BUBBLES IN THE TUBA...
WHAT BUBBLES WHERE..?!
ER... WHAT'S UP, MR. A?
WELL, EVER SINCE YOU PLAYED THAT BENEFIT CONCERT AT THE CHOWHOUSE FOR THE CHERYL BLOSSOM FOUNDA-TION--
--WE'VE GOTTEN A BUNCH OF CALLS FROM PEOPLE ASKING ABOUT BOOKING YOUR BAND, CHEERLEADER!

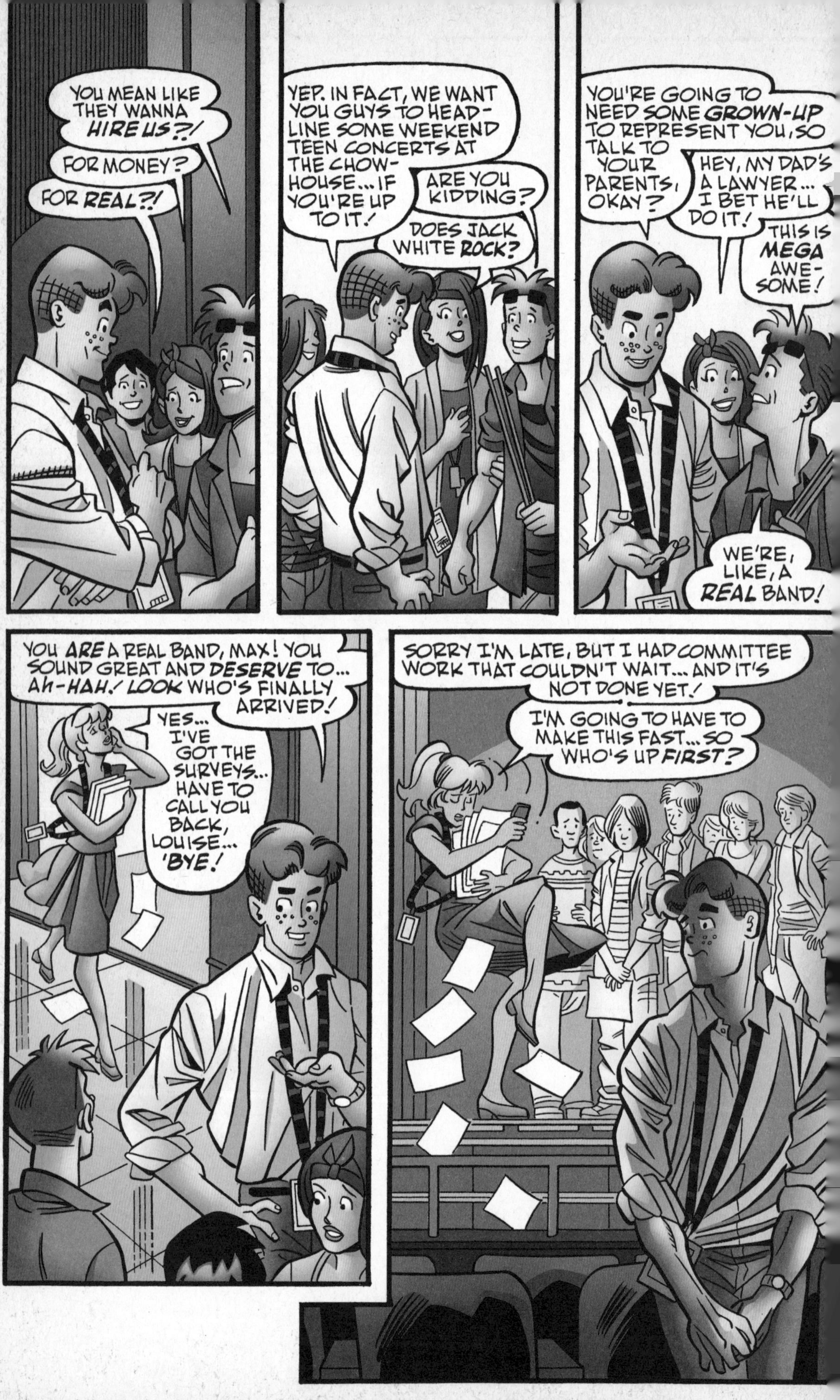
YOU MEAN LIKE THEY WANNA HIRE US?!
FOR MONEY?
FOR REAL?!
YEP. IN FACT, WE WANT YOU GUYS TO HEAD-LINE SOME WEEKEND TEEN CONCERTS AT THE CHOW-HOUSE... IF YOU'RE UP TO IT!
ARE YOU KIDDING?
DOES JACK WHITE ROCK?
YOU'RE GOING TO NEED SOME GROWN-UP TO REPRESENT YOU, SO TALK TO YOUR PARENTS, OKAY?
HEY, MY DAD'S A LAWYER... I BET HE'LL DO IT!
THIS IS MEGA AWE-SOME!
WE'RE, LIKE, A REAL BAND!
YOU ARE A REAL BAND, MAX! YOU SOUND GREAT AND DESERVE TO... AH-HAH! LOOK WHO'S FINALLY ARRIVED!
YES... I'VE GOT THE SURVEYS... HAVE TO CALL YOU BACK, LOUISE... 'BYE!
SORRY I'M LATE, BUT I HAD COMMITTEE WORK THAT COULDN'T WAIT... AND IT'S NOT DONE YET!
I'M GOING TO HAVE TO MAKE THIS FAST... SO WHO'S UP FIRST?

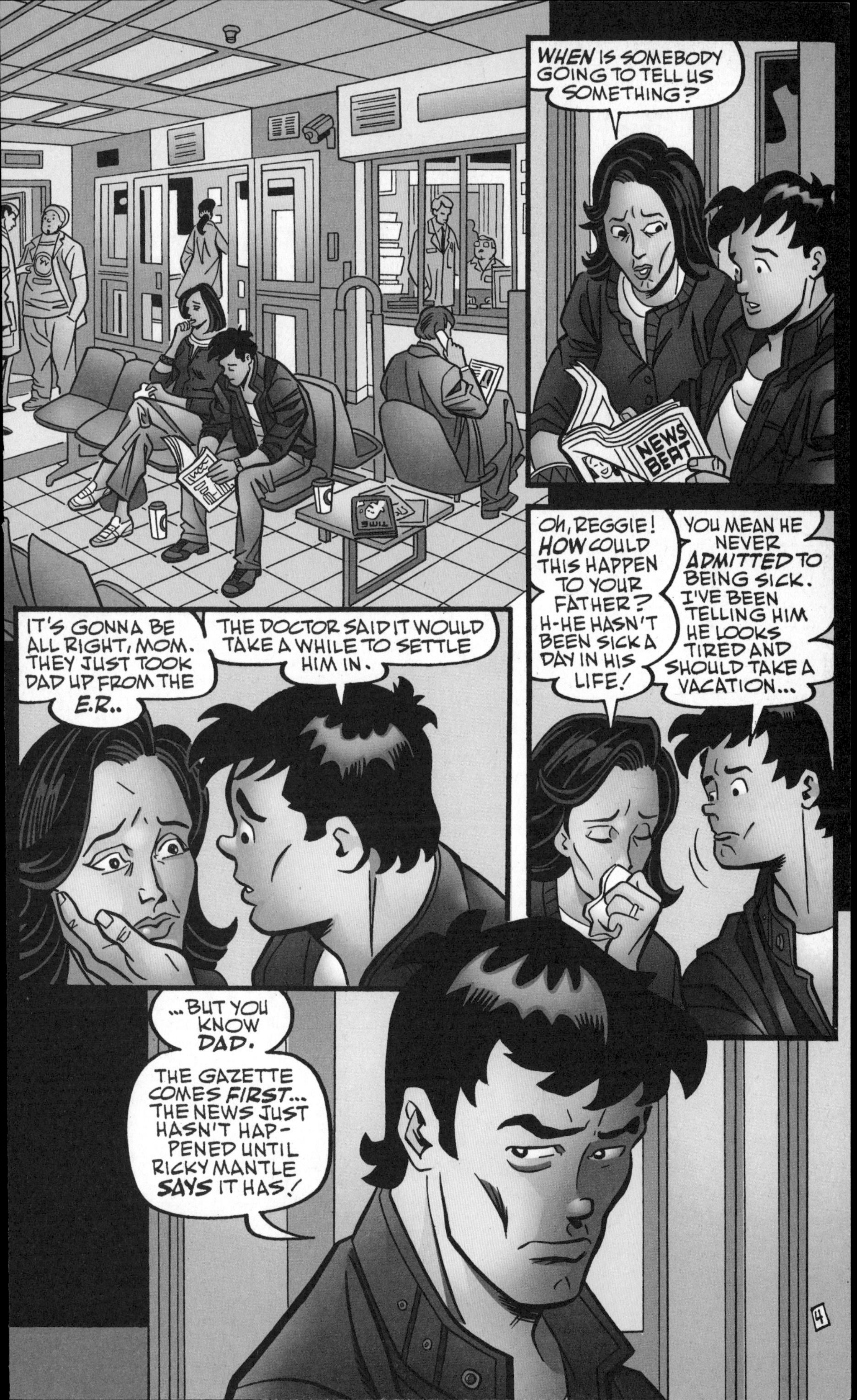
WHEN IS SOMEBODY GOING TO TELL US SOMETHING?
NEWS BEAT
IT'S GONNA BE ALL RIGHT, MOM. THEY JUST TOOK DAD UP FROM THE E.R..
THE DOCTOR SAID IT WOULD TAKE A WHILE TO SETTLE HIM IN.
OH, REGGIE! HOW COULD THIS HAPPEN TO YOUR FATHER? H-HE HASN'T BEEN SICK A DAY IN HIS LIFE!
YOU MEAN HE NEVER ADMITTED TO BEING SICK. I'VE BEEN TELLING HIM HE LOOKS TIRED AND SHOULD TAKE A VACATION...
...BUT YOU KNOW DAD.
THE GAZETTE COMES FIRST... THE NEWS JUST HASN'T HAP-PENED UNTIL RICKY MANTLE SAYS IT HAS!
4

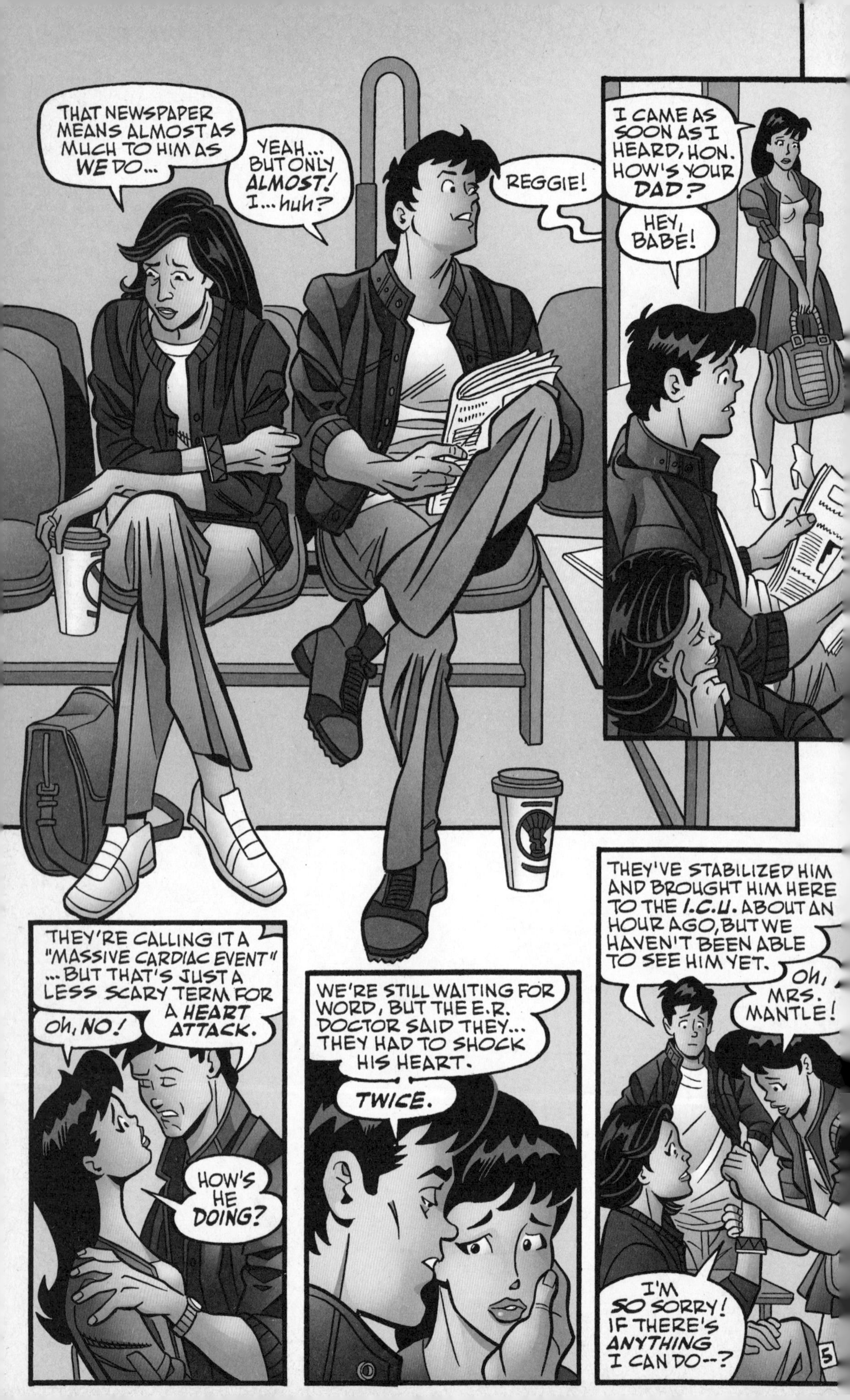
THAT NEWSPAPER MEANS ALMOST AS MUCH TO HIM AS WE DO...
YEAH... BUT ONLY ALMOST! I... huh?
REGGIE!
I CAME AS SOON AS I HEARD, HON. HOW'S YOUR DAD?
HEY, BABE!
THEY'RE CALLING IT A "MASSIVE CARDIAC EVENT" ...BUT THAT'S JUST A LESS SCARY TERM FOR A HEART ATTACK.
Oh, NO!
HOW'S HE DOING?
WE'RE STILL WAITING FOR WORD, BUT THE E.R. DOCTOR SAID THEY... THEY HAD TO SHOCK HIS HEART.
TWICE.
THEY'VE STABILIZED HIM AND BROUGHT HIM HERE TO THE I.C.U. ABOUT AN HOUR AGO, BUT WE HAVEN'T BEEN ABLE TO SEE HIM YET.
Oh, MRS. MANTLE!
I'M SO SORRY! IF THERE'S ANYTHING I CAN DO--?
5

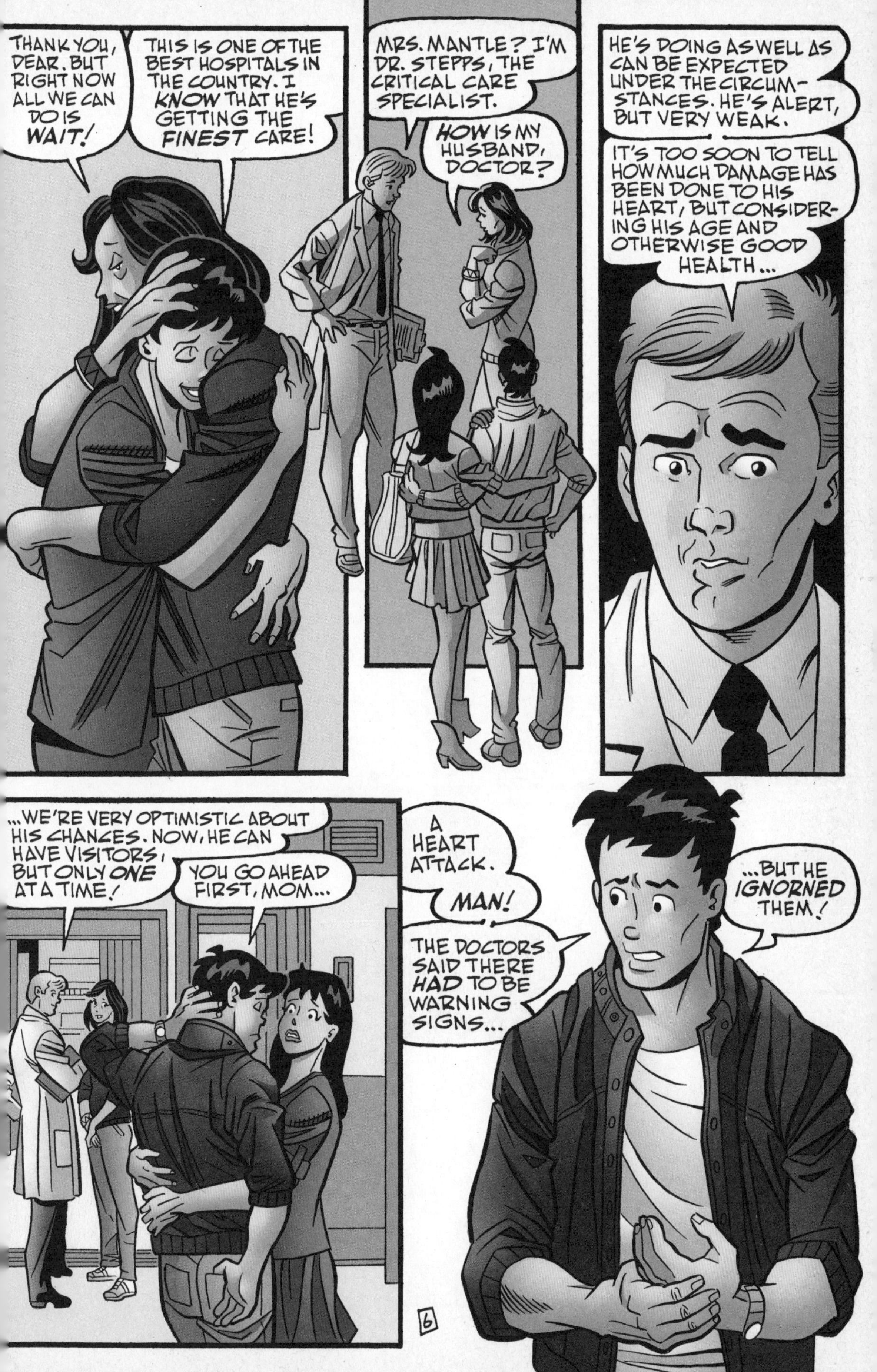

THANK YOU, DEAR. BUT RIGHT NOW ALL WE CAN DO IS WAIT!
THIS IS ONE OF THE BEST HOSPITALS IN THE COUNTRY. I KNOW THAT HE'S GETTING THE FINEST CARE!
MRS. MANTLE? I'M DR. STEPPS, THE CRITICAL CARE SPECIALIST.
HOW IS MY HUSBAND, DOCTOR?
HE'S DOING AS WELL AS CAN BE EXPECTED UNDER THE CIRCUM-STANCES. HE'S ALERT, BUT VERY WEAK.
IT'S TOO SOON TO TELL HOW MUCH DAMAGE HAS BEEN DONE TO HIS HEART, BUT CONSIDER-ING HIS AGE AND OTHERWISE GOOD HEALTH...
...WE'RE VERY OPTIMISTIC ABOUT HIS CHANCES. NOW, HE CAN HAVE VISITORS, BUT ONLY ONE AT A TIME!
YOU GO AHEAD FIRST, MOM...
A HEART ATTACK.
MAN!
THE DOCTORS SAID THERE HAD TO BE WARNING SIGNS...
...BUT HE IGNORNED THEM!

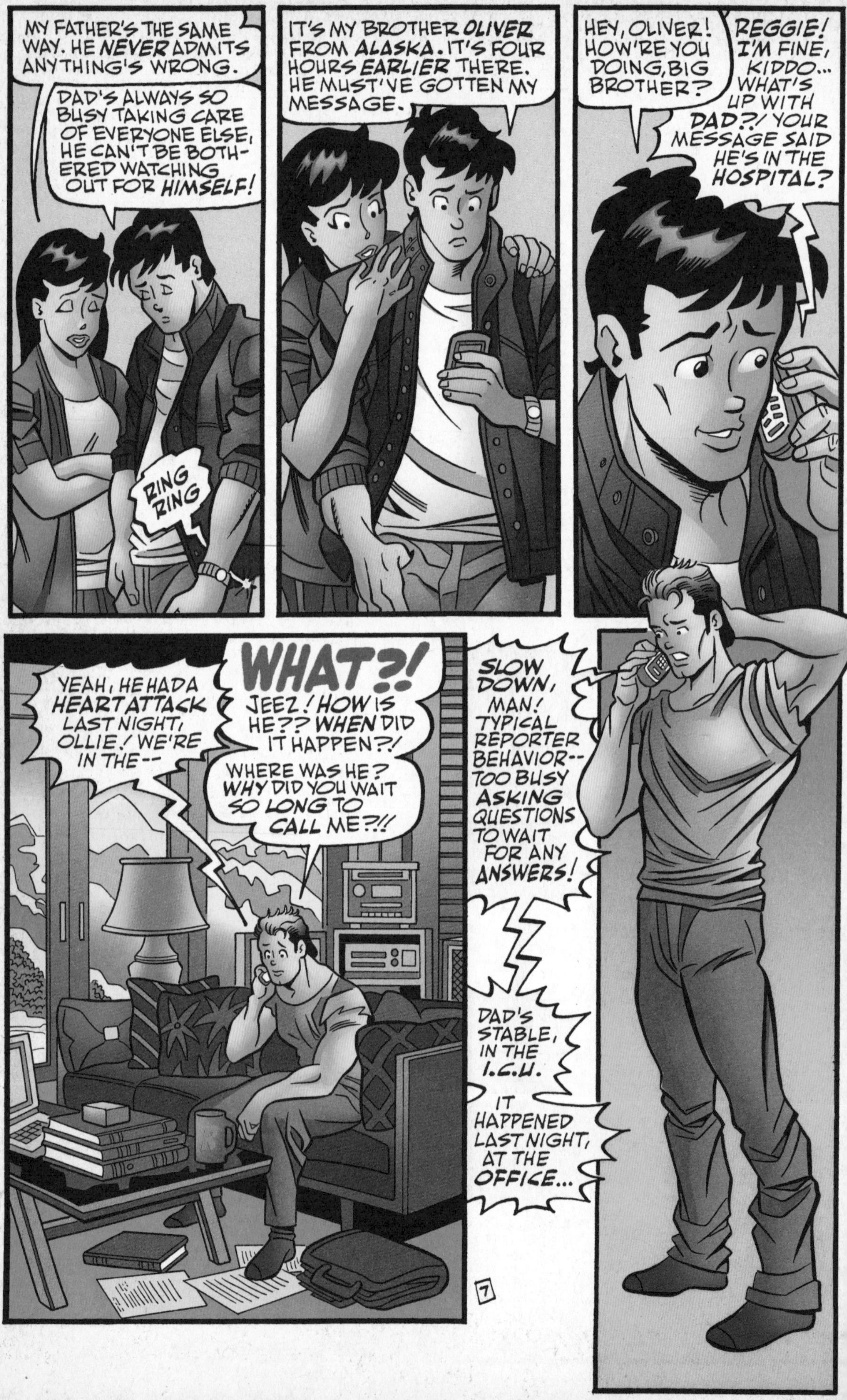

MY FATHER'S THE SAME WAY. HE NEVER ADMITS ANYTHING'S WRONG.
DAD'S ALWAYS SO BUSY TAKING CARE OF EVERYONE ELSE, HE CAN'T BE BOTH-ERED WATCHING OUT FOR HIMSELF!
RING RING
IT'S MY BROTHER OLIVER FROM ALASKA. IT'S FOUR HOURS EARLIER THERE. HE MUST'VE GOTTEN MY MESSAGE.
HEY, OLIVER! HOW'RE YOU DOING, BIG BROTHER?
REGGIE! I'M FINE, KIDDO... WHAT'S UP WITH DAD?! YOUR MESSAGE SAID HE'S IN THE HOSPITAL?
YEAH, HE HAD A HEART ATTACK LAST NIGHT, OLLIE! WE'RE IN THE--
WHAT?!
JEEZ! HOW IS HE?? WHEN DID IT HAPPEN?!
WHERE WAS HE? WHY DID YOU WAIT SO LONG TO CALL ME?!!
SLOW DOWN, MAN! TYPICAL REPORTER BEHAVIOR-- TOO BUSY ASKING QUESTIONS TO WAIT FOR ANY ANSWERS!
DAD'S STABLE, IN THE I.C.U.
IT HAPPENED LAST NIGHT, AT THE OFFICE...
7

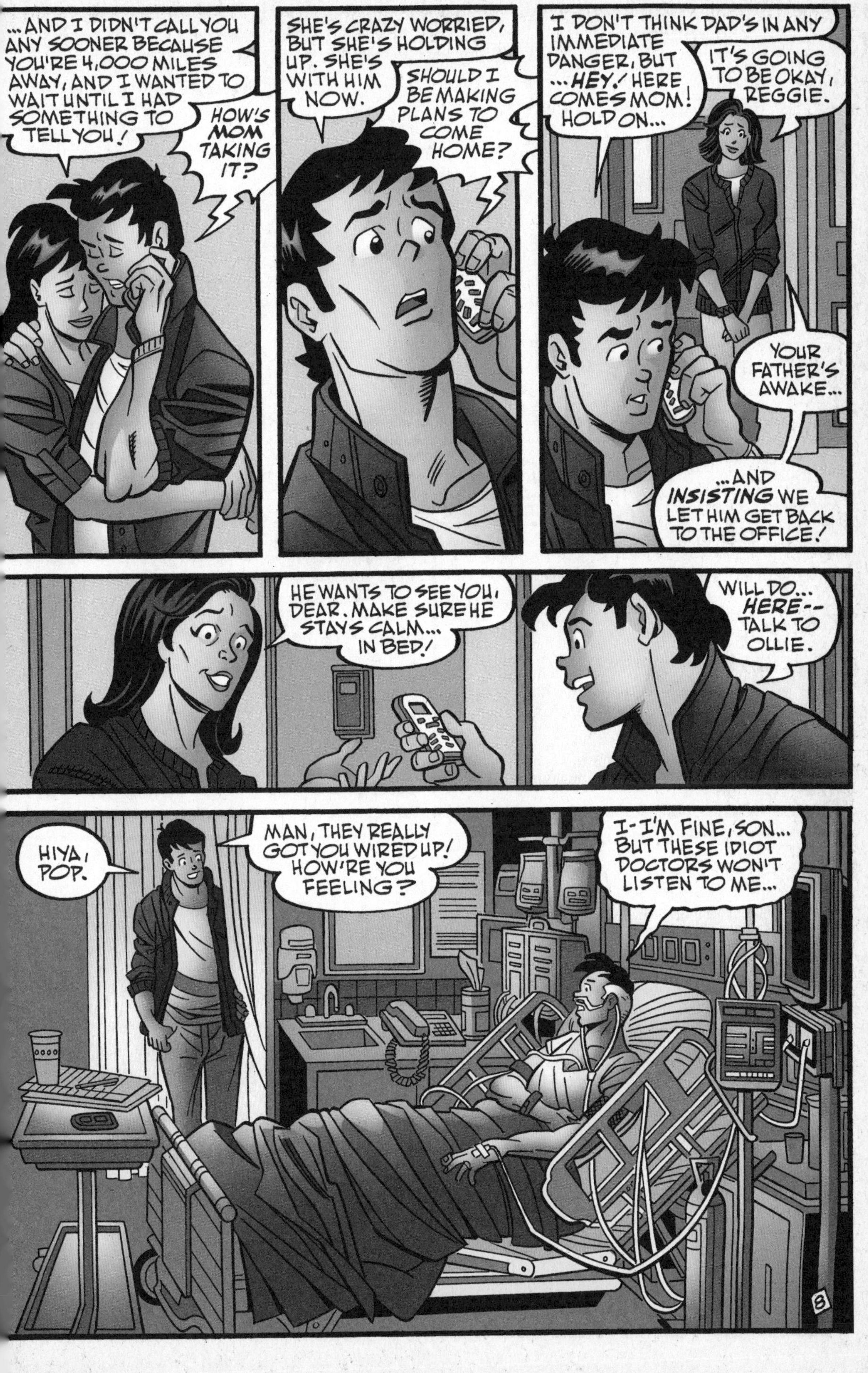
...AND I DIDN'T CALL YOU ANY SOONER BECAUSE YOU'RE 4,000 MILES AWAY, AND I WANTED TO WAIT UNTIL I HAD SOMETHING TO TELL YOU!
HOW'S MOM TAKING IT?
SHE'S CRAZY WORRIED, BUT SHE'S HOLDING UP. SHE'S WITH HIM NOW.
SHOULD I BE MAKING PLANS TO COME HOME?
I DON'T THINK DAD'S IN ANY IMMEDIATE DANGER, BUT ...HEY! HERE COMES MOM! HOLD ON...
IT'S GOING TO BE OKAY, REGGIE.
YOUR FATHER'S AWAKE...
...AND INSISTING WE LET HIM GET BACK TO THE OFFICE!
HE WANTS TO SEE YOU, DEAR. MAKE SURE HE STAYS CALM... IN BED!
WILL DO... HERE-- TALK TO OLLIE.
HIYA, POP.
MAN, THEY REALLY GOT YOU WIRED UP! HOW'RE YOU FEELING?
I-I'M FINE, SON... BUT THESE IDIOT DOCTORS WON'T LISTEN TO ME...
8

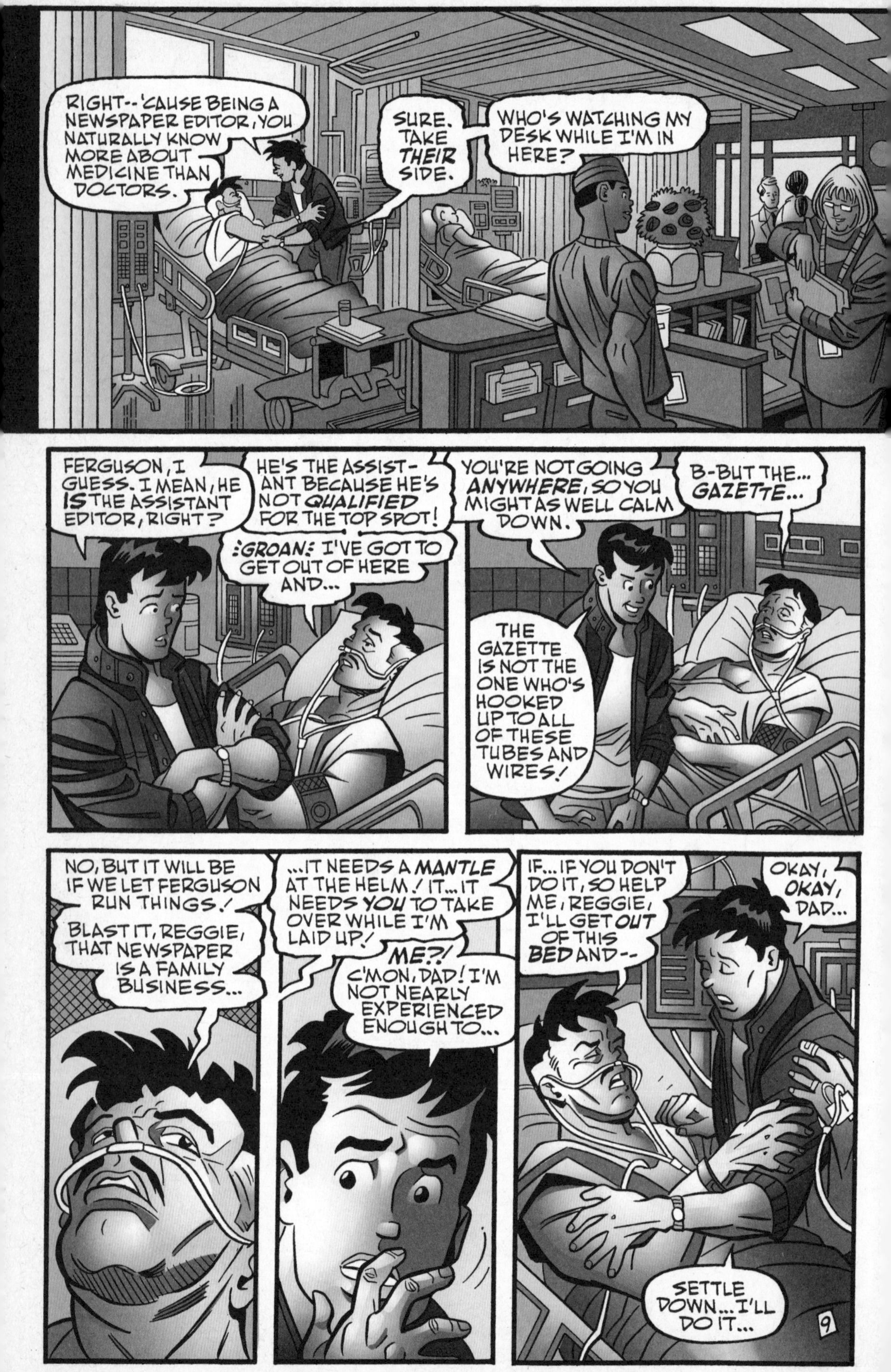
RIGHT--'CAUSE BEING A NEWSPAPER EDITOR, YOU NATURALLY KNOW MORE ABOUT MEDICINE THAN DOCTORS.
SURE. TAKE THEIR SIDE.
WHO'S WATCHING MY DESK WHILE I'M IN HERE?
FERGUSON, I GUESS. I MEAN, HE IS THE ASSISTANT EDITOR, RIGHT?
HE'S THE ASSIST-ANT BECAUSE HE'S NOT QUALIFIED FOR THE TOP SPOT!
:GROAN: I'VE GOT TO GET OUT OF HERE AND...
YOU'RE NOT GOING ANYWHERE, SO YOU MIGHT AS WELL CALM DOWN.
B-BUT THE... GAZETTE...
THE GAZETTE IS NOT THE ONE WHO'S HOOKED UP TO ALL OF THESE TUBES AND WIRES!
NO, BUT IT WILL BE IF WE LET FERGUSON RUN THINGS!
BLAST IT, REGGIE, THAT NEWSPAPER IS A FAMILY BUSINESS...
...IT NEEDS A MANTLE AT THE HELM! IT... IT NEEDS YOU TO TAKE OVER WHILE I'M LAID UP!
ME?! C'MON, DAD! I'M NOT NEARLY EXPERIENCED ENOUGH TO...
IF... IF YOU DON'T DO IT, SO HELP ME, REGGIE, I'LL GET OUT OF THIS BED AND--
OKAY, OKAY, DAD...
SETTLE DOWN... I'LL DO IT...

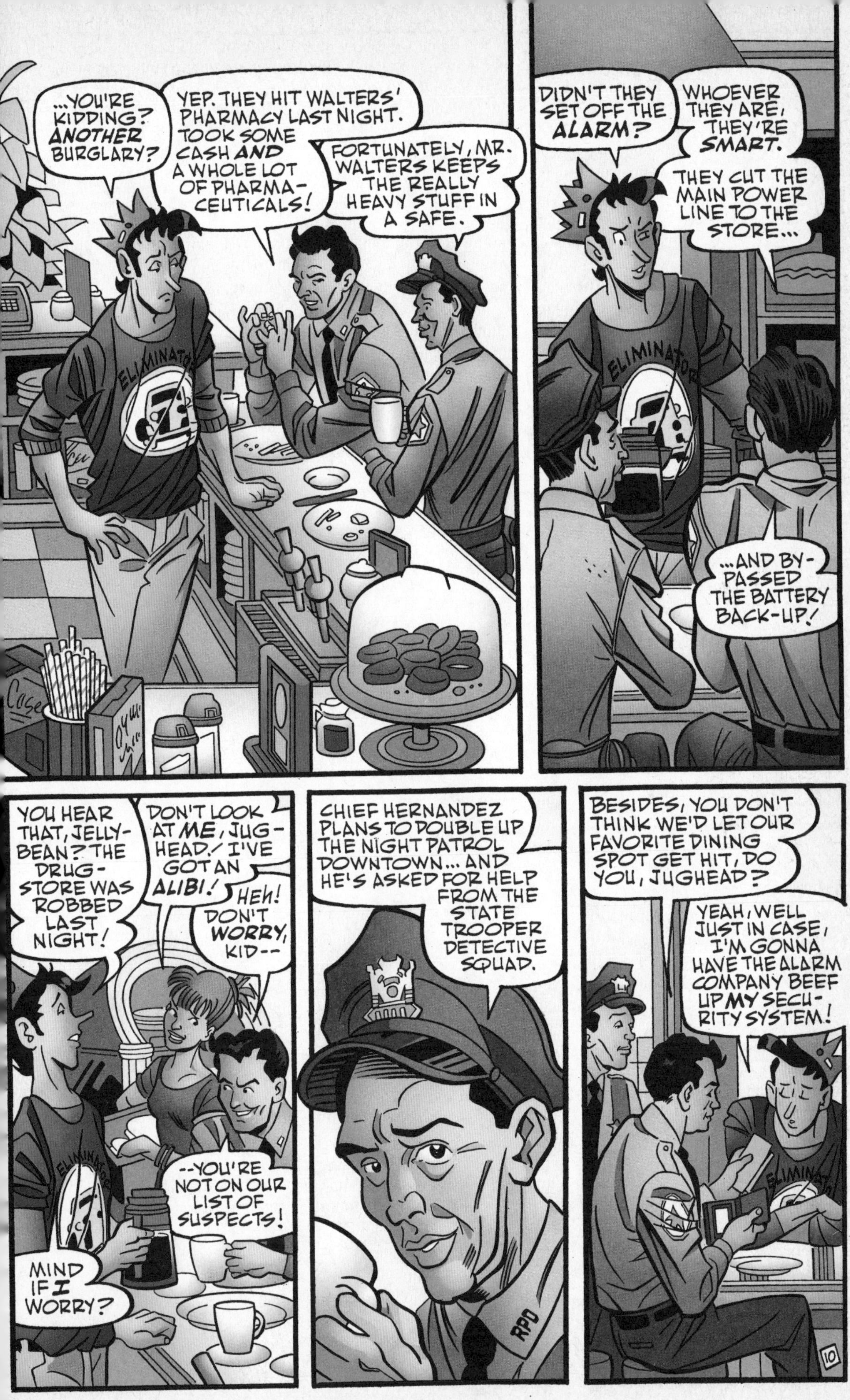
...YOU'RE KIDDING? ANOTHER BURGLARY?
YEP. THEY HIT WALTERS' PHARMACY LAST NIGHT. TOOK SOME CASH AND A WHOLE LOT OF PHARMACEUTICALS!
FORTUNATELY, MR. WALTERS KEEPS THE REALLY HEAVY STUFF IN A SAFE.
DIDN'T THEY SET OFF THE ALARM?
WHOEVER THEY ARE, THEY'RE SMART.
THEY CUT THE MAIN POWER LINE TO THE STORE...
...AND BY-PASSED THE BATTERY BACK-UP!
YOU HEAR THAT, JELLYBEAN? THE DRUGSTORE WAS ROBBED LAST NIGHT!
DON'T LOOK AT ME, JUGHEAD! I'VE GOT AN ALIBI!
HEH! DON'T WORRY, KID--
--YOU'RE NOT ON OUR LIST OF SUSPECTS!
MIND IF I WORRY?
CHIEF HERNANDEZ PLANS TO DOUBLE UP THE NIGHT PATROL DOWNTOWN... AND HE'S ASKED FOR HELP FROM THE STATE TROOPER DETECTIVE SQUAD.
RPD
BESIDES, YOU DON'T THINK WE'D LET OUR FAVORITE DINING SPOT GET HIT, DO YOU, JUGHEAD?
YEAH, WELL JUST IN CASE, I'M GONNA HAVE THE ALARM COMPANY BEEF UP MY SECURITY SYSTEM!

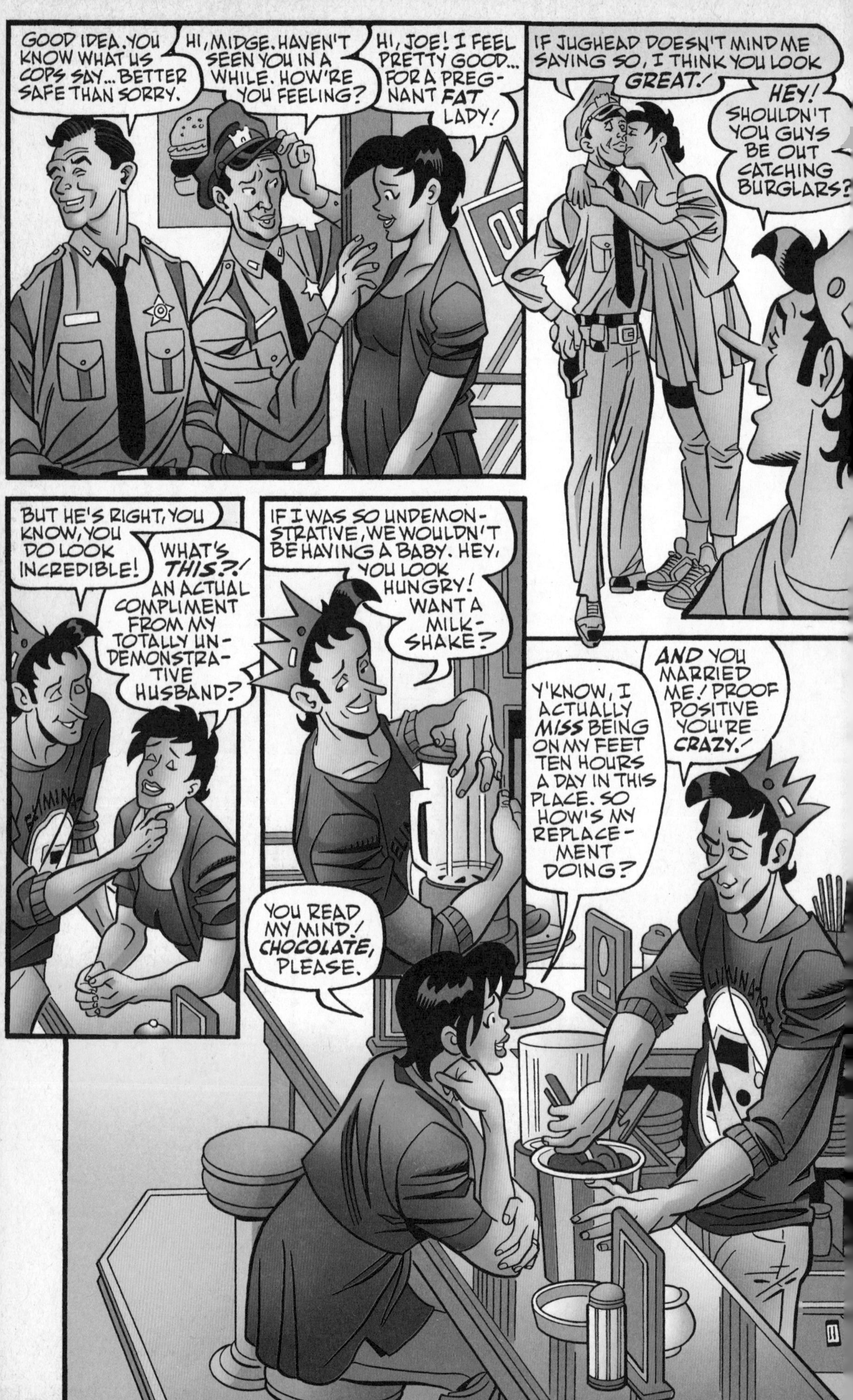
GOOD IDEA. YOU KNOW WHAT US COPS SAY... BETTER SAFE THAN SORRY.
HI, MIDGE. HAVEN'T SEEN YOU IN A WHILE. HOW'RE YOU FEELING?
HI, JOE! I FEEL PRETTY GOOD... FOR A PREGNANT FAT LADY!
IF JUGHEAD DOESN'T MIND ME SAYING SO, I THINK YOU LOOK GREAT!
HEY! SHOULDN'T YOU GUYS BE OUT CATCHING BURGLARS?
BUT HE'S RIGHT, YOU KNOW, YOU DO LOOK INCREDIBLE!
WHAT'S THIS?! AN ACTUAL COMPLIMENT FROM MY TOTALLY UNDEMONSTRATIVE HUSBAND?
IF I WAS SO UNDEMONSTRATIVE, WE WOULDN'T BE HAVING A BABY. HEY, YOU LOOK HUNGRY! WANT A MILKSHAKE?
YOU READ MY MIND! CHOCOLATE, PLEASE.
Y'KNOW, I ACTUALLY MISS BEING ON MY FEET TEN HOURS A DAY IN THIS PLACE. SO HOW'S MY REPLACEMENT DOING?
AND YOU MARRIED ME! PROOF POSITIVE YOU'RE CRAZY!
11

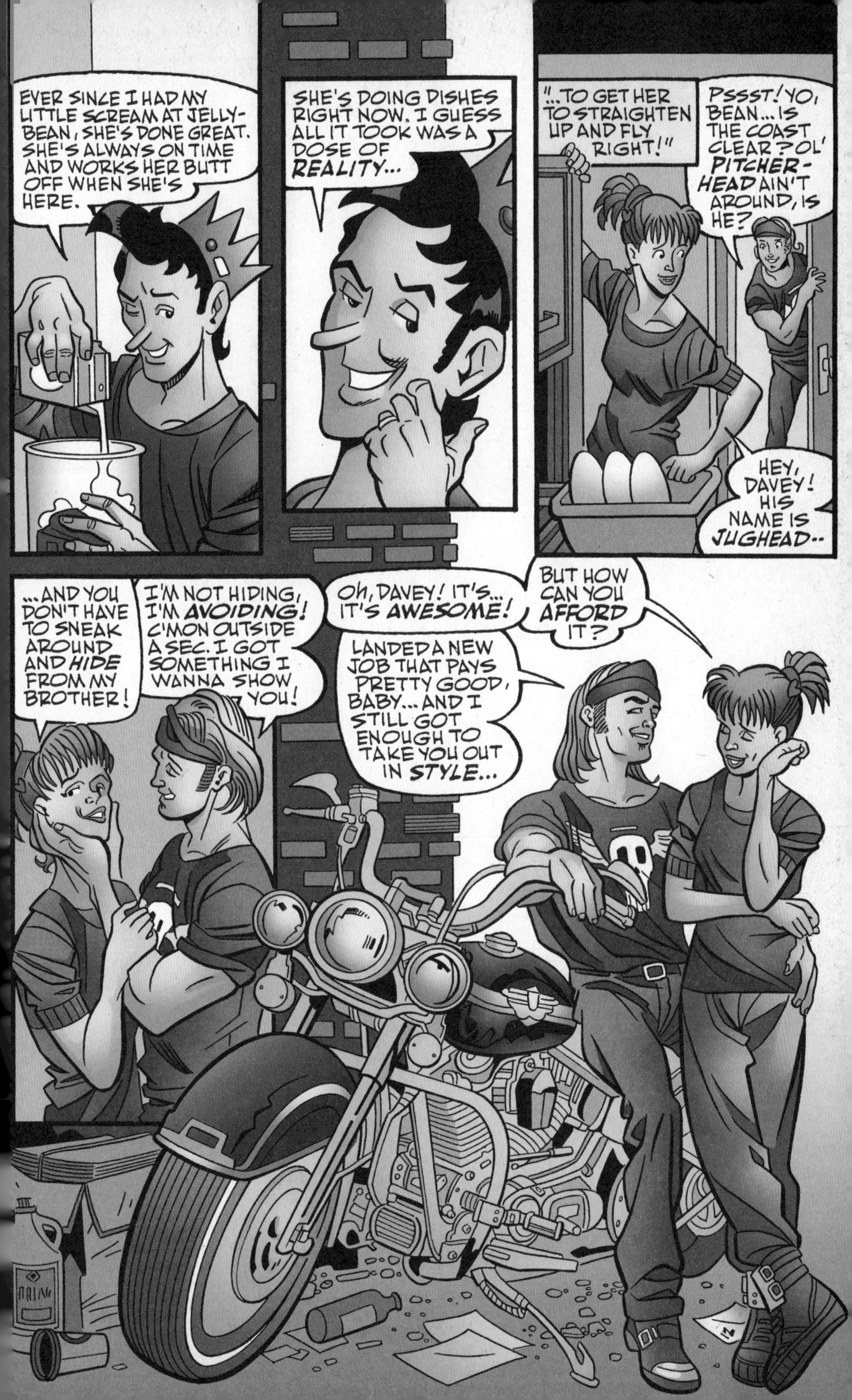
EVER SINCE I HAD MY LITTLE SCREAM AT JELLY-BEAN, SHE'S DONE GREAT. SHE'S ALWAYS ON TIME AND WORKS HER BUTT OFF WHEN SHE'S HERE.
SHE'S DOING DISHES RIGHT NOW. I GUESS ALL IT TOOK WAS A DOSE OF REALITY...
"...TO GET HER TO STRAIGHTEN UP AND FLY RIGHT!"
PSSST! YO, BEAN... IS THE COAST CLEAR? OL' PITCHER-HEAD AIN'T AROUND, IS HE?
HEY, DAVEY! HIS NAME IS JUGHEAD...
...AND YOU DON'T HAVE TO SNEAK AROUND AND HIDE FROM MY BROTHER!
I'M NOT HIDING, I'M AVOIDING! C'MON OUTSIDE A SEC. I GOT SOMETHING I WANNA SHOW YOU!
OH, DAVEY! IT'S... IT'S AWESOME!
BUT HOW CAN YOU AFFORD IT?
LANDED A NEW JOB THAT PAYS PRETTY GOOD, BABY... AND I STILL GOT ENOUGH TO TAKE YOU OUT IN STYLE...

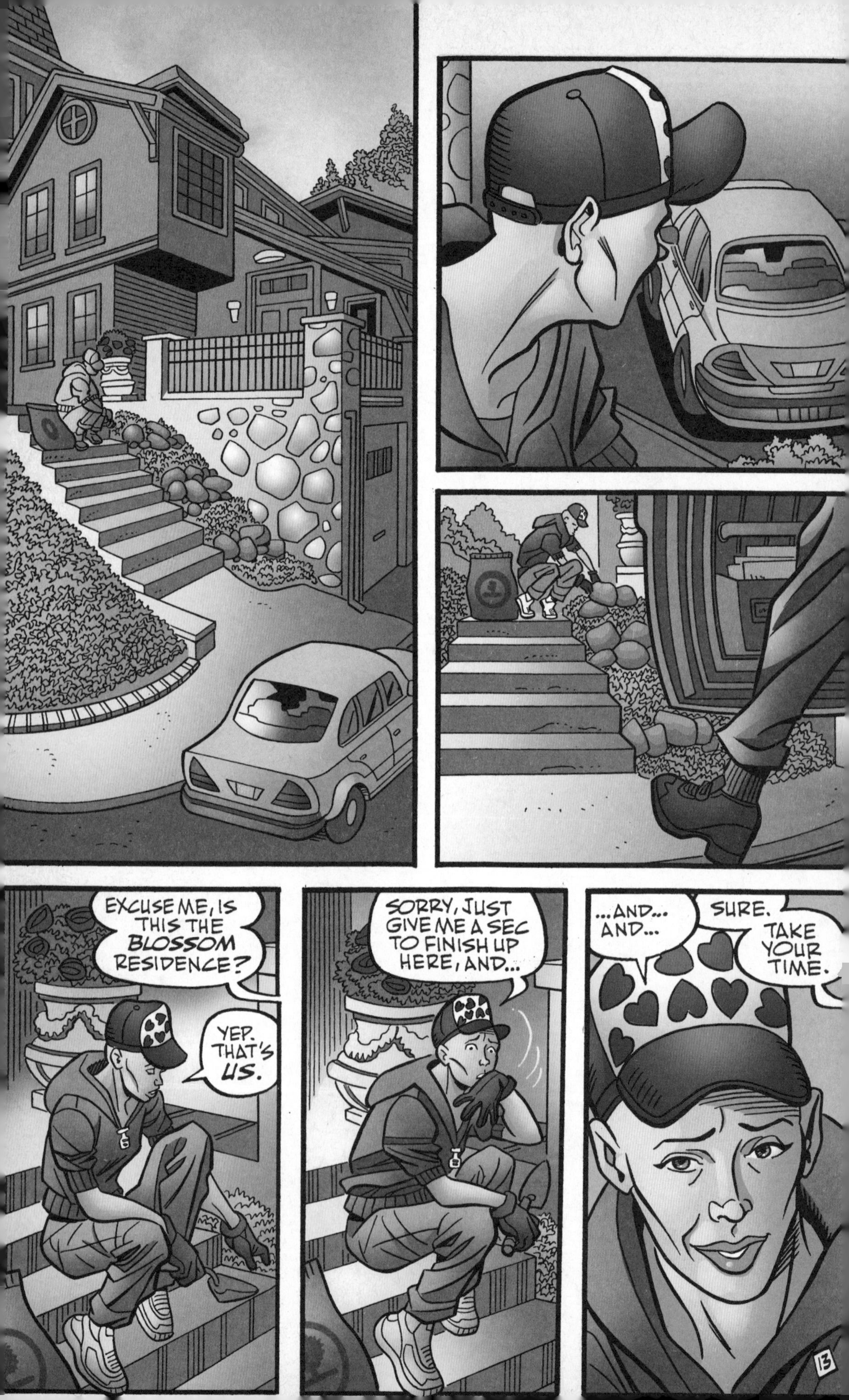

EXCUSE ME, IS THIS THE BLOSSOM RESIDENCE?
YEP. THAT'S US.
SORRY, JUST GIVE ME A SEC TO FINISH UP HERE, AND...
...AND... AND...
SURE.
TAKE YOUR TIME.

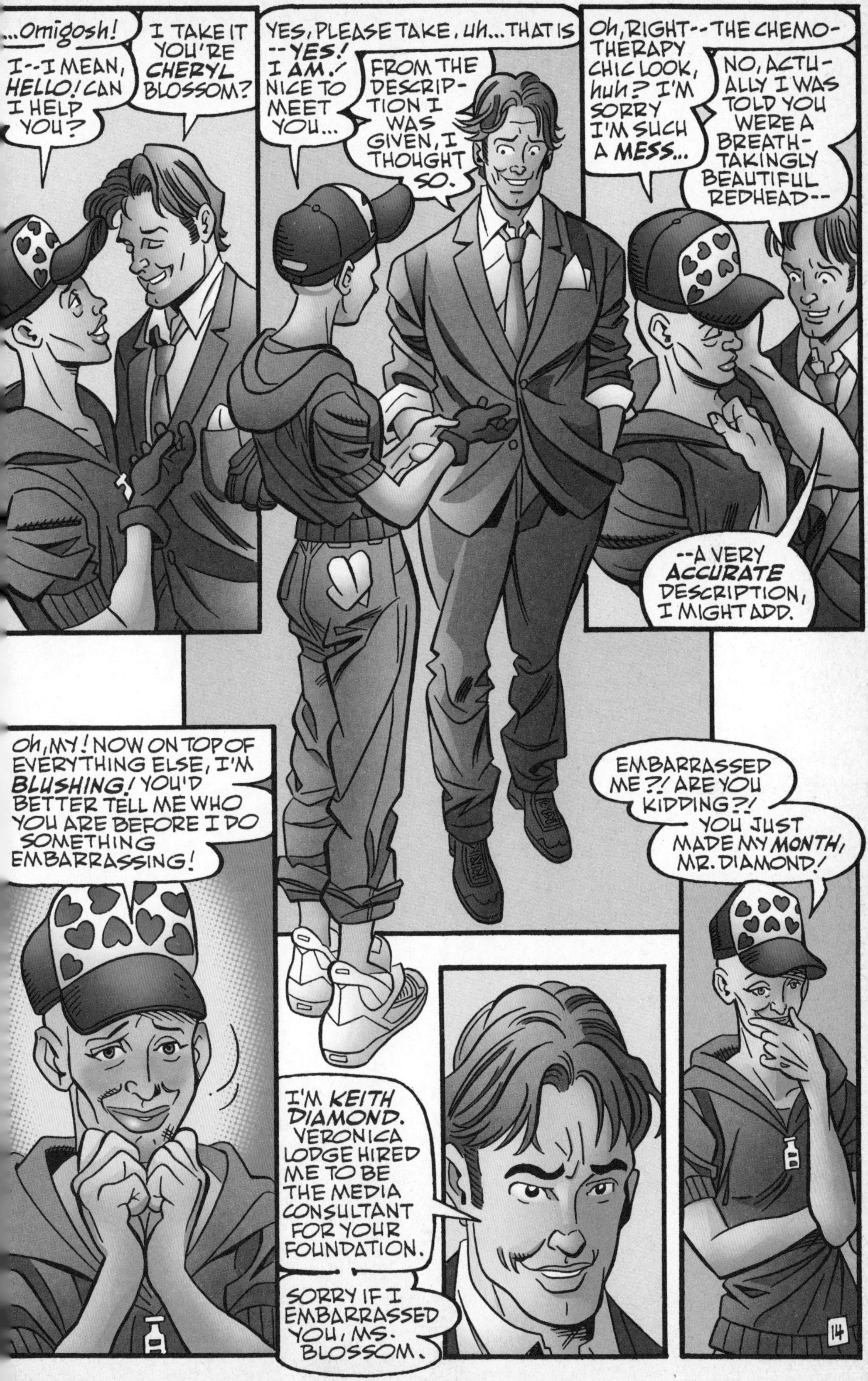
...Omigosh!
I--I MEAN, HELLO! CAN I HELP YOU?
I TAKE IT YOU'RE CHERYL BLOSSOM?
YES, PLEASE TAKE, uh... THAT IS --YES! I AM.! NICE TO MEET YOU...
FROM THE DESCRIPTION I WAS GIVEN, I THOUGHT SO.
Oh, RIGHT-- THE CHEMOTHERAPY CHIC LOOK, huh? I'M SORRY I'M SUCH A MESS...
NO, ACTUALLY I WAS TOLD YOU WERE A BREATHTAKINGLY BEAUTIFUL REDHEAD--
--A VERY ACCURATE DESCRIPTION, I MIGHT ADD.
Oh, MY! NOW ON TOP OF EVERYTHING ELSE, I'M BLUSHING! YOU'D BETTER TELL ME WHO YOU ARE BEFORE I DO SOMETHING EMBARRASSING!
I'M KEITH DIAMOND. VERONICA LODGE HIRED ME TO BE THE MEDIA CONSULTANT FOR YOUR FOUNDATION.
SORRY IF I EMBARRASSED YOU, MS. BLOSSOM.
EMBARRASSED ME?! ARE YOU KIDDING?! YOU JUST MADE MY MONTH, MR. DIAMOND!
14

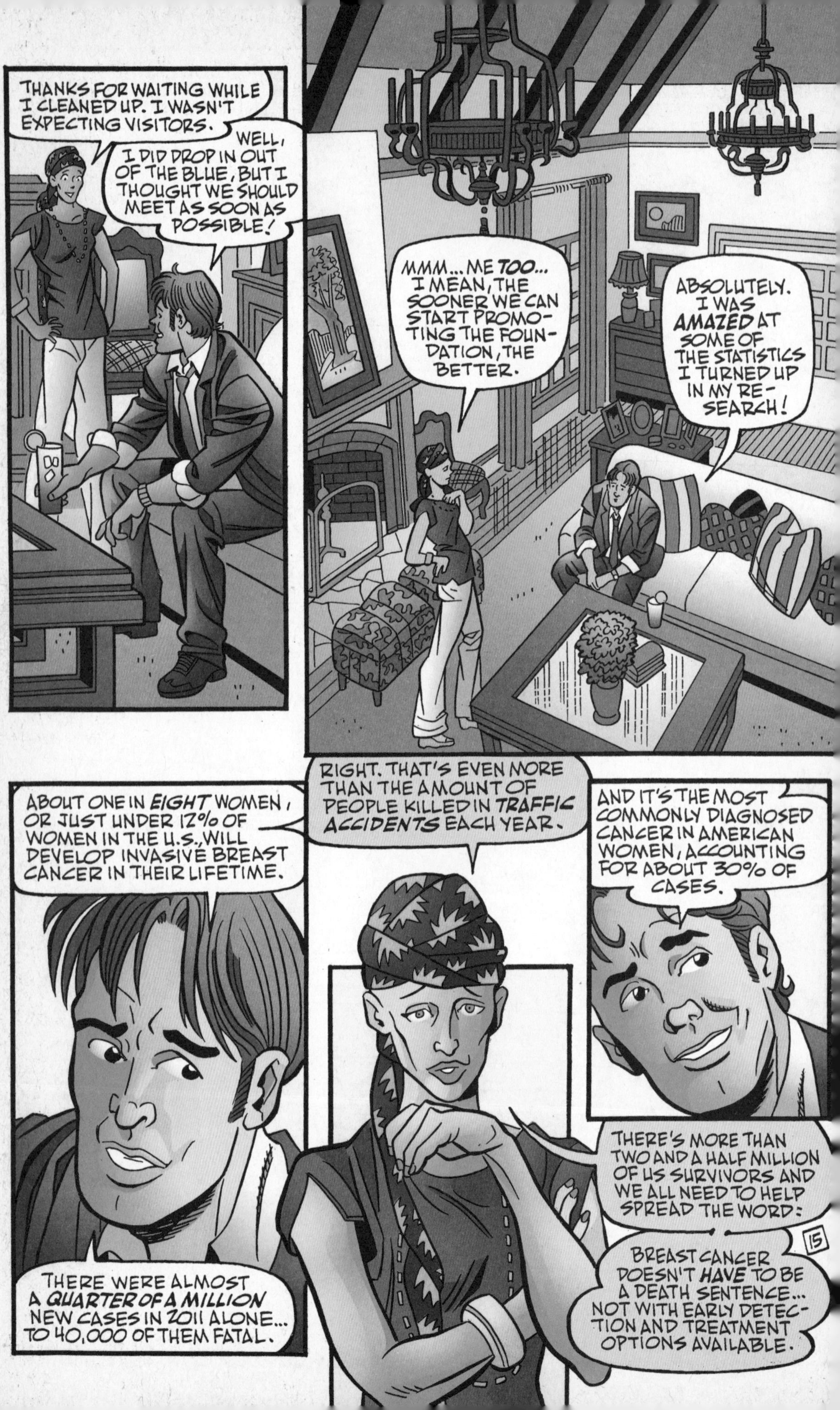
THANKS FOR WAITING WHILE I CLEANED UP. I WASN'T EXPECTING VISITORS.
WELL, I DID DROP IN OUT OF THE BLUE, BUT I THOUGHT WE SHOULD MEET AS SOON AS POSSIBLE!
MMM... ME TOO... I MEAN, THE SOONER WE CAN START PROMOTING THE FOUNDATION, THE BETTER.
ABSOLUTELY. I WAS AMAZED AT SOME OF THE STATISTICS I TURNED UP IN MY RESEARCH!
ABOUT ONE IN EIGHT WOMEN, OR JUST UNDER 12% OF WOMEN IN THE U.S., WILL DEVELOP INVASIVE BREAST CANCER IN THEIR LIFETIME.
RIGHT. THAT'S EVEN MORE THAN THE AMOUNT OF PEOPLE KILLED IN TRAFFIC ACCIDENTS EACH YEAR.
AND IT'S THE MOST COMMONLY DIAGNOSED CANCER IN AMERICAN WOMEN, ACCOUNTING FOR ABOUT 30% OF CASES.
THERE WERE ALMOST A QUARTER OF A MILLION NEW CASES IN 2011 ALONE... TO 40,000 OF THEM FATAL.
THERE'S MORE THAN TWO AND A HALF MILLION OF US SURVIVORS AND WE ALL NEED TO HELP SPREAD THE WORD:
BREAST CANCER DOESN'T HAVE TO BE A DEATH SENTENCE... NOT WITH EARLY DETECTION AND TREATMENT OPTIONS AVAILABLE.
15

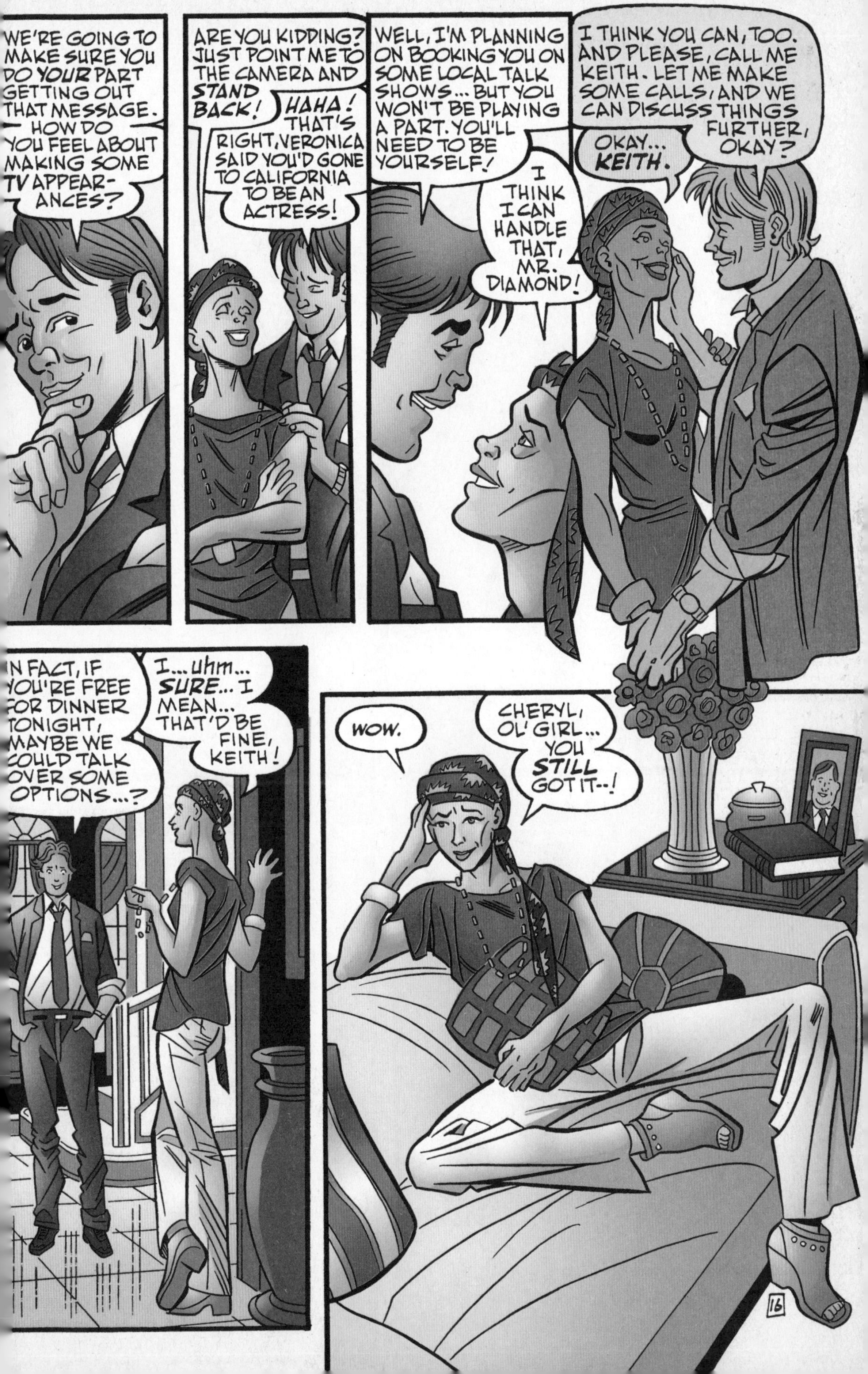

WE'RE GOING TO MAKE SURE YOU DO YOUR PART GETTING OUT THAT MESSAGE. — HOW DO YOU FEEL ABOUT MAKING SOME TV APPEARANCES?
ARE YOU KIDDING? JUST POINT ME TO THE CAMERA AND STAND BACK!
HAHA! THAT'S RIGHT, VERONICA SAID YOU'D GONE TO CALIFORNIA TO BE AN ACTRESS!
WELL, I'M PLANNING ON BOOKING YOU ON SOME LOCAL TALK SHOWS... BUT YOU WON'T BE PLAYING A PART. YOU'LL NEED TO BE YOURSELF!
I THINK I CAN HANDLE THAT, MR. DIAMOND!
I THINK YOU CAN, TOO. AND PLEASE, CALL ME KEITH. LET ME MAKE SOME CALLS, AND WE CAN DISCUSS THINGS FURTHER, OKAY?
OKAY... KEITH.
IN FACT, IF YOU'RE FREE FOR DINNER TONIGHT, MAYBE WE COULD TALK OVER SOME OPTIONS...?
I... uhm... SURE... I MEAN... THAT'D BE FINE, KEITH!
WOW.
CHERYL, OL' GIRL... YOU STILL GOT IT--!
16

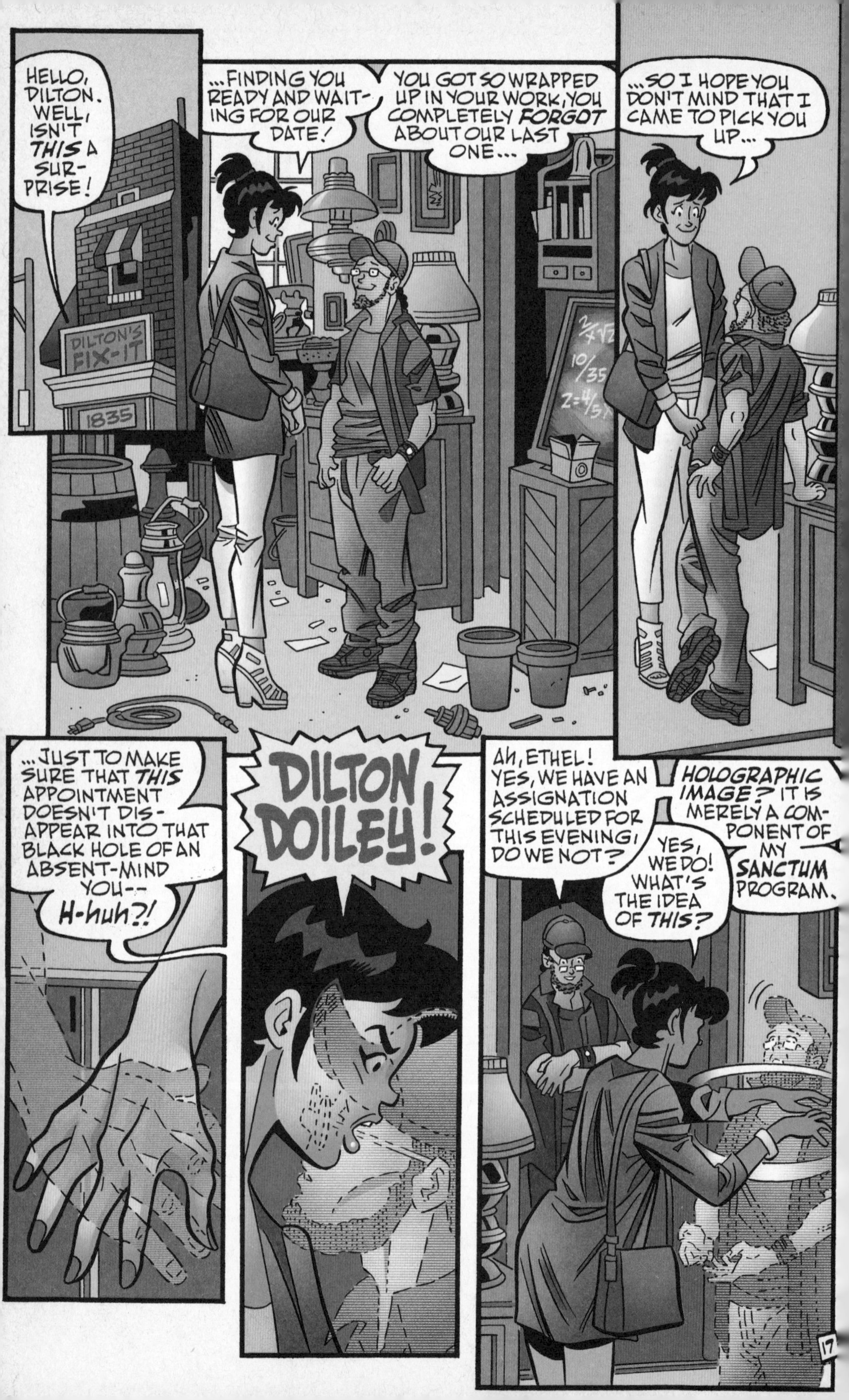
HELLO, DILTON. WELL, ISN'T THIS A SUR-PRISE!
DILTON'S FIX-IT
1835
...FINDING YOU READY AND WAIT-ING FOR OUR DATE!
YOU GOT SO WRAPPED UP IN YOUR WORK, YOU COMPLETELY FORGOT ABOUT OUR LAST ONE...
...SO I HOPE YOU DON'T MIND THAT I CAME TO PICK YOU UP...
...JUST TO MAKE SURE THAT THIS APPOINTMENT DOESN'T DIS-APPEAR INTO THAT BLACK HOLE OF AN ABSENT-MIND YOU-- H-huh?!
DILTON DOILEY!
Ah, ETHEL! YES, WE HAVE AN ASSIGNATION SCHEDULED FOR THIS EVENING, DO WE NOT?
YES, WE DO! WHAT'S THE IDEA OF THIS?
HOLOGRAPHIC IMAGE? IT IS MERELY A COM-PONENT OF MY SANCTUM PROGRAM.

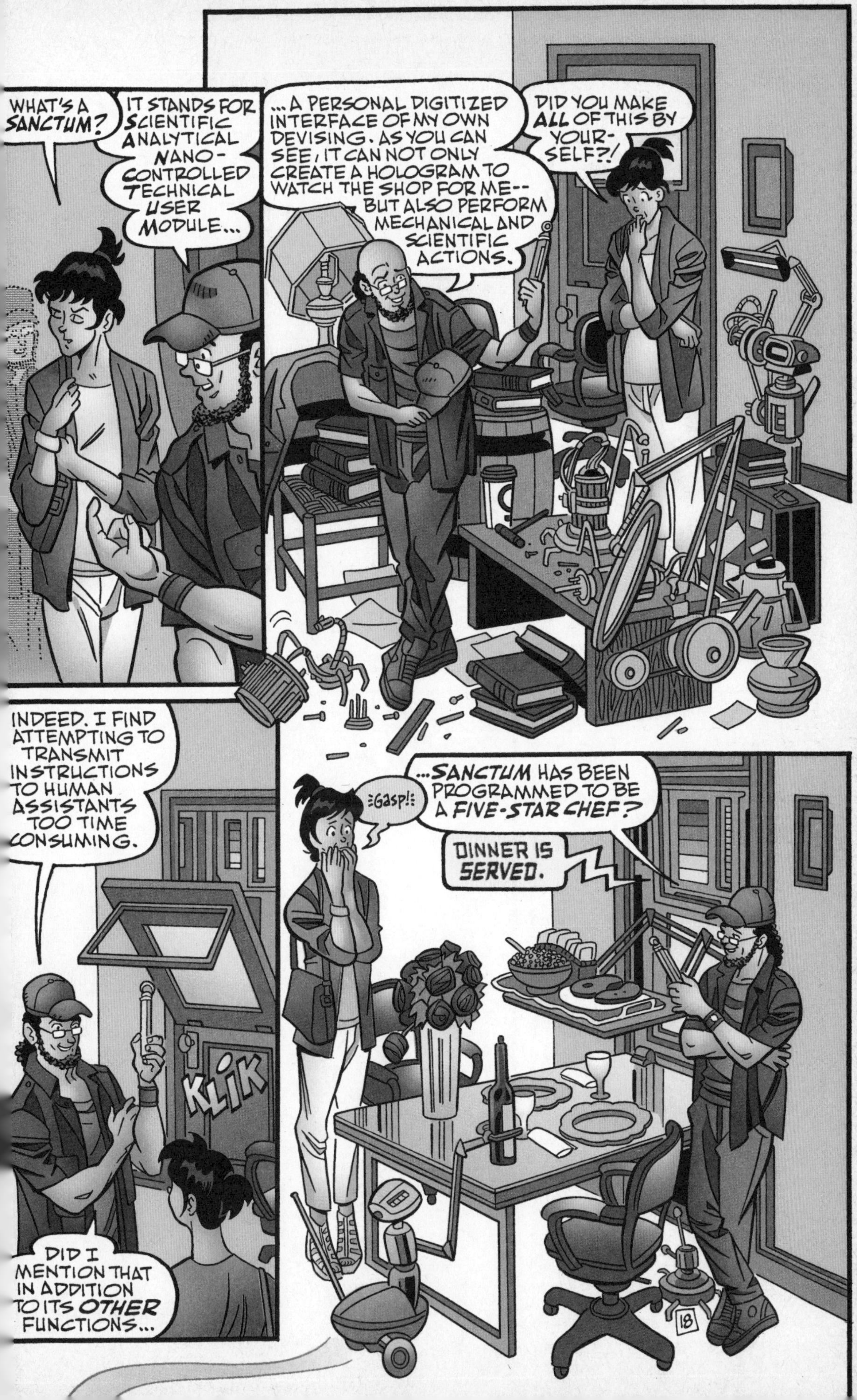

WHAT'S A SANCTUM?
IT STANDS FOR SCIENTIFIC ANALYTICAL NANO-CONTROLLED TECHNICAL USER MODULE...
...A PERSONAL DIGITIZED INTERFACE OF MY OWN DEVISING. AS YOU CAN SEE, IT CAN NOT ONLY CREATE A HOLOGRAM TO WATCH THE SHOP FOR ME-- BUT ALSO PERFORM MECHANICAL AND SCIENTIFIC ACTIONS.
DID YOU MAKE ALL OF THIS BY YOUR-SELF?!
INDEED. I FIND ATTEMPTING TO TRANSMIT INSTRUCTIONS TO HUMAN ASSISTANTS TOO TIME CONSUMING.
KLIK
DID I MENTION THAT IN ADDITION TO ITS OTHER FUNCTIONS...
:GASP!:
...SANCTUM HAS BEEN PROGRAMMED TO BE A FIVE-STAR CHEF?
DINNER IS SERVED.
18

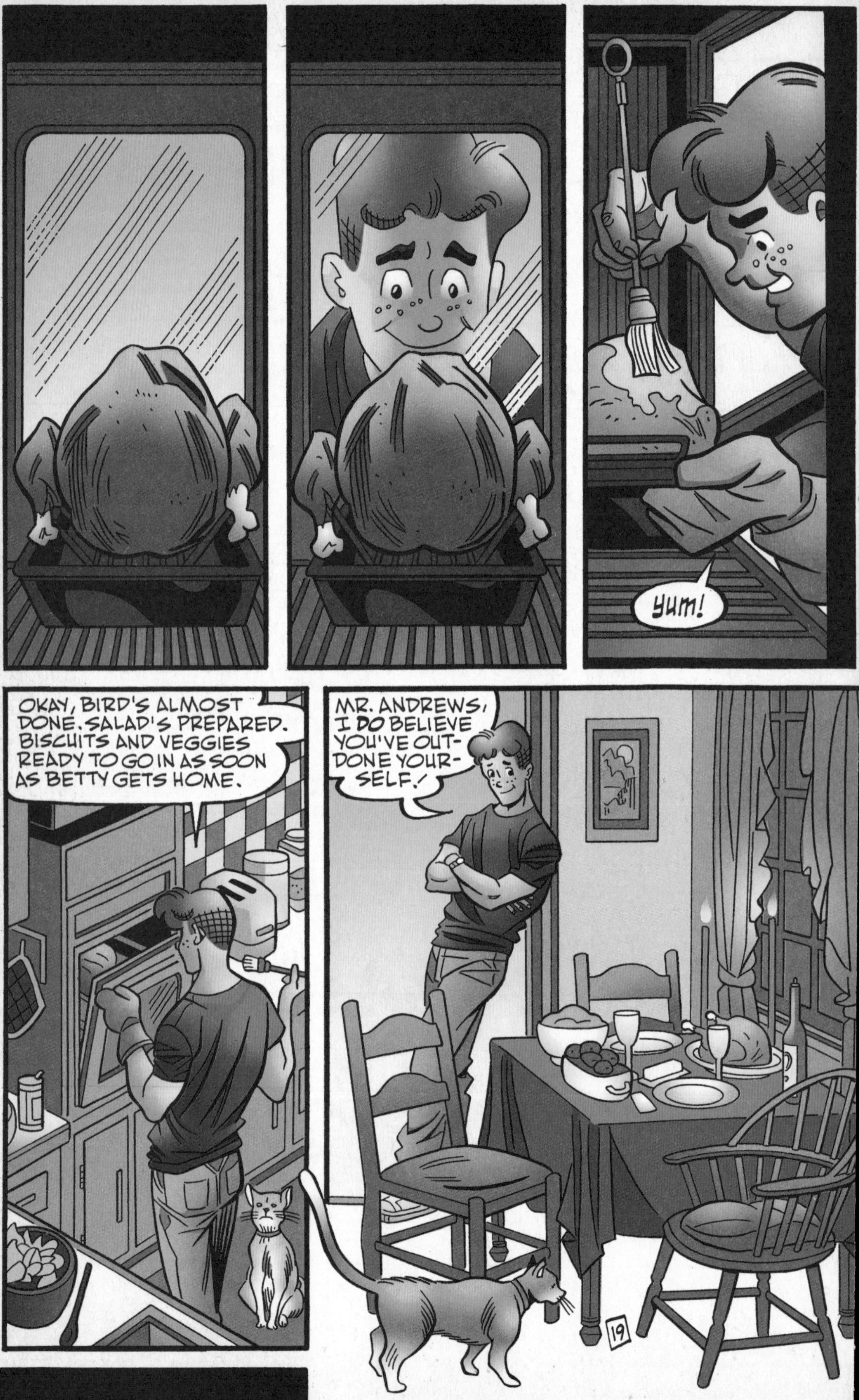
YUM!
OKAY, BIRD'S ALMOST DONE. SALAD'S PREPARED. BISCUITS AND VEGGIES READY TO GO IN AS SOON AS BETTY GETS HOME.
MR. ANDREWS, I DO BELIEVE YOU'VE OUT-DONE YOUR-SELF!
19

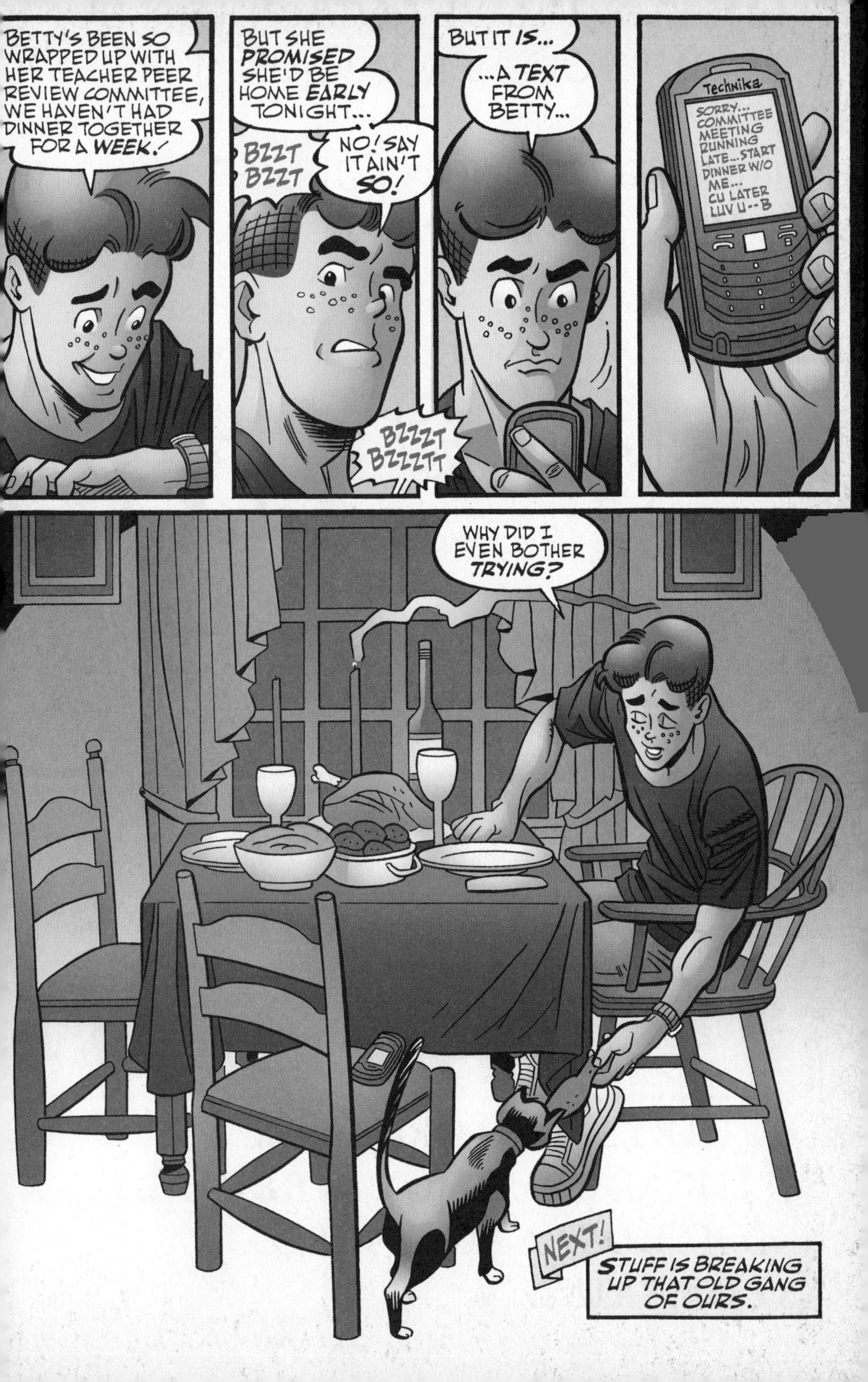
BETTY'S BEEN SO WRAPPED UP WITH HER TEACHER PEER REVIEW COMMITTEE, WE HAVEN'T HAD DINNER TOGETHER FOR A WEEK!
BUT SHE PROMISED SHE'D BE HOME EARLY TONIGHT...
BZZT BZZT
NO! SAY IT AIN'T SO!
BUT IT IS...
...A TEXT FROM BETTY...
BZZZT BZZZTT
Technika
SORRY... COMMITTEE MEETING RUNNING LATE...START DINNER W/O ME... CU LATER LUV U--B
WHY DID I EVEN BOTHER TRYING?
NEXT!
STUFF IS BREAKING UP THAT OLD GANG OF OURS.

"I **COULDN'T** HAVE GOTTEN THIS DONE WITHOUT YOU, VERONICA!"

"I THOUGHT BEING A SOLDIER WAS THE HARDEST JOB I'D EVER HAVE..."

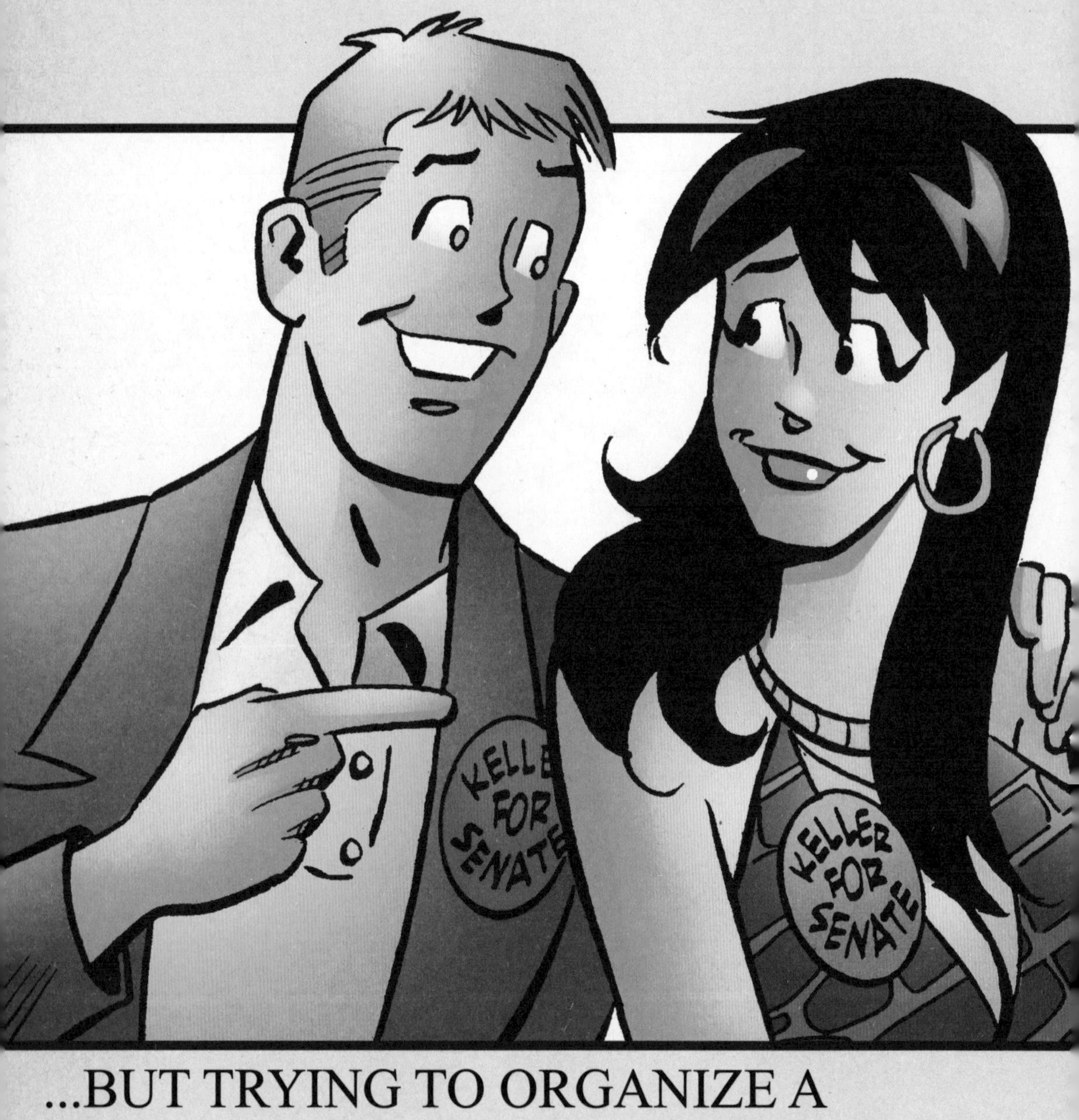
KELLER FOR SENATE
KELLER FOR SENATE

...BUT TRYING TO ORGANIZE A POLITICAL CAMPAIGN IS **BRUTAL** -- AND ***ALMOST*** AS CUTTHROAT AS COMBAT!"

-KEVIN KELLER

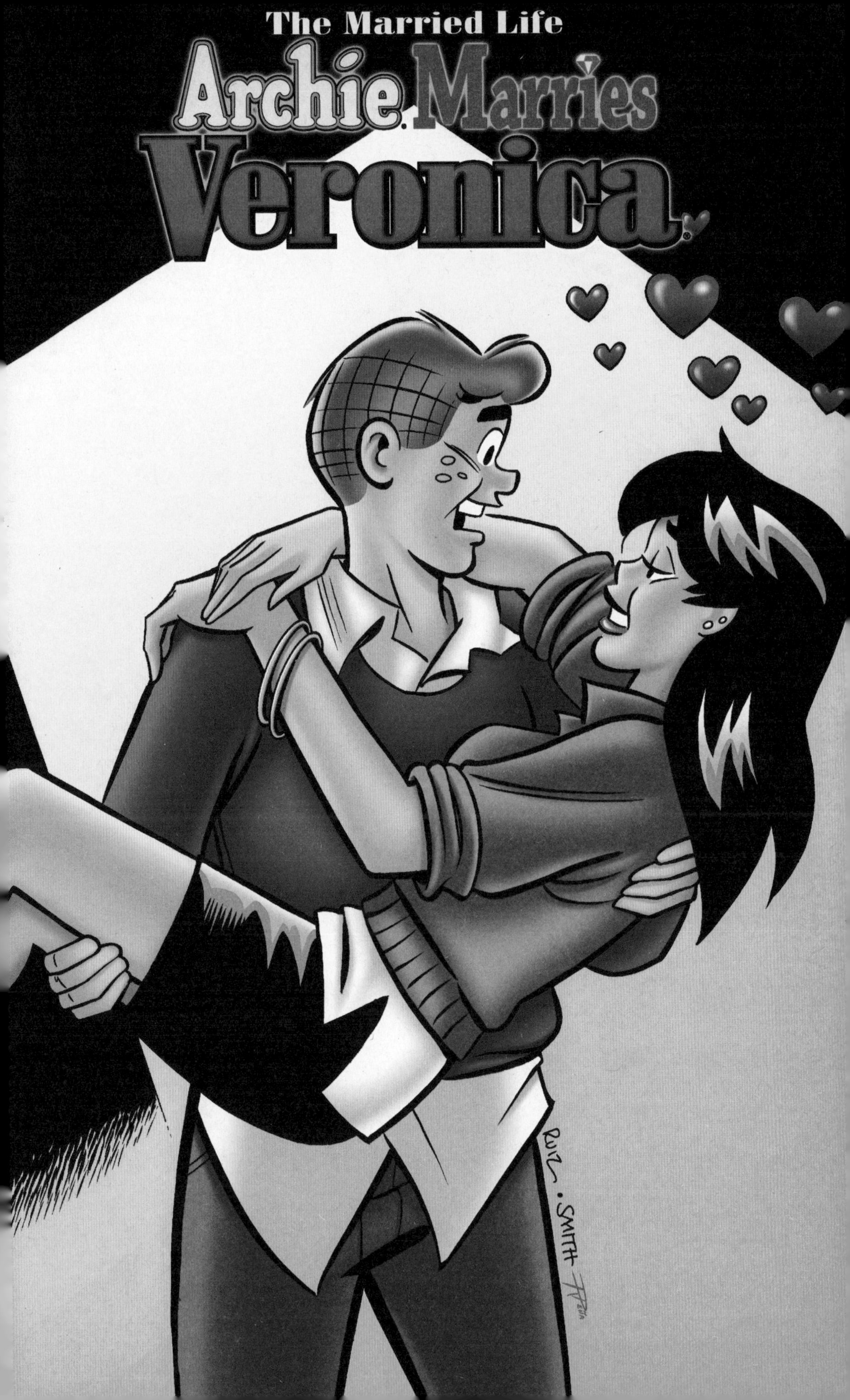
The Married Life
Archie Marries
Veronica
RUIZ
SMITH

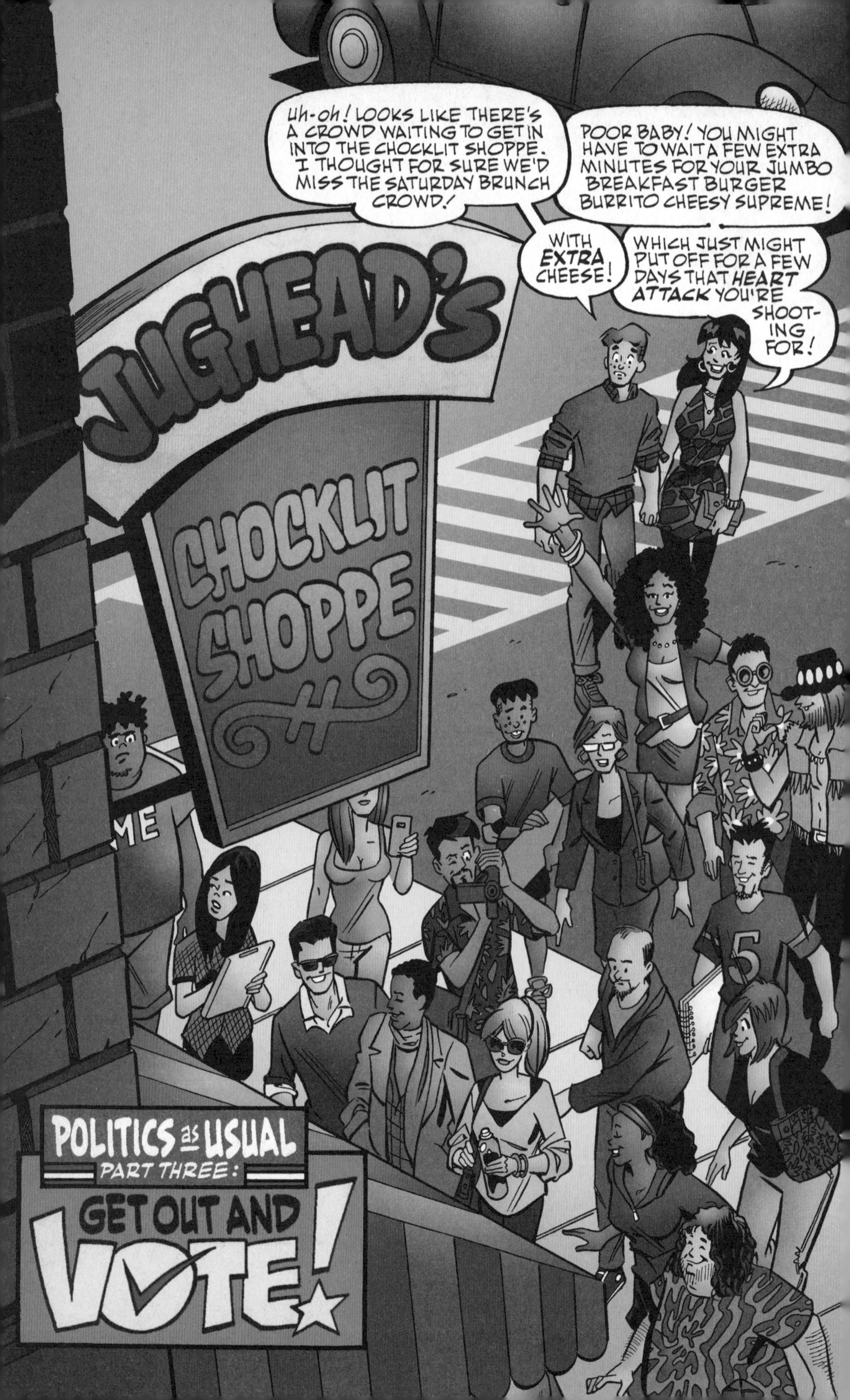
JUGHEAD'S
CHOCKLIT SHOPPE
UH-OH! LOOKS LIKE THERE'S A CROWD WAITING TO GET IN INTO THE CHOCKLIT SHOPPE. I THOUGHT FOR SURE WE'D MISS THE SATURDAY BRUNCH CROWD!
POOR BABY! YOU MIGHT HAVE TO WAIT A FEW EXTRA MINUTES FOR YOUR JUMBO BREAKFAST BURGER BURRITO CHEESY SUPREME!
WITH EXTRA CHEESE!
WHICH JUST MIGHT PUT OFF FOR A FEW DAYS THAT HEART ATTACK YOU'RE SHOOTING FOR!
POLITICS as USUAL
PART THREE:
GET OUT AND VOTE!

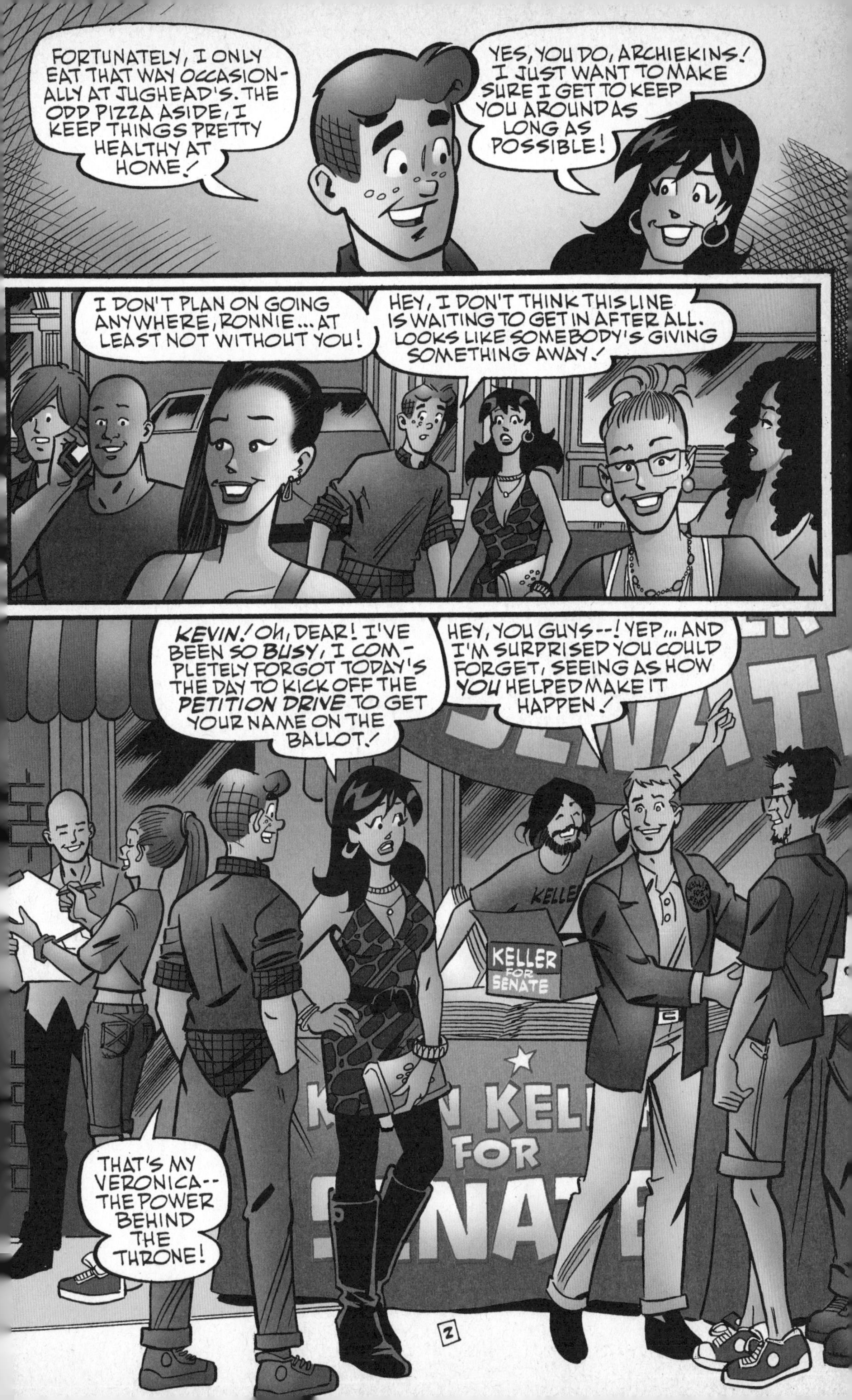
FORTUNATELY, I ONLY EAT THAT WAY OCCASION-ALLY AT JUGHEAD'S. THE ODD PIZZA ASIDE, I KEEP THINGS PRETTY HEALTHY AT HOME!
YES, YOU DO, ARCHIEKINS! I JUST WANT TO MAKE SURE I GET TO KEEP YOU AROUND AS LONG AS POSSIBLE!
I DON'T PLAN ON GOING ANYWHERE, RONNIE... AT LEAST NOT WITHOUT YOU!
HEY, I DON'T THINK THIS LINE IS WAITING TO GET IN AFTER ALL. LOOKS LIKE SOMEBODY'S GIVING SOMETHING AWAY!
KEVIN! OH, DEAR! I'VE BEEN SO BUSY, I COM-PLETELY FORGOT TODAY'S THE DAY TO KICK OFF THE PETITION DRIVE TO GET YOUR NAME ON THE BALLOT!
HEY, YOU GUYS--! YEP... AND I'M SURPRISED YOU COULD FORGET, SEEING AS HOW YOU HELPED MAKE IT HAPPEN!
KELLER
KELLER FOR SENATE
FOR
THAT'S MY VERONICA-- THE POWER BEHIND THE THRONE!

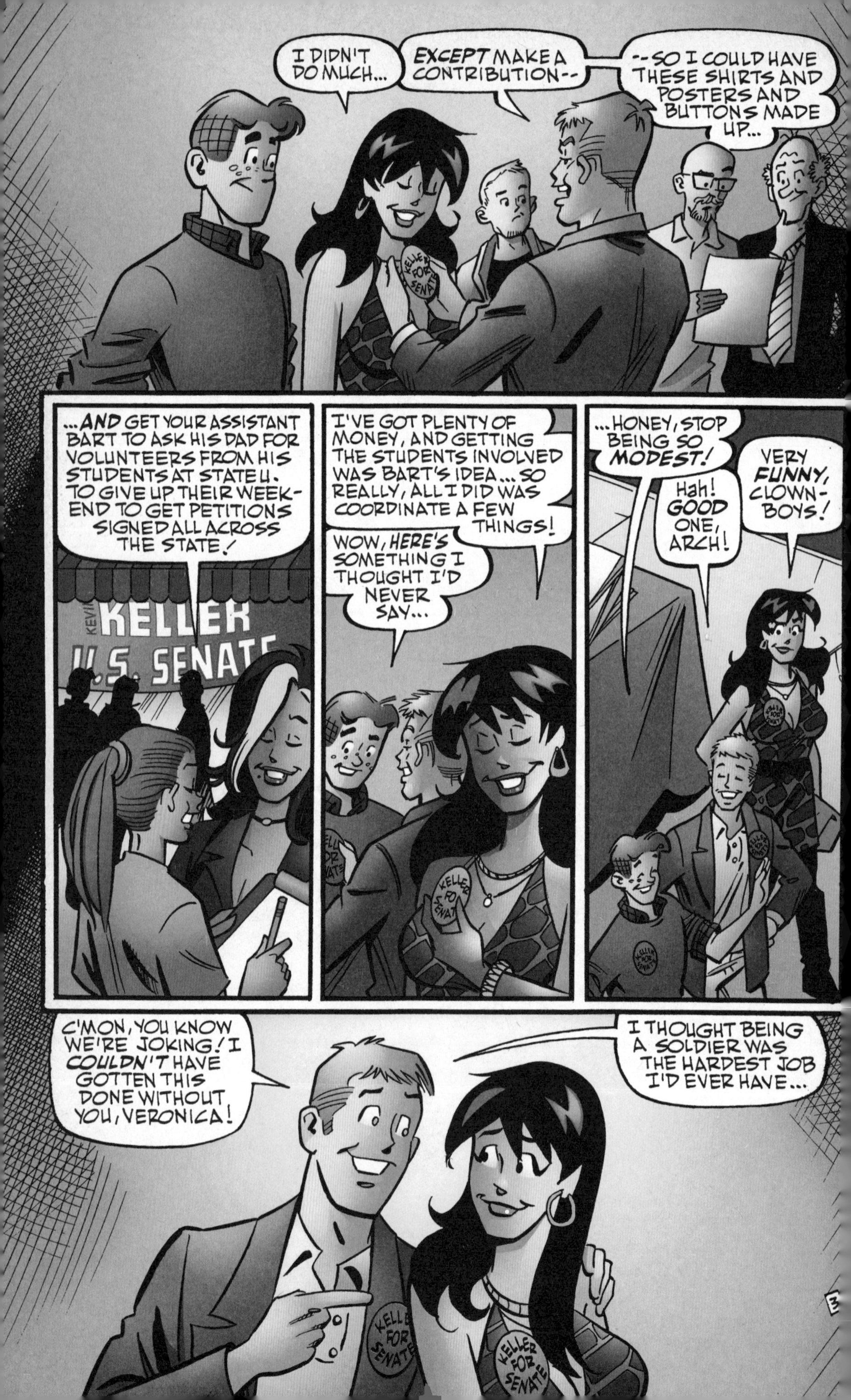
I DIDN'T DO MUCH...
EXCEPT MAKE A CONTRIBUTION--
--SO I COULD HAVE THESE SHIRTS AND POSTERS AND BUTTONS MADE UP...
KELLER FOR SENATE
...AND GET YOUR ASSISTANT BART TO ASK HIS DAD FOR VOLUNTEERS FROM HIS STUDENTS AT STATE U. TO GIVE UP THEIR WEEK-END TO GET PETITIONS SIGNED ALL ACROSS THE STATE!
KELLER
I'VE GOT PLENTY OF MONEY, AND GETTING THE STUDENTS INVOLVED WAS BART'S IDEA... SO REALLY, ALL I DID WAS COORDINATE A FEW THINGS!
WOW, HERE'S SOMETHING I THOUGHT I'D NEVER SAY...
...HONEY, STOP BEING SO MODEST!
Hah! GOOD ONE, ARCH!
VERY FUNNY, CLOWN-BOYS!
C'MON, YOU KNOW WE'RE JOKING! I COULDN'T HAVE GOTTEN THIS DONE WITHOUT YOU, VERONICA!
I THOUGHT BEING A SOLDIER WAS THE HARDEST JOB I'D EVER HAVE...
KELLER FOR SENATE
3

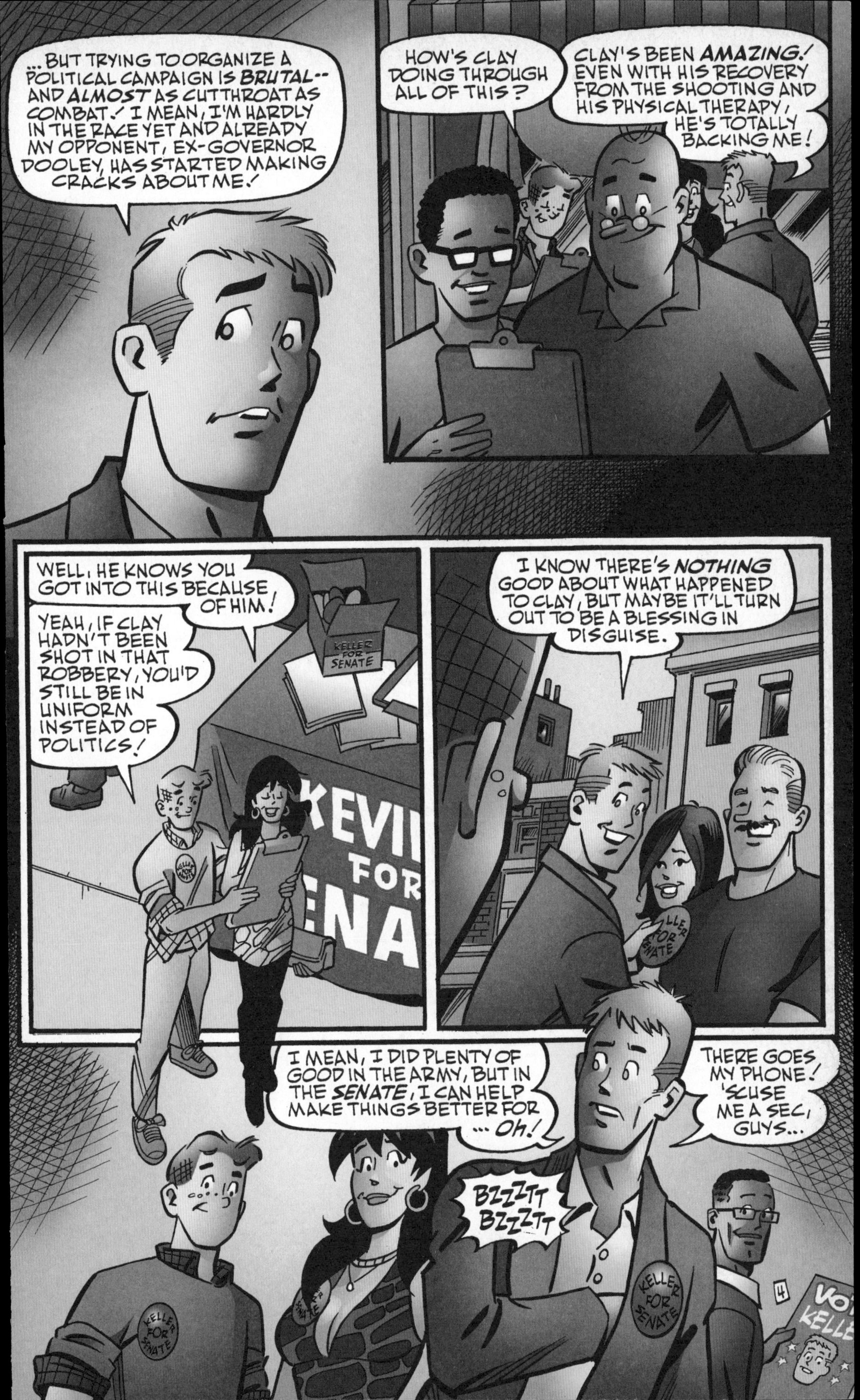
...BUT TRYING TO ORGANIZE A POLITICAL CAMPAIGN IS BRUTAL-- AND ALMOST AS CUTTHROAT AS COMBAT! I MEAN, I'M HARDLY IN THE RACE YET AND ALREADY MY OPPONENT, EX-GOVERNOR DOOLEY, HAS STARTED MAKING CRACKS ABOUT ME!
HOW'S CLAY DOING THROUGH ALL OF THIS?
CLAY'S BEEN AMAZING! EVEN WITH HIS RECOVERY FROM THE SHOOTING AND HIS PHYSICAL THERAPY, HE'S TOTALLY BACKING ME!
WELL, HE KNOWS YOU GOT INTO THIS BECAUSE OF HIM!
YEAH, IF CLAY HADN'T BEEN SHOT IN THAT ROBBERY, YOU'D STILL BE IN UNIFORM INSTEAD OF POLITICS!
KELLER FOR SENATE
KEVI FOR ENA
I KNOW THERE'S NOTHING GOOD ABOUT WHAT HAPPENED TO CLAY, BUT MAYBE IT'LL TURN OUT TO BE A BLESSING IN DISGUISE.
I MEAN, I DID PLENTY OF GOOD IN THE ARMY, BUT IN THE SENATE, I CAN HELP MAKE THINGS BETTER FOR ...Oh!
THERE GOES MY PHONE! 'SCUSE ME A SEC, GUYS...
BZZZTT BZZZTT
KELLER FOR SENATE
KELLER FOR SENATE
VOT KELLE

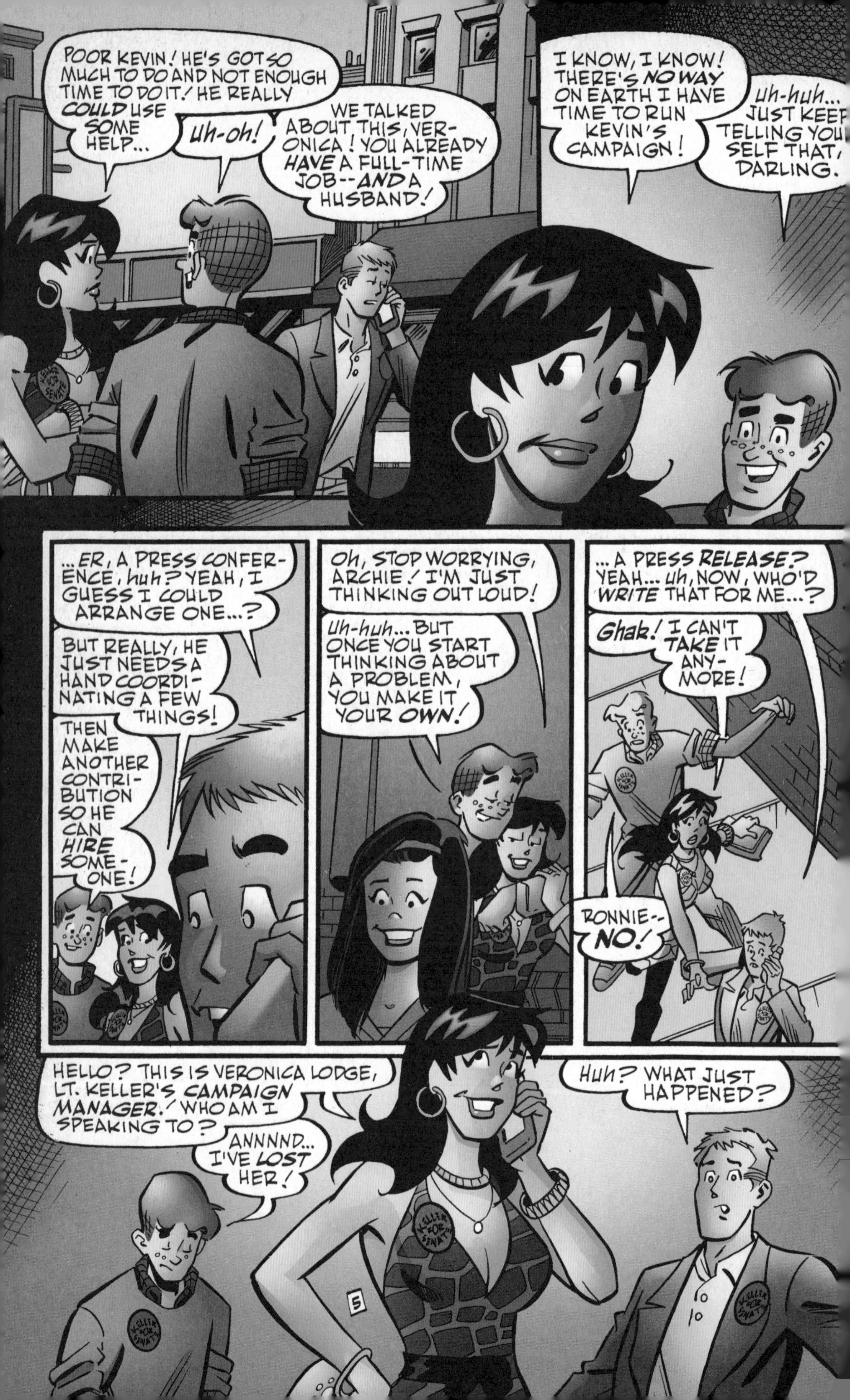
POOR KEVIN! HE'S GOT SO MUCH TO DO AND NOT ENOUGH TIME TO DO IT! HE REALLY COULD USE SOME HELP...
Uh-oh!
WE TALKED ABOUT THIS, VERONICA! YOU ALREADY HAVE A FULL-TIME JOB--AND A HUSBAND!
I KNOW, I KNOW! THERE'S NO WAY ON EARTH I HAVE TIME TO RUN KEVIN'S CAMPAIGN!
Uh-huh... JUST KEEP TELLING YOURSELF THAT, DARLING.
...ER, A PRESS CONFERENCE, huh? YEAH, I GUESS I COULD ARRANGE ONE...?
BUT REALLY, HE JUST NEEDS A HAND COORDINATING A FEW THINGS!
THEN MAKE ANOTHER CONTRIBUTION SO HE CAN HIRE SOMEONE!
Oh, STOP WORRYING, ARCHIE! I'M JUST THINKING OUT LOUD!
Uh-huh... BUT ONCE YOU START THINKING ABOUT A PROBLEM, YOU MAKE IT YOUR OWN!
...A PRESS RELEASE? YEAH... uh, NOW, WHO'D WRITE THAT FOR ME...?
Ghak! I CAN'T TAKE IT ANYMORE!
RONNIE-- NO!
HELLO? THIS IS VERONICA LODGE, LT. KELLER'S CAMPAIGN MANAGER! WHO AM I SPEAKING TO?
ANNNND... I'VE LOST HER!
Huh? WHAT JUST HAPPENED?
5

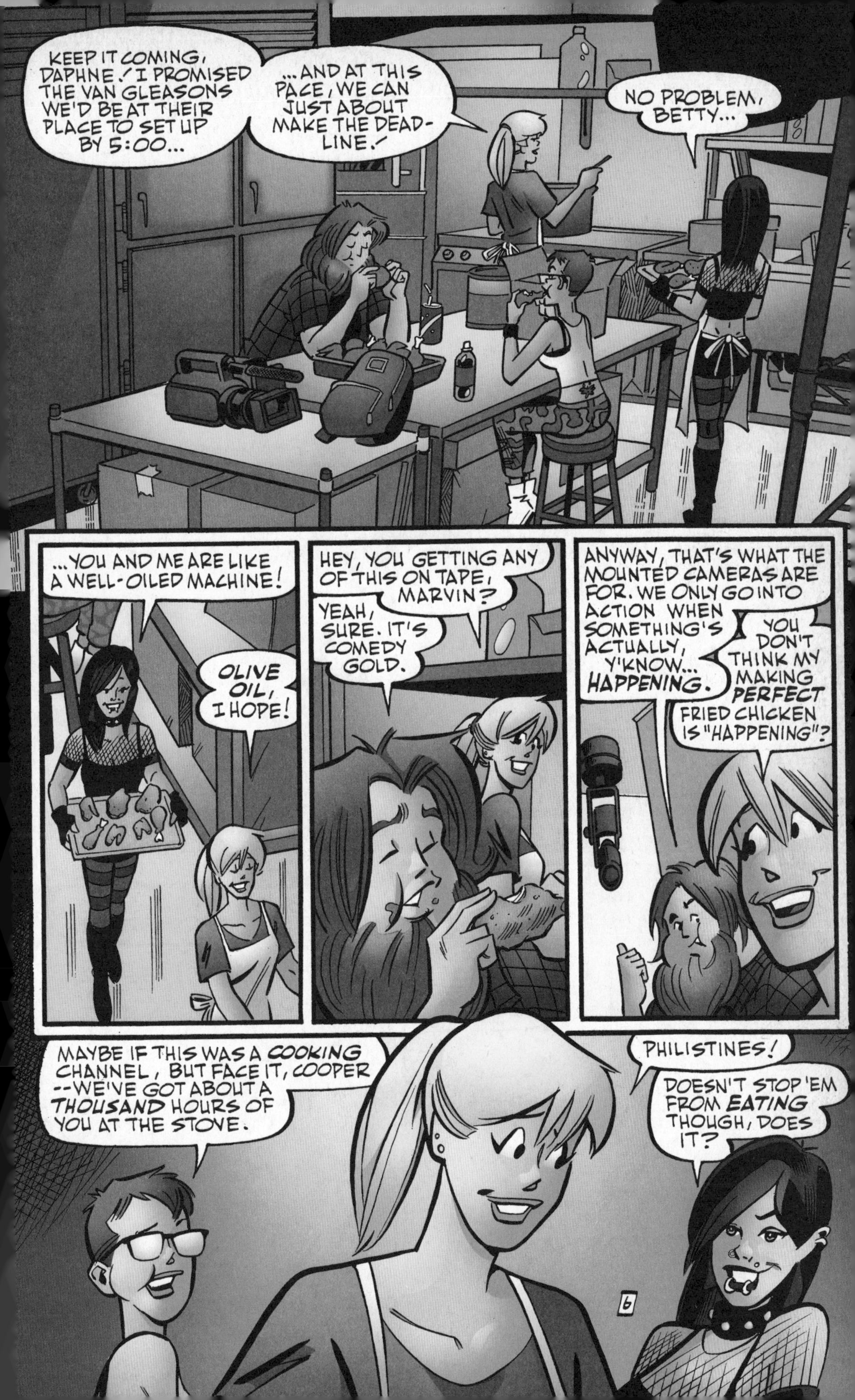
KEEP IT COMING, DAPHNE! I PROMISED THE VAN GLEASONS WE'D BE AT THEIR PLACE TO SET UP BY 5:00...
...AND AT THIS PACE, WE CAN JUST ABOUT MAKE THE DEAD-LINE!
NO PROBLEM, BETTY...
...YOU AND ME ARE LIKE A WELL-OILED MACHINE!
OLIVE OIL, I HOPE!
HEY, YOU GETTING ANY OF THIS ON TAPE, MARVIN?
YEAH, SURE. IT'S COMEDY GOLD.
ANYWAY, THAT'S WHAT THE MOUNTED CAMERAS ARE FOR. WE ONLY GO INTO ACTION WHEN SOMETHING'S ACTUALLY, Y'KNOW... HAPPENING.
YOU DON'T THINK MY MAKING PERFECT FRIED CHICKEN IS "HAPPENING"?
MAYBE IF THIS WAS A COOKING CHANNEL, BUT FACE IT, COOPER --WE'VE GOT ABOUT A THOUSAND HOURS OF YOU AT THE STOVE.
PHILISTINES!
DOESN'T STOP 'EM FROM EATING THOUGH, DOES IT?
6

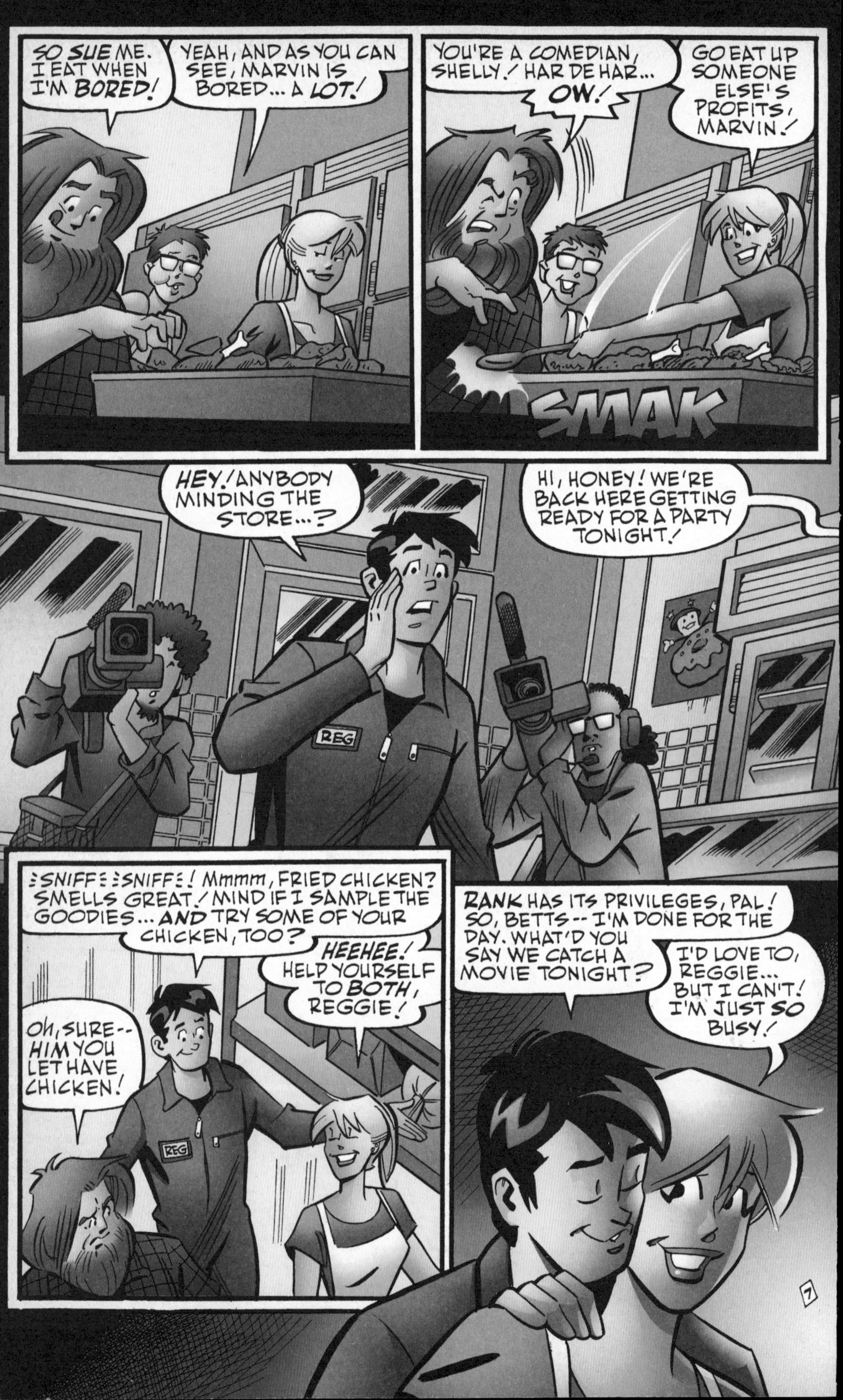
SO SUE ME. I EAT WHEN I'M BORED!
YEAH, AND AS YOU CAN SEE, MARVIN IS BORED... A LOT!
YOU'RE A COMEDIAN, SHELLY! HAR DE HAR... OW!
GO EAT UP SOMEONE ELSE'S PROFITS, MARVIN!
SMAK
HEY! ANYBODY MINDING THE STORE...?
HI, HONEY! WE'RE BACK HERE GETTING READY FOR A PARTY TONIGHT!
REG
:SNIFF: :SNIFF:! Mmmm, FRIED CHICKEN? SMELLS GREAT! MIND IF I SAMPLE THE GOODIES... AND TRY SOME OF YOUR CHICKEN, TOO?
HEEHEE! HELP YOURSELF TO BOTH, REGGIE!
Oh, SURE-- HIM YOU LET HAVE CHICKEN!
REG
RANK HAS ITS PRIVILEGES, PAL! SO, BETTS -- I'M DONE FOR THE DAY. WHAT'D YOU SAY WE CATCH A MOVIE TONIGHT?
I'D LOVE TO, REGGIE... BUT I CAN'T! I'M JUST SO BUSY!
7

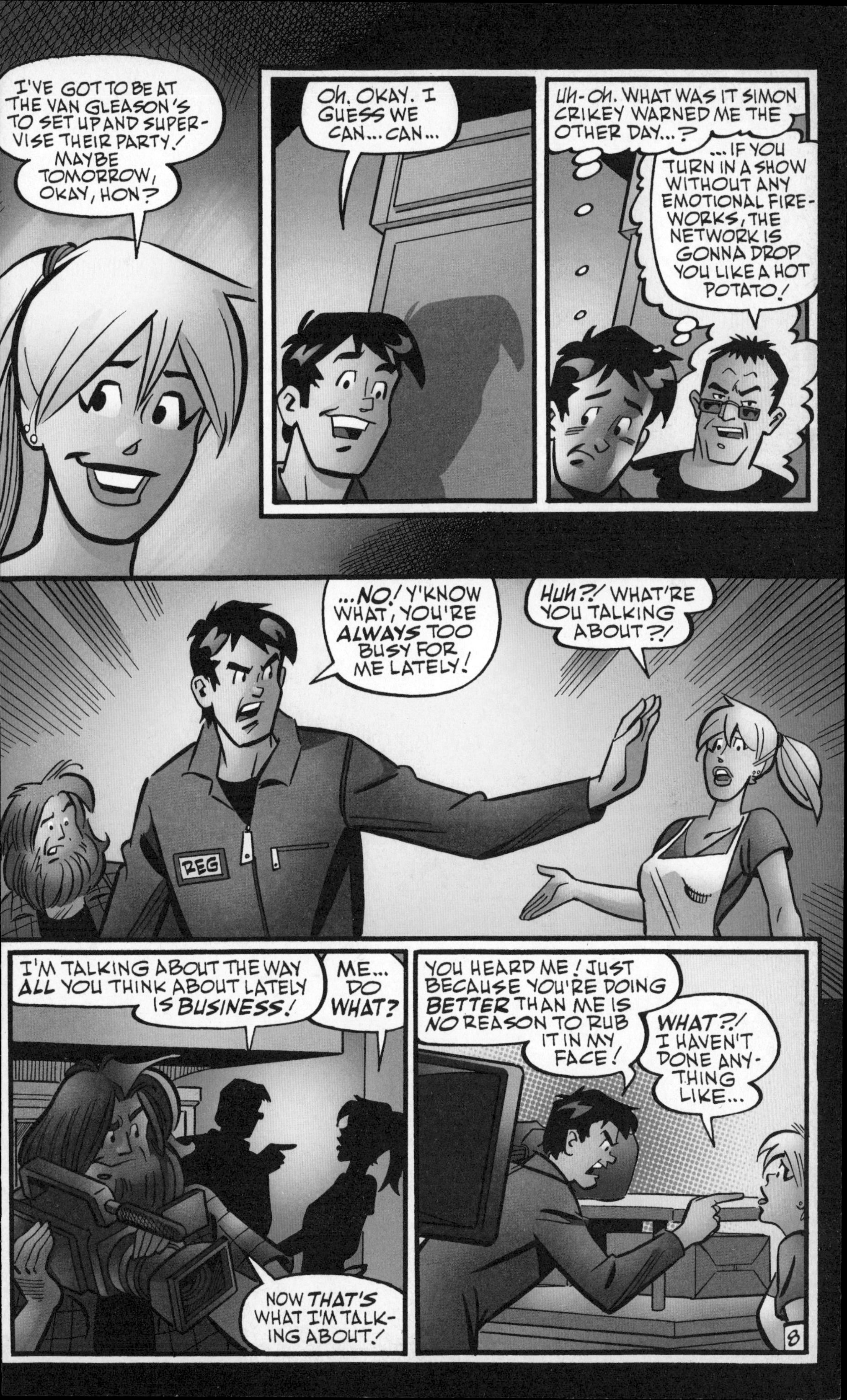
I'VE GOT TO BE AT THE VAN GLEASON'S TO SET UP AND SUPER-VISE THEIR PARTY! MAYBE TOMORROW, OKAY, HON?
OH, OKAY. I GUESS WE CAN... CAN...
UH-OH. WHAT WAS IT SIMON CRIKEY WARNED ME THE OTHER DAY...?
...IF YOU TURN IN A SHOW WITHOUT ANY EMOTIONAL FIRE-WORKS, THE NETWORK IS GONNA DROP YOU LIKE A HOT POTATO!
...NO! Y'KNOW WHAT, YOU'RE ALWAYS TOO BUSY FOR ME LATELY!
HUH?! WHAT'RE YOU TALKING ABOUT?!
REG
I'M TALKING ABOUT THE WAY ALL YOU THINK ABOUT LATELY IS BUSINESS!
ME... DO WHAT?
NOW THAT'S WHAT I'M TALK-ING ABOUT!
YOU HEARD ME! JUST BECAUSE YOU'RE DOING BETTER THAN ME IS NO REASON TO RUB IT IN MY FACE!
WHAT?! I HAVEN'T DONE ANY-THING LIKE...
8

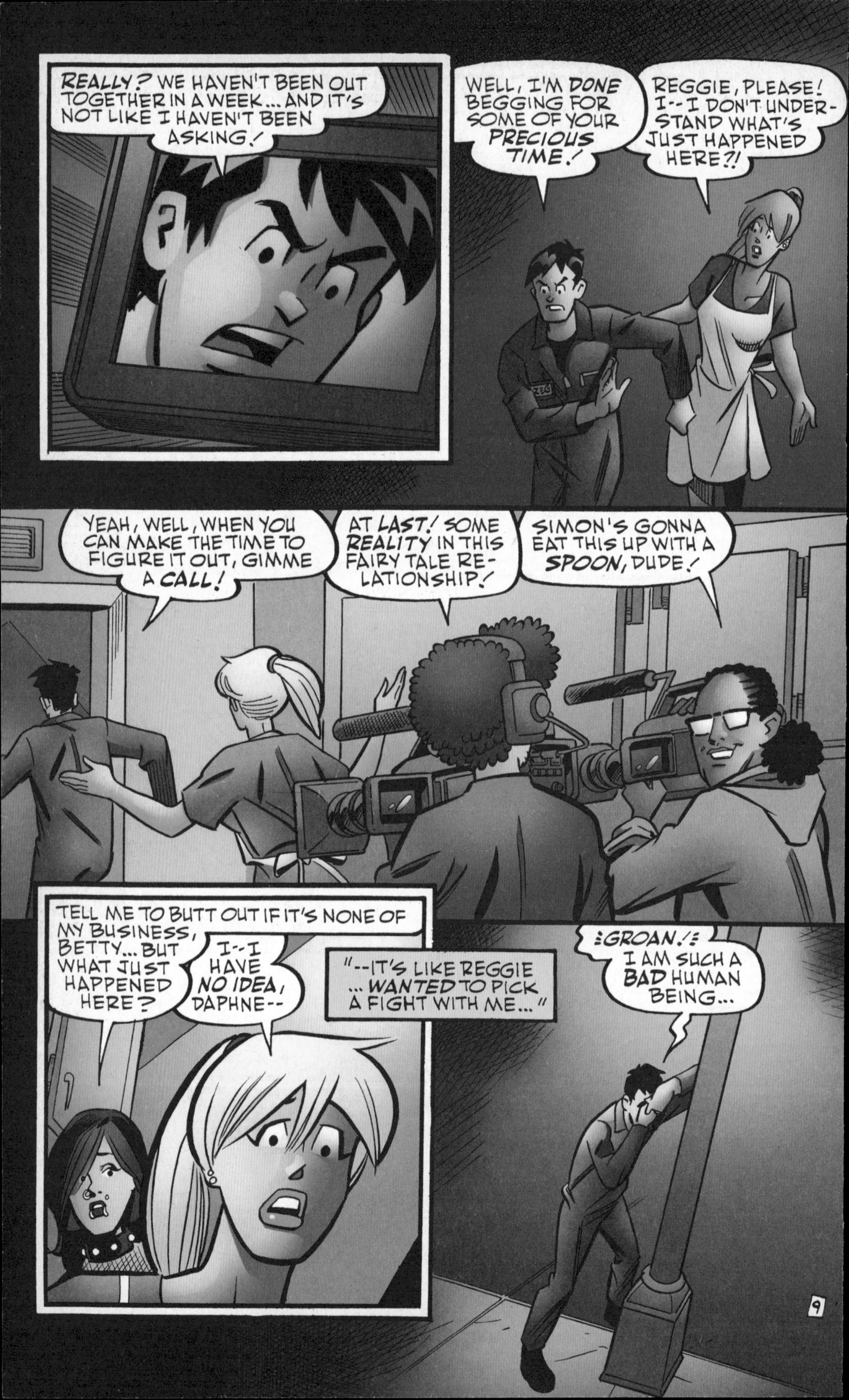

REALLY? WE HAVEN'T BEEN OUT TOGETHER IN A WEEK... AND IT'S NOT LIKE I HAVEN'T BEEN ASKING!
WELL, I'M DONE BEGGING FOR SOME OF YOUR PRECIOUS TIME!
REGGIE, PLEASE! I-- I DON'T UNDERSTAND WHAT'S JUST HAPPENED HERE?!
YEAH, WELL, WHEN YOU CAN MAKE THE TIME TO FIGURE IT OUT, GIMME A CALL!
AT LAST! SOME REALITY IN THIS FAIRY TALE RELATIONSHIP!
SIMON'S GONNA EAT THIS UP WITH A SPOON, DUDE!
TELL ME TO BUTT OUT IF IT'S NONE OF MY BUSINESS, BETTY... BUT WHAT JUST HAPPENED HERE?
I-- I HAVE NO IDEA, DAPHNE--
"--IT'S LIKE REGGIE ... WANTED TO PICK A FIGHT WITH ME..."
GROAN!
I AM SUCH A BAD HUMAN BEING...

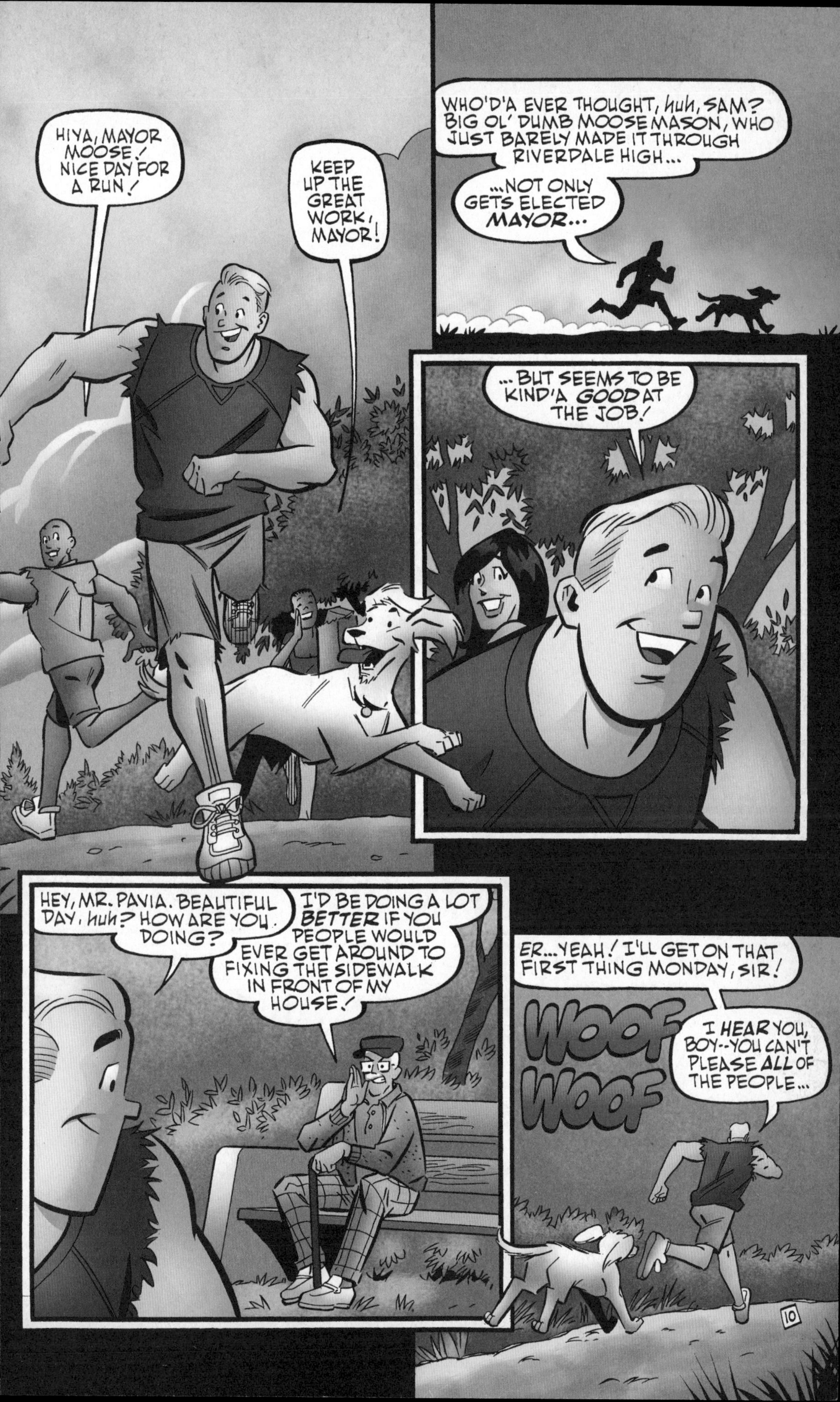

HIYA, MAYOR MOOSE! NICE DAY FOR A RUN!
KEEP UP THE GREAT WORK, MAYOR!
WHO'D'A EVER THOUGHT, huh, SAM? BIG OL' DUMB MOOSE MASON, WHO JUST BARELY MADE IT THROUGH RIVERDALE HIGH...
...NOT ONLY GETS ELECTED MAYOR...
...BUT SEEMS TO BE KIND'A GOOD AT THE JOB!
HEY, MR. PAVIA. BEAUTIFUL DAY, huh? HOW ARE YOU DOING?
I'D BE DOING A LOT BETTER IF YOU PEOPLE WOULD EVER GET AROUND TO FIXING THE SIDEWALK IN FRONT OF MY HOUSE!
ER...YEAH! I'LL GET ON THAT FIRST THING MONDAY, SIR!
WOOF WOOF
I HEAR YOU, BOY--YOU CAN'T PLEASE ALL OF THE PEOPLE...
10

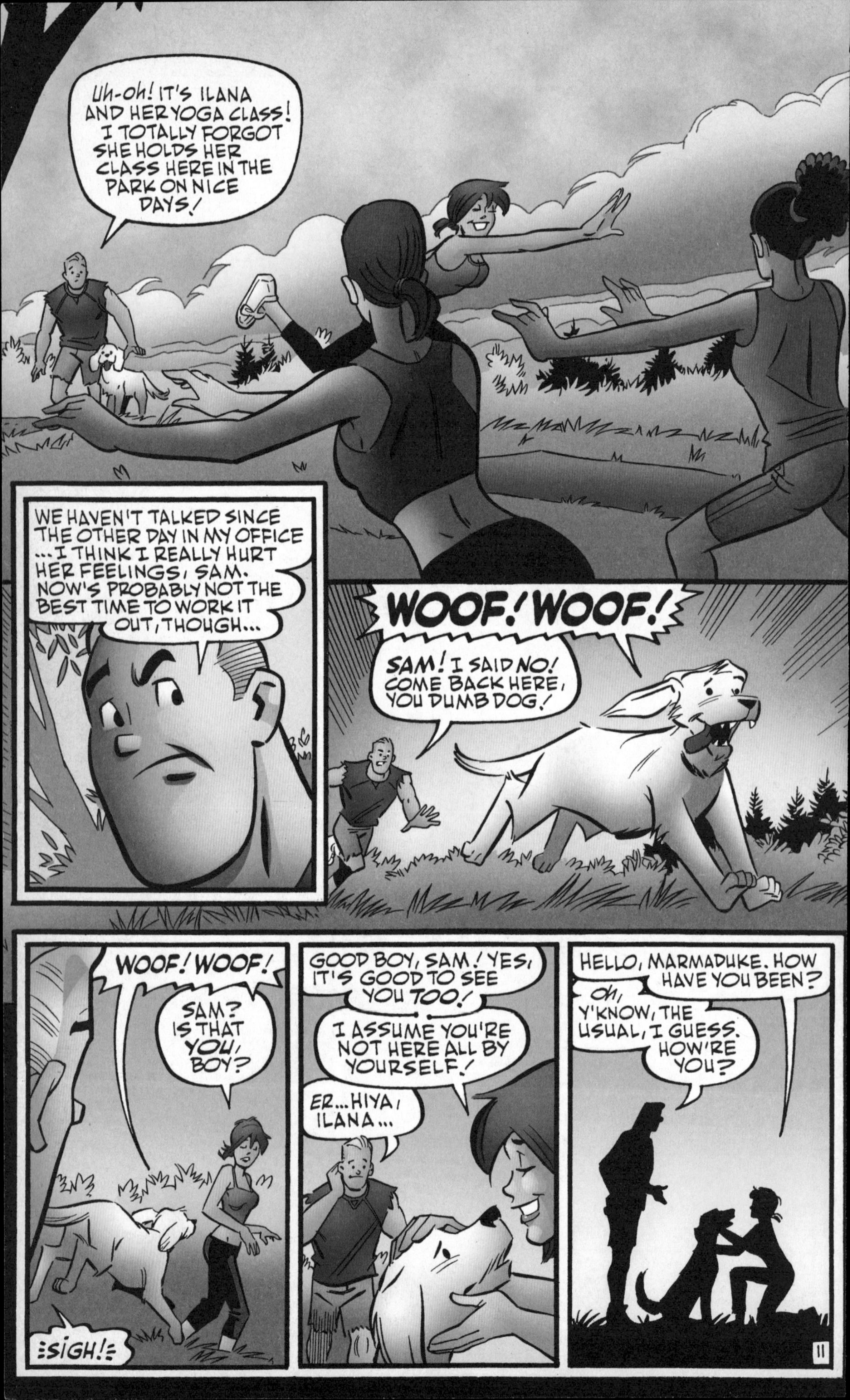
UH-OH! IT'S ILANA AND HER YOGA CLASS! I TOTALLY FORGOT SHE HOLDS HER CLASS HERE IN THE PARK ON NICE DAYS!
WE HAVEN'T TALKED SINCE THE OTHER DAY IN MY OFFICE ...I THINK I REALLY HURT HER FEELINGS, SAM. NOW'S PROBABLY NOT THE BEST TIME TO WORK IT OUT, THOUGH...
WOOF! WOOF!
SAM! I SAID NO! COME BACK HERE, YOU DUMB DOG!
WOOF! WOOF!
SAM? IS THAT YOU, BOY?
SIGH!
GOOD BOY, SAM! YES, IT'S GOOD TO SEE YOU TOO!
I ASSUME YOU'RE NOT HERE ALL BY YOURSELF!
ER...HIYA, ILANA...
HELLO, MARMADUKE. HOW HAVE YOU BEEN?
OH, Y'KNOW, THE USUAL, I GUESS. HOW'RE YOU?
11

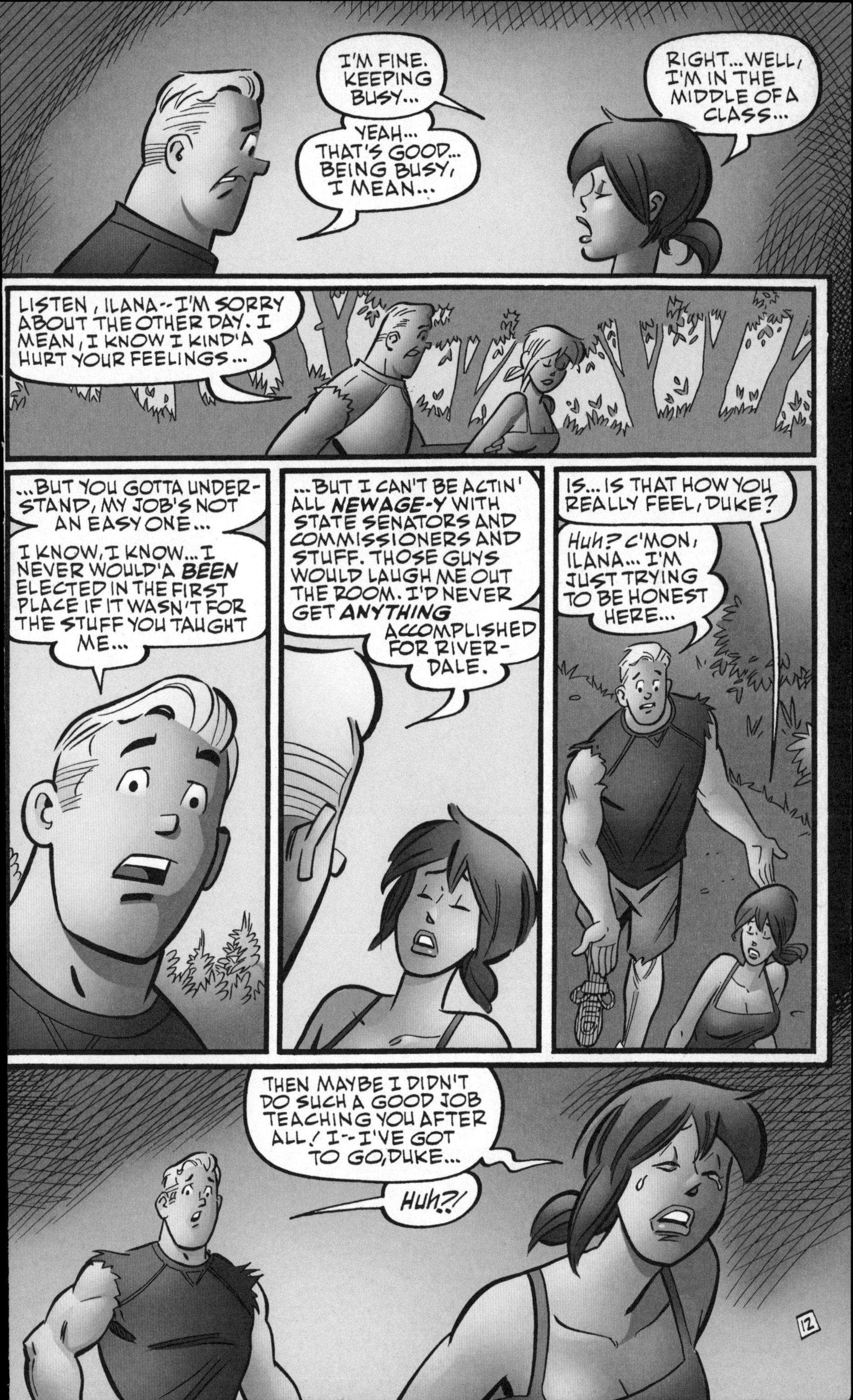
I'M FINE. KEEPING BUSY...
YEAH... THAT'S GOOD... BEING BUSY, I MEAN...
RIGHT... WELL, I'M IN THE MIDDLE OF A CLASS...
LISTEN, ILANA--I'M SORRY ABOUT THE OTHER DAY. I MEAN, I KNOW I KIND'A HURT YOUR FEELINGS...
...BUT YOU GOTTA UNDER-STAND, MY JOB'S NOT AN EASY ONE...
I KNOW, I KNOW... I NEVER WOULD'A *BEEN* ELECTED IN THE FIRST PLACE IF IT WASN'T FOR THE STUFF YOU TAUGHT ME...
...BUT I CAN'T BE ACTIN' ALL *NEWAGE-Y* WITH STATE SENATORS AND COMMISSIONERS AND STUFF. THOSE GUYS WOULD LAUGH ME OUT THE ROOM. I'D NEVER GET *ANYTHING* ACCOMPLISHED FOR RIVER-DALE.
IS... IS THAT HOW YOU REALLY FEEL, DUKE?
HUH? C'MON, ILANA... I'M JUST TRYING TO BE HONEST HERE...
THEN MAYBE I DIDN'T DO SUCH A GOOD JOB TEACHING YOU AFTER ALL! I--I'VE GOT TO GO, DUKE...
HUH?!
12

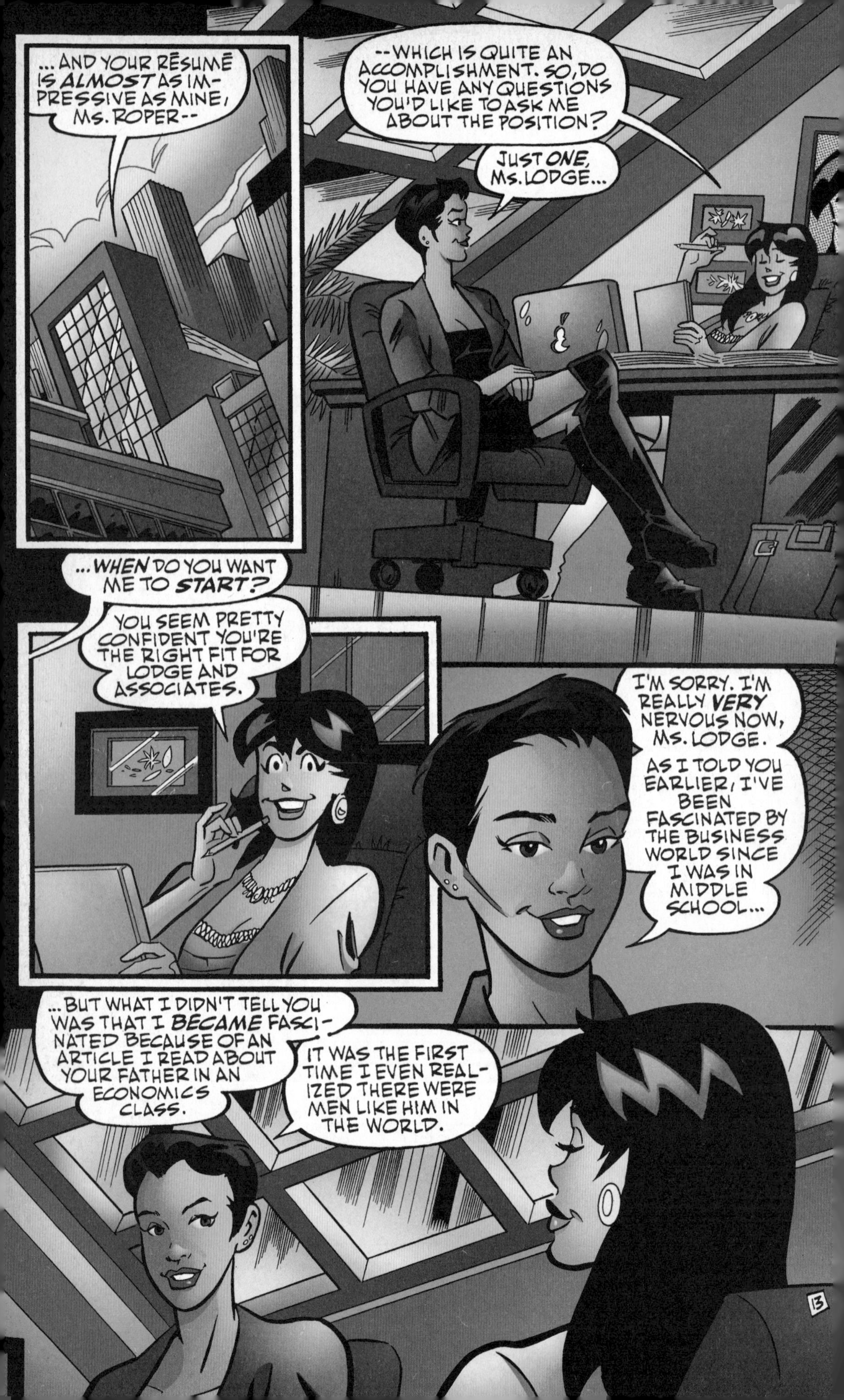
...AND YOUR RÉSUMÉ IS ALMOST AS IMPRESSIVE AS MINE, MS. ROPER--
--WHICH IS QUITE AN ACCOMPLISHMENT. SO, DO YOU HAVE ANY QUESTIONS YOU'D LIKE TO ASK ME ABOUT THE POSITION?
JUST ONE, MS. LODGE...
...WHEN DO YOU WANT ME TO START?
YOU SEEM PRETTY CONFIDENT YOU'RE THE RIGHT FIT FOR LODGE AND ASSOCIATES.
I'M SORRY. I'M REALLY VERY NERVOUS NOW, MS. LODGE.
AS I TOLD YOU EARLIER, I'VE BEEN FASCINATED BY THE BUSINESS WORLD SINCE I WAS IN MIDDLE SCHOOL...
...BUT WHAT I DIDN'T TELL YOU WAS THAT I BECAME FASCINATED BECAUSE OF AN ARTICLE I READ ABOUT YOUR FATHER IN AN ECONOMICS CLASS.
IT WAS THE FIRST TIME I EVEN REALIZED THERE WERE MEN LIKE HIM IN THE WORLD.
13

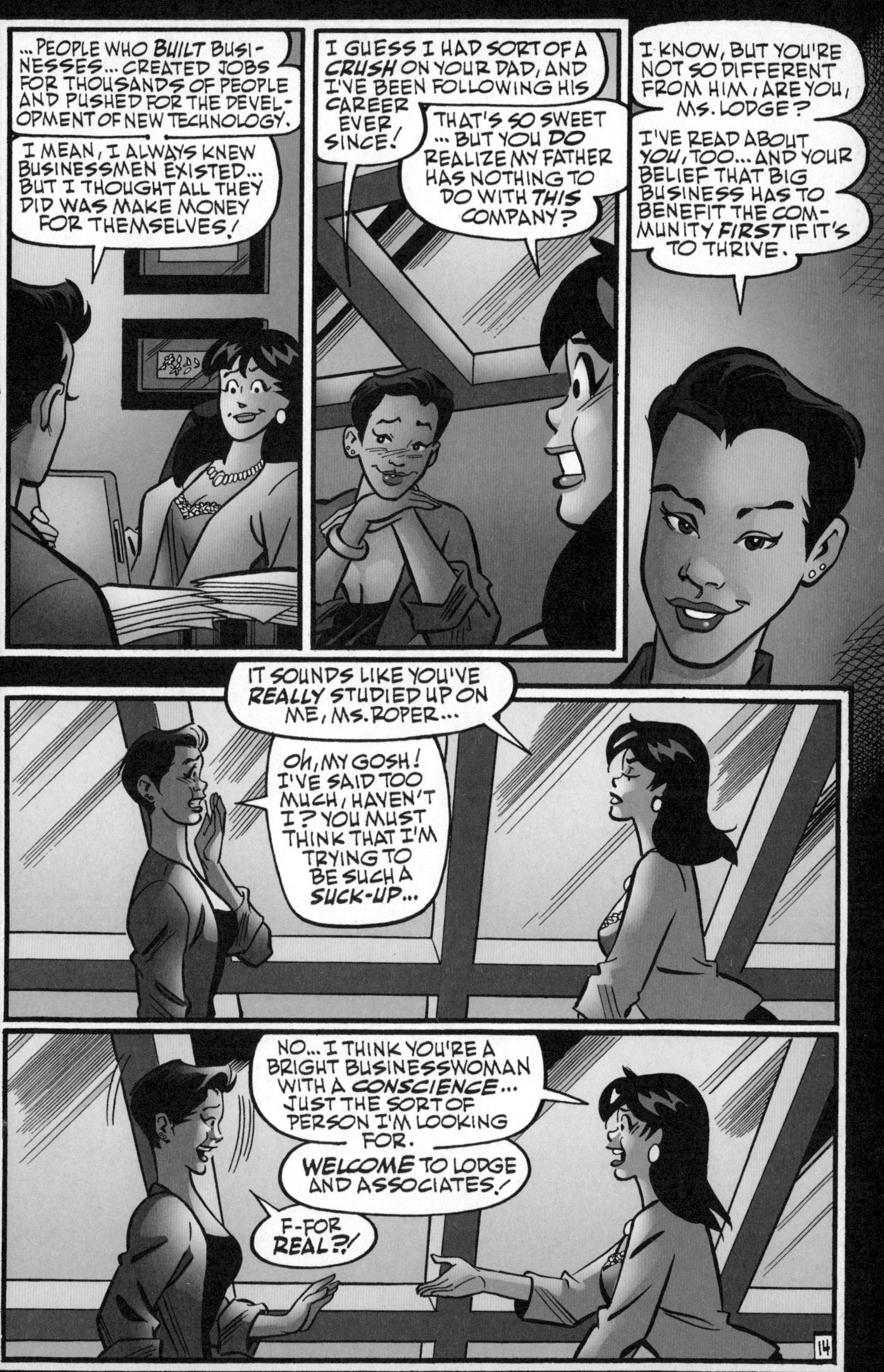
...PEOPLE WHO BUILT BUSINESSES... CREATED JOBS FOR THOUSANDS OF PEOPLE AND PUSHED FOR THE DEVELOPMENT OF NEW TECHNOLOGY.
I MEAN, I ALWAYS KNEW BUSINESSMEN EXISTED... BUT I THOUGHT ALL THEY DID WAS MAKE MONEY FOR THEMSELVES!
I GUESS I HAD SORT OF A CRUSH ON YOUR DAD, AND I'VE BEEN FOLLOWING HIS CAREER EVER SINCE!
THAT'S SO SWEET ...BUT YOU DO REALIZE MY FATHER HAS NOTHING TO DO WITH THIS COMPANY?
I KNOW, BUT YOU'RE NOT SO DIFFERENT FROM HIM, ARE YOU, MS. LODGE?
I'VE READ ABOUT YOU, TOO... AND YOUR BELIEF THAT BIG BUSINESS HAS TO BENEFIT THE COMMUNITY FIRST IF IT'S TO THRIVE.
IT SOUNDS LIKE YOU'VE REALLY STUDIED UP ON ME, MS. ROPER...
OH, MY GOSH! I'VE SAID TOO MUCH, HAVEN'T I? YOU MUST THINK THAT I'M TRYING TO BE SUCH A SUCK-UP...
NO... I THINK YOU'RE A BRIGHT BUSINESSWOMAN WITH A CONSCIENCE... JUST THE SORT OF PERSON I'M LOOKING FOR.
WELCOME TO LODGE AND ASSOCIATES!
F-FOR REAL?!

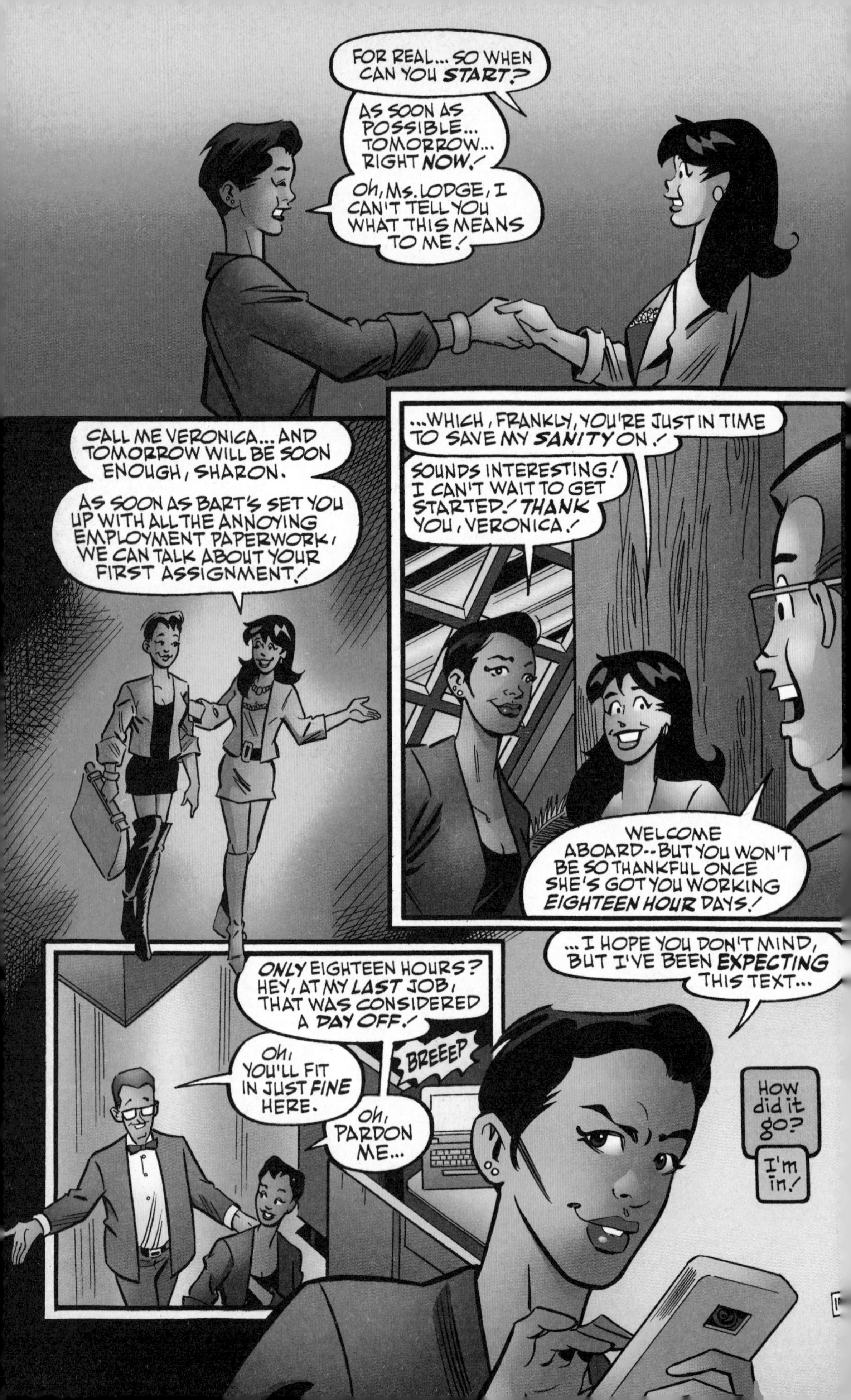
FOR REAL... SO WHEN CAN YOU START?
AS SOON AS POSSIBLE... TOMORROW... RIGHT NOW!
OH, MS. LODGE, I CAN'T TELL YOU WHAT THIS MEANS TO ME!
CALL ME VERONICA... AND TOMORROW WILL BE SOON ENOUGH, SHARON.
AS SOON AS BART'S SET YOU UP WITH ALL THE ANNOYING EMPLOYMENT PAPERWORK, WE CAN TALK ABOUT YOUR FIRST ASSIGNMENT!
...WHICH, FRANKLY, YOU'RE JUST IN TIME TO SAVE MY SANITY ON!
SOUNDS INTERESTING! I CAN'T WAIT TO GET STARTED! THANK YOU, VERONICA!
WELCOME ABOARD--BUT YOU WON'T BE SO THANKFUL ONCE SHE'S GOT YOU WORKING EIGHTEEN HOUR DAYS!
ONLY EIGHTEEN HOURS? HEY, AT MY LAST JOB, THAT WAS CONSIDERED A DAY OFF!
OH, YOU'LL FIT IN JUST FINE HERE.
BREEEP
OH, PARDON ME...
...I HOPE YOU DON'T MIND, BUT I'VE BEEN EXPECTING THIS TEXT...
How did it go?
I'm in!

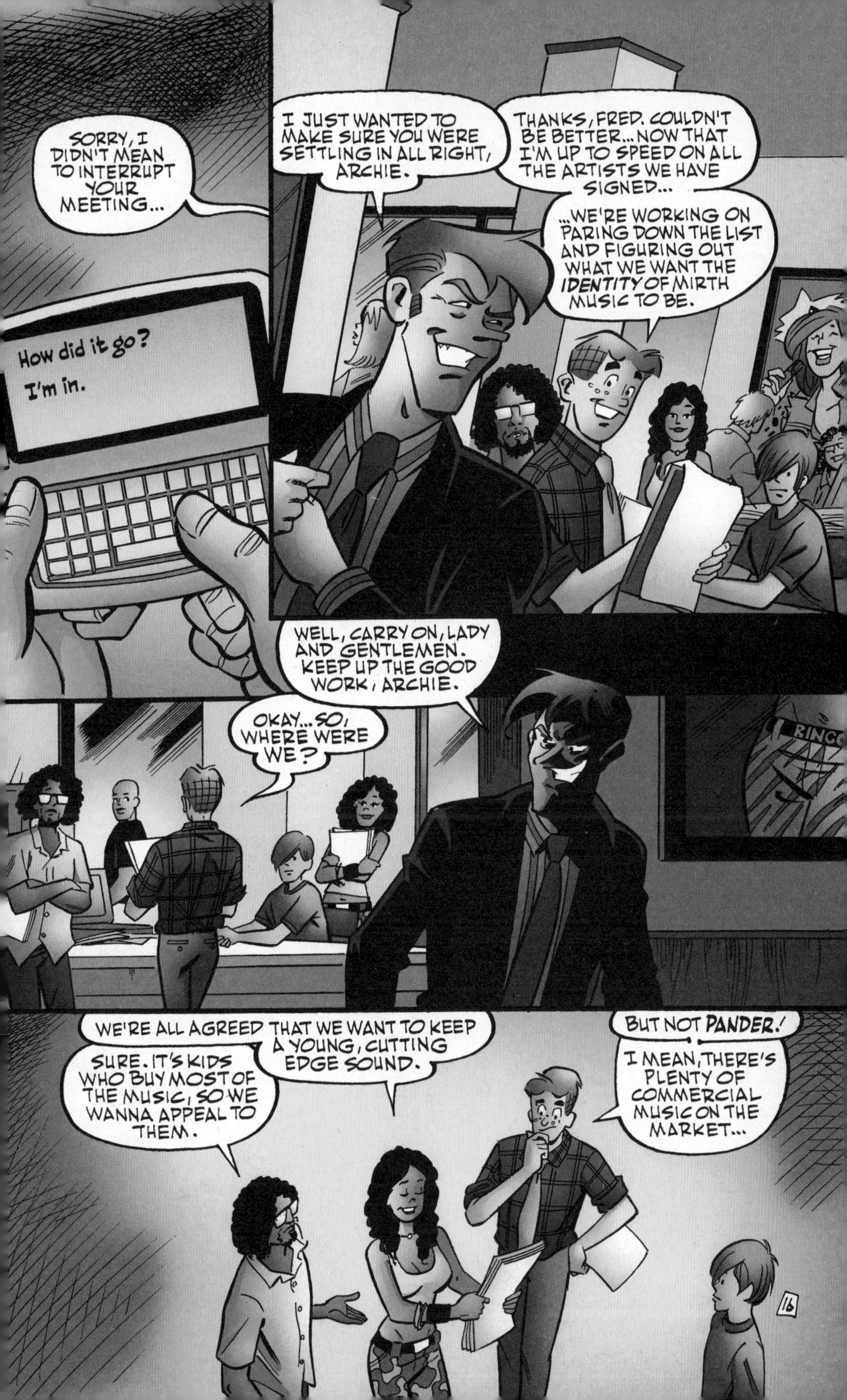
SORRY, I DIDN'T MEAN TO INTERRUPT YOUR MEETING...
How did it go?
I'm in.
I JUST WANTED TO MAKE SURE YOU WERE SETTLING IN ALL RIGHT, ARCHIE.
THANKS, FRED. COULDN'T BE BETTER... NOW THAT I'M UP TO SPEED ON ALL THE ARTISTS WE HAVE SIGNED...
...WE'RE WORKING ON PARING DOWN THE LIST AND FIGURING OUT WHAT WE WANT THE IDENTITY OF MIRTH MUSIC TO BE.
WELL, CARRY ON, LADY AND GENTLEMEN. KEEP UP THE GOOD WORK, ARCHIE.
OKAY... SO, WHERE WERE WE?
WE'RE ALL AGREED THAT WE WANT TO KEEP A YOUNG, CUTTING EDGE SOUND.
SURE. IT'S KIDS WHO BUY MOST OF THE MUSIC, SO WE WANNA APPEAL TO THEM.
BUT NOT PANDER!
I MEAN, THERE'S PLENTY OF COMMERCIAL MUSIC ON THE MARKET...
16

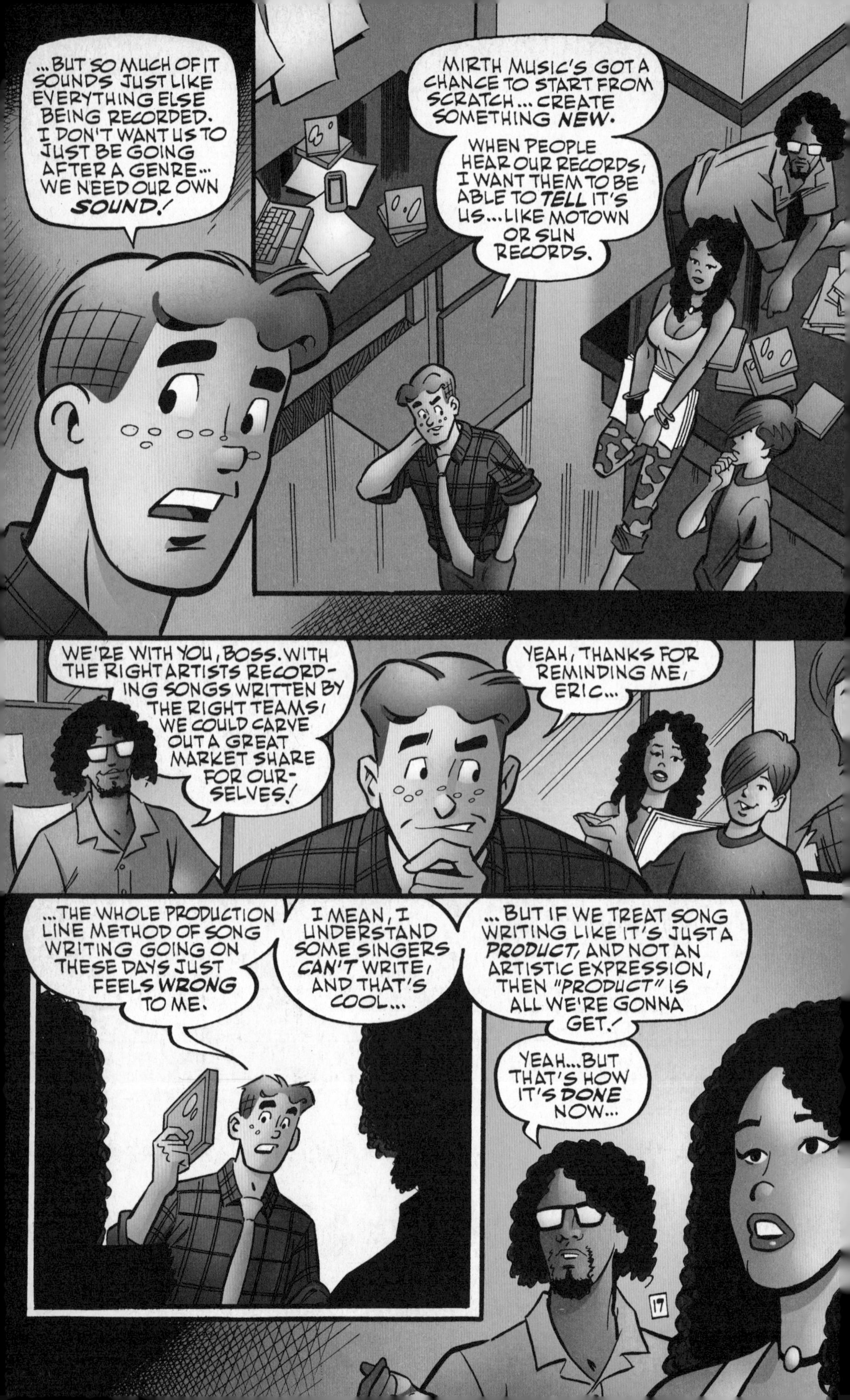
...BUT SO MUCH OF IT SOUNDS JUST LIKE EVERYTHING ELSE BEING RECORDED. I DON'T WANT US TO JUST BE GOING AFTER A GENRE... WE NEED OUR OWN SOUND!
MIRTH MUSIC'S GOT A CHANCE TO START FROM SCRATCH... CREATE SOMETHING NEW.
WHEN PEOPLE HEAR OUR RECORDS, I WANT THEM TO BE ABLE TO TELL IT'S US...LIKE MOTOWN OR SUN RECORDS.
WE'RE WITH YOU, BOSS. WITH THE RIGHT ARTISTS RECORDING SONGS WRITTEN BY THE RIGHT TEAMS, WE COULD CARVE OUT A GREAT MARKET SHARE FOR OURSELVES!
YEAH, THANKS FOR REMINDING ME, ERIC...
...THE WHOLE PRODUCTION LINE METHOD OF SONG WRITING GOING ON THESE DAYS JUST FEELS WRONG TO ME.
I MEAN, I UNDERSTAND SOME SINGERS CAN'T WRITE, AND THAT'S COOL...
...BUT IF WE TREAT SONG WRITING LIKE IT'S JUST A PRODUCT, AND NOT AN ARTISTIC EXPRESSION, THEN "PRODUCT" IS ALL WE'RE GONNA GET!
YEAH...BUT THAT'S HOW IT'S DONE NOW...
17

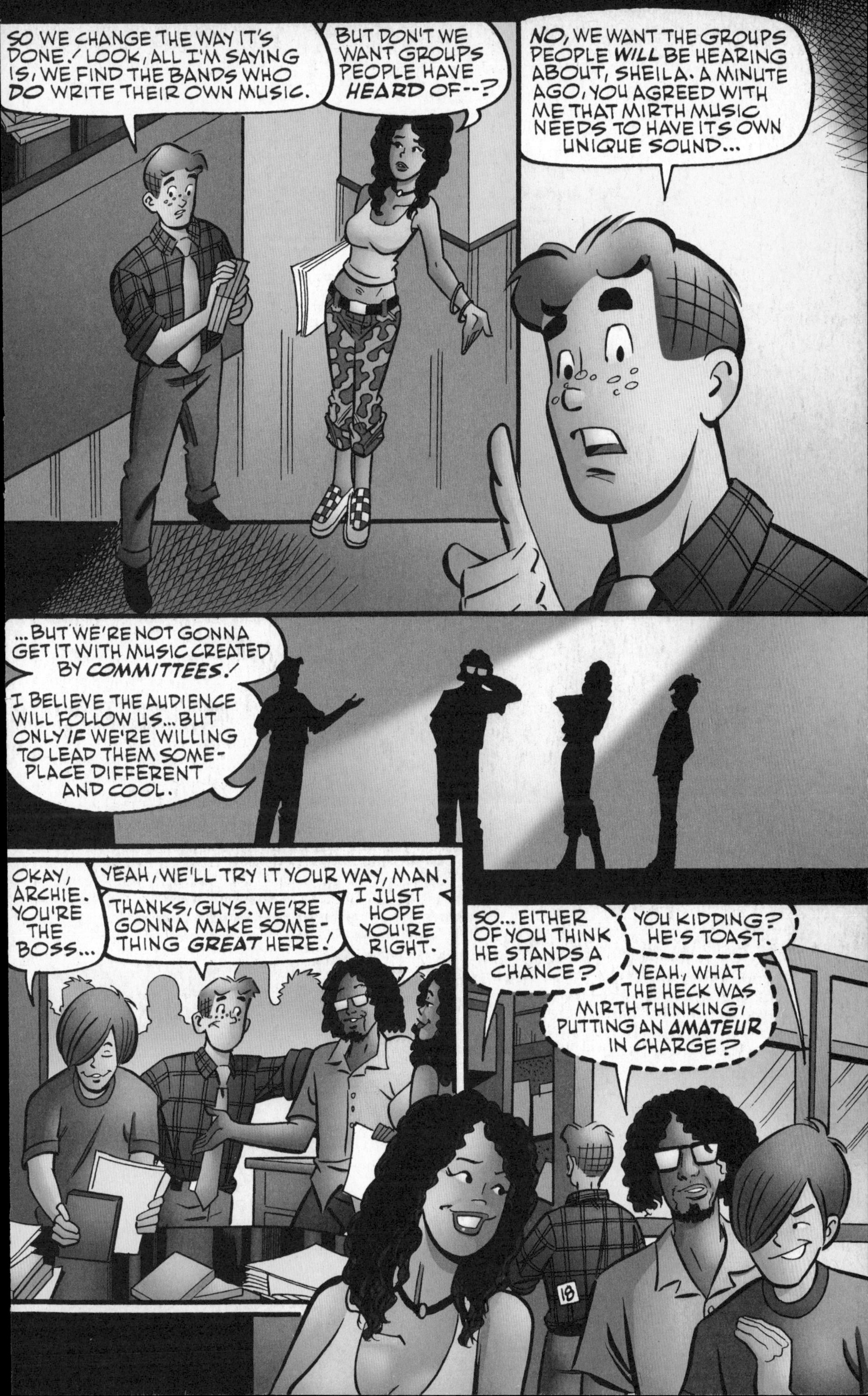
SO WE CHANGE THE WAY IT'S DONE.! LOOK, ALL I'M SAYING IS, WE FIND THE BANDS WHO DO WRITE THEIR OWN MUSIC.
BUT DON'T WE WANT GROUPS PEOPLE HAVE HEARD OF--?
NO, WE WANT THE GROUPS PEOPLE WILL BE HEARING ABOUT, SHEILA. A MINUTE AGO, YOU AGREED WITH ME THAT MIRTH MUSIC NEEDS TO HAVE ITS OWN UNIQUE SOUND...
...BUT WE'RE NOT GONNA GET IT WITH MUSIC CREATED BY COMMITTEES.!
I BELIEVE THE AUDIENCE WILL FOLLOW US... BUT ONLY IF WE'RE WILLING TO LEAD THEM SOMEPLACE DIFFERENT AND COOL.
OKAY, ARCHIE. YOU'RE THE BOSS...
YEAH, WE'LL TRY IT YOUR WAY, MAN.
I JUST HOPE YOU'RE RIGHT.
THANKS, GUYS. WE'RE GONNA MAKE SOMETHING GREAT HERE!
SO... EITHER OF YOU THINK HE STANDS A CHANCE?
YOU KIDDING? HE'S TOAST.
YEAH, WHAT THE HECK WAS MIRTH THINKING, PUTTING AN AMATEUR IN CHARGE?
18

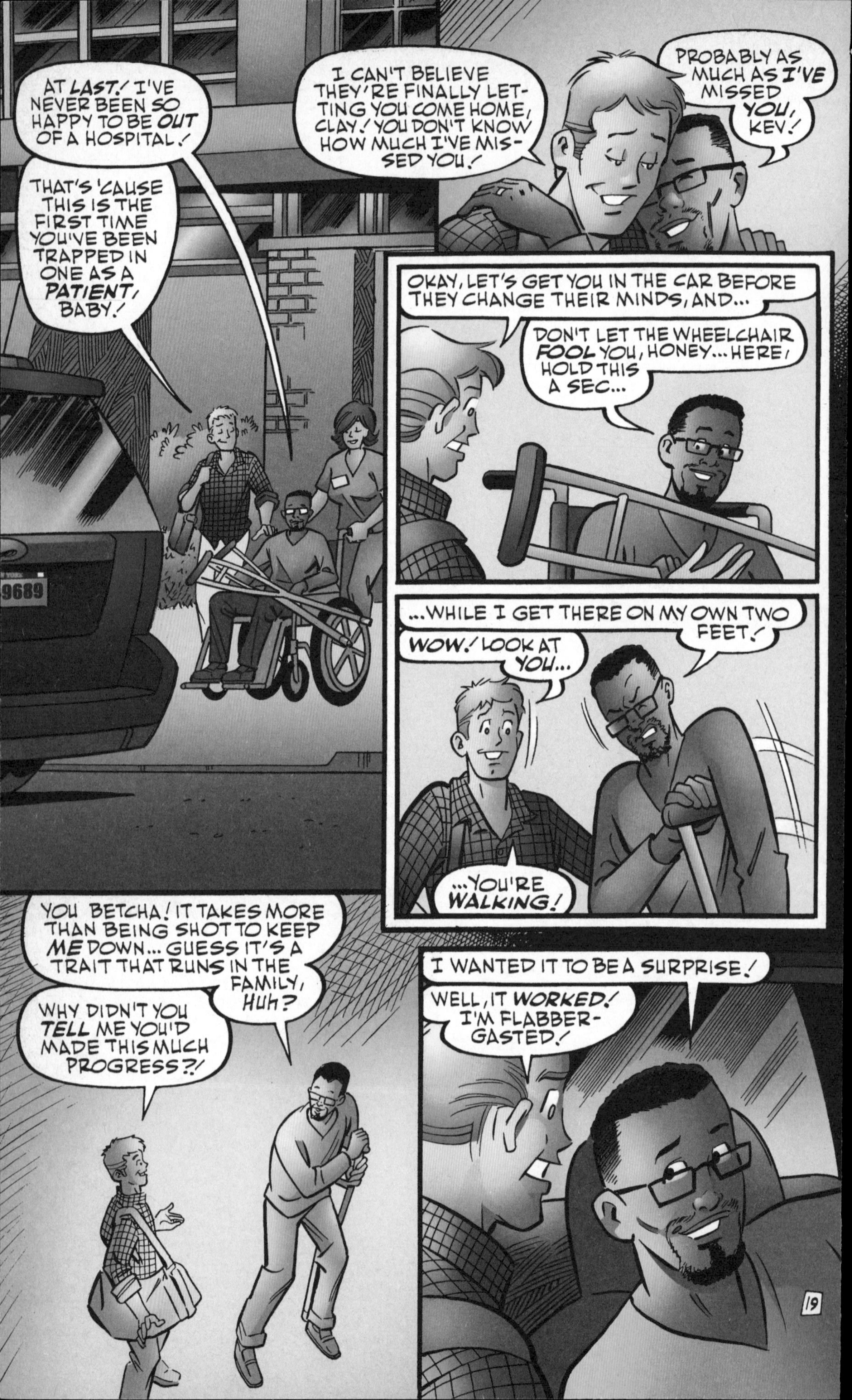
AT LAST! I'VE NEVER BEEN SO HAPPY TO BE OUT OF A HOSPITAL!
THAT'S 'CAUSE THIS IS THE FIRST TIME YOU'VE BEEN TRAPPED IN ONE AS A PATIENT, BABY!
I CAN'T BELIEVE THEY'RE FINALLY LETTING YOU COME HOME, CLAY! YOU DON'T KNOW HOW MUCH I'VE MISSED YOU!
PROBABLY AS MUCH AS I'VE MISSED YOU, KEV!
9689
OKAY, LET'S GET YOU IN THE CAR BEFORE THEY CHANGE THEIR MINDS, AND...
DON'T LET THE WHEELCHAIR FOOL YOU, HONEY... HERE, HOLD THIS A SEC...
...WHILE I GET THERE ON MY OWN TWO FEET!
WOW! LOOK AT YOU...
...YOU'RE WALKING!
YOU BETCHA! IT TAKES MORE THAN BEING SHOT TO KEEP ME DOWN... GUESS IT'S A TRAIT THAT RUNS IN THE FAMILY, HUH?
WHY DIDN'T YOU TELL ME YOU'D MADE THIS MUCH PROGRESS?!
I WANTED IT TO BE A SURPRISE!
WELL, IT WORKED! I'M FLABBERGASTED!

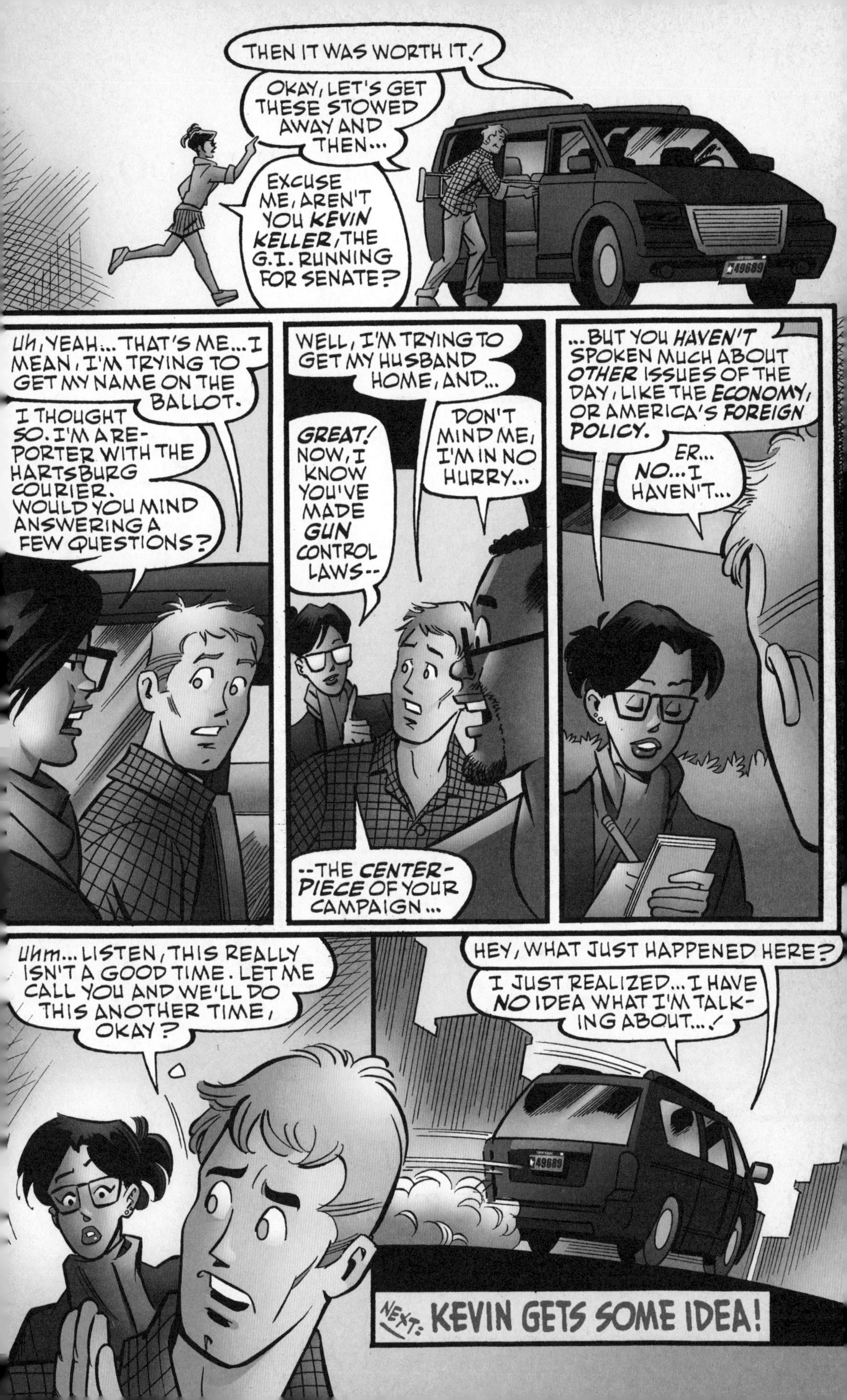
THEN IT WAS WORTH IT!
OKAY, LET'S GET THESE STOWED AWAY AND THEN...
EXCUSE ME, AREN'T YOU KEVIN KELLER, THE G.I. RUNNING FOR SENATE?
UH, YEAH... THAT'S ME... I MEAN, I'M TRYING TO GET MY NAME ON THE BALLOT.
I THOUGHT SO. I'M A REPORTER WITH THE HARTSBURG COURIER. WOULD YOU MIND ANSWERING A FEW QUESTIONS?
WELL, I'M TRYING TO GET MY HUSBAND HOME, AND...
GREAT! NOW, I KNOW YOU'VE MADE GUN CONTROL LAWS--
DON'T MIND ME, I'M IN NO HURRY...
--THE CENTERPIECE OF YOUR CAMPAIGN...
...BUT YOU HAVEN'T SPOKEN MUCH ABOUT OTHER ISSUES OF THE DAY, LIKE THE ECONOMY, OR AMERICA'S FOREIGN POLICY.
ER... NO... I HAVEN'T...
UHM... LISTEN, THIS REALLY ISN'T A GOOD TIME. LET ME CALL YOU AND WE'LL DO THIS ANOTHER TIME, OKAY?
HEY, WHAT JUST HAPPENED HERE?
I JUST REALIZED... I HAVE NO IDEA WHAT I'M TALKING ABOUT...!
NEXT: KEVIN GETS SOME IDEA!

"JEEZ...
THAT JUST AIN'T RIGHT.
I MEAN, WE ALL GOT STUFF TO DO..."

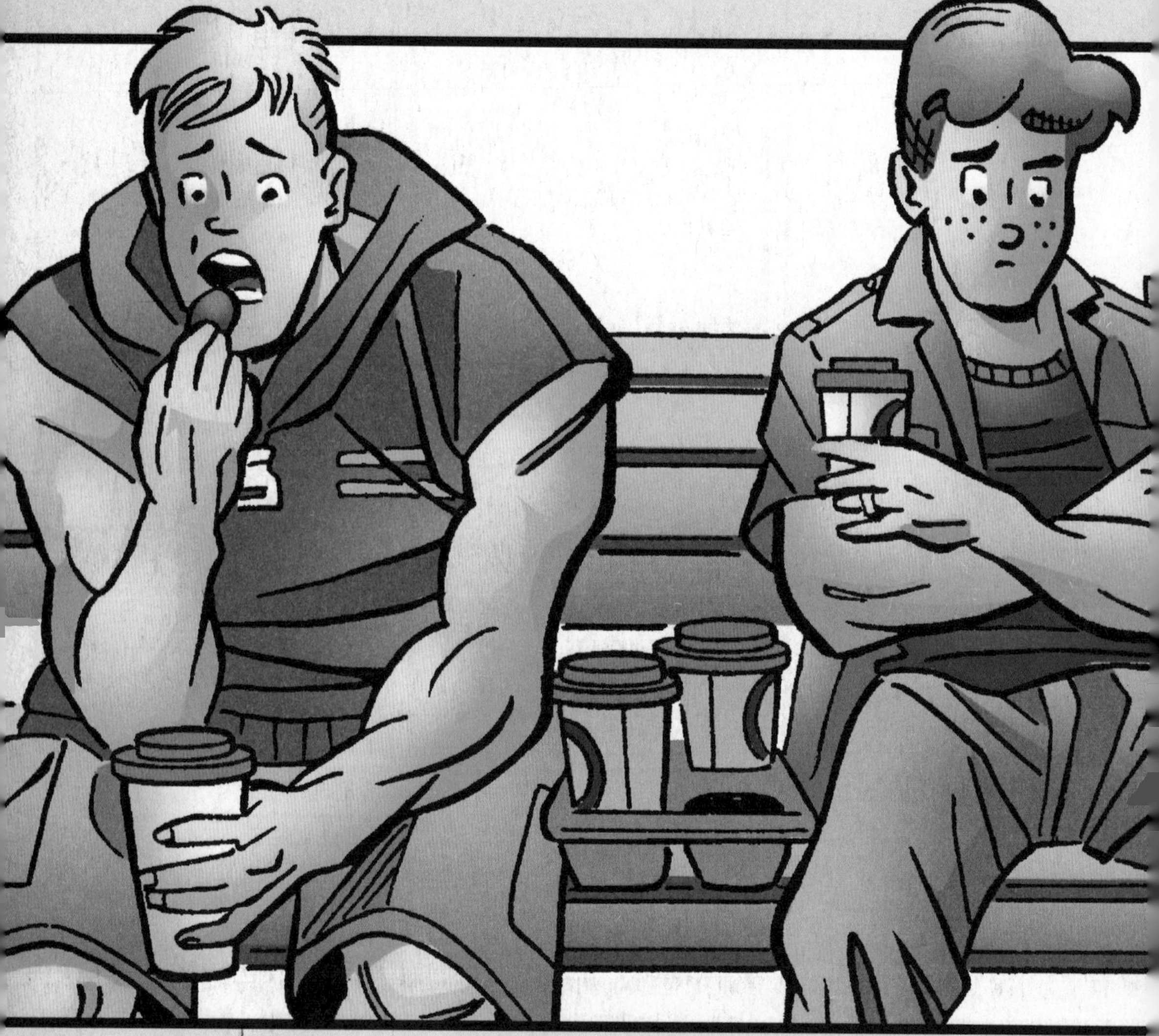

"...BUT WE SHOULD *STILL*
BE ABLE TO MAKE TIME FOR
OUR *FRIENDS*, Y'KNOW?"

-MARMADUKE "MOOSE" MASON

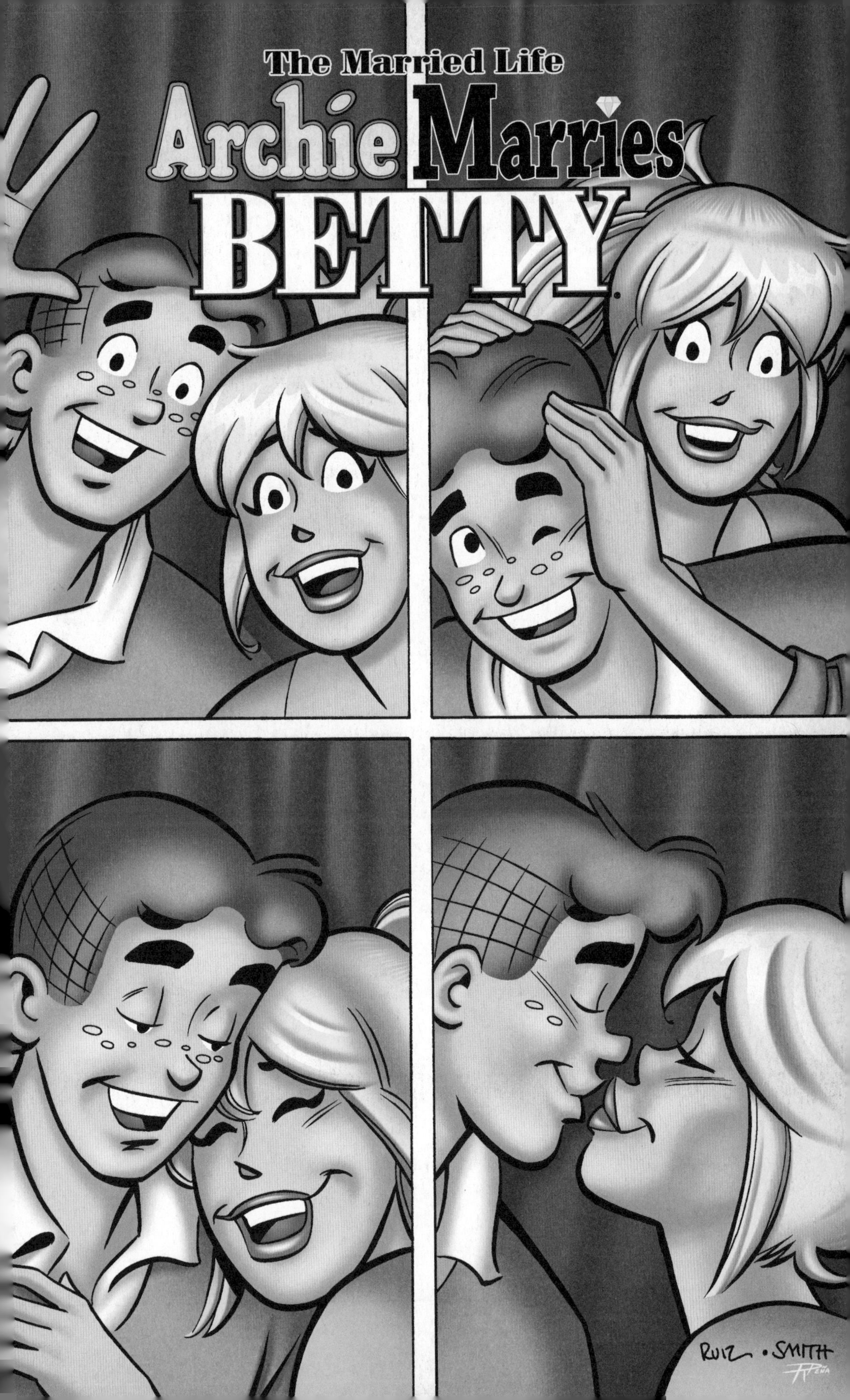
The Married Life
Archie Marries
BETTY
RUIZ • SMITH

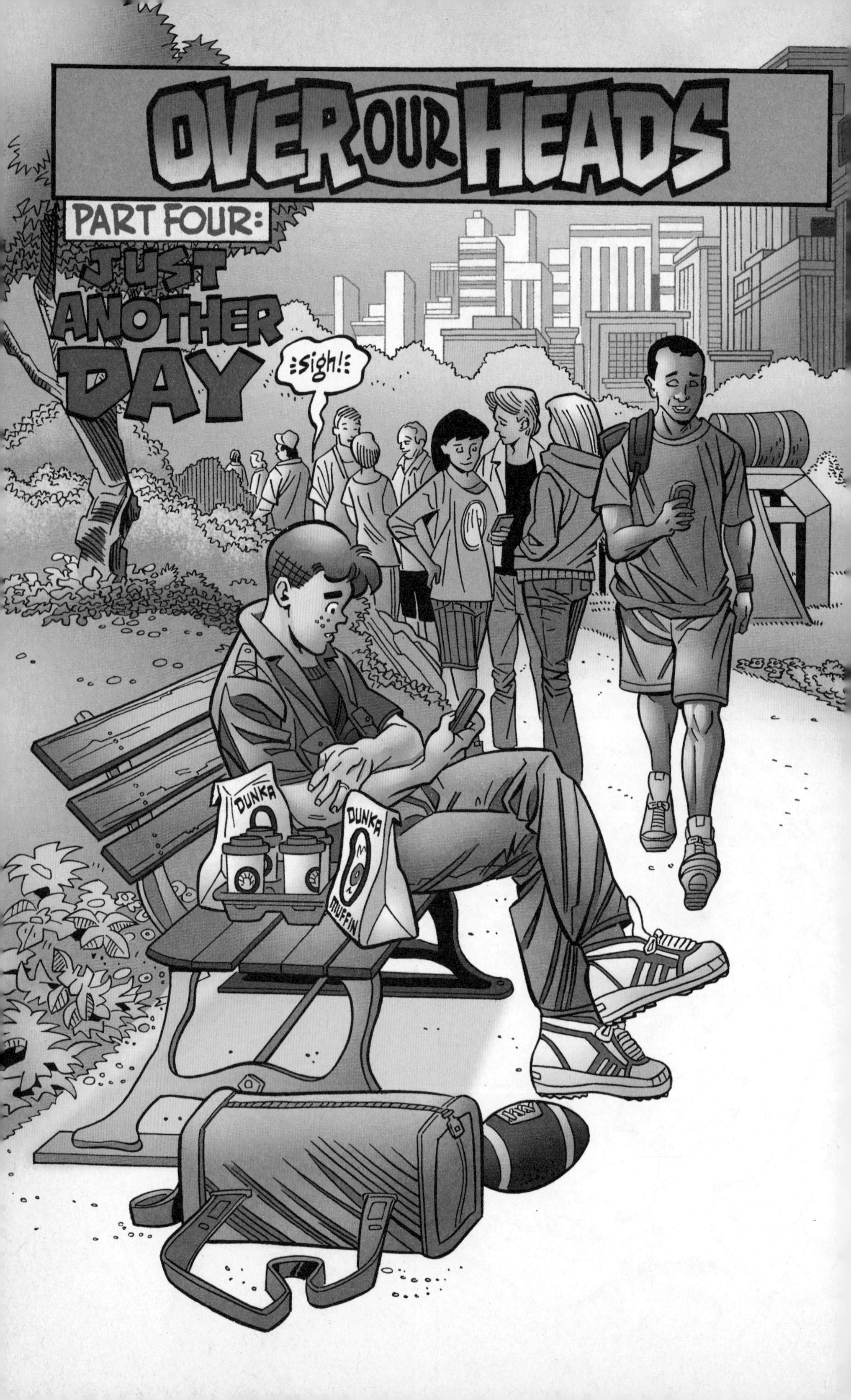
OVER OUR HEADS
PART FOUR:
JUST ANOTHER DAY
sigh!
DUNKA
DUNKA MUFFIN

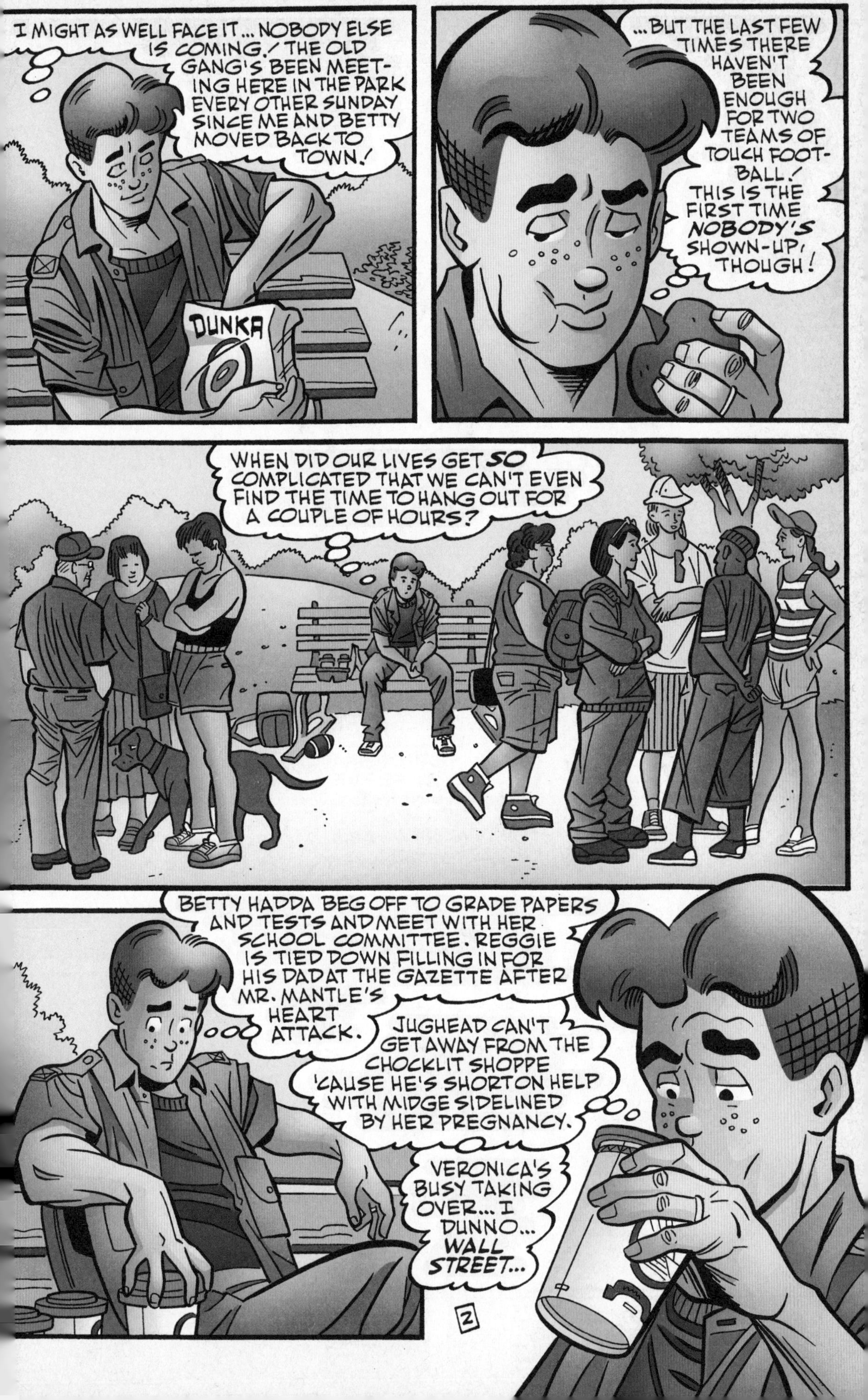
I MIGHT AS WELL FACE IT... NOBODY ELSE IS COMING! THE OLD GANG'S BEEN MEETING HERE IN THE PARK EVERY OTHER SUNDAY SINCE ME AND BETTY MOVED BACK TO TOWN!
DUNKA
...BUT THE LAST FEW TIMES THERE HAVEN'T BEEN ENOUGH FOR TWO TEAMS OF TOUCH FOOTBALL! THIS IS THE FIRST TIME NOBODY'S SHOWN-UP, THOUGH!
WHEN DID OUR LIVES GET SO COMPLICATED THAT WE CAN'T EVEN FIND THE TIME TO HANG OUT FOR A COUPLE OF HOURS?
BETTY HADDA BEG OFF TO GRADE PAPERS AND TESTS AND MEET WITH HER SCHOOL COMMITTEE. REGGIE IS TIED DOWN FILLING IN FOR HIS DAD AT THE GAZETTE AFTER MR. MANTLE'S HEART ATTACK.
JUGHEAD CAN'T GET AWAY FROM THE CHOCKLIT SHOPPE 'CAUSE HE'S SHORT ON HELP WITH MIDGE SIDELINED BY HER PREGNANCY.
VERONICA'S BUSY TAKING OVER... I DUNNO... WALL STREET...
2

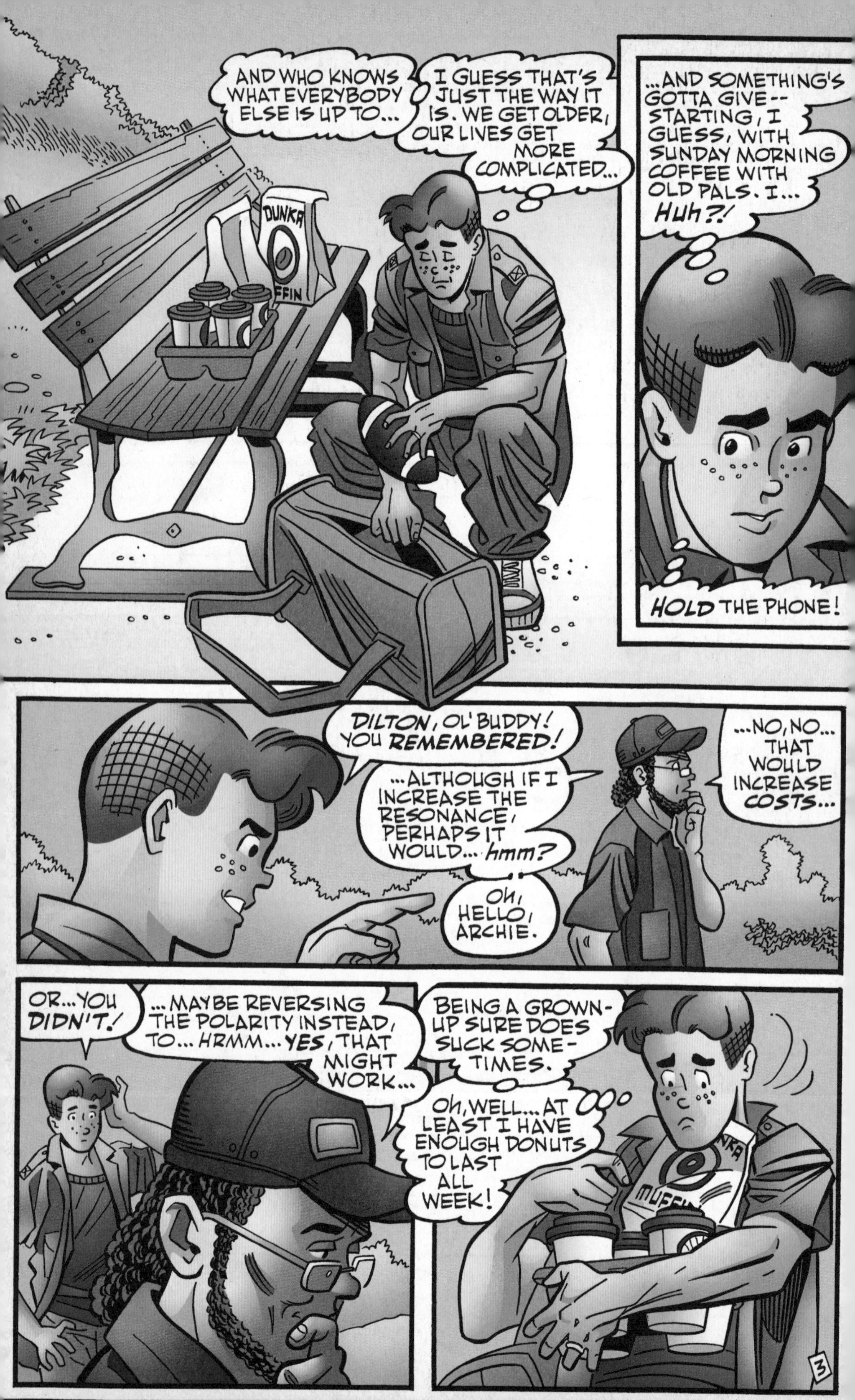

AND WHO KNOWS WHAT EVERYBODY ELSE IS UP TO...
I GUESS THAT'S JUST THE WAY IT IS. WE GET OLDER, OUR LIVES GET MORE COMPLICATED...
DUNKA
...AND SOMETHING'S GOTTA GIVE -- STARTING, I GUESS, WITH SUNDAY MORNING COFFEE WITH OLD PALS. I... Huh?!
HOLD THE PHONE!
DILTON, OL' BUDDY! YOU REMEMBERED!
...ALTHOUGH IF I INCREASE THE RESONANCE, PERHAPS IT WOULD... hmm?
OH, HELLO, ARCHIE.
...NO, NO... THAT WOULD INCREASE COSTS...
OR... YOU DIDN'T!
...MAYBE REVERSING THE POLARITY INSTEAD, TO... HRMM... YES, THAT MIGHT WORK...
BEING A GROWN-UP SURE DOES SUCK SOME-TIMES.
OH, WELL... AT LEAST I HAVE ENOUGH DONUTS TO LAST ALL WEEK!
3

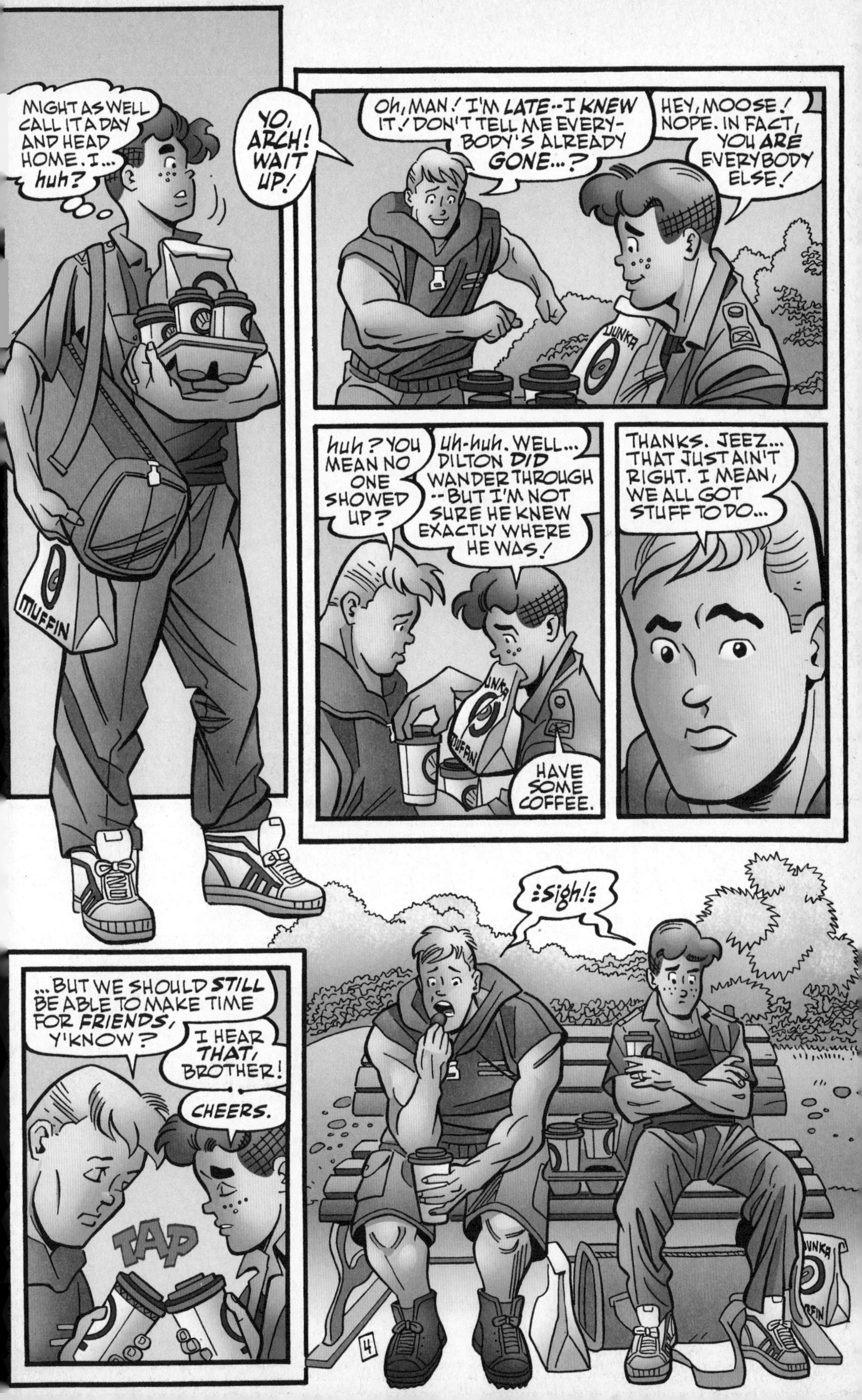
MIGHT AS WELL CALL IT A DAY AND HEAD HOME. I... huh?
YO, ARCH! WAIT UP!
MUFFIN
Oh, MAN! I'M LATE--I KNEW IT! DON'T TELL ME EVERYBODY'S ALREADY GONE...?
HEY, MOOSE! NOPE. IN FACT, YOU ARE EVERYBODY ELSE!
DUNKA
huh? YOU MEAN NO ONE SHOWED UP?
uh-huh. WELL... DILTON DID WANDER THROUGH --BUT I'M NOT SURE HE KNEW EXACTLY WHERE HE WAS!
HAVE SOME COFFEE.
THANKS. JEEZ... THAT JUST AIN'T RIGHT. I MEAN, WE ALL GOT STUFF TO DO...
...BUT WE SHOULD STILL BE ABLE TO MAKE TIME FOR FRIENDS, Y'KNOW?
I HEAR THAT, BROTHER!
CHEERS.
TAP
SIGH!
4

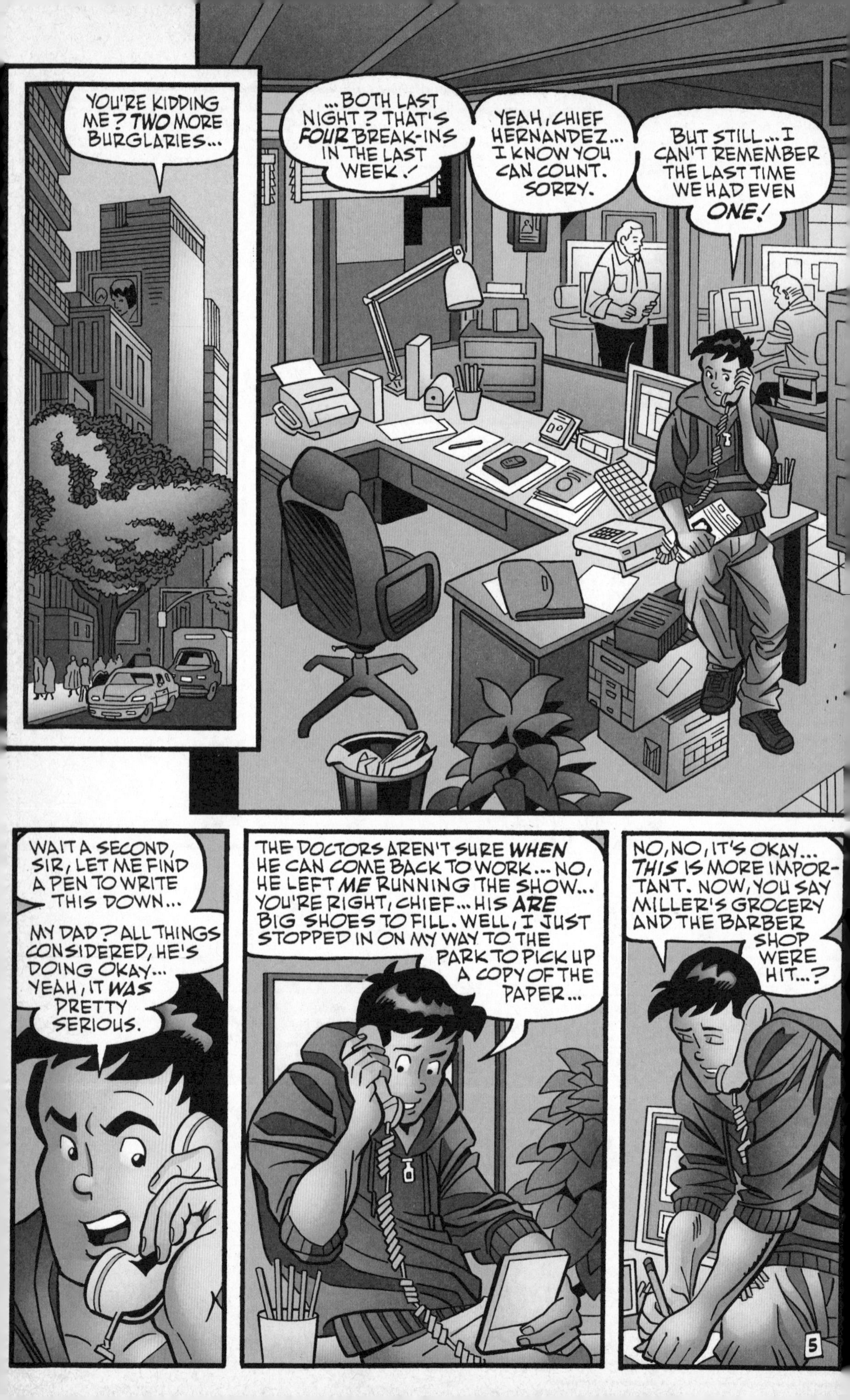
YOU'RE KIDDING ME? TWO MORE BURGLARIES...
...BOTH LAST NIGHT? THAT'S FOUR BREAK-INS IN THE LAST WEEK!
YEAH, CHIEF HERNANDEZ... I KNOW YOU CAN COUNT. SORRY.
BUT STILL... I CAN'T REMEMBER THE LAST TIME WE HAD EVEN ONE!
WAIT A SECOND, SIR, LET ME FIND A PEN TO WRITE THIS DOWN...
MY DAD? ALL THINGS CONSIDERED, HE'S DOING OKAY... YEAH, IT WAS PRETTY SERIOUS.
THE DOCTORS AREN'T SURE WHEN HE CAN COME BACK TO WORK... NO, HE LEFT ME RUNNING THE SHOW... YOU'RE RIGHT, CHIEF... HIS ARE BIG SHOES TO FILL. WELL, I JUST STOPPED IN ON MY WAY TO THE PARK TO PICK UP A COPY OF THE PAPER...
NO, NO, IT'S OKAY... THIS IS MORE IMPORTANT. NOW, YOU SAY MILLER'S GROCERY AND THE BARBER SHOP WERE HIT...?
5

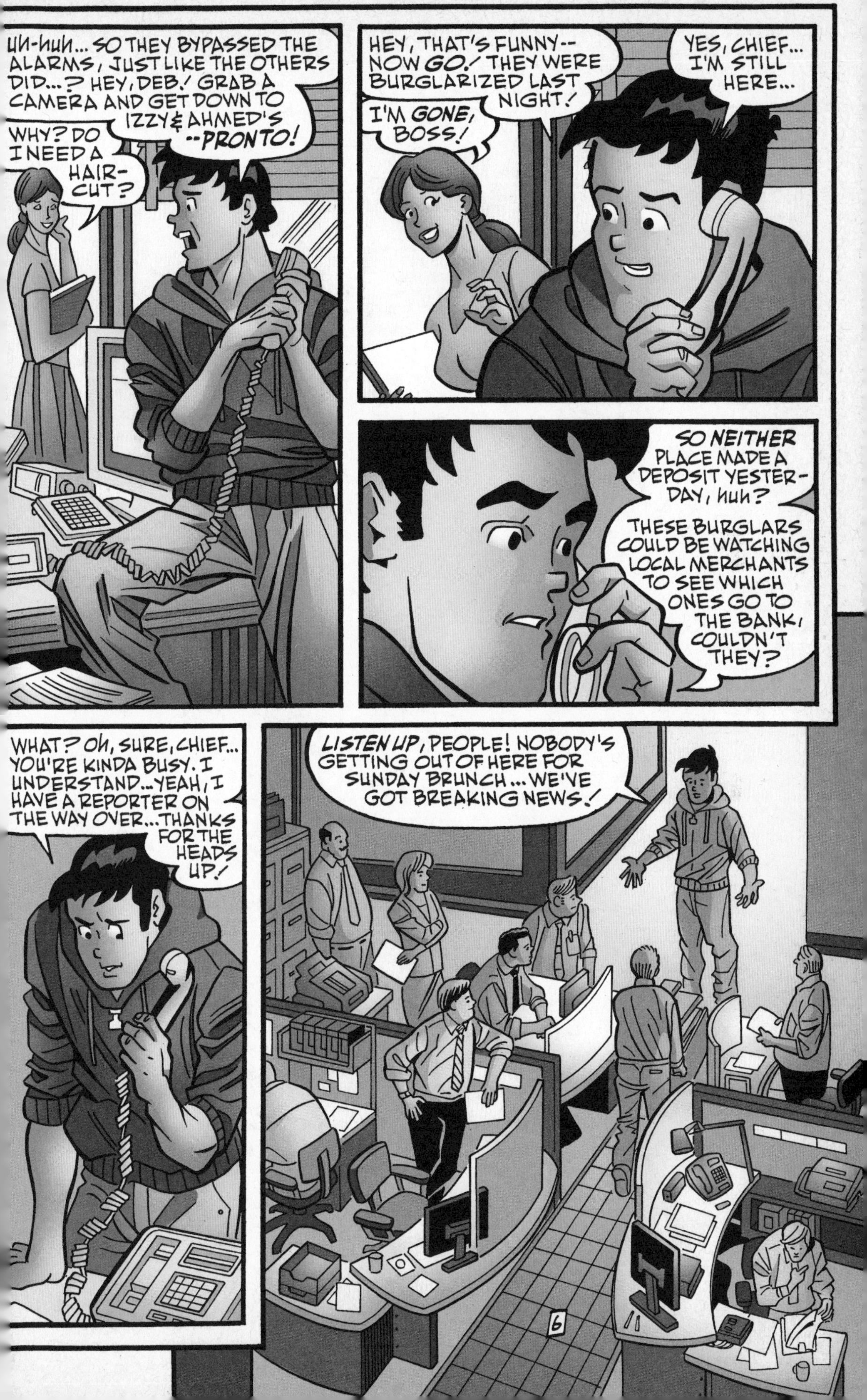
UH-HUH... SO THEY BYPASSED THE ALARMS, JUST LIKE THE OTHERS DID...? HEY, DEB! GRAB A CAMERA AND GET DOWN TO IZZY & AHMED'S --PRONTO!
WHY? DO I NEED A HAIR-CUT?
HEY, THAT'S FUNNY-- NOW GO! THEY WERE BURGLARIZED LAST NIGHT!
I'M GONE, BOSS!
YES, CHIEF... I'M STILL HERE...
SO NEITHER PLACE MADE A DEPOSIT YESTER-DAY, HUH?
THESE BURGLARS COULD BE WATCHING LOCAL MERCHANTS TO SEE WHICH ONES GO TO THE BANK, COULDN'T THEY?
WHAT? OH, SURE, CHIEF... YOU'RE KINDA BUSY. I UNDERSTAND...YEAH, I HAVE A REPORTER ON THE WAY OVER...THANKS FOR THE HEADS UP!
LISTEN UP, PEOPLE! NOBODY'S GETTING OUT OF HERE FOR SUNDAY BRUNCH... WE'VE GOT BREAKING NEWS!
6

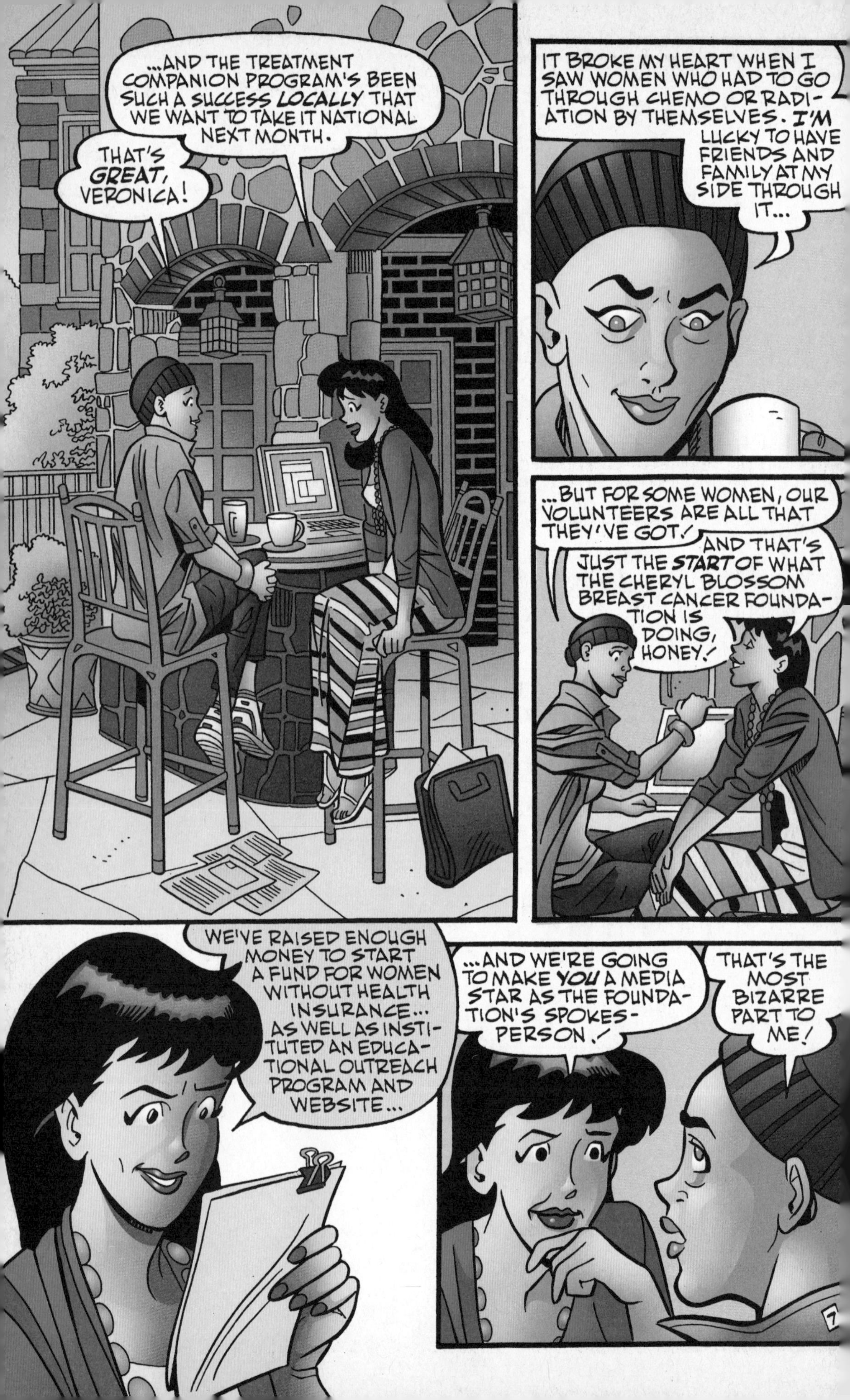
...AND THE TREATMENT COMPANION PROGRAM'S BEEN SUCH A SUCCESS LOCALLY THAT WE WANT TO TAKE IT NATIONAL NEXT MONTH.
THAT'S GREAT, VERONICA!
IT BROKE MY HEART WHEN I SAW WOMEN WHO HAD TO GO THROUGH CHEMO OR RADIATION BY THEMSELVES. I'M LUCKY TO HAVE FRIENDS AND FAMILY AT MY SIDE THROUGH IT...
...BUT FOR SOME WOMEN, OUR VOLUNTEERS ARE ALL THAT THEY'VE GOT!
AND THAT'S JUST THE START OF WHAT THE CHERYL BLOSSOM BREAST CANCER FOUNDATION IS DOING, HONEY!
WE'VE RAISED ENOUGH MONEY TO START A FUND FOR WOMEN WITHOUT HEALTH INSURANCE... AS WELL AS INSTITUTED AN EDUCATIONAL OUTREACH PROGRAM AND WEBSITE...
...AND WE'RE GOING TO MAKE YOU A MEDIA STAR AS THE FOUNDATION'S SPOKESPERSON!
THAT'S THE MOST BIZARRE PART TO ME!
7

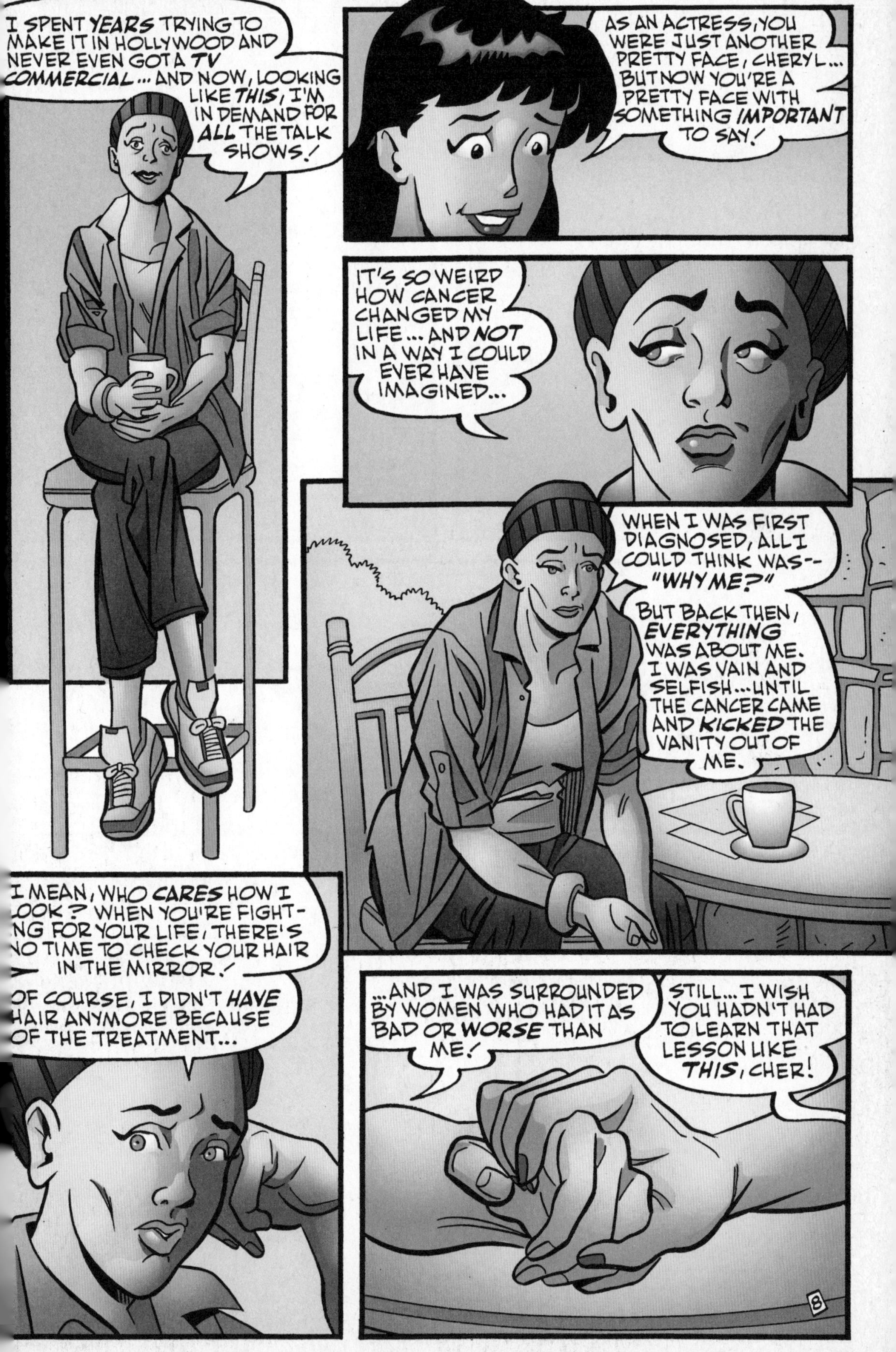
I SPENT YEARS TRYING TO MAKE IT IN HOLLYWOOD AND NEVER EVEN GOT A TV COMMERCIAL... AND NOW, LOOKING LIKE THIS, I'M IN DEMAND FOR ALL THE TALK SHOWS!
AS AN ACTRESS, YOU WERE JUST ANOTHER PRETTY FACE, CHERYL... BUT NOW YOU'RE A PRETTY FACE WITH SOMETHING IMPORTANT TO SAY!
IT'S SO WEIRD HOW CANCER CHANGED MY LIFE... AND NOT IN A WAY I COULD EVER HAVE IMAGINED...
WHEN I WAS FIRST DIAGNOSED, ALL I COULD THINK WAS-- "WHY ME?"
BUT BACK THEN, EVERYTHING WAS ABOUT ME. I WAS VAIN AND SELFISH... UNTIL THE CANCER CAME AND KICKED THE VANITY OUT OF ME.
I MEAN, WHO CARES HOW I LOOK? WHEN YOU'RE FIGHTING FOR YOUR LIFE, THERE'S NO TIME TO CHECK YOUR HAIR IN THE MIRROR!
OF COURSE, I DIDN'T HAVE HAIR ANYMORE BECAUSE OF THE TREATMENT...
...AND I WAS SURROUNDED BY WOMEN WHO HAD IT AS BAD OR WORSE THAN ME!
STILL... I WISH YOU HADN'T HAD TO LEARN THAT LESSON LIKE THIS, CHER!
8

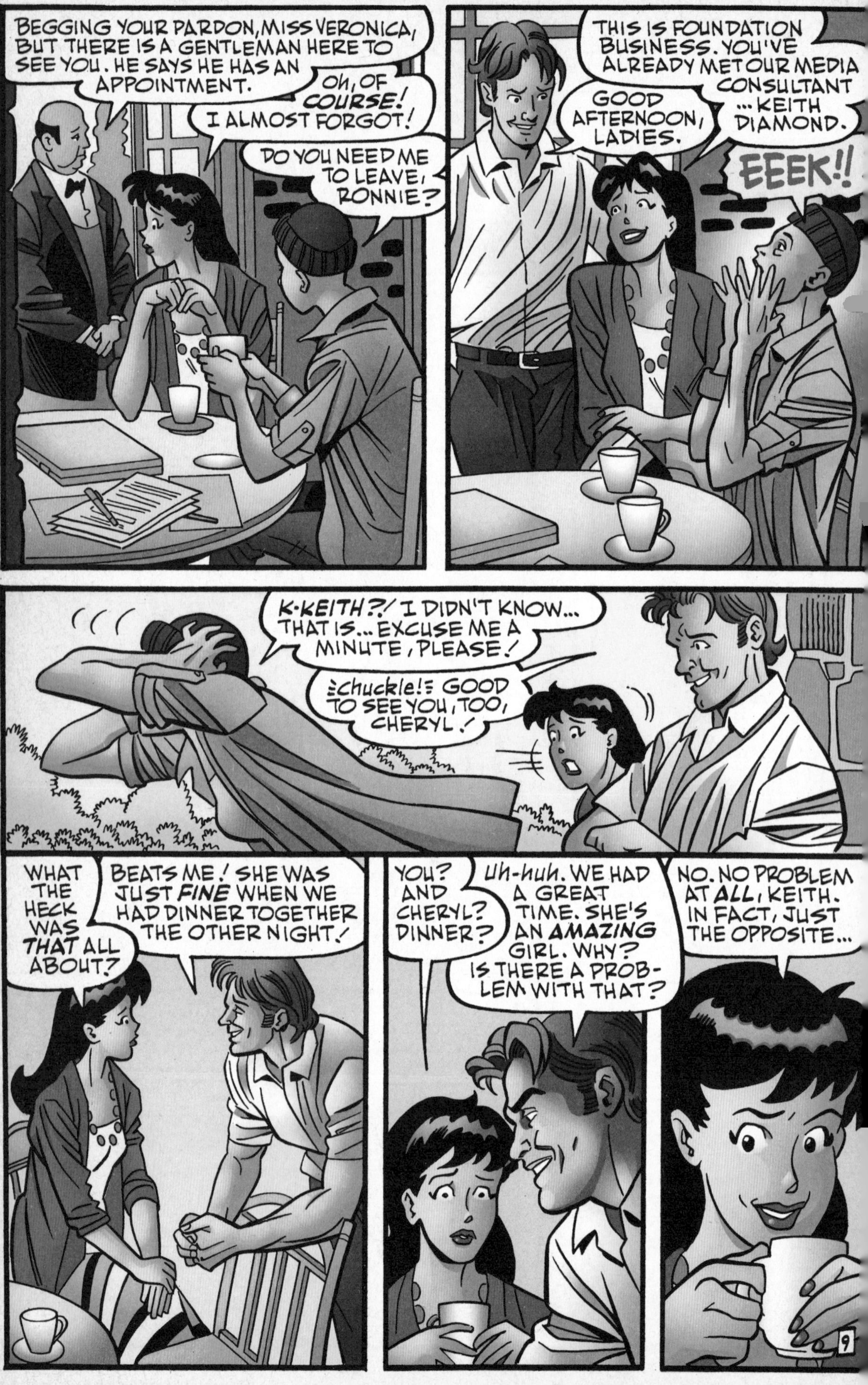
BEGGING YOUR PARDON, MISS VERONICA, BUT THERE IS A GENTLEMAN HERE TO SEE YOU. HE SAYS HE HAS AN APPOINTMENT.
OH, OF COURSE! I ALMOST FORGOT!
DO YOU NEED ME TO LEAVE, RONNIE?
THIS IS FOUNDATION BUSINESS. YOU'VE ALREADY MET OUR MEDIA CONSULTANT ...KEITH DIAMOND.
GOOD AFTERNOON, LADIES.
EEEK!!
K-KEITH?!! I DIDN'T KNOW... THAT IS... EXCUSE ME A MINUTE, PLEASE!
chuckle! GOOD TO SEE YOU, TOO, CHERYL!
WHAT THE HECK WAS THAT ALL ABOUT?
BEATS ME! SHE WAS JUST FINE WHEN WE HAD DINNER TOGETHER THE OTHER NIGHT!
YOU? AND CHERYL? DINNER?
UH-HUH. WE HAD A GREAT TIME. SHE'S AN AMAZING GIRL. WHY? IS THERE A PROBLEM WITH THAT?
NO. NO PROBLEM AT ALL, KEITH. IN FACT, JUST THE OPPOSITE...

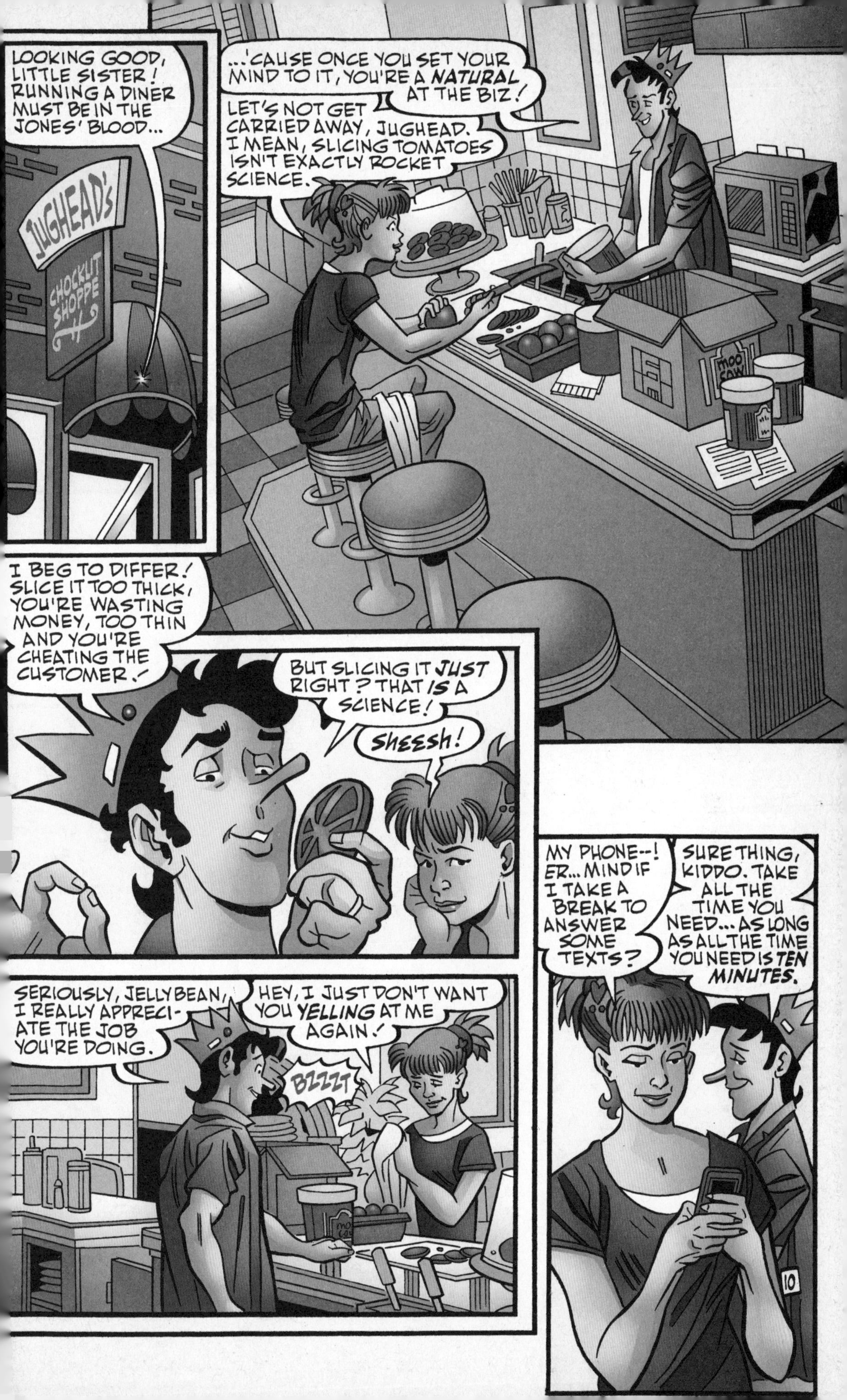
LOOKING GOOD, LITTLE SISTER! RUNNING A DINER MUST BE IN THE JONES' BLOOD...
JUGHEAD'S
CHOCKLIT SHOPPE
...'CAUSE ONCE YOU SET YOUR MIND TO IT, YOU'RE A **NATURAL** AT THE BIZ!
LET'S NOT GET CARRIED AWAY, JUGHEAD. I MEAN, SLICING TOMATOES ISN'T EXACTLY ROCKET SCIENCE.
MOO COW
I BEG TO DIFFER! SLICE IT TOO THICK, YOU'RE WASTING MONEY, TOO THIN AND YOU'RE CHEATING THE CUSTOMER!
BUT SLICING IT **JUST** RIGHT? THAT **IS** A SCIENCE!
SHEESH!
SERIOUSLY, JELLYBEAN, I REALLY APPRECIATE THE JOB YOU'RE DOING.
HEY, I JUST DON'T WANT YOU **YELLING** AT ME AGAIN!
BZZZT
MY PHONE--! ER... MIND IF I TAKE A BREAK TO ANSWER SOME TEXTS?
SURE THING, KIDDO. TAKE ALL THE TIME YOU NEED... AS LONG AS ALL THE TIME YOU NEED IS **TEN MINUTES**.
10

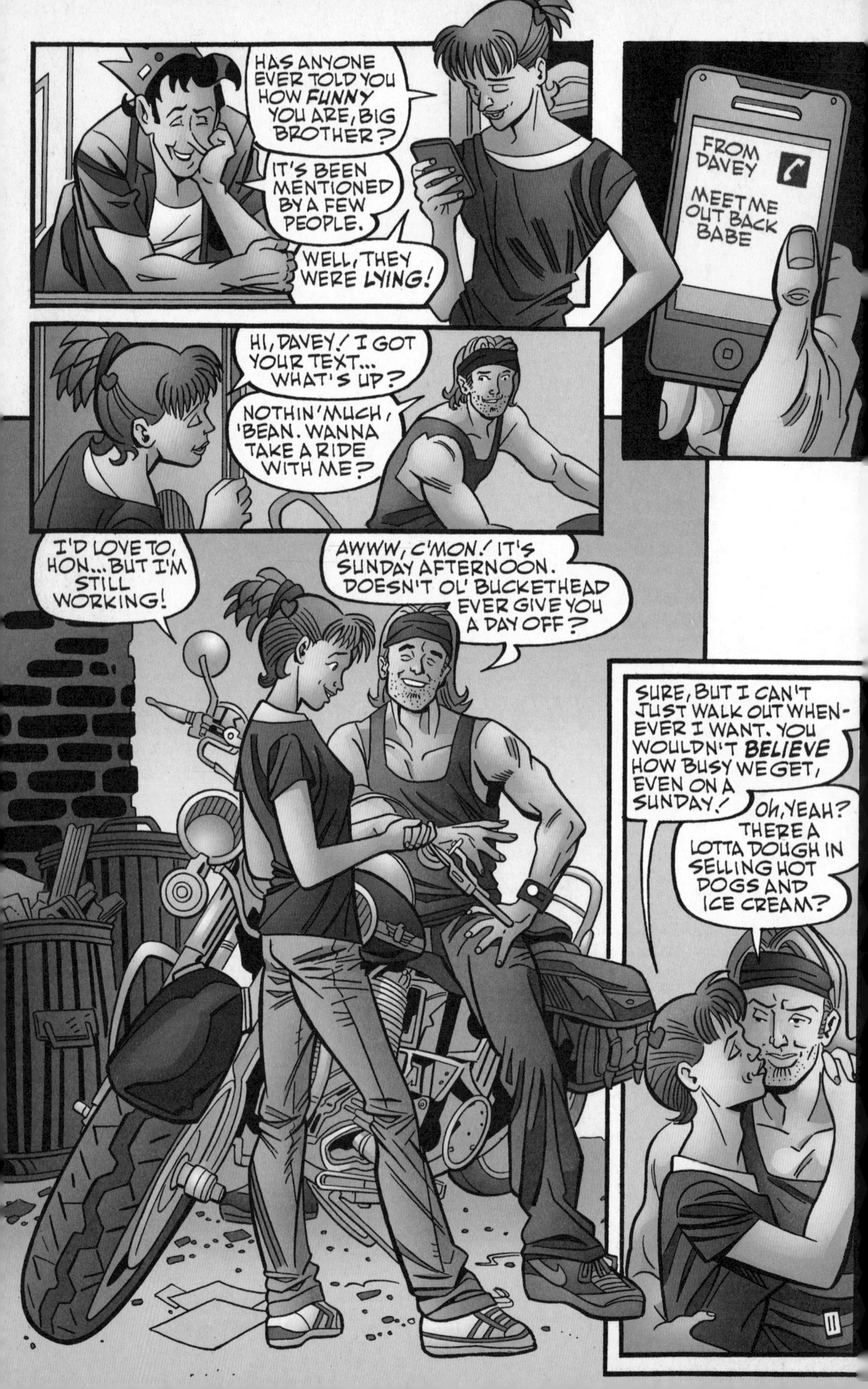
HAS ANYONE EVER TOLD YOU HOW FUNNY YOU ARE, BIG BROTHER?
IT'S BEEN MENTIONED BY A FEW PEOPLE.
WELL, THEY WERE LYING!
FROM DAVEY
MEET ME OUT BACK BABE
HI, DAVEY! I GOT YOUR TEXT... WHAT'S UP?
NOTHIN' MUCH, 'BEAN. WANNA TAKE A RIDE WITH ME?
I'D LOVE TO, HON... BUT I'M STILL WORKING!
AWWW, C'MON! IT'S SUNDAY AFTERNOON. DOESN'T OL' BUCKETHEAD EVER GIVE YOU A DAY OFF?
SURE, BUT I CAN'T JUST WALK OUT WHEN-EVER I WANT. YOU WOULDN'T BELIEVE HOW BUSY WE GET, EVEN ON A SUNDAY!
OH, YEAH? THERE A LOTTA DOUGH IN SELLING HOT DOGS AND ICE CREAM?
11

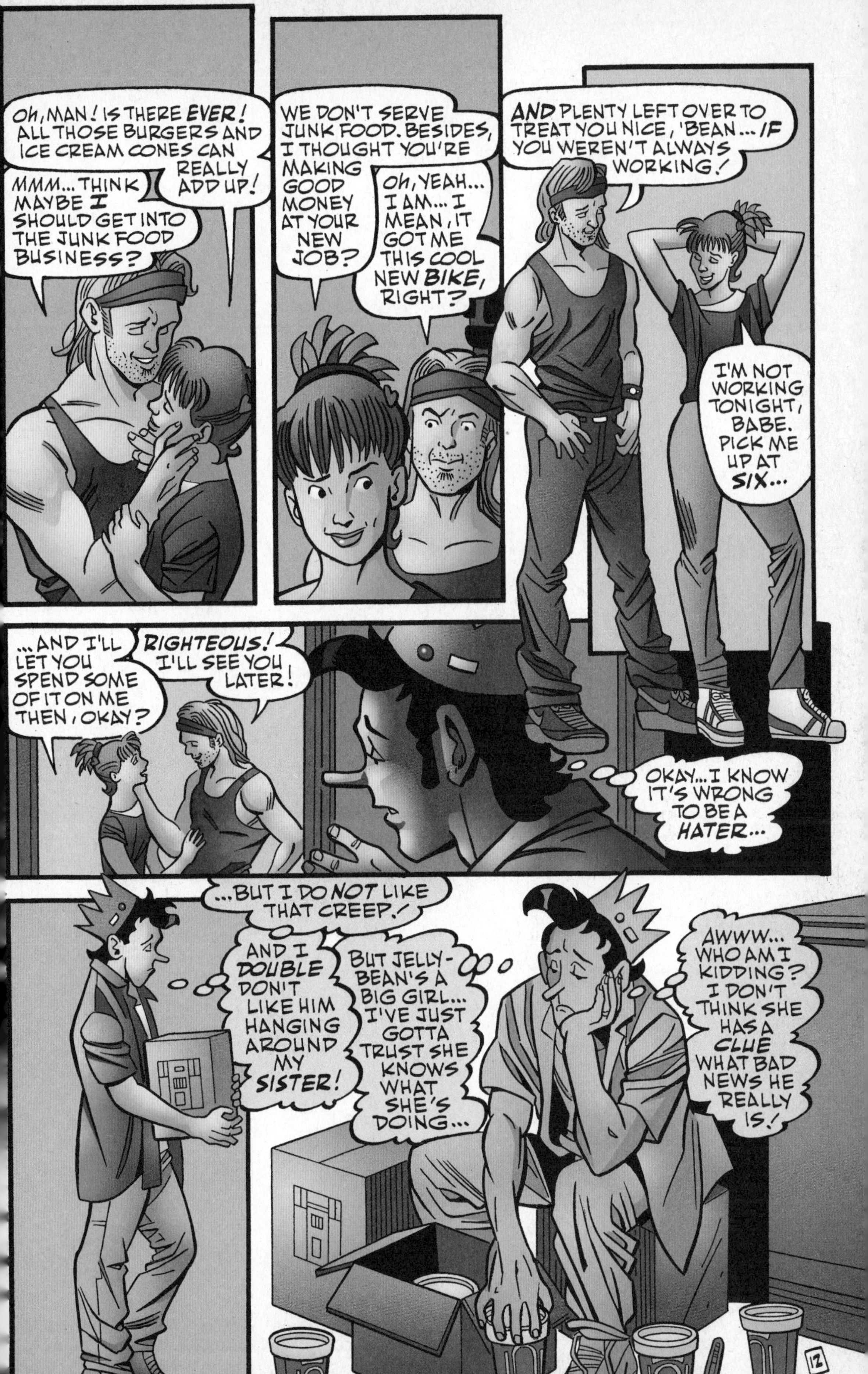

Oh, MAN! IS THERE EVER! ALL THOSE BURGERS AND ICE CREAM CONES CAN REALLY ADD UP!
MMM... THINK MAYBE I SHOULD GET INTO THE JUNK FOOD BUSINESS?
WE DON'T SERVE JUNK FOOD. BESIDES, I THOUGHT YOU'RE MAKING GOOD MONEY AT YOUR NEW JOB?
Oh, YEAH... I AM... I MEAN, IT GOT ME THIS COOL NEW BIKE, RIGHT?
AND PLENTY LEFT OVER TO TREAT YOU NICE, 'BEAN... IF YOU WEREN'T ALWAYS WORKING!
I'M NOT WORKING TONIGHT, BABE. PICK ME UP AT SIX...
...AND I'LL LET YOU SPEND SOME OF IT ON ME THEN, OKAY?
RIGHTEOUS! I'LL SEE YOU LATER!
OKAY... I KNOW IT'S WRONG TO BE A HATER...
...BUT I DO NOT LIKE THAT CREEP!
AND I DOUBLE DON'T LIKE HIM HANGING AROUND MY SISTER!
BUT JELLY-BEAN'S A BIG GIRL... I'VE JUST GOTTA TRUST SHE KNOWS WHAT SHE'S DOING...
AWWW... WHO AM I KIDDING? I DON'T THINK SHE HAS A CLUE WHAT BAD NEWS HE REALLY IS!

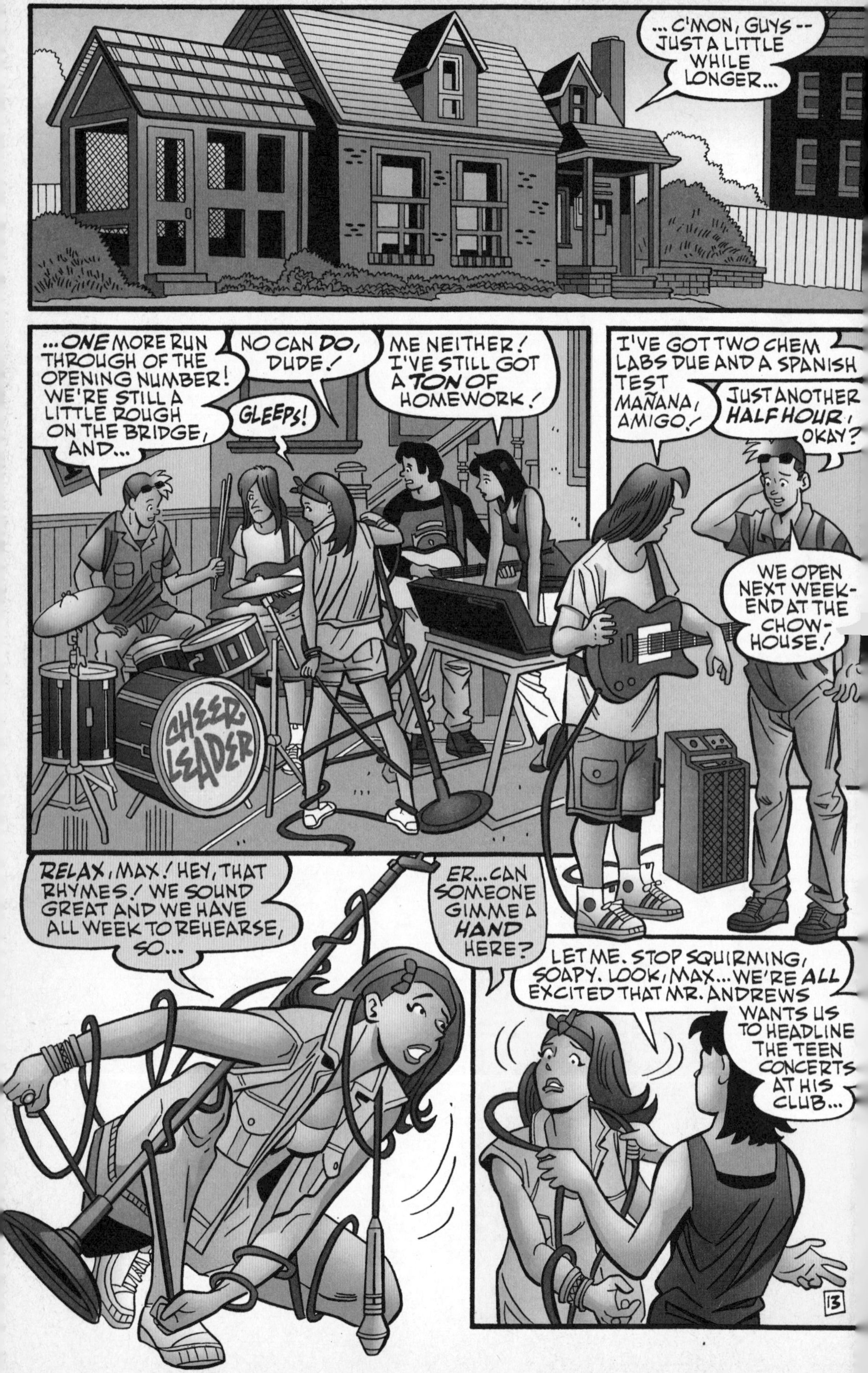
...C'MON, GUYS -- JUST A LITTLE WHILE LONGER...
...ONE MORE RUN THROUGH OF THE OPENING NUMBER! WE'RE STILL A LITTLE ROUGH ON THE BRIDGE, AND...
NO CAN DO, DUDE!
GLEEPS!
ME NEITHER! I'VE STILL GOT A TON OF HOMEWORK!
I'VE GOT TWO CHEM LABS DUE AND A SPANISH TEST MAÑANA, AMIGO!
JUST ANOTHER HALF HOUR, OKAY?
WE OPEN NEXT WEEK-END AT THE CHOW-HOUSE!
CHEER LEADER
RELAX, MAX! HEY, THAT RHYMES! WE SOUND GREAT AND WE HAVE ALL WEEK TO REHEARSE, SO...
ER...CAN SOMEONE GIMME A HAND HERE?
LET ME. STOP SQUIRMING, SOAPY. LOOK, MAX... WE'RE ALL EXCITED THAT MR. ANDREWS WANTS US TO HEADLINE THE TEEN CONCERTS AT HIS CLUB...
13

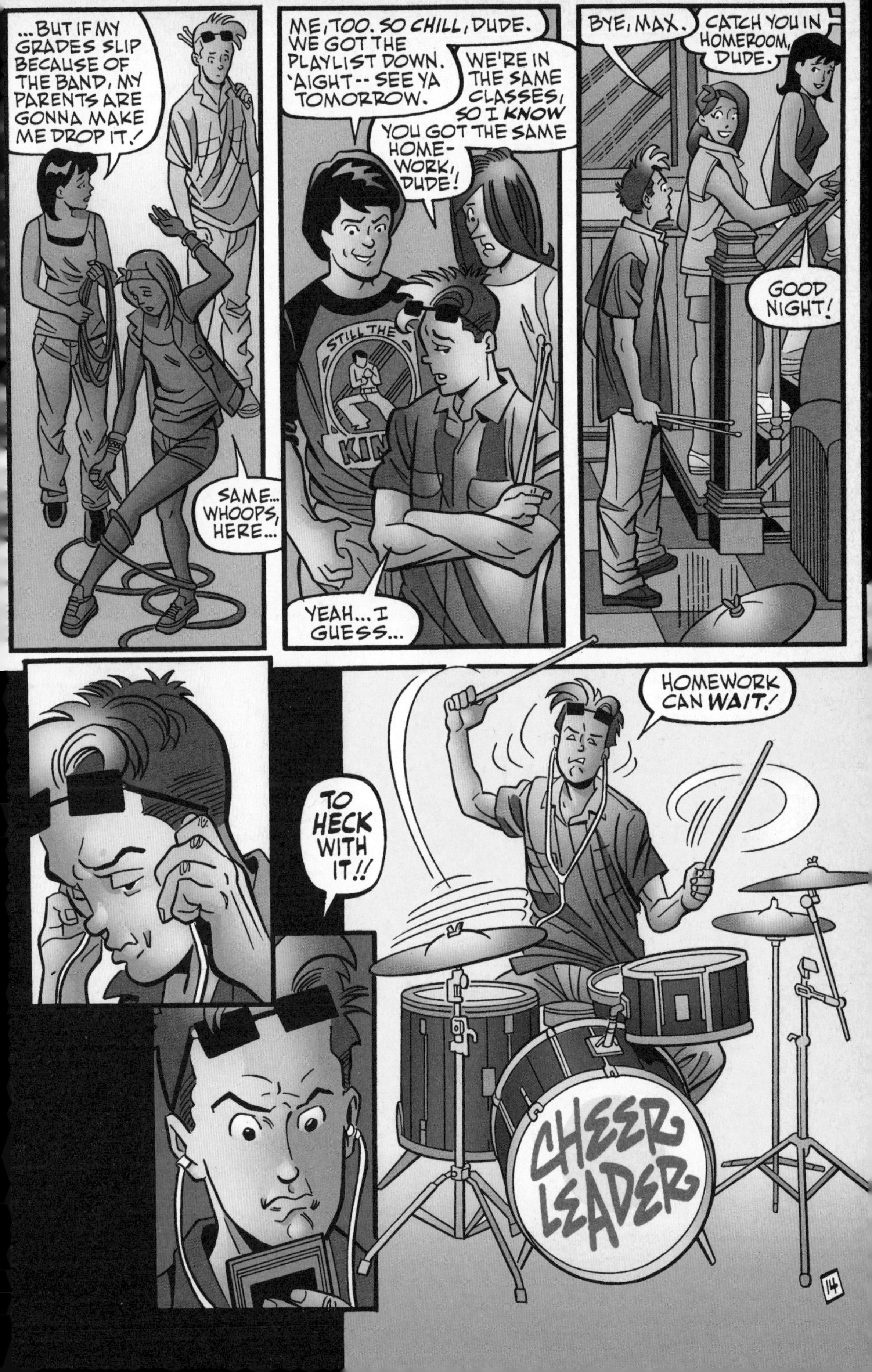
...BUT IF MY GRADES SLIP BECAUSE OF THE BAND, MY PARENTS ARE GONNA MAKE ME DROP IT!
SAME... WHOOPS, HERE...
ME, TOO. SO CHILL, DUDE. WE GOT THE PLAYLIST DOWN. 'AIGHT-- SEE YA TOMORROW.
WE'RE IN THE SAME CLASSES, SO I KNOW YOU GOT THE SAME HOME-WORK, DUDE!
STILL THE KIN
YEAH... I GUESS...
BYE, MAX.
CATCH YOU IN HOMEROOM, DUDE.
GOOD NIGHT!
TO HECK WITH IT!!
HOMEWORK CAN WAIT!
CHEER LEADER
14

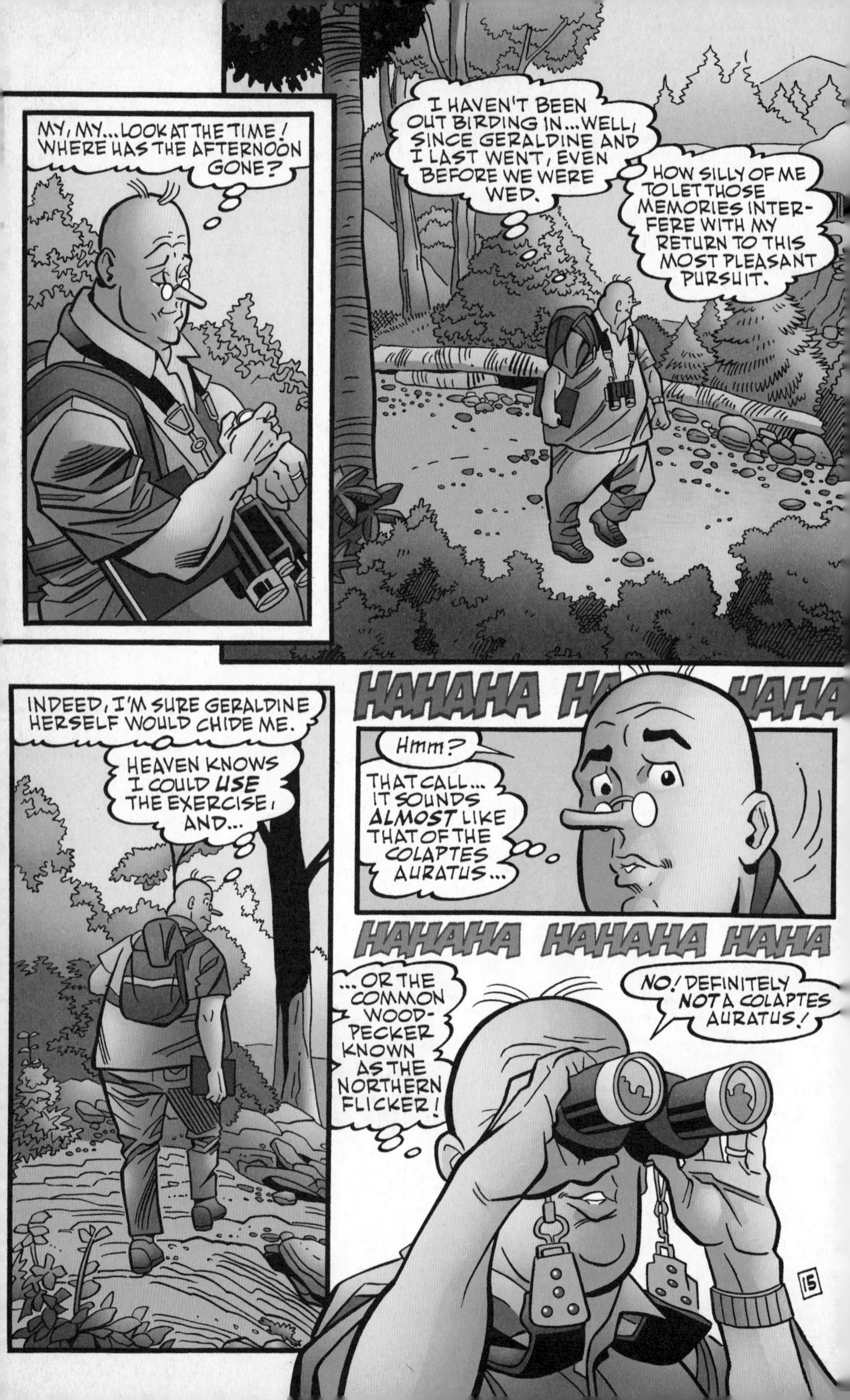
MY, MY...LOOK AT THE TIME! WHERE HAS THE AFTERNOON GONE?
I HAVEN'T BEEN OUT BIRDING IN...WELL, SINCE GERALDINE AND I LAST WENT, EVEN BEFORE WE WERE WED.
HOW SILLY OF ME TO LET THOSE MEMORIES INTER-FERE WITH MY RETURN TO THIS MOST PLEASANT PURSUIT.
INDEED, I'M SURE GERALDINE HERSELF WOULD CHIDE ME.
HEAVEN KNOWS I COULD USE THE EXERCISE, AND...
HAHAHA HA HAHA
Hmm?
THAT CALL... IT SOUNDS ALMOST LIKE THAT OF THE COLAPTES AURATUS...
HAHAHA HAHAHA HAHA
...OR THE COMMON WOOD-PECKER KNOWN AS THE NORTHERN FLICKER!
NO! DEFINITELY NOT A COLAPTES AURATUS!
15

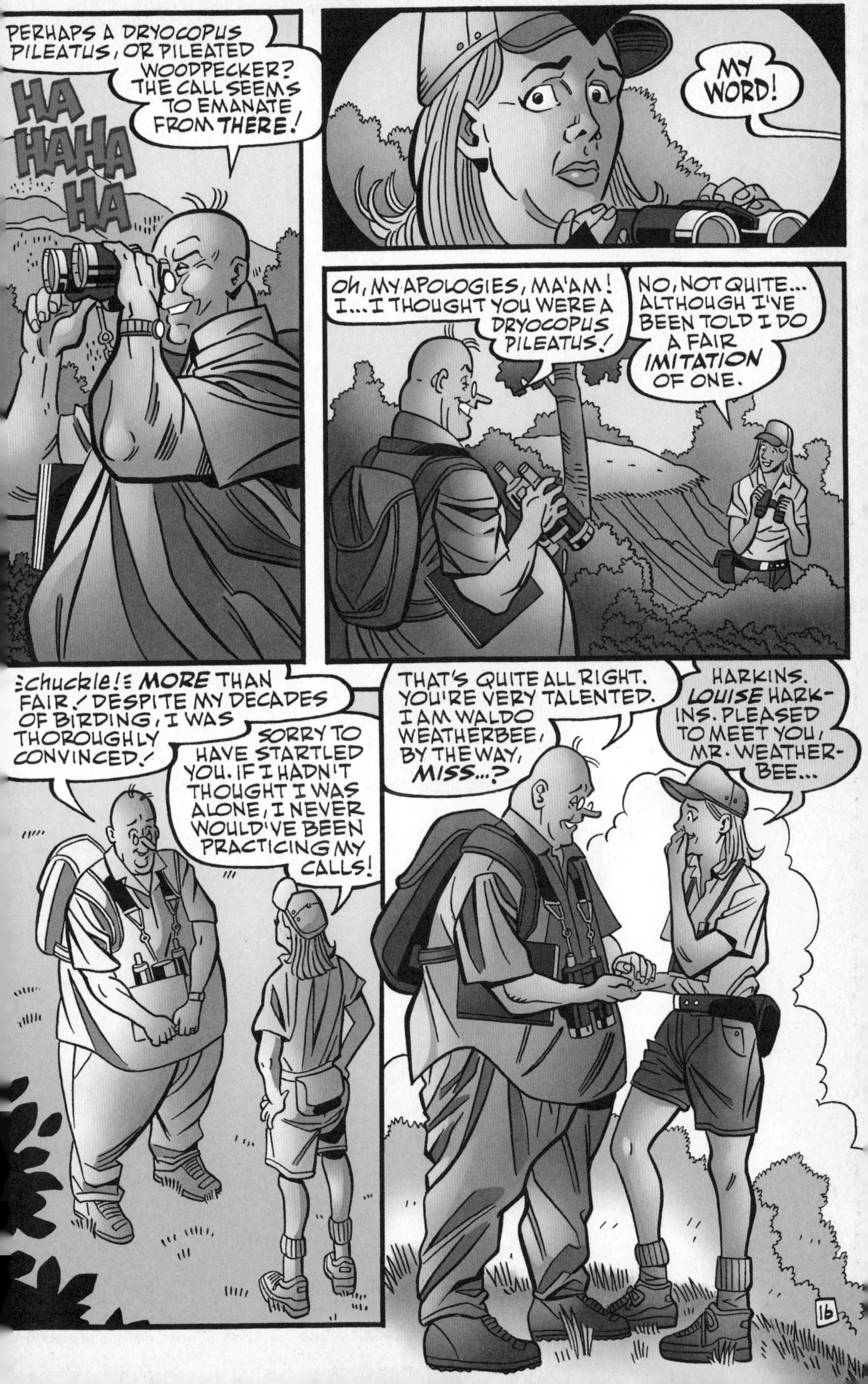
PERHAPS A DRYOCOPUS PILEATUS, OR PILEATED WOODPECKER? THE CALL SEEMS TO EMANATE FROM THERE!
HA HAHAHA HA
MY WORD!
OH, MY APOLOGIES, MA'AM! I... I THOUGHT YOU WERE A DRYOCOPUS PILEATUS!
NO, NOT QUITE... ALTHOUGH I'VE BEEN TOLD I DO A FAIR IMITATION OF ONE.
:CHUCKLE!: MORE THAN FAIR! DESPITE MY DECADES OF BIRDING, I WAS THOROUGHLY CONVINCED!
SORRY TO HAVE STARTLED YOU. IF I HADN'T THOUGHT I WAS ALONE, I NEVER WOULD'VE BEEN PRACTICING MY CALLS!
THAT'S QUITE ALL RIGHT. YOU'RE VERY TALENTED. I AM WALDO WEATHERBEE, BY THE WAY, MISS...?
HARKINS. LOUISE HARKINS. PLEASED TO MEET YOU, MR. WEATHERBEE...
16

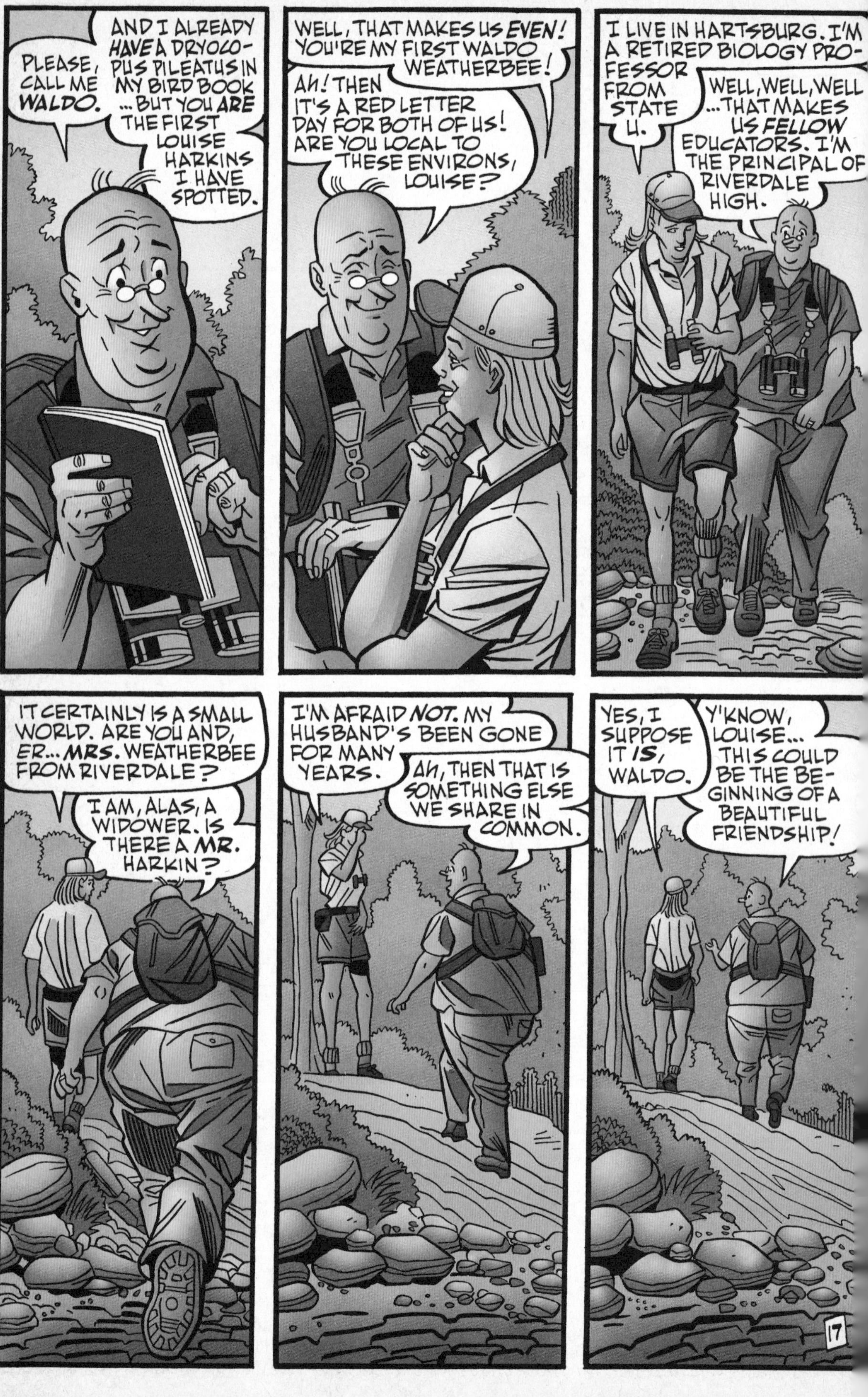
PLEASE, CALL ME WALDO.
AND I ALREADY HAVE A DRYOCOPUS PILEATUS IN MY BIRD BOOK ...BUT YOU ARE THE FIRST LOUISE HARKINS I HAVE SPOTTED.
WELL, THAT MAKES US EVEN! YOU'RE MY FIRST WALDO WEATHERBEE!
AH! THEN IT'S A RED LETTER DAY FOR BOTH OF US! ARE YOU LOCAL TO THESE ENVIRONS, LOUISE?
I LIVE IN HARTSBURG. I'M A RETIRED BIOLOGY PROFESSOR FROM STATE U.
WELL, WELL, WELL ...THAT MAKES US FELLOW EDUCATORS. I'M THE PRINCIPAL OF RIVERDALE HIGH.
IT CERTAINLY IS A SMALL WORLD. ARE YOU AND, ER... MRS. WEATHERBEE FROM RIVERDALE?
I AM, ALAS, A WIDOWER. IS THERE A MR. HARKIN?
I'M AFRAID NOT. MY HUSBAND'S BEEN GONE FOR MANY YEARS.
AH, THEN THAT IS SOMETHING ELSE WE SHARE IN COMMON.
YES, I SUPPOSE IT IS, WALDO.
Y'KNOW, LOUISE... THIS COULD BE THE BEGINNING OF A BEAUTIFUL FRIENDSHIP!
17

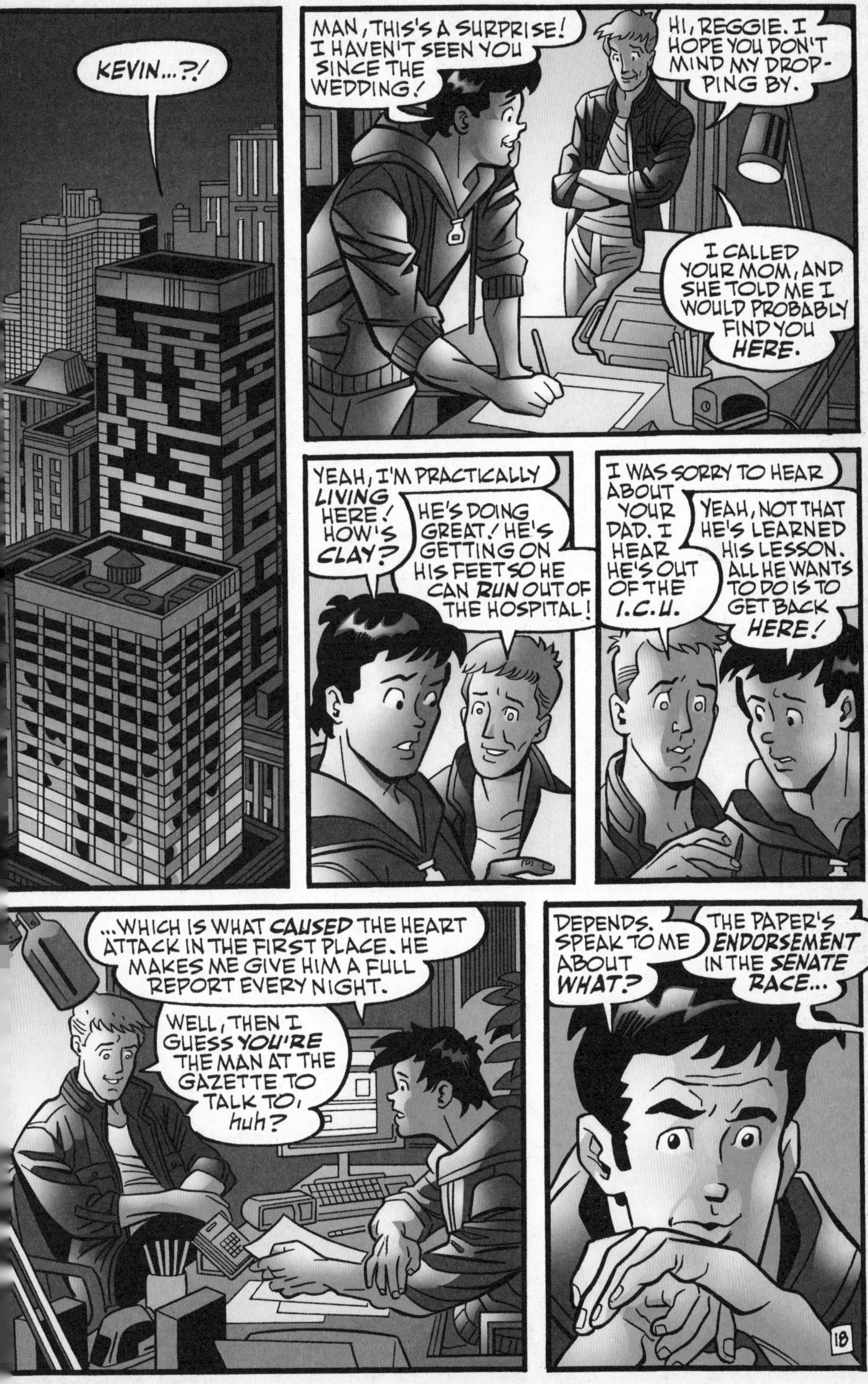
KEVIN...?!
MAN, THIS'S A SURPRISE! I HAVEN'T SEEN YOU SINCE THE WEDDING!
HI, REGGIE. I HOPE YOU DON'T MIND MY DROPPING BY.
I CALLED YOUR MOM, AND SHE TOLD ME I WOULD PROBABLY FIND YOU HERE.
YEAH, I'M PRACTICALLY LIVING HERE! HOW'S CLAY?
HE'S DOING GREAT! HE'S GETTING ON HIS FEET SO HE CAN RUN OUT OF THE HOSPITAL!
I WAS SORRY TO HEAR ABOUT YOUR DAD. I HEAR HE'S OUT OF THE I.C.U.
YEAH, NOT THAT HE'S LEARNED HIS LESSON. ALL HE WANTS TO DO IS TO GET BACK HERE!
...WHICH IS WHAT CAUSED THE HEART ATTACK IN THE FIRST PLACE. HE MAKES ME GIVE HIM A FULL REPORT EVERY NIGHT.
WELL, THEN I GUESS YOU'RE THE MAN AT THE GAZETTE TO TALK TO, huh?
DEPENDS. SPEAK TO ME ABOUT WHAT?
THE PAPER'S ENDORSEMENT IN THE SENATE RACE...
18

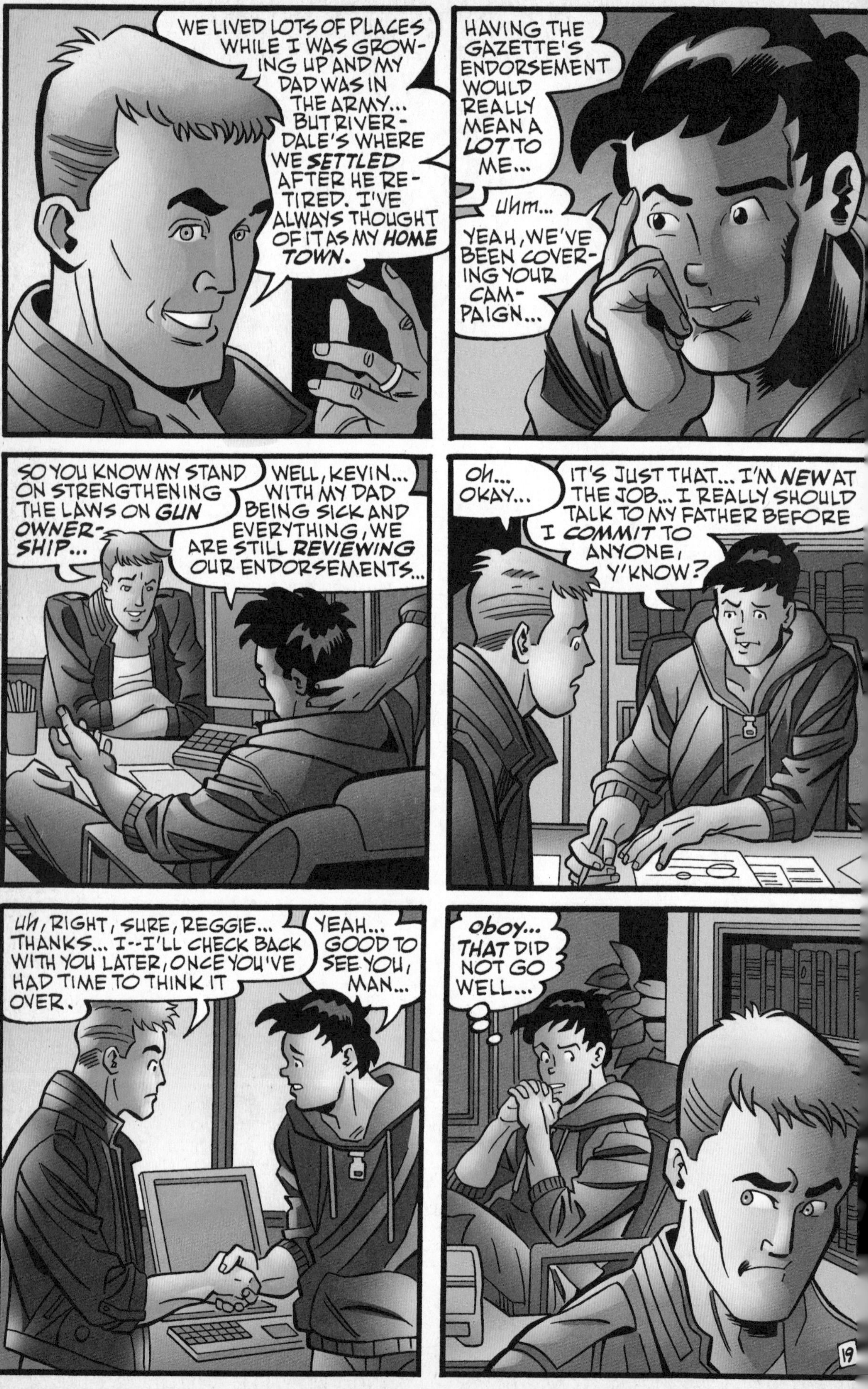
WE LIVED LOTS OF PLACES WHILE I WAS GROWING UP AND MY DAD WAS IN THE ARMY... BUT RIVERDALE'S WHERE WE SETTLED AFTER HE RETIRED. I'VE ALWAYS THOUGHT OF IT AS MY HOME TOWN.
HAVING THE GAZETTE'S ENDORSEMENT WOULD REALLY MEAN A LOT TO ME...
UHM...
YEAH, WE'VE BEEN COVERING YOUR CAMPAIGN...
SO YOU KNOW MY STAND ON STRENGTHENING THE LAWS ON GUN OWNERSHIP...
WELL, KEVIN... WITH MY DAD BEING SICK AND EVERYTHING, WE ARE STILL REVIEWING OUR ENDORSEMENTS...
OH... OKAY...
IT'S JUST THAT... I'M NEW AT THE JOB... I REALLY SHOULD TALK TO MY FATHER BEFORE I COMMIT TO ANYONE, Y'KNOW?
UH, RIGHT, SURE, REGGIE... THANKS... I--I'LL CHECK BACK WITH YOU LATER, ONCE YOU'VE HAD TIME TO THINK IT OVER.
YEAH... GOOD TO SEE YOU, MAN...
OBOY... THAT DID NOT GO WELL...
19

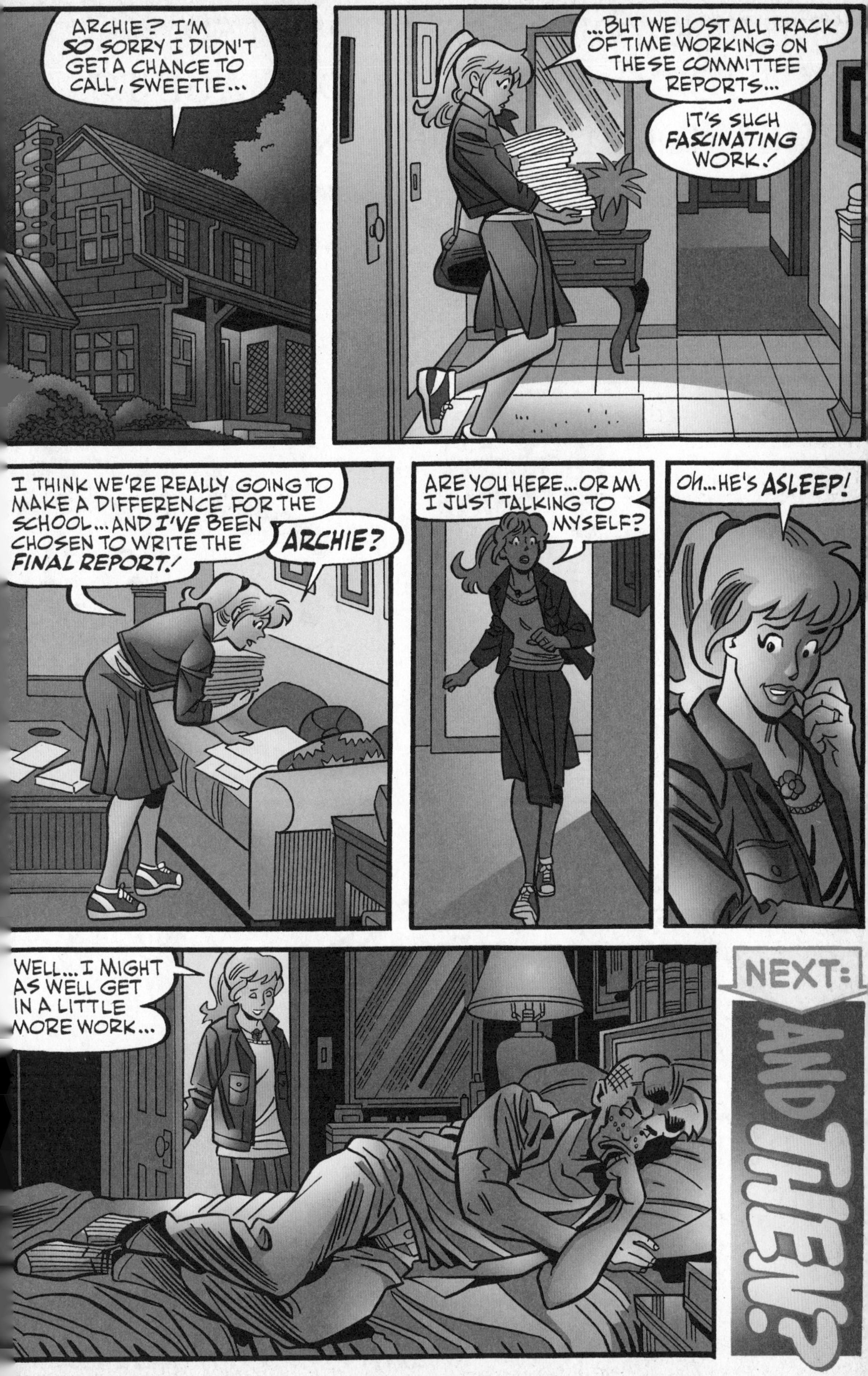
ARCHIE? I'M SO SORRY I DIDN'T GET A CHANCE TO CALL, SWEETIE...
...BUT WE LOST ALL TRACK OF TIME WORKING ON THESE COMMITTEE REPORTS...
IT'S SUCH FASCINATING WORK!
I THINK WE'RE REALLY GOING TO MAKE A DIFFERENCE FOR THE SCHOOL... AND I'VE BEEN CHOSEN TO WRITE THE FINAL REPORT!
ARCHIE?
ARE YOU HERE... OR AM I JUST TALKING TO MYSELF?
Oh... HE'S ASLEEP!
WELL... I MIGHT AS WELL GET IN A LITTLE MORE WORK...
NEXT:
AND THEN?

"I THINK YOU CAN BE TRUSTED NOT TO DO ANY *MAJOR* DAMAGE TO THE CHOCKLIT SHOPPE NOW, JUGHEAD..."

"...BUT I'M NOT SO SURE THE SAME CAN BE SAID FOR *FRED MIRTH*."

-TERRY "POP" TATE

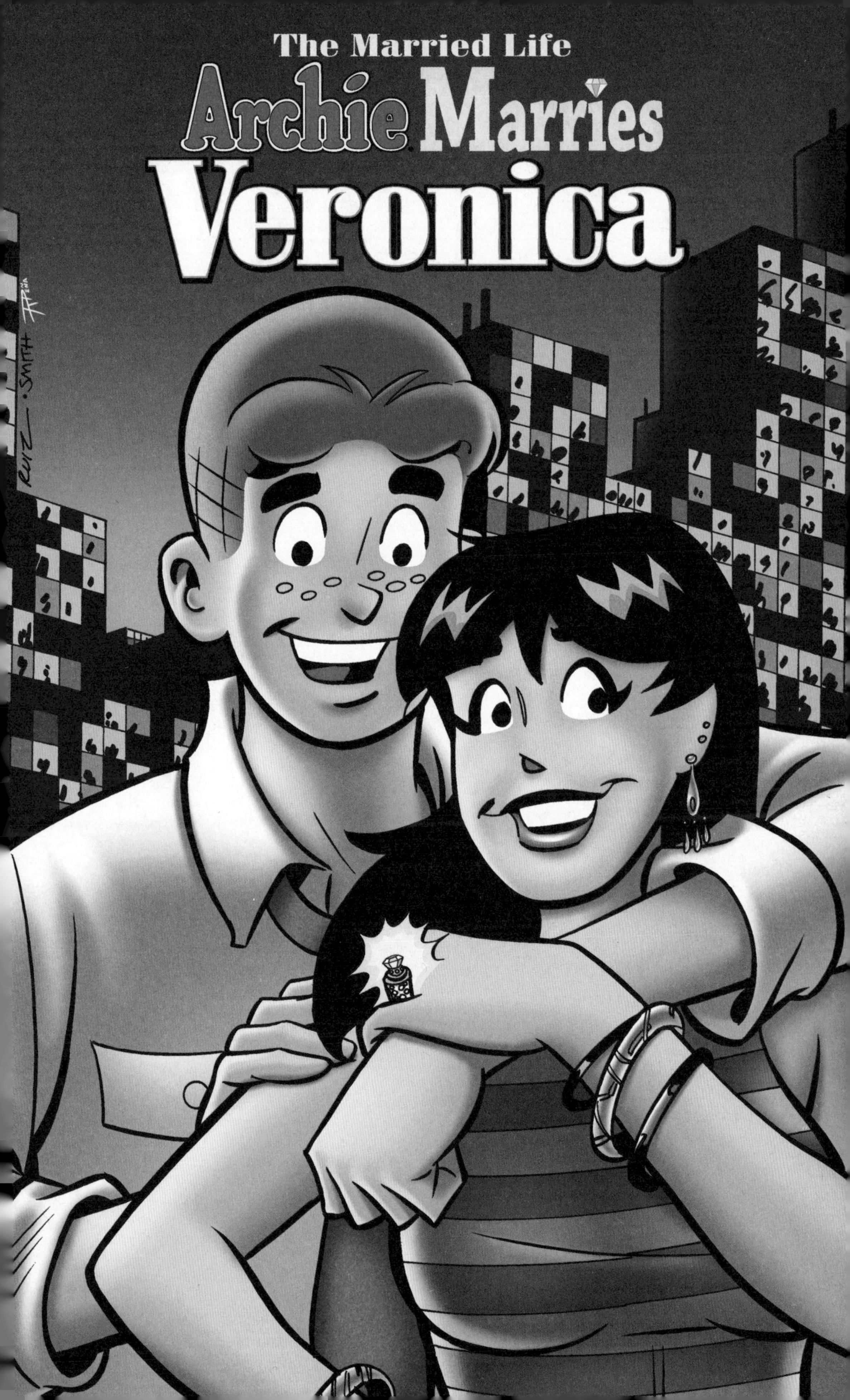
The Married Life
Archie Marries
Veronica

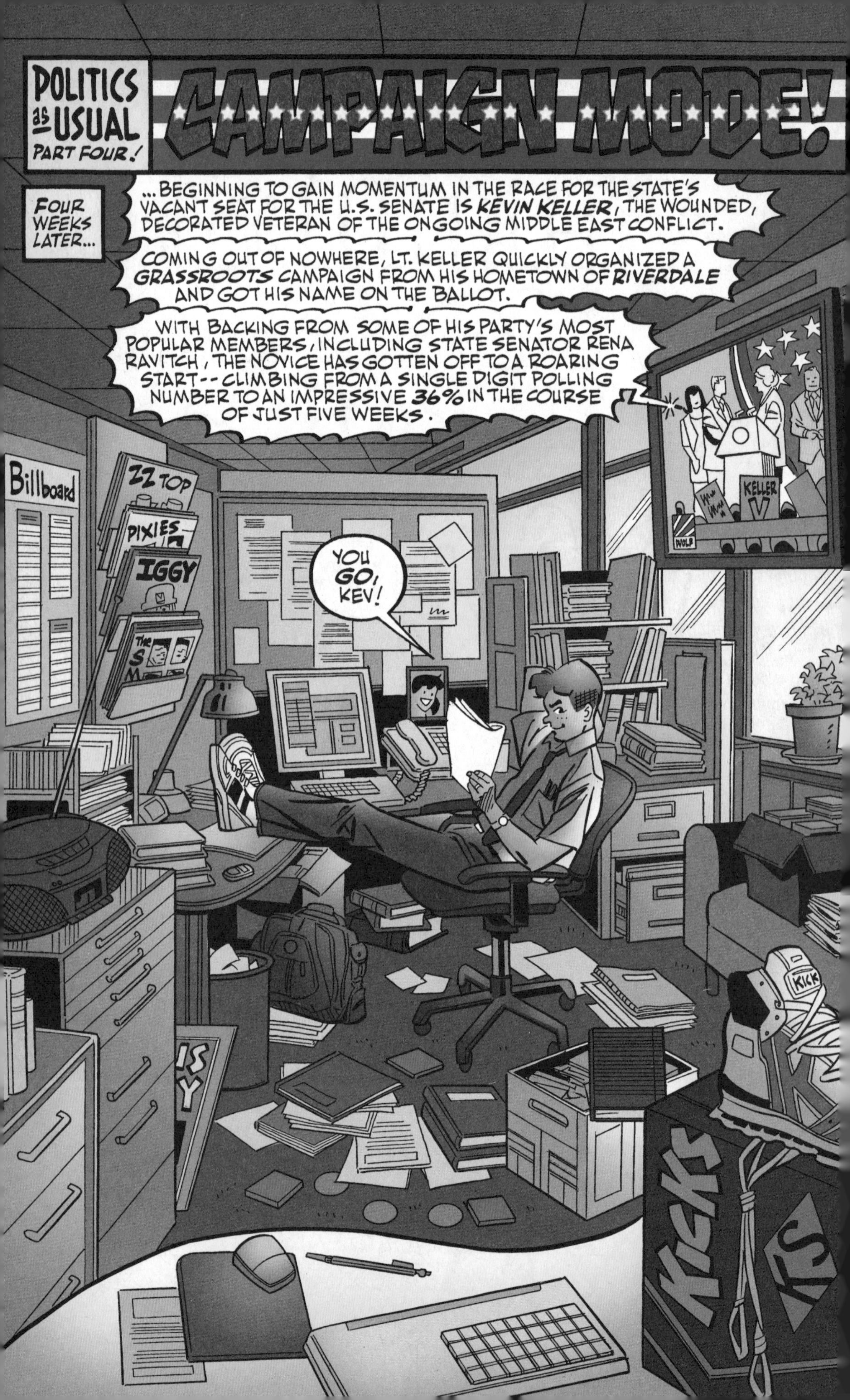
POLITICS as USUAL PART FOUR!
CAMPAIGN MODE!
FOUR WEEKS LATER...
...BEGINNING TO GAIN MOMENTUM IN THE RACE FOR THE STATE'S VACANT SEAT FOR THE U.S. SENATE IS KEVIN KELLER, THE WOUNDED, DECORATED VETERAN OF THE ONGOING MIDDLE EAST CONFLICT.
COMING OUT OF NOWHERE, LT. KELLER QUICKLY ORGANIZED A GRASSROOTS CAMPAIGN FROM HIS HOMETOWN OF RIVERDALE AND GOT HIS NAME ON THE BALLOT.
WITH BACKING FROM SOME OF HIS PARTY'S MOST POPULAR MEMBERS, INCLUDING STATE SENATOR RENA RAVITCH, THE NOVICE HAS GOTTEN OFF TO A ROARING START--CLIMBING FROM A SINGLE DIGIT POLLING NUMBER TO AN IMPRESSIVE 36% IN THE COURSE OF JUST FIVE WEEKS.
KELLER
WOLF
Billboard
ZZ TOP
PIXIES
IGGY
YOU GO, KEV!
KICK
KICKS

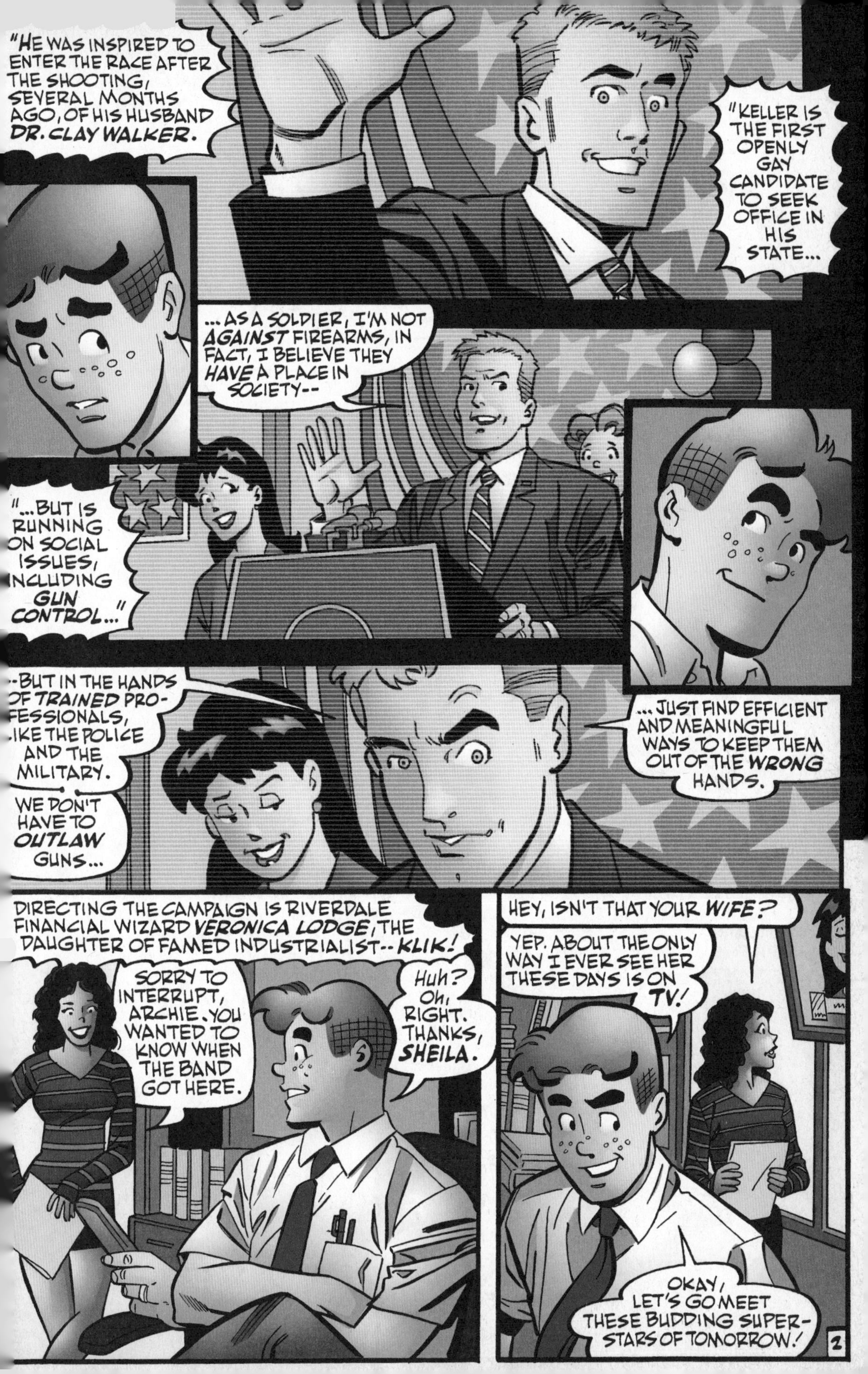
"HE WAS INSPIRED TO ENTER THE RACE AFTER THE SHOOTING, SEVERAL MONTHS AGO, OF HIS HUSBAND DR. CLAY WALKER.
"KELLER IS THE FIRST OPENLY GAY CANDIDATE TO SEEK OFFICE IN HIS STATE...
...AS A SOLDIER, I'M NOT AGAINST FIREARMS, IN FACT, I BELIEVE THEY HAVE A PLACE IN SOCIETY--
"...BUT IS RUNNING ON SOCIAL ISSUES, INCLUDING GUN CONTROL..."
--BUT IN THE HANDS OF TRAINED PRO-FESSIONALS, LIKE THE POLICE AND THE MILITARY.
WE DON'T HAVE TO OUTLAW GUNS...
...JUST FIND EFFICIENT AND MEANINGFUL WAYS TO KEEP THEM OUT OF THE WRONG HANDS.
DIRECTING THE CAMPAIGN IS RIVERDALE FINANCIAL WIZARD VERONICA LODGE, THE DAUGHTER OF FAMED INDUSTRIALIST-- KLIK!
SORRY TO INTERRUPT, ARCHIE. YOU WANTED TO KNOW WHEN THE BAND GOT HERE.
Huh? Oh, RIGHT. THANKS, SHEILA.
HEY, ISN'T THAT YOUR WIFE?
YEP. ABOUT THE ONLY WAY I EVER SEE HER THESE DAYS IS ON TV!
OKAY, LET'S GO MEET THESE BUDDING SUPER-STARS OF TOMORROW!
2

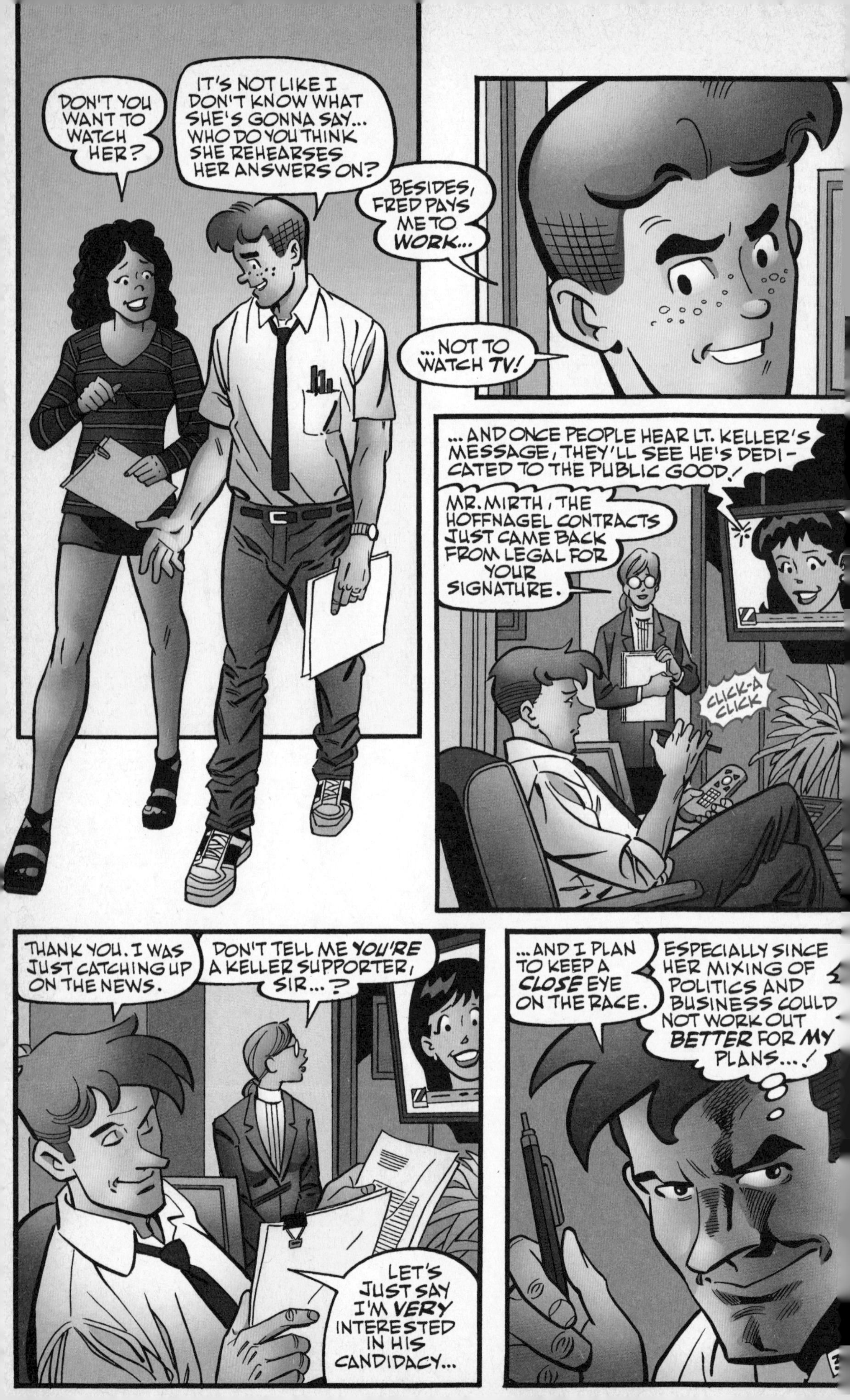
DON'T YOU WANT TO WATCH HER?
IT'S NOT LIKE I DON'T KNOW WHAT SHE'S GONNA SAY... WHO DO YOU THINK SHE REHEARSES HER ANSWERS ON?
BESIDES, FRED PAYS ME TO WORK...
...NOT TO WATCH TV!
...AND ONCE PEOPLE HEAR LT. KELLER'S MESSAGE, THEY'LL SEE HE'S DEDICATED TO THE PUBLIC GOOD!
MR. MIRTH, THE HOFFNAGEL CONTRACTS JUST CAME BACK FROM LEGAL FOR YOUR SIGNATURE.
CLICK-A CLICK
THANK YOU. I WAS JUST CATCHING UP ON THE NEWS.
DON'T TELL ME YOU'RE A KELLER SUPPORTER, SIR...?
LET'S JUST SAY I'M VERY INTERESTED IN HIS CANDIDACY...
...AND I PLAN TO KEEP A CLOSE EYE ON THE RACE.
ESPECIALLY SINCE HER MIXING OF POLITICS AND BUSINESS COULD NOT WORK OUT BETTER FOR MY PLANS...!

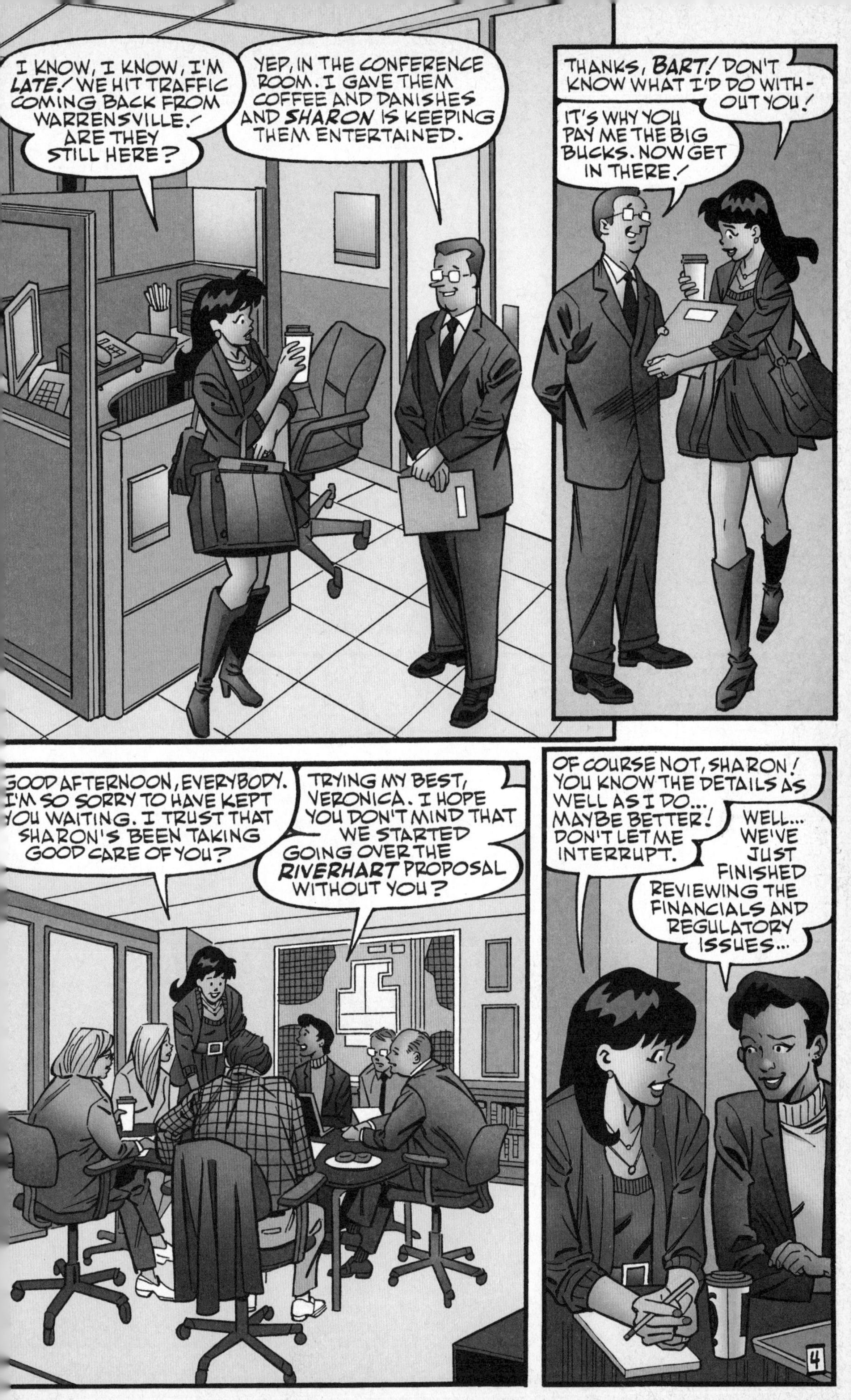

I KNOW, I KNOW, I'M LATE! WE HIT TRAFFIC COMING BACK FROM WARRENSVILLE! ARE THEY STILL HERE?
YEP, IN THE CONFERENCE ROOM. I GAVE THEM COFFEE AND DANISHES AND SHARON IS KEEPING THEM ENTERTAINED.
THANKS, BART! DON'T KNOW WHAT I'D DO WITH-OUT YOU!
IT'S WHY YOU PAY ME THE BIG BUCKS. NOW GET IN THERE!
GOOD AFTERNOON, EVERYBODY. I'M SO SORRY TO HAVE KEPT YOU WAITING. I TRUST THAT SHARON'S BEEN TAKING GOOD CARE OF YOU?
TRYING MY BEST, VERONICA. I HOPE YOU DON'T MIND THAT WE STARTED GOING OVER THE RIVERHART PROPOSAL WITHOUT YOU?
OF COURSE NOT, SHARON! YOU KNOW THE DETAILS AS WELL AS I DO... MAYBE BETTER! DON'T LET ME INTERRUPT.
WELL... WE'VE JUST FINISHED REVIEWING THE FINANCIALS AND REGULATORY ISSUES...
4

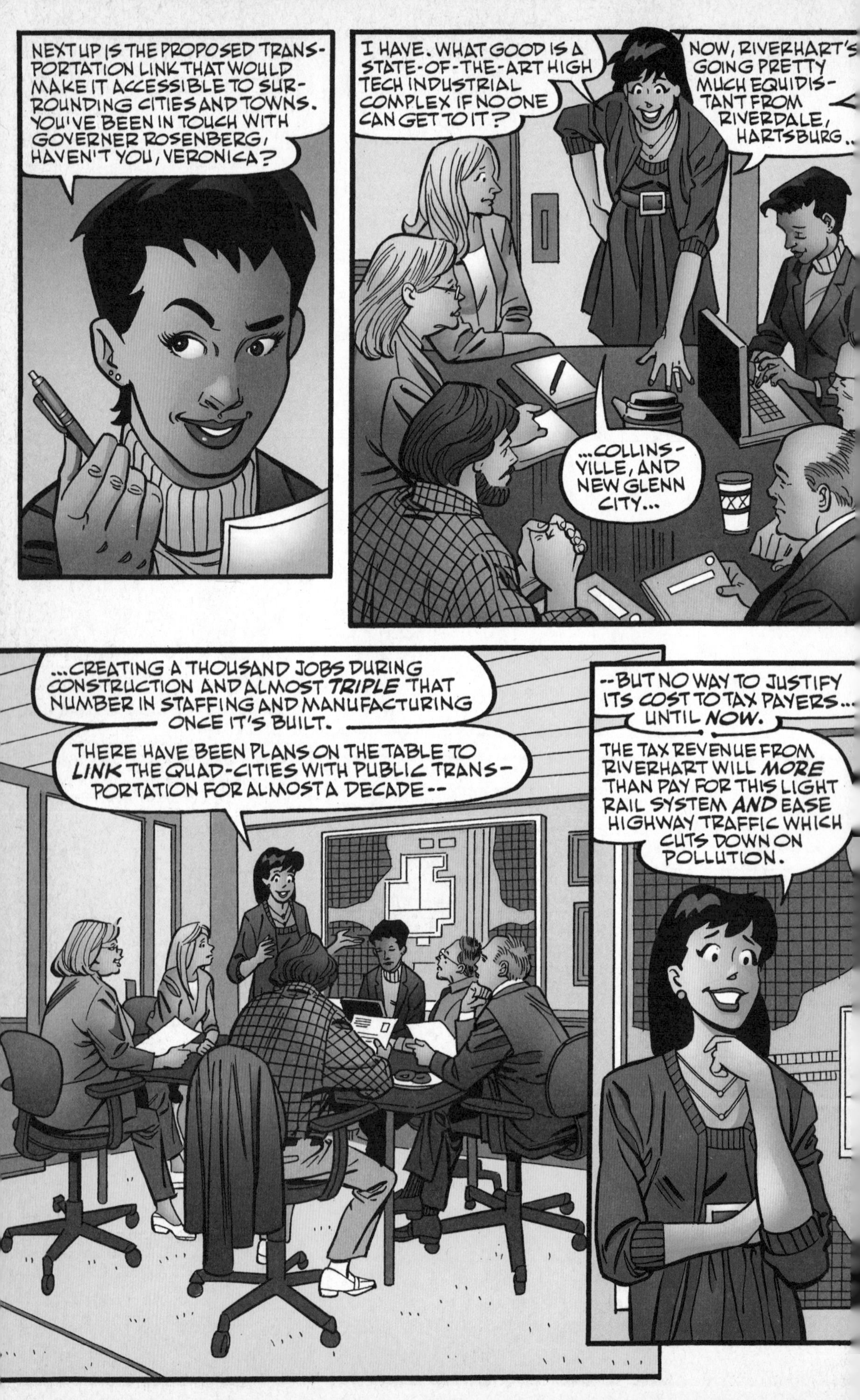

NEXT UP IS THE PROPOSED TRANSPORTATION LINK THAT WOULD MAKE IT ACCESSIBLE TO SURROUNDING CITIES AND TOWNS. YOU'VE BEEN IN TOUCH WITH GOVERNER ROSENBERG, HAVEN'T YOU, VERONICA?
I HAVE. WHAT GOOD IS A STATE-OF-THE-ART HIGH TECH INDUSTRIAL COMPLEX IF NO ONE CAN GET TO IT?
NOW, RIVERHART'S GOING PRETTY MUCH EQUIDISTANT FROM RIVERDALE, HARTSBURG...
...COLLINSVILLE, AND NEW GLENN CITY...
...CREATING A THOUSAND JOBS DURING CONSTRUCTION AND ALMOST TRIPLE THAT NUMBER IN STAFFING AND MANUFACTURING ONCE IT'S BUILT.
THERE HAVE BEEN PLANS ON THE TABLE TO LINK THE QUAD-CITIES WITH PUBLIC TRANSPORTATION FOR ALMOST A DECADE--
--BUT NO WAY TO JUSTIFY ITS COST TO TAX PAYERS... UNTIL NOW.
THE TAX REVENUE FROM RIVERHART WILL MORE THAN PAY FOR THIS LIGHT RAIL SYSTEM AND EASE HIGHWAY TRAFFIC WHICH CUTS DOWN ON POLLUTION.

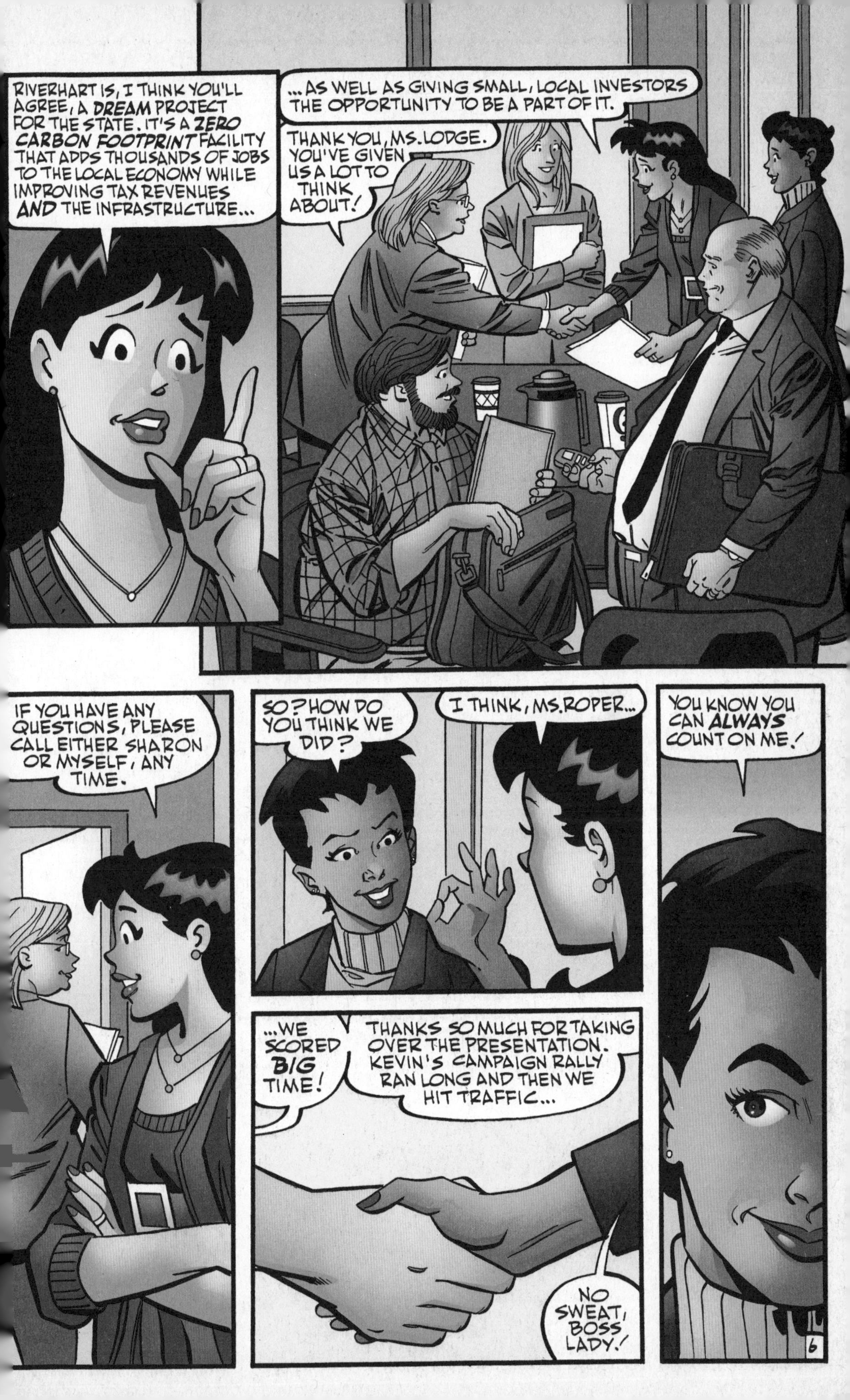

RIVERHART IS, I THINK YOU'LL AGREE, A DREAM PROJECT FOR THE STATE. IT'S A ZERO CARBON FOOTPRINT FACILITY THAT ADDS THOUSANDS OF JOBS TO THE LOCAL ECONOMY WHILE IMPROVING TAX REVENUES AND THE INFRASTRUCTURE...
...AS WELL AS GIVING SMALL, LOCAL INVESTORS THE OPPORTUNITY TO BE A PART OF IT.
THANK YOU, MS. LODGE. YOU'VE GIVEN US A LOT TO THINK ABOUT!
IF YOU HAVE ANY QUESTIONS, PLEASE CALL EITHER SHARON OR MYSELF, ANY TIME.
SO? HOW DO YOU THINK WE DID?
I THINK, MS. ROPER...
...WE SCORED BIG TIME!
THANKS SO MUCH FOR TAKING OVER THE PRESENTATION. KEVIN'S CAMPAIGN RALLY RAN LONG AND THEN WE HIT TRAFFIC...
NO SWEAT, BOSS LADY!
YOU KNOW YOU CAN ALWAYS COUNT ON ME!
6

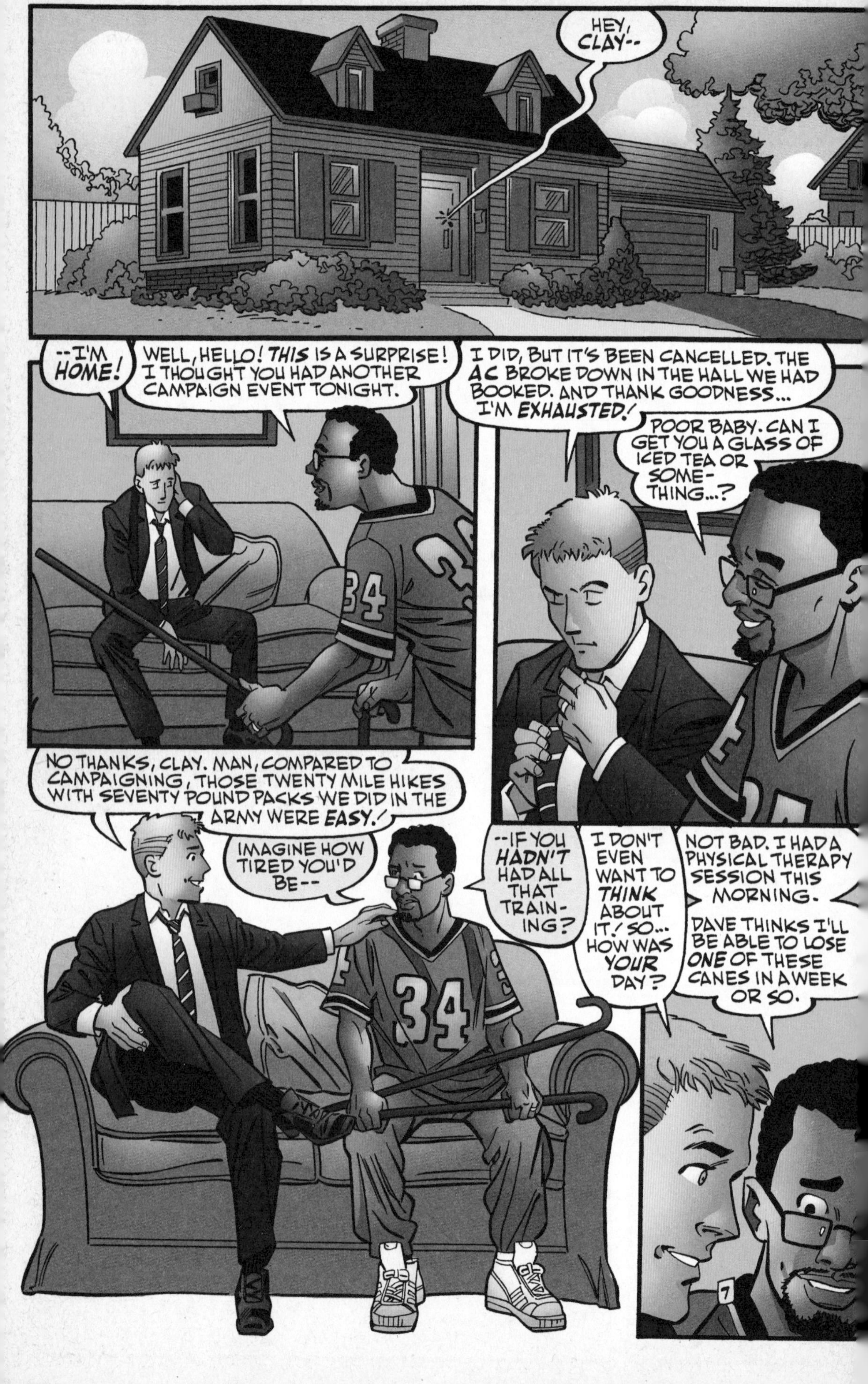
HEY, CLAY--
--I'M HOME!
WELL, HELLO! THIS IS A SURPRISE! I THOUGHT YOU HAD ANOTHER CAMPAIGN EVENT TONIGHT.
I DID, BUT IT'S BEEN CANCELLED. THE AC BROKE DOWN IN THE HALL WE HAD BOOKED. AND THANK GOODNESS... I'M EXHAUSTED!
POOR BABY. CAN I GET YOU A GLASS OF ICED TEA OR SOME-THING...?
NO THANKS, CLAY. MAN, COMPARED TO CAMPAIGNING, THOSE TWENTY MILE HIKES WITH SEVENTY POUND PACKS WE DID IN THE ARMY WERE EASY!
IMAGINE HOW TIRED YOU'D BE--
--IF YOU HADN'T HAD ALL THAT TRAIN-ING?
I DON'T EVEN WANT TO THINK ABOUT IT! SO... HOW WAS YOUR DAY?
NOT BAD. I HAD A PHYSICAL THERAPY SESSION THIS MORNING.
DAVE THINKS I'LL BE ABLE TO LOSE ONE OF THESE CANES IN A WEEK OR SO.

THAT'S *AWESOME!* PRETTY SOON YOU'LL BE *DANCING* AGAIN!

I DON'T KNOW ABOUT THAT... BUT I *WILL* BE ABLE TO CAMPAIGN WITH YOU.

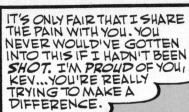

IT'S ONLY FAIR THAT I SHARE THE PAIN WITH YOU. YOU NEVER WOULD'VE GOTTEN INTO THIS IF I HADN'T BEEN *SHOT.* I'M *PROUD* OF YOU, KEV... YOU'RE REALLY TRYING TO MAKE A DIFFERENCE.

SOMEBODY'S GOT TO. I JUST HAPPENED TO FIND A REASON WHY IT SHOULD BE ME.

HEY, DID YOU HEAR? MY OPPONENT, GOVERNOR DOOLEY, HAS FINALLY AGREED TO A *DEBATE!*

ABOUT *TIME!* HE'S BEEN DOING PLENTY OF SNIP-ING AT YOU... BUT LET'S SEE HOW TOUGH HE'LL BE FACE-TO-FACE!

HE WON'T HAVE TO BE TOUGH AT ALL IF I DON'T GET IN A *HEAP* MORE STUDYING AND DEBATE PREP THAN I'VE BEEN DOING!

THEN WHAT'RE WE WAITING FOR?! LET'S HIT THOSE BRIEFING BOOKS!

ABSOLUTELY...

... BUT *AFTER* I GIVE MYSELF JUST *TEN* MINUTES OF DOING NOTHING, OKAY?

Heh-heh! MAKE IT *FIVE*, SOLDIER!

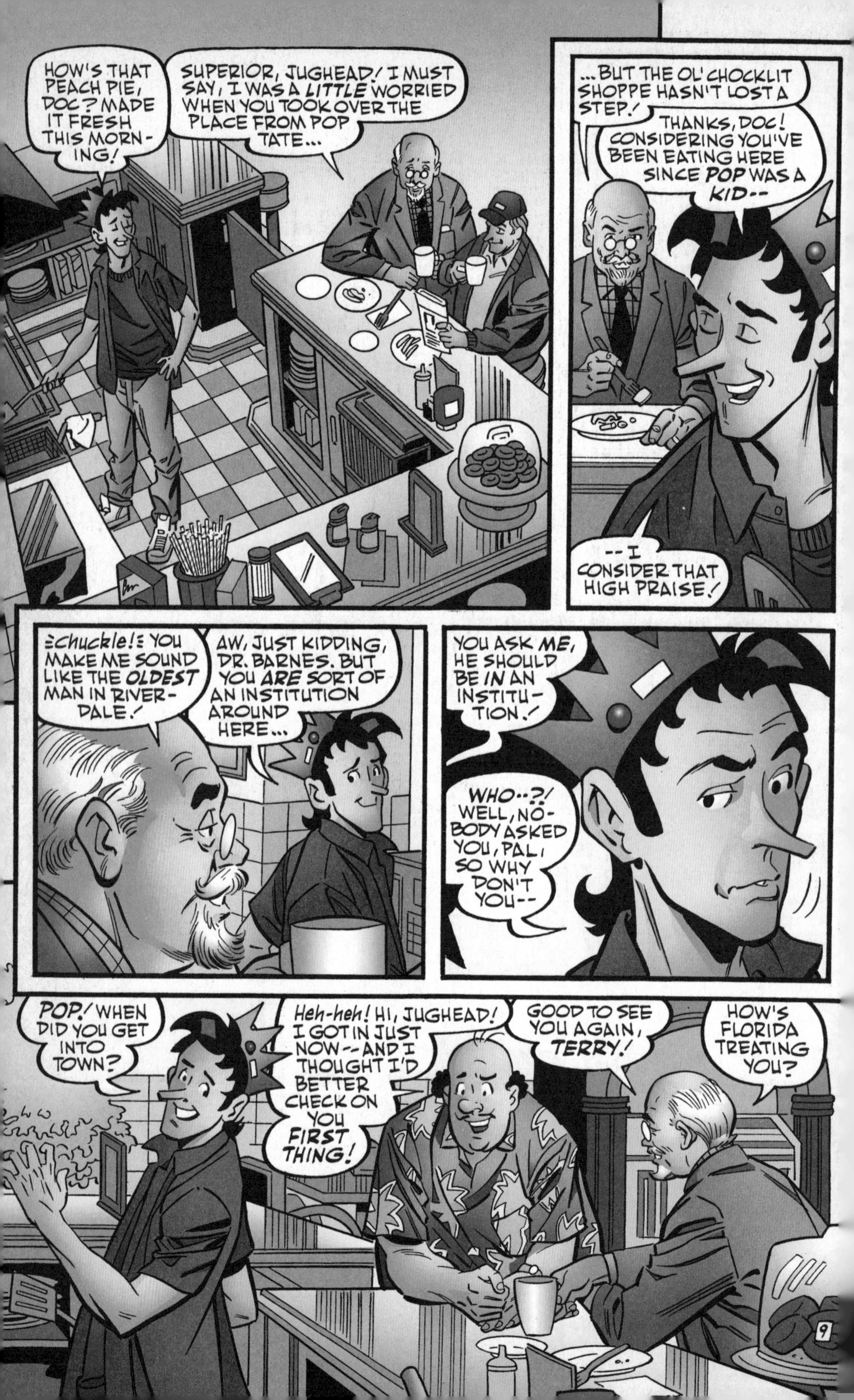

HOW'S THAT PEACH PIE, DOC? MADE IT FRESH THIS MORNING!
SUPERIOR, JUGHEAD! I MUST SAY, I WAS A *LITTLE* WORRIED WHEN YOU TOOK OVER THE PLACE FROM POP TATE...
...BUT THE OL' CHOCKLIT SHOPPE HASN'T LOST A STEP!
THANKS, DOC! CONSIDERING YOU'VE BEEN EATING HERE SINCE *POP* WAS A *KID*--
--I CONSIDER THAT HIGH PRAISE!
:Chuckle!: YOU MAKE ME SOUND LIKE THE *OLDEST* MAN IN RIVERDALE!
AW, JUST KIDDING, DR. BARNES. BUT YOU *ARE* SORT OF AN INSTITUTION AROUND HERE...
YOU ASK *ME*, HE SHOULD BE *IN* AN INSTITUTION!
WHO--?! WELL, NOBODY ASKED YOU, PAL, SO WHY DON'T YOU--
POP! WHEN DID YOU GET INTO TOWN?
Heh-heh! HI, JUGHEAD! I GOT IN JUST NOW--AND I THOUGHT I'D BETTER CHECK ON YOU *FIRST THING!*
GOOD TO SEE YOU AGAIN, *TERRY!*
HOW'S FLORIDA TREATING YOU?
9

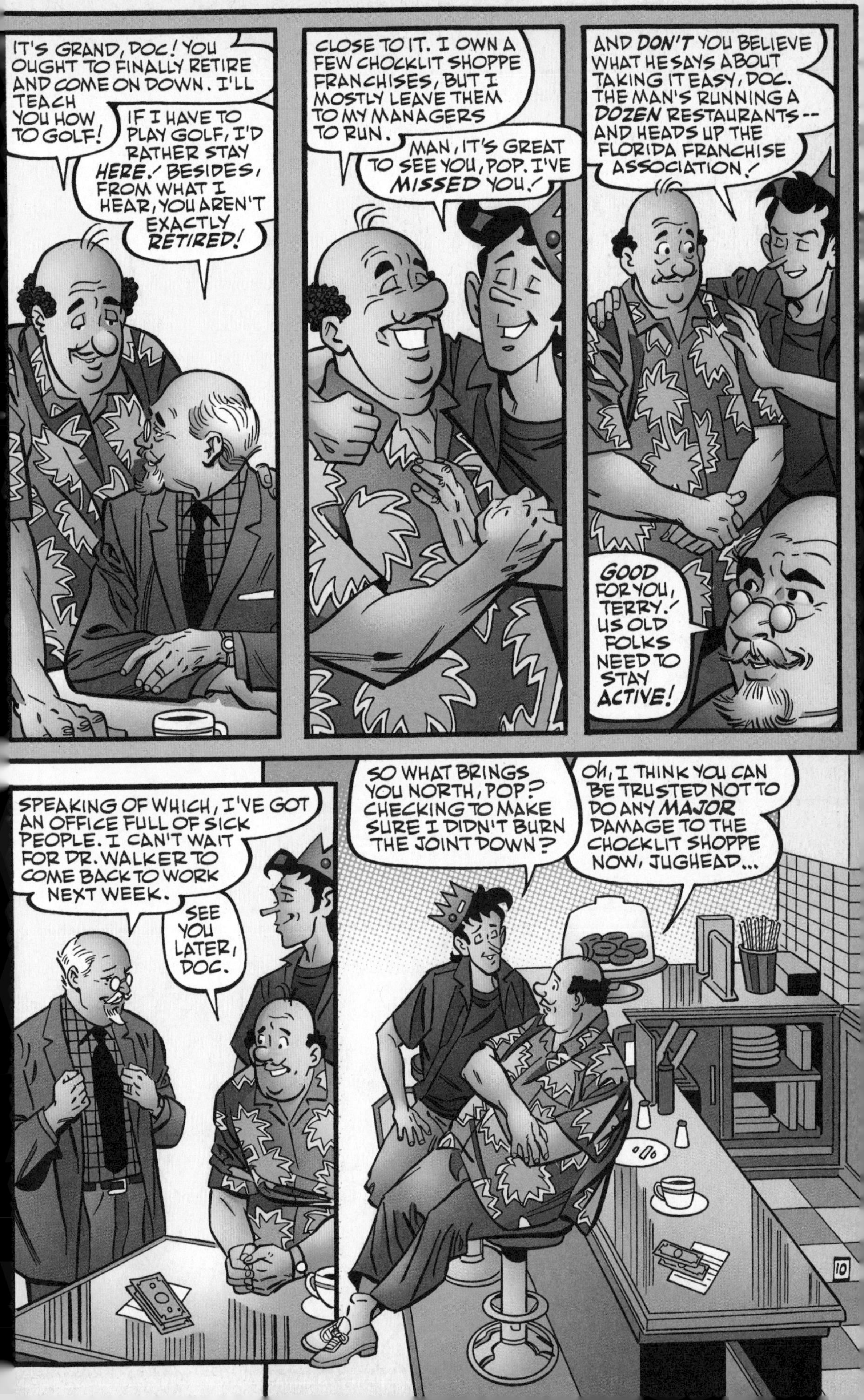
IT'S GRAND, DOC! YOU OUGHT TO FINALLY RETIRE AND COME ON DOWN. I'LL TEACH YOU HOW TO GOLF!
IF I HAVE TO PLAY GOLF, I'D RATHER STAY HERE! BESIDES, FROM WHAT I HEAR, YOU AREN'T EXACTLY RETIRED!
CLOSE TO IT. I OWN A FEW CHOCKLIT SHOPPE FRANCHISES, BUT I MOSTLY LEAVE THEM TO MY MANAGERS TO RUN.
MAN, IT'S GREAT TO SEE YOU, POP. I'VE MISSED YOU!
AND DON'T YOU BELIEVE WHAT HE SAYS ABOUT TAKING IT EASY, DOC. THE MAN'S RUNNING A DOZEN RESTAURANTS -- AND HEADS UP THE FLORIDA FRANCHISE ASSOCIATION!
GOOD FOR YOU, TERRY! US OLD FOLKS NEED TO STAY ACTIVE!
SPEAKING OF WHICH, I'VE GOT AN OFFICE FULL OF SICK PEOPLE. I CAN'T WAIT FOR DR. WALKER TO COME BACK TO WORK NEXT WEEK.
SEE YOU LATER, DOC.
SO WHAT BRINGS YOU NORTH, POP? CHECKING TO MAKE SURE I DIDN'T BURN THE JOINT DOWN?
OH, I THINK YOU CAN BE TRUSTED NOT TO DO ANY MAJOR DAMAGE TO THE CHOCKLIT SHOPPE NOW, JUGHEAD...
10

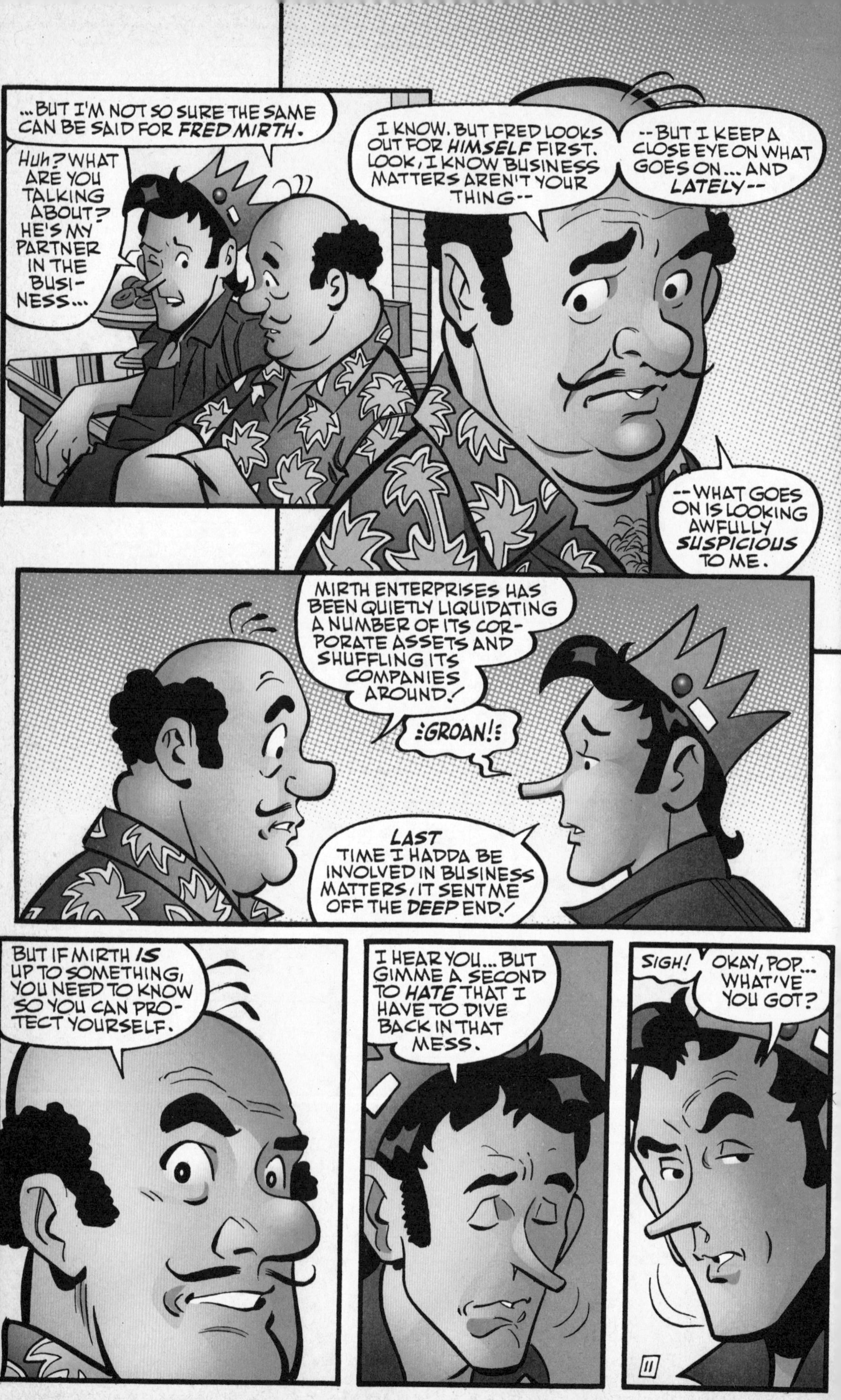
...BUT I'M NOT SO SURE THE SAME CAN BE SAID FOR FRED MIRTH.
Huh? WHAT ARE YOU TALKING ABOUT? HE'S MY PARTNER IN THE BUSINESS...
I KNOW. BUT FRED LOOKS OUT FOR HIMSELF FIRST. LOOK, I KNOW BUSINESS MATTERS AREN'T YOUR THING--
--BUT I KEEP A CLOSE EYE ON WHAT GOES ON... AND LATELY--
--WHAT GOES ON IS LOOKING AWFULLY SUSPICIOUS TO ME.
MIRTH ENTERPRISES HAS BEEN QUIETLY LIQUIDATING A NUMBER OF ITS CORPORATE ASSETS AND SHUFFLING ITS COMPANIES AROUND!
GROAN!
LAST TIME I HADDA BE INVOLVED IN BUSINESS MATTERS, IT SENT ME OFF THE DEEP END!
BUT IF MIRTH IS UP TO SOMETHING, YOU NEED TO KNOW SO YOU CAN PROTECT YOURSELF.
I HEAR YOU... BUT GIMME A SECOND TO HATE THAT I HAVE TO DIVE BACK IN THAT MESS.
SIGH!
OKAY, POP... WHAT'VE YOU GOT?
11

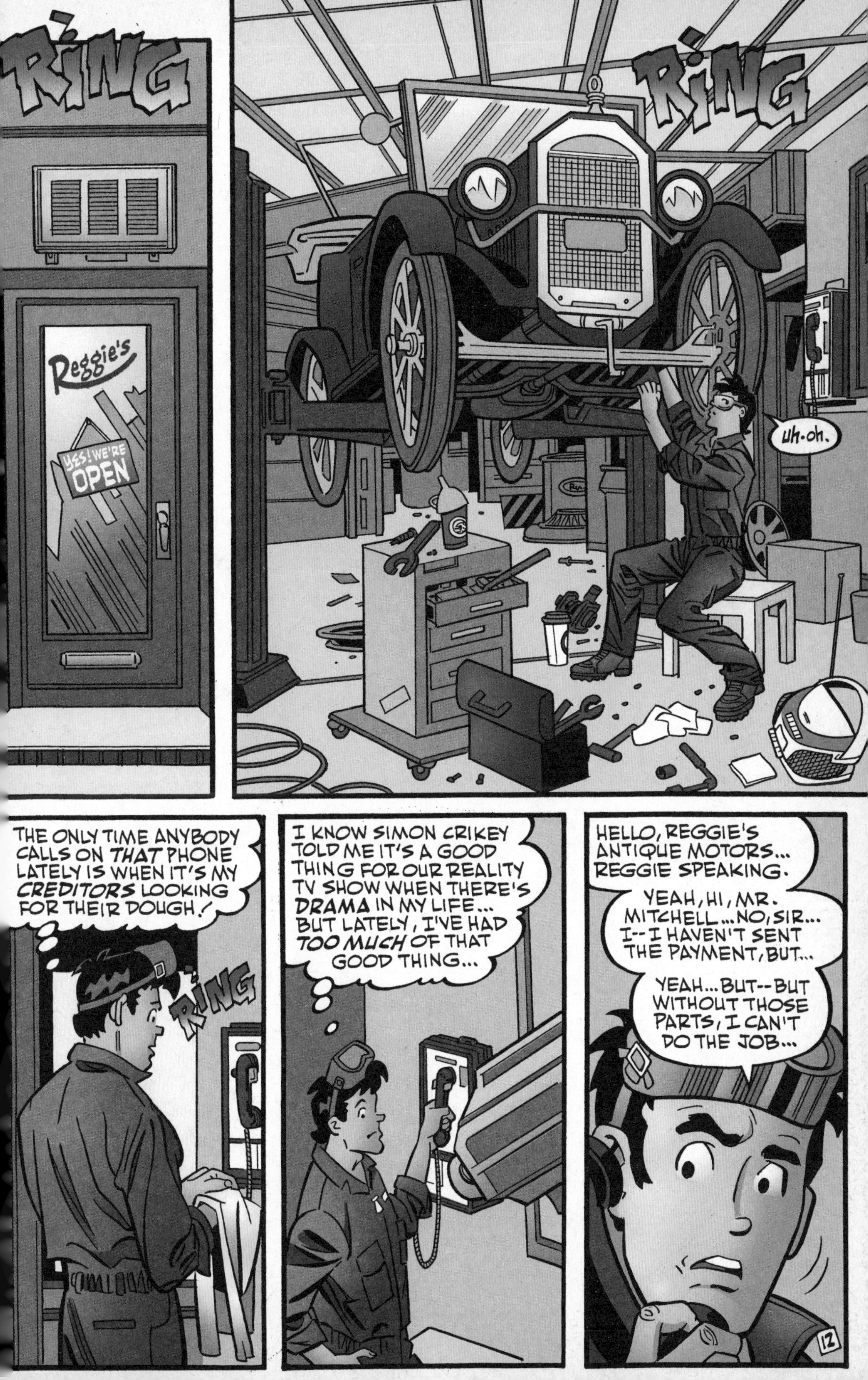
RING
Reggie's
YES! WE'RE OPEN
RING
UH-OH.
THE ONLY TIME ANYBODY CALLS ON THAT PHONE LATELY IS WHEN IT'S MY CREDITORS LOOKING FOR THEIR DOUGH!
RING
I KNOW SIMON CRIKEY TOLD ME IT'S A GOOD THING FOR OUR REALITY TV SHOW WHEN THERE'S DRAMA IN MY LIFE... BUT LATELY, I'VE HAD TOO MUCH OF THAT GOOD THING...
HELLO, REGGIE'S ANTIQUE MOTORS... REGGIE SPEAKING.
YEAH, HI, MR. MITCHELL... NO, SIR... I-- I HAVEN'T SENT THE PAYMENT, BUT...
YEAH... BUT-- BUT WITHOUT THOSE PARTS, I CAN'T DO THE JOB...

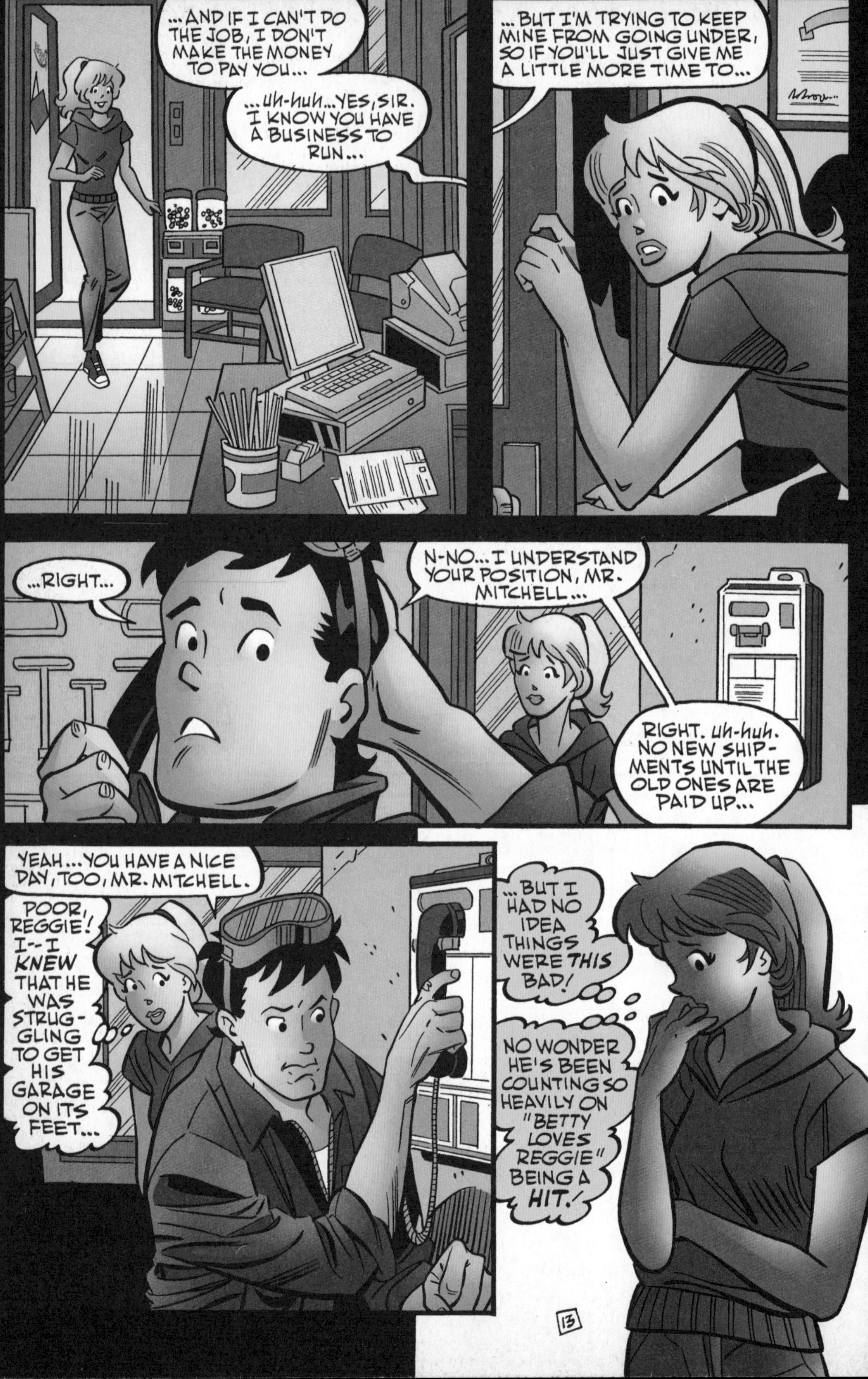

...AND IF I CAN'T DO THE JOB, I DON'T MAKE THE MONEY TO PAY YOU...
...uh-huh...YES, SIR. I KNOW YOU HAVE A BUSINESS TO RUN...
...BUT I'M TRYING TO KEEP MINE FROM GOING UNDER, SO IF YOU'LL JUST GIVE ME A LITTLE MORE TIME TO...
...RIGHT...
N-NO... I UNDERSTAND YOUR POSITION, MR. MITCHELL...
RIGHT. uh-huh. NO NEW SHIP-MENTS UNTIL THE OLD ONES ARE PAID UP...
YEAH... YOU HAVE A NICE DAY, TOO, MR. MITCHELL.
POOR, REGGIE! I--I KNEW THAT HE WAS STRUG-GLING TO GET HIS GARAGE ON ITS FEET...
...BUT I HAD NO IDEA THINGS WERE THIS BAD!
NO WONDER HE'S BEEN COUNTING SO HEAVILY ON "BETTY LOVES REGGIE" BEING A HIT!

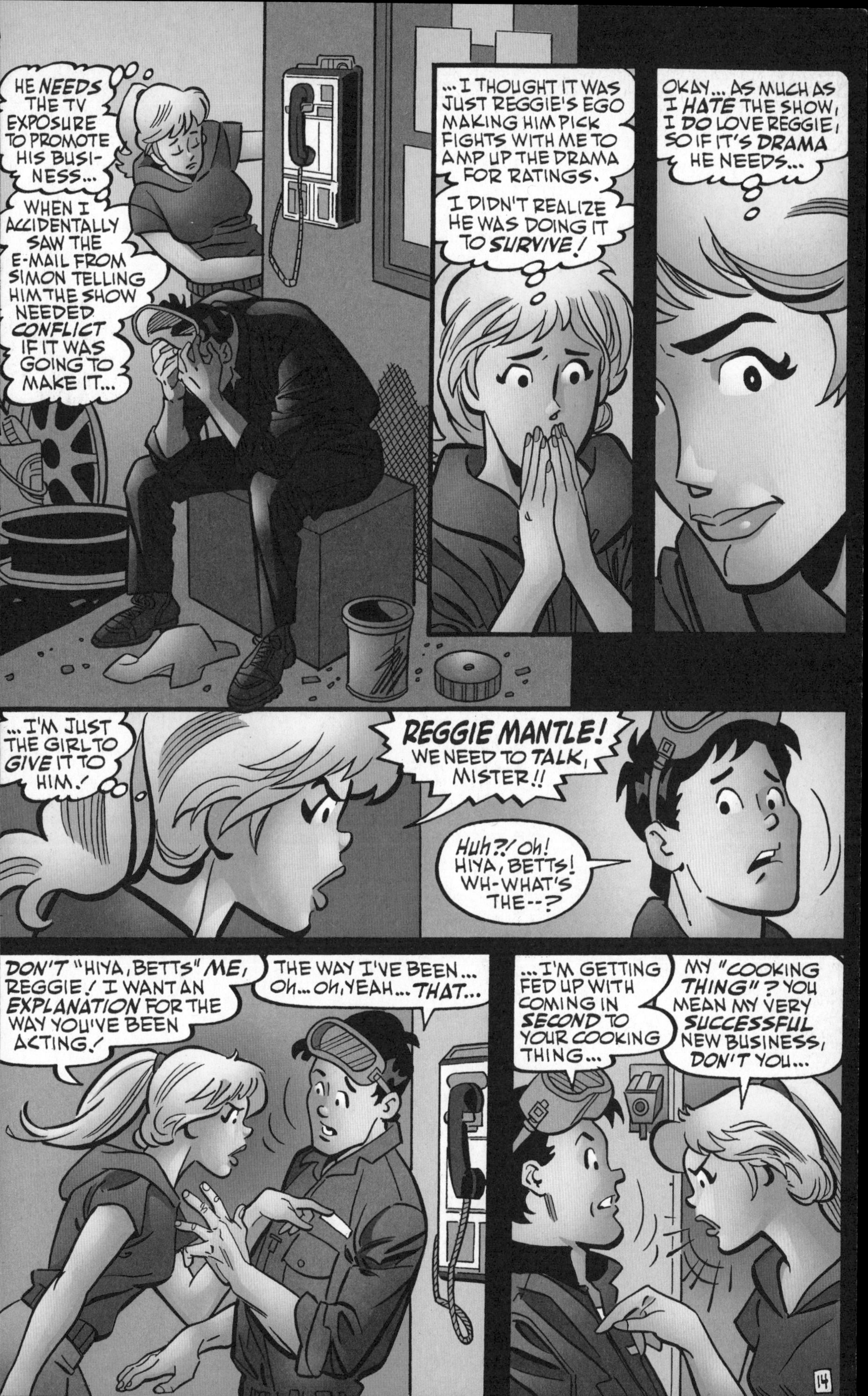
HE NEEDS THE TV EXPOSURE TO PROMOTE HIS BUSI-NESS...
WHEN I ACCIDENTALLY SAW THE E-MAIL FROM SIMON TELLING HIM THE SHOW NEEDED CONFLICT IF IT WAS GOING TO MAKE IT...
...I THOUGHT IT WAS JUST REGGIE'S EGO MAKING HIM PICK FIGHTS WITH ME TO AMP UP THE DRAMA FOR RATINGS.
I DIDN'T REALIZE HE WAS DOING IT TO SURVIVE!
OKAY... AS MUCH AS I HATE THE SHOW, I DO LOVE REGGIE, SO IF IT'S DRAMA HE NEEDS...
...I'M JUST THE GIRL TO GIVE IT TO HIM!
REGGIE MANTLE! WE NEED TO TALK, MISTER!!
HUH?! OH! HIYA, BETTS! WH-WHAT'S THE--?
DON'T "HIYA, BETTS" ME, REGGIE! I WANT AN EXPLANATION FOR THE WAY YOU'VE BEEN ACTING!
THE WAY I'VE BEEN... OH... OH, YEAH... THAT...
...I'M GETTING FED UP WITH COMING IN SECOND TO YOUR COOKING THING...
MY "COOKING THING"? YOU MEAN MY VERY SUCCESSFUL NEW BUSINESS, DON'T YOU...
14

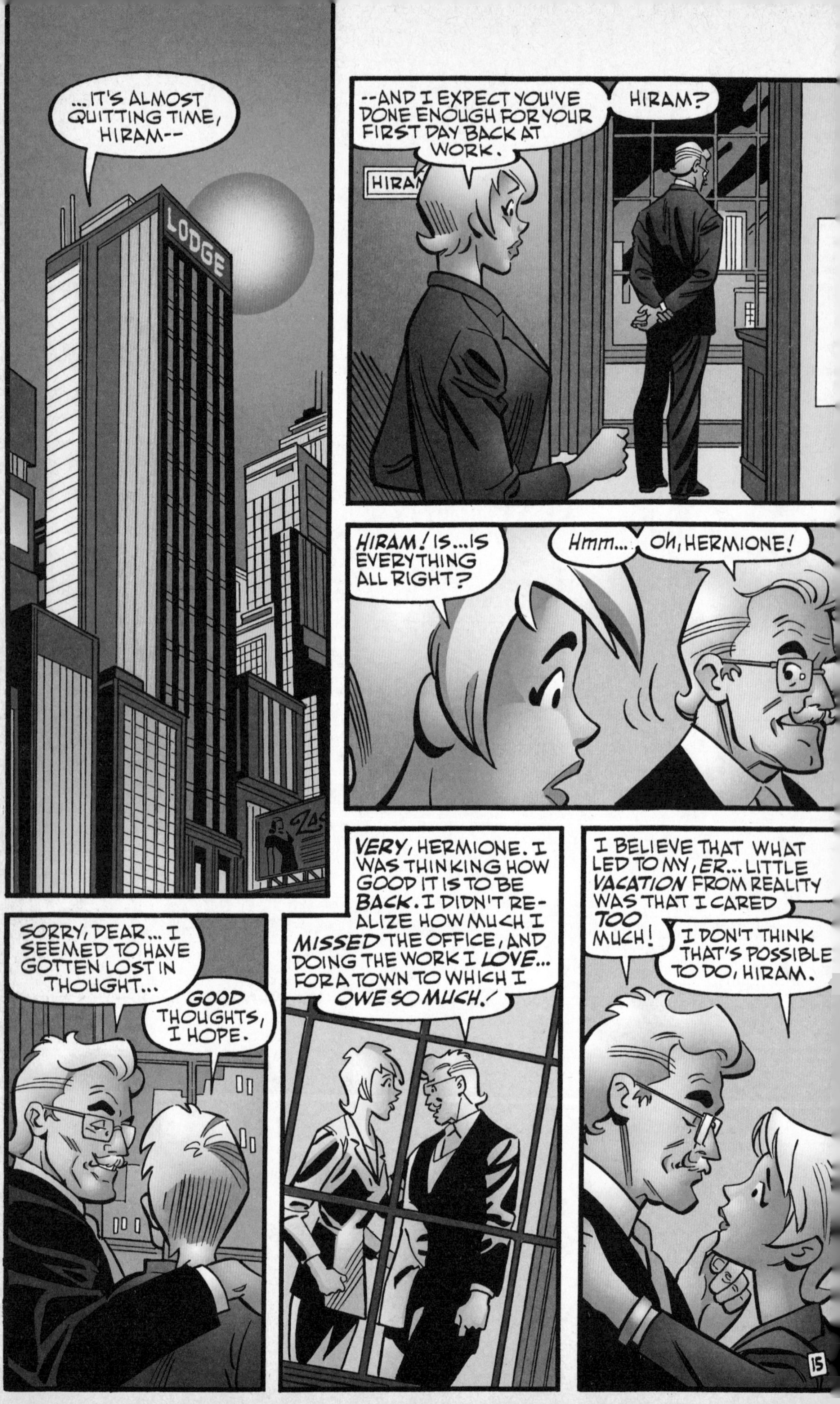
...IT'S ALMOST QUITTING TIME, HIRAM--
LODGE
--AND I EXPECT YOU'VE DONE ENOUGH FOR YOUR FIRST DAY BACK AT WORK.
HIRAM?
HIRAM! IS...IS EVERYTHING ALL RIGHT?
Hmm...
Oh, HERMIONE!
SORRY, DEAR... I SEEMED TO HAVE GOTTEN LOST IN THOUGHT...
GOOD THOUGHTS, I HOPE.
VERY, HERMIONE. I WAS THINKING HOW GOOD IT IS TO BE BACK. I DIDN'T REALIZE HOW MUCH I MISSED THE OFFICE, AND DOING THE WORK I LOVE... FOR A TOWN TO WHICH I OWE SO MUCH!
I BELIEVE THAT WHAT LED TO MY, ER... LITTLE VACATION FROM REALITY WAS THAT I CARED TOO MUCH!
I DON'T THINK THAT'S POSSIBLE TO DO, HIRAM.
15

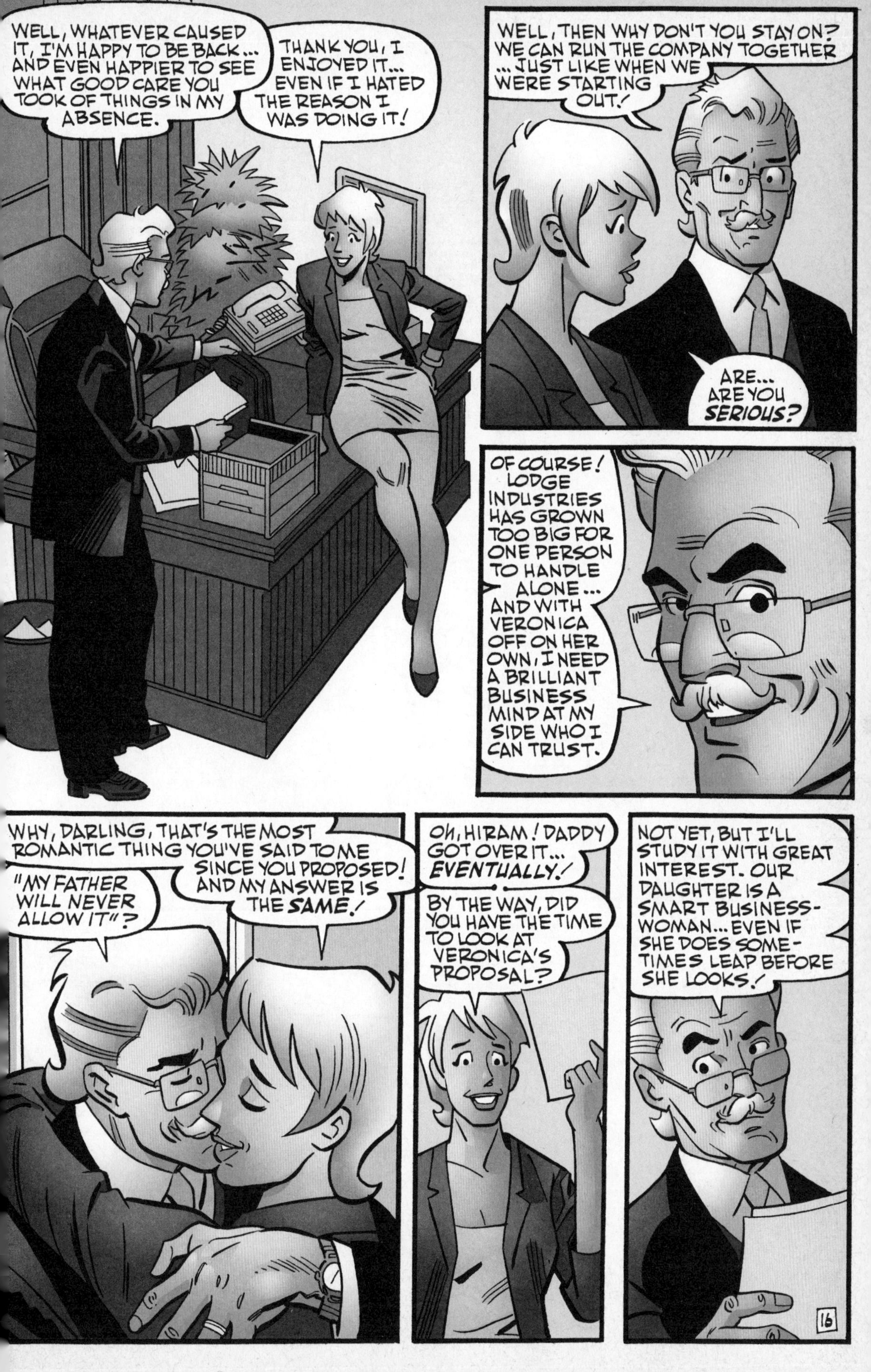
WELL, WHATEVER CAUSED IT, I'M HAPPY TO BE BACK... AND EVEN HAPPIER TO SEE WHAT GOOD CARE YOU TOOK OF THINGS IN MY ABSENCE.
THANK YOU, I ENJOYED IT... EVEN IF I HATED THE REASON I WAS DOING IT!
WELL, THEN WHY DON'T YOU STAY ON? WE CAN RUN THE COMPANY TOGETHER ...JUST LIKE WHEN WE WERE STARTING OUT!
ARE... ARE YOU SERIOUS?
OF COURSE! LODGE INDUSTRIES HAS GROWN TOO BIG FOR ONE PERSON TO HANDLE ALONE... AND WITH VERONICA OFF ON HER OWN, I NEED A BRILLIANT BUSINESS MIND AT MY SIDE WHO I CAN TRUST.
WHY, DARLING, THAT'S THE MOST ROMANTIC THING YOU'VE SAID TO ME SINCE YOU PROPOSED! AND MY ANSWER IS THE SAME!
"MY FATHER WILL NEVER ALLOW IT"?
OH, HIRAM! DADDY GOT OVER IT... EVENTUALLY!
BY THE WAY, DID YOU HAVE THE TIME TO LOOK AT VERONICA'S PROPOSAL?
NOT YET, BUT I'LL STUDY IT WITH GREAT INTEREST. OUR DAUGHTER IS A SMART BUSINESS-WOMAN... EVEN IF SHE DOES SOME-TIMES LEAP BEFORE SHE LOOKS!
16

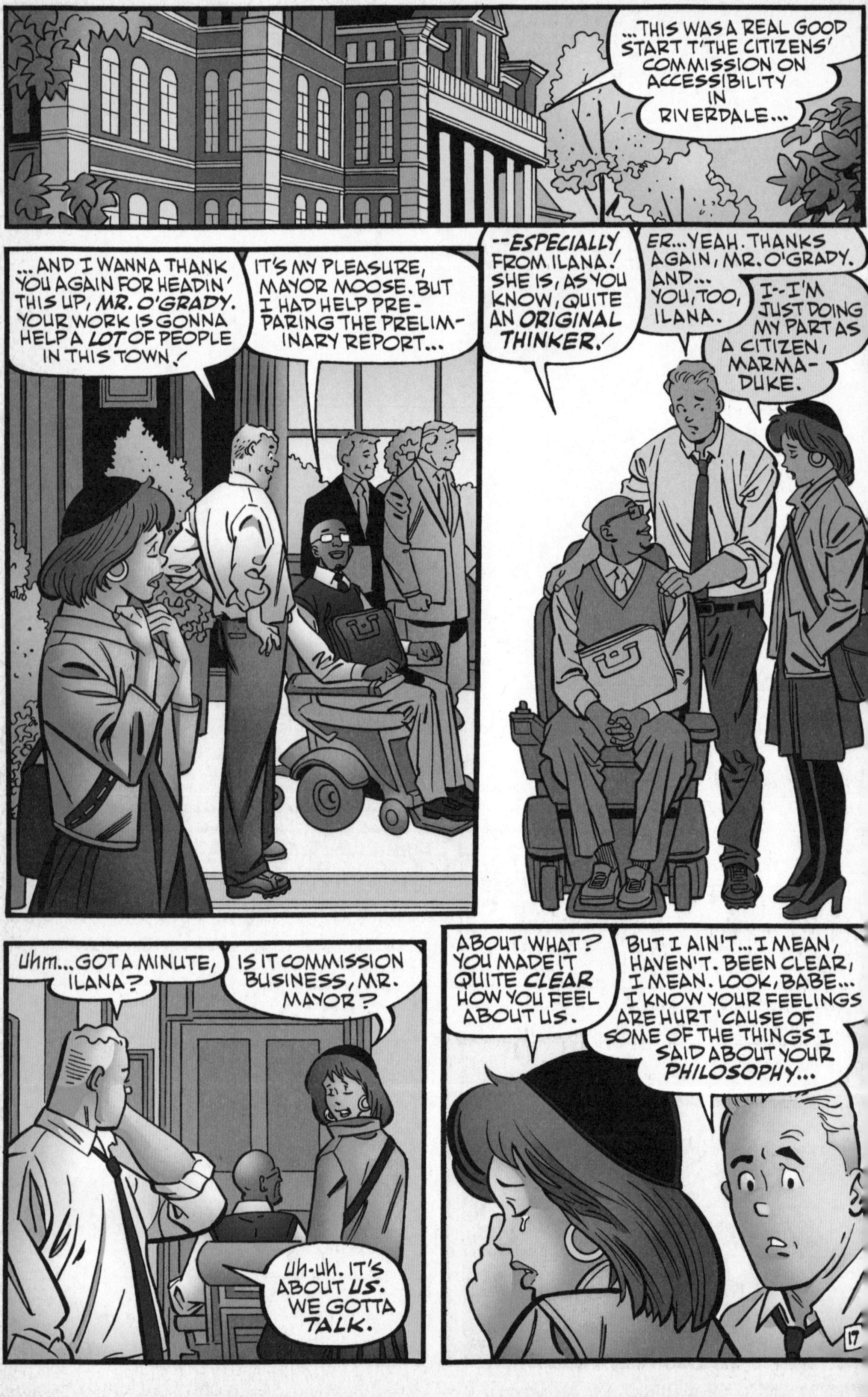
...THIS WAS A REAL GOOD START T'THE CITIZENS' COMMISSION ON ACCESSIBILITY IN RIVERDALE...
...AND I WANNA THANK YOU AGAIN FOR HEADIN' THIS UP, MR. O'GRADY. YOUR WORK IS GONNA HELP A LOT OF PEOPLE IN THIS TOWN!
IT'S MY PLEASURE, MAYOR MOOSE. BUT I HAD HELP PRE-PARING THE PRELIM-INARY REPORT...
--ESPECIALLY FROM ILANA! SHE IS, AS YOU KNOW, QUITE AN ORIGINAL THINKER!
ER...YEAH. THANKS AGAIN, MR. O'GRADY. AND... YOU, TOO, ILANA.
I--I'M JUST DOING MY PART AS A CITIZEN, MARMA-DUKE.
UHM...GOT A MINUTE, ILANA?
IS IT COMMISSION BUSINESS, MR. MAYOR?
UH-UH. IT'S ABOUT US. WE GOTTA TALK.
ABOUT WHAT? YOU MADE IT QUITE CLEAR HOW YOU FEEL ABOUT US.
BUT I AIN'T... I MEAN, HAVEN'T. BEEN CLEAR, I MEAN. LOOK, BABE... I KNOW YOUR FEELINGS ARE HURT 'CAUSE OF SOME OF THE THINGS I SAID ABOUT YOUR PHILOSOPHY...
17

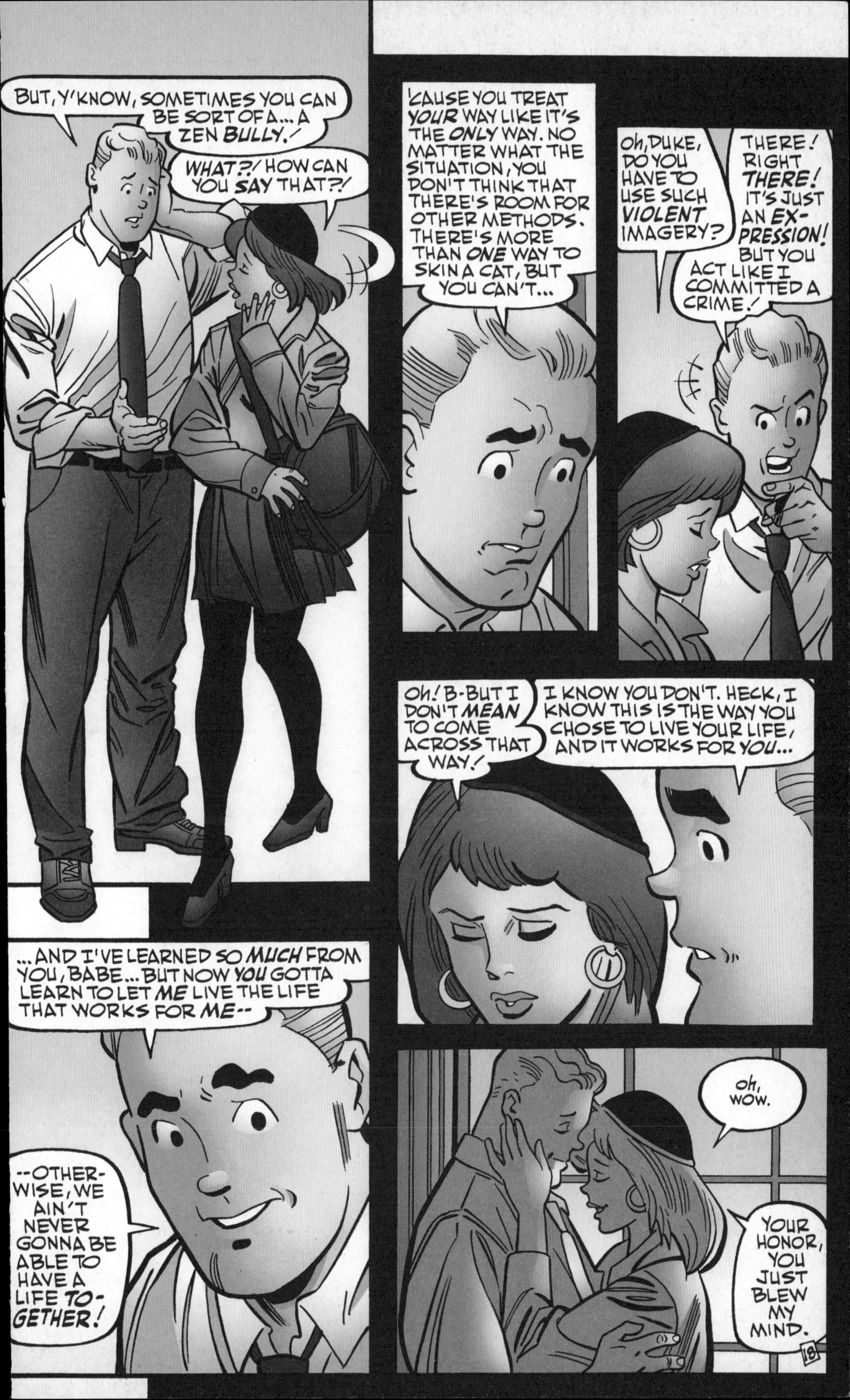

BUT, Y'KNOW, SOMETIMES YOU CAN BE SORT OF A... A ZEN BULLY!
WHAT?! HOW CAN YOU SAY THAT?!
'CAUSE YOU TREAT YOUR WAY LIKE IT'S THE ONLY WAY. NO MATTER WHAT THE SITUATION, YOU DON'T THINK THAT THERE'S ROOM FOR OTHER METHODS. THERE'S MORE THAN ONE WAY TO SKIN A CAT, BUT YOU CAN'T...
OH, DUKE, DO YOU HAVE TO USE SUCH VIOLENT IMAGERY?
THERE! RIGHT THERE! IT'S JUST AN EX-PRESSION! BUT YOU ACT LIKE I COMMITTED A CRIME!
OH! B-BUT I DON'T MEAN TO COME ACROSS THAT WAY!
I KNOW YOU DON'T. HECK, I KNOW THIS IS THE WAY YOU CHOSE TO LIVE YOUR LIFE, AND IT WORKS FOR YOU...
...AND I'VE LEARNED SO MUCH FROM YOU, BABE... BUT NOW YOU GOTTA LEARN TO LET ME LIVE THE LIFE THAT WORKS FOR ME--
--OTHER-WISE, WE AIN'T NEVER GONNA BE ABLE TO HAVE A LIFE TO-GETHER!
OH, WOW.
YOUR HONOR, YOU JUST BLEW MY MIND.
18

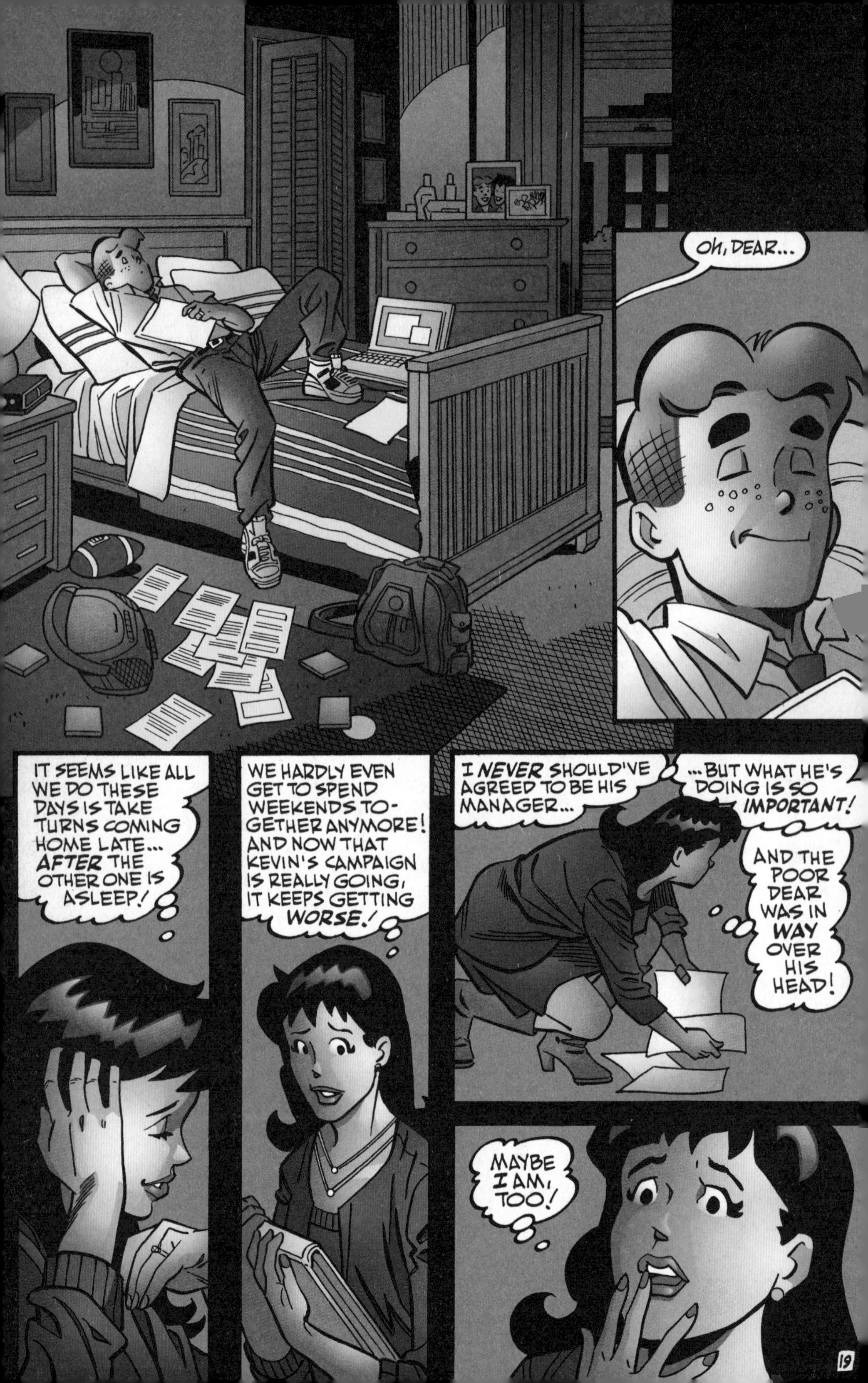
OH, DEAR...
IT SEEMS LIKE ALL WE DO THESE DAYS IS TAKE TURNS COMING HOME LATE... AFTER THE OTHER ONE IS ASLEEP!
WE HARDLY EVEN GET TO SPEND WEEKENDS TOGETHER ANYMORE! AND NOW THAT KEVIN'S CAMPAIGN IS REALLY GOING, IT KEEPS GETTING WORSE!
I NEVER SHOULD'VE AGREED TO BE HIS MANAGER...
...BUT WHAT HE'S DOING IS SO IMPORTANT!
AND THE POOR DEAR WAS IN WAY OVER HIS HEAD!
MAYBE I AM, TOO!

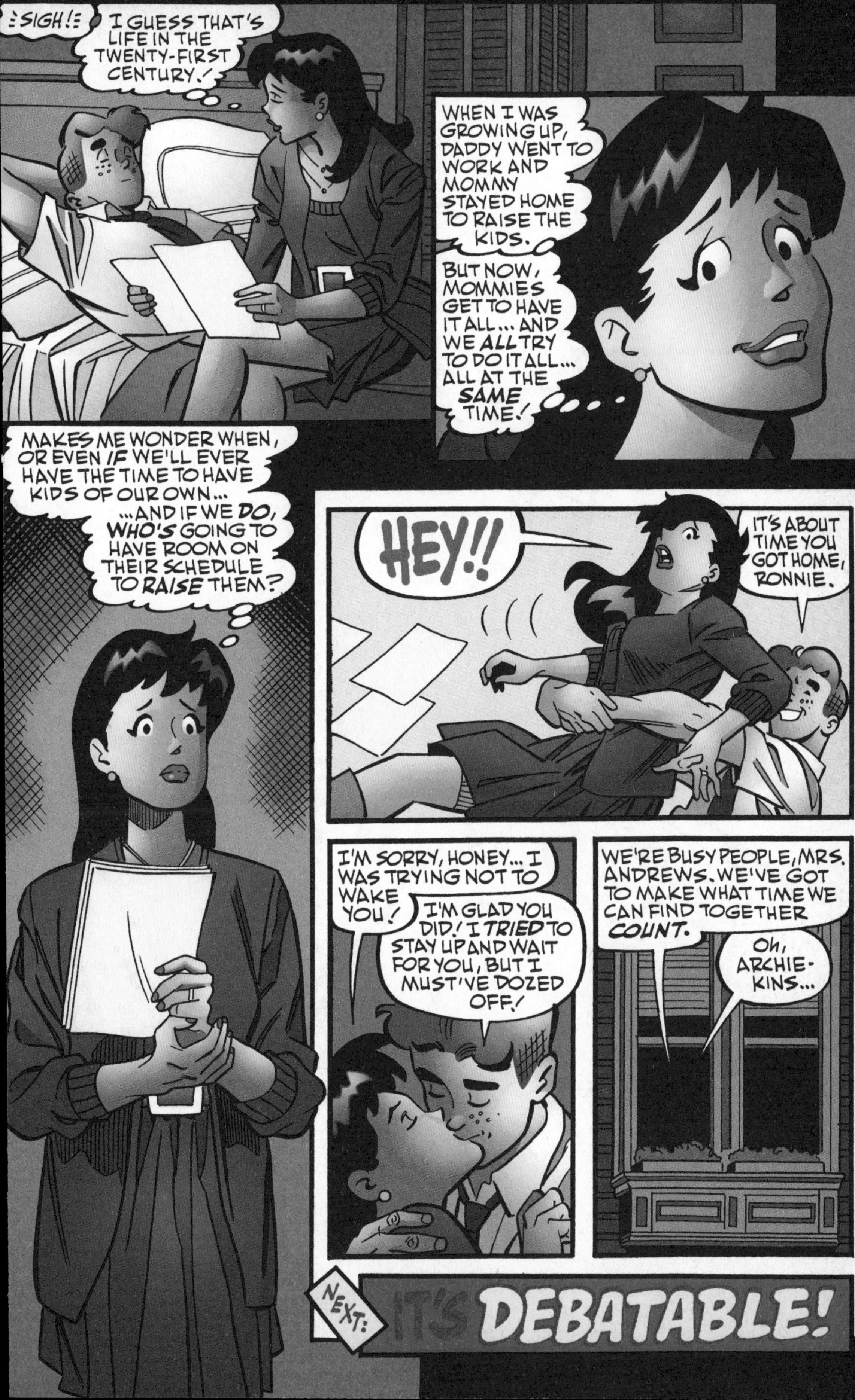
:SIGH!:
I GUESS THAT'S LIFE IN THE TWENTY-FIRST CENTURY!
WHEN I WAS GROWING UP, DADDY WENT TO WORK AND MOMMY STAYED HOME TO RAISE THE KIDS.
BUT NOW, MOMMIES GET TO HAVE IT ALL... AND WE ALL TRY TO DO IT ALL... ALL AT THE SAME TIME!
MAKES ME WONDER WHEN, OR EVEN IF WE'LL EVER HAVE THE TIME TO HAVE KIDS OF OUR OWN...
...AND IF WE DO, WHO'S GOING TO HAVE ROOM ON THEIR SCHEDULE TO RAISE THEM?
HEY!!
IT'S ABOUT TIME YOU GOT HOME, RONNIE.
I'M SORRY, HONEY... I WAS TRYING NOT TO WAKE YOU!
I'M GLAD YOU DID! I TRIED TO STAY UP AND WAIT FOR YOU, BUT I MUST'VE DOZED OFF!
WE'RE BUSY PEOPLE, MRS. ANDREWS. WE'VE GOT TO MAKE WHAT TIME WE CAN FIND TOGETHER COUNT.
Oh, ARCHIE-KINS...
NEXT: IT'S DEBATABLE!

"AH, *GERALDINE*. OUR TIME TOGETHER WAS SO *SHORT*..."

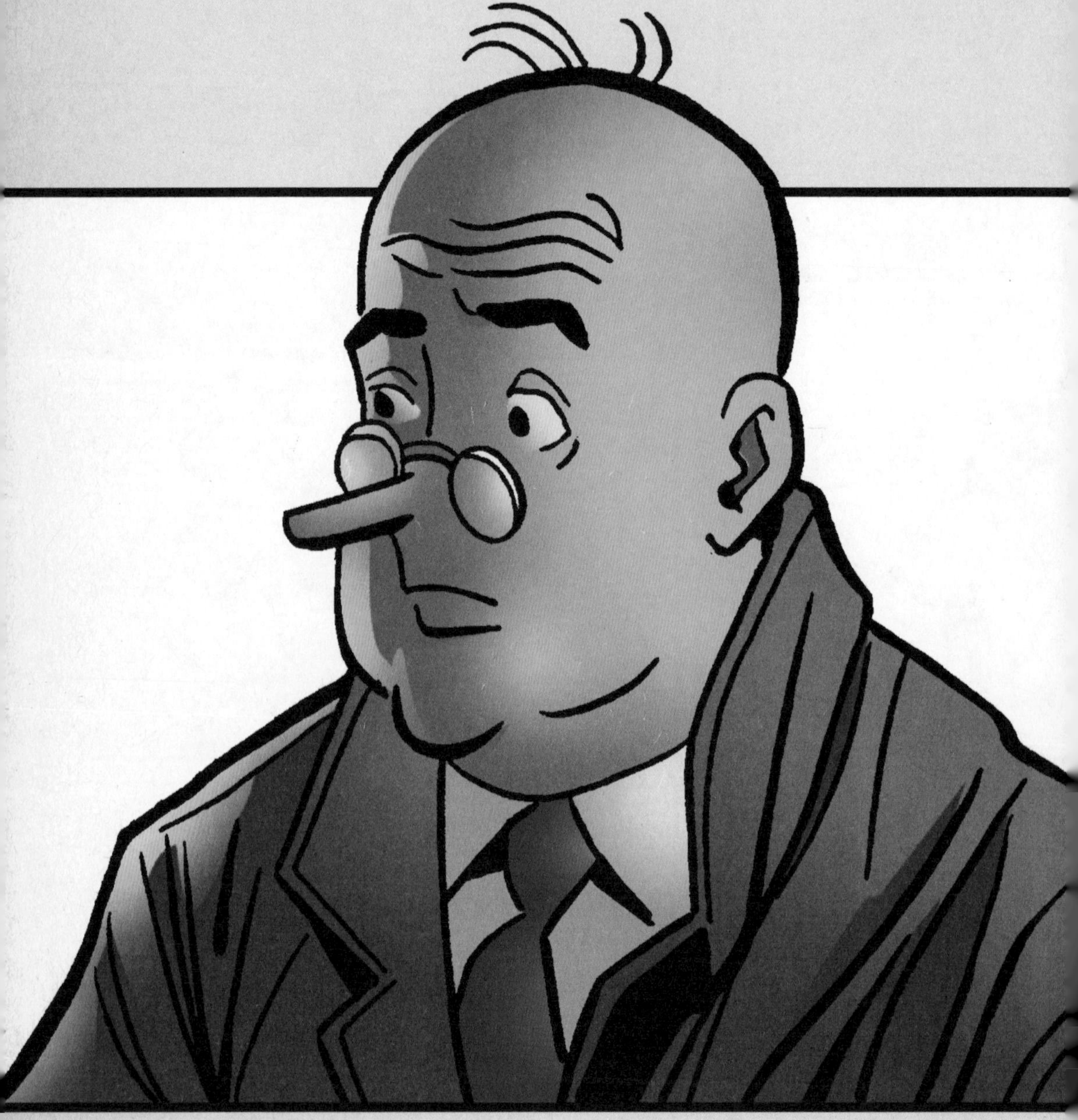

"...BUT SO ***RIGHT!***"

-WALDO WEATHERBEE

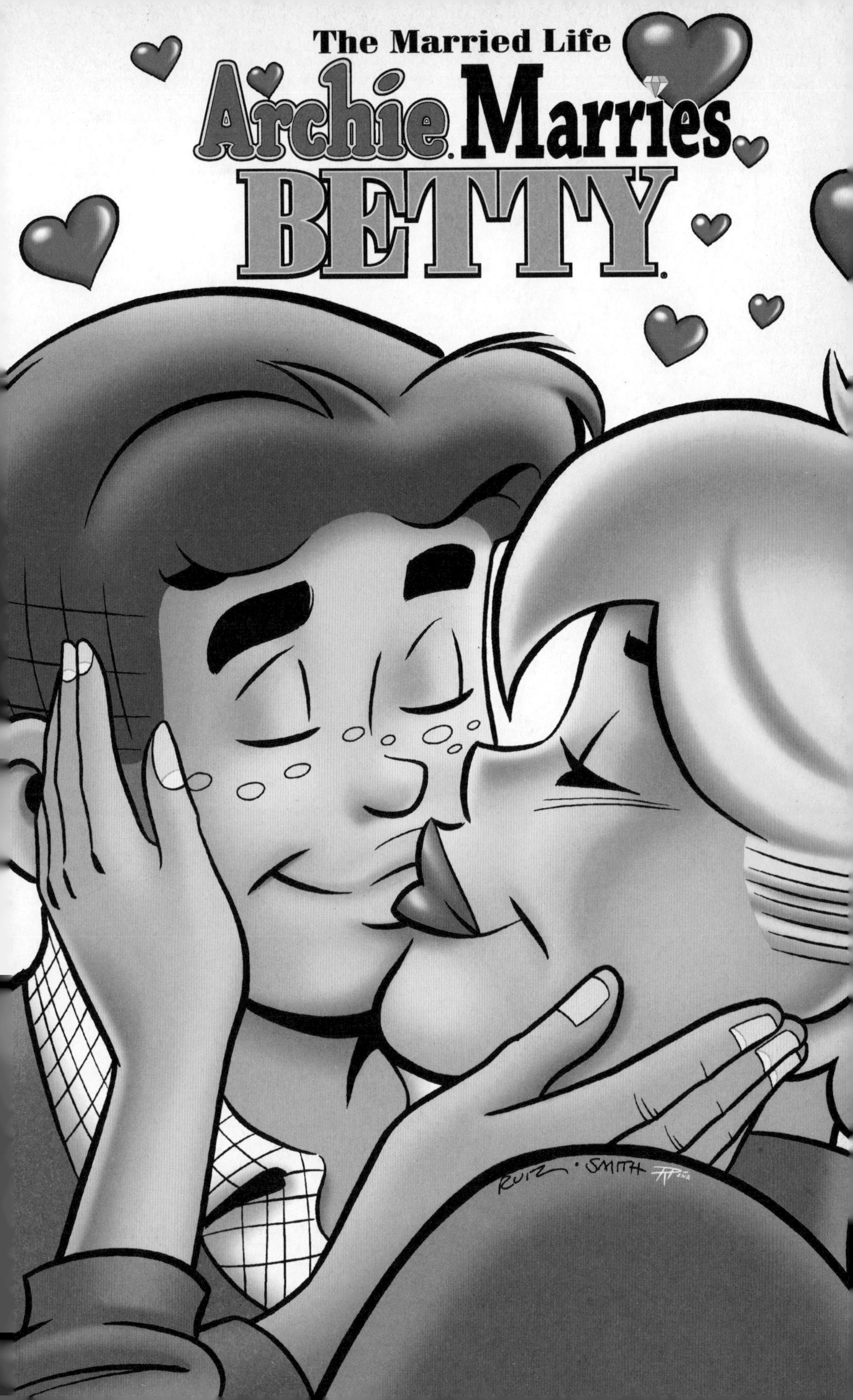
The Married Life
Archie Marries BETTY
RUIZ · SMITH

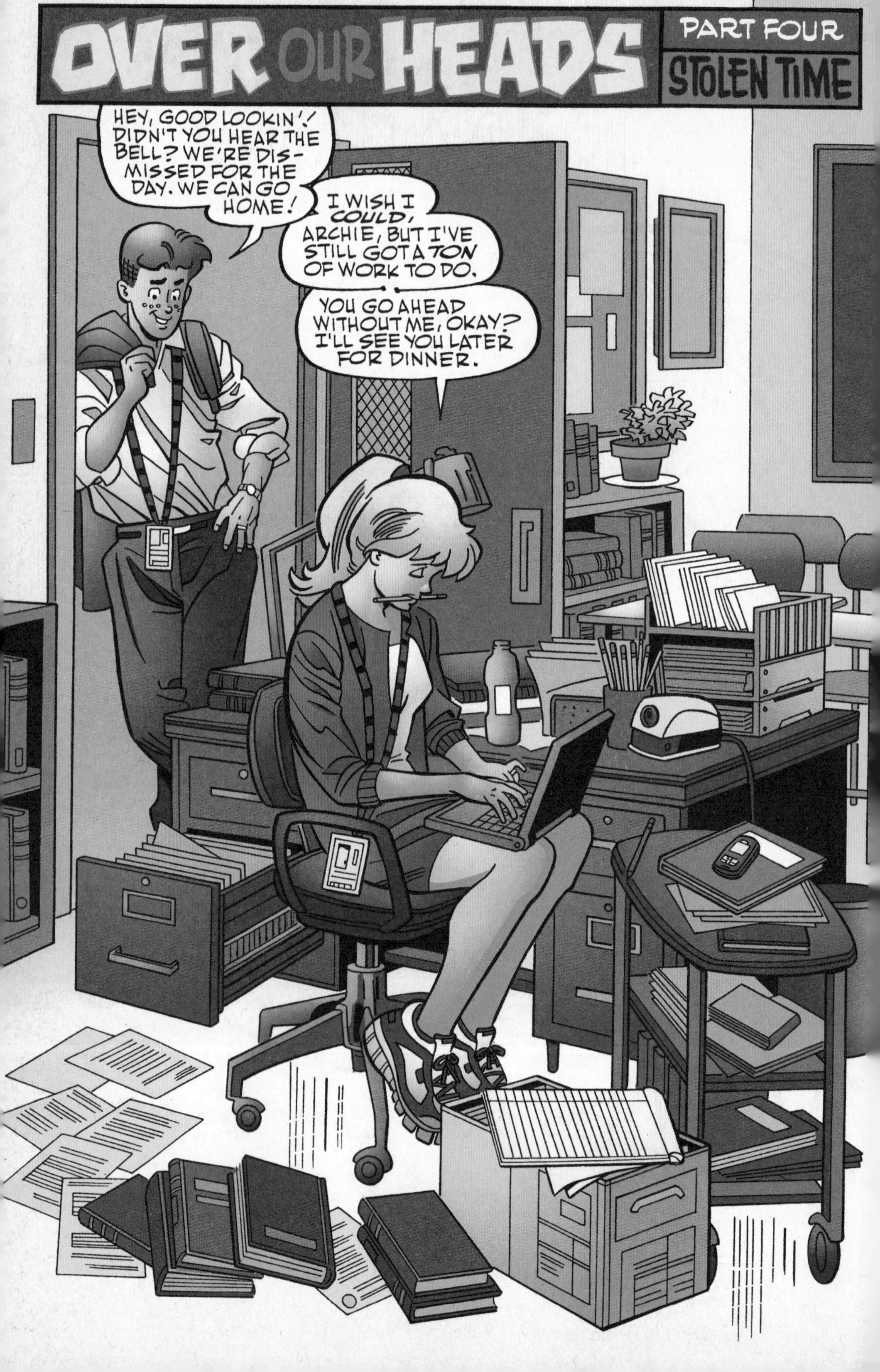
OVER OUR HEADS
PART FOUR
STOLEN TIME
HEY, GOOD LOOKIN'! DIDN'T YOU HEAR THE BELL? WE'RE DISMISSED FOR THE DAY. WE CAN GO HOME!
I WISH I COULD, ARCHIE, BUT I'VE STILL GOT A TON OF WORK TO DO.
YOU GO AHEAD WITHOUT ME, OKAY? I'LL SEE YOU LATER FOR DINNER.

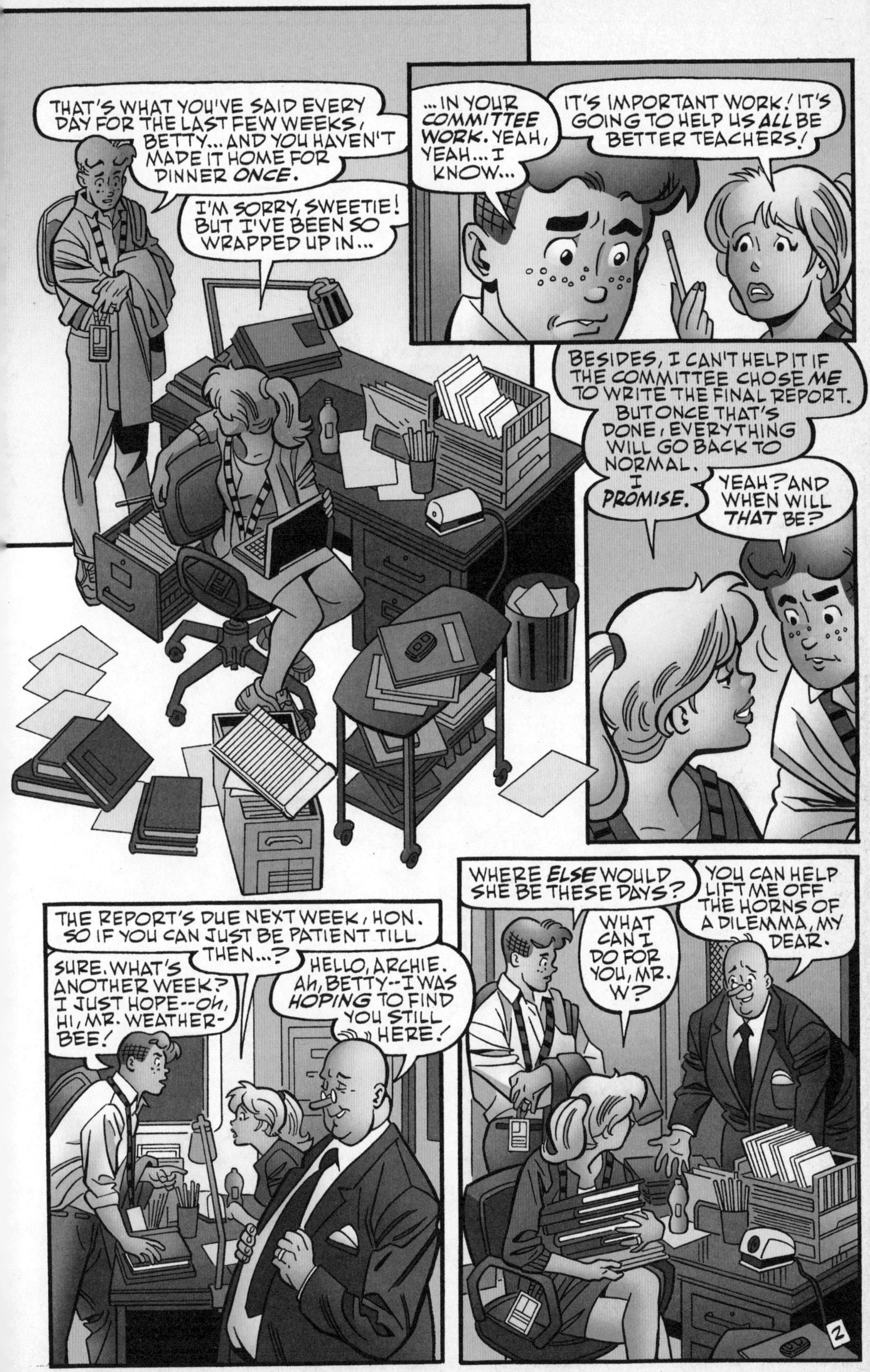
THAT'S WHAT YOU'VE SAID EVERY DAY FOR THE LAST FEW WEEKS, BETTY... AND YOU HAVEN'T MADE IT HOME FOR DINNER ONCE.
I'M SORRY, SWEETIE! BUT I'VE BEEN SO WRAPPED UP IN...
...IN YOUR COMMITTEE WORK. YEAH, YEAH... I KNOW...
IT'S IMPORTANT WORK! IT'S GOING TO HELP US ALL BE BETTER TEACHERS!
BESIDES, I CAN'T HELP IT IF THE COMMITTEE CHOSE ME TO WRITE THE FINAL REPORT. BUT ONCE THAT'S DONE, EVERYTHING WILL GO BACK TO NORMAL. I PROMISE.
YEAH? AND WHEN WILL THAT BE?
THE REPORT'S DUE NEXT WEEK, HON. SO IF YOU CAN JUST BE PATIENT TILL THEN...?
SURE. WHAT'S ANOTHER WEEK? I JUST HOPE--OH, HI, MR. WEATHERBEE!
HELLO, ARCHIE. AH, BETTY--I WAS HOPING TO FIND YOU STILL HERE!
WHERE ELSE WOULD SHE BE THESE DAYS?
WHAT CAN I DO FOR YOU, MR. W?
YOU CAN HELP LIFT ME OFF THE HORNS OF A DILEMMA, MY DEAR.
2

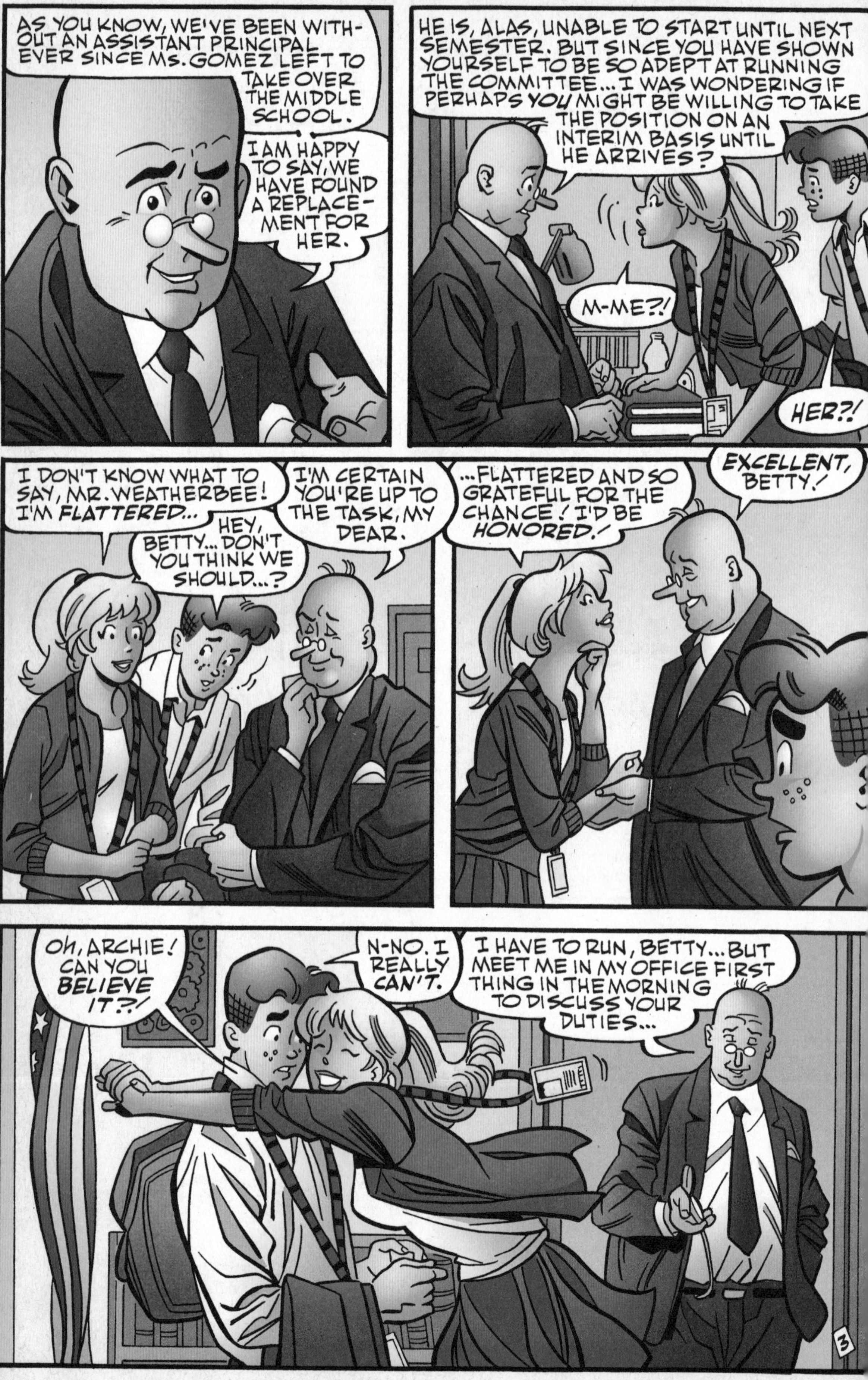
AS YOU KNOW, WE'VE BEEN WITHOUT AN ASSISTANT PRINCIPAL EVER SINCE MS. GOMEZ LEFT TO TAKE OVER THE MIDDLE SCHOOL.
I AM HAPPY TO SAY, WE HAVE FOUND A REPLACEMENT FOR HER.
HE IS, ALAS, UNABLE TO START UNTIL NEXT SEMESTER. BUT SINCE YOU HAVE SHOWN YOURSELF TO BE SO ADEPT AT RUNNING THE COMMITTEE... I WAS WONDERING IF PERHAPS YOU MIGHT BE WILLING TO TAKE THE POSITION ON AN INTERIM BASIS UNTIL HE ARRIVES?
M-ME?!
HER?!
I DON'T KNOW WHAT TO SAY, MR. WEATHERBEE! I'M FLATTERED...
HEY, BETTY... DON'T YOU THINK WE SHOULD...?
I'M CERTAIN YOU'RE UP TO THE TASK, MY DEAR.
...FLATTERED AND SO GRATEFUL FOR THE CHANCE! I'D BE HONORED!
EXCELLENT, BETTY!
Oh, ARCHIE! CAN YOU BELIEVE IT?!
N-NO. I REALLY CAN'T.
I HAVE TO RUN, BETTY... BUT MEET ME IN MY OFFICE FIRST THING IN THE MORNING TO DISCUSS YOUR DUTIES...

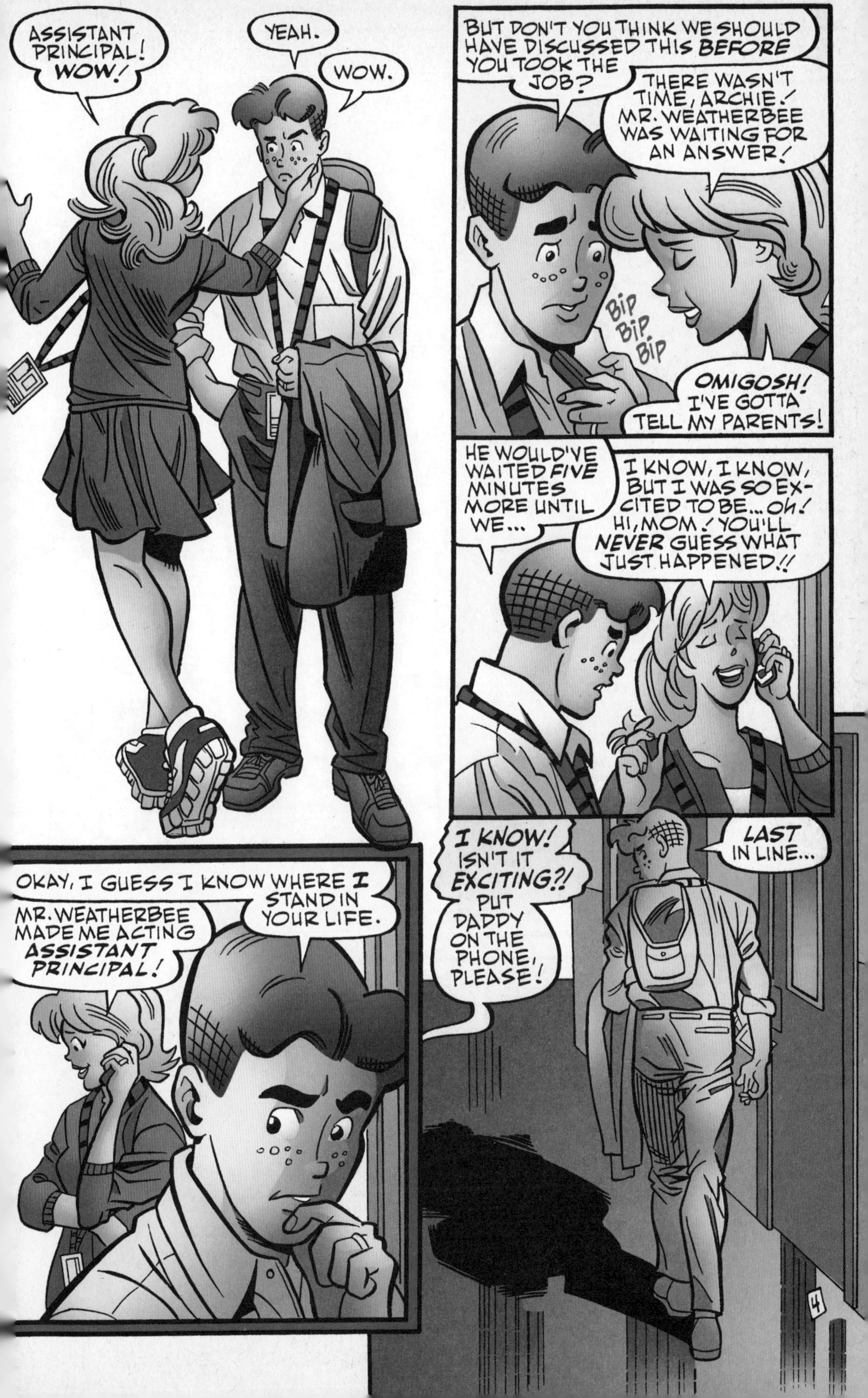
ASSISTANT PRINCIPAL! WOW!
YEAH.
WOW.
BUT DON'T YOU THINK WE SHOULD HAVE DISCUSSED THIS BEFORE YOU TOOK THE JOB?
THERE WASN'T TIME, ARCHIE! MR. WEATHERBEE WAS WAITING FOR AN ANSWER!
BIP BIP BIP
OMIGOSH! I'VE GOTTA TELL MY PARENTS!
HE WOULD'VE WAITED FIVE MINUTES MORE UNTIL WE...
I KNOW, I KNOW, BUT I WAS SO EXCITED TO BE... OH! HI, MOM! YOU'LL NEVER GUESS WHAT JUST HAPPENED!!
MR. WEATHERBEE MADE ME ACTING ASSISTANT PRINCIPAL!
OKAY, I GUESS I KNOW WHERE I STAND IN YOUR LIFE.
I KNOW! ISN'T IT EXCITING?! PUT DADDY ON THE PHONE, PLEASE!
LAST IN LINE...
4

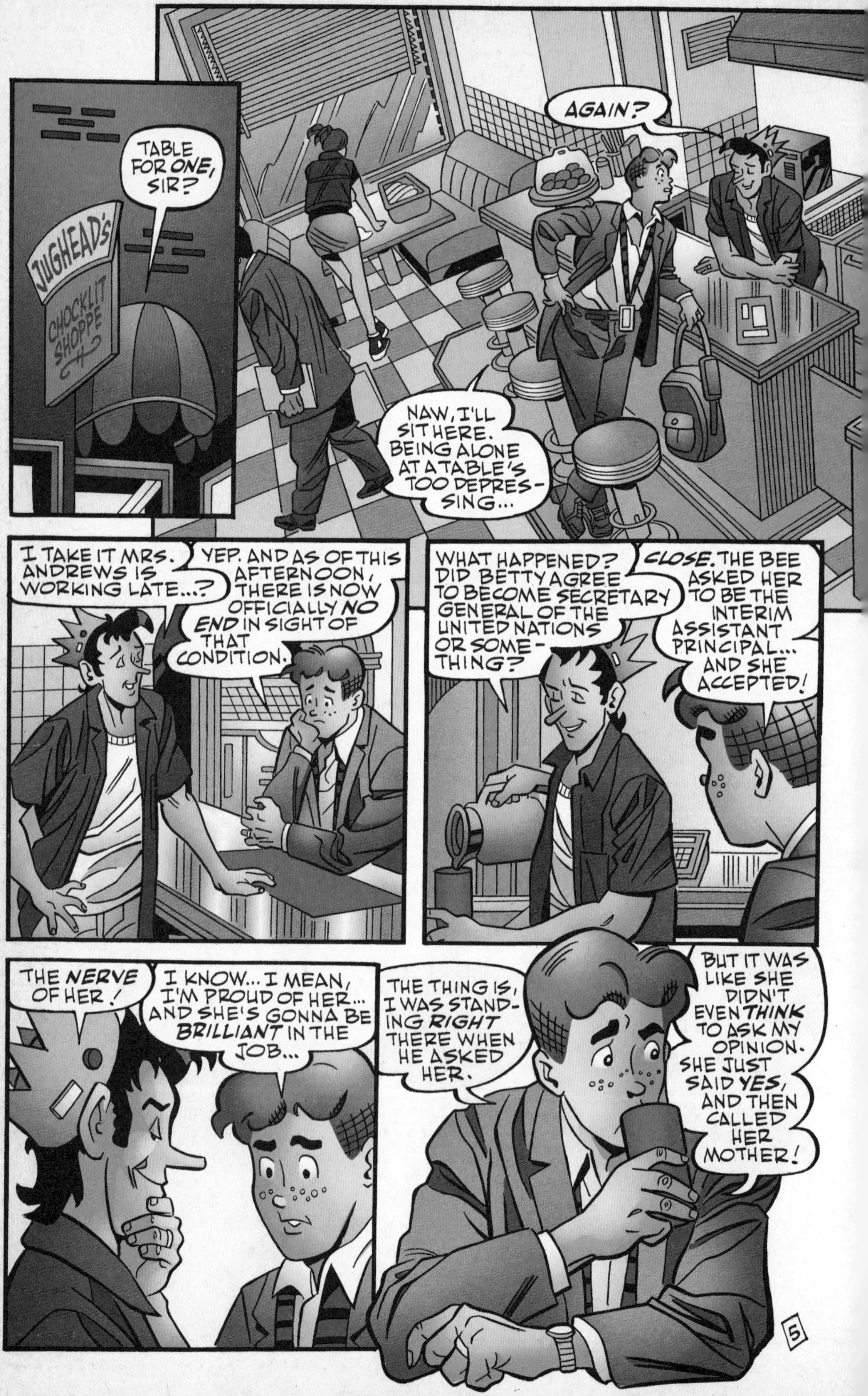
TABLE FOR ONE, SIR?
JUGHEAD'S
CHOCKLIT SHOPPE
AGAIN?
NAW, I'LL SIT HERE. BEING ALONE AT A TABLE'S TOO DEPRES-SING...
I TAKE IT MRS. ANDREWS IS WORKING LATE...?
YEP. AND AS OF THIS AFTERNOON, THERE IS NOW OFFICIALLY NO END IN SIGHT OF THAT CONDITION.
WHAT HAPPENED? DID BETTY AGREE TO BECOME SECRETARY GENERAL OF THE UNITED NATIONS OR SOME-THING?
CLOSE. THE BEE ASKED HER TO BE THE INTERIM ASSISTANT PRINCIPAL... AND SHE ACCEPTED!
THE NERVE OF HER!
I KNOW... I MEAN, I'M PROUD OF HER... AND SHE'S GONNA BE BRILLIANT IN THE JOB...
THE THING IS, I WAS STAND-ING RIGHT THERE WHEN HE ASKED HER.
BUT IT WAS LIKE SHE DIDN'T EVEN THINK TO ASK MY OPINION. SHE JUST SAID YES, AND THEN CALLED HER MOTHER!
5

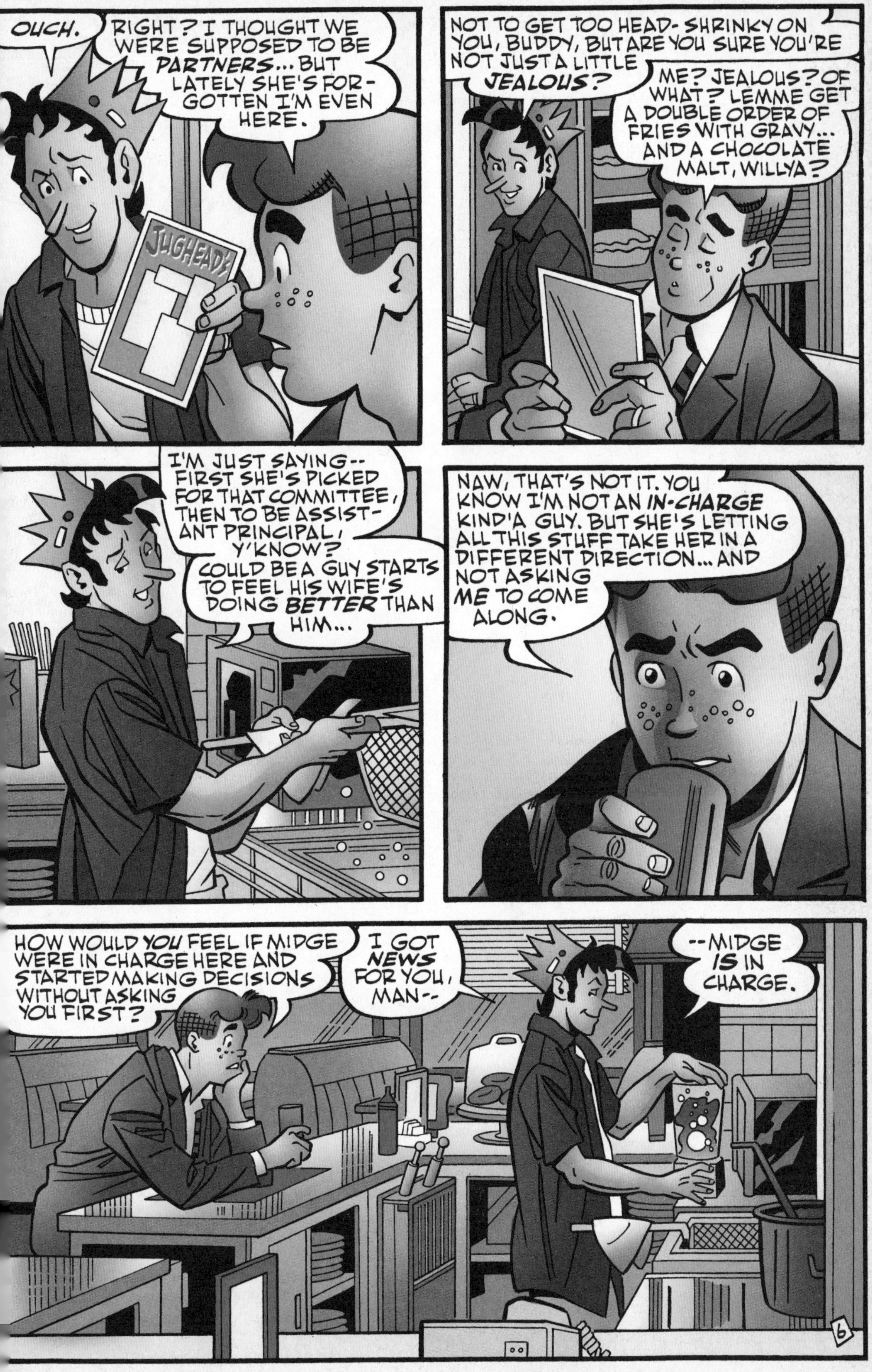
OUCH.
RIGHT? I THOUGHT WE WERE SUPPOSED TO BE PARTNERS... BUT LATELY SHE'S FORGOTTEN I'M EVEN HERE.
JUGHEAD'S
NOT TO GET TOO HEAD-SHRINKY ON YOU, BUDDY, BUT ARE YOU SURE YOU'RE NOT JUST A LITTLE JEALOUS?
ME? JEALOUS? OF WHAT? LEMME GET A DOUBLE ORDER OF FRIES WITH GRAVY... AND A CHOCOLATE MALT, WILLYA?
I'M JUST SAYING-- FIRST SHE'S PICKED FOR THAT COMMITTEE, THEN TO BE ASSISTANT PRINCIPAL, Y'KNOW?
COULD BE A GUY STARTS TO FEEL HIS WIFE'S DOING BETTER THAN HIM...
NAW, THAT'S NOT IT. YOU KNOW I'M NOT AN IN-CHARGE KIND'A GUY. BUT SHE'S LETTING ALL THIS STUFF TAKE HER IN A DIFFERENT DIRECTION... AND NOT ASKING ME TO COME ALONG.
HOW WOULD YOU FEEL IF MIDGE WERE IN CHARGE HERE AND STARTED MAKING DECISIONS WITHOUT ASKING YOU FIRST?
I GOT NEWS FOR YOU, MAN--
--MIDGE IS IN CHARGE.
6

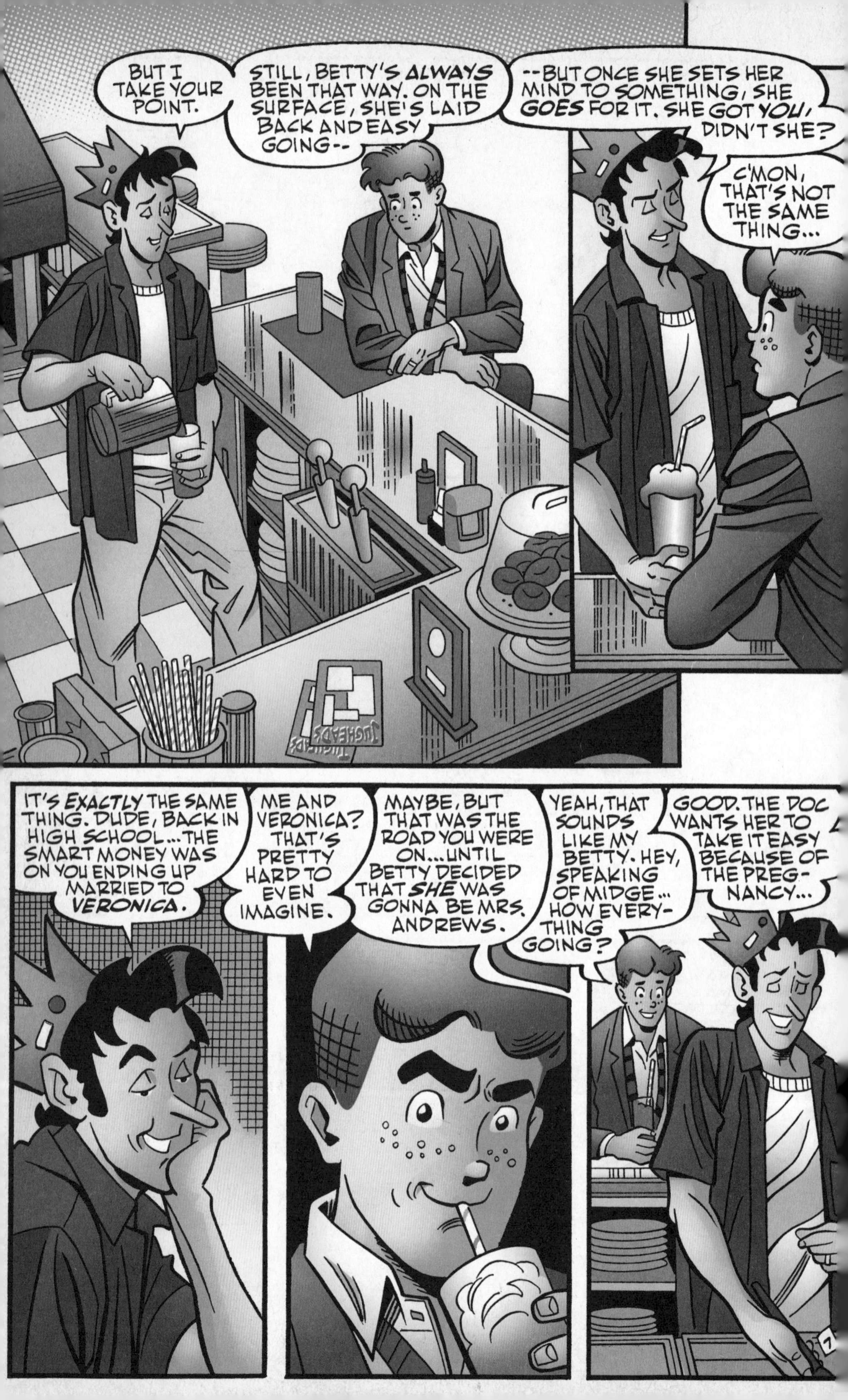
BUT I TAKE YOUR POINT.
STILL, BETTY'S ALWAYS BEEN THAT WAY. ON THE SURFACE, SHE'S LAID BACK AND EASY GOING--
--BUT ONCE SHE SETS HER MIND TO SOMETHING, SHE GOES FOR IT. SHE GOT YOU, DIDN'T SHE?
C'MON, THAT'S NOT THE SAME THING...
IT'S EXACTLY THE SAME THING. DUDE, BACK IN HIGH SCHOOL... THE SMART MONEY WAS ON YOU ENDING UP MARRIED TO VERONICA.
ME AND VERONICA? THAT'S PRETTY HARD TO EVEN IMAGINE.
MAYBE, BUT THAT WAS THE ROAD YOU WERE ON... UNTIL BETTY DECIDED THAT SHE WAS GONNA BE MRS. ANDREWS.
YEAH, THAT SOUNDS LIKE MY BETTY. HEY, SPEAKING OF MIDGE... HOW EVERY-THING GOING?
GOOD. THE DOC WANTS HER TO TAKE IT EASY BECAUSE OF THE PREG-NANCY...
7

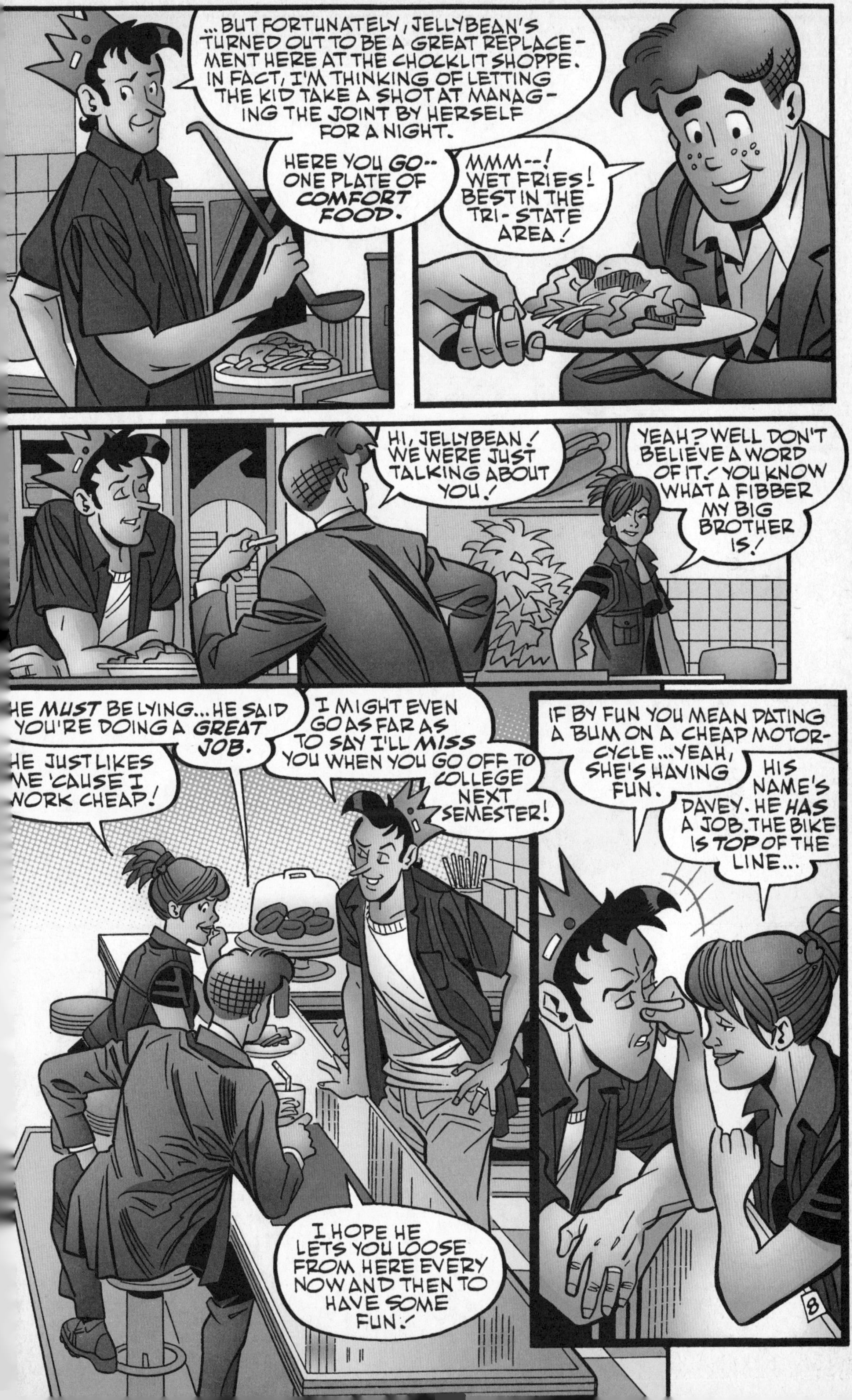
...BUT FORTUNATELY, JELLYBEAN'S TURNED OUT TO BE A GREAT REPLACEMENT HERE AT THE CHOCKLIT SHOPPE. IN FACT, I'M THINKING OF LETTING THE KID TAKE A SHOT AT MANAGING THE JOINT BY HERSELF FOR A NIGHT.
HERE YOU GO-- ONE PLATE OF COMFORT FOOD.
MMM--! WET FRIES! BEST IN THE TRI-STATE AREA!
HI, JELLYBEAN! WE WERE JUST TALKING ABOUT YOU!
YEAH? WELL DON'T BELIEVE A WORD OF IT! YOU KNOW WHAT A FIBBER MY BIG BROTHER IS!
HE MUST BE LYING... HE SAID YOU'RE DOING A GREAT JOB.
HE JUST LIKES ME 'CAUSE I WORK CHEAP!
I MIGHT EVEN GO AS FAR AS TO SAY I'LL MISS YOU WHEN YOU GO OFF TO COLLEGE NEXT SEMESTER!
I HOPE HE LETS YOU LOOSE FROM HERE EVERY NOW AND THEN TO HAVE SOME FUN!
IF BY FUN YOU MEAN DATING A BUM ON A CHEAP MOTORCYCLE...YEAH, SHE'S HAVING FUN.
HIS NAME'S DAVEY. HE HAS A JOB. THE BIKE IS TOP OF THE LINE...
8

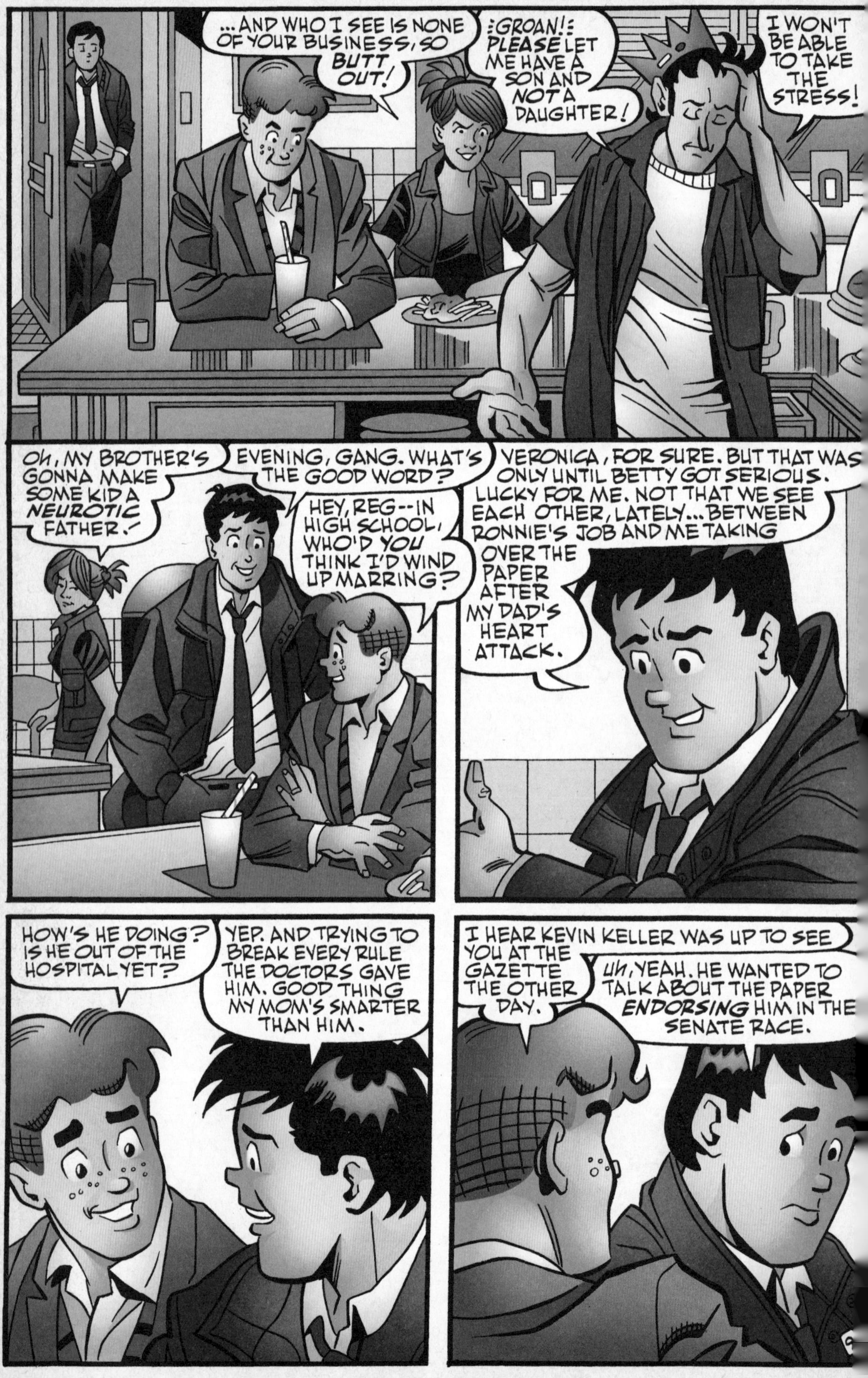
...AND WHO I SEE IS NONE OF YOUR BUSINESS, SO BUTT OUT!
:GROAN!: PLEASE LET ME HAVE A SON AND NOT A DAUGHTER!
I WON'T BE ABLE TO TAKE THE STRESS!
OH, MY BROTHER'S GONNA MAKE SOME KID A NEUROTIC FATHER.
EVENING, GANG. WHAT'S THE GOOD WORD?
HEY, REG--IN HIGH SCHOOL, WHO'D YOU THINK I'D WIND UP MARRING?
VERONICA, FOR SURE. BUT THAT WAS ONLY UNTIL BETTY GOT SERIOUS. LUCKY FOR ME. NOT THAT WE SEE EACH OTHER, LATELY... BETWEEN RONNIE'S JOB AND ME TAKING OVER THE PAPER AFTER MY DAD'S HEART ATTACK.
HOW'S HE DOING? IS HE OUT OF THE HOSPITAL YET?
YEP. AND TRYING TO BREAK EVERY RULE THE DOCTORS GAVE HIM. GOOD THING MY MOM'S SMARTER THAN HIM.
I HEAR KEVIN KELLER WAS UP TO SEE YOU AT THE GAZETTE THE OTHER DAY.
UH, YEAH. HE WANTED TO TALK ABOUT THE PAPER ENDORSING HIM IN THE SENATE RACE.
9

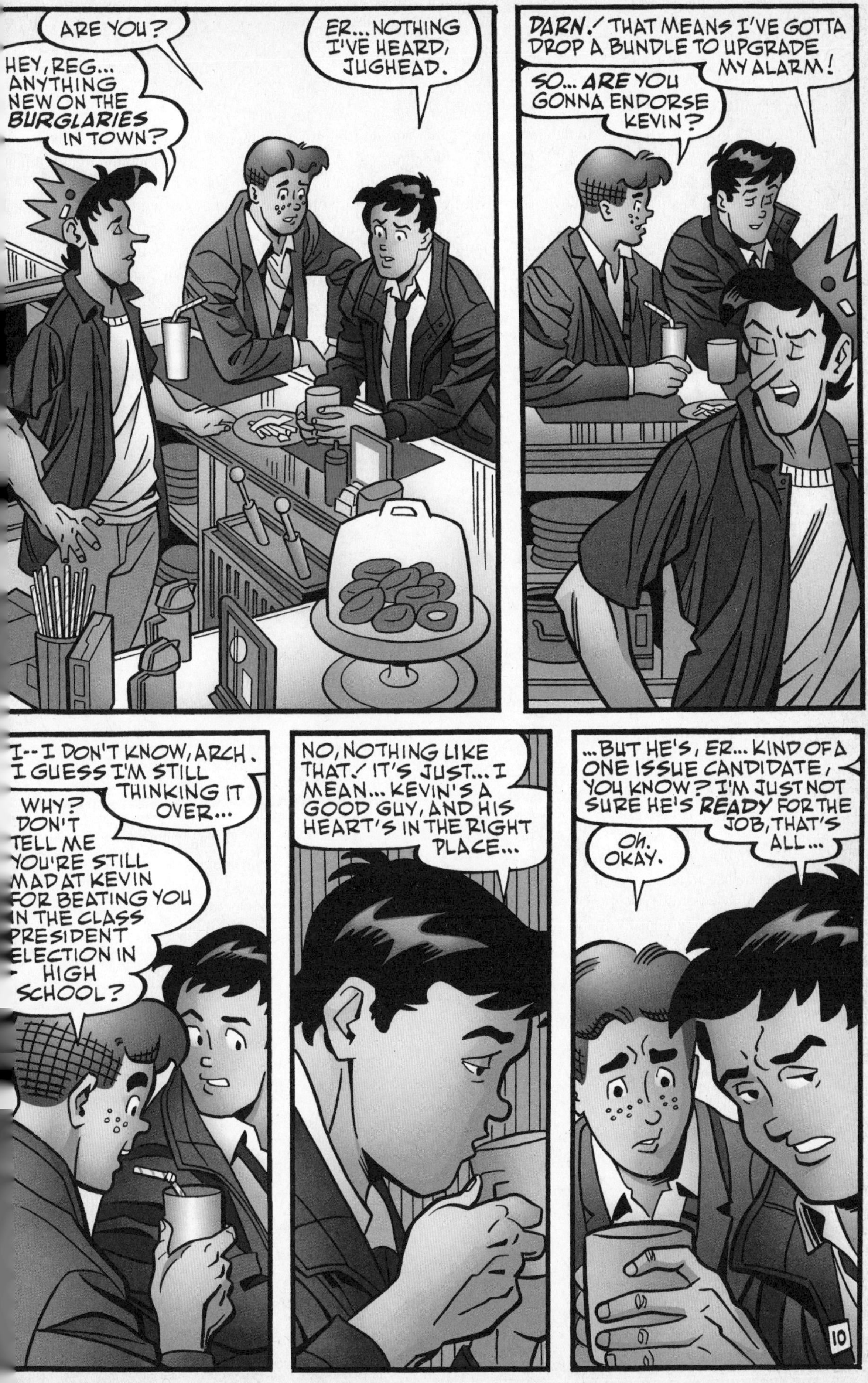
HEY, REG... ANYTHING NEW ON THE BURGLARIES IN TOWN?
ARE YOU?
ER... NOTHING I'VE HEARD, JUGHEAD.
DARN.! THAT MEANS I'VE GOTTA DROP A BUNDLE TO UPGRADE MY ALARM!
SO... ARE YOU GONNA ENDORSE KEVIN?
WHY? DON'T TELL ME YOU'RE STILL MAD AT KEVIN FOR BEATING YOU IN THE CLASS PRESIDENT ELECTION IN HIGH SCHOOL?
I-- I DON'T KNOW, ARCH. I GUESS I'M STILL THINKING IT OVER...
NO, NOTHING LIKE THAT.! IT'S JUST... I MEAN... KEVIN'S A GOOD GUY, AND HIS HEART'S IN THE RIGHT PLACE...
...BUT HE'S, ER... KIND OF A ONE ISSUE CANDIDATE, YOU KNOW? I'M JUST NOT SURE HE'S READY FOR THE JOB, THAT'S ALL...
Oh. OKAY.
10

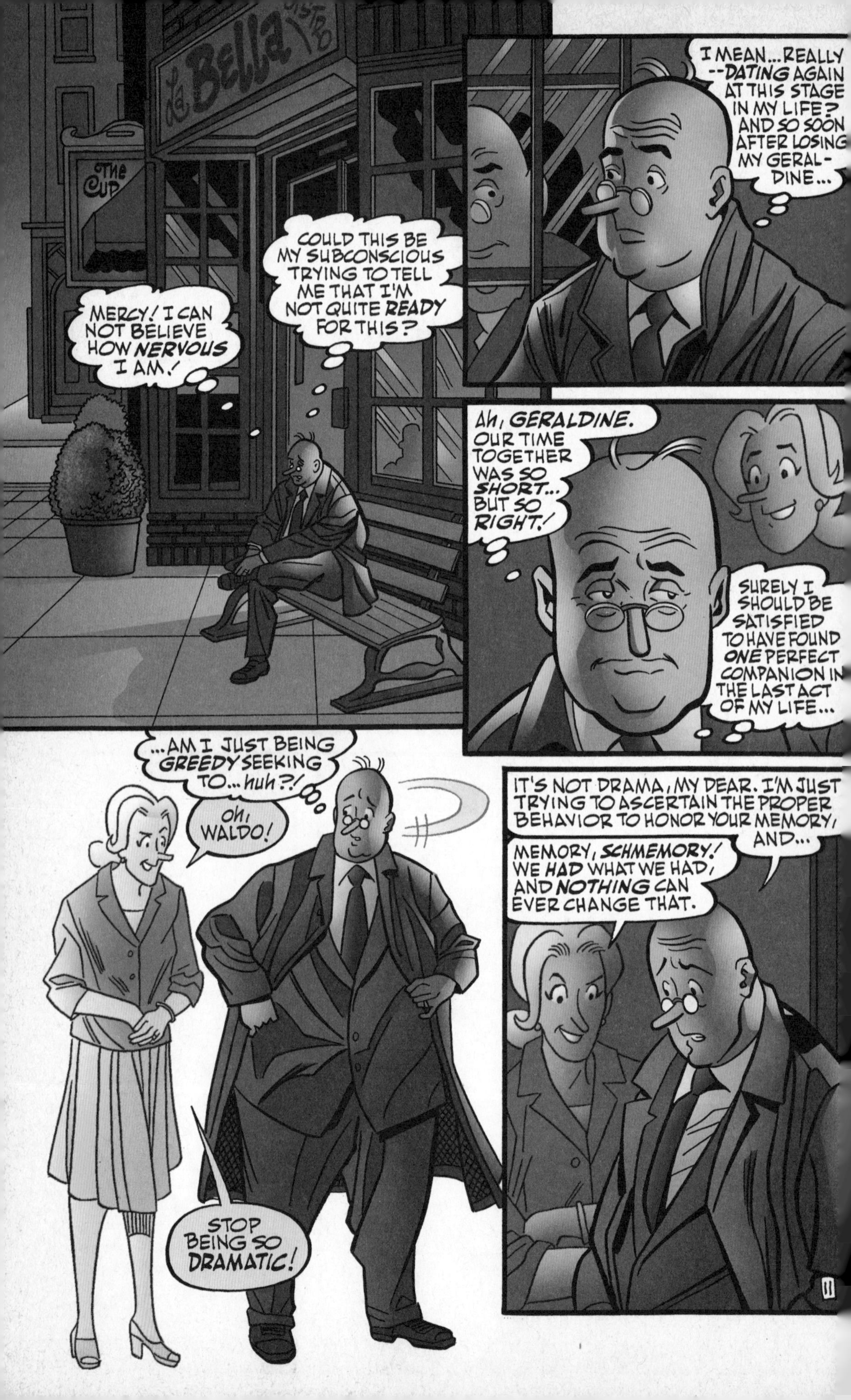
La Bella Bistro
The Cup
MERCY! I CAN NOT BELIEVE HOW NERVOUS I AM!
COULD THIS BE MY SUBCONSCIOUS TRYING TO TELL ME THAT I'M NOT QUITE READY FOR THIS?
I MEAN... REALLY --DATING AGAIN AT THIS STAGE IN MY LIFE? AND SO SOON AFTER LOSING MY GERAL-DINE...
Ah, GERALDINE. OUR TIME TOGETHER WAS SO SHORT... BUT SO RIGHT!
SURELY I SHOULD BE SATISFIED TO HAVE FOUND ONE PERFECT COMPANION IN THE LAST ACT OF MY LIFE...
...AM I JUST BEING GREEDY SEEKING TO... huh?!
oh, WALDO!
STOP BEING SO DRAMATIC!
IT'S NOT DRAMA, MY DEAR. I'M JUST TRYING TO ASCERTAIN THE PROPER BEHAVIOR TO HONOR YOUR MEMORY, AND...
MEMORY, SCHMEMORY! WE HAD WHAT WE HAD, AND NOTHING CAN EVER CHANGE THAT.
11

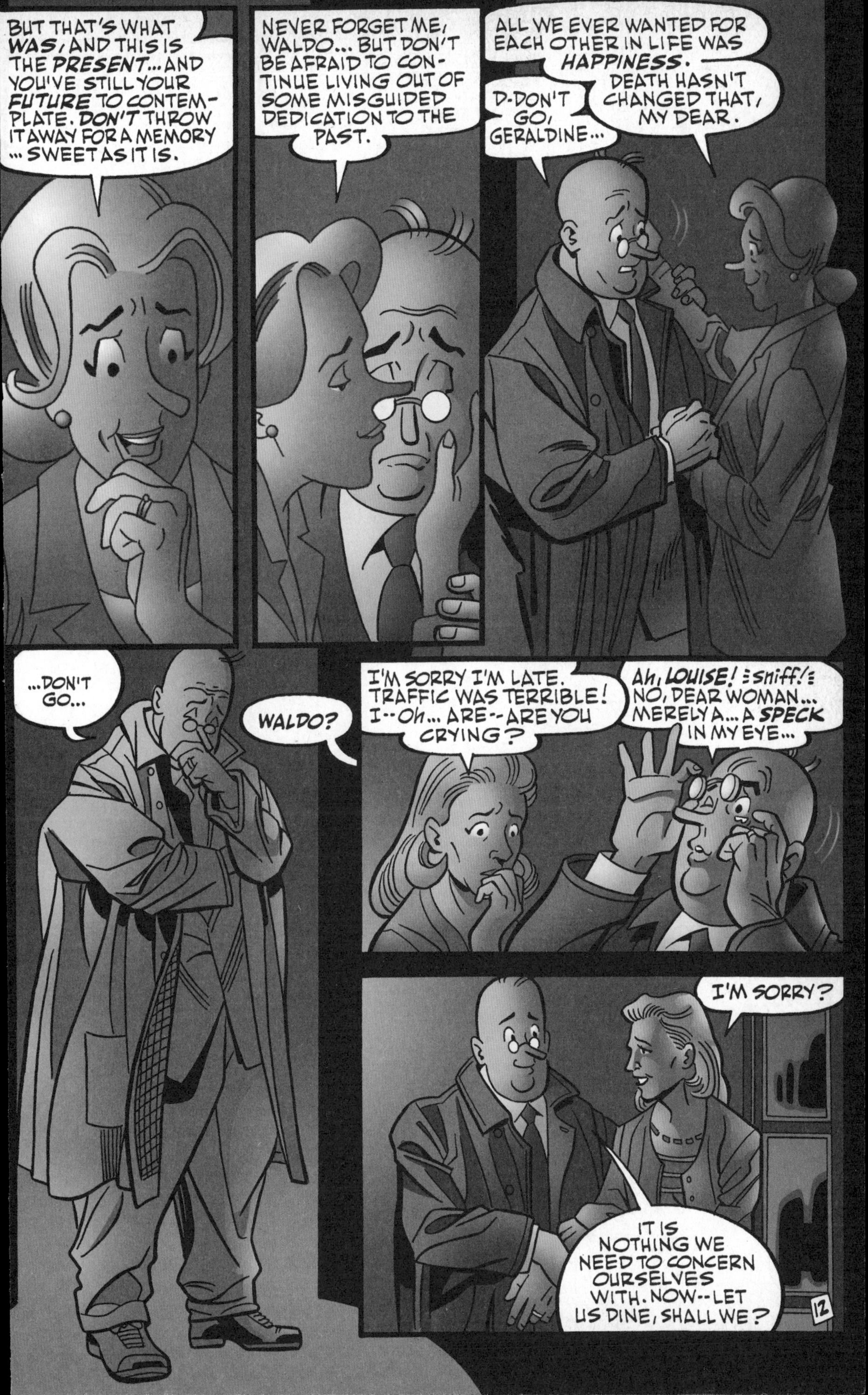
BUT THAT'S WHAT *WAS*, AND THIS IS THE *PRESENT*... AND YOU'VE STILL YOUR *FUTURE* TO CONTEMPLATE. *DON'T* THROW IT AWAY FOR A MEMORY ... SWEET AS IT IS.
NEVER FORGET ME, WALDO... BUT DON'T BE AFRAID TO CONTINUE LIVING OUT OF SOME MISGUIDED DEDICATION TO THE PAST.
ALL WE EVER WANTED FOR EACH OTHER IN LIFE WAS *HAPPINESS*.
D-DON'T GO, GERALDINE...
DEATH HASN'T CHANGED THAT, MY DEAR.
...DON'T GO...
WALDO?
I'M SORRY I'M LATE. TRAFFIC WAS TERRIBLE! I--OH... ARE--ARE YOU CRYING?
AH, *LOUISE!* :SNIFF!: NO, DEAR WOMAN... MERELY A... A *SPECK* IN MY EYE...
I'M SORRY?
IT IS NOTHING WE NEED TO CONCERN OURSELVES WITH. NOW--LET US DINE, SHALL WE?
12

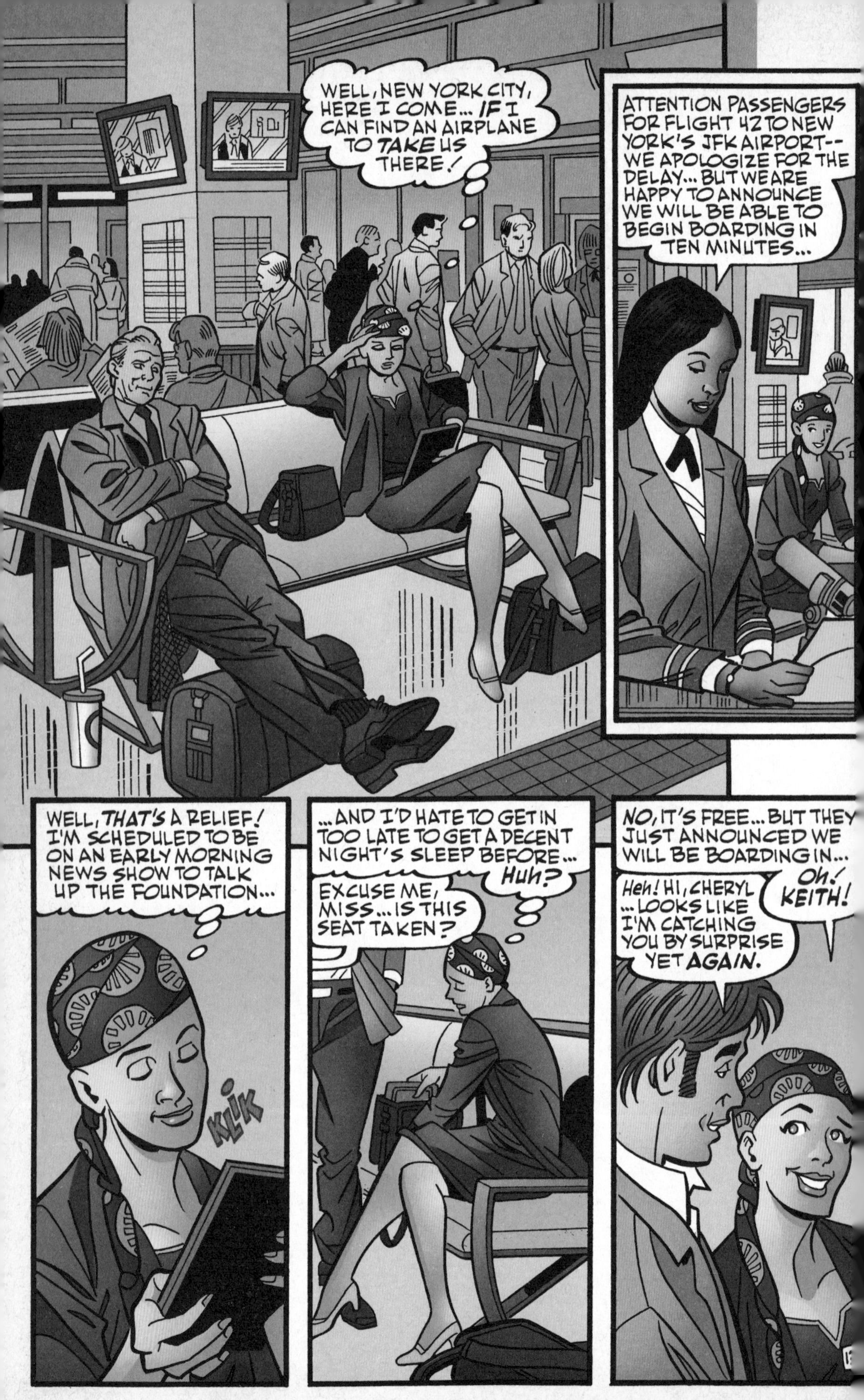
WELL, NEW YORK CITY, HERE I COME... IF I CAN FIND AN AIRPLANE TO TAKE US THERE!
ATTENTION PASSENGERS FOR FLIGHT 42 TO NEW YORK'S JFK AIRPORT-- WE APOLOGIZE FOR THE DELAY... BUT WE ARE HAPPY TO ANNOUNCE WE WILL BE ABLE TO BEGIN BOARDING IN TEN MINUTES...
WELL, THAT'S A RELIEF! I'M SCHEDULED TO BE ON AN EARLY MORNING NEWS SHOW TO TALK UP THE FOUNDATION...
KLIK
...AND I'D HATE TO GET IN TOO LATE TO GET A DECENT NIGHT'S SLEEP BEFORE...
Huh?
EXCUSE ME, MISS... IS THIS SEAT TAKEN?
NO, IT'S FREE... BUT THEY JUST ANNOUNCED WE WILL BE BOARDING IN...
Oh! KEITH!
Heh! HI, CHERYL ...LOOKS LIKE I'M CATCHING YOU BY SURPRISE YET AGAIN.

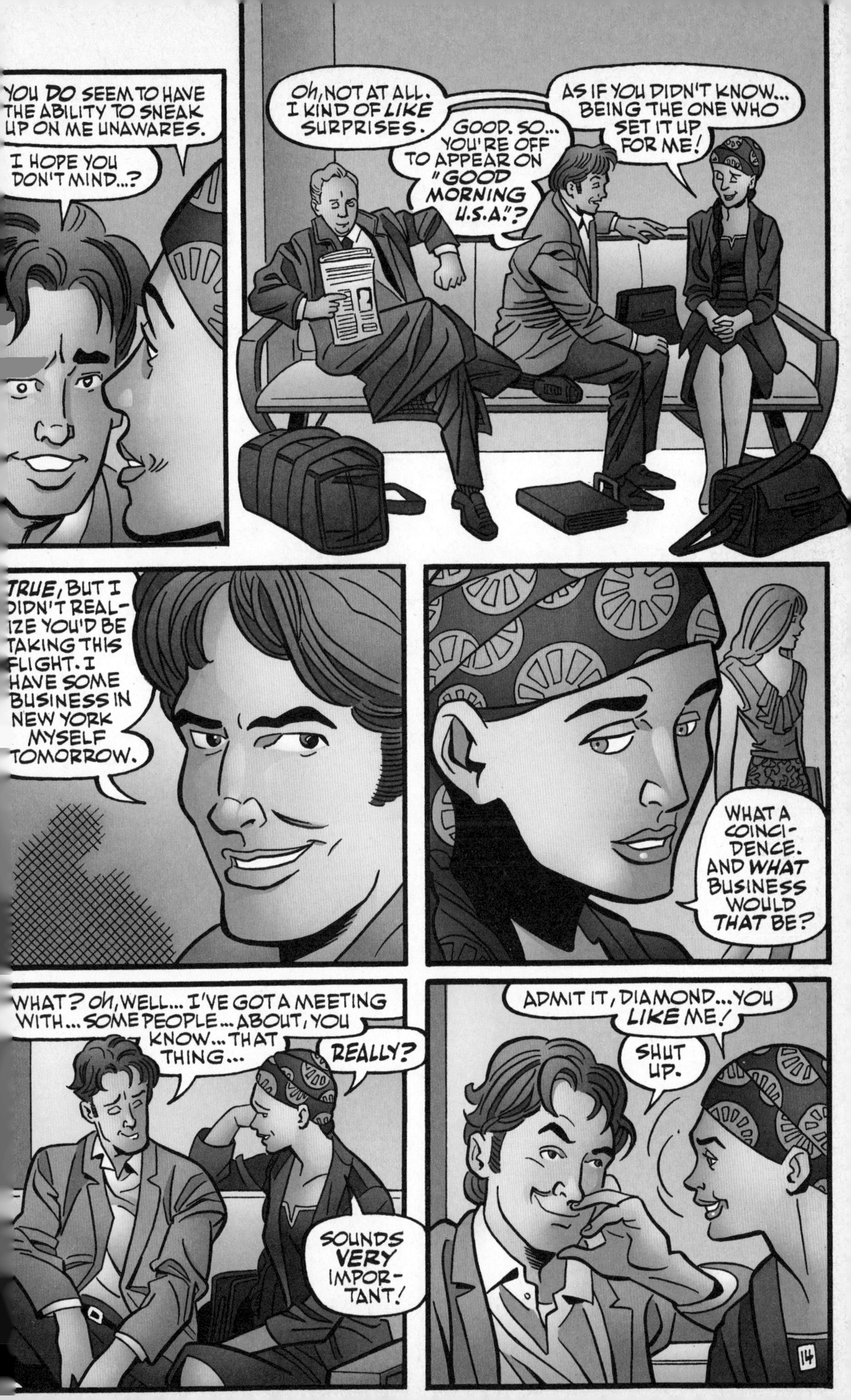
YOU DO SEEM TO HAVE THE ABILITY TO SNEAK UP ON ME UNAWARES.
I HOPE YOU DON'T MIND...?
Oh, NOT AT ALL. I KIND OF LIKE SURPRISES.
GOOD. SO... YOU'RE OFF TO APPEAR ON "GOOD MORNING U.S.A."?
AS IF YOU DIDN'T KNOW... BEING THE ONE WHO SET IT UP FOR ME!
TRUE, BUT I DIDN'T REALIZE YOU'D BE TAKING THIS FLIGHT. I HAVE SOME BUSINESS IN NEW YORK MYSELF TOMORROW.
WHAT A COINCIDENCE. AND WHAT BUSINESS WOULD THAT BE?
WHAT? Oh, WELL... I'VE GOT A MEETING WITH... SOME PEOPLE... ABOUT, YOU KNOW... THAT THING...
REALLY?
SOUNDS VERY IMPORTANT!
ADMIT IT, DIAMOND... YOU LIKE ME!
SHUT UP.
14

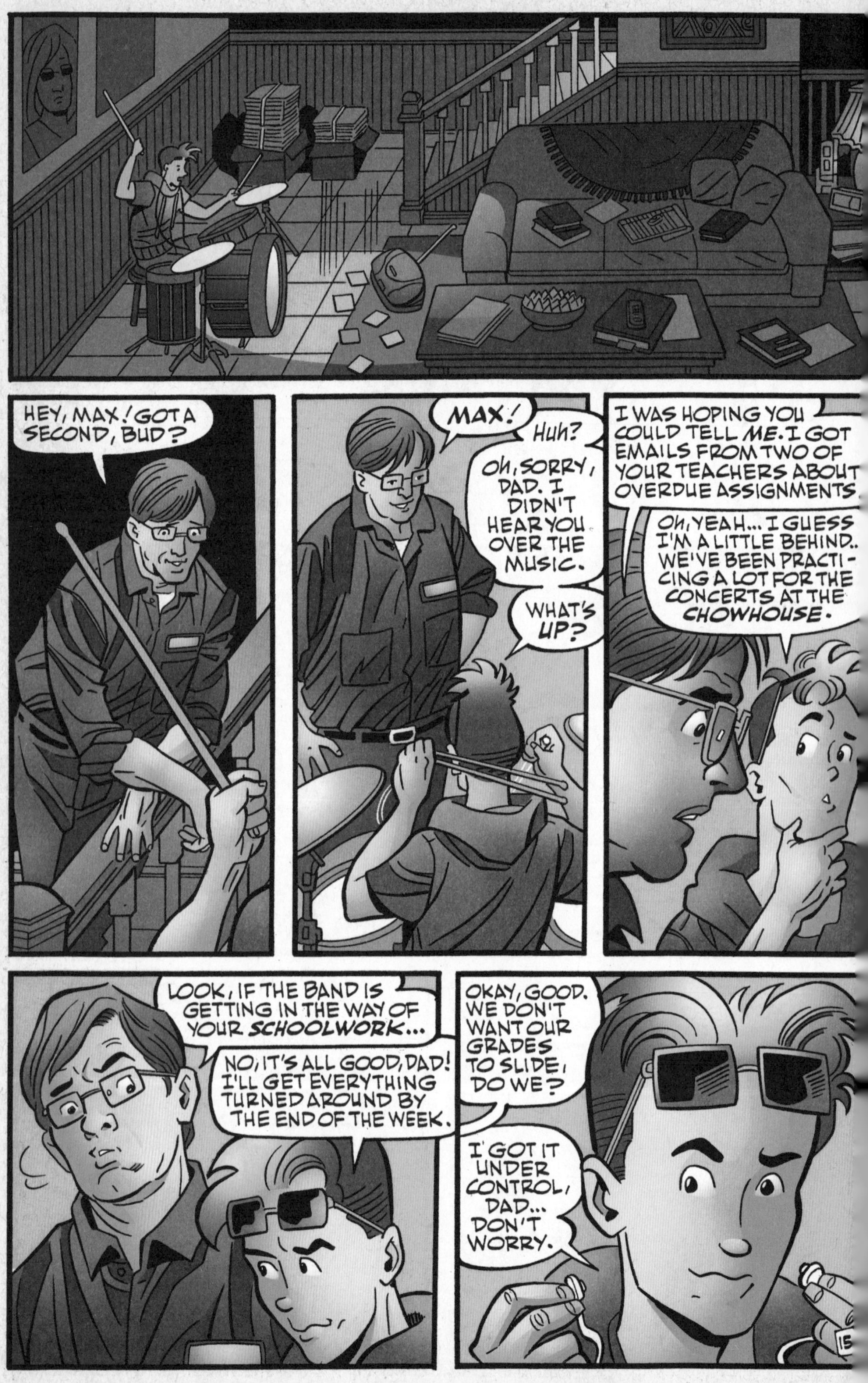
HEY, MAX! GOT A SECOND, BUD?
MAX!
Huh?
Oh, SORRY, DAD. I DIDN'T HEAR YOU OVER THE MUSIC.
WHAT'S UP?
I WAS HOPING YOU COULD TELL ME. I GOT EMAILS FROM TWO OF YOUR TEACHERS ABOUT OVERDUE ASSIGNMENTS.
Oh, YEAH... I GUESS I'M A LITTLE BEHIND.. WE'VE BEEN PRACTICING A LOT FOR THE CONCERTS AT THE CHOWHOUSE.
LOOK, IF THE BAND IS GETTING IN THE WAY OF YOUR SCHOOLWORK...
NO, IT'S ALL GOOD, DAD! I'LL GET EVERYTHING TURNED AROUND BY THE END OF THE WEEK.
OKAY, GOOD. WE DON'T WANT OUR GRADES TO SLIDE, DO WE?
I GOT IT UNDER CONTROL, DAD... DON'T WORRY.

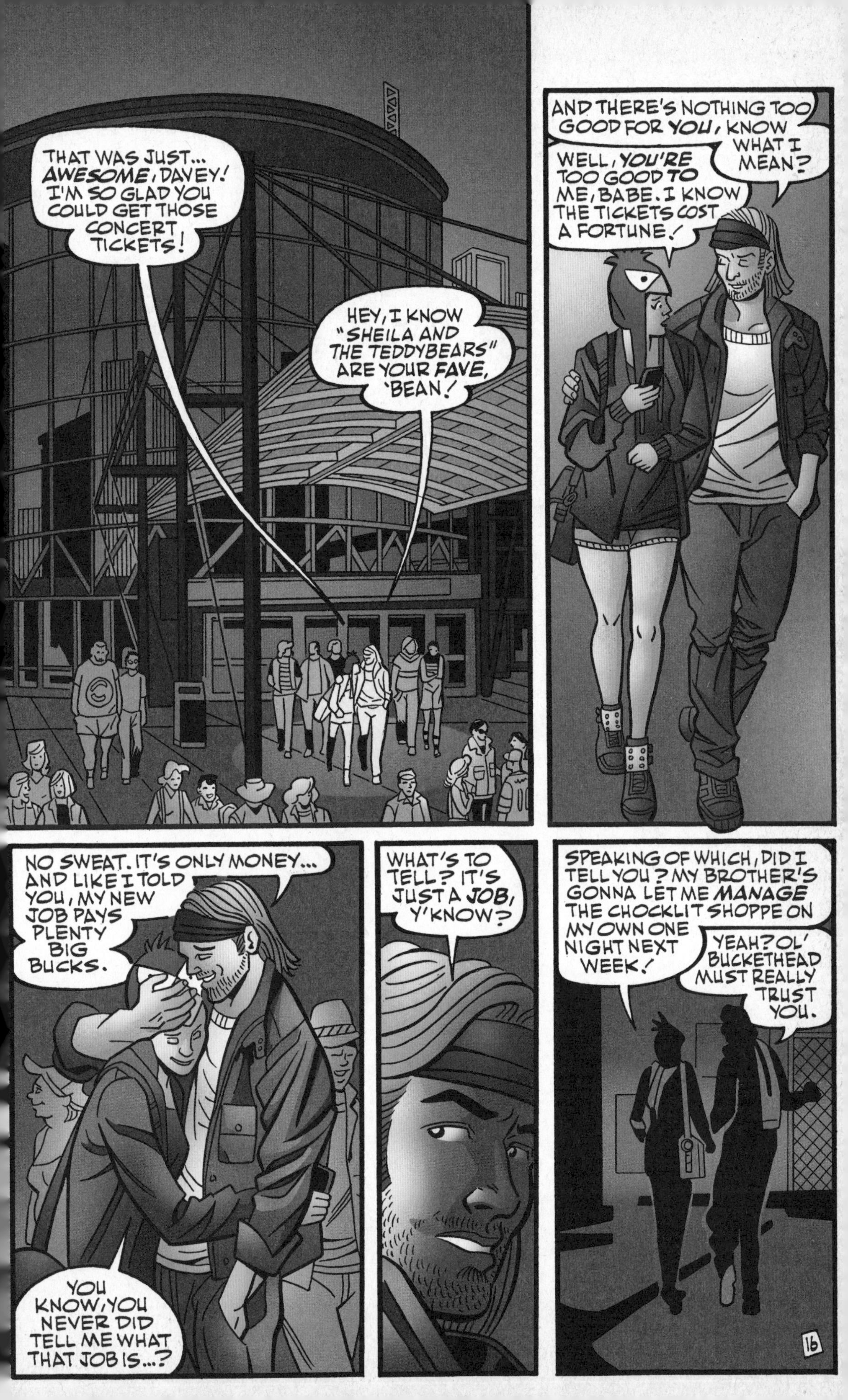
THAT WAS JUST... AWESOME, DAVEY! I'M SO GLAD YOU COULD GET THOSE CONCERT TICKETS!
HEY, I KNOW "SHEILA AND THE TEDDYBEARS" ARE YOUR FAVE, 'BEAN!
AND THERE'S NOTHING TOO GOOD FOR YOU, KNOW WHAT I MEAN?
WELL, YOU'RE TOO GOOD TO ME, BABE. I KNOW THE TICKETS COST A FORTUNE!
NO SWEAT. IT'S ONLY MONEY... AND LIKE I TOLD YOU, MY NEW JOB PAYS PLENTY BIG BUCKS.
YOU KNOW, YOU NEVER DID TELL ME WHAT THAT JOB IS...?
WHAT'S TO TELL? IT'S JUST A JOB, Y'KNOW?
SPEAKING OF WHICH, DID I TELL YOU? MY BROTHER'S GONNA LET ME MANAGE THE CHOCKLIT SHOPPE ON MY OWN ONE NIGHT NEXT WEEK!
YEAH? OL' BUCKETHEAD MUST REALLY TRUST YOU.
16

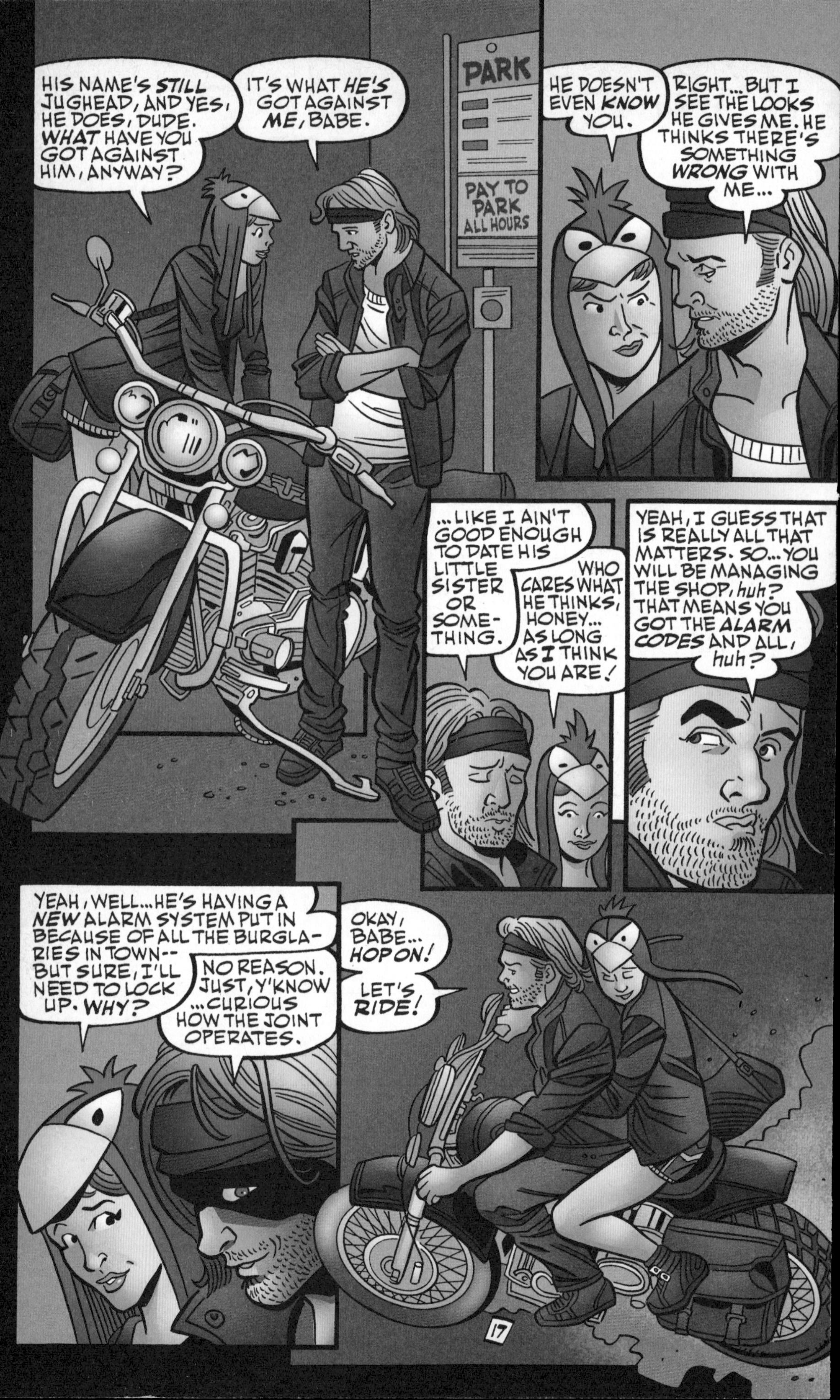

HIS NAME'S STILL JUGHEAD, AND YES, HE DOES, DUDE. WHAT HAVE YOU GOT AGAINST HIM, ANYWAY?
IT'S WHAT HE'S GOT AGAINST ME, BABE.
PARK
PAY TO PARK ALL HOURS
HE DOESN'T EVEN KNOW YOU.
RIGHT... BUT I SEE THE LOOKS HE GIVES ME. HE THINKS THERE'S SOMETHING WRONG WITH ME...
...LIKE I AIN'T GOOD ENOUGH TO DATE HIS LITTLE SISTER OR SOME-THING.
WHO CARES WHAT HE THINKS, HONEY... AS LONG AS I THINK YOU ARE!
YEAH, I GUESS THAT IS REALLY ALL THAT MATTERS. SO... YOU WILL BE MANAGING THE SHOP, huh? THAT MEANS YOU GOT THE ALARM CODES AND ALL, huh?
YEAH, WELL... HE'S HAVING A NEW ALARM SYSTEM PUT IN BECAUSE OF ALL THE BURGLA-RIES IN TOWN-- BUT SURE, I'LL NEED TO LOCK UP. WHY?
NO REASON. JUST, Y'KNOW ...CURIOUS HOW THE JOINT OPERATES.
OKAY, BABE... HOP ON!
LET'S RIDE!
17

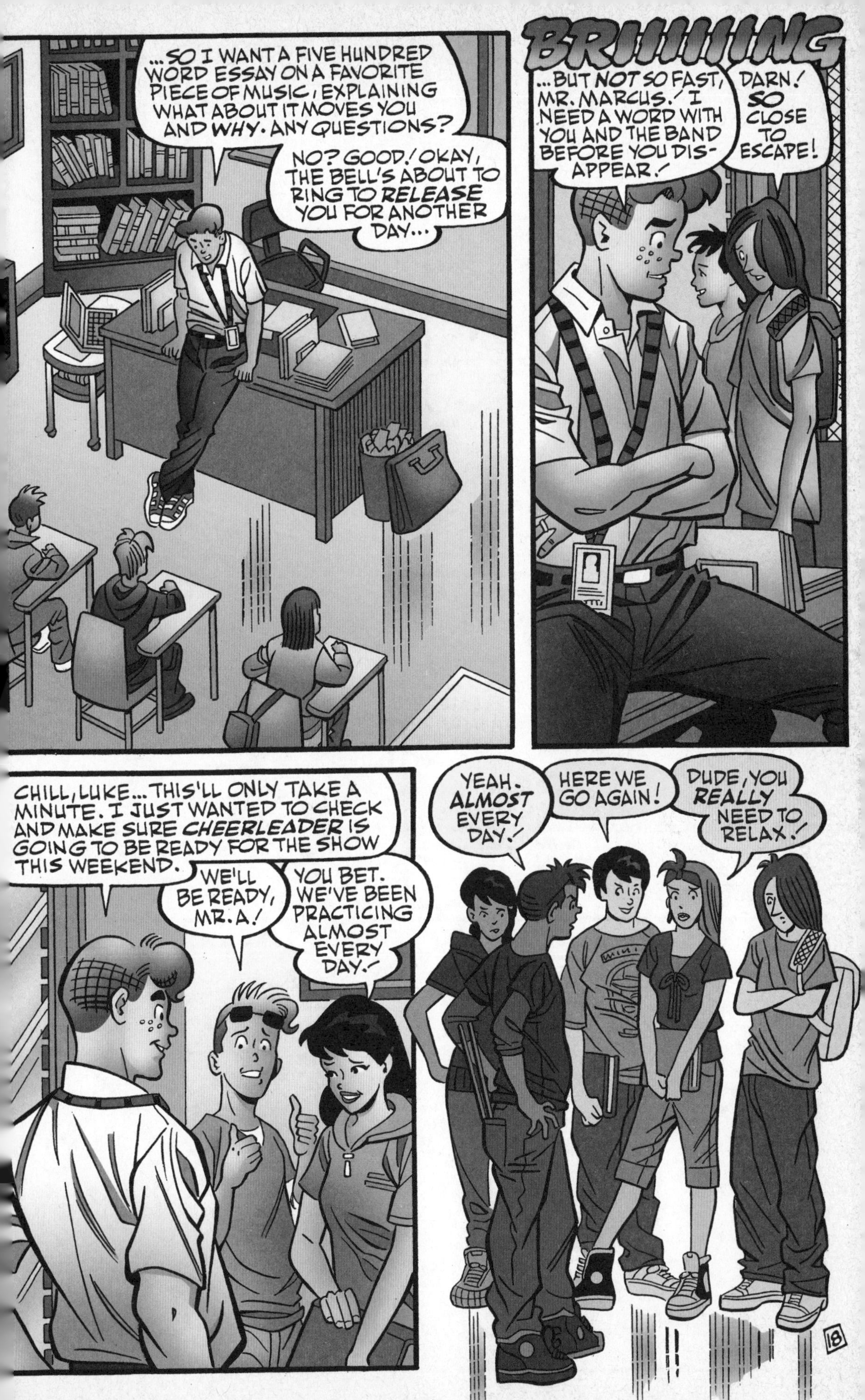
...SO I WANT A FIVE HUNDRED WORD ESSAY ON A FAVORITE PIECE OF MUSIC, EXPLAINING WHAT ABOUT IT MOVES YOU AND WHY. ANY QUESTIONS?
NO? GOOD! OKAY, THE BELL'S ABOUT TO RING TO RELEASE YOU FOR ANOTHER DAY...
BRIIIIIING
...BUT NOT SO FAST, MR. MARCUS.! I NEED A WORD WITH YOU AND THE BAND BEFORE YOU DIS-APPEAR.!
DARN! SO CLOSE TO ESCAPE!
CHILL, LUKE... THIS'LL ONLY TAKE A MINUTE. I JUST WANTED TO CHECK AND MAKE SURE CHEERLEADER IS GOING TO BE READY FOR THE SHOW THIS WEEKEND.
WE'LL BE READY, MR. A!
YOU BET. WE'VE BEEN PRACTICING ALMOST EVERY DAY.!
YEAH. ALMOST EVERY DAY.!
HERE WE GO AGAIN!
DUDE, YOU REALLY NEED TO RELAX.!
18

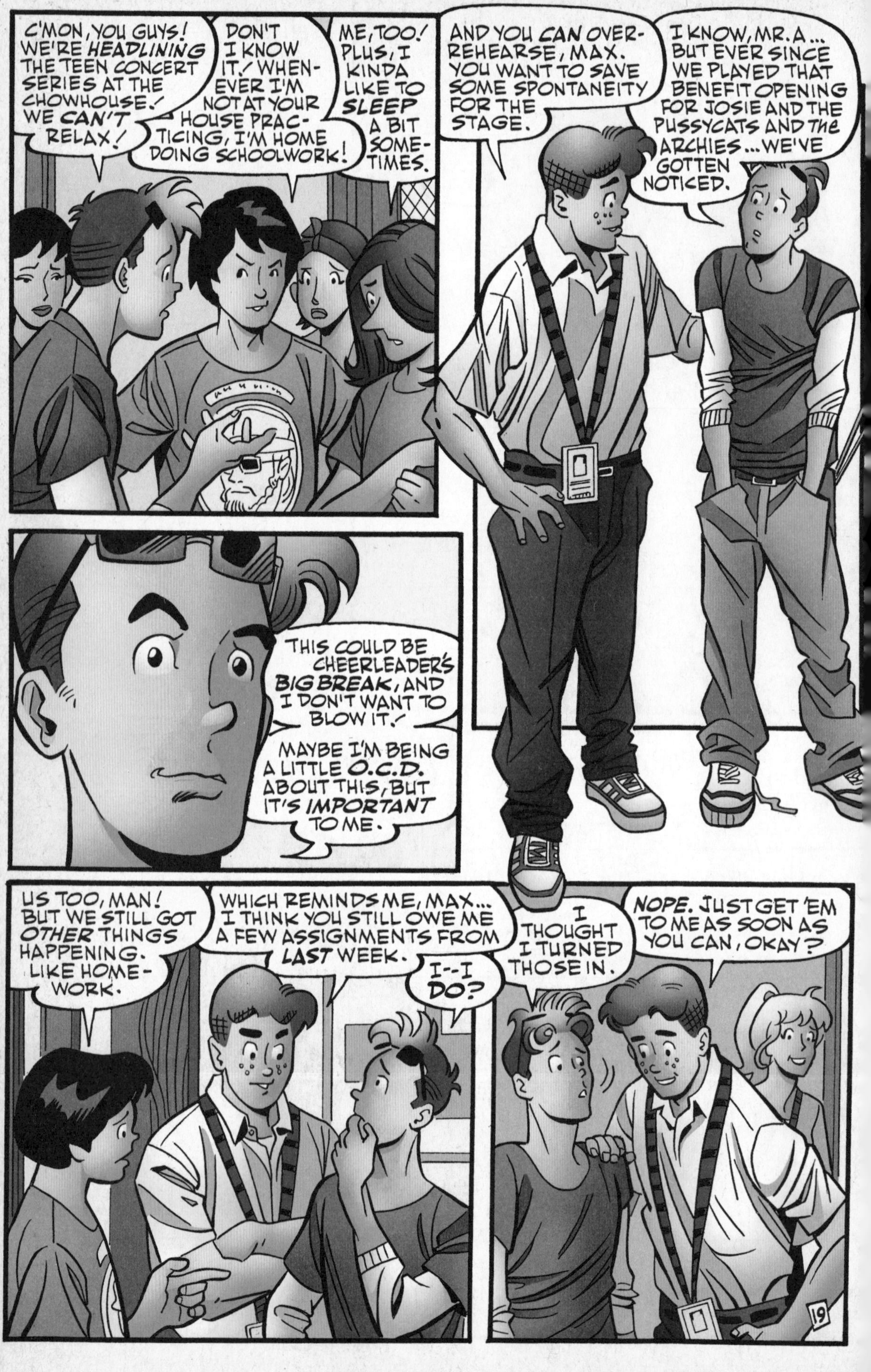
C'MON, YOU GUYS! WE'RE HEADLINING THE TEEN CONCERT SERIES AT THE CHOWHOUSE! WE CAN'T RELAX!
DON'T I KNOW IT! WHENEVER I'M NOT AT YOUR HOUSE PRACTICING, I'M HOME DOING SCHOOLWORK!
ME, TOO! PLUS, I KINDA LIKE TO SLEEP A BIT SOMETIMES.
THIS COULD BE CHEERLEADER'S BIG BREAK, AND I DON'T WANT TO BLOW IT!
MAYBE I'M BEING A LITTLE O.C.D. ABOUT THIS, BUT IT'S IMPORTANT TO ME.
AND YOU CAN OVER-REHEARSE, MAX. YOU WANT TO SAVE SOME SPONTANEITY FOR THE STAGE.
I KNOW, MR. A ... BUT EVER SINCE WE PLAYED THAT BENEFIT OPENING FOR JOSIE AND THE PUSSYCATS AND THE ARCHIES ... WE'VE GOTTEN NOTICED.
US TOO, MAN! BUT WE STILL GOT OTHER THINGS HAPPENING. LIKE HOMEWORK.
WHICH REMINDS ME, MAX... I THINK YOU STILL OWE ME A FEW ASSIGNMENTS FROM LAST WEEK.
I--I DO?
I THOUGHT I TURNED THOSE IN.
NOPE. JUST GET 'EM TO ME AS SOON AS YOU CAN, OKAY?
19

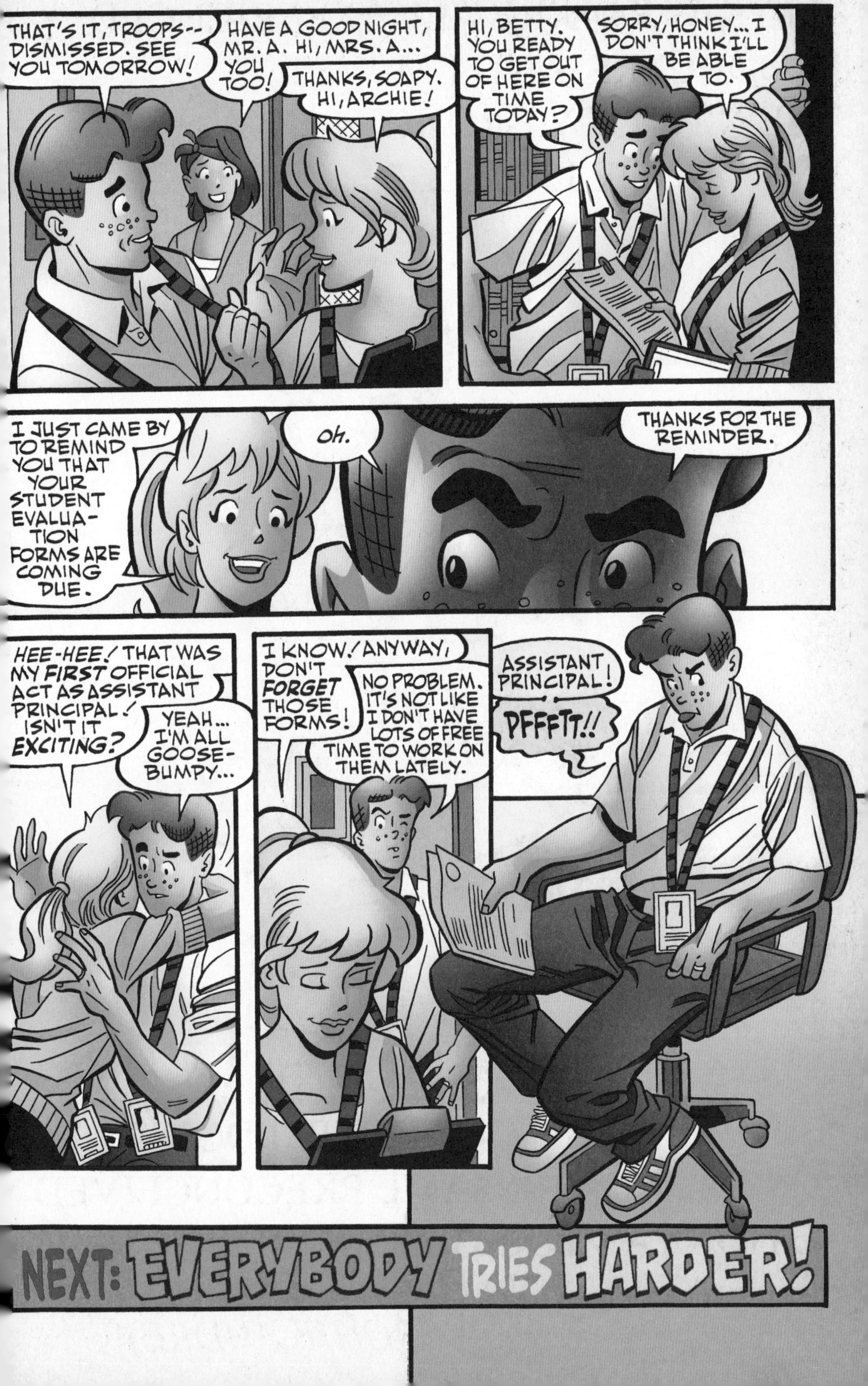
THAT'S IT, TROOPS--DISMISSED. SEE YOU TOMORROW!
HAVE A GOOD NIGHT, MR. A. HI, MRS. A... YOU TOO!
THANKS, SOAPY. HI, ARCHIE!
HI, BETTY. YOU READY TO GET OUT OF HERE ON TIME TODAY?
SORRY, HONEY... I DON'T THINK I'LL BE ABLE TO.
I JUST CAME BY TO REMIND YOU THAT YOUR STUDENT EVALUATION FORMS ARE COMING DUE.
oh.
THANKS FOR THE REMINDER.
HEE-HEE! THAT WAS MY FIRST OFFICIAL ACT AS ASSISTANT PRINCIPAL! ISN'T IT EXCITING?
YEAH... I'M ALL GOOSE-BUMPY...
I KNOW! ANYWAY, DON'T FORGET THOSE FORMS!
NO PROBLEM. IT'S NOT LIKE I DON'T HAVE LOTS OF FREE TIME TO WORK ON THEM LATELY.
ASSISTANT PRINCIPAL!
PFFFTT!!
NEXT: EVERYBODY TRIES HARDER!

"I KNOW YOU'RE ALL EXPERIENCED PRODUCERS, AND I'M JUST THE NEW GUY BROUGHT IN TO RUN THE LABEL..."

"BUT BEING AN OUTSIDER, I DON'T COME WITH THE SAME PRECONCEIVED NOTIONS AS YOU GUYS."

-ARCHIE ANDREWS

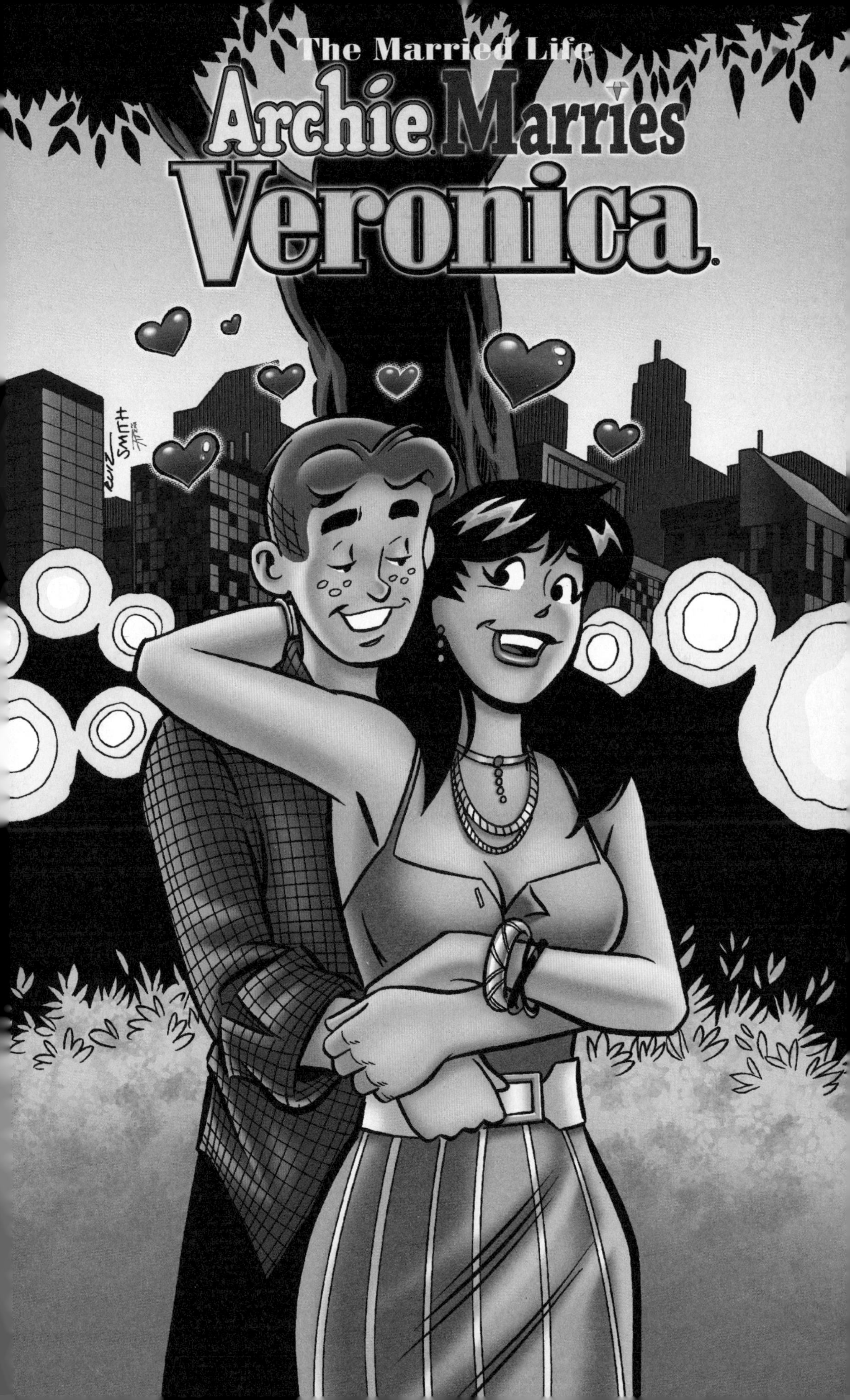
The Married Life
Archie Marries Veronica
RUIZ SMITH

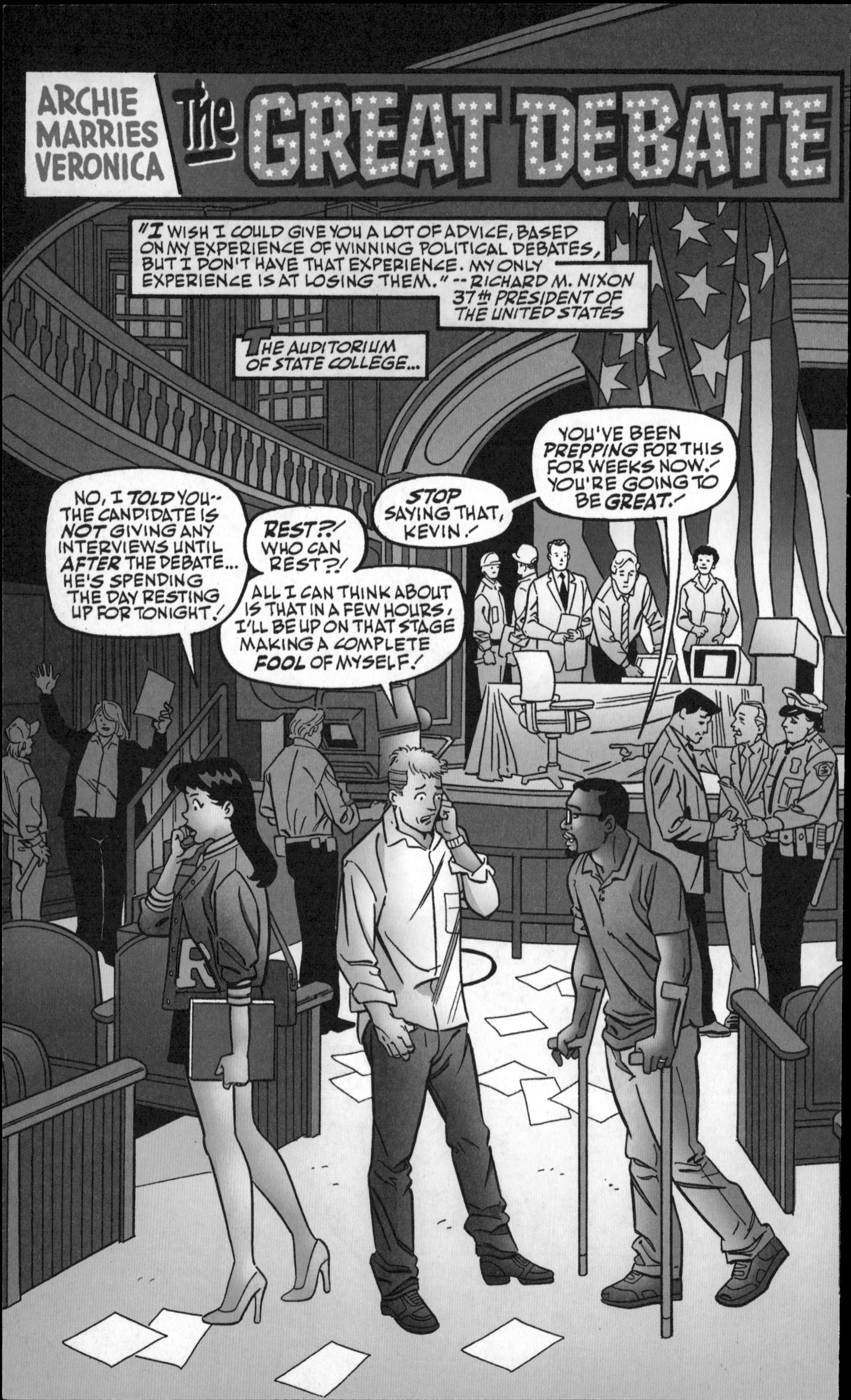
ARCHIE MARRIES VERONICA
The GREAT DEBATE
"I WISH I COULD GIVE YOU A LOT OF ADVICE, BASED ON MY EXPERIENCE OF WINNING POLITICAL DEBATES, BUT I DON'T HAVE THAT EXPERIENCE. MY ONLY EXPERIENCE IS AT LOSING THEM." -- RICHARD M. NIXON 37th PRESIDENT OF THE UNITED STATES
THE AUDITORIUM OF STATE COLLEGE...
NO, I TOLD YOU-- THE CANDIDATE IS NOT GIVING ANY INTERVIEWS UNTIL AFTER THE DEBATE... HE'S SPENDING THE DAY RESTING UP FOR TONIGHT!
REST?! WHO CAN REST?!
ALL I CAN THINK ABOUT IS THAT IN A FEW HOURS, I'LL BE UP ON THAT STAGE MAKING A COMPLETE FOOL OF MYSELF!
STOP SAYING THAT, KEVIN!
YOU'VE BEEN PREPPING FOR THIS FOR WEEKS NOW! YOU'RE GOING TO BE GREAT!

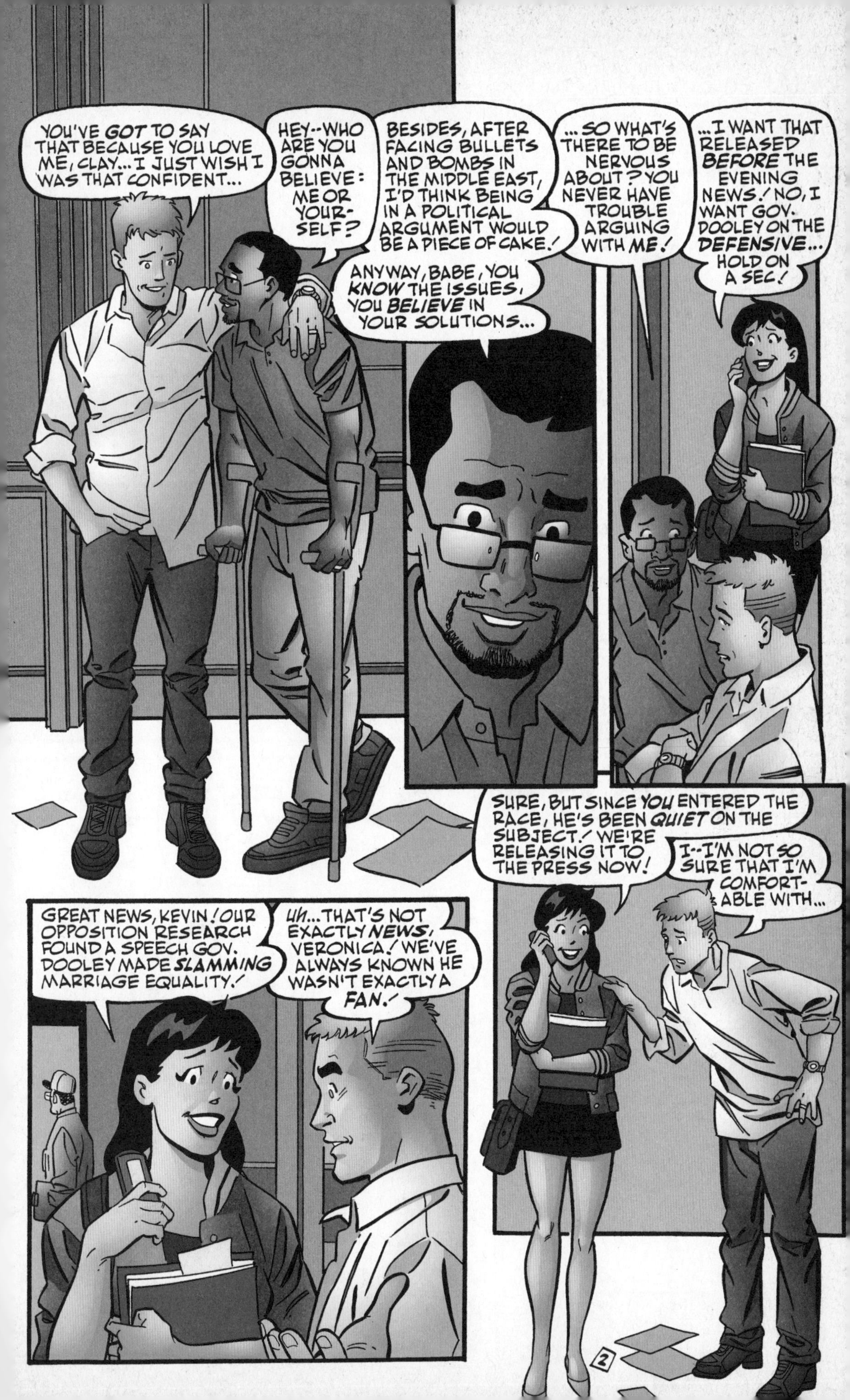

YOU'VE GOT TO SAY THAT BECAUSE YOU LOVE ME, CLAY... I JUST WISH I WAS THAT CONFIDENT...
HEY--WHO ARE YOU GONNA BELIEVE: ME OR YOURSELF?
BESIDES, AFTER FACING BULLETS AND BOMBS IN THE MIDDLE EAST, I'D THINK BEING IN A POLITICAL ARGUMENT WOULD BE A PIECE OF CAKE!
ANYWAY, BABE, YOU KNOW THE ISSUES, YOU BELIEVE IN YOUR SOLUTIONS...
...SO WHAT'S THERE TO BE NERVOUS ABOUT? YOU NEVER HAVE TROUBLE ARGUING WITH ME!
...I WANT THAT RELEASED BEFORE THE EVENING NEWS! NO, I WANT GOV. DOOLEY ON THE DEFENSIVE... HOLD ON A SEC!
GREAT NEWS, KEVIN! OUR OPPOSITION RESEARCH FOUND A SPEECH GOV. DOOLEY MADE SLAMMING MARRIAGE EQUALITY!
UH... THAT'S NOT EXACTLY NEWS, VERONICA! WE'VE ALWAYS KNOWN HE WASN'T EXACTLY A FAN!
SURE, BUT SINCE YOU ENTERED THE RACE, HE'S BEEN QUIET ON THE SUBJECT! WE'RE RELEASING IT TO THE PRESS NOW!
I--I'M NOT SO SURE THAT I'M COMFORTABLE WITH...
2

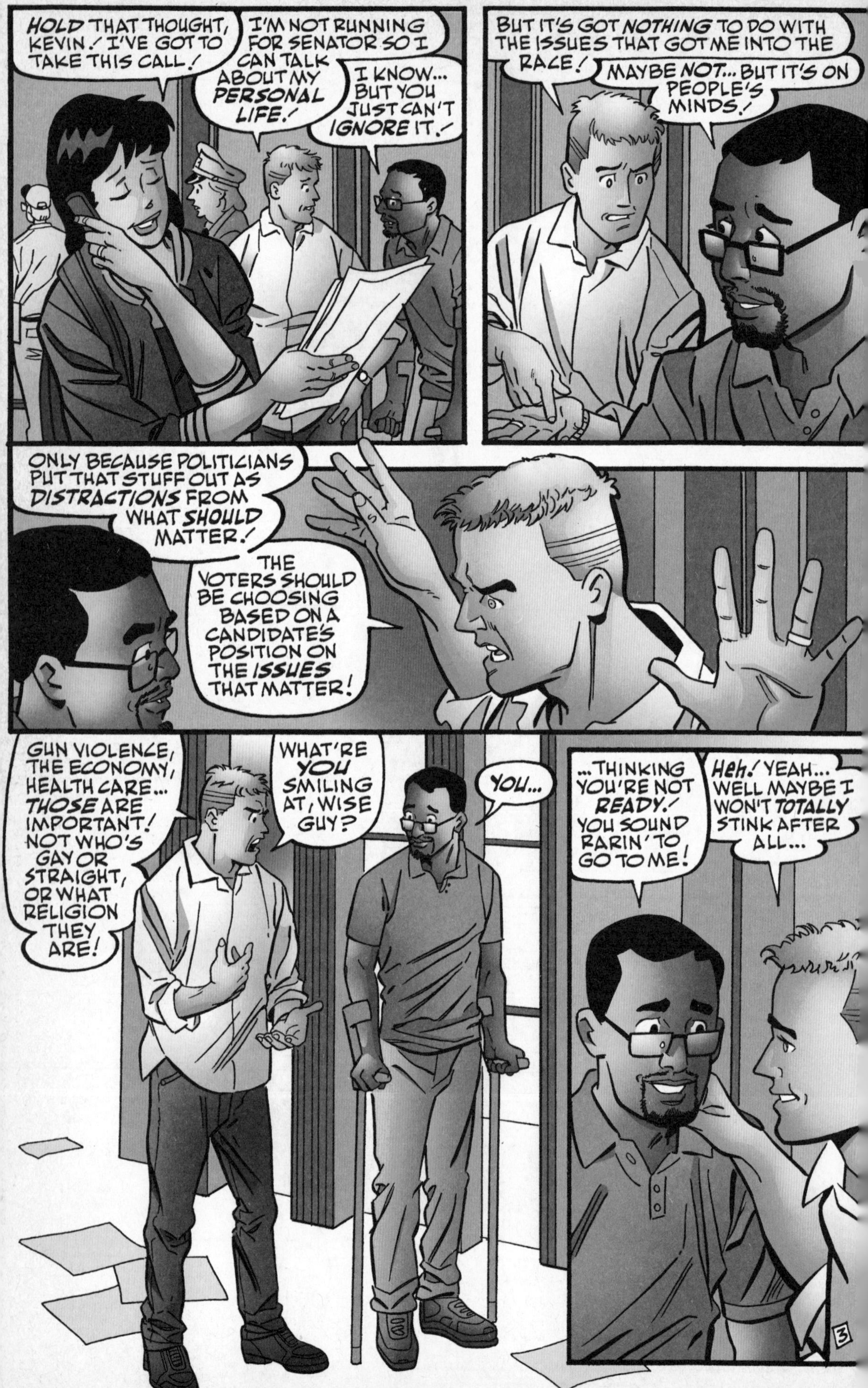
HOLD THAT THOUGHT, KEVIN! I'VE GOT TO TAKE THIS CALL!
I'M NOT RUNNING FOR SENATOR SO I CAN TALK ABOUT MY PERSONAL LIFE!
I KNOW... BUT YOU JUST CAN'T IGNORE IT!
BUT IT'S GOT NOTHING TO DO WITH THE ISSUES THAT GOT ME INTO THE RACE!
MAYBE NOT... BUT IT'S ON PEOPLE'S MINDS!
ONLY BECAUSE POLITICIANS PUT THAT STUFF OUT AS DISTRACTIONS FROM WHAT SHOULD MATTER!
THE VOTERS SHOULD BE CHOOSING BASED ON A CANDIDATE'S POSITION ON THE ISSUES THAT MATTER!
GUN VIOLENCE, THE ECONOMY, HEALTH CARE... THOSE ARE IMPORTANT! NOT WHO'S GAY OR STRAIGHT, OR WHAT RELIGION THEY ARE!
WHAT'RE YOU SMILING AT, WISE GUY?
YOU...
...THINKING YOU'RE NOT READY! YOU SOUND RARIN' TO GO TO ME!
Heh! YEAH... WELL MAYBE I WON'T TOTALLY STINK AFTER ALL...

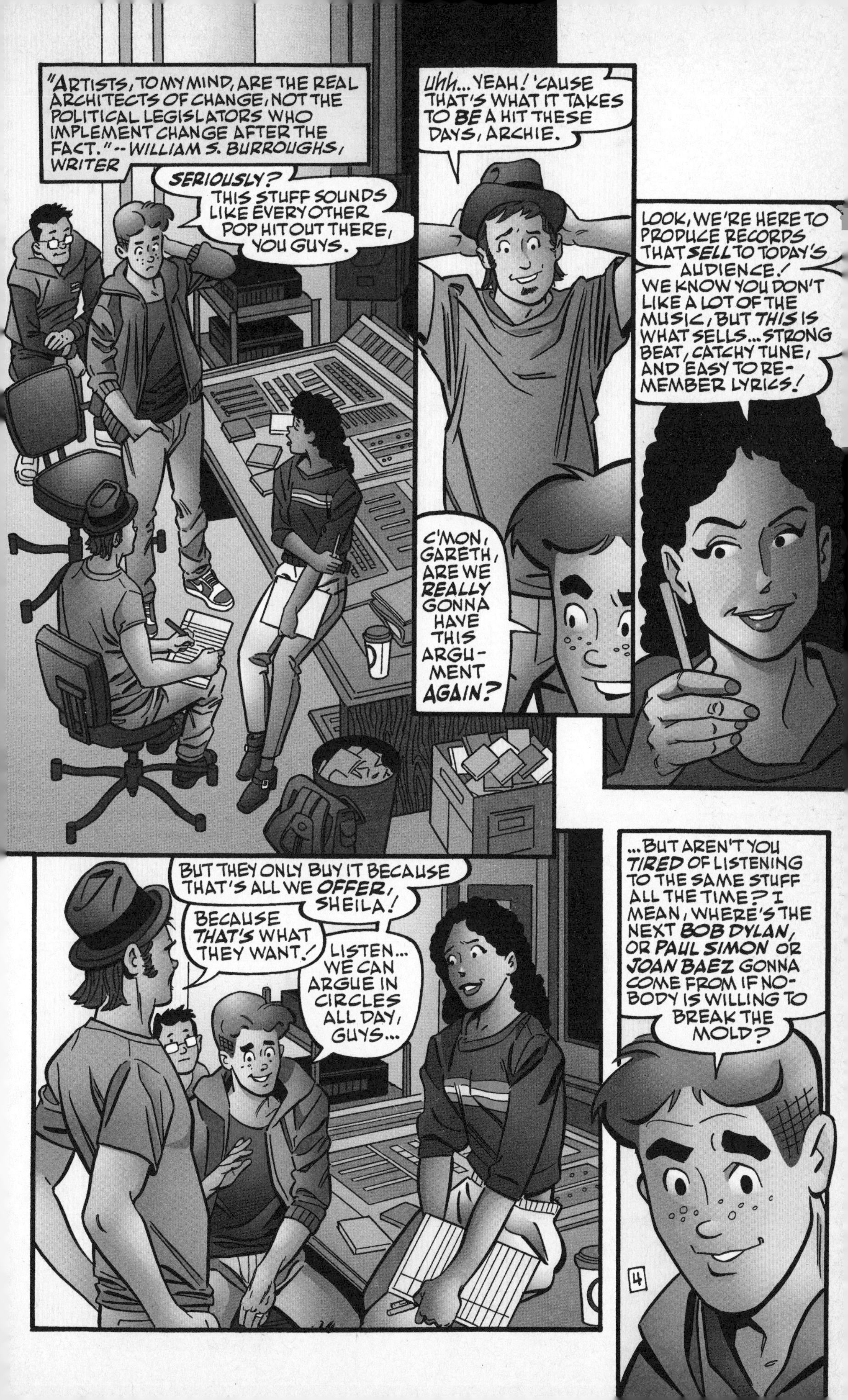
"ARTISTS, TO MY MIND, ARE THE REAL ARCHITECTS OF CHANGE, NOT THE POLITICAL LEGISLATORS WHO IMPLEMENT CHANGE AFTER THE FACT." -- WILLIAM S. BURROUGHS, WRITER
SERIOUSLY? THIS STUFF SOUNDS LIKE EVERY OTHER POP HIT OUT THERE, YOU GUYS.
UHH... YEAH! 'CAUSE THAT'S WHAT IT TAKES TO BE A HIT THESE DAYS, ARCHIE.
C'MON, GARETH, ARE WE REALLY GONNA HAVE THIS ARGUMENT AGAIN?
LOOK, WE'RE HERE TO PRODUCE RECORDS THAT SELL TO TODAY'S AUDIENCE! WE KNOW YOU DON'T LIKE A LOT OF THE MUSIC, BUT THIS IS WHAT SELLS... STRONG BEAT, CATCHY TUNE, AND EASY TO RE-MEMBER LYRICS!
BUT THEY ONLY BUY IT BECAUSE THAT'S ALL WE OFFER, SHEILA!
BECAUSE THAT'S WHAT THEY WANT!
LISTEN... WE CAN ARGUE IN CIRCLES ALL DAY, GUYS...
...BUT AREN'T YOU TIRED OF LISTENING TO THE SAME STUFF ALL THE TIME? I MEAN, WHERE'S THE NEXT BOB DYLAN, OR PAUL SIMON OR JOAN BAEZ GONNA COME FROM IF NO-BODY IS WILLING TO BREAK THE MOLD?
4

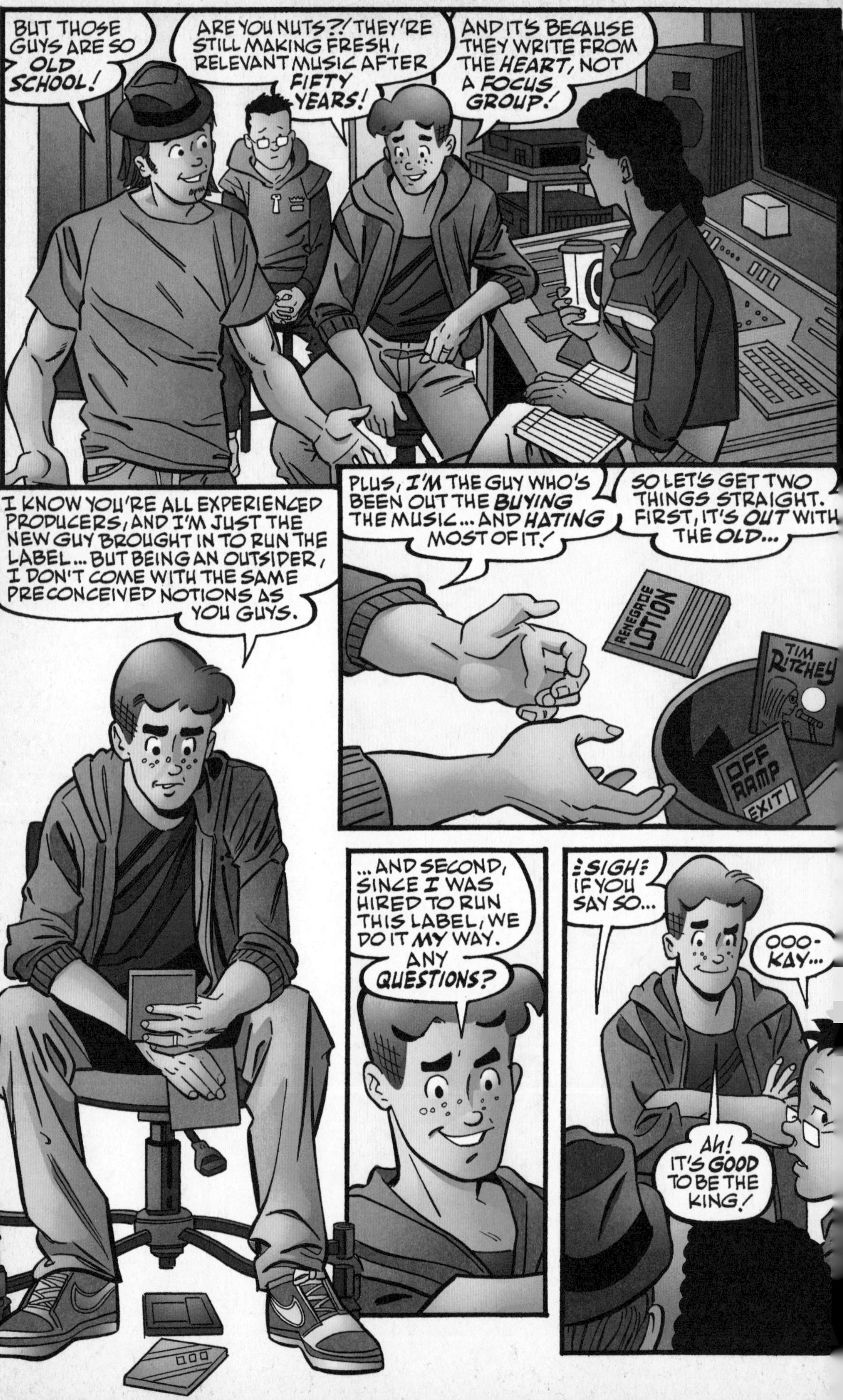
BUT THOSE GUYS ARE SO OLD SCHOOL!
ARE YOU NUTS?! THEY'RE STILL MAKING FRESH, RELEVANT MUSIC AFTER FIFTY YEARS!
AND IT'S BECAUSE THEY WRITE FROM THE HEART, NOT A FOCUS GROUP!
I KNOW YOU'RE ALL EXPERIENCED PRODUCERS, AND I'M JUST THE NEW GUY BROUGHT IN TO RUN THE LABEL... BUT BEING AN OUTSIDER, I DON'T COME WITH THE SAME PRECONCEIVED NOTIONS AS YOU GUYS.
PLUS, I'M THE GUY WHO'S BEEN OUT THE BUYING THE MUSIC... AND HATING MOST OF IT!
SO LET'S GET TWO THINGS STRAIGHT. FIRST, IT'S OUT WITH THE OLD...
RENEGADE LOTION
TIM RITCHEY
OFF RAMP
EXIT
...AND SECOND, SINCE I WAS HIRED TO RUN THIS LABEL, WE DO IT MY WAY.
ANY QUESTIONS?
SIGH IF YOU SAY SO...
OOO-KAY...
AH! IT'S GOOD TO BE THE KING!

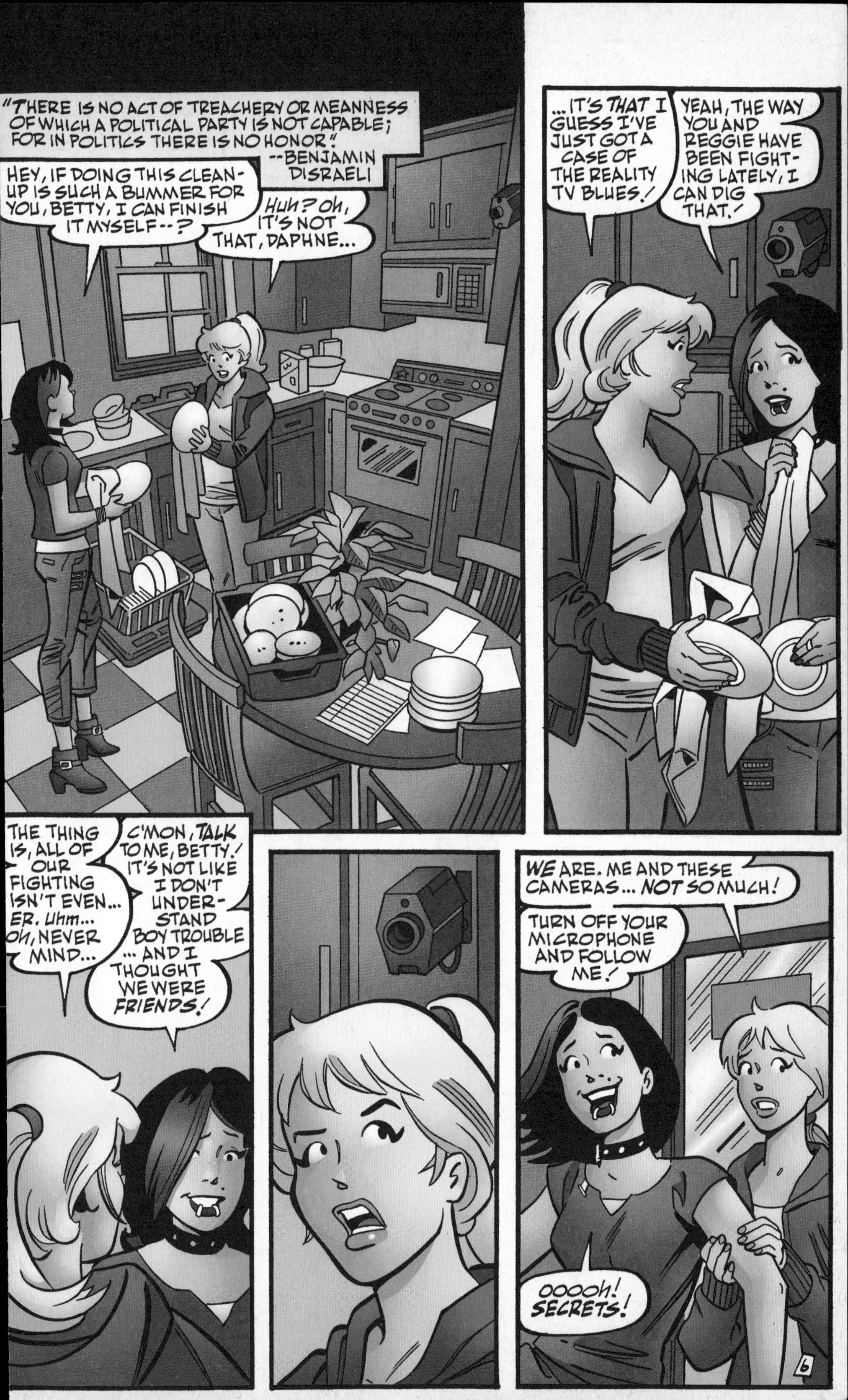
"THERE IS NO ACT OF TREACHERY OR MEANNESS OF WHICH A POLITICAL PARTY IS NOT CAPABLE; FOR IN POLITICS THERE IS NO HONOR!" --BENJAMIN DISRAELI
HEY, IF DOING THIS CLEAN-UP IS SUCH A BUMMER FOR YOU, BETTY, I CAN FINISH IT MYSELF--?
HUH? OH, IT'S NOT THAT, DAPHNE...
...IT'S THAT I GUESS I'VE JUST GOT A CASE OF THE REALITY TV BLUES!
YEAH, THE WAY YOU AND REGGIE HAVE BEEN FIGHTING LATELY, I CAN DIG THAT.!
THE THING IS, ALL OF OUR FIGHTING ISN'T EVEN... ER. UHM... OH, NEVER MIND...
C'MON, TALK TO ME, BETTY! IT'S NOT LIKE I DON'T UNDERSTAND BOY TROUBLE ... AND I THOUGHT WE WERE FRIENDS!
WE ARE. ME AND THESE CAMERAS... NOT SO MUCH!
TURN OFF YOUR MICROPHONE AND FOLLOW ME!
OOOOH! SECRETS!
6

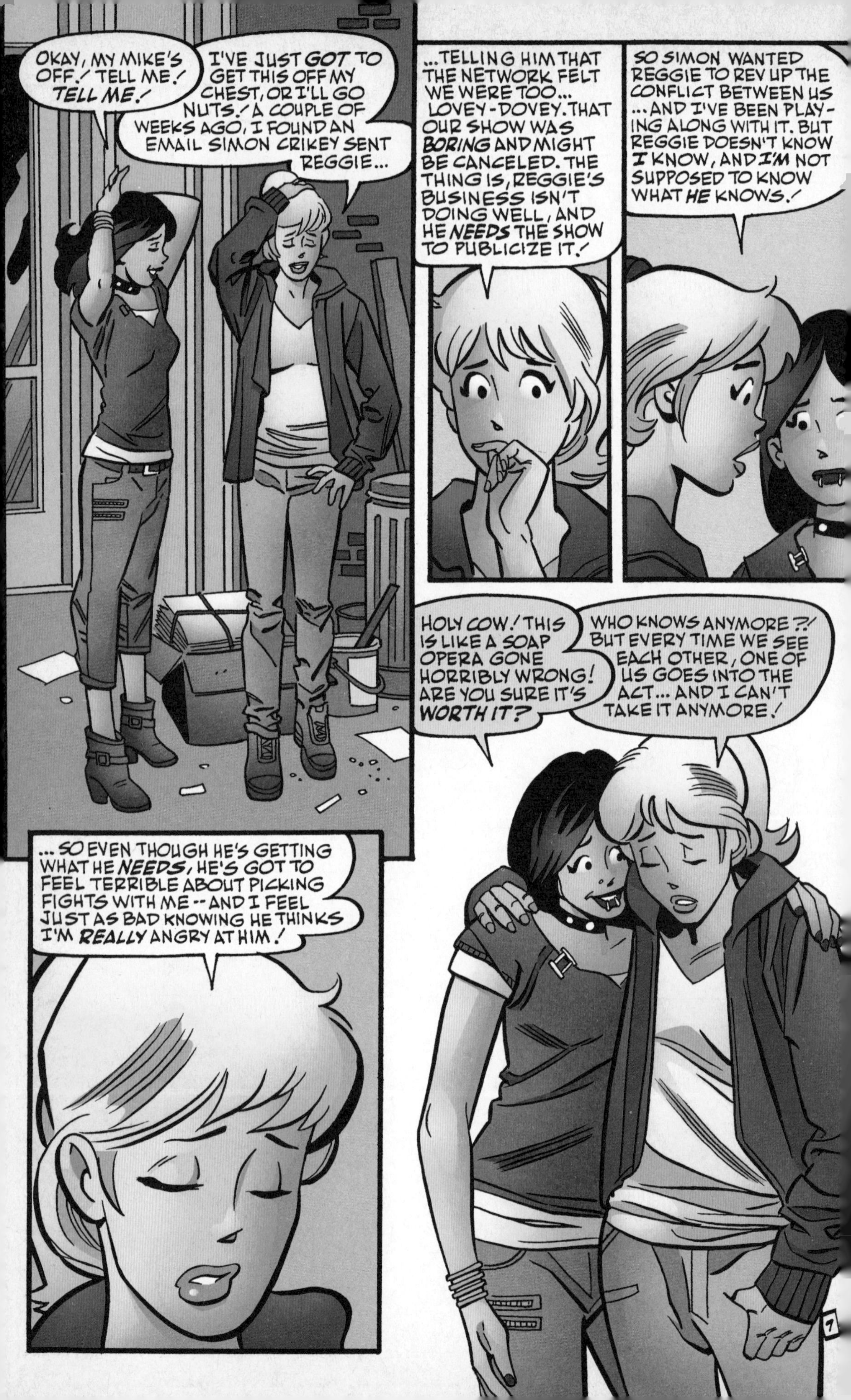
OKAY, MY MIKE'S OFF! TELL ME! TELL ME!
I'VE JUST GOT TO GET THIS OFF MY CHEST, OR I'LL GO NUTS! A COUPLE OF WEEKS AGO, I FOUND AN EMAIL SIMON CRIKEY SENT REGGIE...
...TELLING HIM THAT THE NETWORK FELT WE WERE TOO... LOVEY-DOVEY. THAT OUR SHOW WAS BORING AND MIGHT BE CANCELED. THE THING IS, REGGIE'S BUSINESS ISN'T DOING WELL, AND HE NEEDS THE SHOW TO PUBLICIZE IT!
SO SIMON WANTED REGGIE TO REV UP THE CONFLICT BETWEEN US ...AND I'VE BEEN PLAYING ALONG WITH IT. BUT REGGIE DOESN'T KNOW I KNOW, AND I'M NOT SUPPOSED TO KNOW WHAT HE KNOWS!
...SO EVEN THOUGH HE'S GETTING WHAT HE NEEDS, HE'S GOT TO FEEL TERRIBLE ABOUT PICKING FIGHTS WITH ME -- AND I FEEL JUST AS BAD KNOWING HE THINKS I'M REALLY ANGRY AT HIM!
HOLY COW! THIS IS LIKE A SOAP OPERA GONE HORRIBLY WRONG! ARE YOU SURE IT'S WORTH IT?
WHO KNOWS ANYMORE?! BUT EVERY TIME WE SEE EACH OTHER, ONE OF US GOES INTO THE ACT... AND I CAN'T TAKE IT ANYMORE!
7

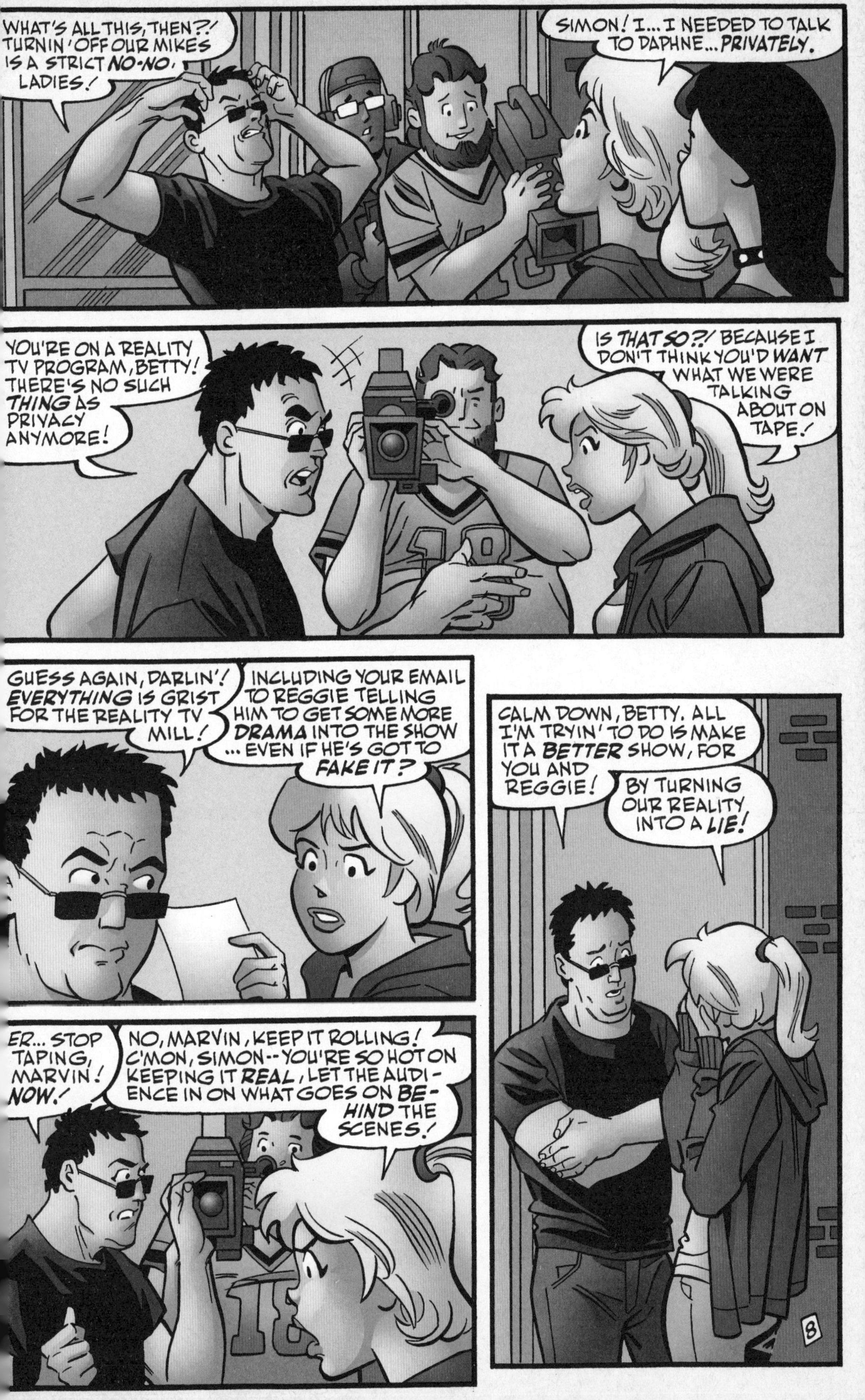
WHAT'S ALL THIS, THEN?! TURNIN' OFF OUR MIKES IS A STRICT NO-NO, LADIES!
SIMON! I... I NEEDED TO TALK TO DAPHNE... PRIVATELY.
YOU'RE ON A REALITY TV PROGRAM, BETTY! THERE'S NO SUCH THING AS PRIVACY ANYMORE!
IS THAT SO?! BECAUSE I DON'T THINK YOU'D WANT WHAT WE WERE TALKING ABOUT ON TAPE!
GUESS AGAIN, DARLIN'! EVERYTHING IS GRIST FOR THE REALITY TV MILL!
INCLUDING YOUR EMAIL TO REGGIE TELLING HIM TO GET SOME MORE DRAMA INTO THE SHOW ... EVEN IF HE'S GOT TO FAKE IT?
CALM DOWN, BETTY. ALL I'M TRYIN' TO DO IS MAKE IT A BETTER SHOW, FOR YOU AND REGGIE!
BY TURNING OUR REALITY INTO A LIE!
ER... STOP TAPING, MARVIN! NOW!
NO, MARVIN, KEEP IT ROLLING! C'MON, SIMON-- YOU'RE SO HOT ON KEEPING IT REAL, LET THE AUDI-ENCE IN ON WHAT GOES ON BE-HIND THE SCENES!
8

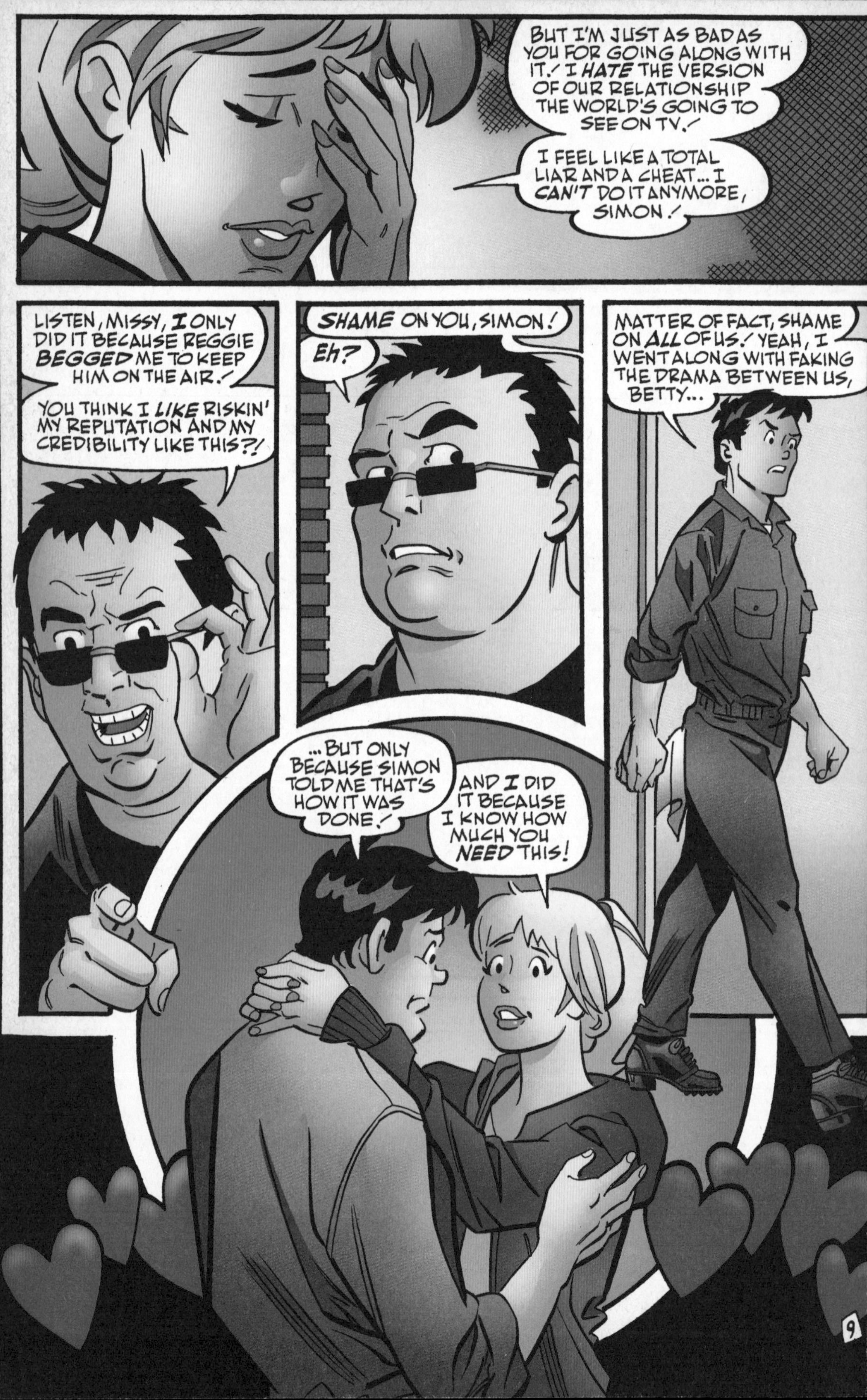

BUT I'M JUST AS BAD AS YOU FOR GOING ALONG WITH IT.! I HATE THE VERSION OF OUR RELATIONSHIP THE WORLD'S GOING TO SEE ON TV.!
I FEEL LIKE A TOTAL LIAR AND A CHEAT... I CAN'T DO IT ANYMORE, SIMON.!
LISTEN, MISSY, I ONLY DID IT BECAUSE REGGIE BEGGED ME TO KEEP HIM ON THE AIR.!
YOU THINK I LIKE RISKIN' MY REPUTATION AND MY CREDIBILITY LIKE THIS?!
SHAME ON YOU, SIMON!
Eh?
MATTER OF FACT, SHAME ON ALL OF US.! YEAH, I WENT ALONG WITH FAKING THE DRAMA BETWEEN US, BETTY...
...BUT ONLY BECAUSE SIMON TOLD ME THAT'S HOW IT WAS DONE.!
AND I DID IT BECAUSE I KNOW HOW MUCH YOU NEED THIS!

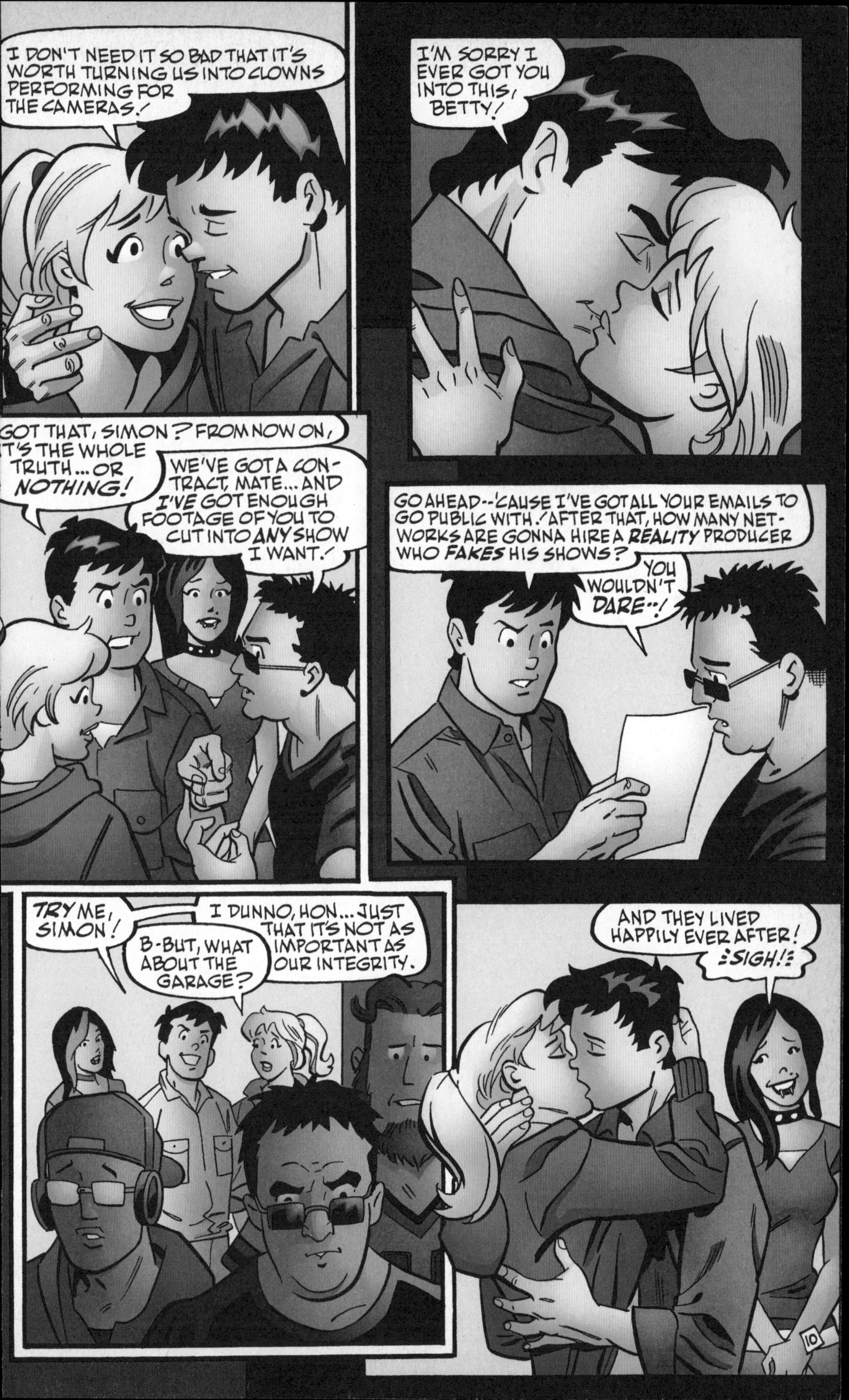
I DON'T NEED IT SO BAD THAT IT'S WORTH TURNING US INTO CLOWNS PERFORMING FOR THE CAMERAS!
I'M SORRY I EVER GOT YOU INTO THIS, BETTY!
GOT THAT, SIMON? FROM NOW ON, IT'S THE WHOLE TRUTH... OR NOTHING!
WE'VE GOT A CONTRACT, MATE... AND I'VE GOT ENOUGH FOOTAGE OF YOU TO CUT INTO ANY SHOW I WANT!
GO AHEAD--'CAUSE I'VE GOT ALL YOUR EMAILS TO GO PUBLIC WITH! AFTER THAT, HOW MANY NETWORKS ARE GONNA HIRE A REALITY PRODUCER WHO FAKES HIS SHOWS?
YOU WOULDN'T DARE..!
TRY ME, SIMON!
B-BUT, WHAT ABOUT THE GARAGE?
I DUNNO, HON... JUST THAT IT'S NOT AS IMPORTANT AS OUR INTEGRITY.
AND THEY LIVED HAPPILY EVER AFTER! SIGH!
10

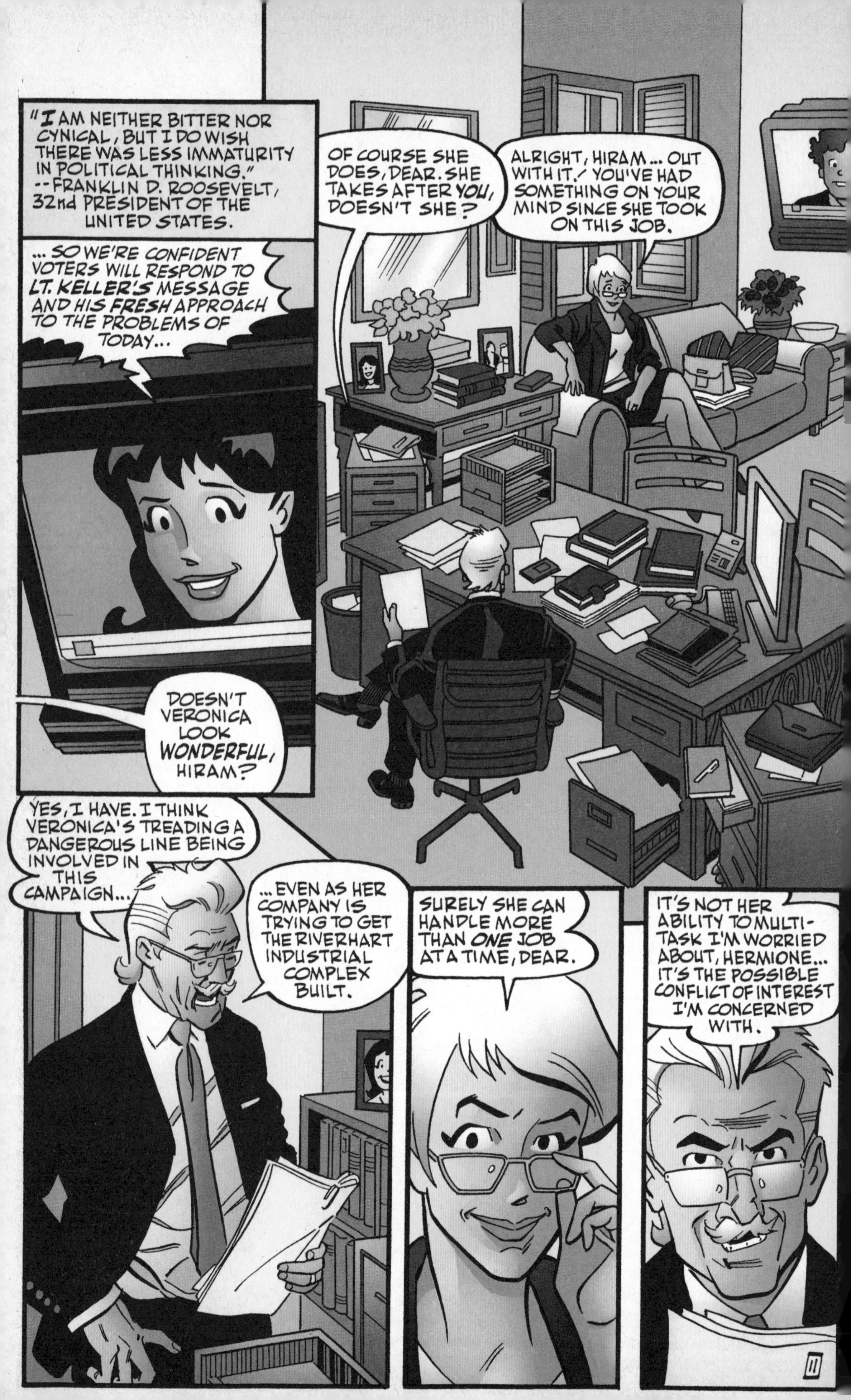
"I AM NEITHER BITTER NOR CYNICAL, BUT I DO WISH THERE WAS LESS IMMATURITY IN POLITICAL THINKING." --FRANKLIN D. ROOSEVELT, 32nd PRESIDENT OF THE UNITED STATES.
...SO WE'RE CONFIDENT VOTERS WILL RESPOND TO LT. KELLER'S MESSAGE AND HIS FRESH APPROACH TO THE PROBLEMS OF TODAY...
DOESN'T VERONICA LOOK WONDERFUL, HIRAM?
OF COURSE SHE DOES, DEAR. SHE TAKES AFTER YOU, DOESN'T SHE?
ALRIGHT, HIRAM... OUT WITH IT.! YOU'VE HAD SOMETHING ON YOUR MIND SINCE SHE TOOK ON THIS JOB.
YES, I HAVE. I THINK VERONICA'S TREADING A DANGEROUS LINE BEING INVOLVED IN THIS CAMPAIGN...
...EVEN AS HER COMPANY IS TRYING TO GET THE RIVERHART INDUSTRIAL COMPLEX BUILT.
SURELY SHE CAN HANDLE MORE THAN ONE JOB AT A TIME, DEAR.
IT'S NOT HER ABILITY TO MULTI-TASK I'M WORRIED ABOUT, HERMIONE... IT'S THE POSSIBLE CONFLICT OF INTEREST I'M CONCERNED WITH.
11

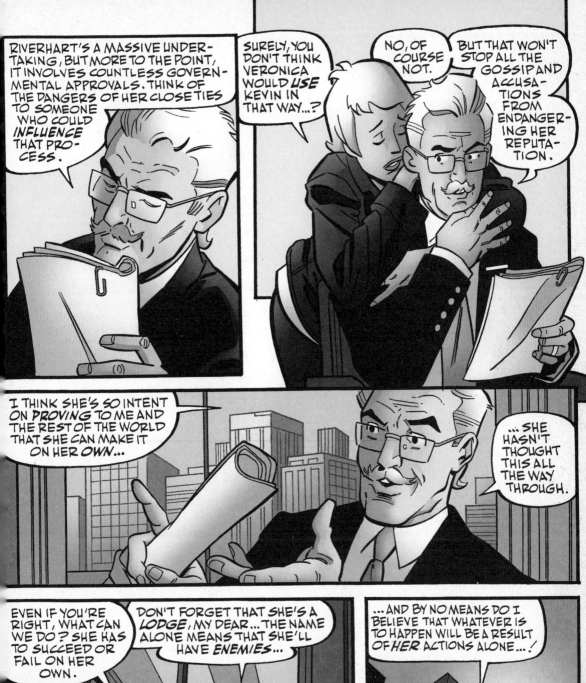

RIVERHART'S A MASSIVE UNDER-TAKING, BUT MORE TO THE POINT, IT INVOLVES COUNTLESS GOVERN-MENTAL APPROVALS. THINK OF THE DANGERS OF HER CLOSE TIES TO SOMEONE WHO COULD *INFLUENCE* THAT PRO-CESS.

SURELY, YOU DON'T THINK VERONICA WOULD *USE* KEVIN IN THAT WAY...?

NO, OF COURSE NOT.

BUT THAT WON'T STOP ALL THE GOSSIP AND ACCUSA-TIONS FROM ENDANGER-ING HER REPUTA-TION.

I THINK SHE'S SO INTENT ON *PROVING* TO ME AND THE REST OF THE WORLD THAT SHE CAN MAKE IT ON HER *OWN*...

...SHE HASN'T THOUGHT THIS ALL THE WAY THROUGH.

EVEN IF YOU'RE RIGHT, WHAT CAN WE DO? SHE HAS TO SUCCEED OR FAIL ON HER OWN.

DON'T FORGET THAT SHE'S A *LODGE*, MY DEAR... THE NAME ALONE MEANS THAT SHE'LL HAVE *ENEMIES*...

...AND BY NO MEANS DO I BELIEVE THAT WHATEVER IS TO HAPPEN WILL BE A RESULT OF *HER* ACTIONS ALONE...!

12

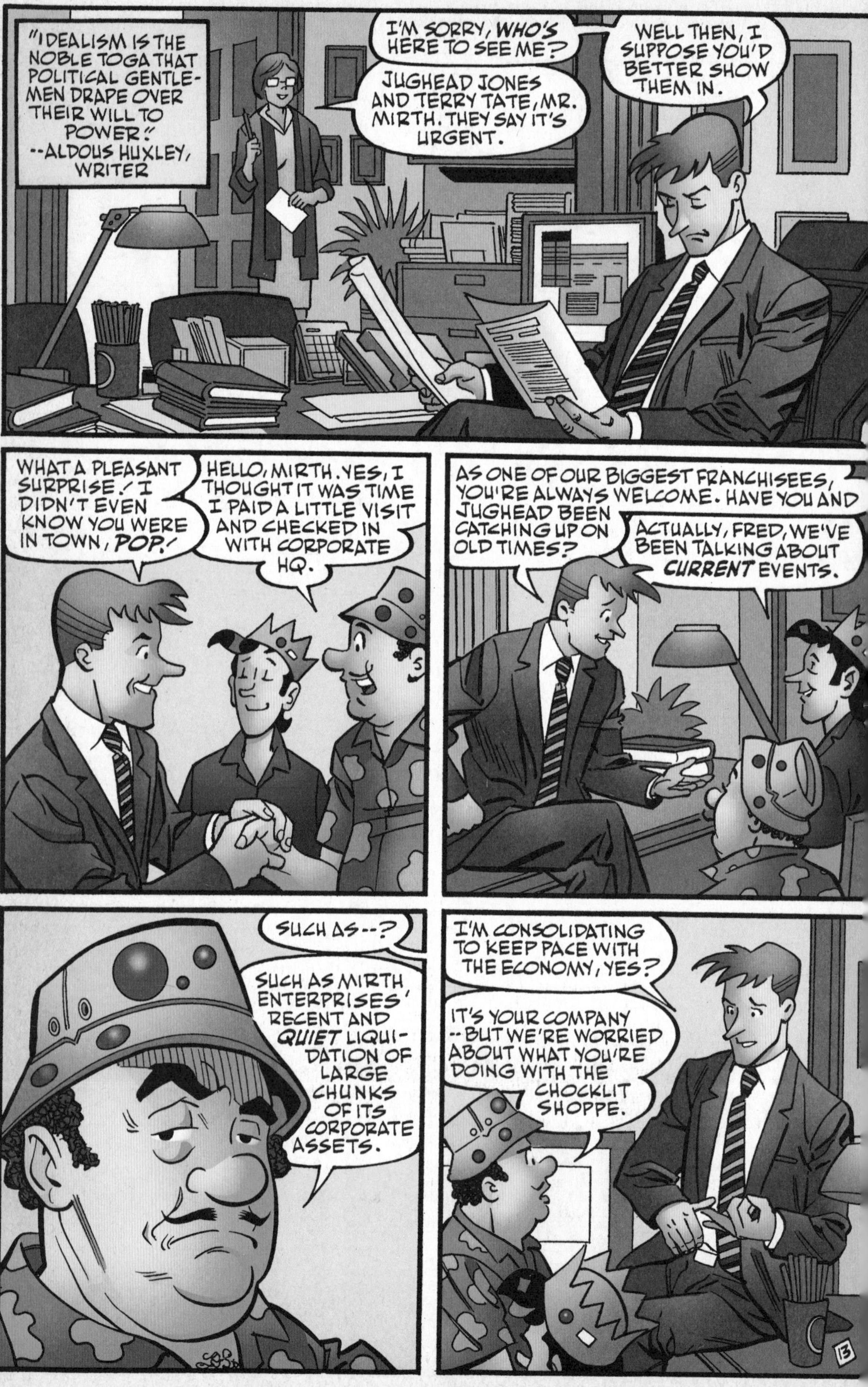
"IDEALISM IS THE NOBLE TOGA THAT POLITICAL GENTLEMEN DRAPE OVER THEIR WILL TO POWER!" --ALDOUS HUXLEY, WRITER
I'M SORRY, WHO'S HERE TO SEE ME?
JUGHEAD JONES AND TERRY TATE, MR. MIRTH. THEY SAY IT'S URGENT.
WELL THEN, I SUPPOSE YOU'D BETTER SHOW THEM IN.
WHAT A PLEASANT SURPRISE! I DIDN'T EVEN KNOW YOU WERE IN TOWN, POP!
HELLO, MIRTH. YES, I THOUGHT IT WAS TIME I PAID A LITTLE VISIT AND CHECKED IN WITH CORPORATE HQ.
AS ONE OF OUR BIGGEST FRANCHISEES, YOU'RE ALWAYS WELCOME. HAVE YOU AND JUGHEAD BEEN CATCHING UP ON OLD TIMES?
ACTUALLY, FRED, WE'VE BEEN TALKING ABOUT CURRENT EVENTS.
SUCH AS--?
SUCH AS MIRTH ENTERPRISES' RECENT AND QUIET LIQUIDATION OF LARGE CHUNKS OF ITS CORPORATE ASSETS.
I'M CONSOLIDATING TO KEEP PACE WITH THE ECONOMY, YES?
IT'S YOUR COMPANY --BUT WE'RE WORRIED ABOUT WHAT YOU'RE DOING WITH THE CHOCKLIT SHOPPE.
13

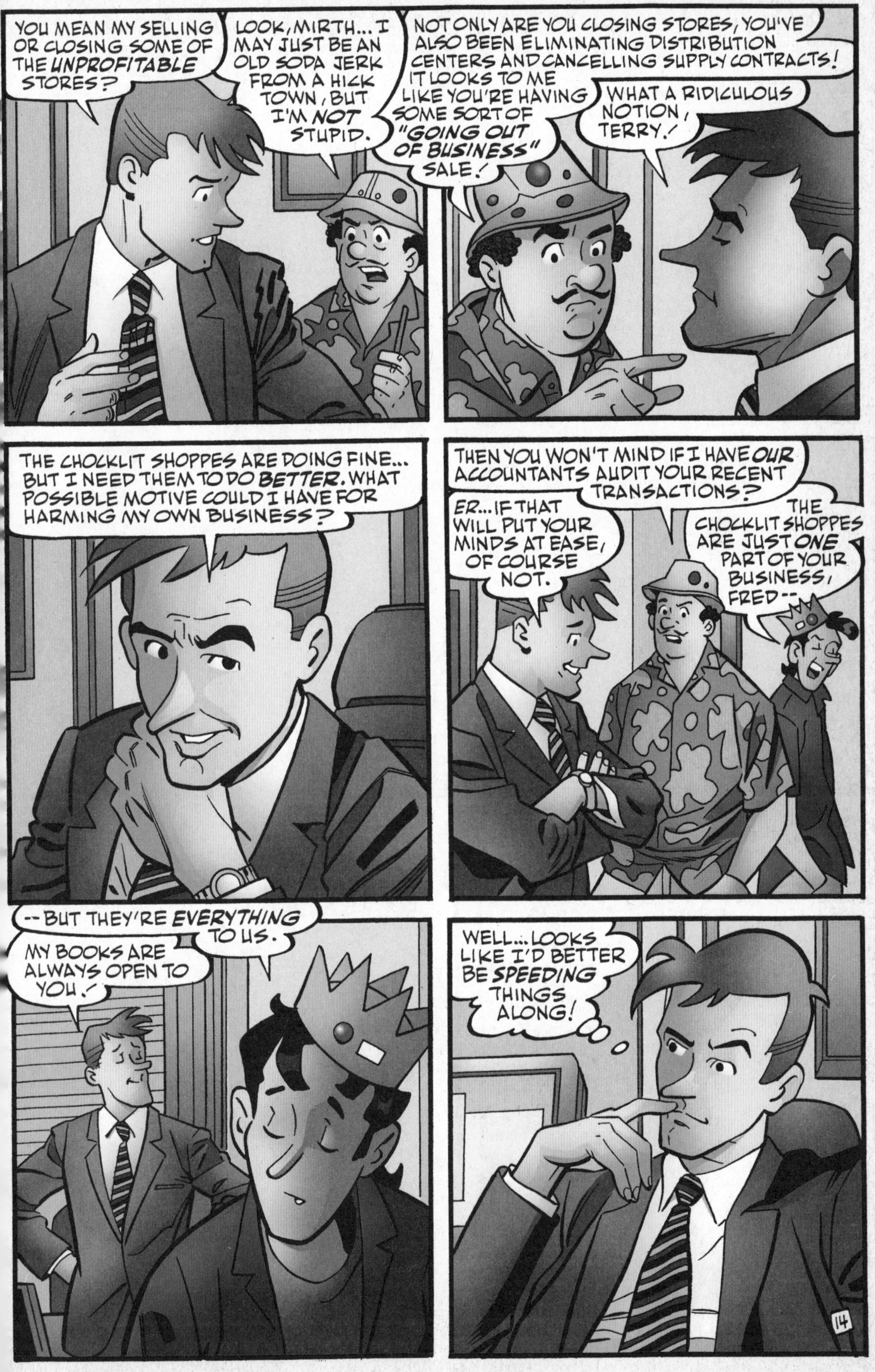
YOU MEAN MY SELLING OR CLOSING SOME OF THE UNPROFITABLE STORES?
LOOK, MIRTH... I MAY JUST BE AN OLD SODA JERK FROM A HICK TOWN, BUT I'M NOT STUPID.
NOT ONLY ARE YOU CLOSING STORES, YOU'VE ALSO BEEN ELIMINATING DISTRIBUTION CENTERS AND CANCELLING SUPPLY CONTRACTS!
IT LOOKS TO ME LIKE YOU'RE HAVING SOME SORT OF "GOING OUT OF BUSINESS" SALE!
WHAT A RIDICULOUS NOTION, TERRY!
THE CHOCKLIT SHOPPES ARE DOING FINE... BUT I NEED THEM TO DO BETTER. WHAT POSSIBLE MOTIVE COULD I HAVE FOR HARMING MY OWN BUSINESS?
THEN YOU WON'T MIND IF I HAVE OUR ACCOUNTANTS AUDIT YOUR RECENT TRANSACTIONS?
ER... IF THAT WILL PUT YOUR MINDS AT EASE, OF COURSE NOT.
THE CHOCKLIT SHOPPES ARE JUST ONE PART OF YOUR BUSINESS, FRED--
--BUT THEY'RE EVERYTHING TO US.
MY BOOKS ARE ALWAYS OPEN TO YOU!
WELL... LOOKS LIKE I'D BETTER BE SPEEDING THINGS ALONG!
14

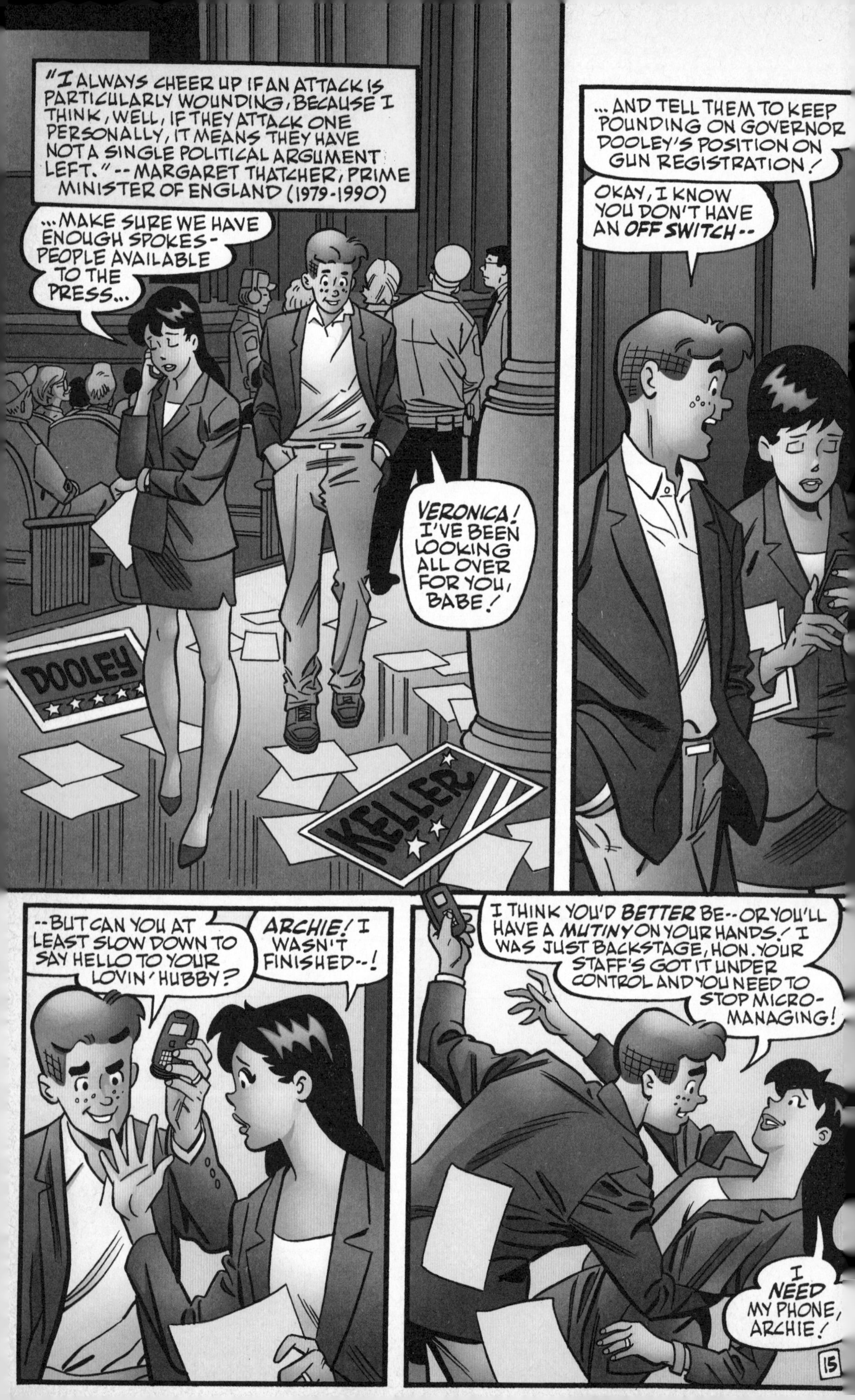
"I ALWAYS CHEER UP IF AN ATTACK IS PARTICULARLY WOUNDING, BECAUSE I THINK, WELL, IF THEY ATTACK ONE PERSONALLY, IT MEANS THEY HAVE NOT A SINGLE POLITICAL ARGUMENT LEFT." -- MARGARET THATCHER, PRIME MINISTER OF ENGLAND (1979-1990)
...MAKE SURE WE HAVE ENOUGH SPOKES-PEOPLE AVAILABLE TO THE PRESS...
VERONICA! I'VE BEEN LOOKING ALL OVER FOR YOU, BABE!
DOOLEY
KELLER
...AND TELL THEM TO KEEP POUNDING ON GOVERNOR DOOLEY'S POSITION ON GUN REGISTRATION!
OKAY, I KNOW YOU DON'T HAVE AN OFF SWITCH--
--BUT CAN YOU AT LEAST SLOW DOWN TO SAY HELLO TO YOUR LOVIN' HUBBY?
ARCHIE! I WASN'T FINISHED--!
I THINK YOU'D BETTER BE--OR YOU'LL HAVE A MUTINY ON YOUR HANDS! I WAS JUST BACKSTAGE, HON. YOUR STAFF'S GOT IT UNDER CONTROL AND YOU NEED TO STOP MICRO-MANAGING!
I NEED MY PHONE, ARCHIE!

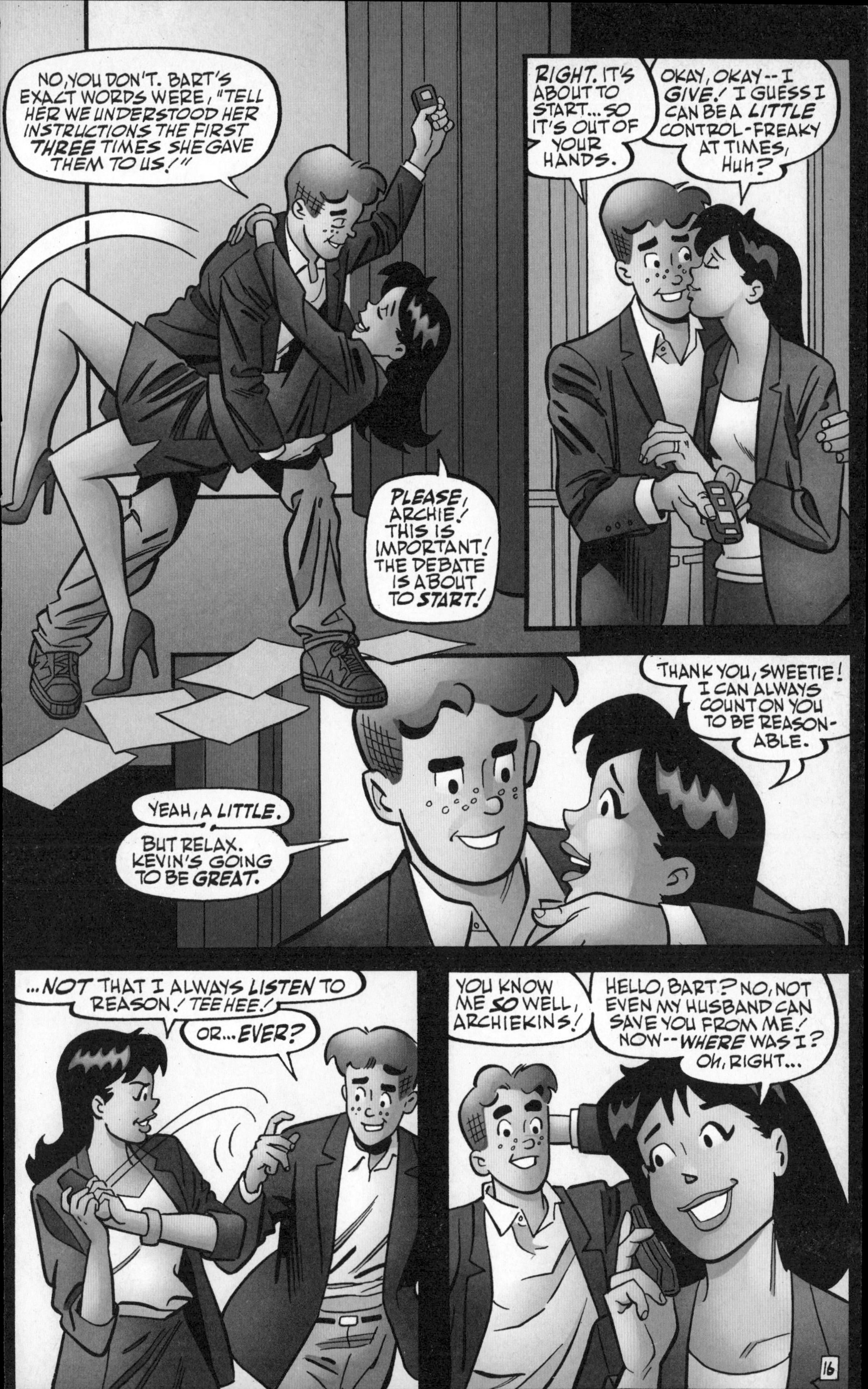
NO, YOU DON'T. BART'S EXACT WORDS WERE, "TELL HER WE UNDERSTOOD HER INSTRUCTIONS THE FIRST THREE TIMES SHE GAVE THEM TO US!"
PLEASE, ARCHIE! THIS IS IMPORTANT! THE DEBATE IS ABOUT TO START!
RIGHT. IT'S ABOUT TO START... SO IT'S OUT OF YOUR HANDS.
OKAY, OKAY -- I GIVE! I GUESS I CAN BE A LITTLE CONTROL-FREAKY AT TIMES, HUH?
YEAH, A LITTLE.
BUT RELAX. KEVIN'S GOING TO BE GREAT.
THANK YOU, SWEETIE! I CAN ALWAYS COUNT ON YOU TO BE REASONABLE.
...NOT THAT I ALWAYS LISTEN TO REASON! TEE HEE!
OR... EVER?
YOU KNOW ME SO WELL, ARCHIEKINS!
HELLO, BART? NO, NOT EVEN MY HUSBAND CAN SAVE YOU FROM ME! NOW -- WHERE WAS I? OH, RIGHT...
16

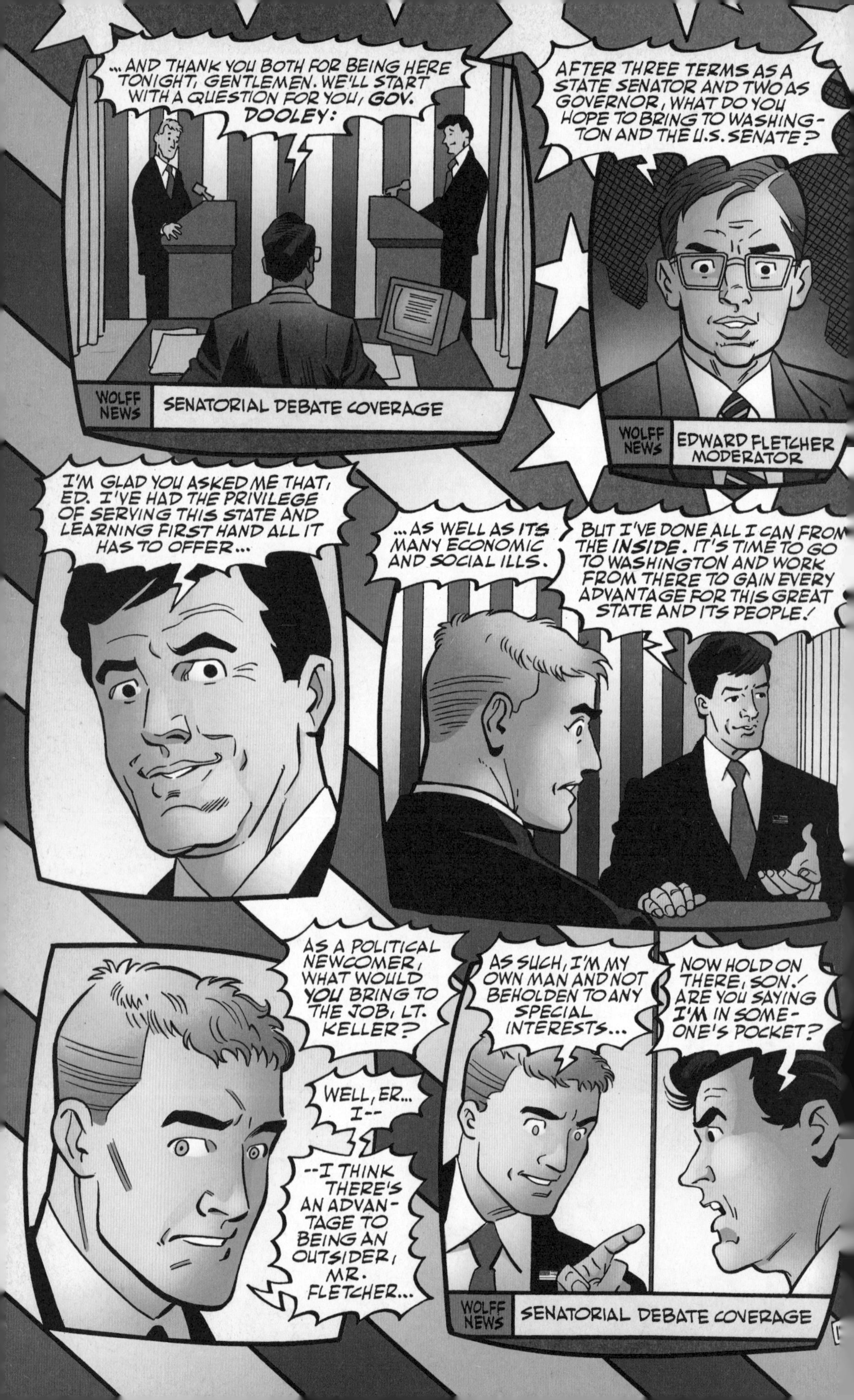
...AND THANK YOU BOTH FOR BEING HERE TONIGHT, GENTLEMEN. WE'LL START WITH A QUESTION FOR YOU, GOV. DOOLEY:
WOLFF NEWS
SENATORIAL DEBATE COVERAGE
AFTER THREE TERMS AS A STATE SENATOR AND TWO AS GOVERNOR, WHAT DO YOU HOPE TO BRING TO WASHINGTON AND THE U.S. SENATE?
WOLFF NEWS
EDWARD FLETCHER MODERATOR
I'M GLAD YOU ASKED ME THAT, ED. I'VE HAD THE PRIVILEGE OF SERVING THIS STATE AND LEARNING FIRST HAND ALL IT HAS TO OFFER...
...AS WELL AS ITS MANY ECONOMIC AND SOCIAL ILLS.
BUT I'VE DONE ALL I CAN FROM THE INSIDE. IT'S TIME TO GO TO WASHINGTON AND WORK FROM THERE TO GAIN EVERY ADVANTAGE FOR THIS GREAT STATE AND ITS PEOPLE!
AS A POLITICAL NEWCOMER, WHAT WOULD YOU BRING TO THE JOB, LT. KELLER?
WELL, ER... I--
--I THINK THERE'S AN ADVANTAGE TO BEING AN OUTSIDER, MR. FLETCHER...
AS SUCH, I'M MY OWN MAN AND NOT BEHOLDEN TO ANY SPECIAL INTERESTS...
NOW HOLD ON THERE, SON! ARE YOU SAYING I'M IN SOMEONE'S POCKET?
WOLFF NEWS
SENATORIAL DEBATE COVERAGE

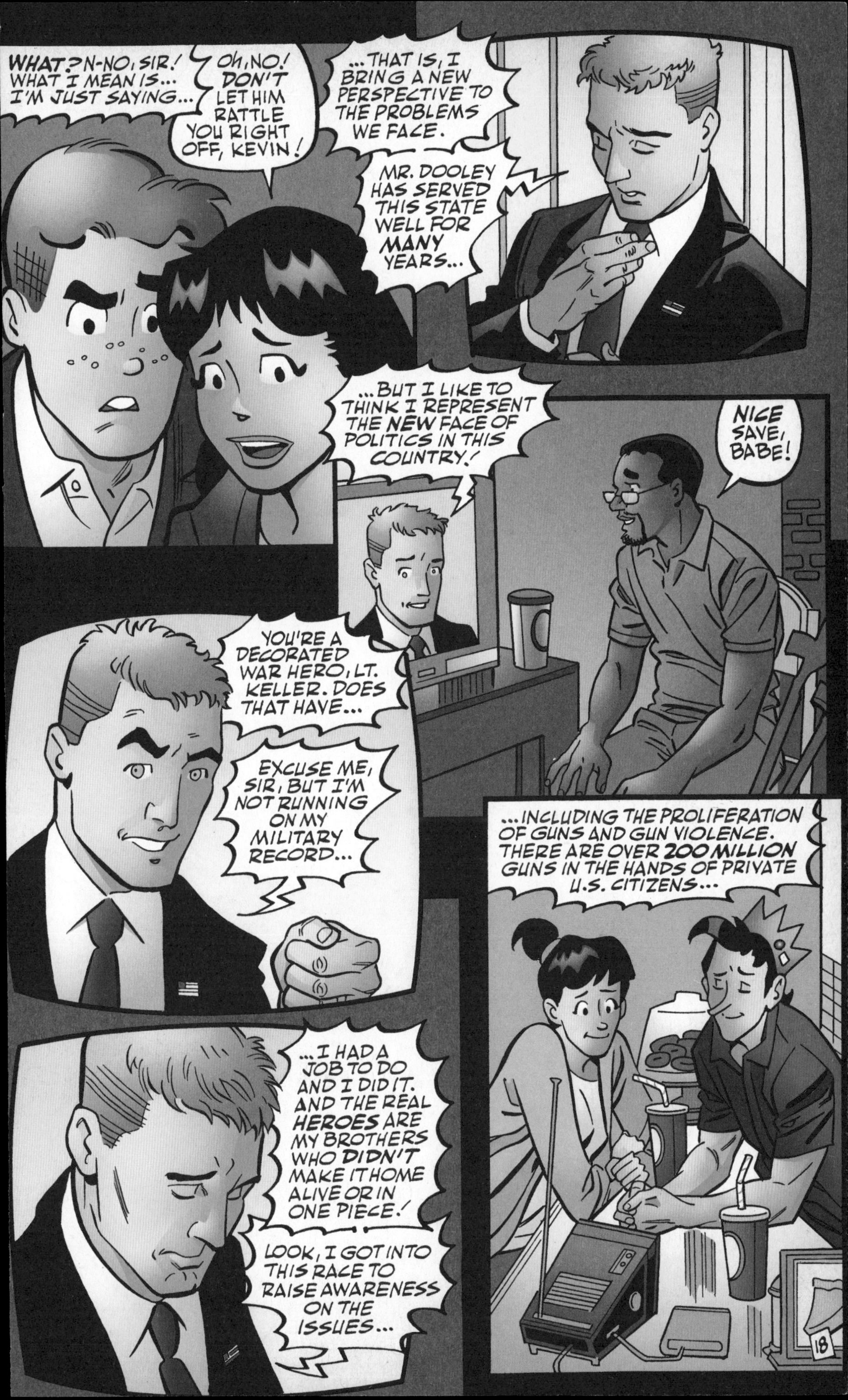
WHAT? N-NO, SIR! WHAT I MEAN IS... I'M JUST SAYING...
OH, NO! DON'T LET HIM RATTLE YOU RIGHT OFF, KEVIN!
...THAT IS, I BRING A NEW PERSPECTIVE TO THE PROBLEMS WE FACE.
MR. DOOLEY HAS SERVED THIS STATE WELL FOR MANY YEARS...
...BUT I LIKE TO THINK I REPRESENT THE NEW FACE OF POLITICS IN THIS COUNTRY!
NICE SAVE, BABE!
YOU'RE A DECORATED WAR HERO, LT. KELLER. DOES THAT HAVE...
EXCUSE ME, SIR, BUT I'M NOT RUNNING ON MY MILITARY RECORD...
...I HAD A JOB TO DO AND I DID IT. AND THE REAL HEROES ARE MY BROTHERS WHO DIDN'T MAKE IT HOME ALIVE OR IN ONE PIECE!
LOOK, I GOT INTO THIS RACE TO RAISE AWARENESS ON THE ISSUES...
...INCLUDING THE PROLIFERATION OF GUNS AND GUN VIOLENCE. THERE ARE OVER 200 MILLION GUNS IN THE HANDS OF PRIVATE U.S. CITIZENS...
18

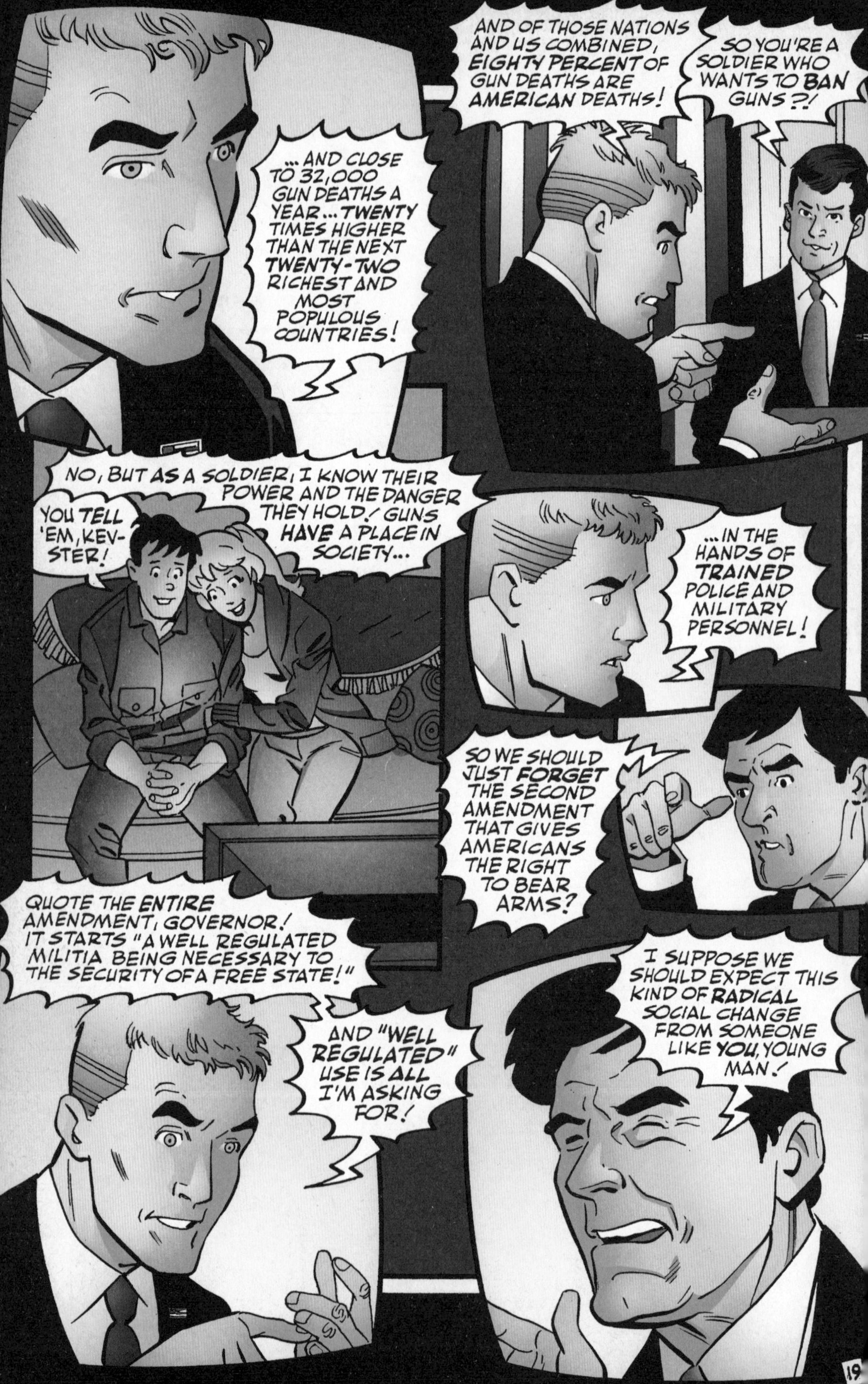
...AND CLOSE TO 32,000 GUN DEATHS A YEAR...TWENTY TIMES HIGHER THAN THE NEXT TWENTY-TWO RICHEST AND MOST POPULOUS COUNTRIES!
AND OF THOSE NATIONS AND US COMBINED, EIGHTY PERCENT OF GUN DEATHS ARE AMERICAN DEATHS!
SO YOU'RE A SOLDIER WHO WANTS TO BAN GUNS?!
NO, BUT AS A SOLDIER, I KNOW THEIR POWER AND THE DANGER THEY HOLD! GUNS HAVE A PLACE IN SOCIETY...
YOU TELL 'EM, KEV-STER!
...IN THE HANDS OF TRAINED POLICE AND MILITARY PERSONNEL!
SO WE SHOULD JUST FORGET THE SECOND AMENDMENT THAT GIVES AMERICANS THE RIGHT TO BEAR ARMS?
QUOTE THE ENTIRE AMENDMENT, GOVERNOR! IT STARTS "A WELL REGULATED MILITIA BEING NECESSARY TO THE SECURITY OF A FREE STATE!"
AND "WELL REGULATED" USE IS ALL I'M ASKING FOR!
I SUPPOSE WE SHOULD EXPECT THIS KIND OF RADICAL SOCIAL CHANGE FROM SOMEONE LIKE YOU, YOUNG MAN!

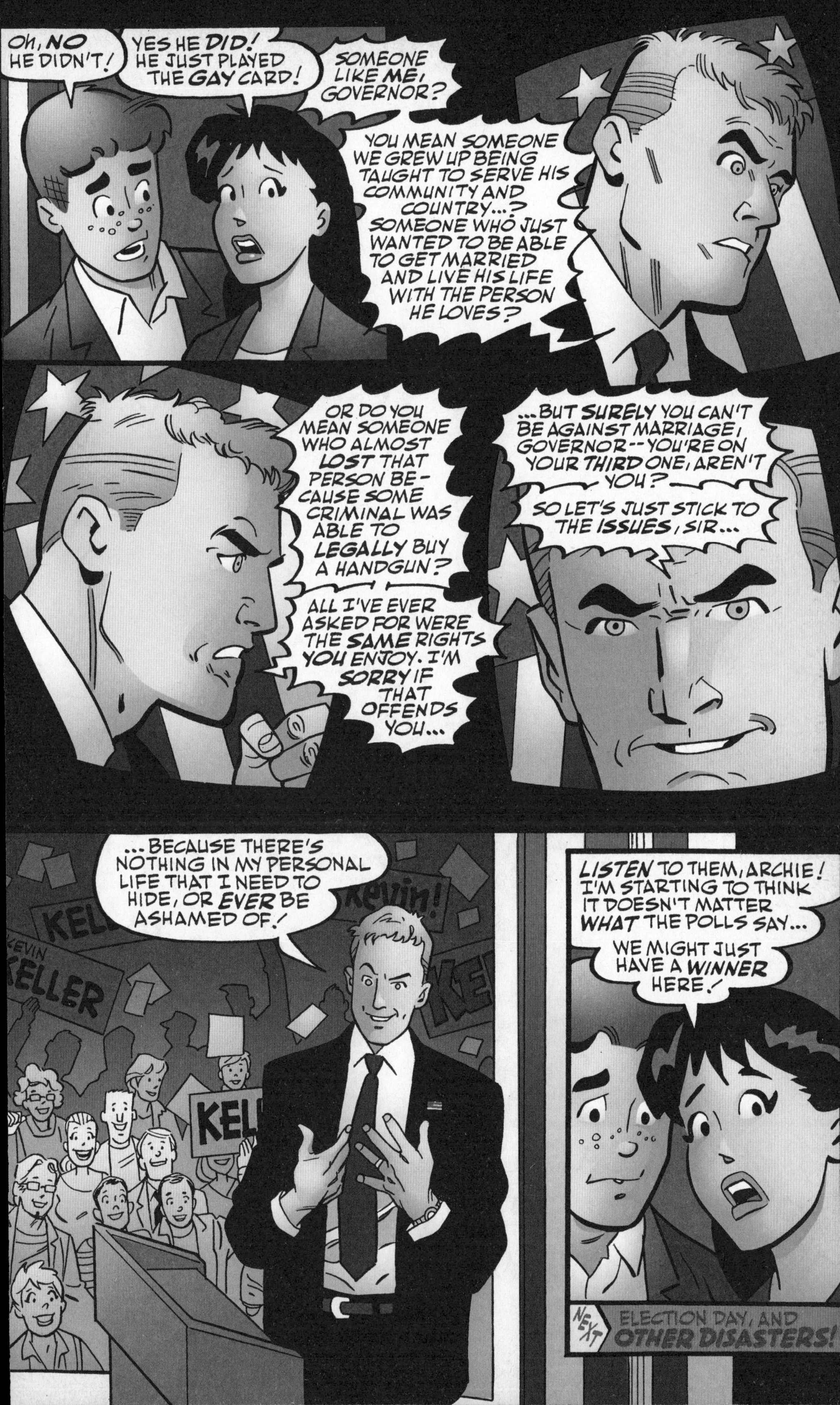
Oh, NO HE DIDN'T!
YES HE DID! HE JUST PLAYED THE GAY CARD!
SOMEONE LIKE ME, GOVERNOR?
YOU MEAN SOMEONE WE GREW UP BEING TAUGHT TO SERVE HIS COMMUNITY AND COUNTRY...? SOMEONE WHO JUST WANTED TO BE ABLE TO GET MARRIED AND LIVE HIS LIFE WITH THE PERSON HE LOVES?
OR DO YOU MEAN SOMEONE WHO ALMOST LOST THAT PERSON BE-CAUSE SOME CRIMINAL WAS ABLE TO LEGALLY BUY A HANDGUN?
ALL I'VE EVER ASKED FOR WERE THE SAME RIGHTS YOU ENJOY. I'M SORRY IF THAT OFFENDS YOU...
...BUT SURELY YOU CAN'T BE AGAINST MARRIAGE, GOVERNOR -- YOU'RE ON YOUR THIRD ONE, AREN'T YOU?
SO LET'S JUST STICK TO THE ISSUES, SIR...
... BECAUSE THERE'S NOTHING IN MY PERSONAL LIFE THAT I NEED TO HIDE, OR EVER BE ASHAMED OF!
KEVIN KELLER
LISTEN TO THEM, ARCHIE! I'M STARTING TO THINK IT DOESN'T MATTER WHAT THE POLLS SAY...
WE MIGHT JUST HAVE A WINNER HERE!
NEXT ELECTION DAY, AND OTHER DISASTERS!

"NO, I'M PRETTY SURE
I'M LOOKING AT *YOU*."

"IN FACT, LATELY, YOU'RE THE
ONLY GIRL I SEEM TO *SEE*,
NO MATTER *WHERE* I LOOK!"

-*KEITH DIAMOND*

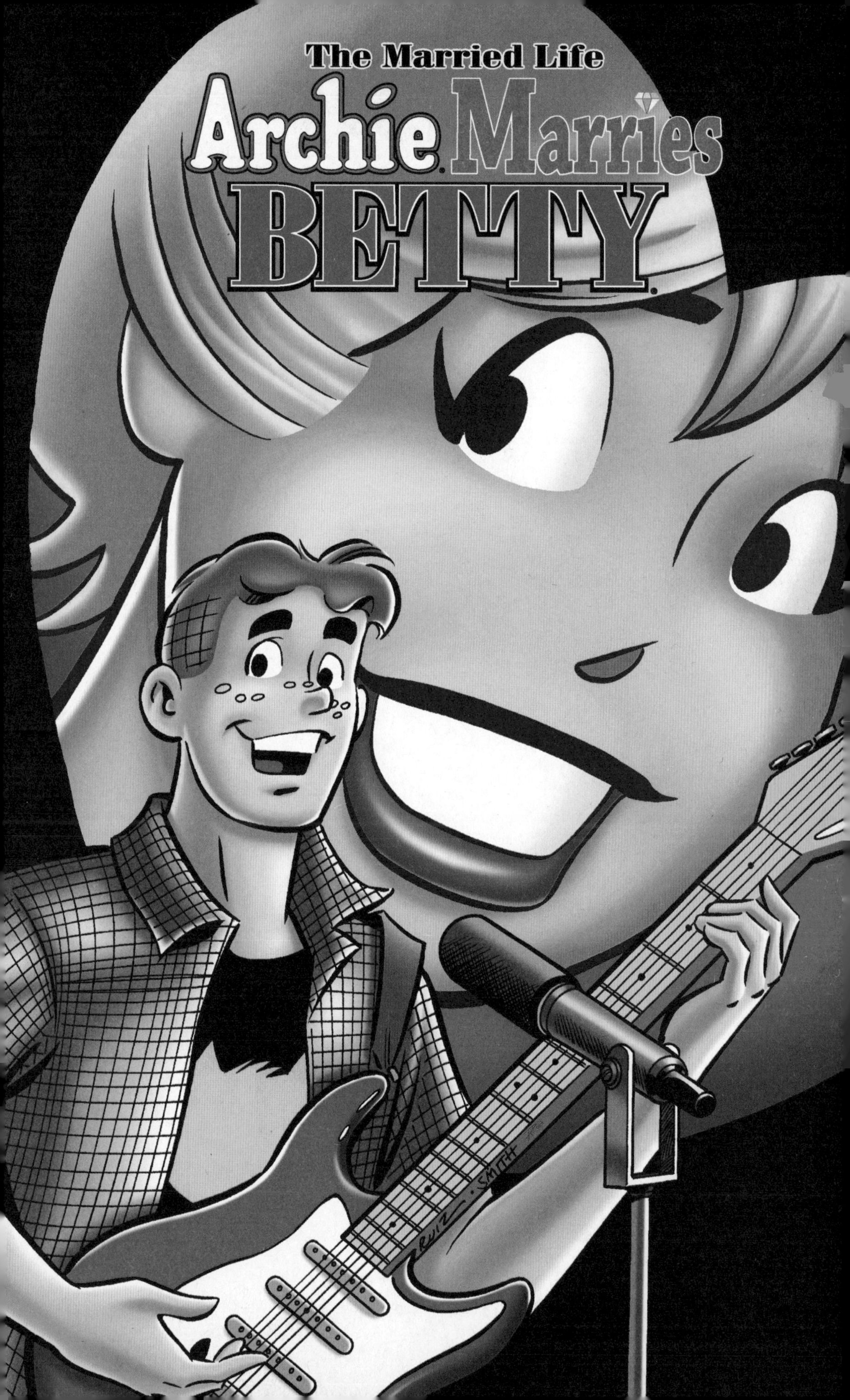
The Married Life
Archie Marries
BETTY

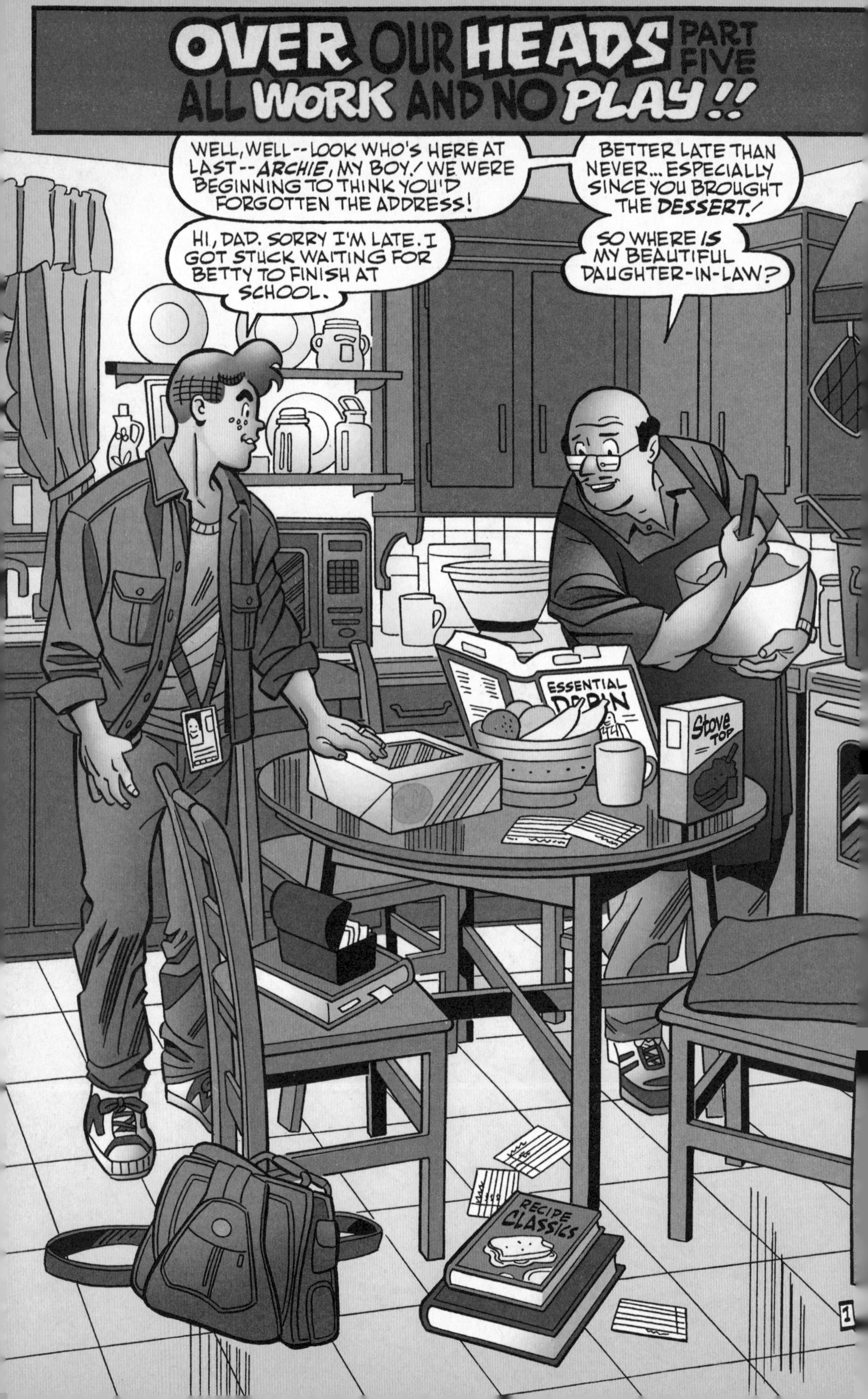
OVER OUR HEADS PART FIVE
ALL WORK AND NO PLAY!!
WELL, WELL--LOOK WHO'S HERE AT LAST--ARCHIE, MY BOY! WE WERE BEGINNING TO THINK YOU'D FORGOTTEN THE ADDRESS!
BETTER LATE THAN NEVER... ESPECIALLY SINCE YOU BROUGHT THE DESSERT!
HI, DAD. SORRY I'M LATE. I GOT STUCK WAITING FOR BETTY TO FINISH AT SCHOOL.
SO WHERE IS MY BEAUTIFUL DAUGHTER-IN-LAW?
ESSENTIAL
Stove TOP
RECIPE CLASSICS
1

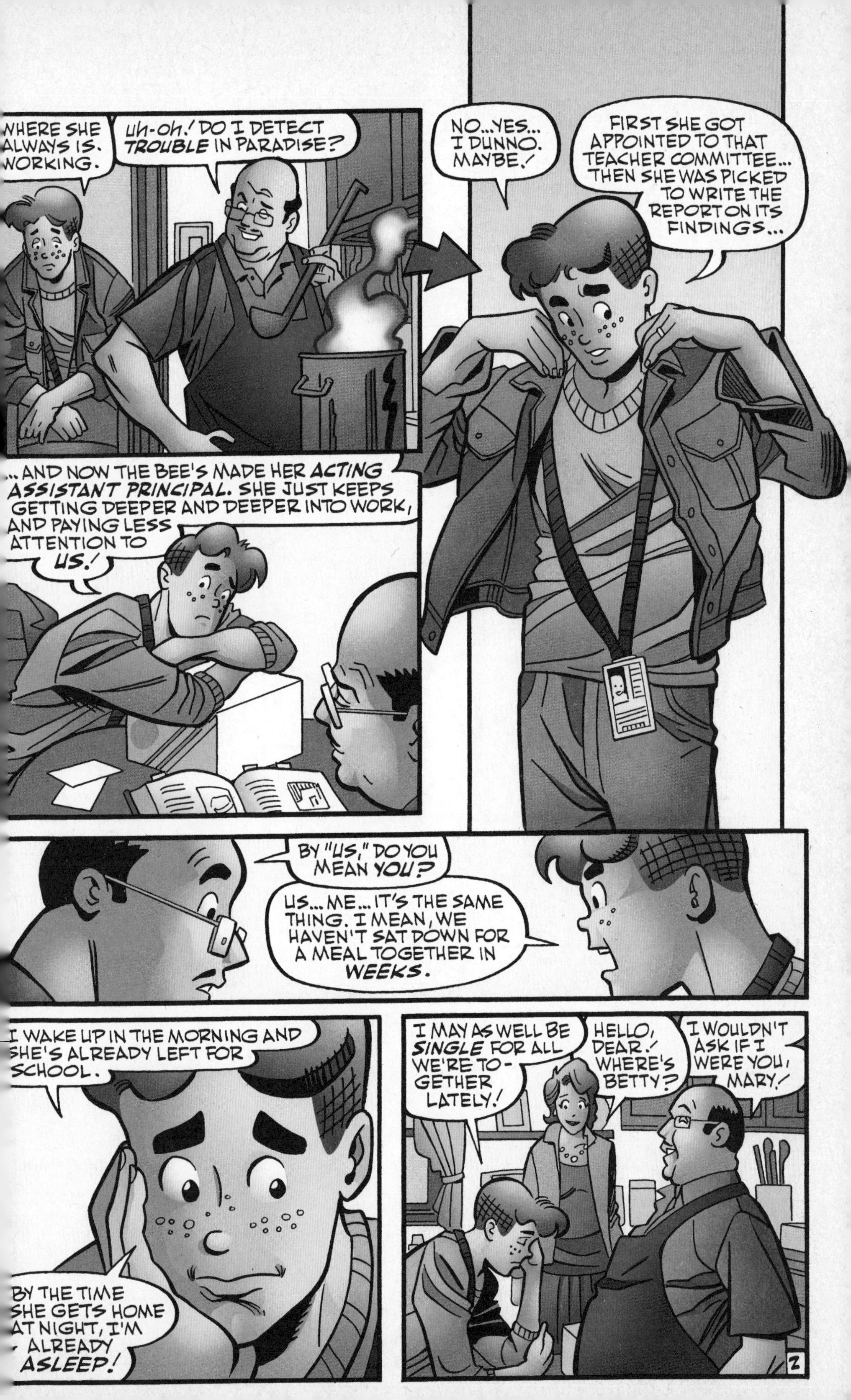
WHERE SHE ALWAYS IS. WORKING.
UH-OH! DO I DETECT TROUBLE IN PARADISE?
NO...YES... I DUNNO. MAYBE!
FIRST SHE GOT APPOINTED TO THAT TEACHER COMMITTEE... THEN SHE WAS PICKED TO WRITE THE REPORT ON ITS FINDINGS...
...AND NOW THE BEE'S MADE HER ACTING ASSISTANT PRINCIPAL. SHE JUST KEEPS GETTING DEEPER AND DEEPER INTO WORK, AND PAYING LESS ATTENTION TO US!
BY "US," DO YOU MEAN YOU?
US... ME... IT'S THE SAME THING. I MEAN, WE HAVEN'T SAT DOWN FOR A MEAL TOGETHER IN WEEKS.
I WAKE UP IN THE MORNING AND SHE'S ALREADY LEFT FOR SCHOOL.
BY THE TIME SHE GETS HOME AT NIGHT, I'M ALREADY ASLEEP!
I MAY AS WELL BE SINGLE FOR ALL WE'RE TOGETHER LATELY!
HELLO, DEAR! WHERE'S BETTY?
I WOULDN'T ASK IF I WERE YOU, MARY!
2

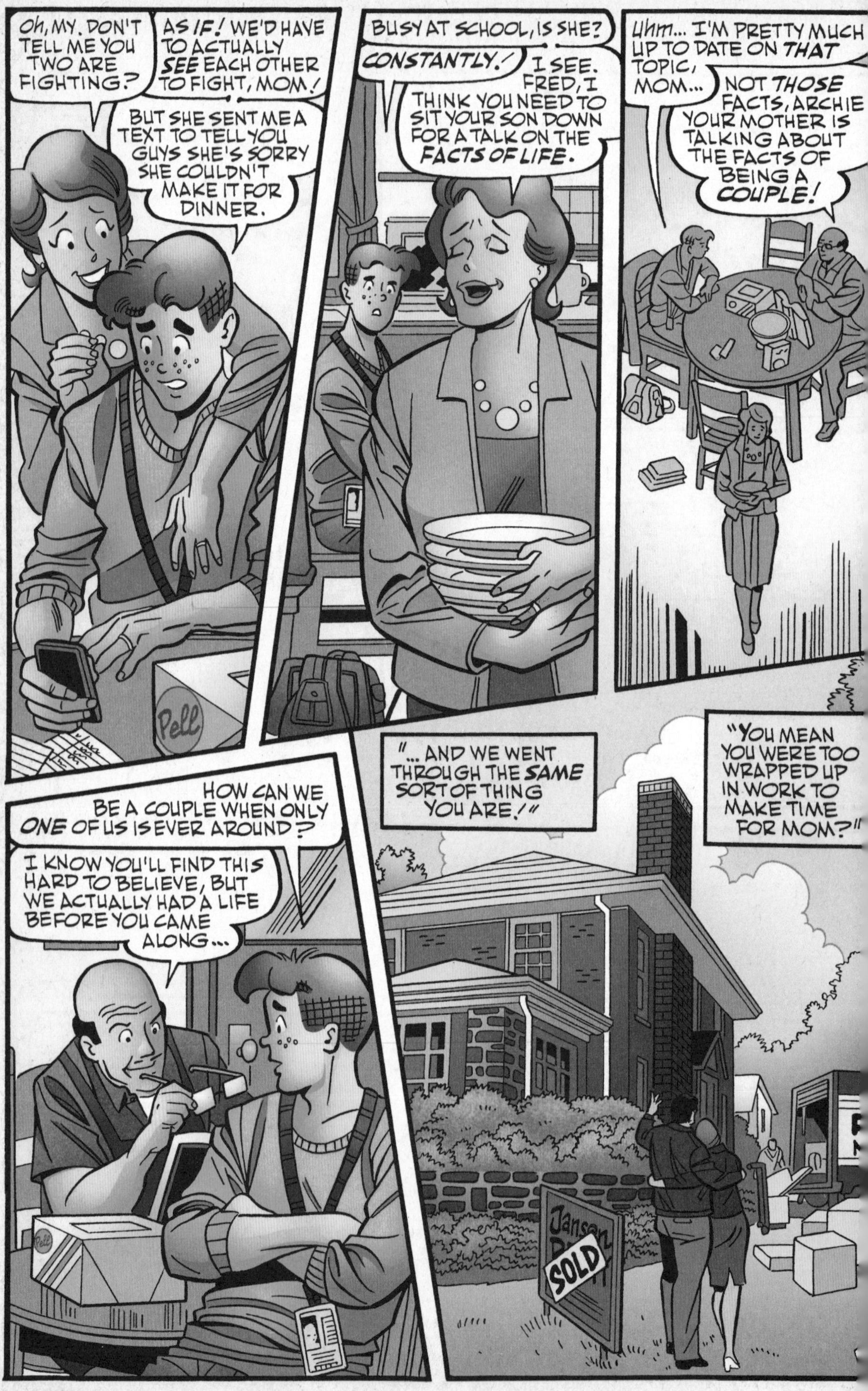
Oh, MY. DON'T TELL ME YOU TWO ARE FIGHTING?
AS IF! WE'D HAVE TO ACTUALLY SEE EACH OTHER TO FIGHT, MOM!
BUT SHE SENT ME A TEXT TO TELL YOU GUYS SHE'S SORRY SHE COULDN'T MAKE IT FOR DINNER.
BUSY AT SCHOOL, IS SHE?
CONSTANTLY!
I SEE. FRED, I THINK YOU NEED TO SIT YOUR SON DOWN FOR A TALK ON THE FACTS OF LIFE.
UHM... I'M PRETTY MUCH UP TO DATE ON THAT TOPIC, MOM...
NOT THOSE FACTS, ARCHIE YOUR MOTHER IS TALKING ABOUT THE FACTS OF BEING A COUPLE!
HOW CAN WE BE A COUPLE WHEN ONLY ONE OF US IS EVER AROUND?
I KNOW YOU'LL FIND THIS HARD TO BELIEVE, BUT WE ACTUALLY HAD A LIFE BEFORE YOU CAME ALONG...
"... AND WE WENT THROUGH THE SAME SORT OF THING YOU ARE!"
"YOU MEAN YOU WERE TOO WRAPPED UP IN WORK TO MAKE TIME FOR MOM?"
SOLD

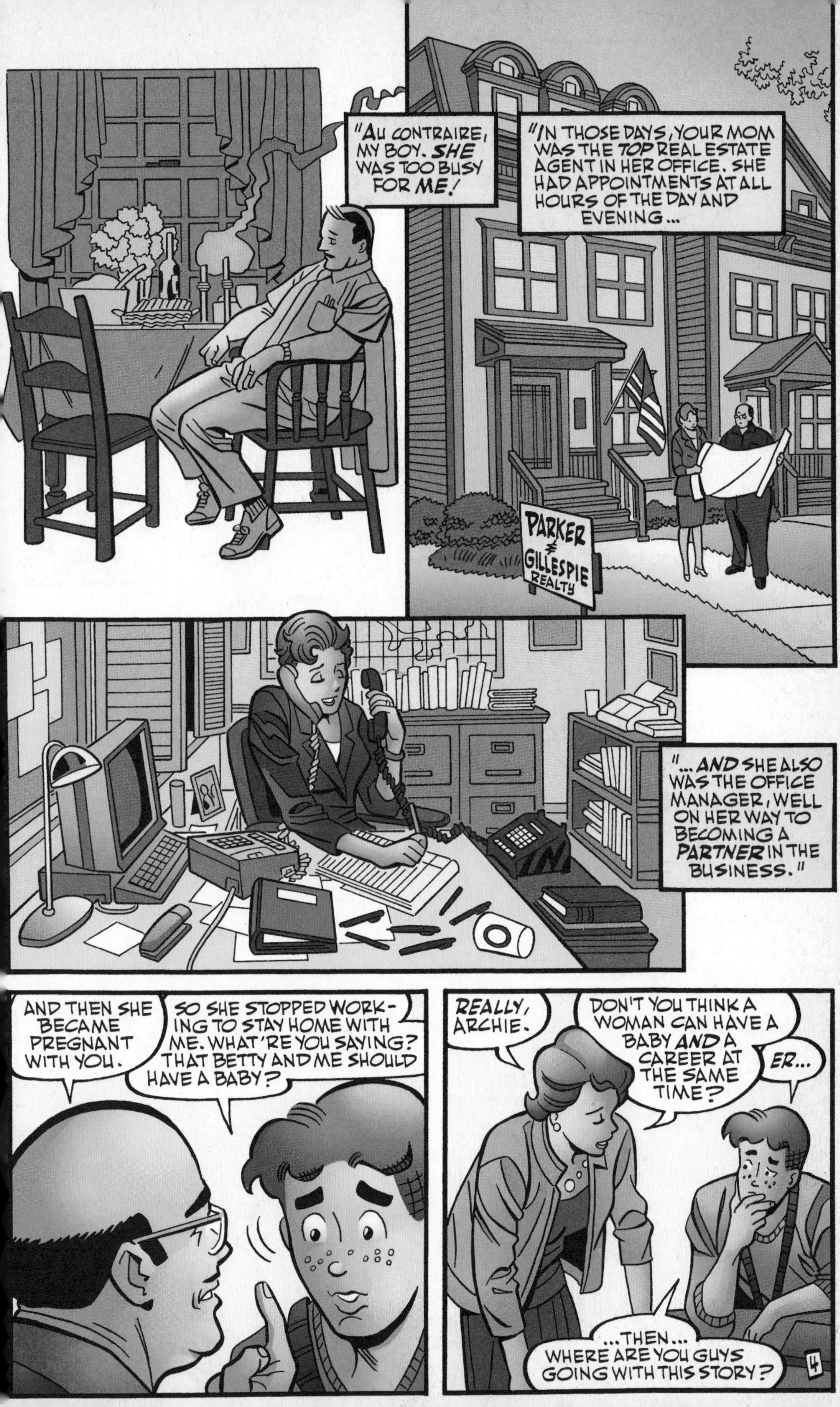
"AU CONTRAIRE, MY BOY. SHE WAS TOO BUSY FOR ME!
"IN THOSE DAYS, YOUR MOM WAS THE TOP REAL ESTATE AGENT IN HER OFFICE. SHE HAD APPOINTMENTS AT ALL HOURS OF THE DAY AND EVENING...
PARKER & GILLESPIE REALTY
"...AND SHE ALSO WAS THE OFFICE MANAGER, WELL ON HER WAY TO BECOMING A PARTNER IN THE BUSINESS."
AND THEN SHE BECAME PREGNANT WITH YOU.
SO SHE STOPPED WORKING TO STAY HOME WITH ME. WHAT'RE YOU SAYING? THAT BETTY AND ME SHOULD HAVE A BABY?
REALLY, ARCHIE.
DON'T YOU THINK A WOMAN CAN HAVE A BABY AND A CAREER AT THE SAME TIME?
ER...
...THEN... WHERE ARE YOU GUYS GOING WITH THIS STORY?
4

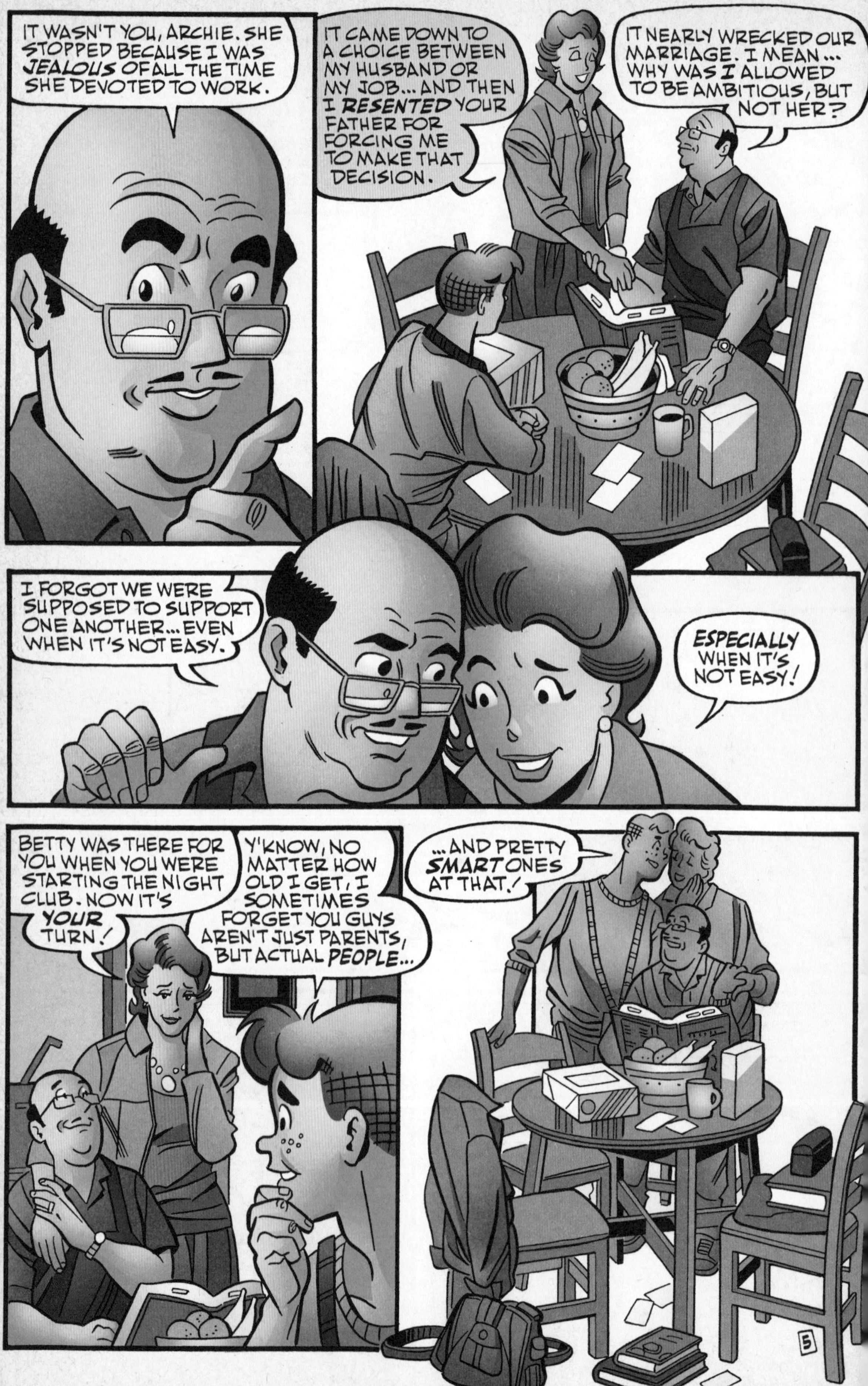
IT WASN'T YOU, ARCHIE. SHE STOPPED BECAUSE I WAS JEALOUS OF ALL THE TIME SHE DEVOTED TO WORK.
IT CAME DOWN TO A CHOICE BETWEEN MY HUSBAND OR MY JOB... AND THEN I RESENTED YOUR FATHER FOR FORCING ME TO MAKE THAT DECISION.
IT NEARLY WRECKED OUR MARRIAGE. I MEAN... WHY WAS I ALLOWED TO BE AMBITIOUS, BUT NOT HER?
I FORGOT WE WERE SUPPOSED TO SUPPORT ONE ANOTHER... EVEN WHEN IT'S NOT EASY.
ESPECIALLY WHEN IT'S NOT EASY!
BETTY WAS THERE FOR YOU WHEN YOU WERE STARTING THE NIGHT CLUB. NOW IT'S YOUR TURN!
Y'KNOW, NO MATTER HOW OLD I GET, I SOMETIMES FORGET YOU GUYS AREN'T JUST PARENTS, BUT ACTUAL PEOPLE...
...AND PRETTY SMART ONES AT THAT!
5

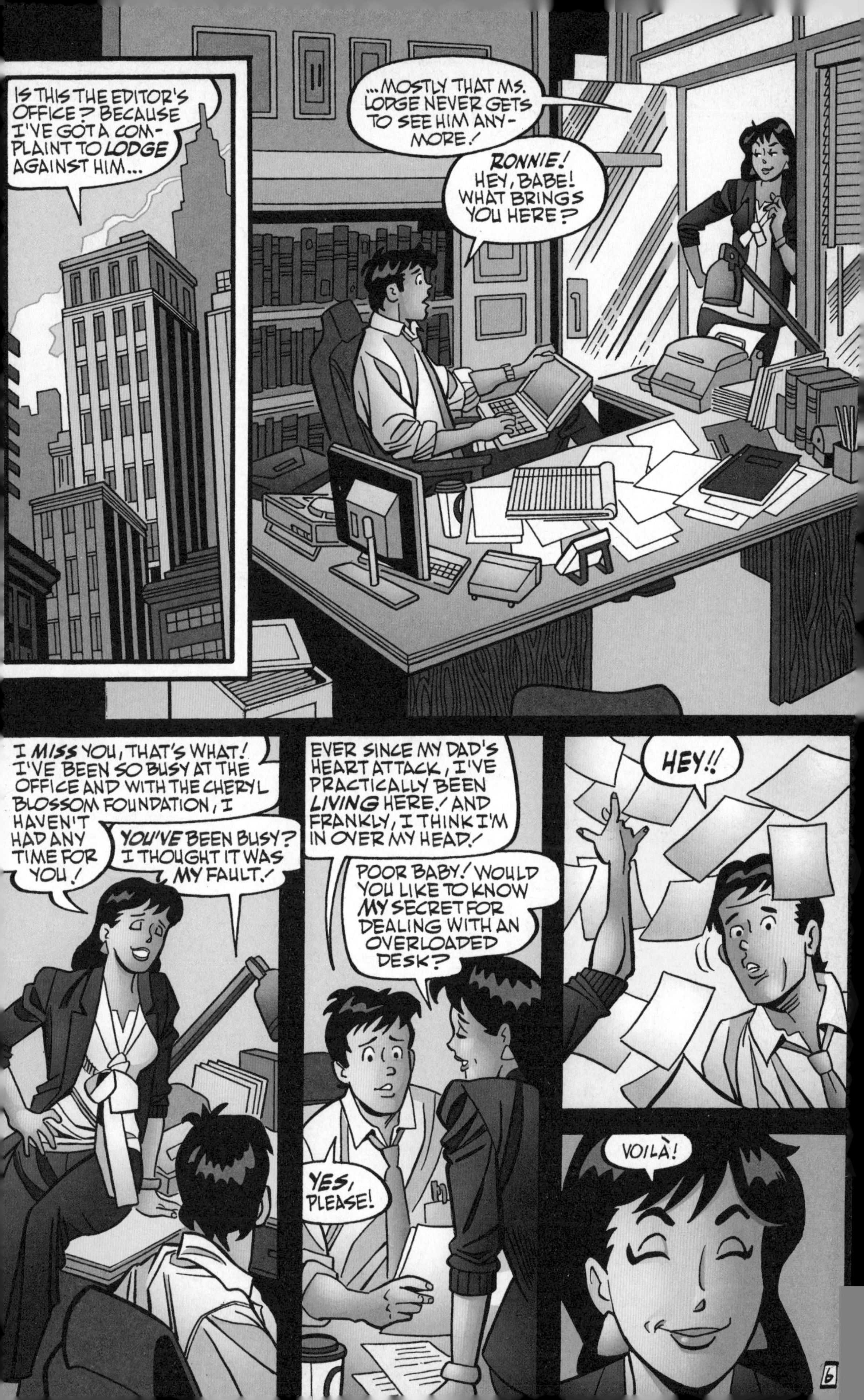

IS THIS THE EDITOR'S OFFICE? BECAUSE I'VE GOT A COMPLAINT TO LODGE AGAINST HIM...
...MOSTLY THAT MS. LODGE NEVER GETS TO SEE HIM ANYMORE!
RONNIE! HEY, BABE! WHAT BRINGS YOU HERE?
I MISS YOU, THAT'S WHAT! I'VE BEEN SO BUSY AT THE OFFICE AND WITH THE CHERYL BLOSSOM FOUNDATION, I HAVEN'T HAD ANY TIME FOR YOU!
YOU'VE BEEN BUSY? I THOUGHT IT WAS MY FAULT!
EVER SINCE MY DAD'S HEART ATTACK, I'VE PRACTICALLY BEEN LIVING HERE! AND FRANKLY, I THINK I'M IN OVER MY HEAD!
POOR BABY! WOULD YOU LIKE TO KNOW MY SECRET FOR DEALING WITH AN OVERLOADED DESK?
YES, PLEASE!
HEY!!
VOILÀ!

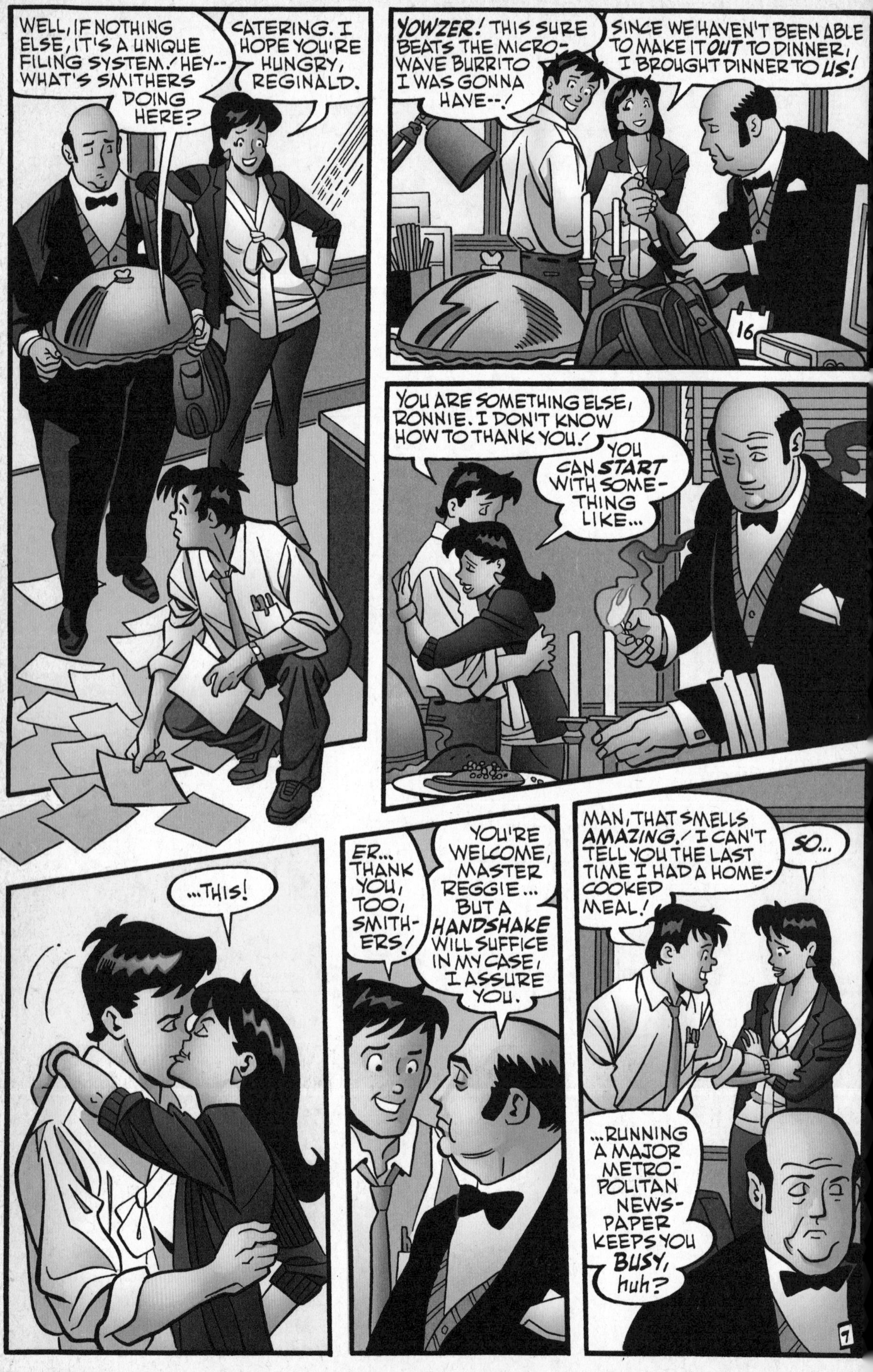
WELL, IF NOTHING ELSE, IT'S A UNIQUE FILING SYSTEM! HEY-- WHAT'S SMITHERS DOING HERE?
CATERING. I HOPE YOU'RE HUNGRY, REGINALD.
YOWZER! THIS SURE BEATS THE MICRO-WAVE BURRITO I WAS GONNA HAVE--!
SINCE WE HAVEN'T BEEN ABLE TO MAKE IT OUT TO DINNER, I BROUGHT DINNER TO US!
16
YOU ARE SOMETHING ELSE, RONNIE. I DON'T KNOW HOW TO THANK YOU!
YOU CAN START WITH SOME-THING LIKE...
...THIS!
ER... THANK YOU, TOO, SMITH-ERS!
YOU'RE WELCOME, MASTER REGGIE... BUT A HANDSHAKE WILL SUFFICE IN MY CASE, I ASSURE YOU.
MAN, THAT SMELLS AMAZING! I CAN'T TELL YOU THE LAST TIME I HAD A HOME-COOKED MEAL!
SO...
...RUNNING A MAJOR METRO-POLITAN NEWS-PAPER KEEPS YOU BUSY, huh?
7

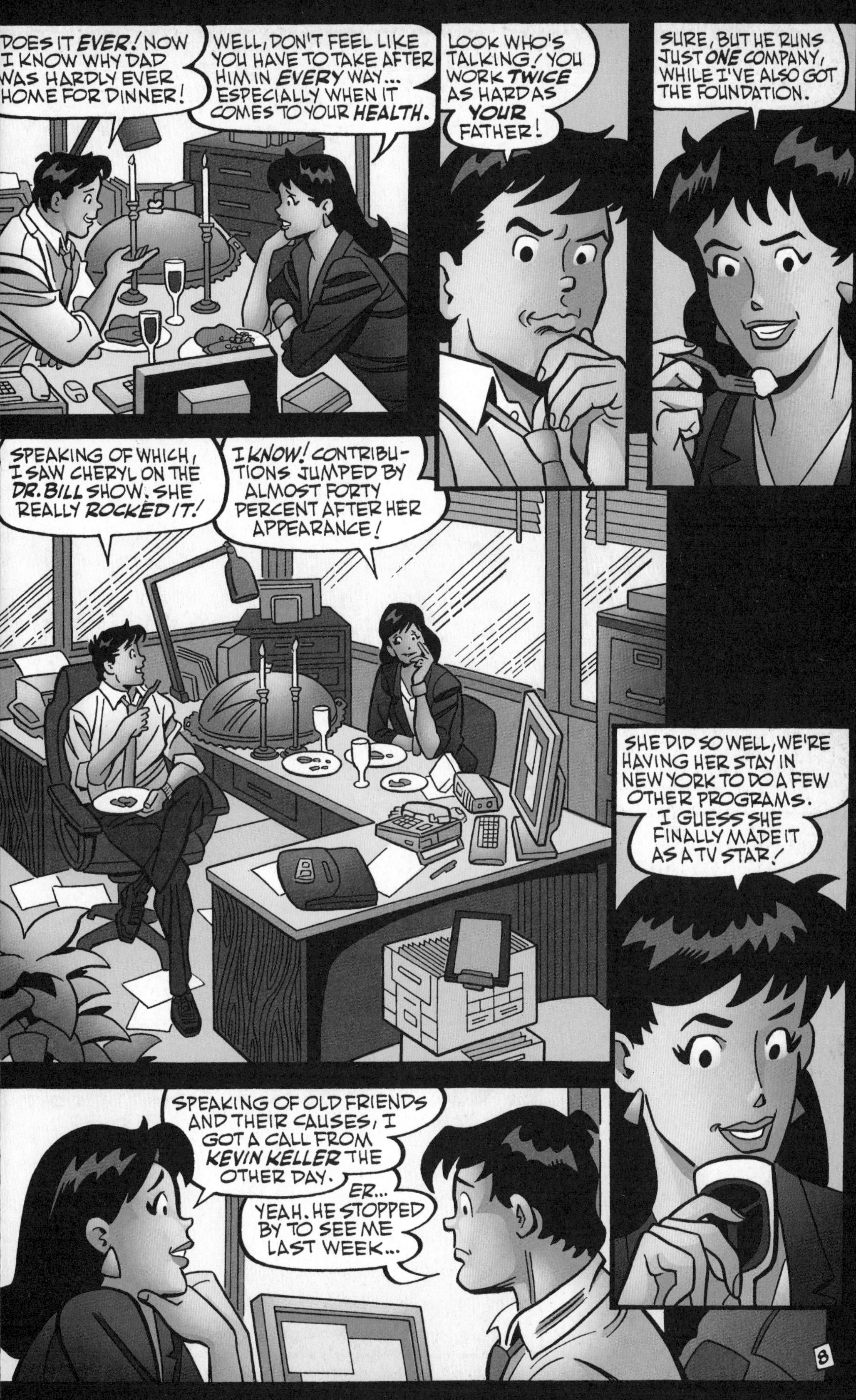
DOES IT EVER! NOW I KNOW WHY DAD WAS HARDLY EVER HOME FOR DINNER!
WELL, DON'T FEEL LIKE YOU HAVE TO TAKE AFTER HIM IN EVERY WAY... ESPECIALLY WHEN IT COMES TO YOUR HEALTH.
LOOK WHO'S TALKING! YOU WORK TWICE AS HARD AS YOUR FATHER!
SURE, BUT HE RUNS JUST ONE COMPANY, WHILE I'VE ALSO GOT THE FOUNDATION.
SPEAKING OF WHICH, I SAW CHERYL ON THE DR. BILL SHOW. SHE REALLY ROCKED IT!
I KNOW! CONTRIBU- TIONS JUMPED BY ALMOST FORTY PERCENT AFTER HER APPEARANCE!
SHE DID SO WELL, WE'RE HAVING HER STAY IN NEW YORK TO DO A FEW OTHER PROGRAMS. I GUESS SHE FINALLY MADE IT AS A TV STAR!
SPEAKING OF OLD FRIENDS AND THEIR CAUSES, I GOT A CALL FROM KEVIN KELLER THE OTHER DAY.
ER... YEAH. HE STOPPED BY TO SEE ME LAST WEEK...
8

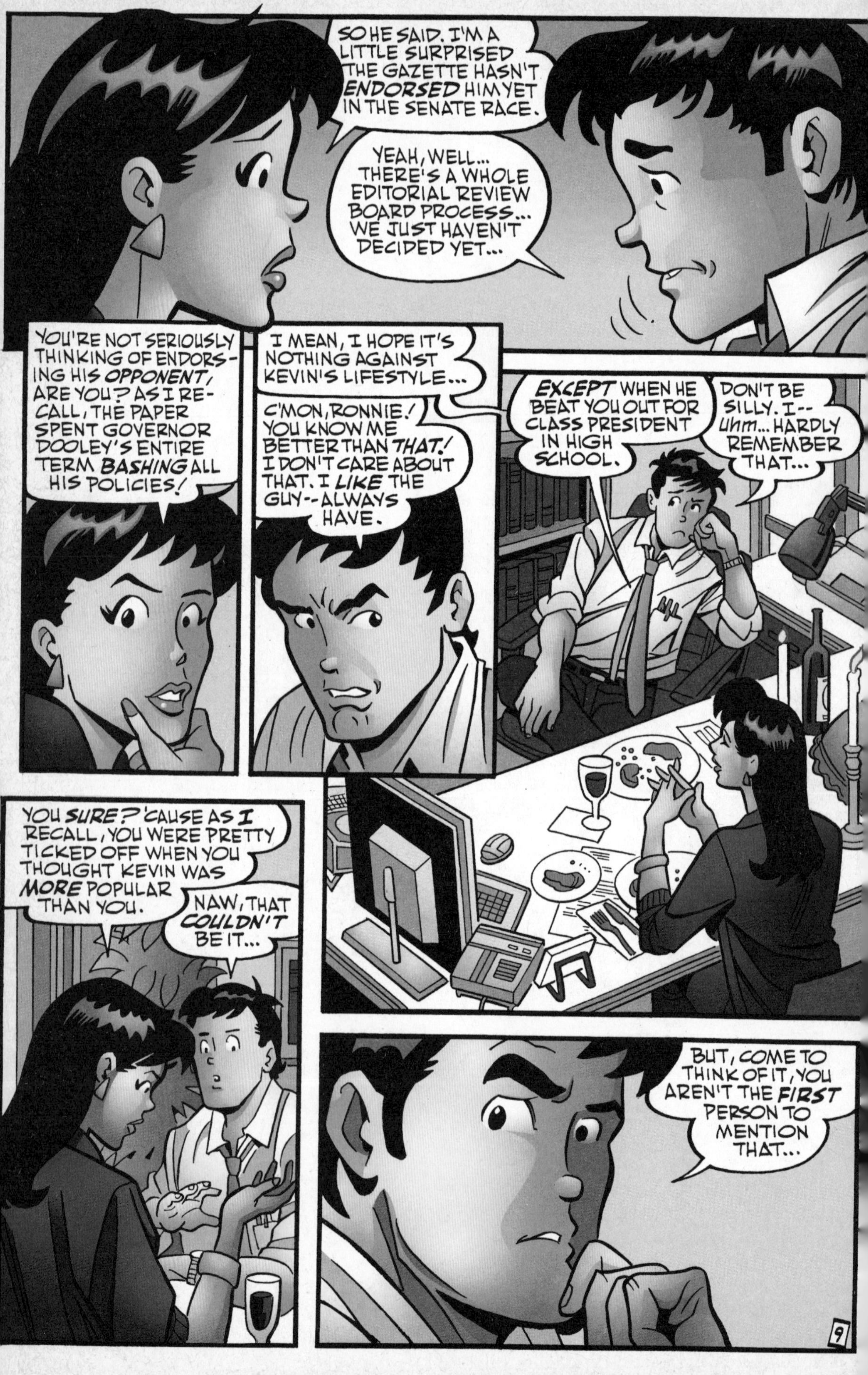
SO HE SAID. I'M A LITTLE SURPRISED THE GAZETTE HASN'T ENDORSED HIM YET IN THE SENATE RACE.
YEAH, WELL... THERE'S A WHOLE EDITORIAL REVIEW BOARD PROCESS... WE JUST HAVEN'T DECIDED YET...
YOU'RE NOT SERIOUSLY THINKING OF ENDORSING HIS OPPONENT, ARE YOU? AS I RECALL, THE PAPER SPENT GOVERNOR DOOLEY'S ENTIRE TERM BASHING ALL HIS POLICIES!
I MEAN, I HOPE IT'S NOTHING AGAINST KEVIN'S LIFESTYLE...
C'MON, RONNIE! YOU KNOW ME BETTER THAN THAT! I DON'T CARE ABOUT THAT. I LIKE THE GUY--ALWAYS HAVE.
EXCEPT WHEN HE BEAT YOU OUT FOR CLASS PRESIDENT IN HIGH SCHOOL.
DON'T BE SILLY. I-- uhm... HARDLY REMEMBER THAT...
YOU SURE? 'CAUSE AS I RECALL, YOU WERE PRETTY TICKED OFF WHEN YOU THOUGHT KEVIN WAS MORE POPULAR THAN YOU.
NAW, THAT COULDN'T BE IT...
BUT, COME TO THINK OF IT, YOU AREN'T THE FIRST PERSON TO MENTION THAT...
9

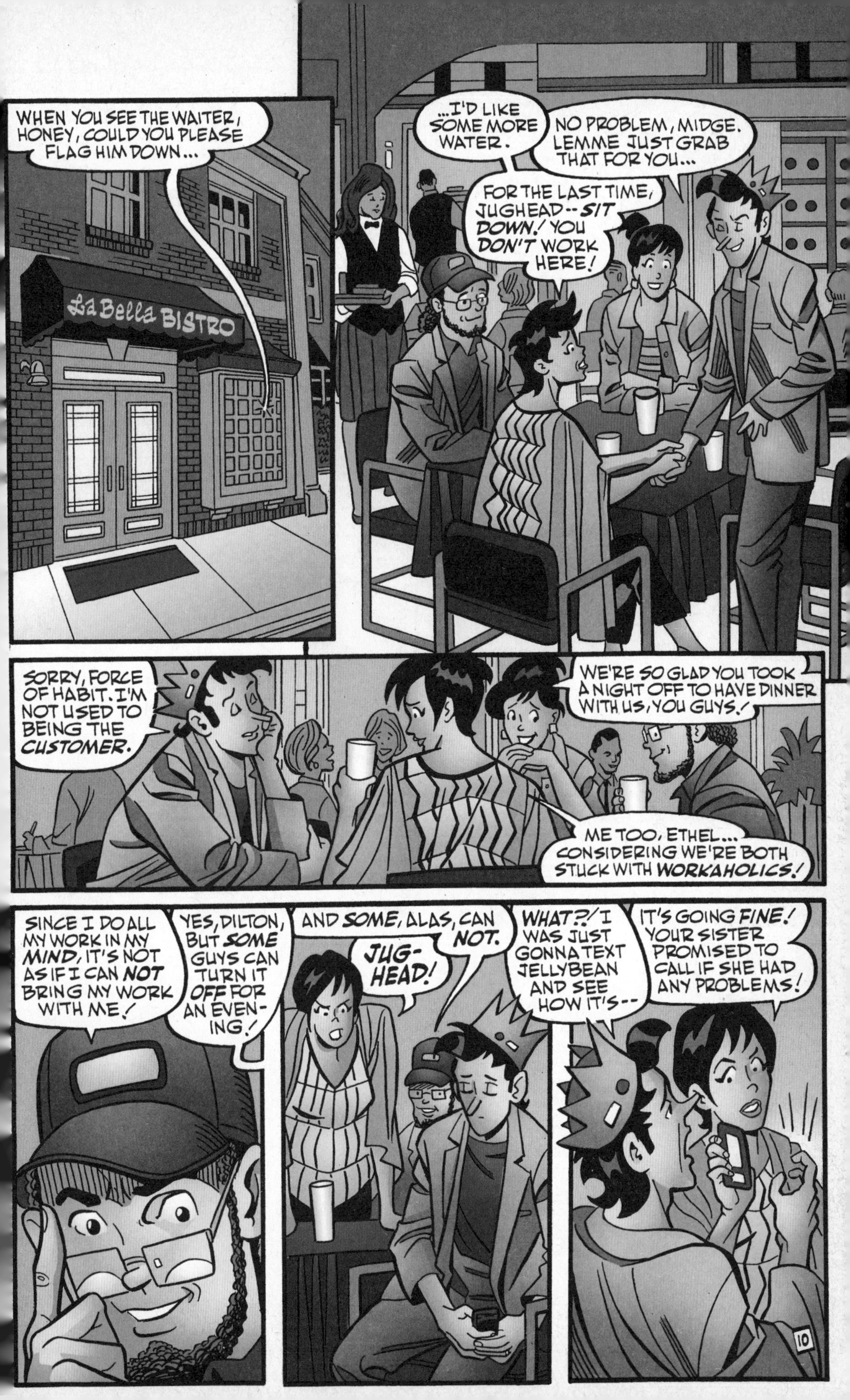
WHEN YOU SEE THE WAITER, HONEY, COULD YOU PLEASE FLAG HIM DOWN...
La Bella BISTRO
...I'D LIKE SOME MORE WATER.
NO PROBLEM, MIDGE. LEMME JUST GRAB THAT FOR YOU...
FOR THE LAST TIME, JUGHEAD--SIT DOWN! YOU DON'T WORK HERE!
SORRY, FORCE OF HABIT. I'M NOT USED TO BEING THE CUSTOMER.
WE'RE SO GLAD YOU TOOK A NIGHT OFF TO HAVE DINNER WITH US, YOU GUYS!
ME TOO, ETHEL... CONSIDERING WE'RE BOTH STUCK WITH WORKAHOLICS!
SINCE I DO ALL MY WORK IN MY MIND, IT'S NOT AS IF I CAN NOT BRING MY WORK WITH ME!
YES, DILTON, BUT SOME GUYS CAN TURN IT OFF FOR AN EVEN-ING!
AND SOME, ALAS, CAN NOT.
JUG-HEAD!
WHAT?! I WAS JUST GONNA TEXT JELLYBEAN AND SEE HOW IT'S--
IT'S GOING FINE! YOUR SISTER PROMISED TO CALL IF SHE HAD ANY PROBLEMS!
10

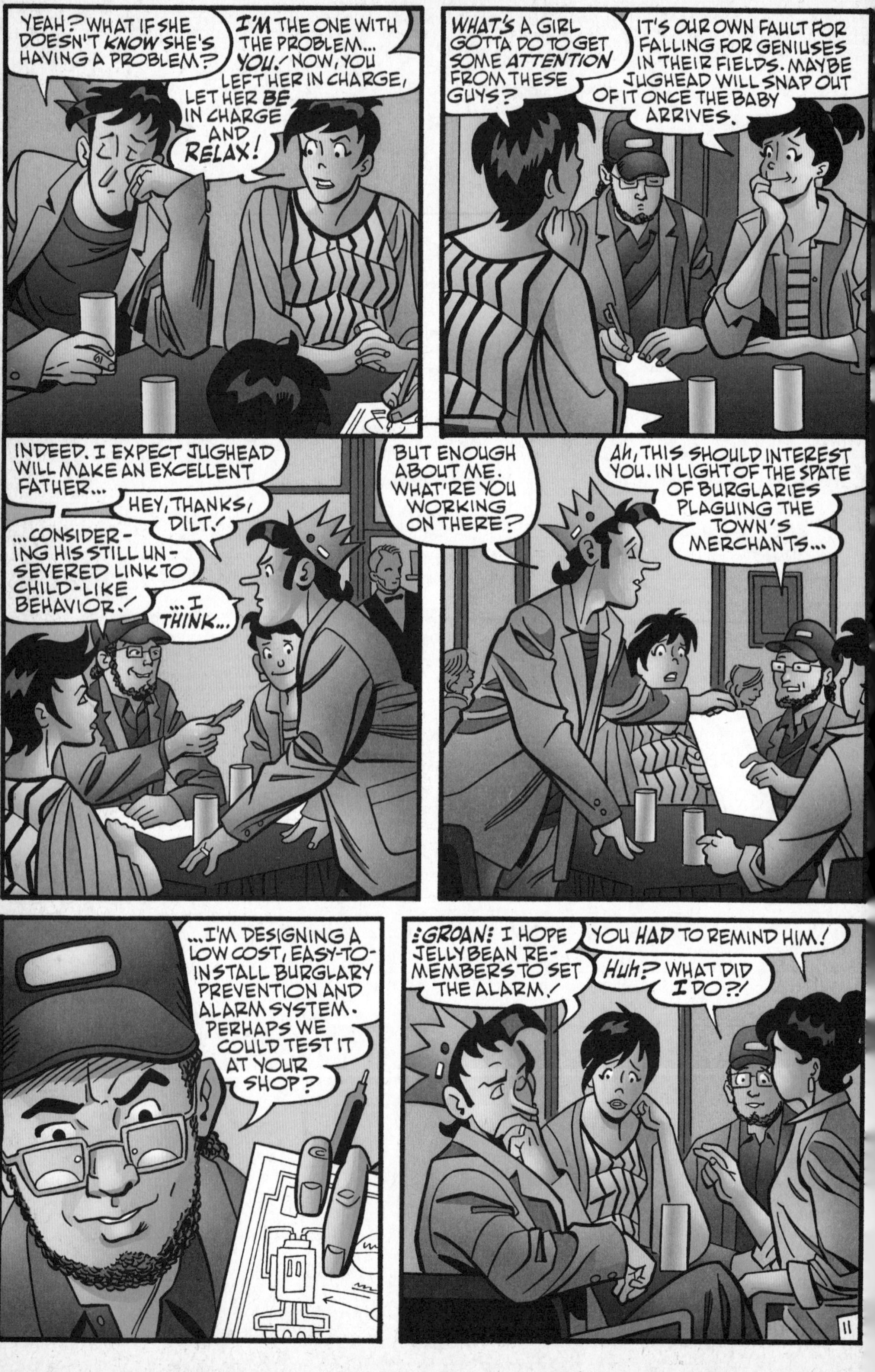
YEAH? WHAT IF SHE DOESN'T KNOW SHE'S HAVING A PROBLEM?
I'M THE ONE WITH THE PROBLEM... YOU! NOW, YOU LEFT HER IN CHARGE, LET HER BE IN CHARGE AND RELAX!
WHAT'S A GIRL GOTTA DO TO GET SOME ATTENTION FROM THESE GUYS?
IT'S OUR OWN FAULT FOR FALLING FOR GENIUSES IN THEIR FIELDS. MAYBE JUGHEAD WILL SNAP OUT OF IT ONCE THE BABY ARRIVES.
INDEED. I EXPECT JUGHEAD WILL MAKE AN EXCELLENT FATHER...
HEY, THANKS, DILT!
...CONSIDERING HIS STILL UNSEVERED LINK TO CHILD-LIKE BEHAVIOR!
...I THINK...
BUT ENOUGH ABOUT ME. WHAT'RE YOU WORKING ON THERE?
AH, THIS SHOULD INTEREST YOU. IN LIGHT OF THE SPATE OF BURGLARIES PLAGUING THE TOWN'S MERCHANTS...
...I'M DESIGNING A LOW COST, EASY-TO-INSTALL BURGLARY PREVENTION AND ALARM SYSTEM. PERHAPS WE COULD TEST IT AT YOUR SHOP?
:GROAN: I HOPE JELLYBEAN REMEMBERS TO SET THE ALARM!
YOU HAD TO REMIND HIM!
HUH? WHAT DID I DO?!
11

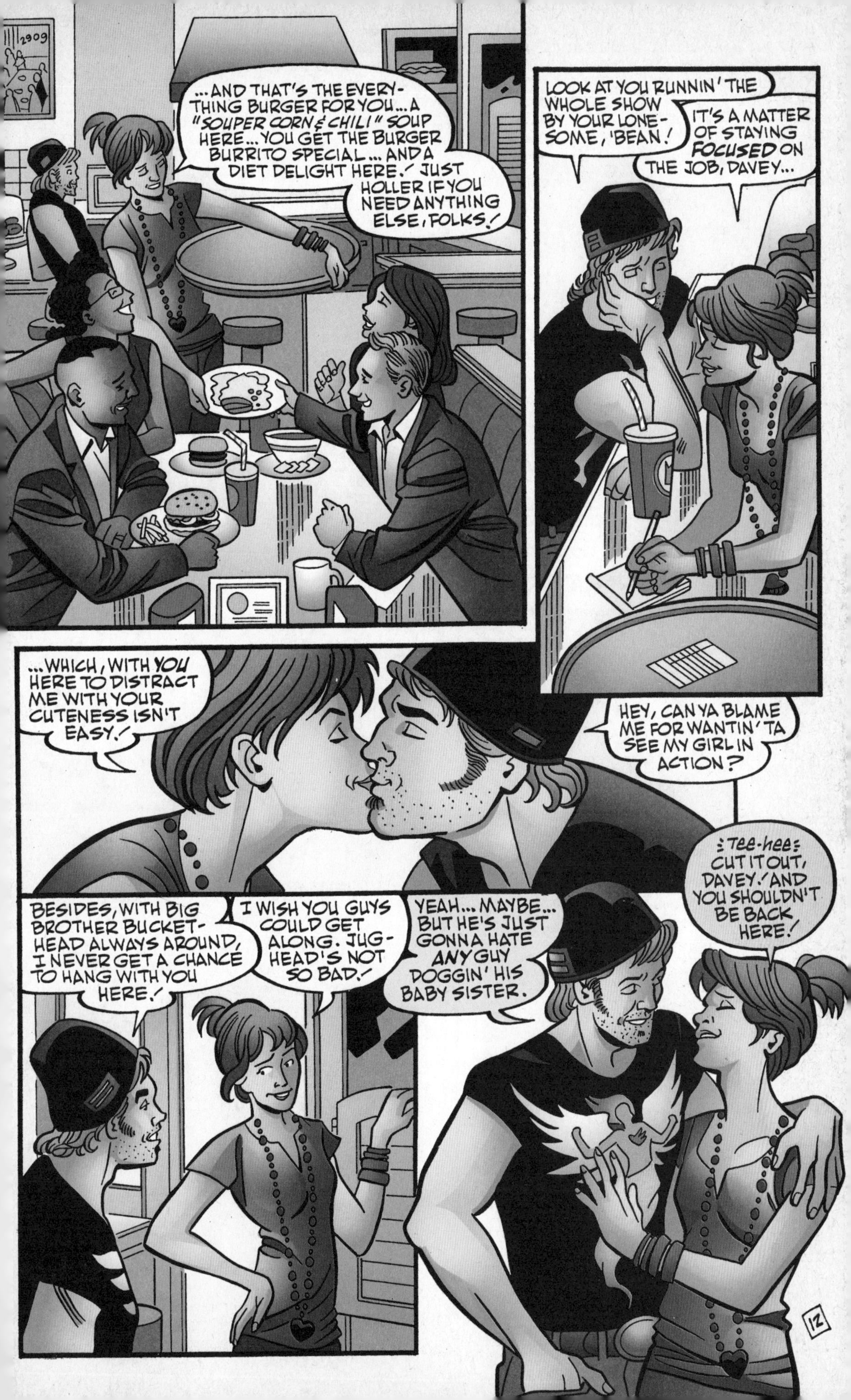
...AND THAT'S THE EVERY-THING BURGER FOR YOU... A "SOUPER CORN & CHILI" SOUP HERE... YOU GET THE BURGER BURRITO SPECIAL... AND A DIET DELIGHT HERE! JUST HOLLER IF YOU NEED ANYTHING ELSE, FOLKS!
LOOK AT YOU RUNNIN' THE WHOLE SHOW BY YOUR LONE-SOME, 'BEAN!
IT'S A MATTER OF STAYING FOCUSED ON THE JOB, DAVEY...
...WHICH, WITH YOU HERE TO DISTRACT ME WITH YOUR CUTENESS ISN'T EASY!
HEY, CAN YA BLAME ME FOR WANTIN' TA SEE MY GIRL IN ACTION?
BESIDES, WITH BIG BROTHER BUCKET-HEAD ALWAYS AROUND, I NEVER GET A CHANCE TO HANG WITH YOU HERE!
I WISH YOU GUYS COULD GET ALONG. JUG-HEAD'S NOT SO BAD!
YEAH... MAYBE... BUT HE'S JUST GONNA HATE ANY GUY DOGGIN' HIS BABY SISTER.
:TEE-HEE: CUT IT OUT, DAVEY! AND YOU SHOULDN'T BE BACK HERE!
12

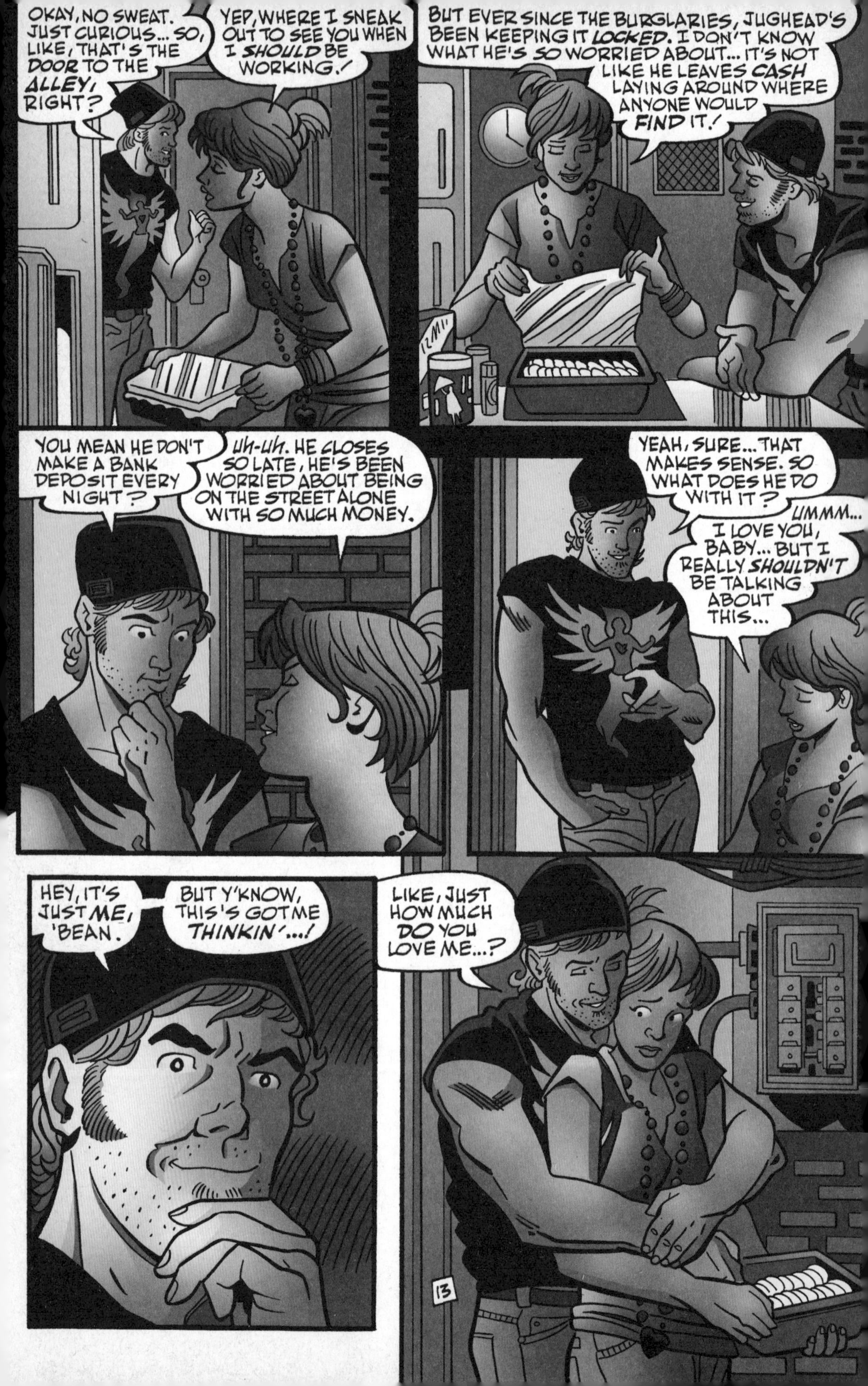
OKAY, NO SWEAT. JUST CURIOUS... SO, LIKE, THAT'S THE DOOR TO THE ALLEY, RIGHT?
YEP, WHERE I SNEAK OUT TO SEE YOU WHEN I SHOULD BE WORKING!
BUT EVER SINCE THE BURGLARIES, JUGHEAD'S BEEN KEEPING IT LOCKED. I DON'T KNOW WHAT HE'S SO WORRIED ABOUT... IT'S NOT LIKE HE LEAVES CASH LAYING AROUND WHERE ANYONE WOULD FIND IT!
YOU MEAN HE DON'T MAKE A BANK DEPOSIT EVERY NIGHT?
UH-UH. HE CLOSES SO LATE, HE'S BEEN WORRIED ABOUT BEING ON THE STREET ALONE WITH SO MUCH MONEY.
YEAH, SURE... THAT MAKES SENSE. SO WHAT DOES HE DO WITH IT?
UMMM... I LOVE YOU, BABY... BUT I REALLY SHOULDN'T BE TALKING ABOUT THIS...
HEY, IT'S JUST ME, 'BEAN.
BUT Y'KNOW, THIS'S GOT ME THINKIN'...!
LIKE, JUST HOW MUCH DO YOU LOVE ME...?
13

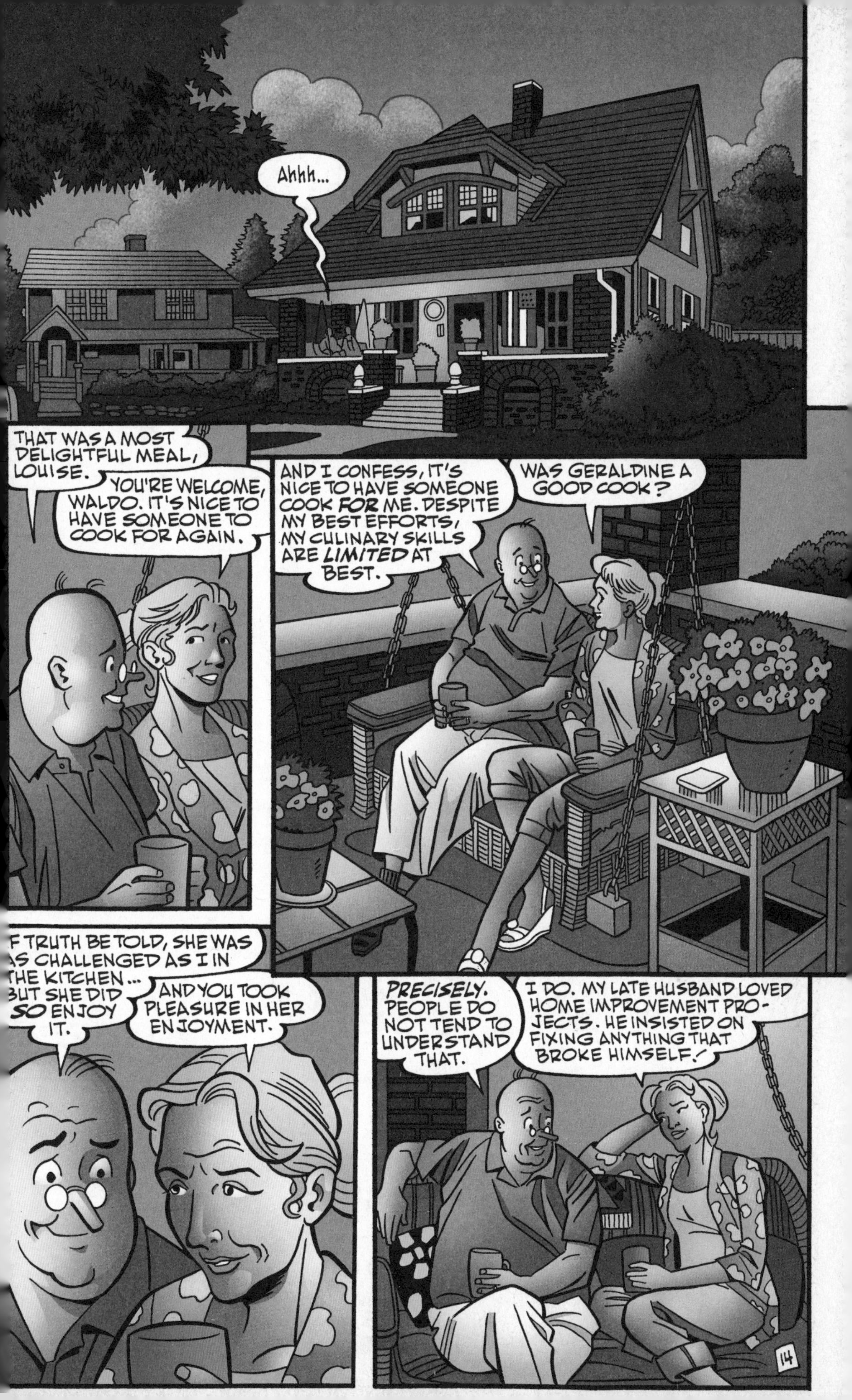
Ahhh...
THAT WAS A MOST DELIGHTFUL MEAL, LOUISE.
YOU'RE WELCOME, WALDO. IT'S NICE TO HAVE SOMEONE TO COOK FOR AGAIN.
AND I CONFESS, IT'S NICE TO HAVE SOMEONE COOK *FOR* ME. DESPITE MY BEST EFFORTS, MY CULINARY SKILLS ARE *LIMITED* AT BEST.
WAS GERALDINE A GOOD COOK?
F TRUTH BE TOLD, SHE WAS AS CHALLENGED AS I IN THE KITCHEN... BUT SHE DID *SO* ENJOY IT.
AND YOU TOOK PLEASURE IN HER ENJOYMENT.
PRECISELY. PEOPLE DO NOT TEND TO UNDERSTAND THAT.
I DO. MY LATE HUSBAND LOVED HOME IMPROVEMENT PRO-JECTS. HE INSISTED ON FIXING ANYTHING THAT BROKE HIMSELF!
14

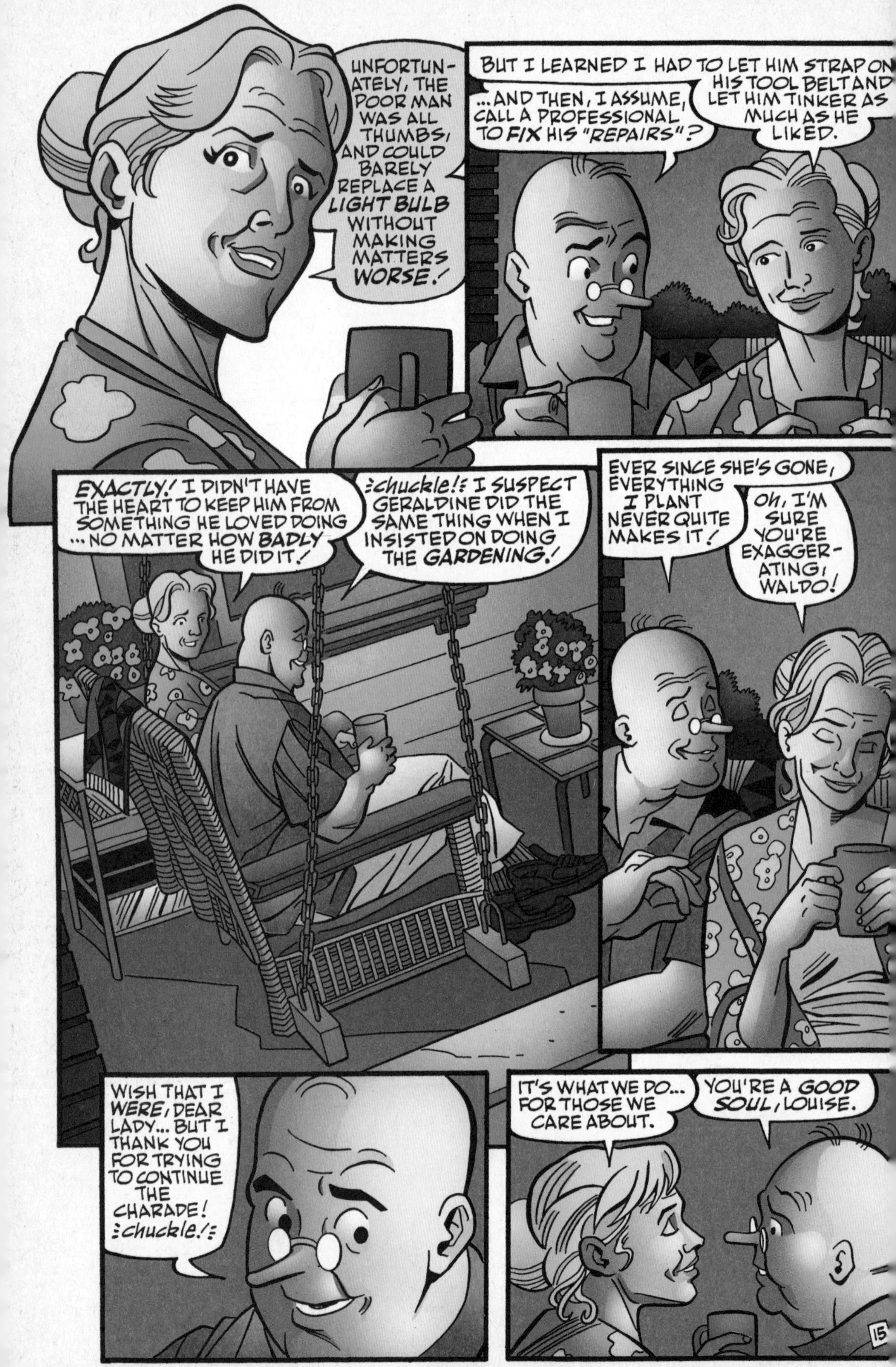

UNFORTUNATELY, THE POOR MAN WAS ALL THUMBS, AND COULD BARELY REPLACE A LIGHT BULB WITHOUT MAKING MATTERS WORSE!
BUT I LEARNED I HAD TO LET HIM STRAP ON HIS TOOL BELT AND LET HIM TINKER AS MUCH AS HE LIKED.
...AND THEN, I ASSUME, CALL A PROFESSIONAL TO FIX HIS "REPAIRS"?
EXACTLY! I DIDN'T HAVE THE HEART TO KEEP HIM FROM SOMETHING HE LOVED DOING ...NO MATTER HOW BADLY HE DID IT!
:chuckle!: I SUSPECT GERALDINE DID THE SAME THING WHEN I INSISTED ON DOING THE GARDENING!
EVER SINCE SHE'S GONE, EVERYTHING I PLANT NEVER QUITE MAKES IT!
OH, I'M SURE YOU'RE EXAGGERATING, WALDO!
WISH THAT I WERE, DEAR LADY... BUT I THANK YOU FOR TRYING TO CONTINUE THE CHARADE! :chuckle!:
IT'S WHAT WE DO... FOR THOSE WE CARE ABOUT.
YOU'RE A GOOD SOUL, LOUISE.
15

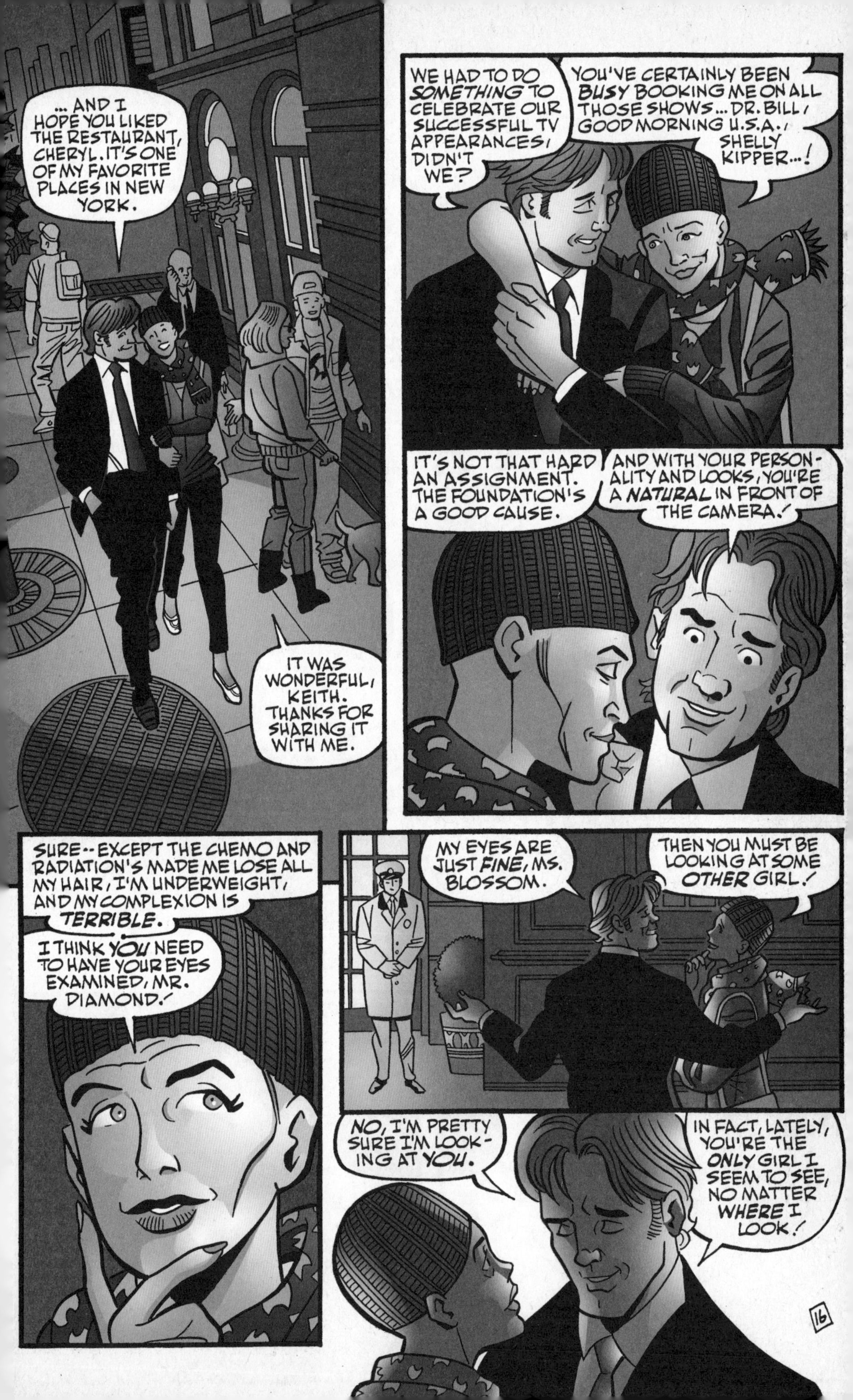

... AND I HOPE YOU LIKED THE RESTAURANT, CHERYL. IT'S ONE OF MY FAVORITE PLACES IN NEW YORK.
IT WAS WONDERFUL, KEITH. THANKS FOR SHARING IT WITH ME.
WE HAD TO DO SOMETHING TO CELEBRATE OUR SUCCESSFUL TV APPEARANCES, DIDN'T WE?
YOU'VE CERTAINLY BEEN BUSY BOOKING ME ON ALL THOSE SHOWS... DR. BILL, GOOD MORNING U.S.A., SHELLY KIPPER...!
IT'S NOT THAT HARD AN ASSIGNMENT. THE FOUNDATION'S A GOOD CAUSE.
AND WITH YOUR PERSONALITY AND LOOKS, YOU'RE A NATURAL IN FRONT OF THE CAMERA!
SURE-- EXCEPT THE CHEMO AND RADIATION'S MADE ME LOSE ALL MY HAIR, I'M UNDERWEIGHT, AND MY COMPLEXION IS TERRIBLE.
I THINK YOU NEED TO HAVE YOUR EYES EXAMINED, MR. DIAMOND!
MY EYES ARE JUST FINE, MS. BLOSSOM.
THEN YOU MUST BE LOOKING AT SOME OTHER GIRL!
NO, I'M PRETTY SURE I'M LOOKING AT YOU.
IN FACT, LATELY, YOU'RE THE ONLY GIRL I SEEM TO SEE, NO MATTER WHERE I LOOK!

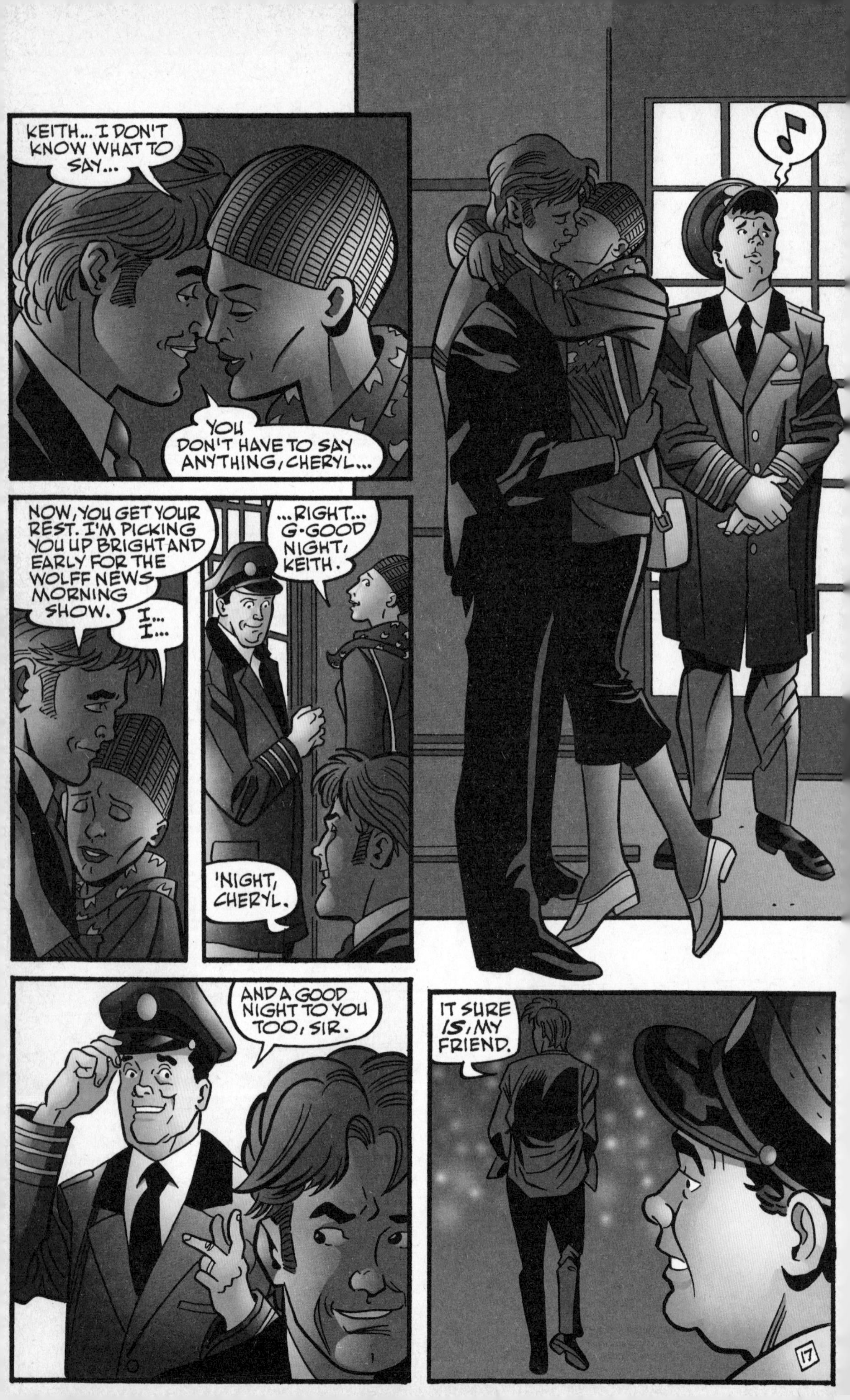

KEITH... I DON'T KNOW WHAT TO SAY...
YOU DON'T HAVE TO SAY ANYTHING, CHERYL...
NOW, YOU GET YOUR REST. I'M PICKING YOU UP BRIGHT AND EARLY FOR THE WOLFF NEWS MORNING SHOW.
I... I...
...RIGHT... G-GOOD NIGHT, KEITH.
'NIGHT, CHERYL.
♪
AND A GOOD NIGHT TO YOU TOO, SIR.
IT SURE *IS*, MY FRIEND.

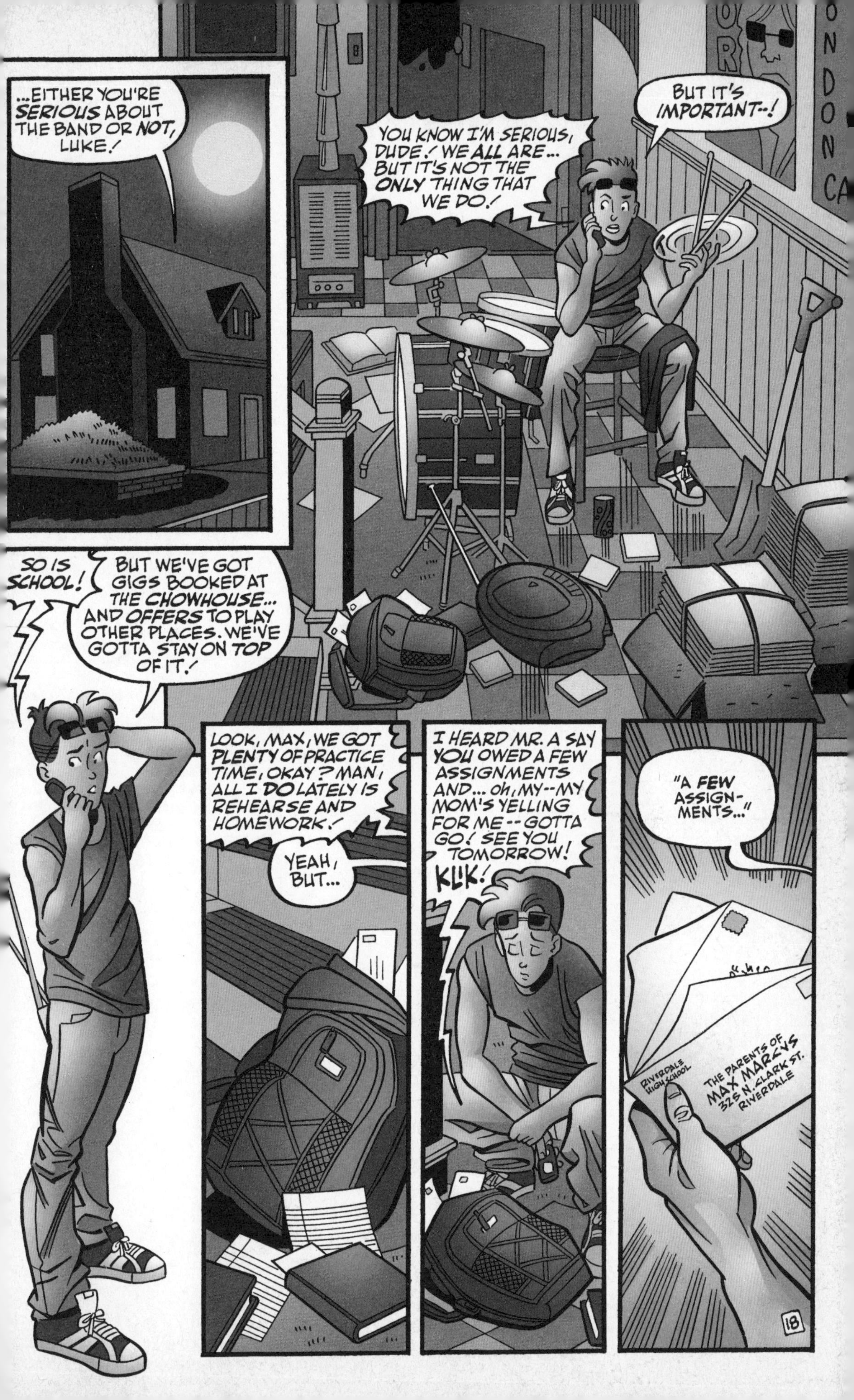

...EITHER YOU'RE SERIOUS ABOUT THE BAND OR NOT, LUKE!
YOU KNOW I'M SERIOUS, DUDE! WE ALL ARE... BUT IT'S NOT THE ONLY THING THAT WE DO!
BUT IT'S IMPORTANT--!
SO IS SCHOOL!
BUT WE'VE GOT GIGS BOOKED AT THE CHOWHOUSE... AND OFFERS TO PLAY OTHER PLACES. WE'VE GOTTA STAY ON TOP OF IT!
LOOK, MAX, WE GOT PLENTY OF PRACTICE TIME, OKAY? MAN, ALL I DO LATELY IS REHEARSE AND HOMEWORK!
YEAH, BUT...
I HEARD MR. A SAY YOU OWED A FEW ASSIGNMENTS AND... oh, MY--MY MOM'S YELLING FOR ME -- GOTTA GO! SEE YOU TOMORROW!
KLIK!
"A FEW ASSIGN-MENTS..."
RIVERDALE HIGH SCHOOL
THE PARENTS OF MAX MARCUS 325 N. CLARK ST. RIVERDALE
18

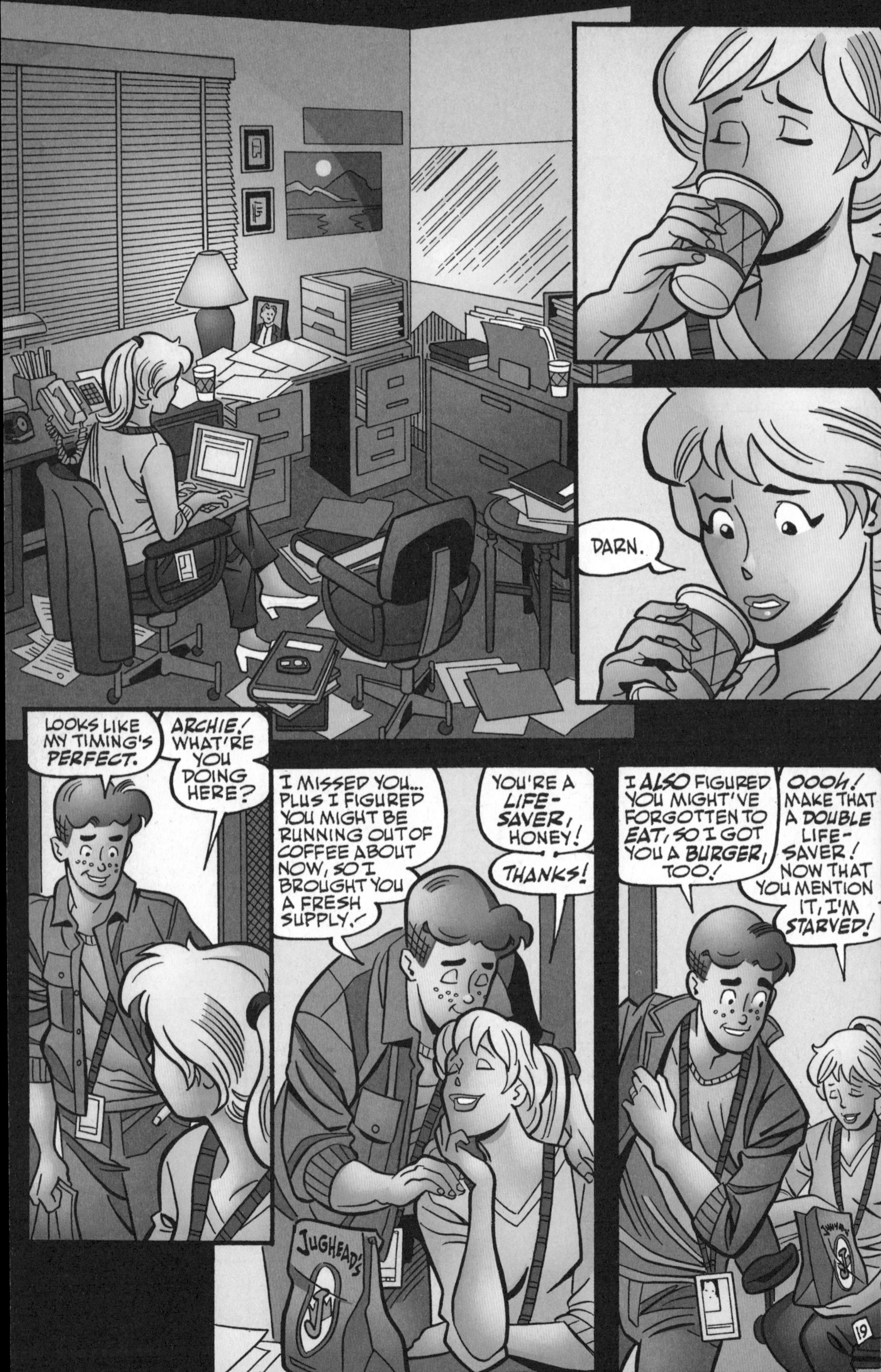
DARN.
LOOKS LIKE MY TIMING'S PERFECT.
ARCHIE! WHAT'RE YOU DOING HERE?
I MISSED YOU... PLUS I FIGURED YOU MIGHT BE RUNNING OUT OF COFFEE ABOUT NOW, SO I BROUGHT YOU A FRESH SUPPLY.
YOU'RE A LIFE-SAVER, HONEY!
THANKS!
JUGHEAD'S
I ALSO FIGURED YOU MIGHT'VE FORGOTTEN TO EAT, SO I GOT YOU A BURGER, TOO!
OOOH! MAKE THAT A DOUBLE LIFE-SAVER! NOW THAT YOU MENTION IT, I'M STARVED!
19

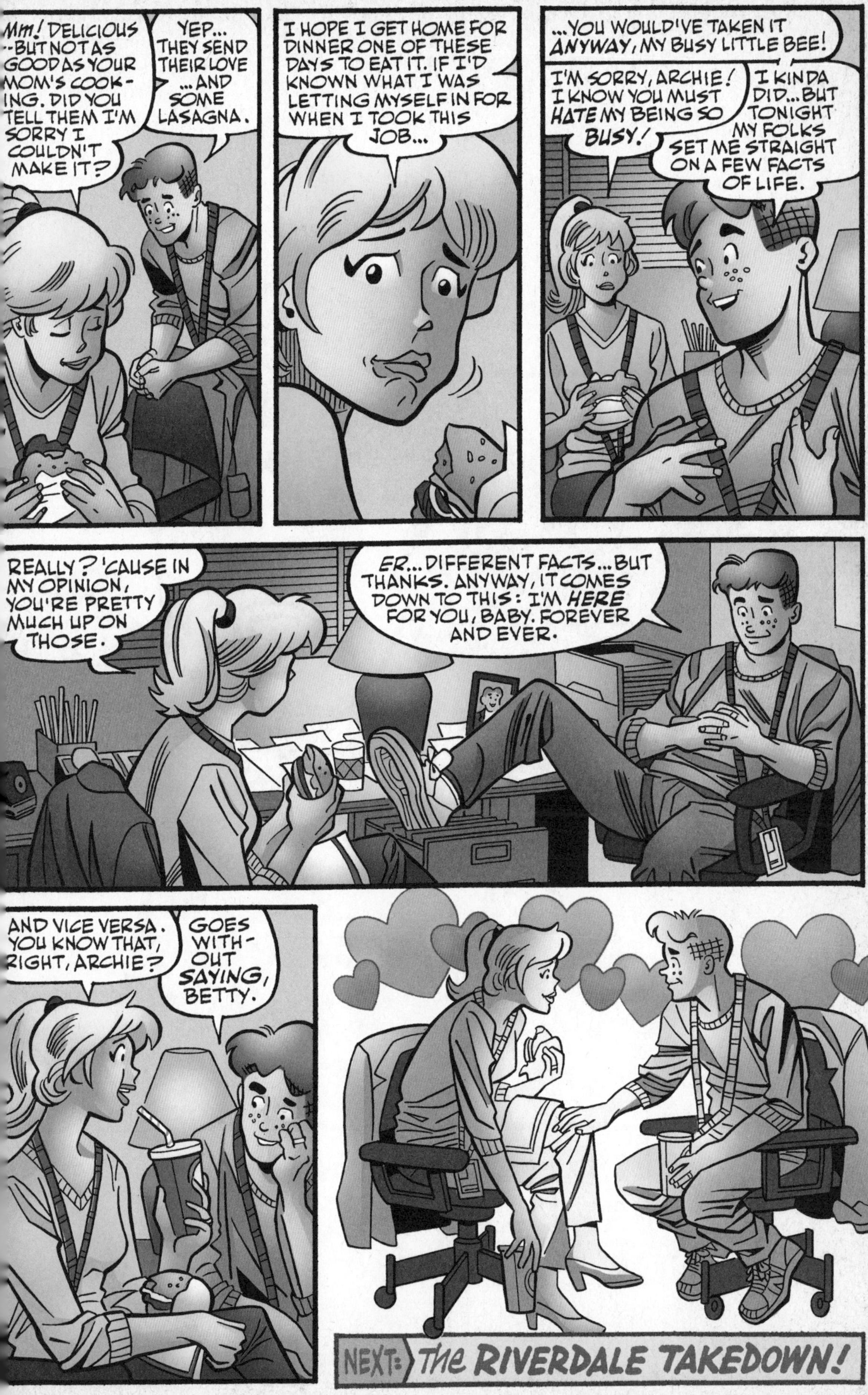
MM! DELICIOUS --BUT NOT AS GOOD AS YOUR MOM'S COOKING. DID YOU TELL THEM I'M SORRY I COULDN'T MAKE IT?
YEP... THEY SEND THEIR LOVE ...AND SOME LASAGNA.
I HOPE I GET HOME FOR DINNER ONE OF THESE DAYS TO EAT IT. IF I'D KNOWN WHAT I WAS LETTING MYSELF IN FOR WHEN I TOOK THIS JOB...
...YOU WOULD'VE TAKEN IT ANYWAY, MY BUSY LITTLE BEE!
I'M SORRY, ARCHIE! I KNOW YOU MUST HATE MY BEING SO BUSY!
I KINDA DID... BUT TONIGHT MY FOLKS SET ME STRAIGHT ON A FEW FACTS OF LIFE.
REALLY? 'CAUSE IN MY OPINION, YOU'RE PRETTY MUCH UP ON THOSE.
ER... DIFFERENT FACTS... BUT THANKS. ANYWAY, IT COMES DOWN TO THIS: I'M HERE FOR YOU, BABY. FOREVER AND EVER.
AND VICE VERSA. YOU KNOW THAT, RIGHT, ARCHIE?
GOES WITH-OUT SAYING, BETTY.
NEXT: The RIVERDALE TAKEDOWN!

"IT'S BEEN A LONG, STRESSFUL MORNING, THE ELECTION IS TOMORROW..."

"...BUT IF I DON'T GET OUT OF HERE FOR A WHILE, I'M GOING TO *SCREAM!*"

-VERONICA LODGE-ANDREWS

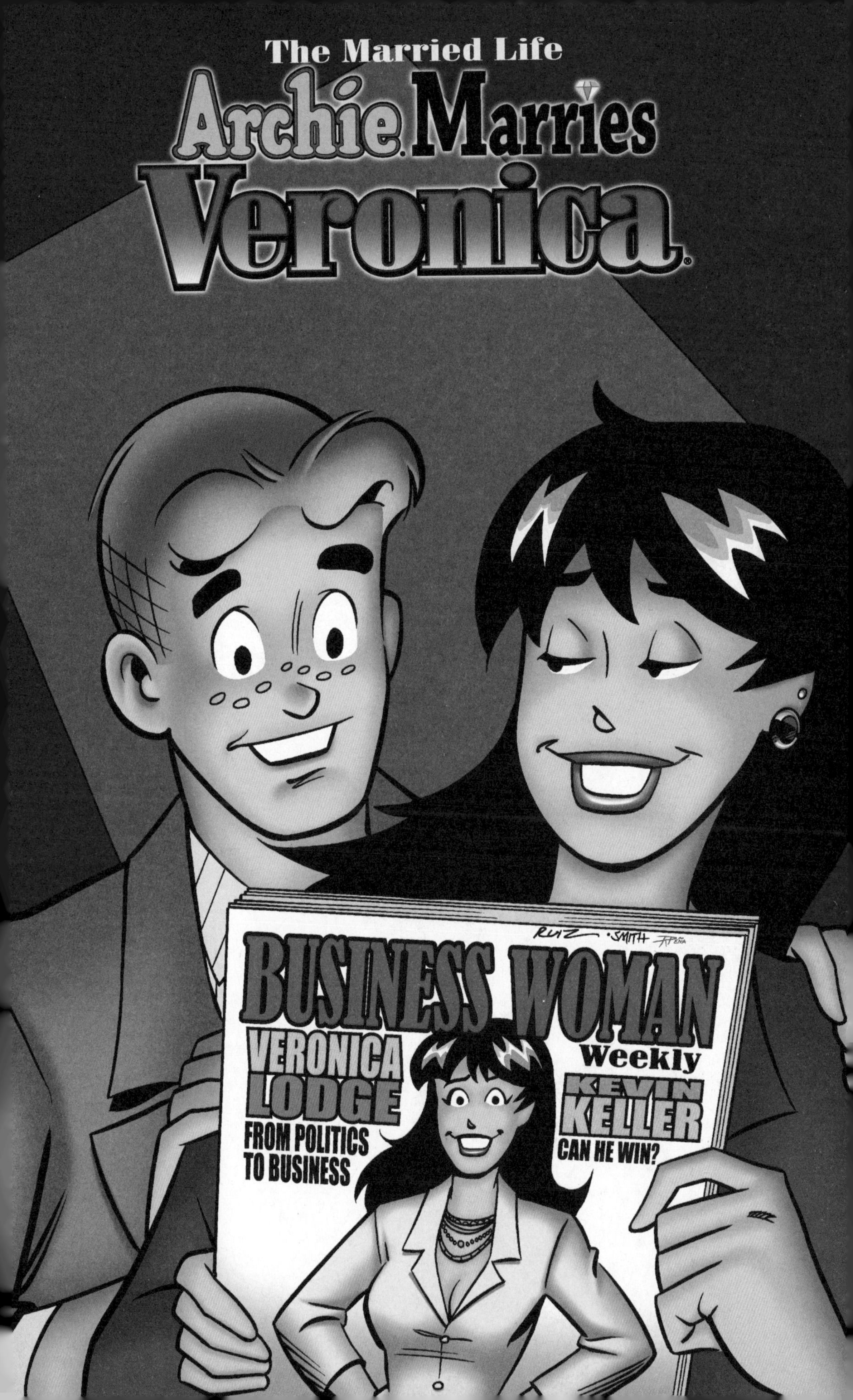
The Married Life
Archie Marries Veronica
BUSINESS WOMAN
Weekly
VERONICA LODGE
FROM POLITICS TO BUSINESS
KEVIN KELLER
CAN HE WIN?

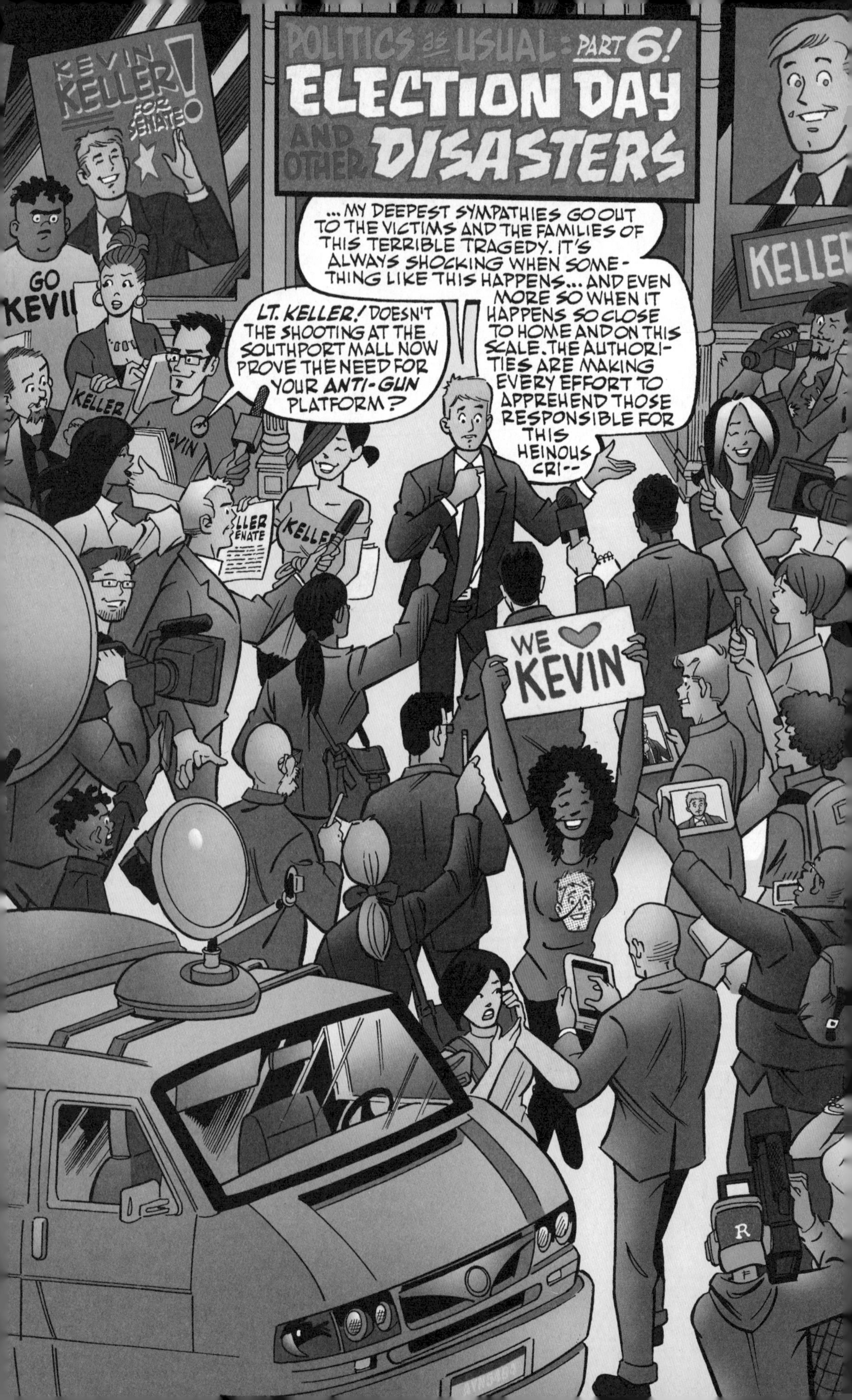

POLITICS AS USUAL: PART 6!
ELECTION DAY AND OTHER DISASTERS
...MY DEEPEST SYMPATHIES GO OUT TO THE VICTIMS AND THE FAMILIES OF THIS TERRIBLE TRAGEDY. IT'S ALWAYS SHOCKING WHEN SOMETHING LIKE THIS HAPPENS... AND EVEN MORE SO WHEN IT HAPPENS SO CLOSE TO HOME AND ON THIS SCALE. THE AUTHORITIES ARE MAKING EVERY EFFORT TO APPREHEND THOSE RESPONSIBLE FOR THIS HEINOUS CRI--
LT. KELLER! DOESN'T THE SHOOTING AT THE SOUTHPORT MALL NOW PROVE THE NEED FOR YOUR ANTI-GUN PLATFORM?
KEVIN KELLER! FOR SENATE
GO KEVI
KELLER
WE ♥ KEVIN

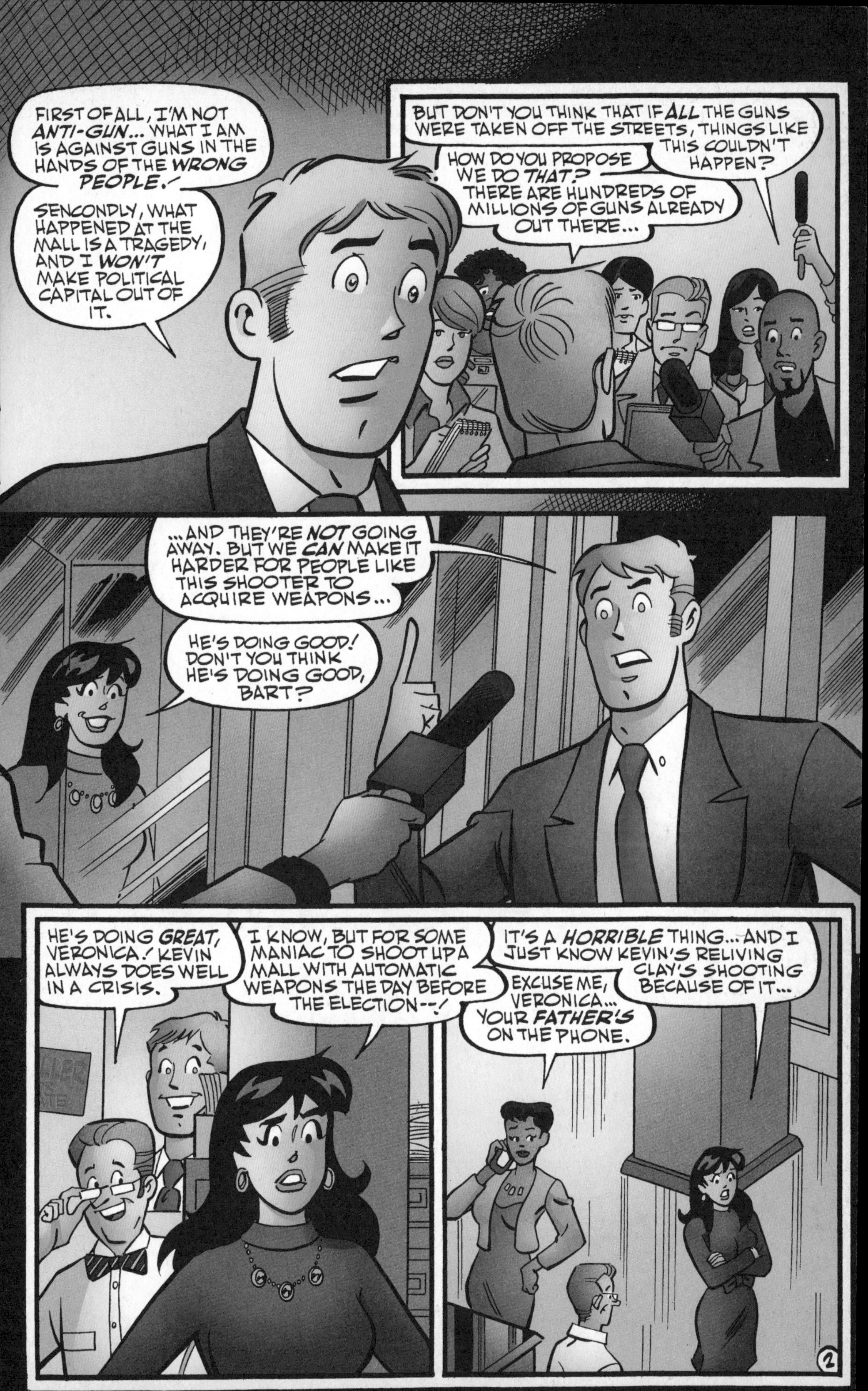
FIRST OF ALL, I'M NOT ANTI-GUN... WHAT I AM IS AGAINST GUNS IN THE HANDS OF THE WRONG PEOPLE.!
SENCONDLY, WHAT HAPPENED AT THE MALL IS A TRAGEDY, AND I WON'T MAKE POLITICAL CAPITAL OUT OF IT.
BUT DON'T YOU THINK THAT IF ALL THE GUNS WERE TAKEN OFF THE STREETS, THINGS LIKE THIS COULDN'T HAPPEN?
HOW DO YOU PROPOSE WE DO THAT? THERE ARE HUNDREDS OF MILLIONS OF GUNS ALREADY OUT THERE...
...AND THEY'RE NOT GOING AWAY. BUT WE CAN MAKE IT HARDER FOR PEOPLE LIKE THIS SHOOTER TO ACQUIRE WEAPONS...
HE'S DOING GOOD! DON'T YOU THINK HE'S DOING GOOD, BART?
HE'S DOING GREAT, VERONICA! KEVIN ALWAYS DOES WELL IN A CRISIS.
I KNOW, BUT FOR SOME MANIAC TO SHOOT UP A MALL WITH AUTOMATIC WEAPONS THE DAY BEFORE THE ELECTION--!
IT'S A HORRIBLE THING... AND I JUST KNOW KEVIN'S RELIVING CLAY'S SHOOTING BECAUSE OF IT...
EXCUSE ME, VERONICA... YOUR FATHER'S ON THE PHONE.
2

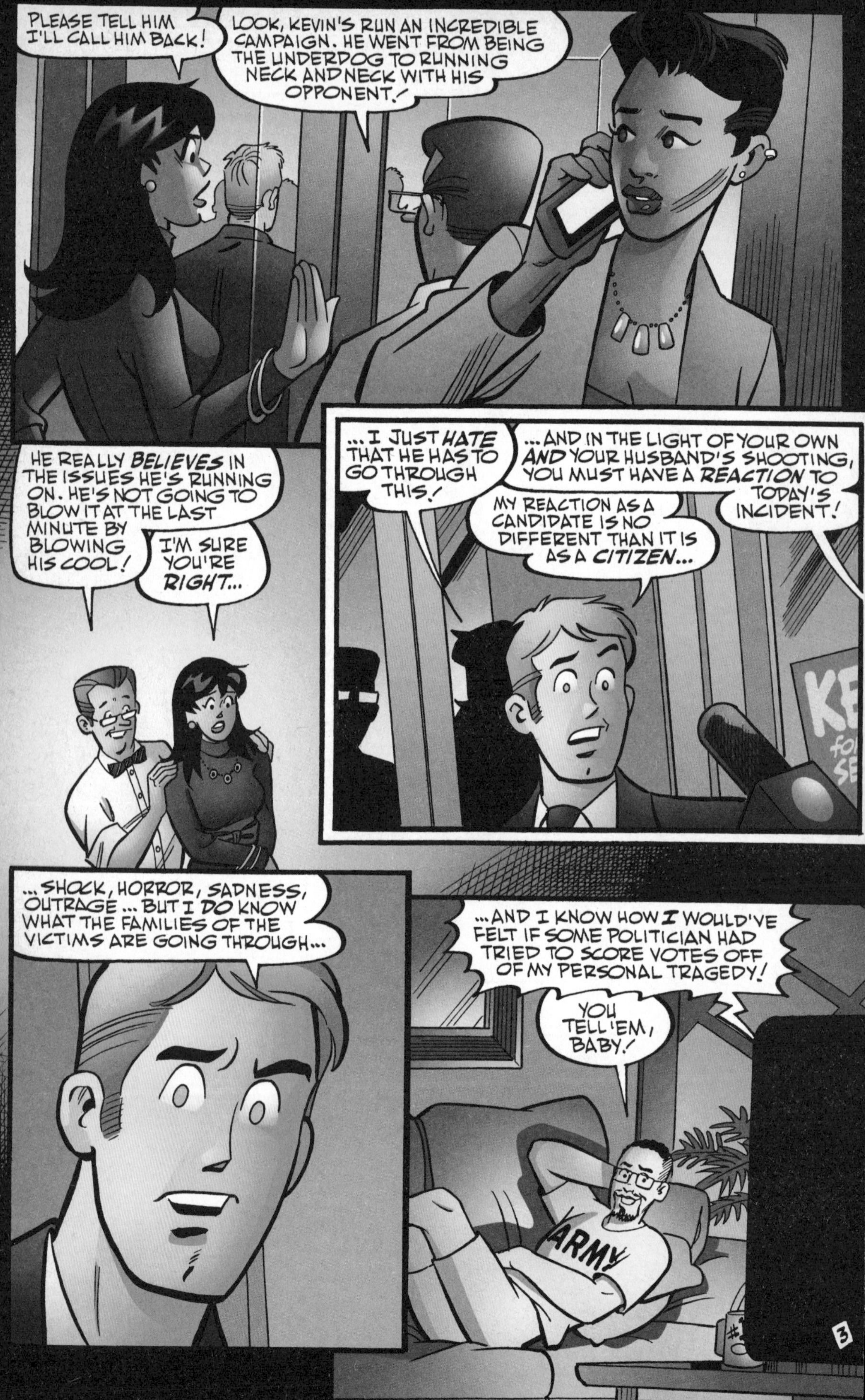
PLEASE TELL HIM I'LL CALL HIM BACK!
LOOK, KEVIN'S RUN AN INCREDIBLE CAMPAIGN. HE WENT FROM BEING THE UNDERDOG TO RUNNING NECK AND NECK WITH HIS OPPONENT!
HE REALLY BELIEVES IN THE ISSUES HE'S RUNNING ON. HE'S NOT GOING TO BLOW IT AT THE LAST MINUTE BY BLOWING HIS COOL!
I'M SURE YOU'RE RIGHT...
...I JUST HATE THAT HE HAS TO GO THROUGH THIS!
...AND IN THE LIGHT OF YOUR OWN AND YOUR HUSBAND'S SHOOTING, YOU MUST HAVE A REACTION TO TODAY'S INCIDENT!
MY REACTION AS A CANDIDATE IS NO DIFFERENT THAN IT IS AS A CITIZEN...
...SHOCK, HORROR, SADNESS, OUTRAGE... BUT I DO KNOW WHAT THE FAMILIES OF THE VICTIMS ARE GOING THROUGH...
...AND I KNOW HOW I WOULD'VE FELT IF SOME POLITICIAN HAD TRIED TO SCORE VOTES OFF OF MY PERSONAL TRAGEDY!
YOU TELL 'EM, BABY!
ARMY
3

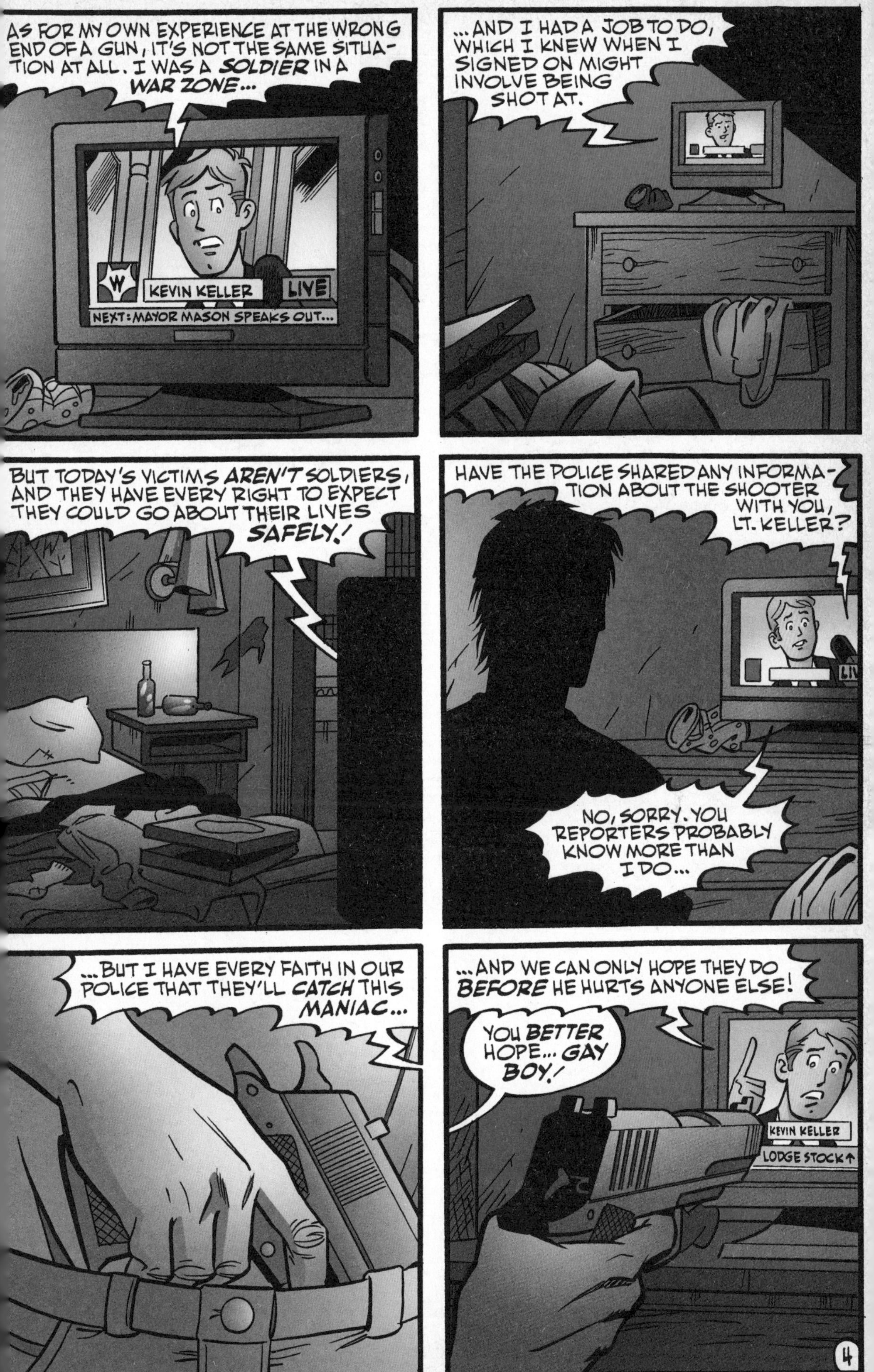
AS FOR MY OWN EXPERIENCE AT THE WRONG END OF A GUN, IT'S NOT THE SAME SITUATION AT ALL. I WAS A SOLDIER IN A WAR ZONE...
KEVIN KELLER
LIVE
NEXT: MAYOR MASON SPEAKS OUT...
...AND I HAD A JOB TO DO, WHICH I KNEW WHEN I SIGNED ON MIGHT INVOLVE BEING SHOT AT.
BUT TODAY'S VICTIMS AREN'T SOLDIERS, AND THEY HAVE EVERY RIGHT TO EXPECT THEY COULD GO ABOUT THEIR LIVES SAFELY!
HAVE THE POLICE SHARED ANY INFORMATION ABOUT THE SHOOTER WITH YOU, LT. KELLER?
NO, SORRY. YOU REPORTERS PROBABLY KNOW MORE THAN I DO...
...BUT I HAVE EVERY FAITH IN OUR POLICE THAT THEY'LL CATCH THIS MANIAC...
...AND WE CAN ONLY HOPE THEY DO BEFORE HE HURTS ANYONE ELSE!
YOU BETTER HOPE... GAY BOY!
KEVIN KELLER
LODGE STOCK ↑

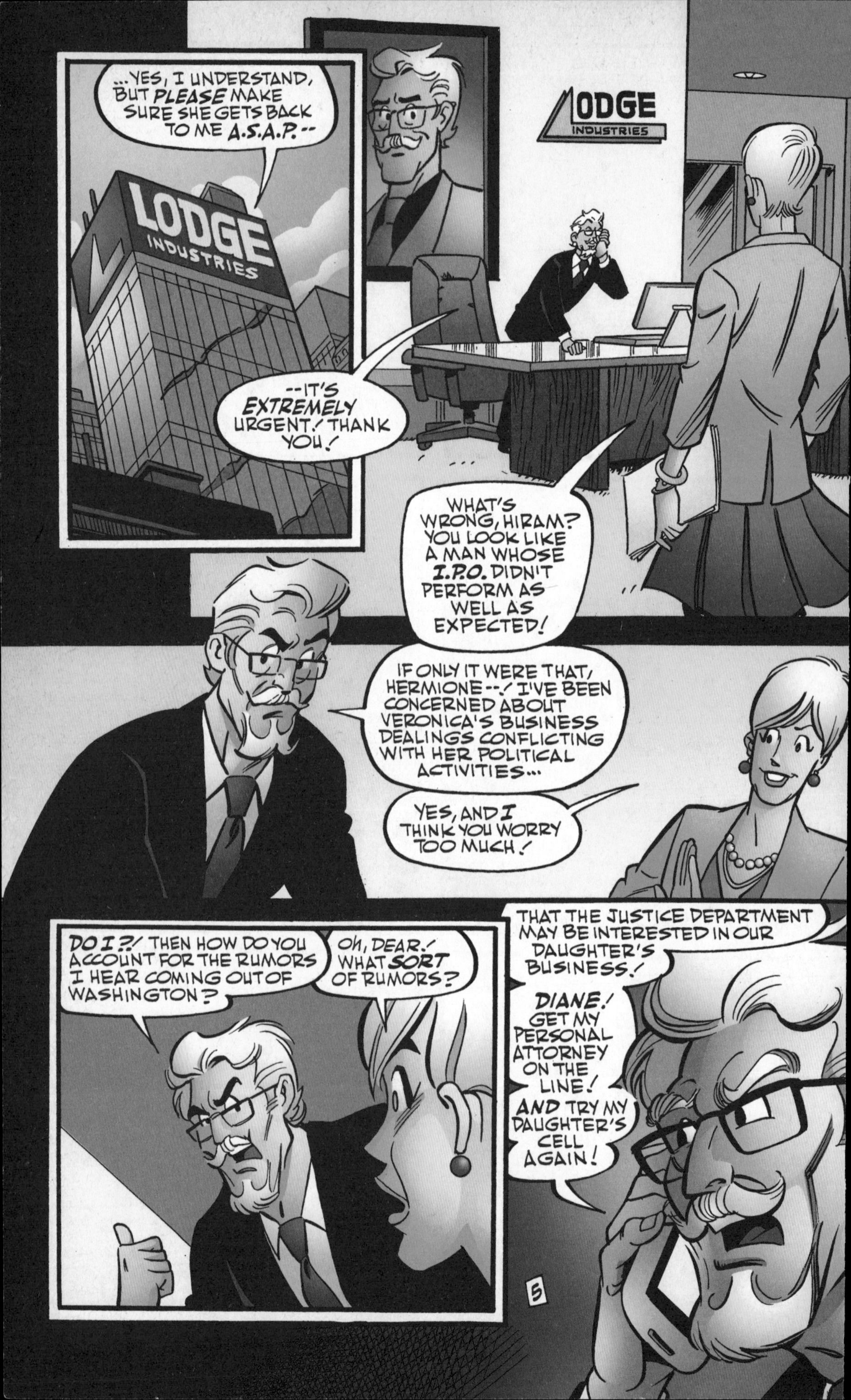

...YES, I UNDERSTAND, BUT PLEASE MAKE SURE SHE GETS BACK TO ME A.S.A.P.--
LODGE INDUSTRIES
LODGE INDUSTRIES
--IT'S EXTREMELY URGENT! THANK YOU!
WHAT'S WRONG, HIRAM? YOU LOOK LIKE A MAN WHOSE I.P.O. DIDN'T PERFORM AS WELL AS EXPECTED!
IF ONLY IT WERE THAT, HERMIONE--! I'VE BEEN CONCERNED ABOUT VERONICA'S BUSINESS DEALINGS CONFLICTING WITH HER POLITICAL ACTIVITIES...
YES, AND I THINK YOU WORRY TOO MUCH!
DO I?! THEN HOW DO YOU ACCOUNT FOR THE RUMORS I HEAR COMING OUT OF WASHINGTON?
OH, DEAR! WHAT SORT OF RUMORS?
THAT THE JUSTICE DEPARTMENT MAY BE INTERESTED IN OUR DAUGHTER'S BUSINESS!
DIANE! GET MY PERSONAL ATTORNEY ON THE LINE!
AND TRY MY DAUGHTER'S CELL AGAIN!
5

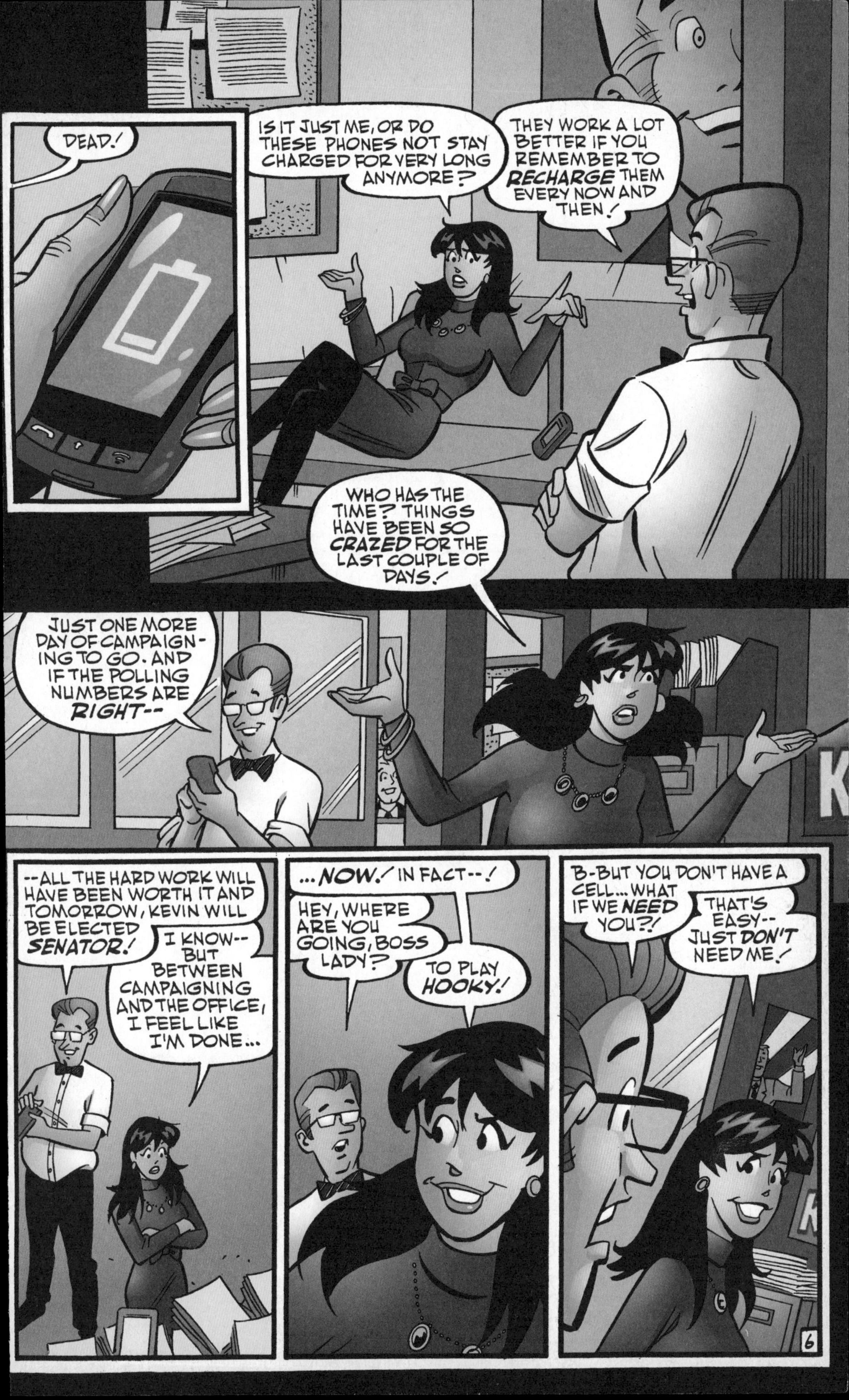
DEAD!
IS IT JUST ME, OR DO THESE PHONES NOT STAY CHARGED FOR VERY LONG ANYMORE?
THEY WORK A LOT BETTER IF YOU REMEMBER TO RECHARGE THEM EVERY NOW AND THEN!
WHO HAS THE TIME? THINGS HAVE BEEN SO CRAZED FOR THE LAST COUPLE OF DAYS!
JUST ONE MORE DAY OF CAMPAIGN-ING TO GO. AND IF THE POLLING NUMBERS ARE RIGHT--
--ALL THE HARD WORK WILL HAVE BEEN WORTH IT AND TOMORROW, KEVIN WILL BE ELECTED SENATOR!
I KNOW-- BUT BETWEEN CAMPAIGNING AND THE OFFICE, I FEEL LIKE I'M DONE...
...NOW! IN FACT--!
HEY, WHERE ARE YOU GOING, BOSS LADY?
TO PLAY HOOKY!
B-BUT YOU DON'T HAVE A CELL... WHAT IF WE NEED YOU?!
THAT'S EASY-- JUST DON'T NEED ME!
6

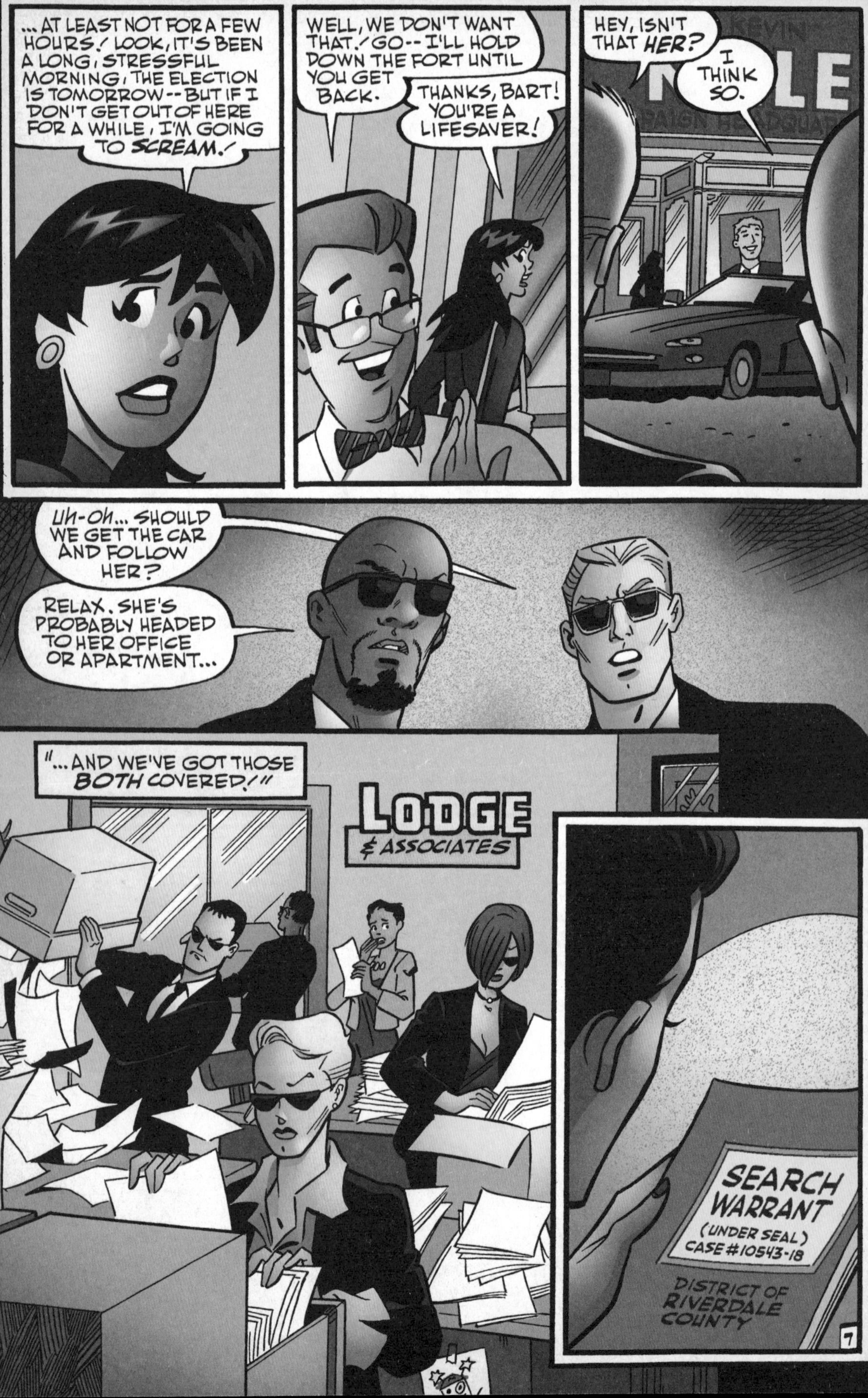
...AT LEAST NOT FOR A FEW HOURS! LOOK, IT'S BEEN A LONG, STRESSFUL MORNING, THE ELECTION IS TOMORROW--BUT IF I DON'T GET OUT OF HERE FOR A WHILE, I'M GOING TO SCREAM!
WELL, WE DON'T WANT THAT! GO--I'LL HOLD DOWN THE FORT UNTIL YOU GET BACK.
THANKS, BART! YOU'RE A LIFESAVER!
HEY, ISN'T THAT HER?
I THINK SO.
UH-OH... SHOULD WE GET THE CAR AND FOLLOW HER?
RELAX. SHE'S PROBABLY HEADED TO HER OFFICE OR APARTMENT...
"...AND WE'VE GOT THOSE BOTH COVERED!"
LODGE & ASSOCIATES
SEARCH WARRANT
(UNDER SEAL)
CASE #10543-18
DISTRICT OF RIVERDALE COUNTY

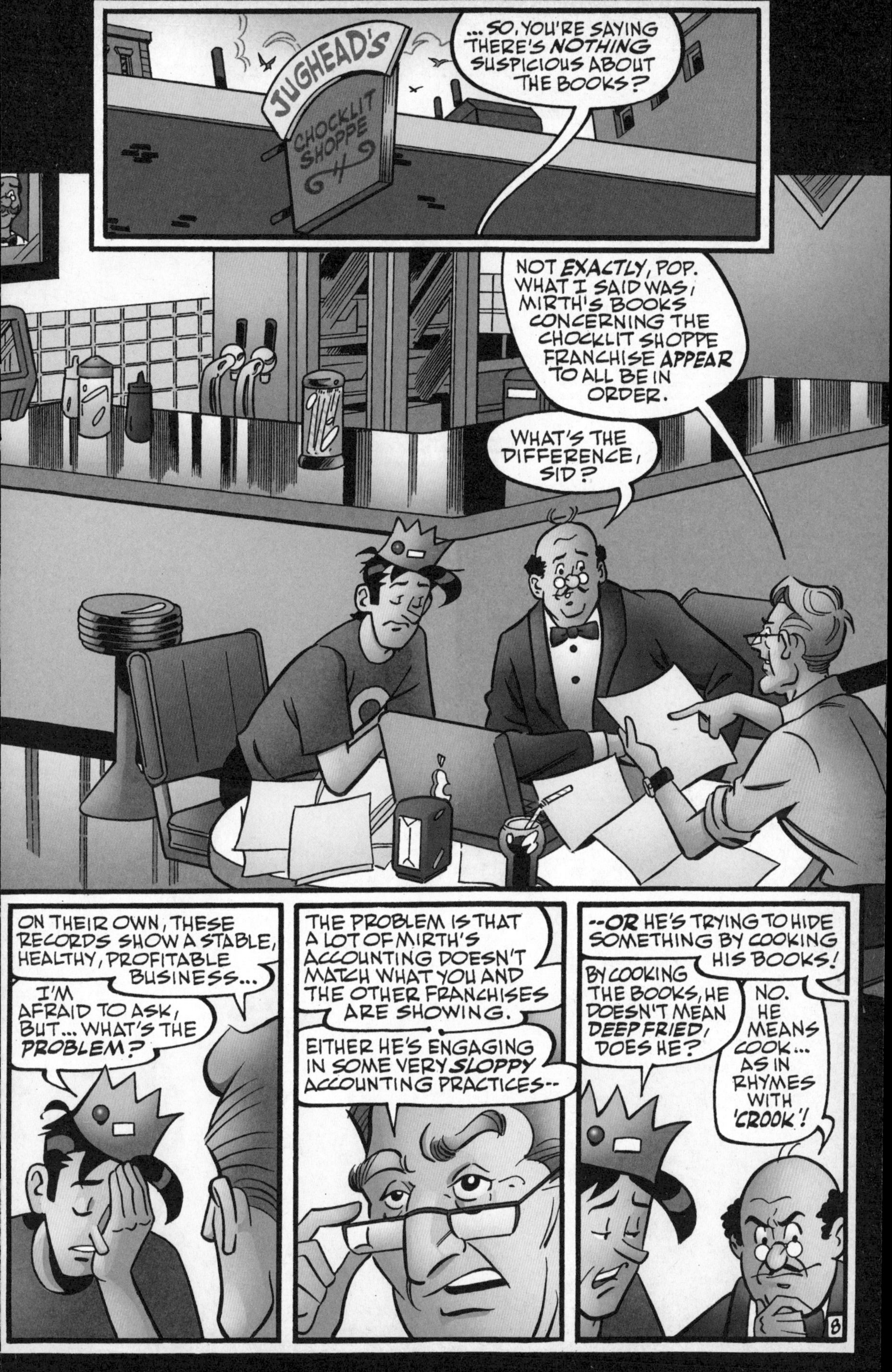
JUGHEAD'S
CHOCKLIT SHOPPE
...SO, YOU'RE SAYING THERE'S *NOTHING* SUSPICIOUS ABOUT THE BOOKS?
NOT *EXACTLY*, POP. WHAT I SAID WAS, MIRTH'S BOOKS CONCERNING THE CHOCKLIT SHOPPE FRANCHISE *APPEAR* TO ALL BE IN ORDER.
WHAT'S THE DIFFERENCE, SID?
ON THEIR OWN, THESE RECORDS SHOW A STABLE, HEALTHY, PROFITABLE BUSINESS...
I'M AFRAID TO ASK, BUT... WHAT'S THE *PROBLEM*?
THE PROBLEM IS THAT A LOT OF MIRTH'S ACCOUNTING DOESN'T MATCH WHAT YOU AND THE OTHER FRANCHISES ARE SHOWING.
EITHER HE'S ENGAGING IN SOME VERY *SLOPPY* ACCOUNTING PRACTICES--
--*OR* HE'S TRYING TO HIDE SOMETHING BY COOKING HIS BOOKS!
BY COOKING THE BOOKS, HE DOESN'T MEAN *DEEP FRIED*, DOES HE?
NO. HE MEANS COOK... AS IN RHYMES WITH '*CROOK*'!
8

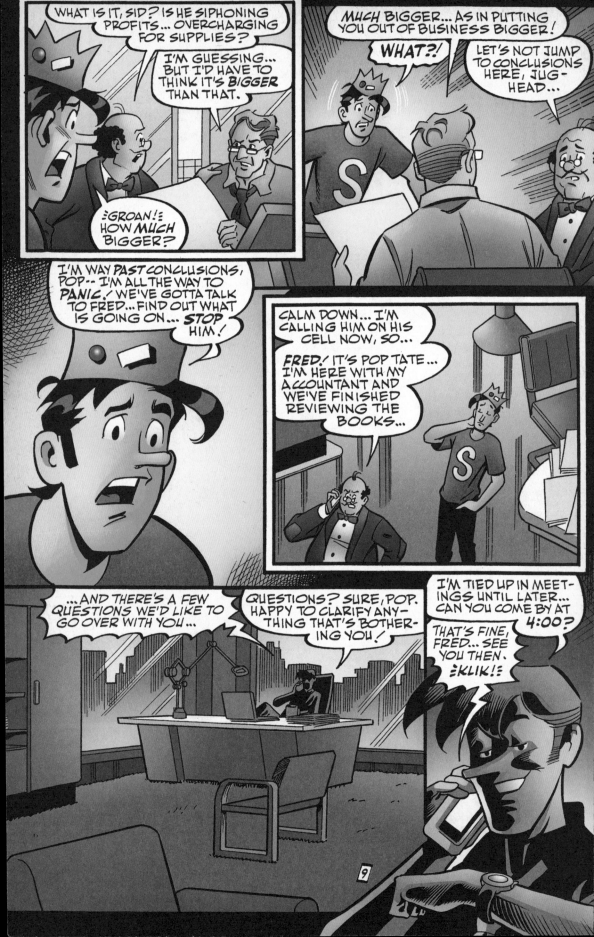

WHAT IS IT, SID? IS HE SIPHONING PROFITS... OVERCHARGING FOR SUPPLIES?

I'M GUESSING... BUT I'D HAVE TO THINK IT'S *BIGGER* THAN THAT.

:GROAN!: HOW *MUCH* BIGGER?

MUCH BIGGER... AS IN PUTTING YOU OUT OF BUSINESS BIGGER!

WHAT?!

LET'S NOT JUMP TO CONCLUSIONS HERE, JUG- HEAD...

I'M WAY *PAST* CONCLUSIONS, POP-- I'M ALL THE WAY TO *PANIC!* WE'VE GOTTA TALK TO FRED... FIND OUT WHAT IS GOING ON... *STOP* HIM!

CALM DOWN... I'M CALLING HIM ON HIS CELL NOW, SO...

FRED! IT'S POP TATE... I'M HERE WITH MY ACCOUNTANT AND WE'VE FINISHED REVIEWING THE BOOKS...

...AND THERE'S A FEW QUESTIONS WE'D LIKE TO GO OVER WITH YOU...

QUESTIONS? SURE, POP. HAPPY TO CLARIFY ANY- THING THAT'S BOTHER- ING YOU!

I'M TIED UP IN MEET- INGS UNTIL LATER... CAN YOU COME BY AT *4:00?*

THAT'S FINE, FRED... SEE YOU THEN. :KLIK!:

9

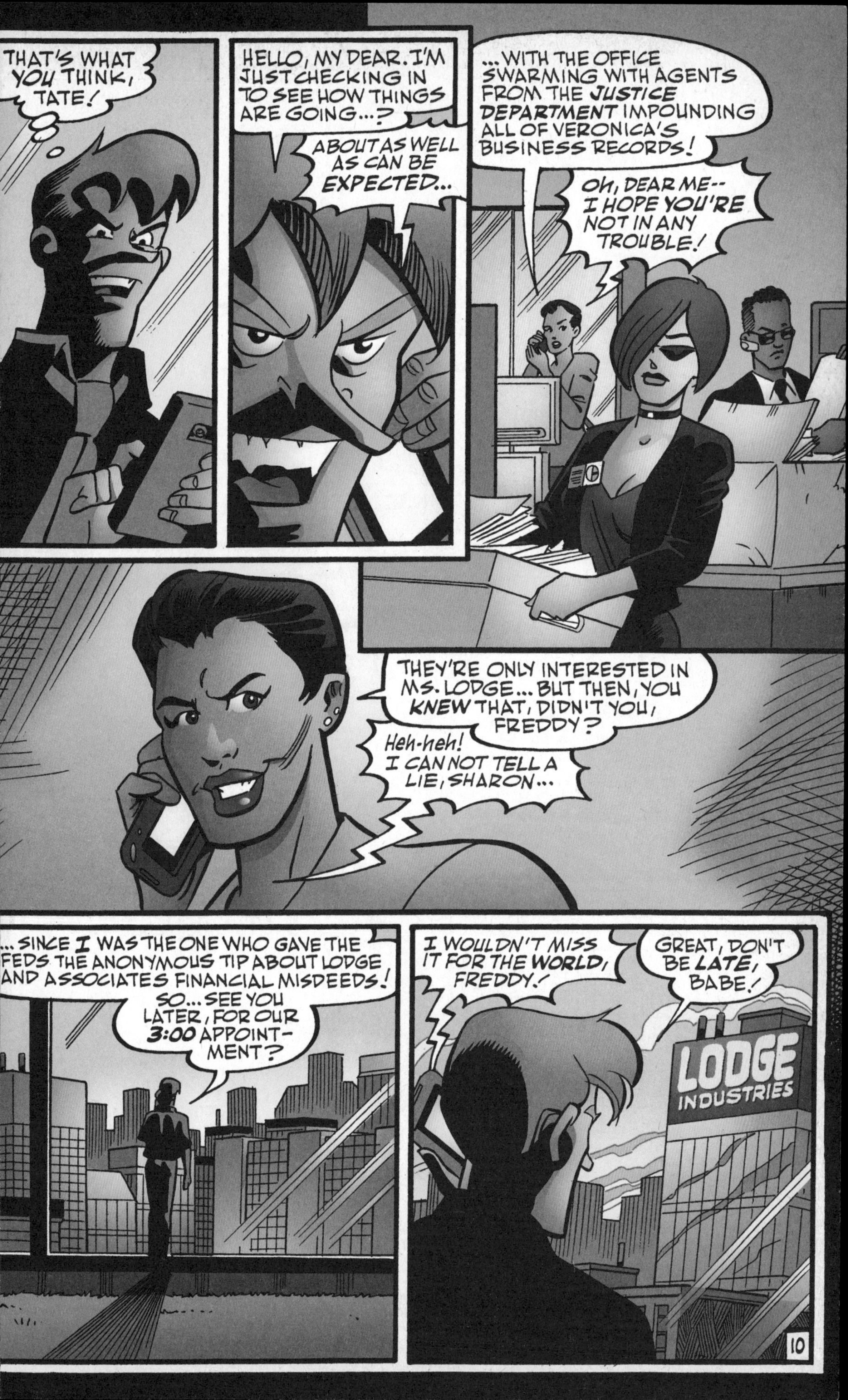
THAT'S WHAT YOU THINK, TATE!
HELLO, MY DEAR. I'M JUST CHECKING IN TO SEE HOW THINGS ARE GOING...?
ABOUT AS WELL AS CAN BE EXPECTED...
...WITH THE OFFICE SWARMING WITH AGENTS FROM THE JUSTICE DEPARTMENT IMPOUNDING ALL OF VERONICA'S BUSINESS RECORDS!
Oh, DEAR ME-- I HOPE YOU'RE NOT IN ANY TROUBLE!
THEY'RE ONLY INTERESTED IN MS. LODGE... BUT THEN, YOU KNEW THAT, DIDN'T YOU, FREDDY?
Heh-heh! I CAN NOT TELL A LIE, SHARON...
...SINCE I WAS THE ONE WHO GAVE THE FEDS THE ANONYMOUS TIP ABOUT LODGE AND ASSOCIATES FINANCIAL MISDEEDS!
SO... SEE YOU LATER, FOR OUR 3:00 APPOINT-MENT?
I WOULDN'T MISS IT FOR THE WORLD, FREDDY!
GREAT, DON'T BE LATE, BABE!
LODGE INDUSTRIES
10

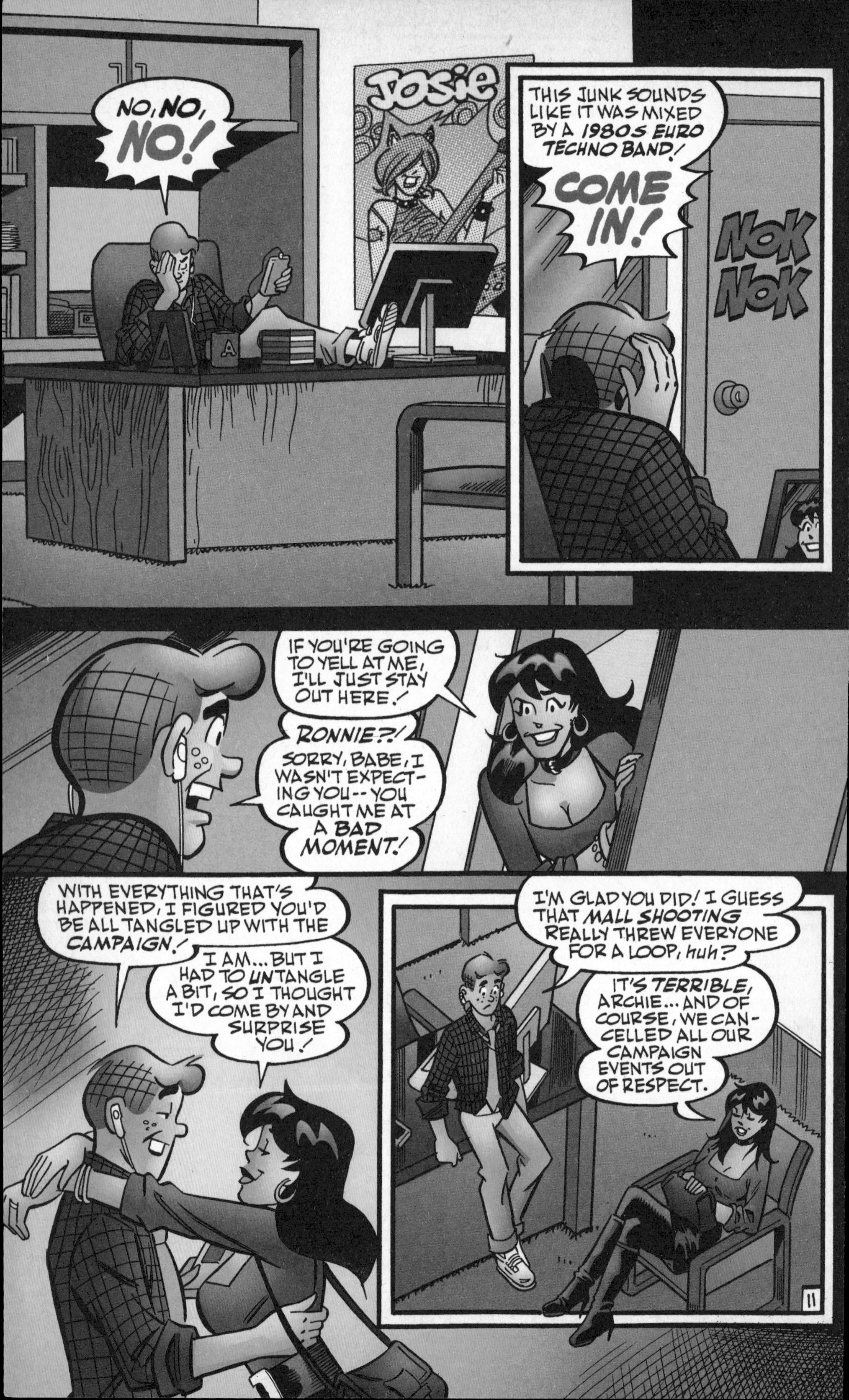
NO, NO, NO!
JOSIE
THIS JUNK SOUNDS LIKE IT WAS MIXED BY A 1980s EURO TECHNO BAND!
COME IN!
NOK NOK
IF YOU'RE GOING TO YELL AT ME, I'LL JUST STAY OUT HERE!
RONNIE?!
SORRY, BABE, I WASN'T EXPECTING YOU-- YOU CAUGHT ME AT A BAD MOMENT!
WITH EVERYTHING THAT'S HAPPENED, I FIGURED YOU'D BE ALL TANGLED UP WITH THE CAMPAIGN!
I AM... BUT I HAD TO UNTANGLE A BIT, SO I THOUGHT I'D COME BY AND SURPRISE YOU!
I'M GLAD YOU DID! I GUESS THAT MALL SHOOTING REALLY THREW EVERYONE FOR A LOOP, huh?
IT'S TERRIBLE, ARCHIE... AND OF COURSE, WE CANCELLED ALL OUR CAMPAIGN EVENTS OUT OF RESPECT.
11

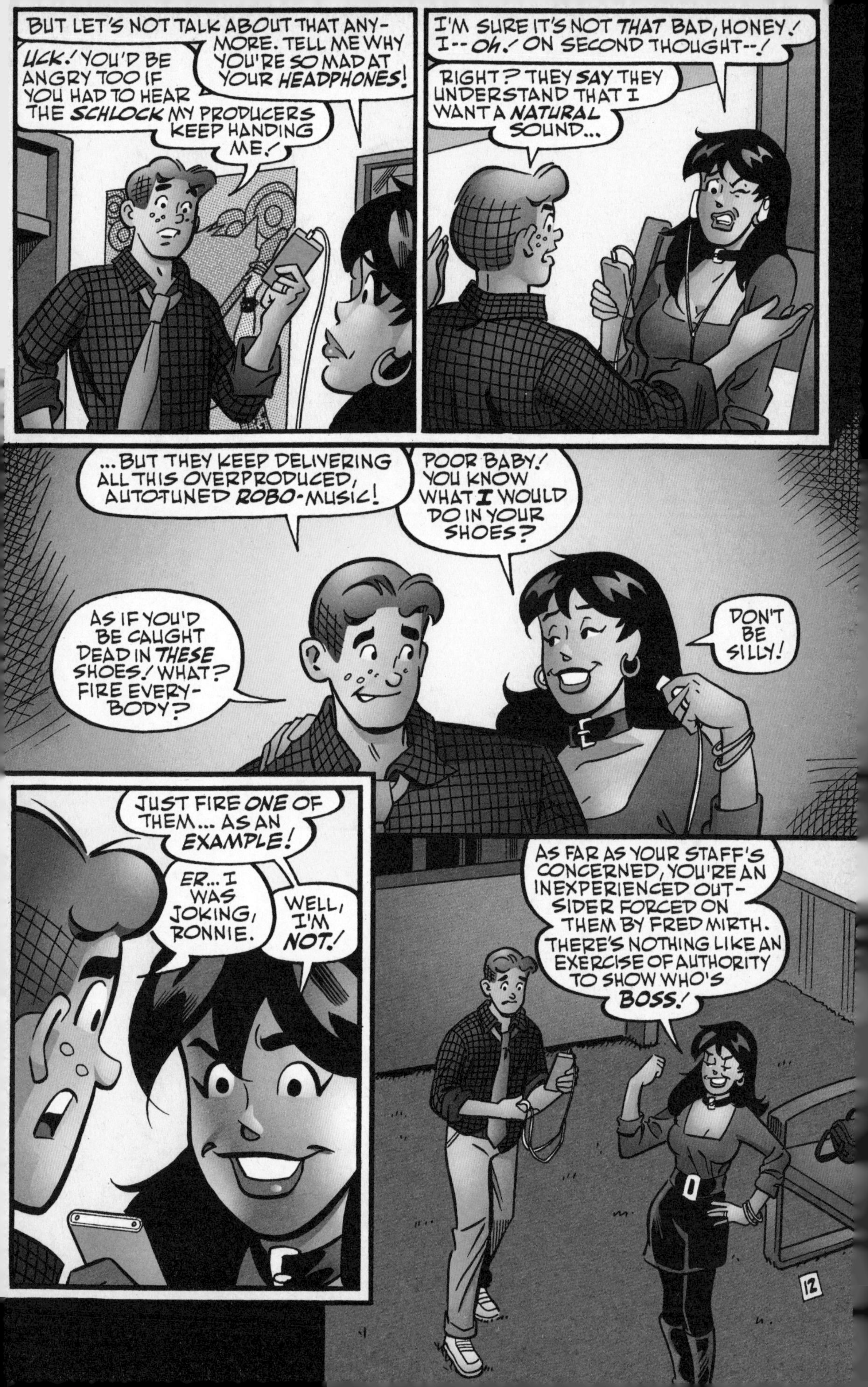
BUT LET'S NOT TALK ABOUT THAT ANY-MORE. TELL ME WHY YOU'RE SO MAD AT YOUR HEADPHONES!
UCK! YOU'D BE ANGRY TOO IF YOU HAD TO HEAR THE SCHLOCK MY PRODUCERS KEEP HANDING ME!
I'M SURE IT'S NOT THAT BAD, HONEY! I-- Oh! ON SECOND THOUGHT--!
RIGHT? THEY SAY THEY UNDERSTAND THAT I WANT A NATURAL SOUND...
...BUT THEY KEEP DELIVERING ALL THIS OVERPRODUCED, AUTOTUNED ROBO-MUSIC!
POOR BABY! YOU KNOW WHAT I WOULD DO IN YOUR SHOES?
AS IF YOU'D BE CAUGHT DEAD IN THESE SHOES! WHAT? FIRE EVERY-BODY?
DON'T BE SILLY!
JUST FIRE ONE OF THEM... AS AN EXAMPLE!
ER... I WAS JOKING, RONNIE.
WELL, I'M NOT!
AS FAR AS YOUR STAFF'S CONCERNED, YOU'RE AN INEXPERIENCED OUT-SIDER FORCED ON THEM BY FRED MIRTH. THERE'S NOTHING LIKE AN EXERCISE OF AUTHORITY TO SHOW WHO'S BOSS!
12

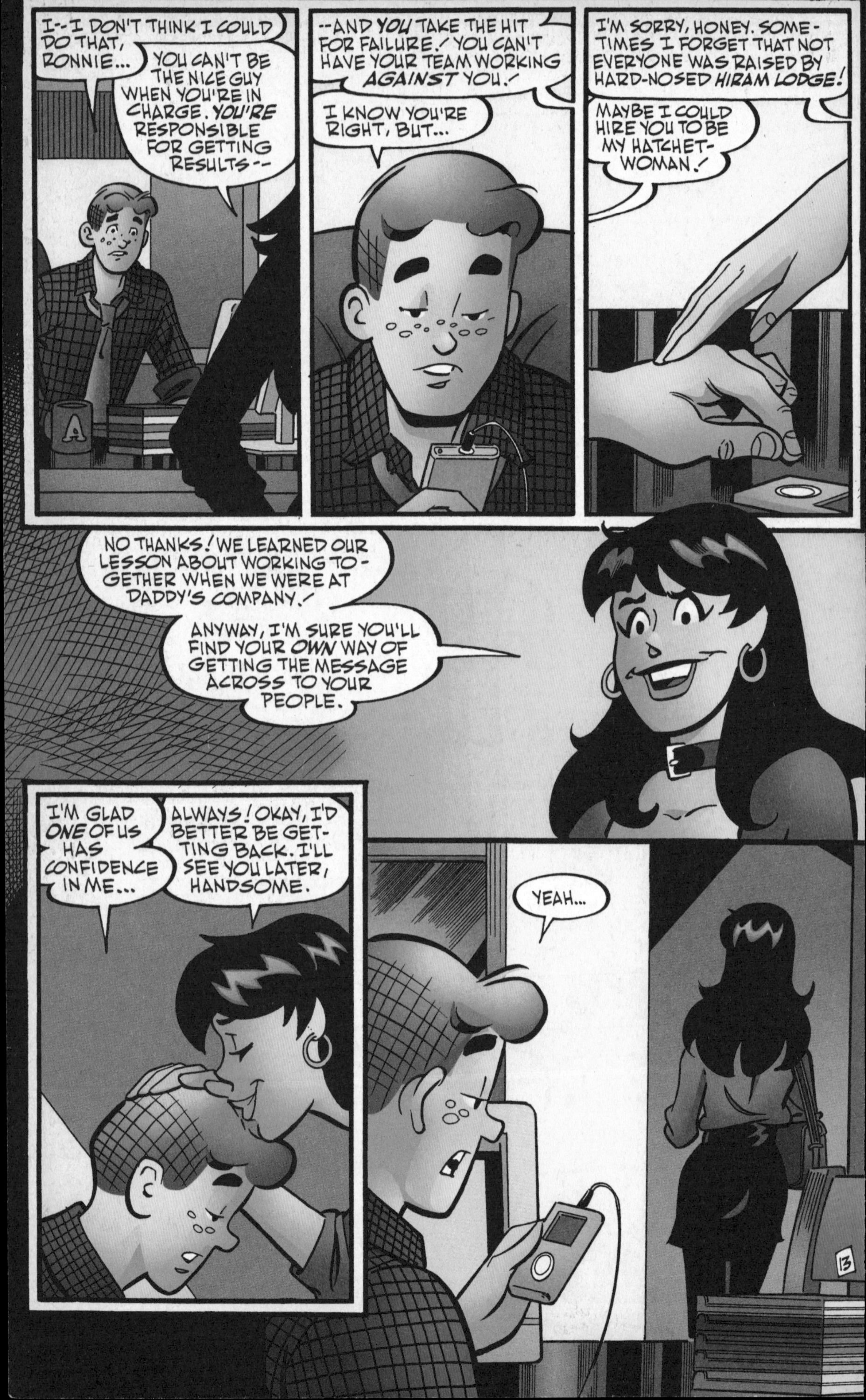
I--I DON'T THINK I COULD DO THAT, RONNIE...
YOU CAN'T BE THE NICE GUY WHEN YOU'RE IN CHARGE. YOU'RE RESPONSIBLE FOR GETTING RESULTS--
--AND YOU TAKE THE HIT FOR FAILURE! YOU CAN'T HAVE YOUR TEAM WORKING AGAINST YOU!
I KNOW YOU'RE RIGHT, BUT...
I'M SORRY, HONEY. SOMETIMES I FORGET THAT NOT EVERYONE WAS RAISED BY HARD-NOSED HIRAM LODGE!
MAYBE I COULD HIRE YOU TO BE MY HATCHET-WOMAN!
NO THANKS! WE LEARNED OUR LESSON ABOUT WORKING TOGETHER WHEN WE WERE AT DADDY'S COMPANY!
ANYWAY, I'M SURE YOU'LL FIND YOUR OWN WAY OF GETTING THE MESSAGE ACROSS TO YOUR PEOPLE.
I'M GLAD ONE OF US HAS CONFIDENCE IN ME...
ALWAYS! OKAY, I'D BETTER BE GETTING BACK. I'LL SEE YOU LATER, HANDSOME.
YEAH...
13

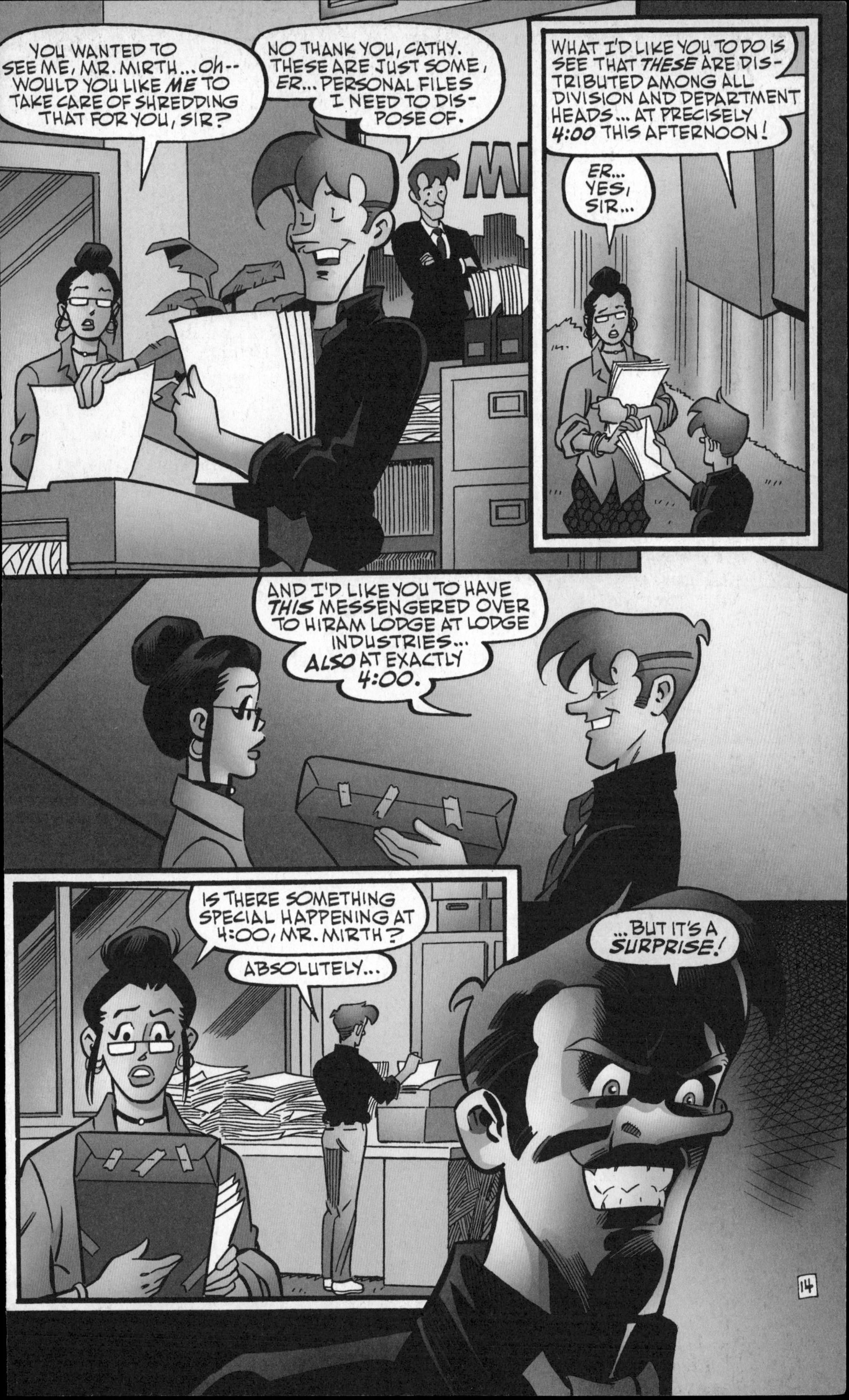
YOU WANTED TO SEE ME, MR. MIRTH... OH-- WOULD YOU LIKE ME TO TAKE CARE OF SHREDDING THAT FOR YOU, SIR?
NO THANK YOU, CATHY. THESE ARE JUST SOME, ER... PERSONAL FILES I NEED TO DISPOSE OF.
WHAT I'D LIKE YOU TO DO IS SEE THAT THESE ARE DISTRIBUTED AMONG ALL DIVISION AND DEPARTMENT HEADS... AT PRECISELY 4:00 THIS AFTERNOON!
ER... YES, SIR...
AND I'D LIKE YOU TO HAVE THIS MESSENGERED OVER TO HIRAM LODGE AT LODGE INDUSTRIES... ALSO AT EXACTLY 4:00.
IS THERE SOMETHING SPECIAL HAPPENING AT 4:00, MR. MIRTH?
ABSOLUTELY...
...BUT IT'S A SURPRISE!
14

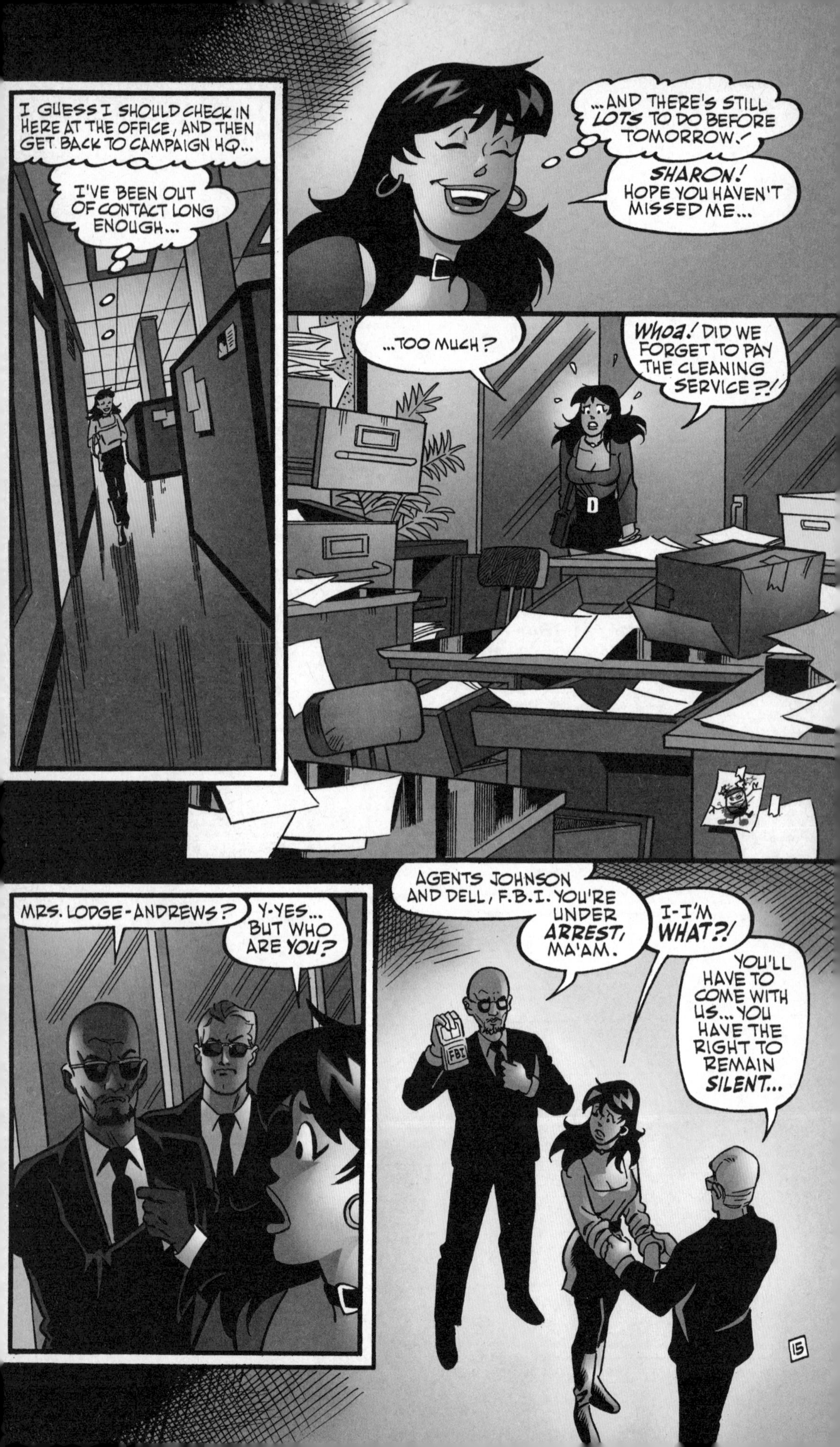
I GUESS I SHOULD CHECK IN HERE AT THE OFFICE, AND THEN GET BACK TO CAMPAIGN HQ...
I'VE BEEN OUT OF CONTACT LONG ENOUGH...
...AND THERE'S STILL LOTS TO DO BEFORE TOMORROW.!
SHARON! HOPE YOU HAVEN'T MISSED ME...
...TOO MUCH?
Whoa! DID WE FORGET TO PAY THE CLEANING SERVICE?!
MRS. LODGE-ANDREWS?
Y-YES... BUT WHO ARE YOU?
AGENTS JOHNSON AND DELL, F.B.I. YOU'RE UNDER ARREST, MA'AM.
I-I'M WHAT?!
YOU'LL HAVE TO COME WITH US... YOU HAVE THE RIGHT TO REMAIN SILENT...
FBI
15

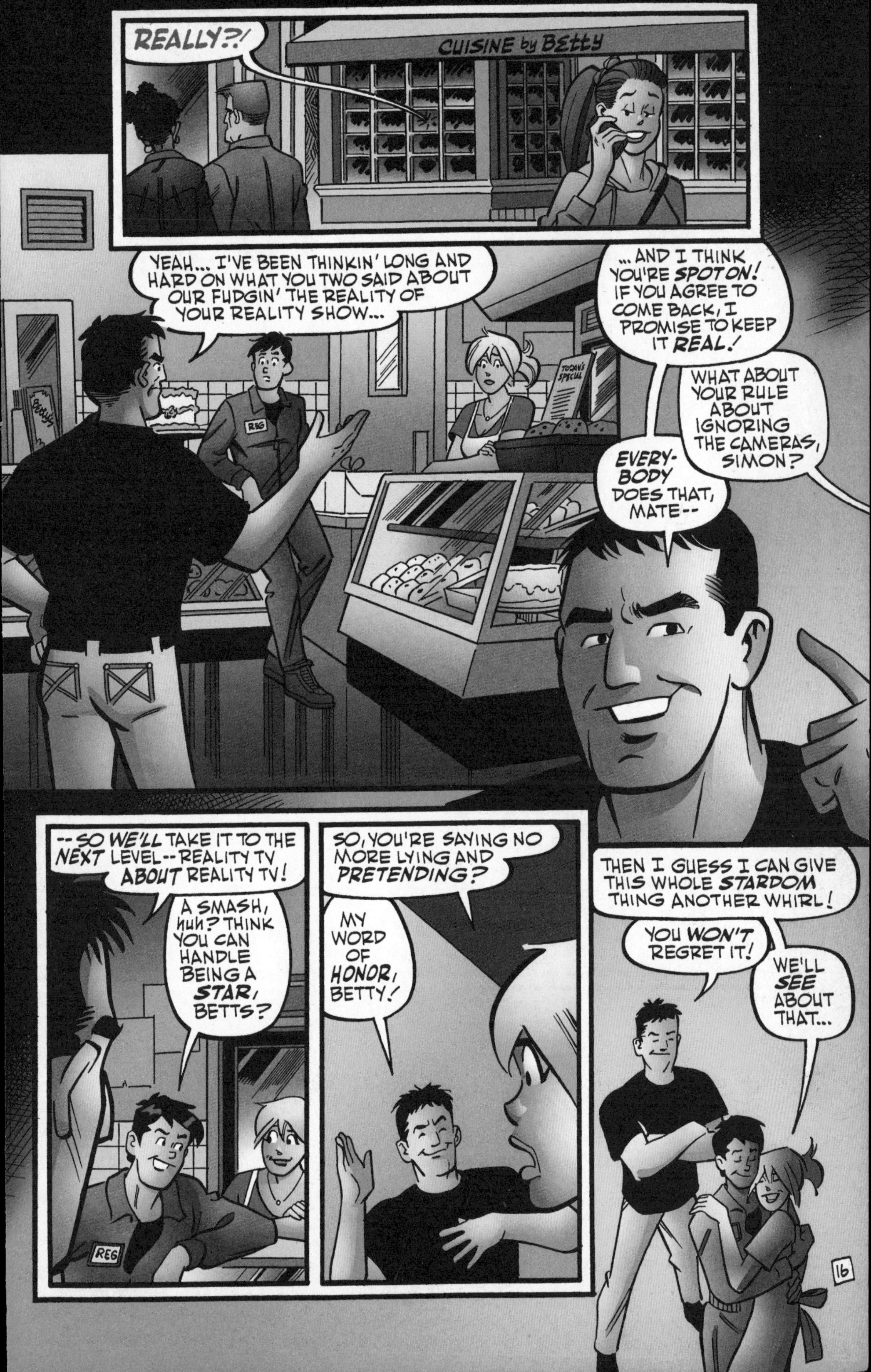
REALLY?!
CUISINE by BETTY
YEAH... I'VE BEEN THINKIN' LONG AND HARD ON WHAT YOU TWO SAID ABOUT OUR FUDGIN' THE REALITY OF YOUR REALITY SHOW...
...AND I THINK YOU'RE SPOT ON! IF YOU AGREE TO COME BACK, I PROMISE TO KEEP IT REAL!
WHAT ABOUT YOUR RULE ABOUT IGNORING THE CAMERAS, SIMON?
EVERYBODY DOES THAT, MATE--
--SO WE'LL TAKE IT TO THE NEXT LEVEL--REALITY TV ABOUT REALITY TV!
A SMASH, huh? THINK YOU CAN HANDLE BEING A STAR, BETTS?
SO, YOU'RE SAYING NO MORE LYING AND PRETENDING?
MY WORD OF HONOR, BETTY!
THEN I GUESS I CAN GIVE THIS WHOLE STARDOM THING ANOTHER WHIRL!
YOU WON'T REGRET IT!
WE'LL SEE ABOUT THAT...
16

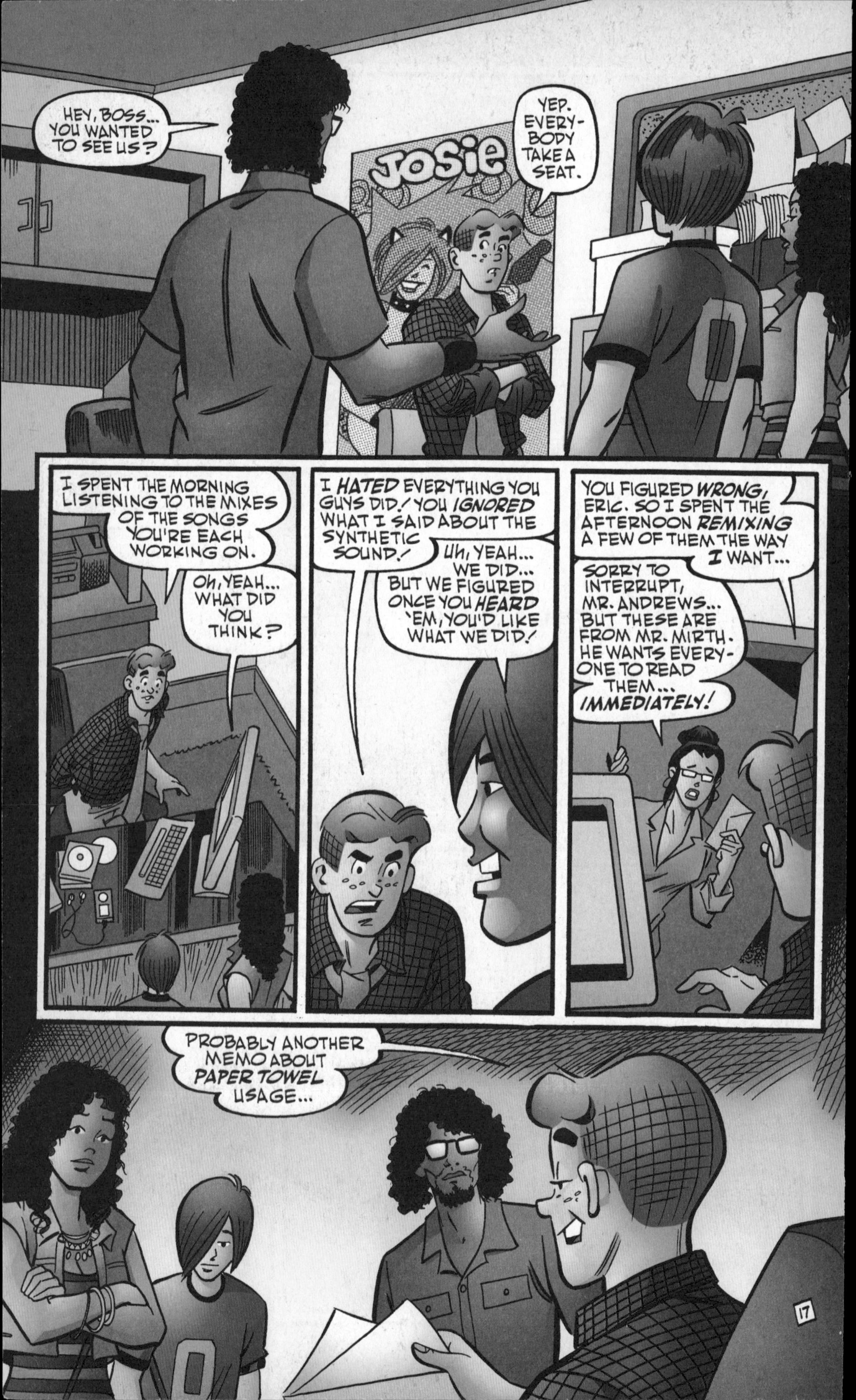

HEY, BOSS... YOU WANTED TO SEE US?
YEP. EVERYBODY TAKE A SEAT.
JOSIE
I SPENT THE MORNING LISTENING TO THE MIXES OF THE SONGS YOU'RE EACH WORKING ON.
OH, YEAH... WHAT DID YOU THINK?
I HATED EVERYTHING YOU GUYS DID! YOU IGNORED WHAT I SAID ABOUT THE SYNTHETIC SOUND!
UH, YEAH... WE DID... BUT WE FIGURED ONCE YOU HEARD 'EM, YOU'D LIKE WHAT WE DID!
YOU FIGURED WRONG, ERIC. SO I SPENT THE AFTERNOON REMIXING A FEW OF THEM THE WAY I WANT...
SORRY TO INTERRUPT, MR. ANDREWS... BUT THESE ARE FROM MR. MIRTH. HE WANTS EVERYONE TO READ THEM... IMMEDIATELY!
PROBABLY ANOTHER MEMO ABOUT PAPER TOWEL USAGE...
17

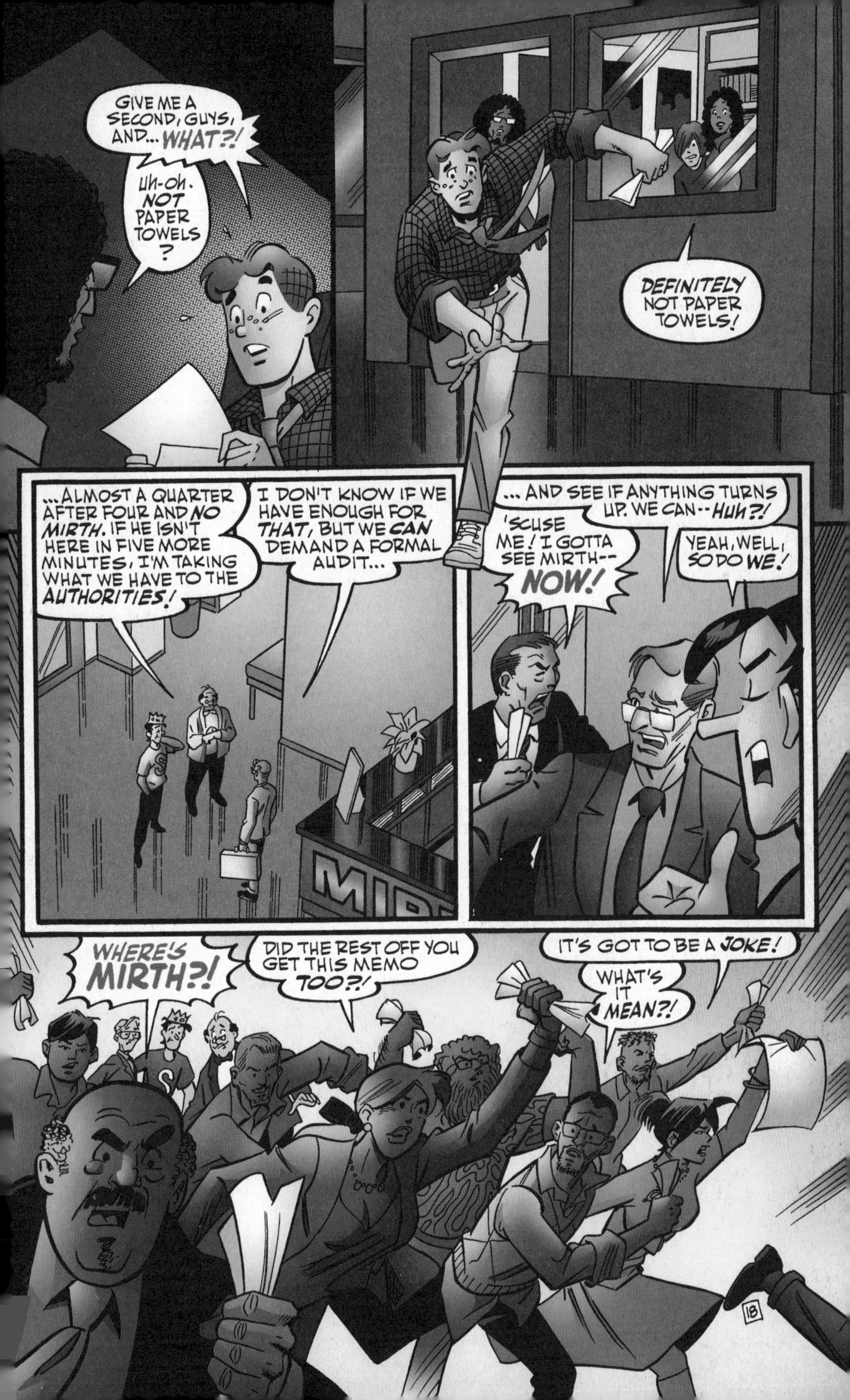
GIVE ME A SECOND, GUYS, AND... WHAT?!
UH-OH. NOT PAPER TOWELS?
DEFINITELY NOT PAPER TOWELS!
...ALMOST A QUARTER AFTER FOUR AND NO MIRTH. IF HE ISN'T HERE IN FIVE MORE MINUTES, I'M TAKING WHAT WE HAVE TO THE AUTHORITIES!
I DON'T KNOW IF WE HAVE ENOUGH FOR THAT, BUT WE CAN DEMAND A FORMAL AUDIT...
...AND SEE IF ANYTHING TURNS UP. WE CAN-- HUH?!
'SCUSE ME! I GOTTA SEE MIRTH-- NOW!
YEAH, WELL, SO DO WE!
WHERE'S MIRTH?!
DID THE REST OFF YOU GET THIS MEMO TOO?!
IT'S GOT TO BE A JOKE!
WHAT'S IT MEAN?!
18

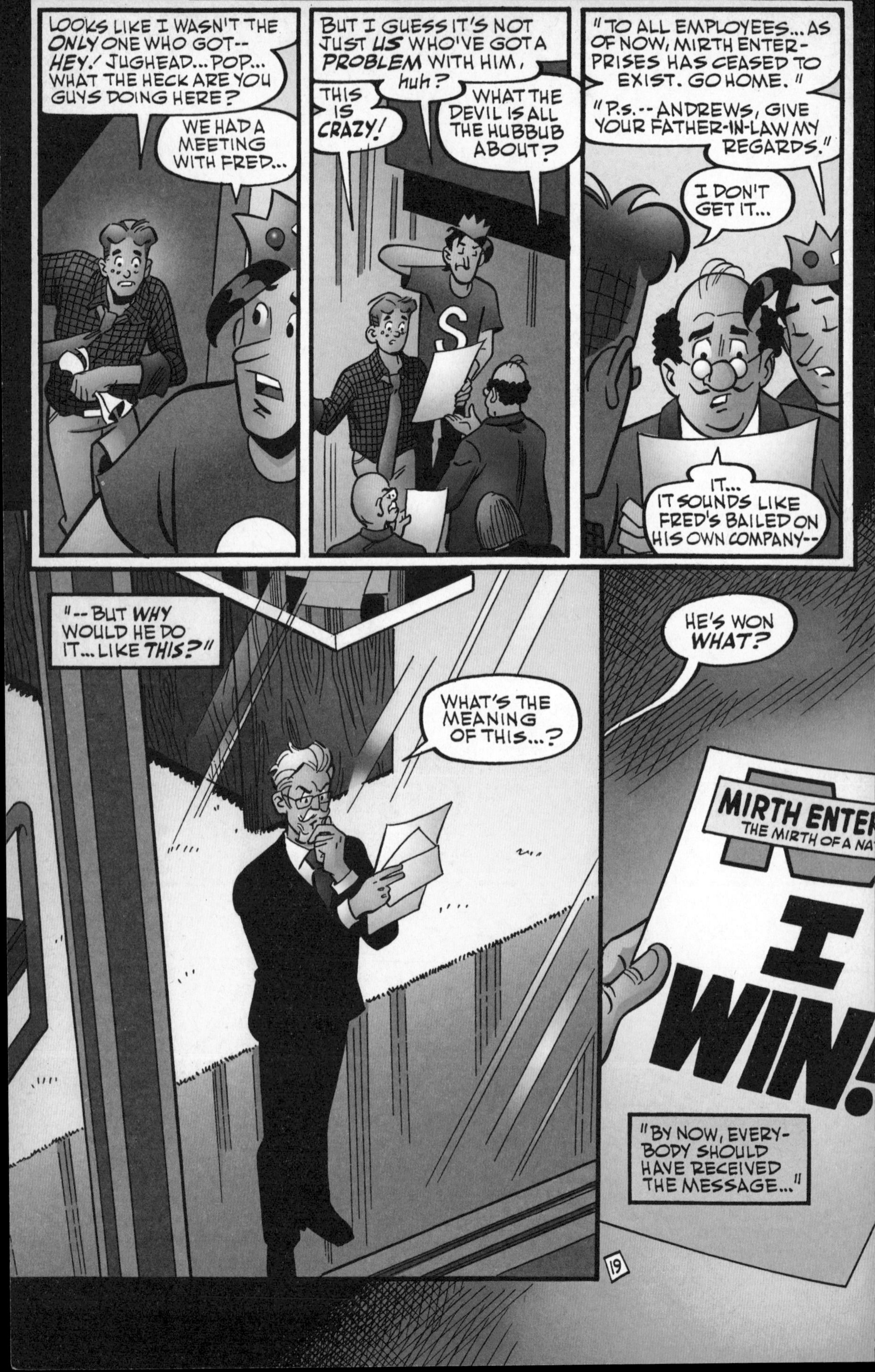
LOOKS LIKE I WASN'T THE ONLY ONE WHO GOT-- HEY! JUGHEAD...POP... WHAT THE HECK ARE YOU GUYS DOING HERE?
WE HAD A MEETING WITH FRED...
BUT I GUESS IT'S NOT JUST US WHO'VE GOT A PROBLEM WITH HIM, huh?
THIS IS CRAZY!
WHAT THE DEVIL IS ALL THE HUBBUB ABOUT?
"TO ALL EMPLOYEES...AS OF NOW, MIRTH ENTERPRISES HAS CEASED TO EXIST. GO HOME."
"P.S.--ANDREWS, GIVE YOUR FATHER-IN-LAW MY REGARDS."
I DON'T GET IT...
IT... IT SOUNDS LIKE FRED'S BAILED ON HIS OWN COMPANY--
"--BUT WHY WOULD HE DO IT...LIKE THIS?"
WHAT'S THE MEANING OF THIS...?
HE'S WON WHAT?
MIRTH ENTE
THE MIRTH OF A NA
I WIN!
"BY NOW, EVERYBODY SHOULD HAVE RECEIVED THE MESSAGE..."
19

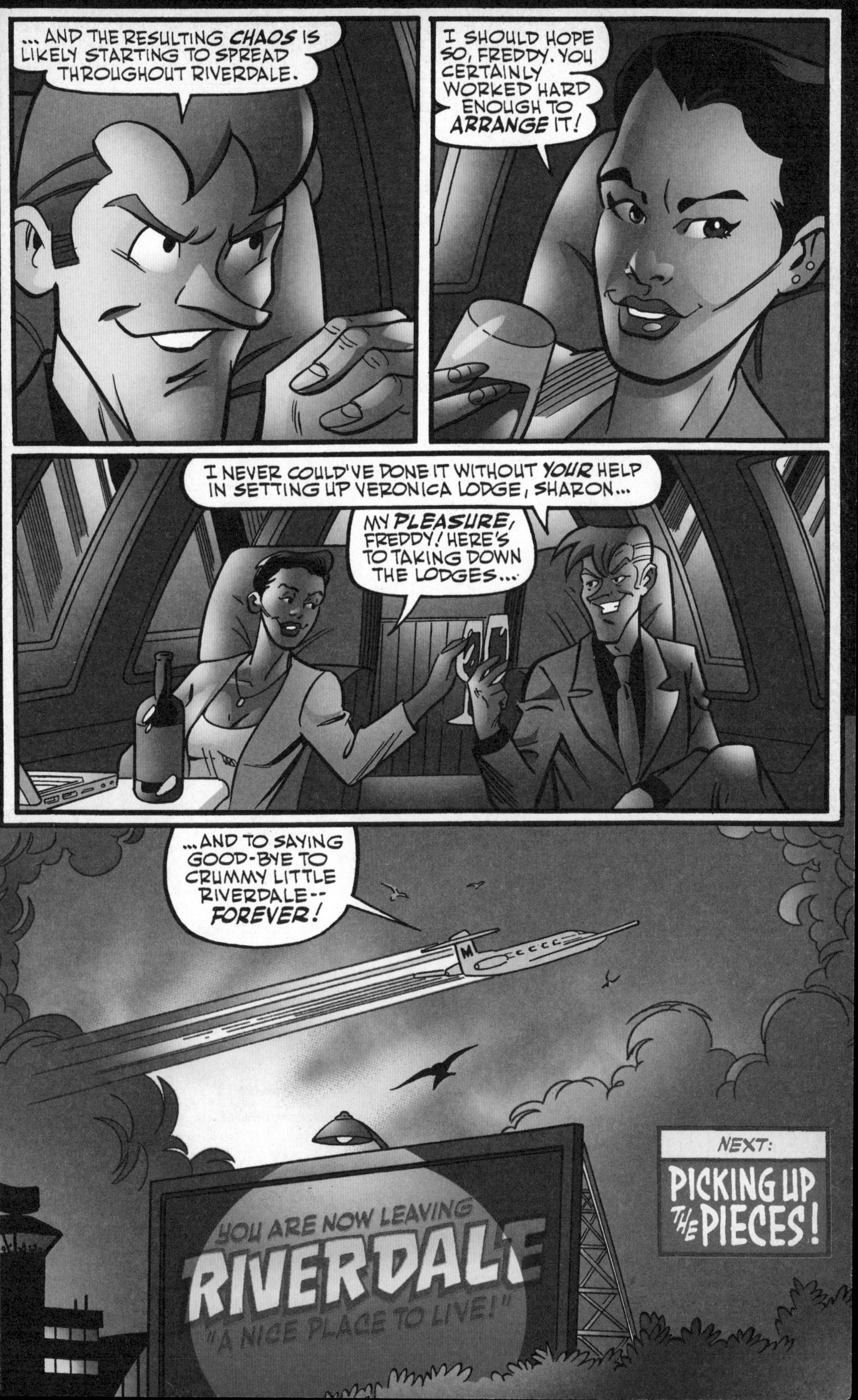
...AND THE RESULTING CHAOS IS LIKELY STARTING TO SPREAD THROUGHOUT RIVERDALE.
I SHOULD HOPE SO, FREDDY. YOU CERTAINLY WORKED HARD ENOUGH TO ARRANGE IT!
I NEVER COULD'VE DONE IT WITHOUT YOUR HELP IN SETTING UP VERONICA LODGE, SHARON...
MY PLEASURE, FREDDY! HERE'S TO TAKING DOWN THE LODGES...
...AND TO SAYING GOOD-BYE TO CRUMMY LITTLE RIVERDALE-- FOREVER!
YOU ARE NOW LEAVING RIVERDAL
"A NICE PLACE TO LIVE!"
NEXT:
PICKING UP THE PIECES!

"MAN, I CAN'T TELL YOU HOW *COOL* IT IS TO HAVE SOMEONE I CAN ***RELY*** ON TO RUN THIS PLACE FOR ME."

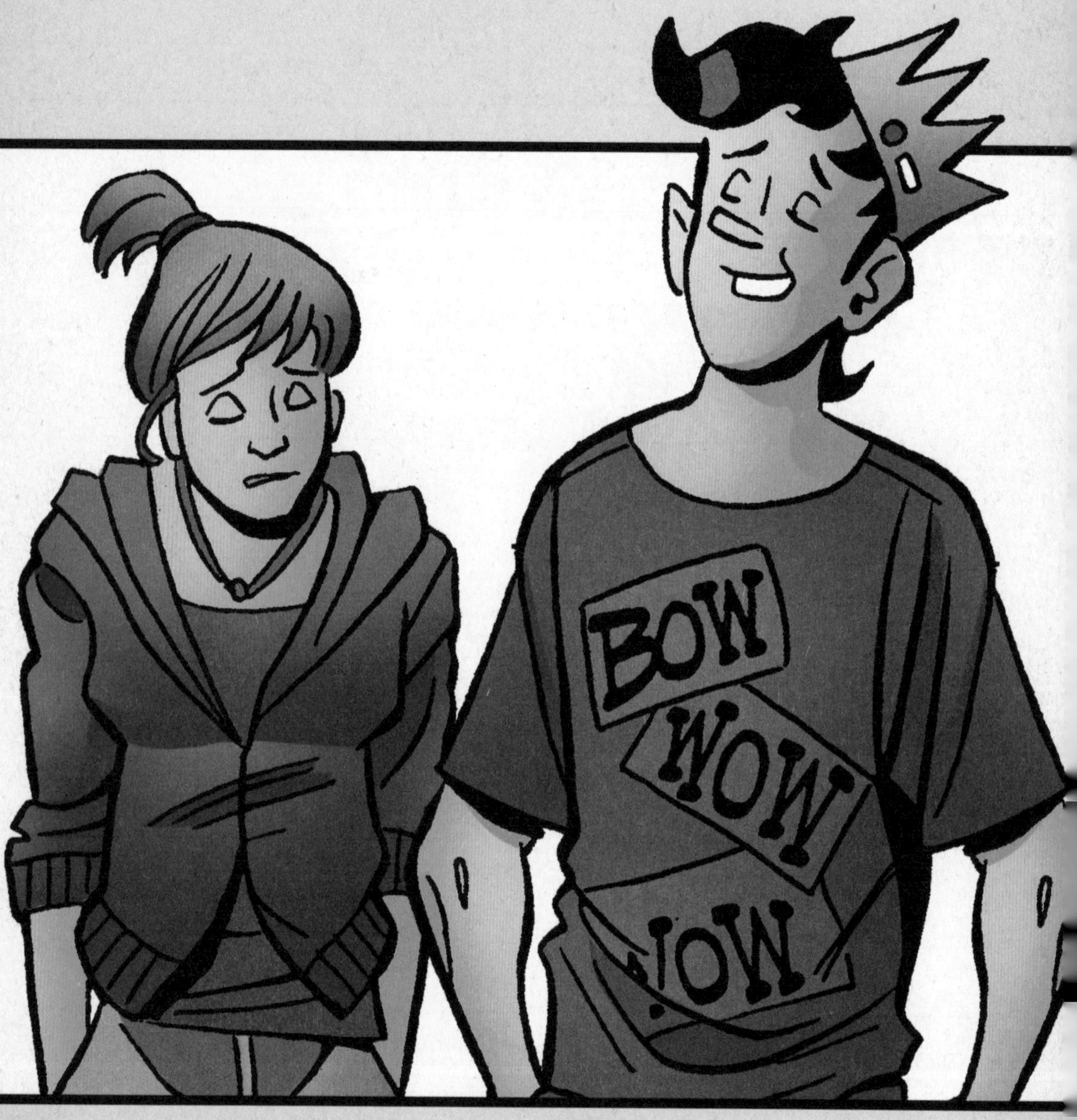
BOW
WOW

"WITH THE BABY ON THE WAY, I DON'T KNOW WHAT I'D DO ***WITHOUT*** YOU!"

-FORSYTHE "JUGHEAD" JONES

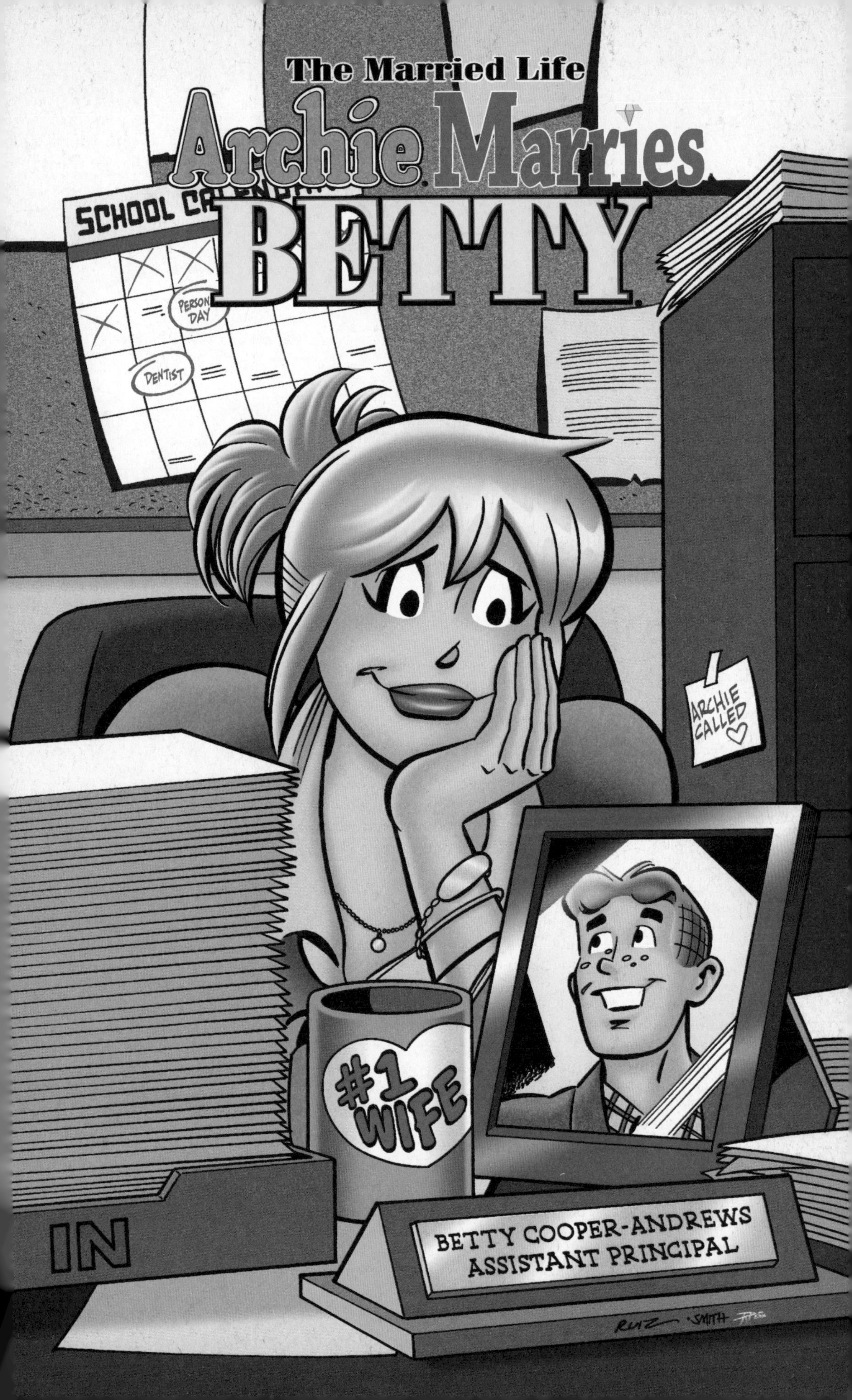

The Married Life
Archie Marries
BETTY
SCHOOL CA
PERSON DAY
DENTIST
ARCHIE CALLED
#1 WIFE
IN
BETTY COOPER-ANDREWS
ASSISTANT PRINCIPAL

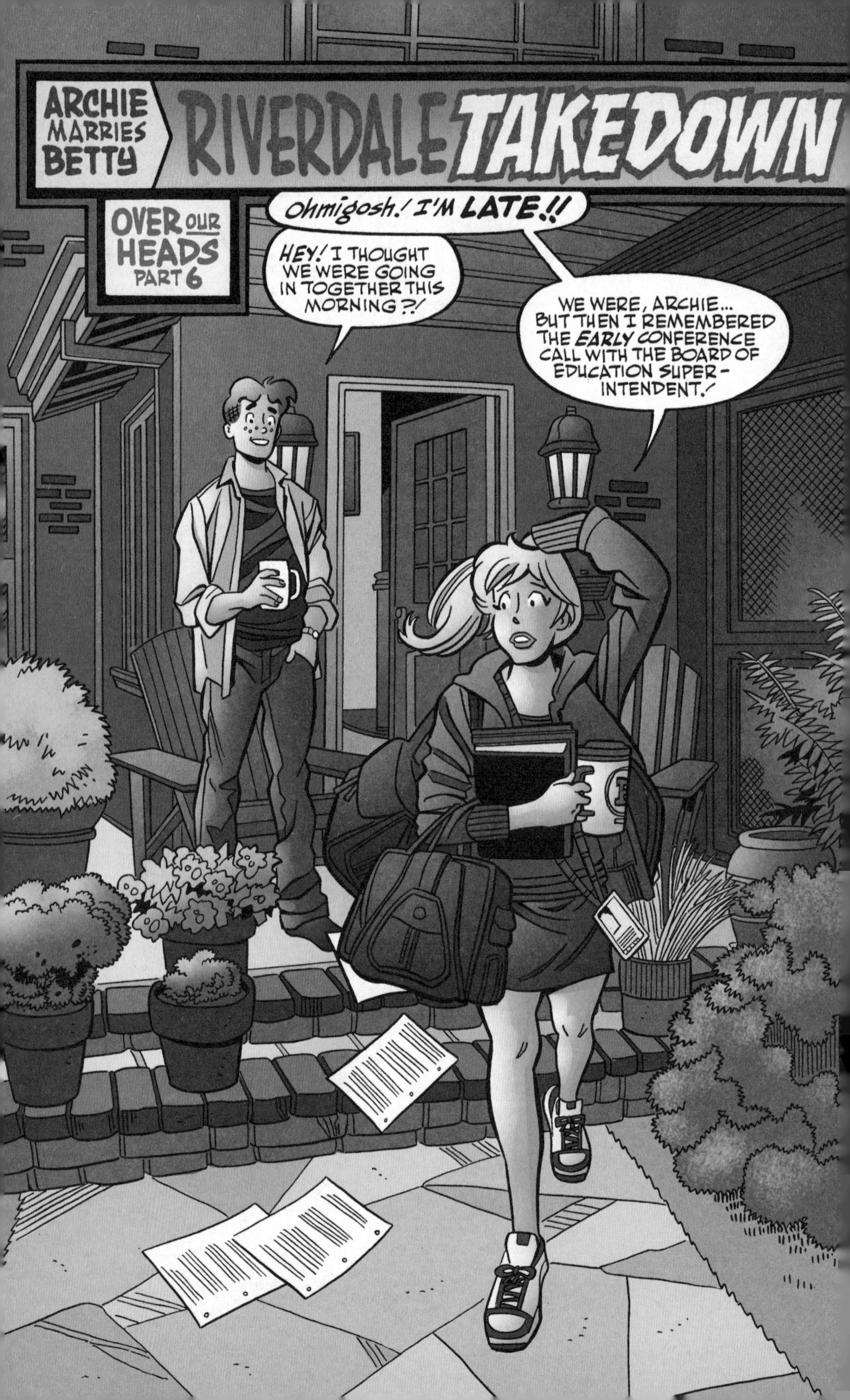
ARCHIE MARRIES BETTY
RIVERDALE TAKEDOWN
OVER OUR HEADS PART 6
Ohmigosh! I'M LATE!!
HEY! I THOUGHT WE WERE GOING IN TOGETHER THIS MORNING?!
WE WERE, ARCHIE... BUT THEN I REMEMBERED THE EARLY CONFERENCE CALL WITH THE BOARD OF EDUCATION SUPER-INTENDENT!

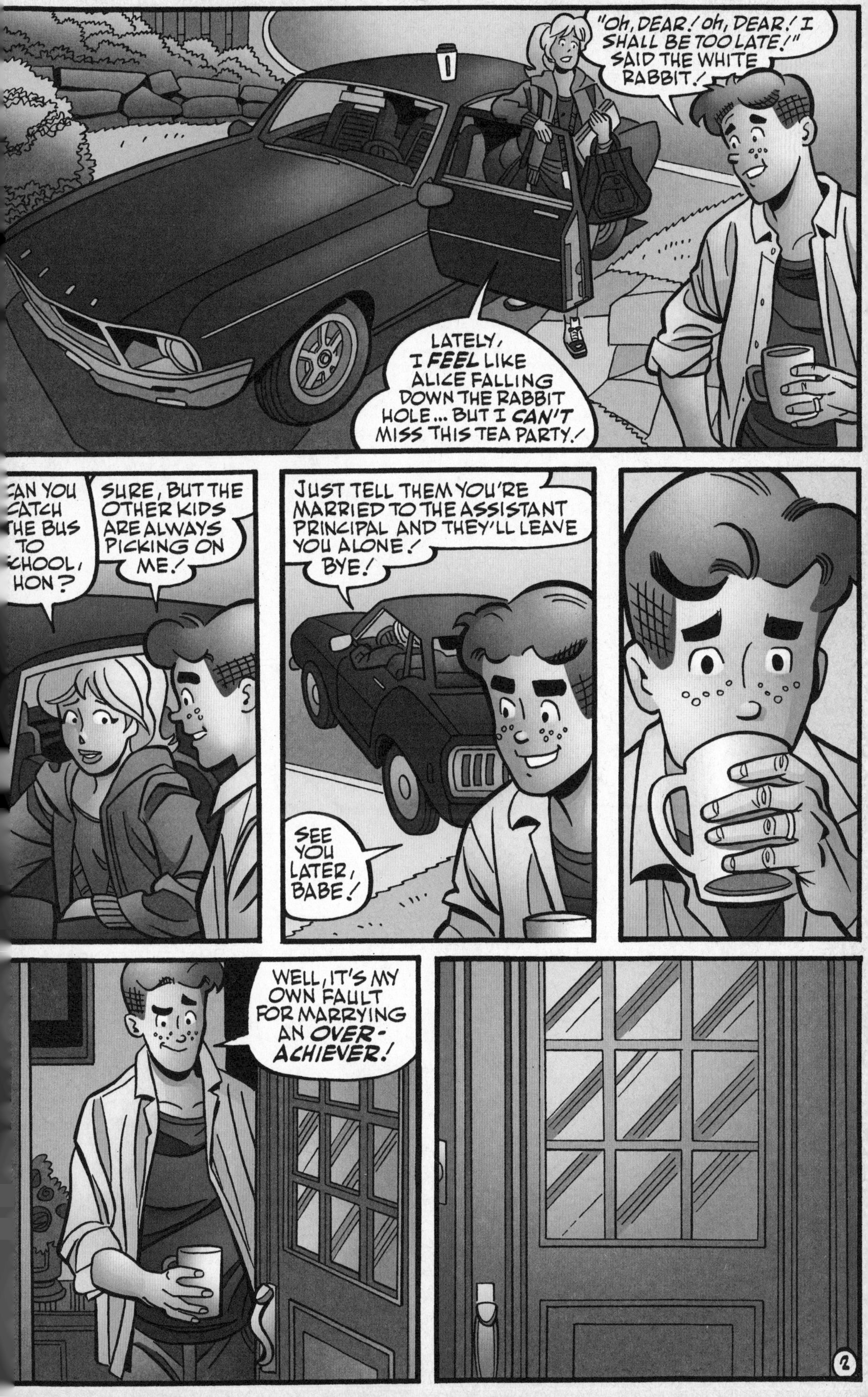
"Oh, DEAR! Oh, DEAR! I SHALL BE TOO LATE!" SAID THE WHITE RABBIT!
LATELY, I FEEL LIKE ALICE FALLING DOWN THE RABBIT HOLE... BUT I CAN'T MISS THIS TEA PARTY!
AN YOU ATCH HE BUS TO CHOOL, HON?
SURE, BUT THE OTHER KIDS ARE ALWAYS PICKING ON ME!
JUST TELL THEM YOU'RE MARRIED TO THE ASSISTANT PRINCIPAL AND THEY'LL LEAVE YOU ALONE! BYE!
SEE YOU LATER, BABE!
WELL, IT'S MY OWN FAULT FOR MARRYING AN OVER-ACHIEVER!

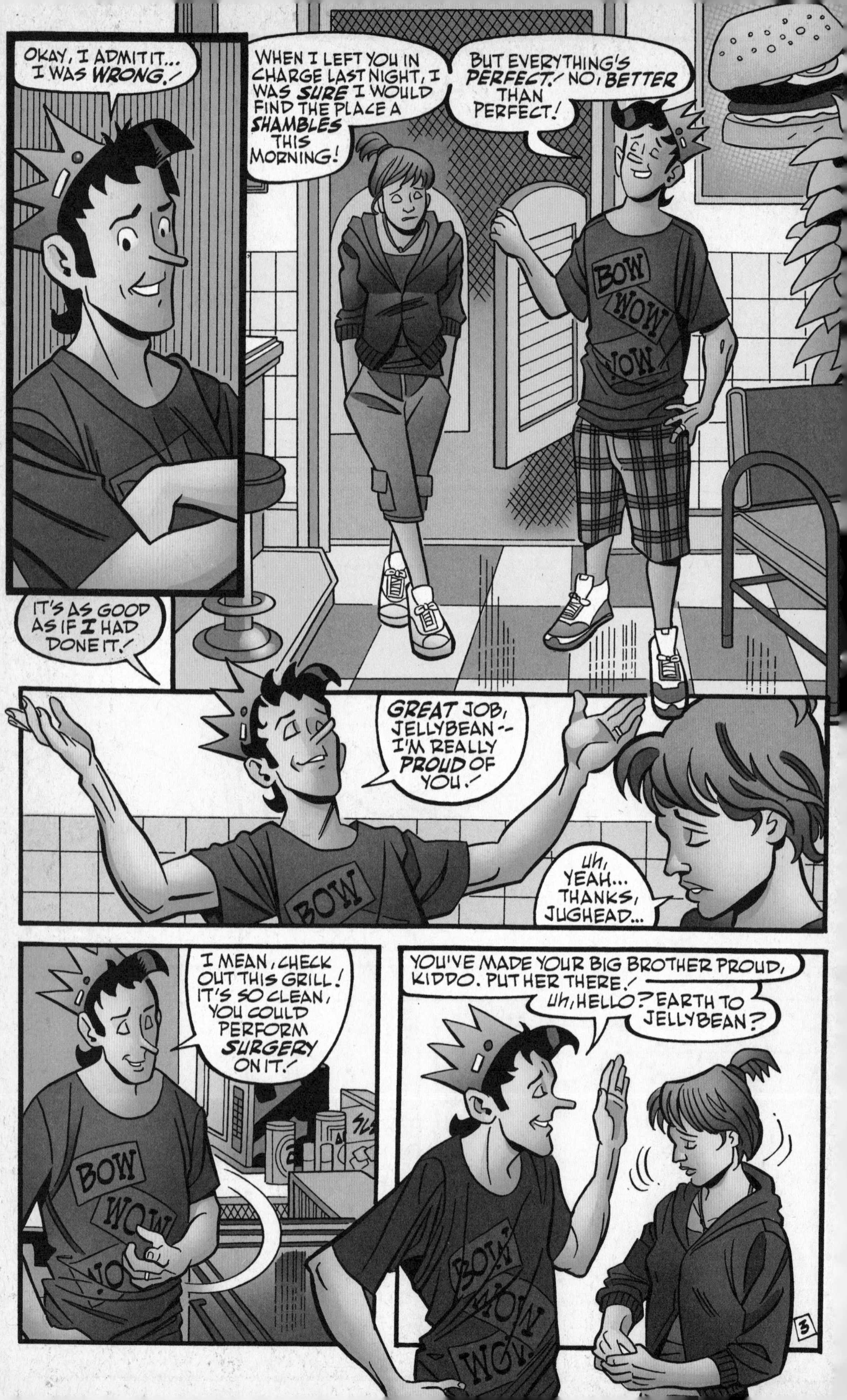
OKAY, I ADMIT IT... I WAS WRONG.!
WHEN I LEFT YOU IN CHARGE LAST NIGHT, I WAS SURE I WOULD FIND THE PLACE A SHAMBLES THIS MORNING!
BUT EVERYTHING'S PERFECT.! NO, BETTER THAN PERFECT!
BOW WOW WOW
IT'S AS GOOD AS IF I HAD DONE IT.!
GREAT JOB, JELLYBEAN-- I'M REALLY PROUD OF YOU.!
UH, YEAH... THANKS, JUGHEAD...
I MEAN, CHECK OUT THIS GRILL! IT'S SO CLEAN, YOU COULD PERFORM SURGERY ON IT.!
YOU'VE MADE YOUR BIG BROTHER PROUD, KIDDO. PUT HER THERE.!
UH, HELLO? EARTH TO JELLYBEAN?
3

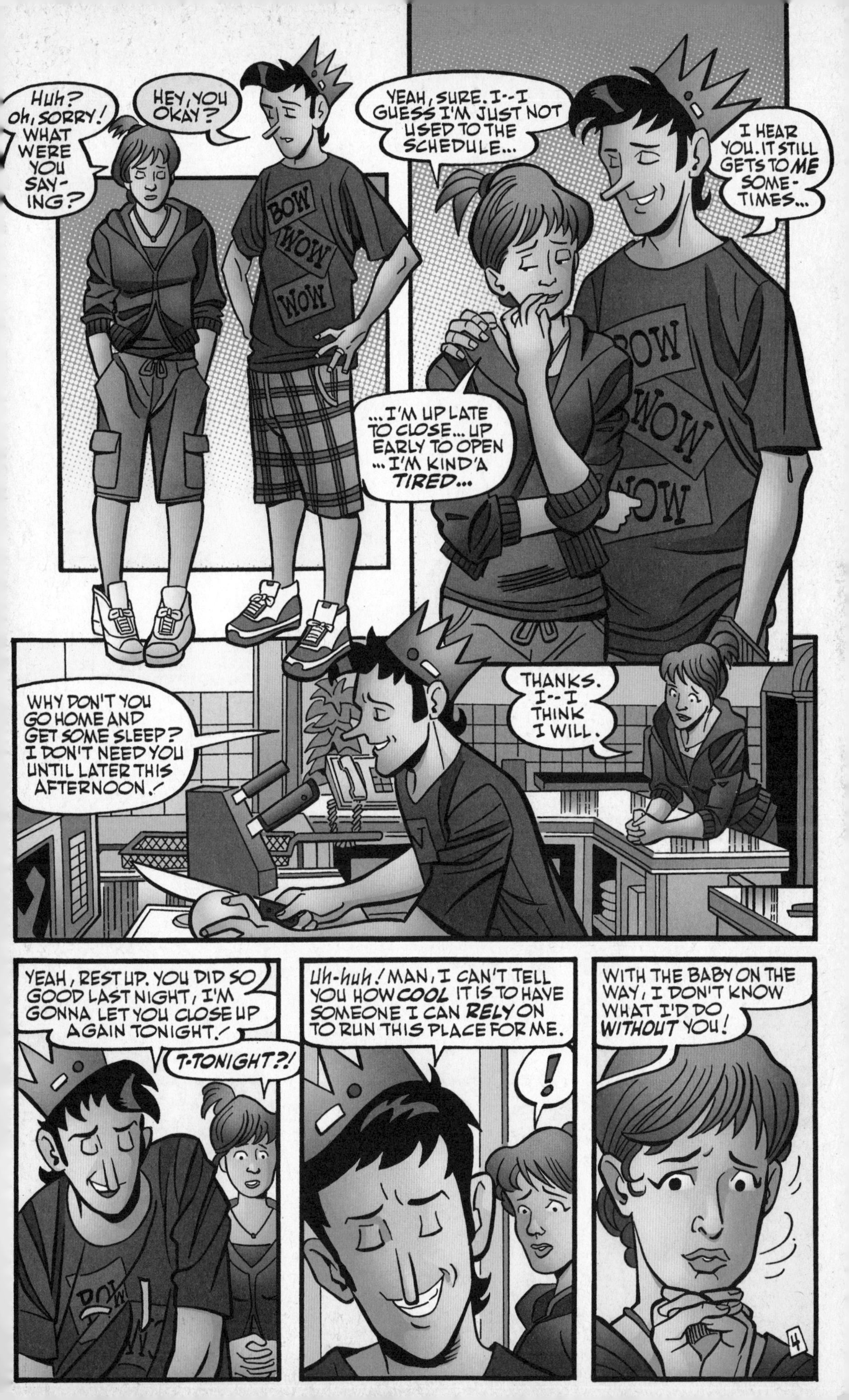

HEY, YOU OKAY?
Huh? oh, SORRY! WHAT WERE YOU SAY-ING?
BOW WOW WOW
YEAH, SURE. I--I GUESS I'M JUST NOT USED TO THE SCHEDULE...
I HEAR YOU. IT STILL GETS TO ME SOME-TIMES...
...I'M UP LATE TO CLOSE... UP EARLY TO OPEN ...I'M KIND'A TIRED...
WHY DON'T YOU GO HOME AND GET SOME SLEEP? I DON'T NEED YOU UNTIL LATER THIS AFTERNOON.
THANKS. I-- I THINK I WILL.
YEAH, REST UP. YOU DID SO GOOD LAST NIGHT, I'M GONNA LET YOU CLOSE UP AGAIN TONIGHT.
T-TONIGHT?!
Uh-huh! MAN, I CAN'T TELL YOU HOW COOL IT IS TO HAVE SOMEONE I CAN RELY ON TO RUN THIS PLACE FOR ME.
!
WITH THE BABY ON THE WAY, I DON'T KNOW WHAT I'D DO WITHOUT YOU!
4

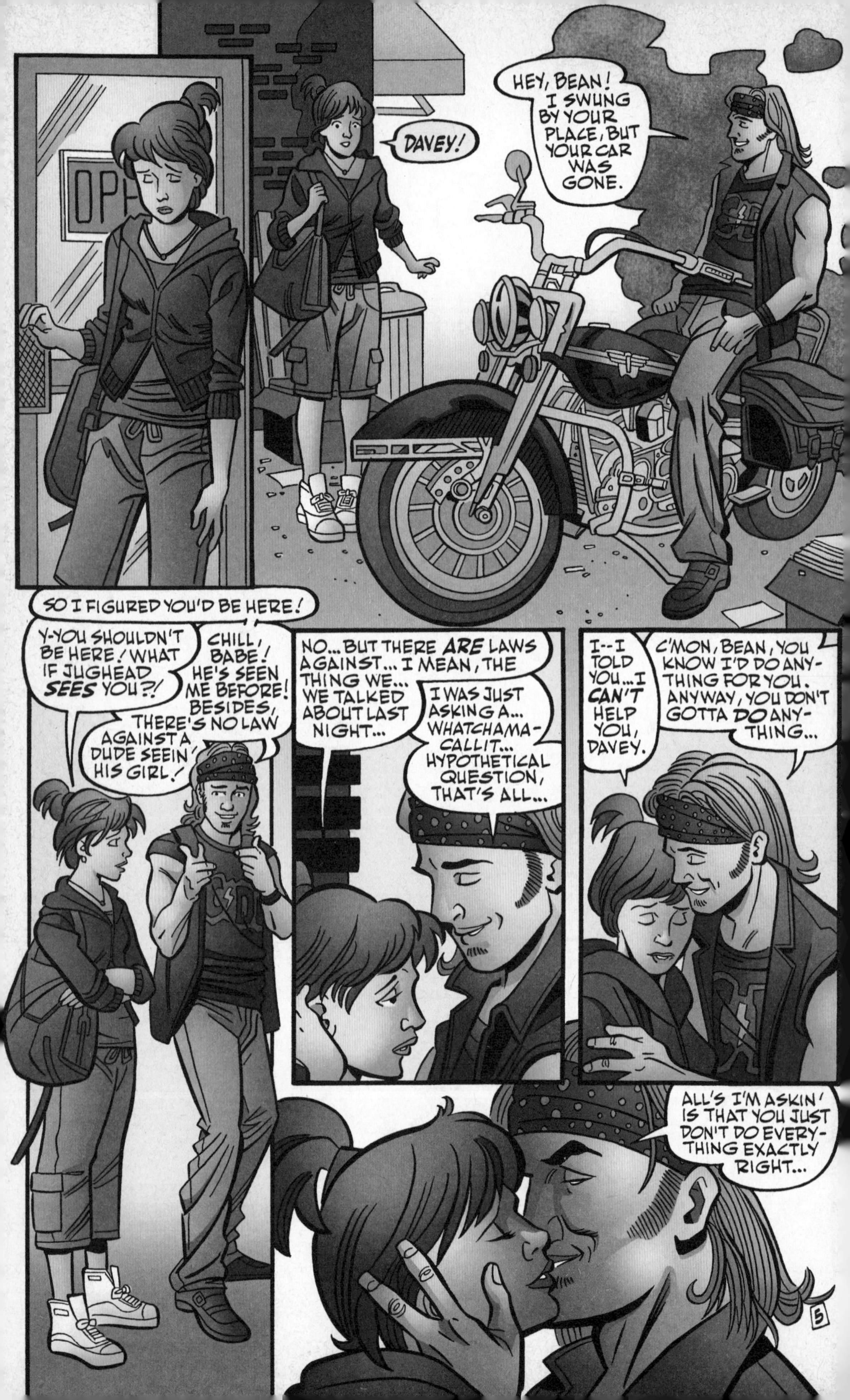
DAVEY!
HEY, BEAN! I SWUNG BY YOUR PLACE, BUT YOUR CAR WAS GONE.
SO I FIGURED YOU'D BE HERE!
Y-YOU SHOULDN'T BE HERE! WHAT IF JUGHEAD **SEES** YOU?!
CHILL, BABE! HE'S SEEN ME BEFORE! BESIDES, THERE'S NO LAW AGAINST A DUDE SEEIN' HIS GIRL!
NO... BUT THERE **ARE** LAWS AGAINST... I MEAN, THE THING WE... WE TALKED ABOUT LAST NIGHT...
I WAS JUST ASKING A... WHATCHAMA-CALLIT... HYPOTHETICAL QUESTION, THAT'S ALL...
I--I TOLD YOU... I **CAN'T** HELP YOU, DAVEY.
C'MON, BEAN, YOU KNOW I'D DO ANYTHING FOR YOU. ANYWAY, YOU DON'T GOTTA **DO** ANYTHING...
ALL'S I'M ASKIN' IS THAT YOU JUST DON'T DO EVERYTHING EXACTLY RIGHT...

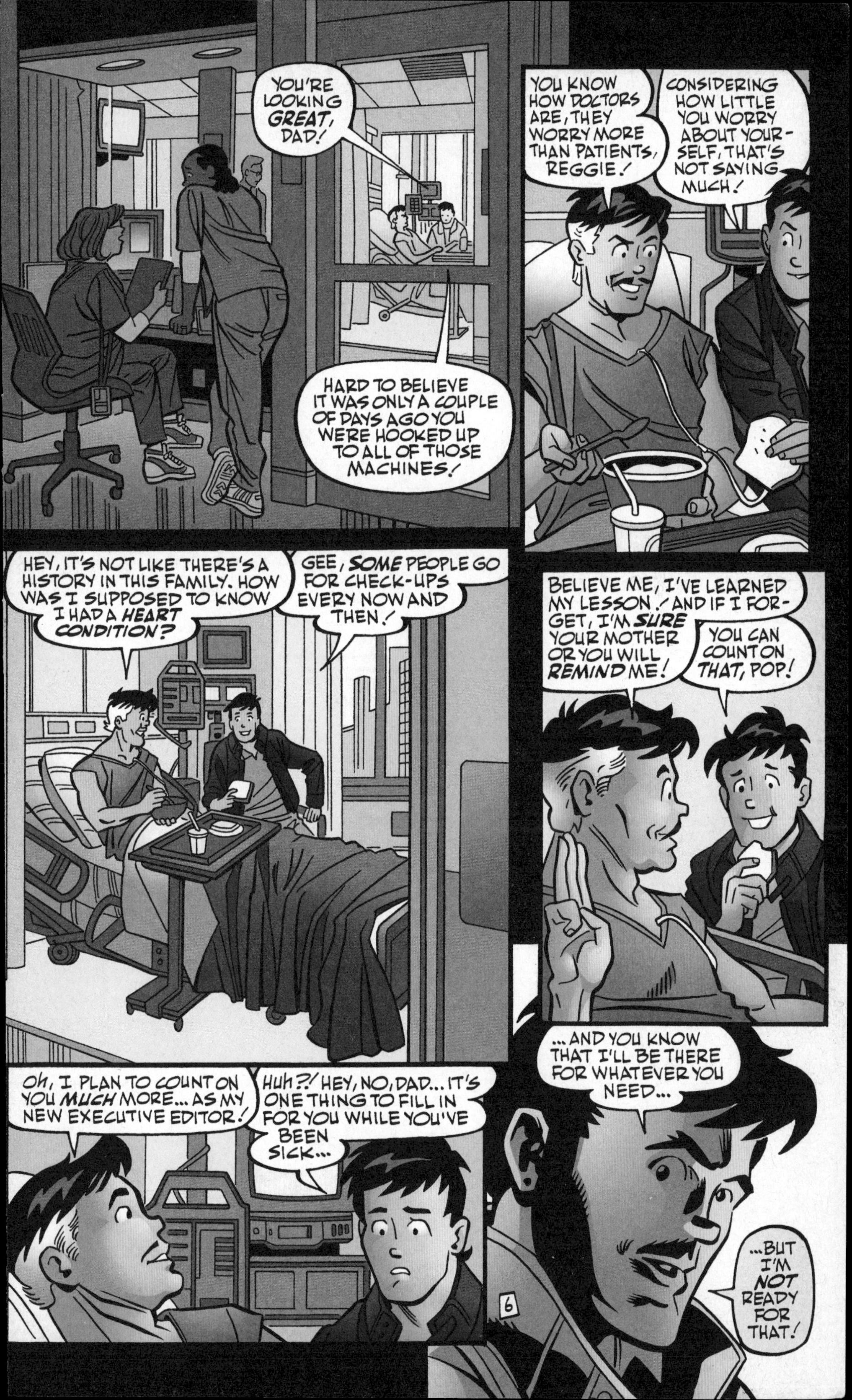

YOU'RE LOOKING GREAT, DAD!
HARD TO BELIEVE IT WAS ONLY A COUPLE OF DAYS AGO YOU WERE HOOKED UP TO ALL OF THOSE MACHINES!
YOU KNOW HOW DOCTORS ARE, THEY WORRY MORE THAN PATIENTS, REGGIE!
CONSIDERING HOW LITTLE YOU WORRY ABOUT YOURSELF, THAT'S NOT SAYING MUCH!
HEY, IT'S NOT LIKE THERE'S A HISTORY IN THIS FAMILY. HOW WAS I SUPPOSED TO KNOW I HAD A HEART CONDITION?
GEE, SOME PEOPLE GO FOR CHECK-UPS EVERY NOW AND THEN!
BELIEVE ME, I'VE LEARNED MY LESSON! AND IF I FORGET, I'M SURE YOUR MOTHER OR YOU WILL REMIND ME!
YOU CAN COUNT ON THAT, POP!
OH, I PLAN TO COUNT ON YOU MUCH MORE... AS MY NEW EXECUTIVE EDITOR!
HUH?! HEY, NO, DAD... IT'S ONE THING TO FILL IN FOR YOU WHILE YOU'VE BEEN SICK...
...AND YOU KNOW THAT I'LL BE THERE FOR WHATEVER YOU NEED...
...BUT I'M NOT READY FOR THAT!
6

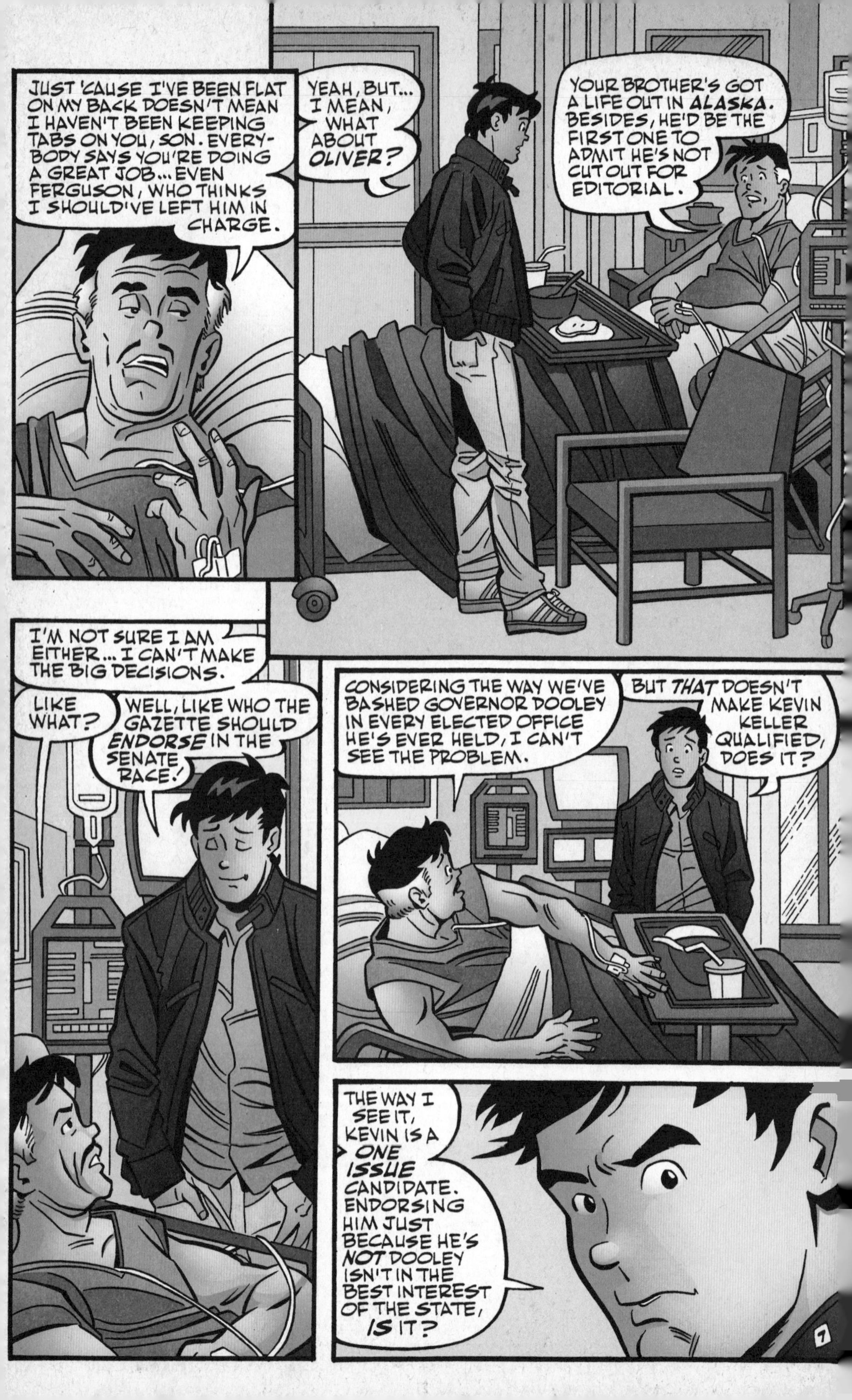
JUST 'CAUSE I'VE BEEN FLAT ON MY BACK DOESN'T MEAN I HAVEN'T BEEN KEEPING TABS ON YOU, SON. EVERYBODY SAYS YOU'RE DOING A GREAT JOB... EVEN FERGUSON, WHO THINKS I SHOULD'VE LEFT HIM IN CHARGE.
YEAH, BUT... I MEAN, WHAT ABOUT OLIVER?
YOUR BROTHER'S GOT A LIFE OUT IN ALASKA. BESIDES, HE'D BE THE FIRST ONE TO ADMIT HE'S NOT CUT OUT FOR EDITORIAL.
I'M NOT SURE I AM EITHER... I CAN'T MAKE THE BIG DECISIONS.
LIKE WHAT?
WELL, LIKE WHO THE GAZETTE SHOULD ENDORSE IN THE SENATE RACE!
CONSIDERING THE WAY WE'VE BASHED GOVERNOR DOOLEY IN EVERY ELECTED OFFICE HE'S EVER HELD, I CAN'T SEE THE PROBLEM.
BUT THAT DOESN'T MAKE KEVIN KELLER QUALIFIED, DOES IT?
THE WAY I SEE IT, KEVIN IS A ONE ISSUE CANDIDATE. ENDORSING HIM JUST BECAUSE HE'S NOT DOOLEY ISN'T IN THE BEST INTEREST OF THE STATE, IS IT?
7

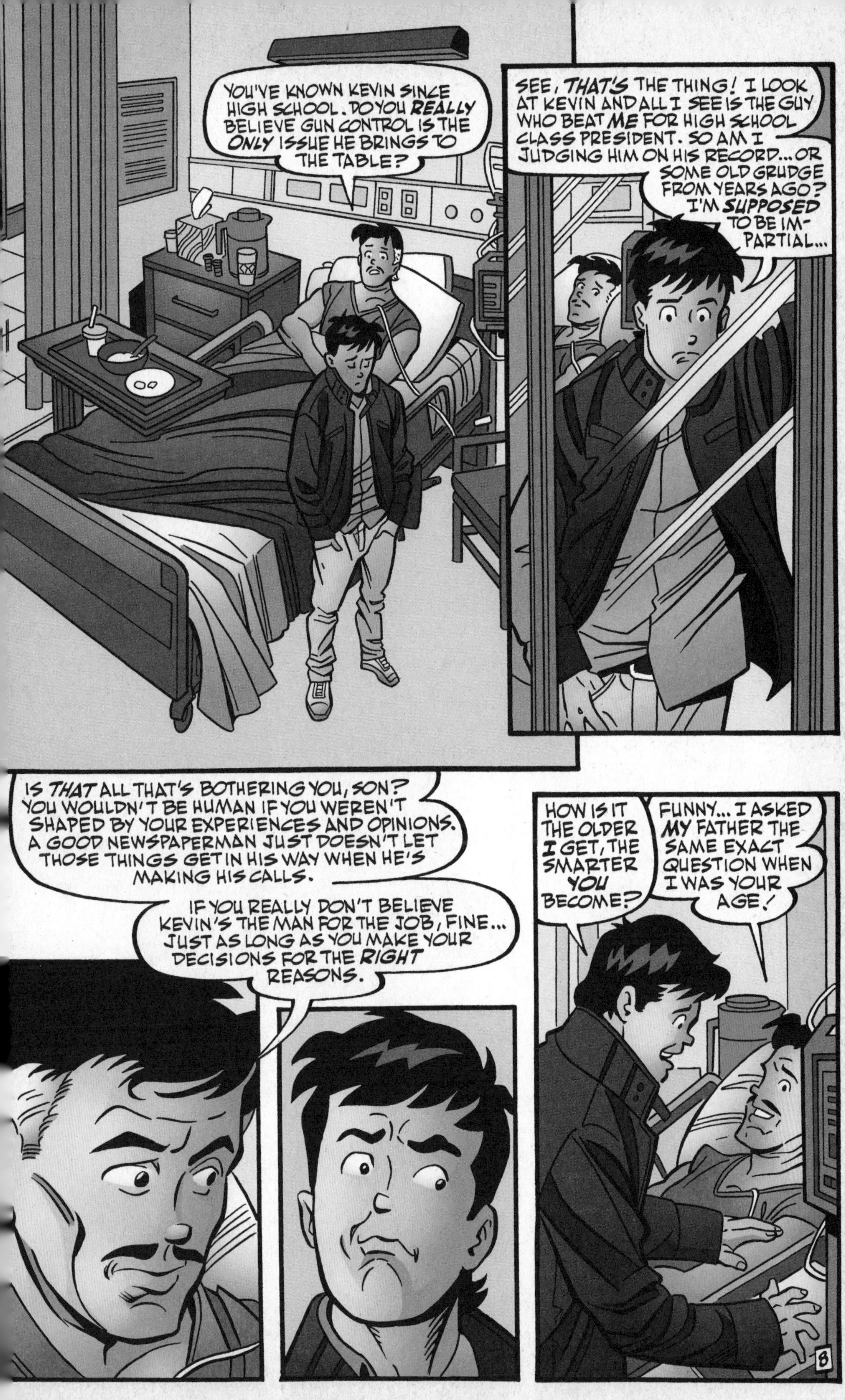
YOU'VE KNOWN KEVIN SINCE HIGH SCHOOL. DO YOU REALLY BELIEVE GUN CONTROL IS THE ONLY ISSUE HE BRINGS TO THE TABLE?
SEE, THAT'S THE THING! I LOOK AT KEVIN AND ALL I SEE IS THE GUY WHO BEAT ME FOR HIGH SCHOOL CLASS PRESIDENT. SO AM I JUDGING HIM ON HIS RECORD...OR SOME OLD GRUDGE FROM YEARS AGO? I'M SUPPOSED TO BE IM-PARTIAL...
IS THAT ALL THAT'S BOTHERING YOU, SON? YOU WOULDN'T BE HUMAN IF YOU WEREN'T SHAPED BY YOUR EXPERIENCES AND OPINIONS. A GOOD NEWSPAPERMAN JUST DOESN'T LET THOSE THINGS GET IN HIS WAY WHEN HE'S MAKING HIS CALLS.
IF YOU REALLY DON'T BELIEVE KEVIN'S THE MAN FOR THE JOB, FINE... JUST AS LONG AS YOU MAKE YOUR DECISIONS FOR THE RIGHT REASONS.
HOW IS IT THE OLDER I GET, THE SMARTER YOU BECOME?
FUNNY... I ASKED MY FATHER THE SAME EXACT QUESTION WHEN I WAS YOUR AGE!
8

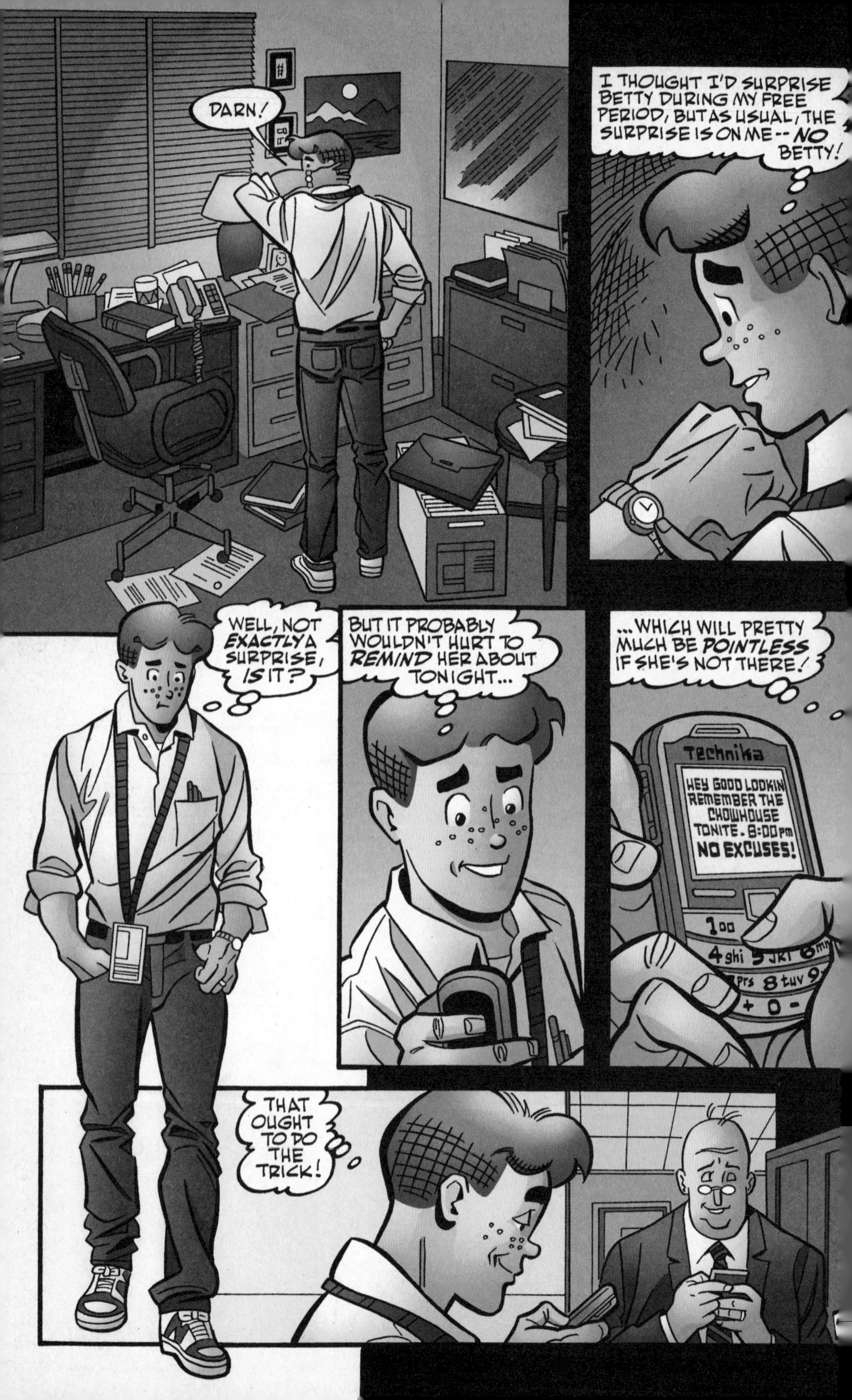
DARN!
I THOUGHT I'D SURPRISE BETTY DURING MY FREE PERIOD, BUT AS USUAL, THE SURPRISE IS ON ME -- NO BETTY!
WELL, NOT EXACTLY A SURPRISE, IS IT?
BUT IT PROBABLY WOULDN'T HURT TO REMIND HER ABOUT TONIGHT...
...WHICH WILL PRETTY MUCH BE POINTLESS IF SHE'S NOT THERE!
Technika
HEY GOOD LOOKIN REMEMBER THE CHOWHOUSE TONITE. 8:00pm NO EXCUSES!
THAT OUGHT TO DO THE TRICK!

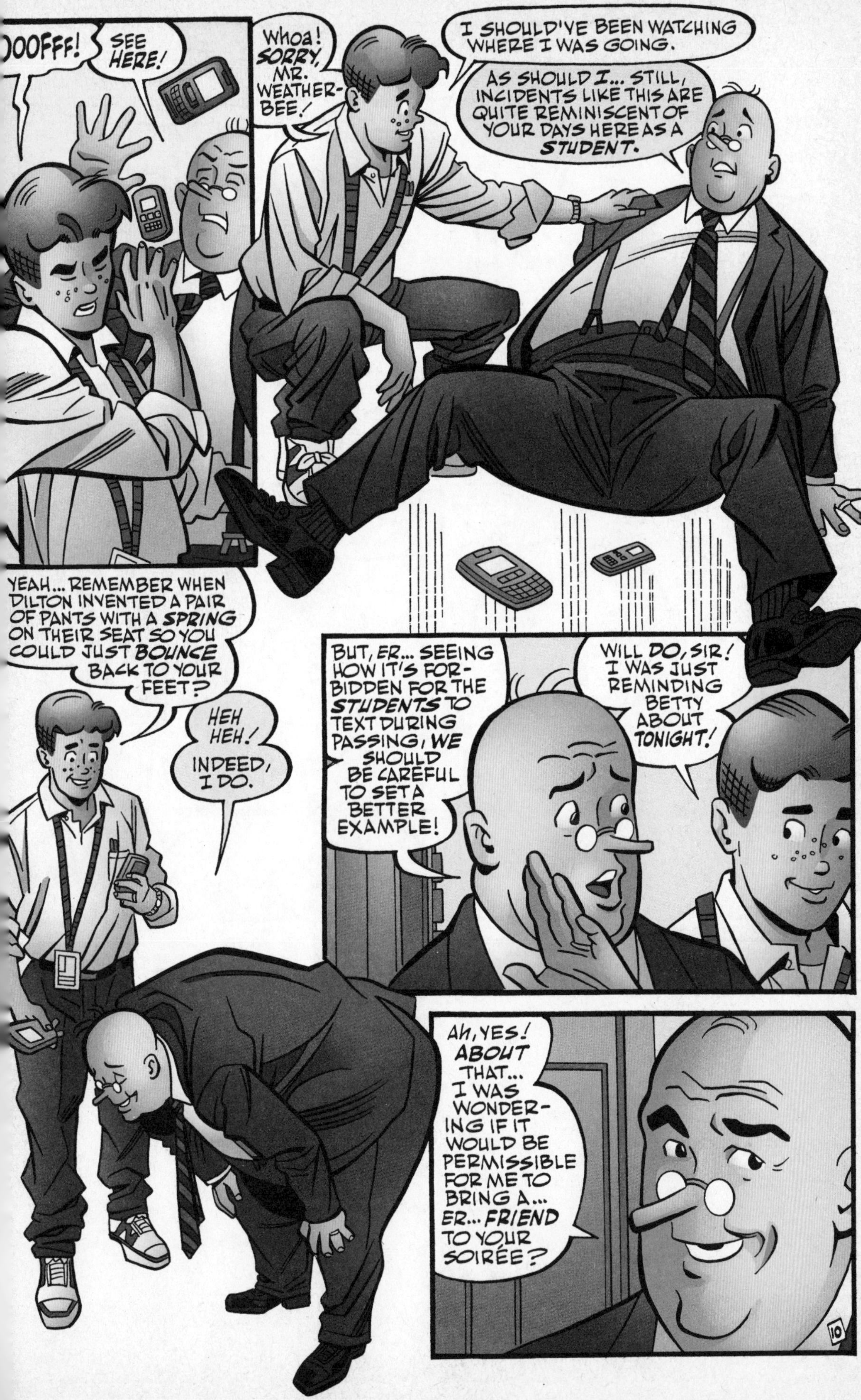
OOOFFF!
SEE HERE!
Whoa! SORRY, MR. WEATHERBEE!
I SHOULD'VE BEEN WATCHING WHERE I WAS GOING.
AS SHOULD I... STILL, INCIDENTS LIKE THIS ARE QUITE REMINISCENT OF YOUR DAYS HERE AS A STUDENT.
YEAH... REMEMBER WHEN DILTON INVENTED A PAIR OF PANTS WITH A SPRING ON THEIR SEAT SO YOU COULD JUST BOUNCE BACK TO YOUR FEET?
HEH HEH!
INDEED, I DO.
BUT, ER... SEEING HOW IT'S FORBIDDEN FOR THE STUDENTS TO TEXT DURING PASSING, WE SHOULD BE CAREFUL TO SET A BETTER EXAMPLE!
WILL DO, SIR! I WAS JUST REMINDING BETTY ABOUT TONIGHT!
AH, YES! ABOUT THAT... I WAS WONDERING IF IT WOULD BE PERMISSIBLE FOR ME TO BRING A... ER... FRIEND TO YOUR SOIRÉE?
10

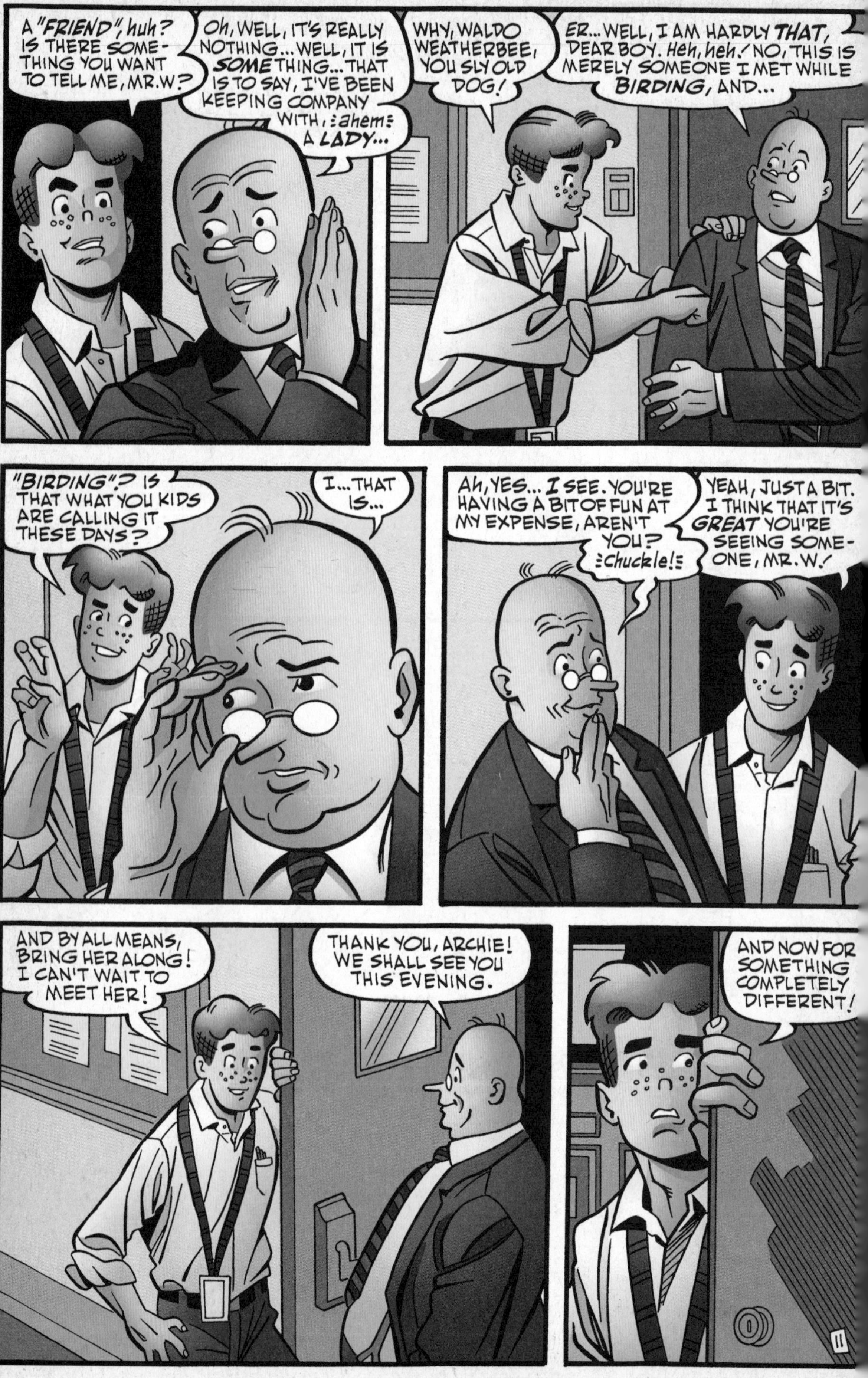
A "FRIEND", huh? IS THERE SOMETHING YOU WANT TO TELL ME, MR. W?
Oh, WELL, IT'S REALLY NOTHING... WELL, IT IS SOMETHING... THAT IS TO SAY, I'VE BEEN KEEPING COMPANY WITH, :ahem: A LADY...
WHY, WALDO WEATHERBEE, YOU SLY OLD DOG!
ER... WELL, I AM HARDLY THAT, DEAR BOY. Heh, heh! NO, THIS IS MERELY SOMEONE I MET WHILE BIRDING, AND...
"BIRDING"? IS THAT WHAT YOU KIDS ARE CALLING IT THESE DAYS?
I... THAT IS...
Ah, YES... I SEE. YOU'RE HAVING A BIT OF FUN AT MY EXPENSE, AREN'T YOU? :Chuckle!:
YEAH, JUST A BIT. I THINK THAT IT'S GREAT YOU'RE SEEING SOMEONE, MR. W!
AND BY ALL MEANS, BRING HER ALONG! I CAN'T WAIT TO MEET HER!
THANK YOU, ARCHIE! WE SHALL SEE YOU THIS EVENING.
AND NOW FOR SOMETHING COMPLETELY DIFFERENT!
11

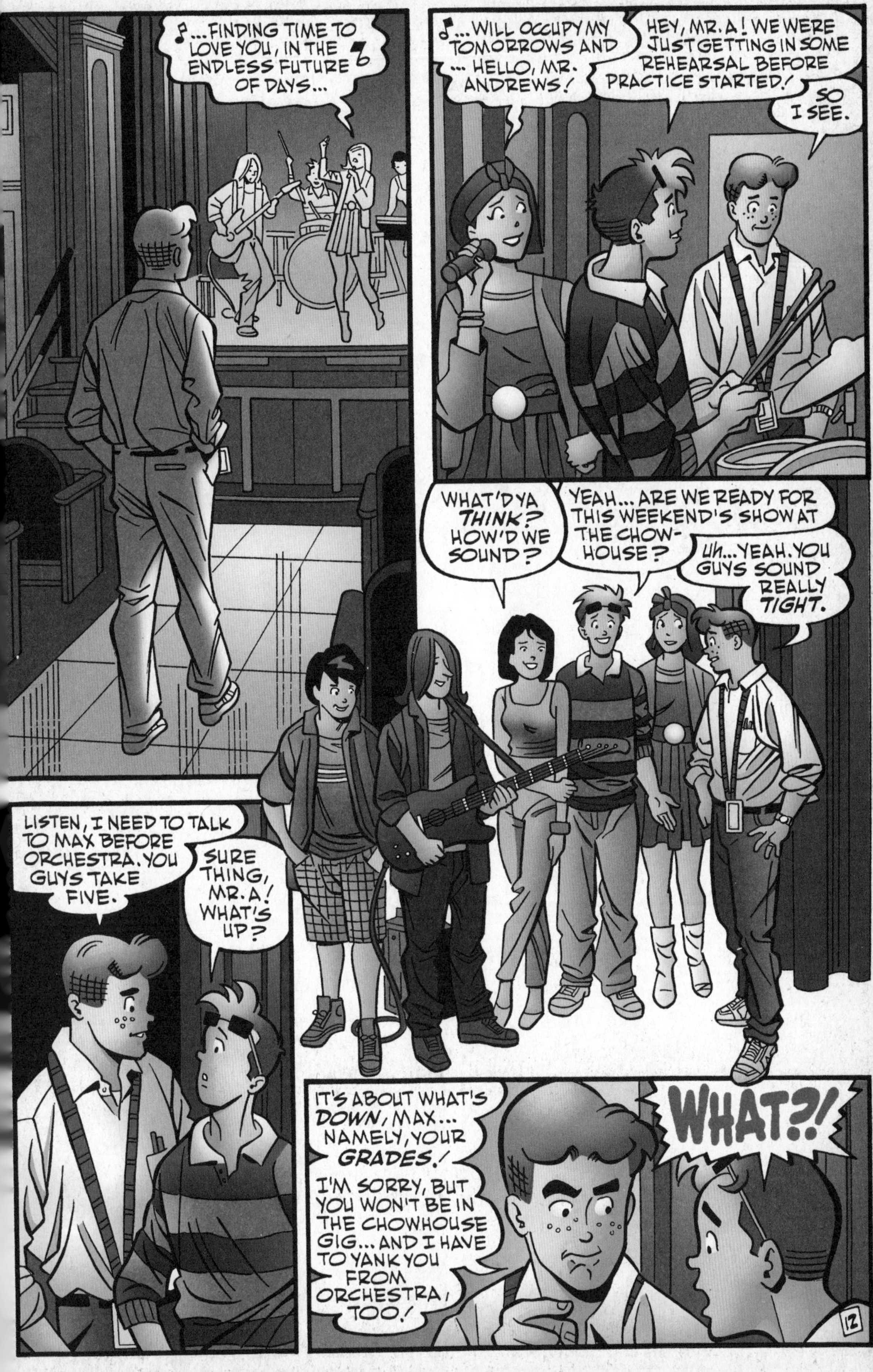
♪... FINDING TIME TO LOVE YOU, IN THE ENDLESS FUTURE OF DAYS...
♪... WILL OCCUPY MY TOMORROWS AND ... HELLO, MR. ANDREWS!
HEY, MR. A! WE WERE JUST GETTING IN SOME REHEARSAL BEFORE PRACTICE STARTED!
SO I SEE.
WHAT'D YA *THINK*? HOW'D WE SOUND?
YEAH... ARE WE READY FOR THIS WEEKEND'S SHOW AT THE CHOW-HOUSE?
UH... YEAH. YOU GUYS SOUND REALLY *TIGHT*.
LISTEN, I NEED TO TALK TO MAX BEFORE ORCHESTRA. YOU GUYS TAKE FIVE.
SURE THING, MR. A! WHAT'S UP?
IT'S ABOUT WHAT'S *DOWN*, MAX... NAMELY, YOUR *GRADES*!
I'M SORRY, BUT YOU WON'T BE IN THE CHOWHOUSE GIG... AND I HAVE TO YANK YOU FROM ORCHESTRA, TOO!
WHAT?!
12

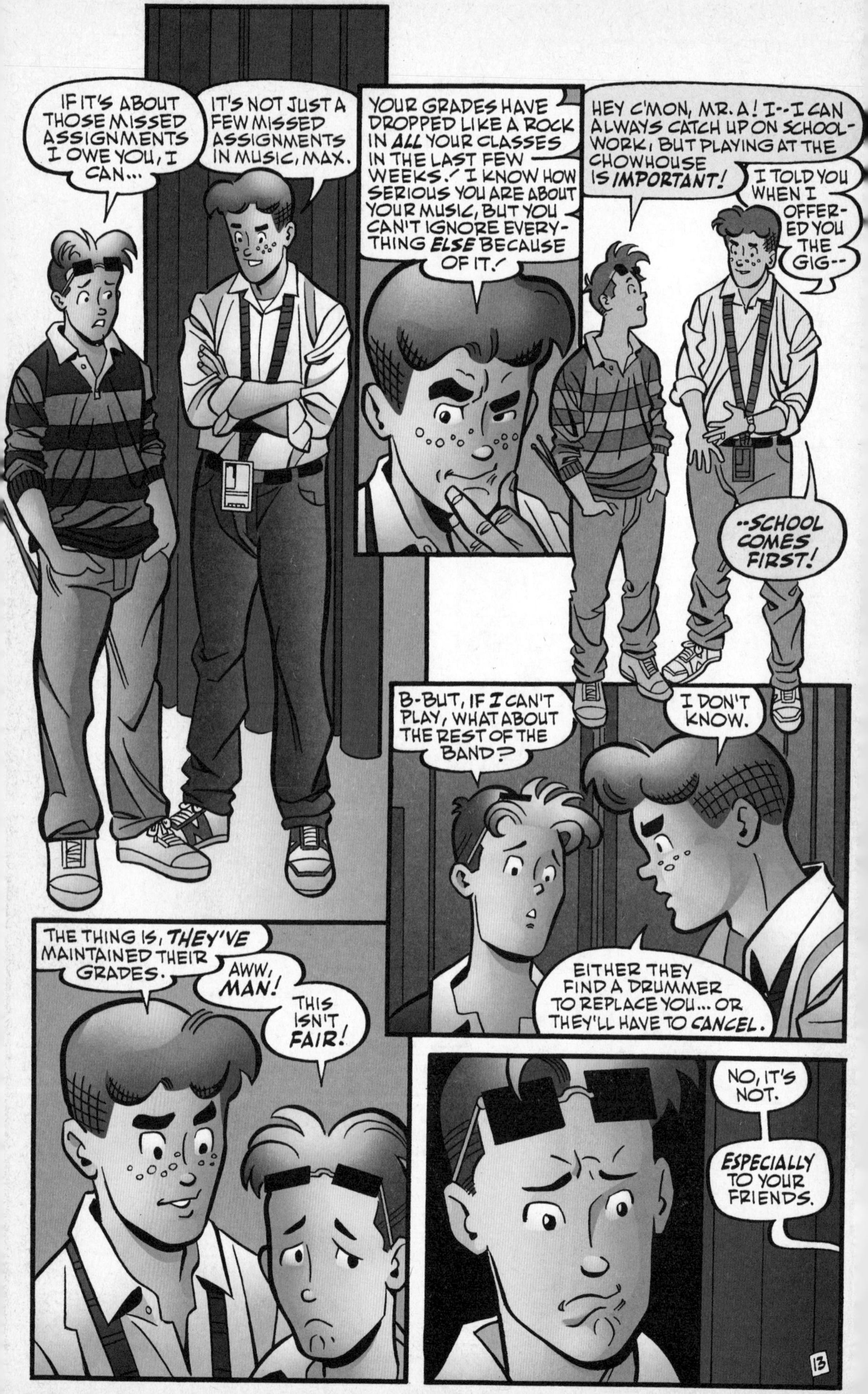
IF IT'S ABOUT THOSE MISSED ASSIGNMENTS I OWE YOU, I CAN...
IT'S NOT JUST A FEW MISSED ASSIGNMENTS IN MUSIC, MAX.
YOUR GRADES HAVE DROPPED LIKE A ROCK IN ALL YOUR CLASSES IN THE LAST FEW WEEKS! I KNOW HOW SERIOUS YOU ARE ABOUT YOUR MUSIC, BUT YOU CAN'T IGNORE EVERYTHING ELSE BECAUSE OF IT!
HEY C'MON, MR. A! I--I CAN ALWAYS CATCH UP ON SCHOOLWORK, BUT PLAYING AT THE CHOWHOUSE IS IMPORTANT!
I TOLD YOU WHEN I OFFERED YOU THE GIG--
--SCHOOL COMES FIRST!
B-BUT, IF I CAN'T PLAY, WHAT ABOUT THE REST OF THE BAND?
I DON'T KNOW.
EITHER THEY FIND A DRUMMER TO REPLACE YOU... OR THEY'LL HAVE TO CANCEL.
THE THING IS, THEY'VE MAINTAINED THEIR GRADES.
AWW, MAN!
THIS ISN'T FAIR!
NO, IT'S NOT.
ESPECIALLY TO YOUR FRIENDS.
13

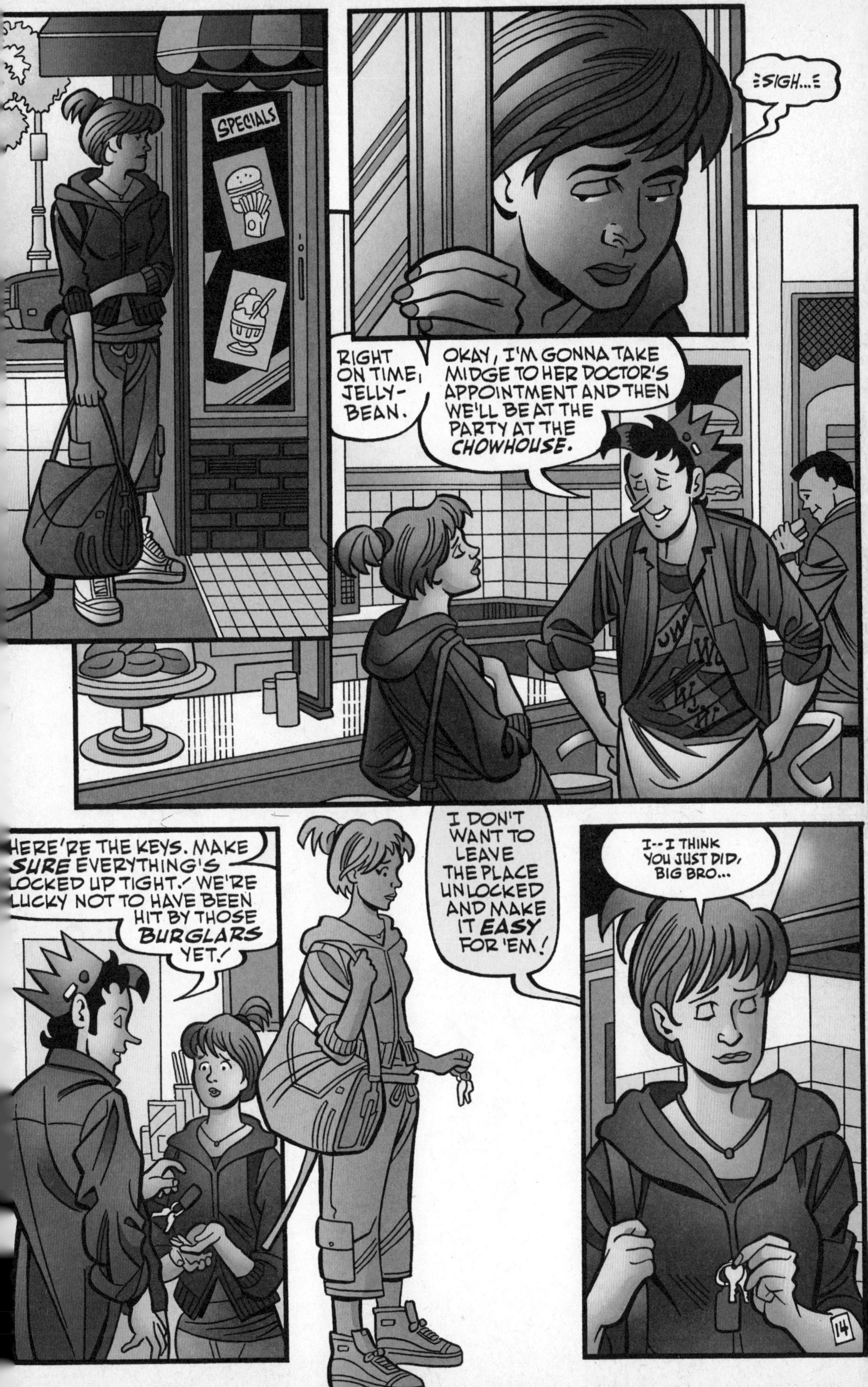

SIGH...
RIGHT ON TIME, JELLY-BEAN.
OKAY, I'M GONNA TAKE MIDGE TO HER DOCTOR'S APPOINTMENT AND THEN WE'LL BE AT THE PARTY AT THE CHOWHOUSE.
HERE'RE THE KEYS. MAKE SURE EVERYTHING'S LOCKED UP TIGHT! WE'RE LUCKY NOT TO HAVE BEEN HIT BY THOSE BURGLARS YET!
I DON'T WANT TO LEAVE THE PLACE UNLOCKED AND MAKE IT EASY FOR 'EM!
I--I THINK YOU JUST DID, BIG BRO...
14

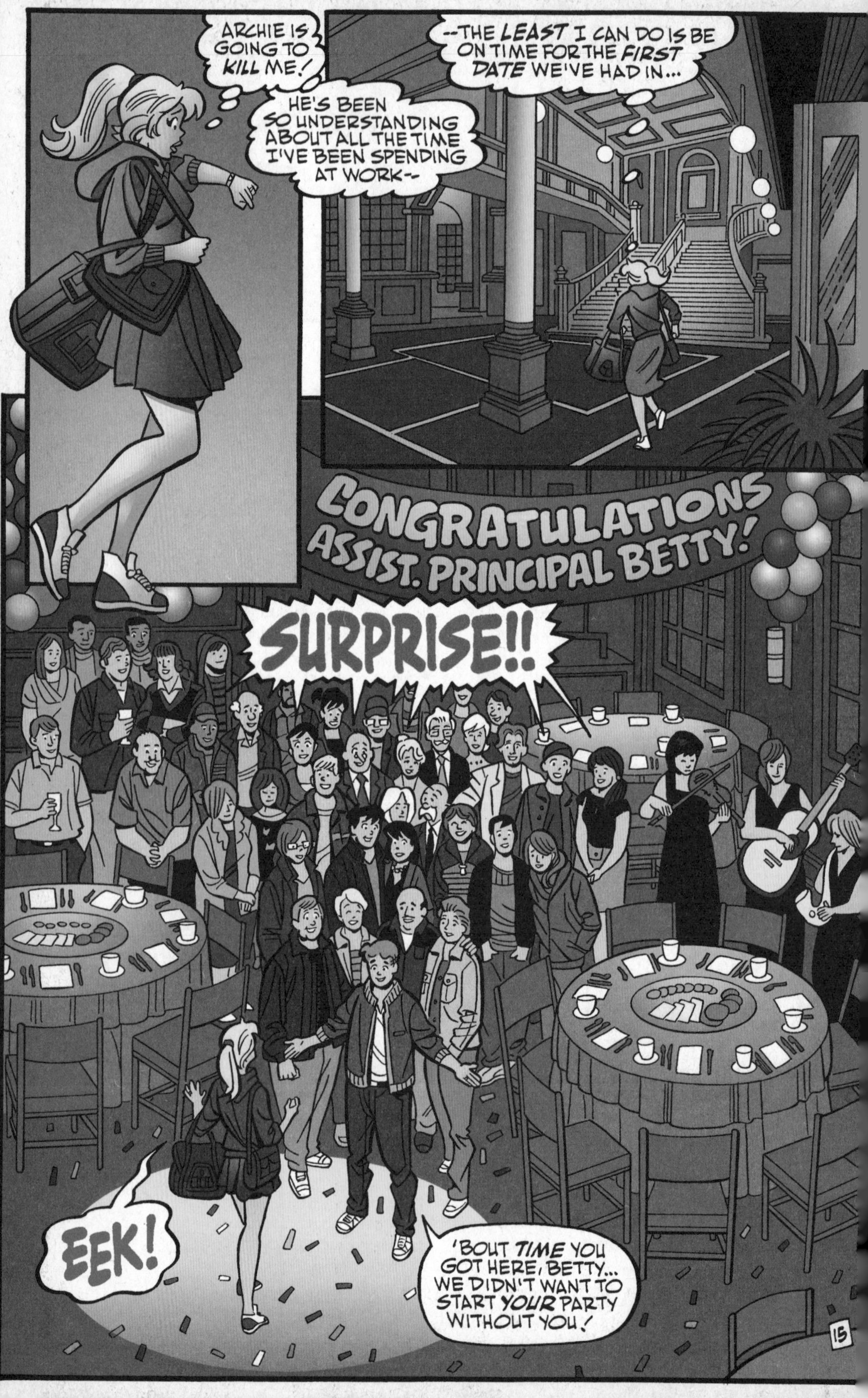
ARCHIE IS GOING TO KILL ME!
HE'S BEEN SO UNDERSTANDING ABOUT ALL THE TIME I'VE BEEN SPENDING AT WORK--
--THE LEAST I CAN DO IS BE ON TIME FOR THE FIRST DATE WE'VE HAD IN...
CONGRATULATIONS ASSIST. PRINCIPAL BETTY!
SURPRISE!!
EEK!
'BOUT TIME YOU GOT HERE, BETTY... WE DIDN'T WANT TO START YOUR PARTY WITHOUT YOU!
15

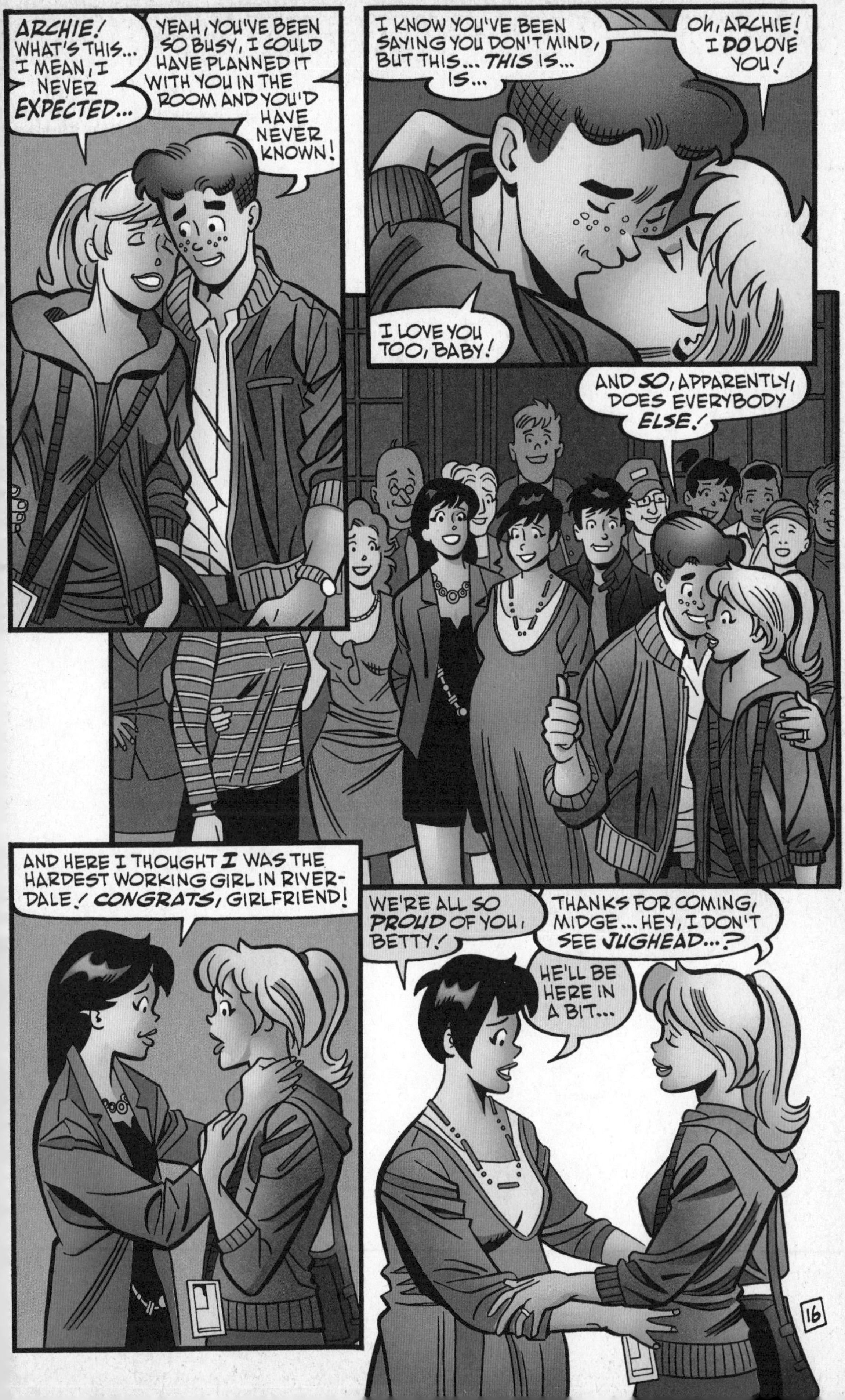

ARCHIE! WHAT'S THIS... I MEAN, I NEVER EXPECTED...
YEAH, YOU'VE BEEN SO BUSY, I COULD HAVE PLANNED IT WITH YOU IN THE ROOM AND YOU'D HAVE NEVER KNOWN!
I KNOW YOU'VE BEEN SAYING YOU DON'T MIND, BUT THIS... THIS IS... IS...
OH, ARCHIE! I DO LOVE YOU!
I LOVE YOU TOO, BABY!
AND SO, APPARENTLY, DOES EVERYBODY ELSE!
AND HERE I THOUGHT I WAS THE HARDEST WORKING GIRL IN RIVER-DALE! CONGRATS, GIRLFRIEND!
WE'RE ALL SO PROUD OF YOU, BETTY!
THANKS FOR COMING, MIDGE... HEY, I DON'T SEE JUGHEAD...?
HE'LL BE HERE IN A BIT...
16

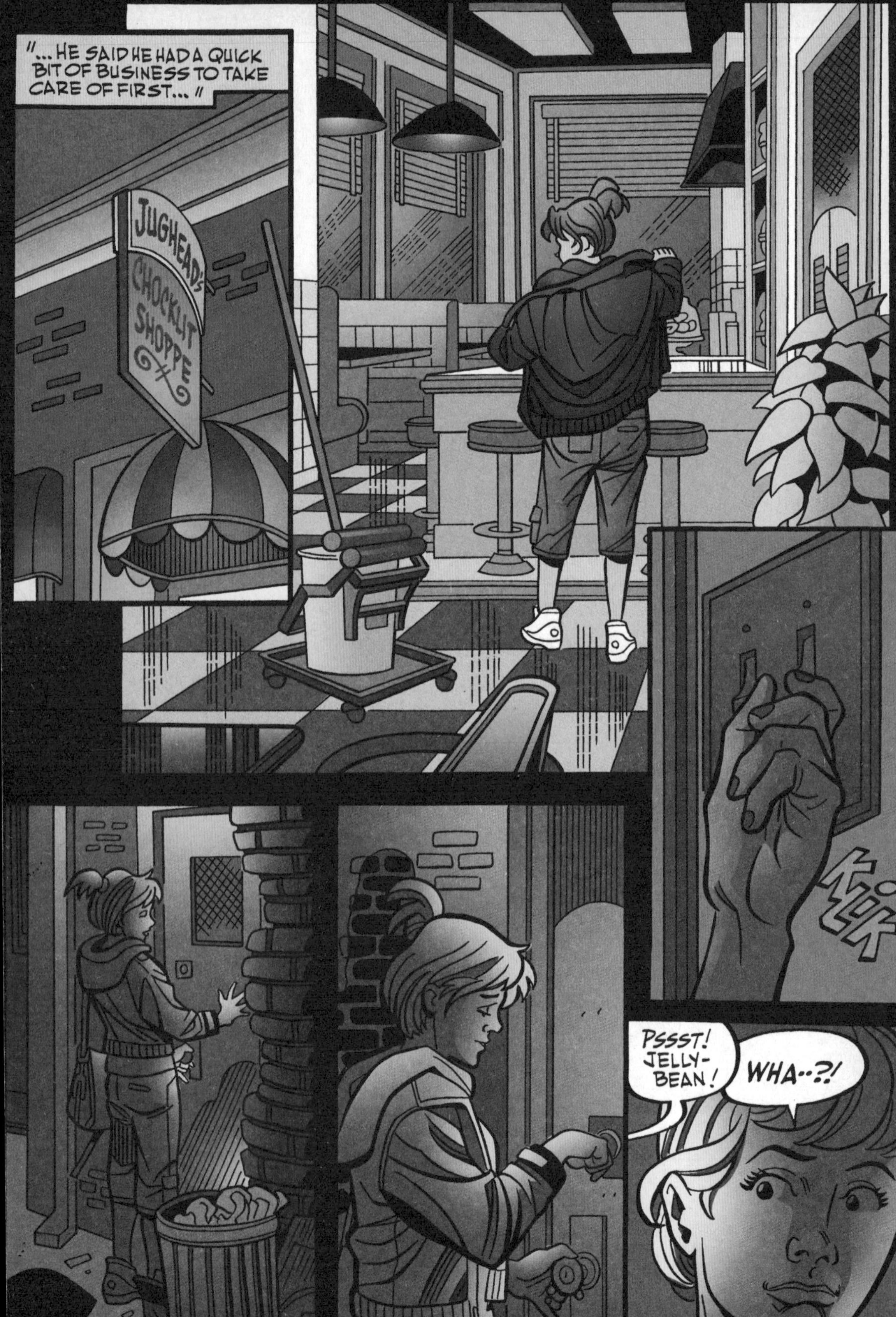
"...HE SAID HE HAD A QUICK BIT OF BUSINESS TO TAKE CARE OF FIRST..."
JUGHEAD'S CHOCKLIT SHOPPE
KLIK
PSSST! JELLY-BEAN!
WHA--?!

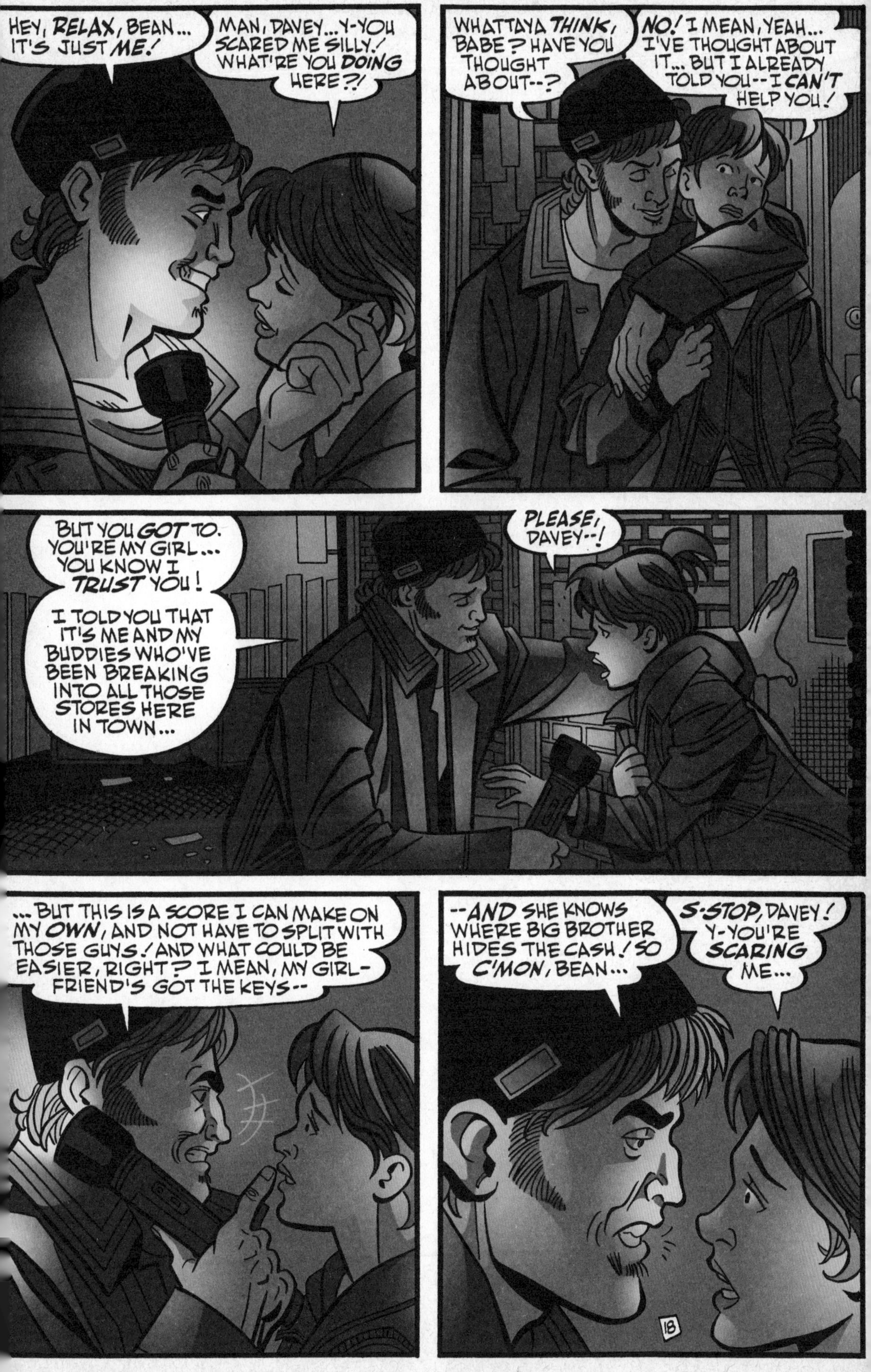
HEY, RELAX, BEAN... IT'S JUST ME!
MAN, DAVEY... Y-YOU SCARED ME SILLY! WHAT'RE YOU DOING HERE?!
WHATTAYA THINK, BABE? HAVE YOU THOUGHT ABOUT--?
NO! I MEAN, YEAH... I'VE THOUGHT ABOUT IT... BUT I ALREADY TOLD YOU-- I CAN'T HELP YOU!
BUT YOU GOT TO. YOU'RE MY GIRL... YOU KNOW I TRUST YOU!
I TOLD YOU THAT IT'S ME AND MY BUDDIES WHO'VE BEEN BREAKING INTO ALL THOSE STORES HERE IN TOWN...
PLEASE, DAVEY--!
...BUT THIS IS A SCORE I CAN MAKE ON MY OWN, AND NOT HAVE TO SPLIT WITH THOSE GUYS! AND WHAT COULD BE EASIER, RIGHT? I MEAN, MY GIRL-FRIEND'S GOT THE KEYS--
--AND SHE KNOWS WHERE BIG BROTHER HIDES THE CASH! SO C'MON, BEAN...
S-STOP, DAVEY! Y-YOU'RE SCARING ME...
18

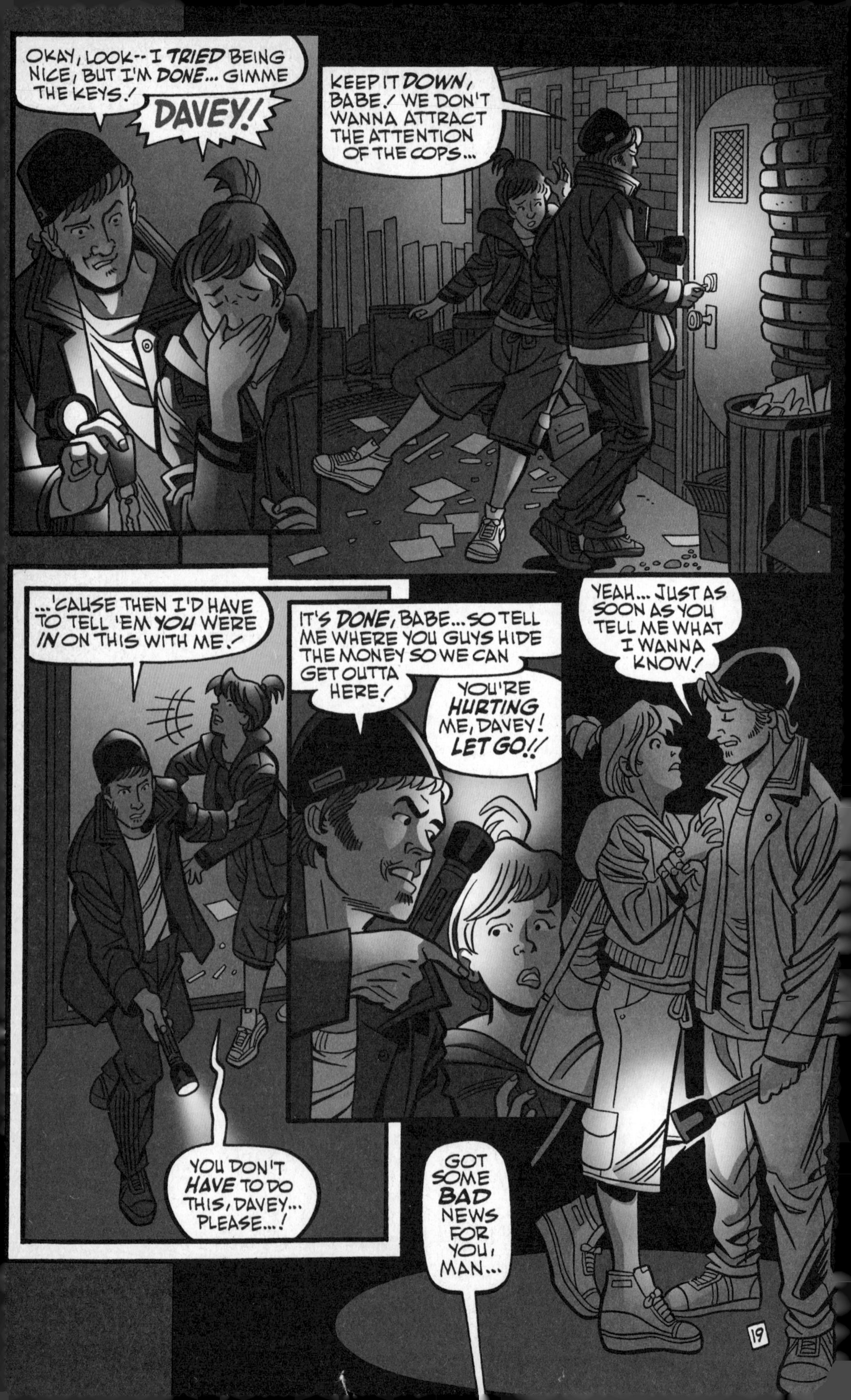
OKAY, LOOK-- I TRIED BEING NICE, BUT I'M DONE... GIMME THE KEYS.!
DAVEY!
KEEP IT DOWN, BABE.! WE DON'T WANNA ATTRACT THE ATTENTION OF THE COPS...
...'CAUSE THEN I'D HAVE TO TELL 'EM YOU WERE IN ON THIS WITH ME.!
YOU DON'T HAVE TO DO THIS, DAVEY... PLEASE...!
IT'S DONE, BABE... SO TELL ME WHERE YOU GUYS HIDE THE MONEY SO WE CAN GET OUTTA HERE!
YOU'RE HURTING ME, DAVEY! LET GO!!
YEAH... JUST AS SOON AS YOU TELL ME WHAT I WANNA KNOW!
GOT SOME BAD NEWS FOR YOU, MAN...
19

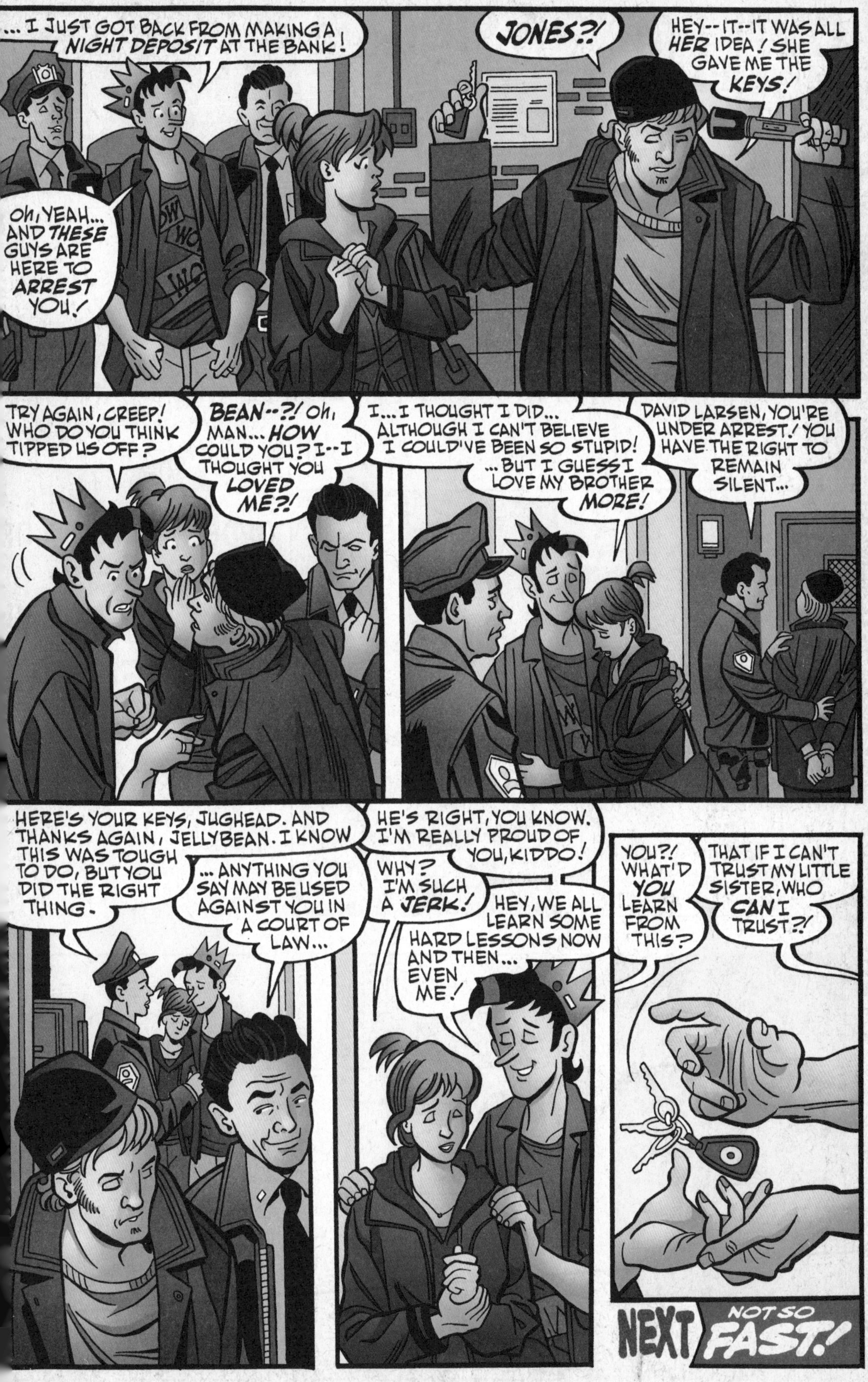
... I JUST GOT BACK FROM MAKING A NIGHT DEPOSIT AT THE BANK!
JONES?!
HEY--IT--IT WAS ALL HER IDEA! SHE GAVE ME THE KEYS!
OH, YEAH... AND THESE GUYS ARE HERE TO ARREST YOU!
TRY AGAIN, CREEP! WHO DO YOU THINK TIPPED US OFF?
BEAN--?! OH, MAN... HOW COULD YOU? I--I THOUGHT YOU LOVED ME?!
I... I THOUGHT I DID... ALTHOUGH I CAN'T BELIEVE I COULD'VE BEEN SO STUPID!
... BUT I GUESS I LOVE MY BROTHER MORE!
DAVID LARSEN, YOU'RE UNDER ARREST! YOU HAVE THE RIGHT TO REMAIN SILENT...
HERE'S YOUR KEYS, JUGHEAD. AND THANKS AGAIN, JELLYBEAN. I KNOW THIS WAS TOUGH TO DO, BUT YOU DID THE RIGHT THING.
... ANYTHING YOU SAY MAY BE USED AGAINST YOU IN A COURT OF LAW...
HE'S RIGHT, YOU KNOW. I'M REALLY PROUD OF YOU, KIDDO!
WHY? I'M SUCH A JERK!
HEY, WE ALL LEARN SOME HARD LESSONS NOW AND THEN... EVEN ME!
YOU?! WHAT'D YOU LEARN FROM THIS?
THAT IF I CAN'T TRUST MY LITTLE SISTER, WHO CAN I TRUST?!
NEXT NOT SO FAST!

DON'T MISS A SINGLE MOMENT OF THE FINALE MAKING HEADLINES AROUND THE WORLD.

THIS IS THE END!

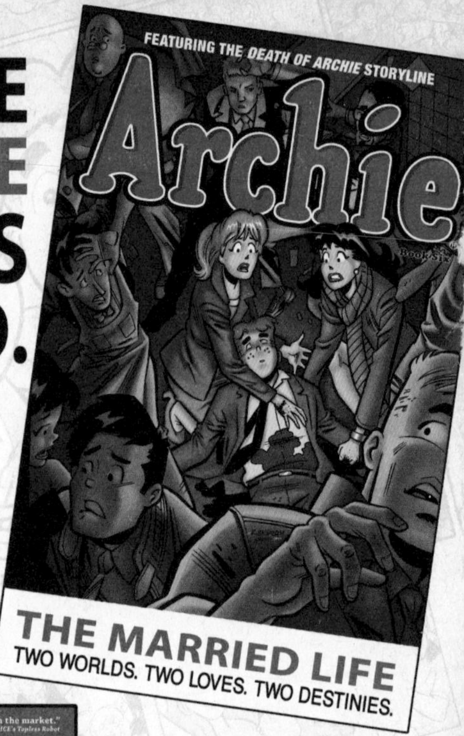
FEATURING THE DEATH OF ARCHIE STORYLINE
Archie
Book Six
THE MARRIED LIFE
TWO WORLDS. TWO LOVES. TWO DESTINIES.

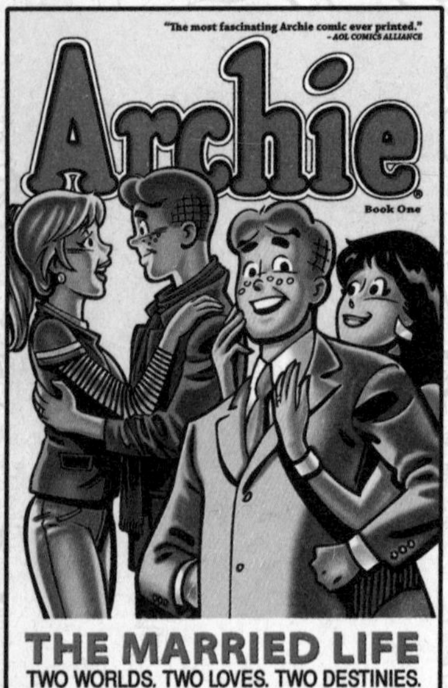
"The most fascinating Archie comic ever printed."
- AOL COMICS ALLIANCE
Archie
Book One
THE MARRIED LIFE
TWO WORLDS. TWO LOVES. TWO DESTINIES.

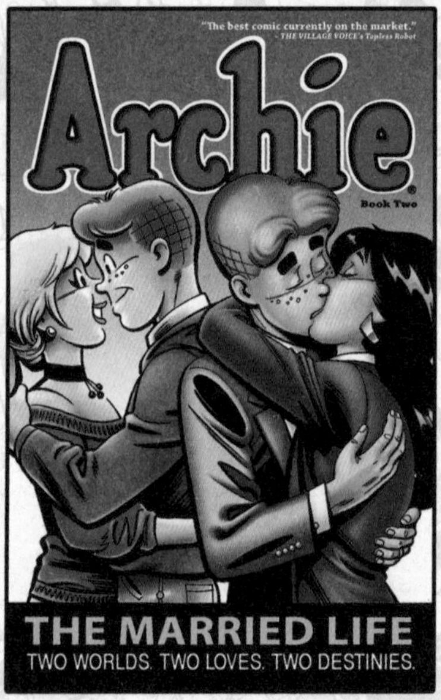
"The best comic currently on the market."
- THE VILLAGE VOICE's Topless Robot
Archie
Book Two
THE MARRIED LIFE
TWO WORLDS. TWO LOVES. TWO DESTINIES.

ORDER YOUR COPY OF THE MARRIED LIFE BOOK 6 TODAY!

AND BE SURE TO LOOK FOR BOOKS 1-5 ON SALE NOW!

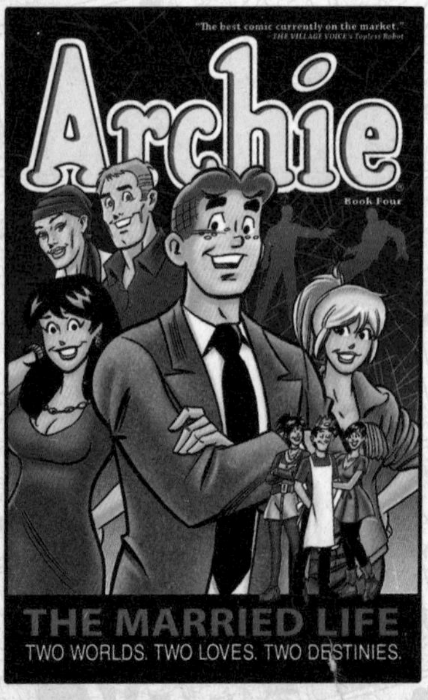
"The best comic currently on the market."
- THE VILLAGE VOICE's Topless Robot
Archie
Book Four
THE MARRIED LIFE
TWO WORLDS. TWO LOVES. TWO DESTINIES.

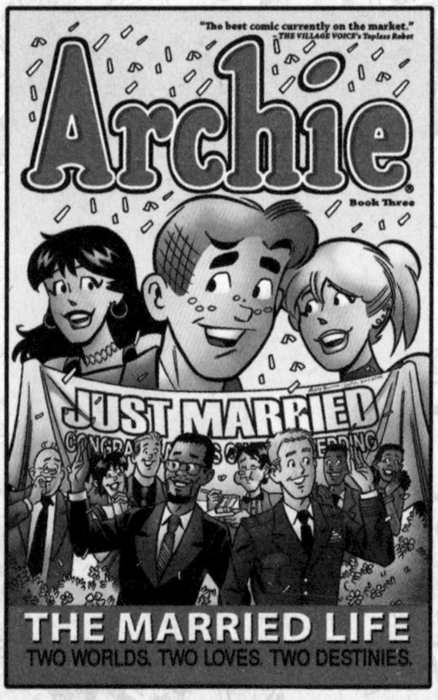
"The best comic currently on the market."
- THE VILLAGE VOICE's Topless Robot
Archie
Book Three
JUST MARRIED
THE MARRIED LIFE
TWO WORLDS. TWO LOVES. TWO DESTINIES.

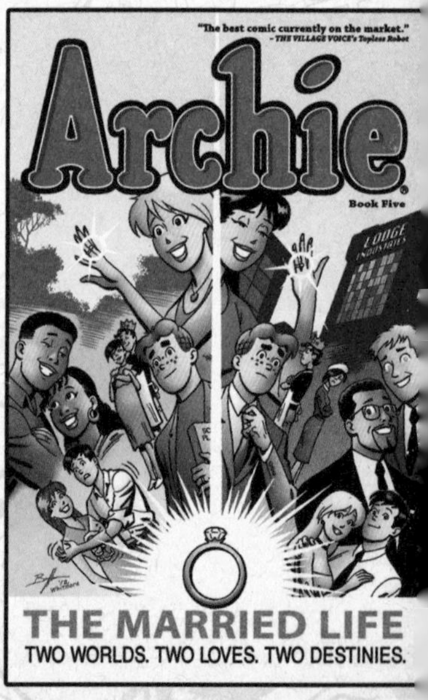
"The best comic currently on the market."
- THE VILLAGE VOICE's Topless Robot
Archie
Book Five
LODGE INDUSTRIES
THE MARRIED LIFE
TWO WORLDS. TWO LOVES. TWO DESTINIES.